THE STRUCTURE OF POLITICS
AT THE ACCESSION OF
GEORGE III

γαμψωνύχων τε πτῆσιν οἰωνῶν σκεθρῶς
διώρισ᾽, οἵτινές τε δεξιοὶ φύσιν
εὐωνύμους τε, καὶ δίαιταν ἥντινα
ἔχουσ᾽ ἕκαστοι, καὶ πρὸς ἀλλήλους τίνες
ἔχθραι τε καὶ στέργηθρα καὶ συνεδρίαι.

AESCHYLUS, *Prometheus Vinctus*, 488-492.

I took pains to determine the flight of crook-taloned birds, marking which were of the right by nature, and which of the left, and what were their ways of living, each after his kind, and the enmities and affections that were between them, and how they consorted together.

THE
STRUCTURE OF POLITICS
AT THE ACCESSION OF
GEORGE III

BY

SIR LEWIS NAMIER

SECOND EDITION

LONDON

MACMILLAN & CO LTD

NEW YORK · ST MARTIN'S PRESS

1961

MACMILLAN AND COMPANY LIMITED
London Bombay Calcutta Madras Melbourne

THE MACMILLAN COMPANY OF CANADA LIMITED
Toronto

ST MARTIN'S PRESS INC
New York

PRINTED IN GREAT BRITAIN

23625

PREFACE TO SECOND EDITION

UNDERTAKING a revision of the book after a lapse of thirty years, I had to ask myself what measure of change would improve and not deform it. During the intervening period, and especially since work started on the *History of Parliament* five years ago, I have examined scores of collections of MSS. — how much of the new material was I to fit into the book? It seemed to me best to leave the basic structure unchanged : had I started pulling down and replacing bits of the fabric, architectonic chaos might have resulted, while stuck on additions would have disfigured it. I have corrected mistakes, clarified points in the light of new information, and have made minor additions : the sum total of these alterations has wrought much greater change than appears on the surface. Still, only in exceptional cases have I made more extensive additions — for instance in the essay on Harwich : material in the Devonshire Papers and the Townshend MSS. in the possession of the Duke of Buccleuch has supplied me with the other side of the story. New wine has not been poured into old bottles but old wine has been allowed to mature.

I beg to express my dutiful thanks for permission to make use of the papers of King George III in the Royal Archives at Windsor Castle.

I further wish to thank the owners and custodians of private collections of manuscripts listed below for generous permission to quote from them.

I am particularly indebted to John Brooke for having read the proofs and made valuable suggestions. For helping me with information on particular points I have to thank Ian Christie, K. L. Ellis, Lady Haden-Guest, Alan Hardy, Brian Hayes, Aubrey Newman, J. B. Owen, and John Tomlinson.

L. B. NAMIER

60 THE GRAMPIANS, LONDON, W.6
14 *Aug.* 1956

v

MANUSCRIPTS QUOTED

BRITISH MUSEUM

Additional Manuscripts :

Musgrave MS (5726)
Fairfax MSS (11325 and 30306)
Calcraft MSS (17493-17496)
Newcastle MSS (32689-33201)
West MSS (34728-34747)
Hardwicke MSS (35349-36278)
Register of Bute Correspondence (36796)
Liverpool MSS (38237-38302)
Samuel Martin MSS (41348-41360)
Egmont MSS (unbound)

Egerton MSS :

Douglas MS (2186)
Cavendish Debates (215-262)

BODLEIAN LIBRARY, OXFORD :

Bowdler MSS (Top. Salop. c. 3)
North MSS

COUNTY RECORD OFFICE, TRURO :

Rashleigh MSS

HUNTINGTON LIBRARY, CALIFORNIA :

George Grenville's Letter Books

NORTHAMPTONSHIRE RECORD OFFICE :

Fitzwilliam (Milton) MSS

PUBLIC RECORD OFFICE :

Chatham Papers

ROYAL INSTITUTION OF CORNWALL :

Hawkins MSS

PRIVATE COLLECTIONS :

The Duke of Bedford's MSS at Woburn
The Lady Berwick's and the National Trust's MSS (Attingham Collection, Thomas Hill's Papers) at the Salop Record Office

The Duke of Buccleuch's MSS (Townshend Papers) at Dalkeith House

The Marquess of Bute's MSS at Mount Stuart

The Duke of Devonshire's MSS at Chatsworth

The Earl Fitzwilliam's and the Wentworth Woodhouse Trustees' MSS (Rockingham MSS) at the Sheffield City Library

The Viscount Gage's MSS at Firle

Mr. Alan Godsal's transcripts of Charles Garth's Letter Books at Haines Hill

The Duke of Grafton's MSS at the West Suffolk Record Office

The Viscount Hinchingbrooke's MSS (Sandwich Papers) at Hinchingbrooke

The Marquess of Lansdowne's MSS (Shelburne Papers) at Bowood

Mr. G. F. Luttrell's MSS at Dunster Castle

The Earl of Malmesbury's MSS (James Harris Papers) at Newnham House

Mr. R. E. Money-Kyrle's MSS (Ernle Papers) at Whetham

Mr. Jasper More's MSS at Linley Hall

Sir John Murray's MSS (Grenville Papers) at 50 Albemarle Street, London W.1

Mr. Humphrey FitzRoy Newdegate's MSS at the Warwickshire Record Office

The Earl of Powis's MSS (Clive Papers) in the India Office Library, and Powis MSS at Powis Castle

The Lord Rayleigh's MSS (Strutt Papers) at Terling Place

The Viscount Ridley's MSS at Blagdon

The Duke of Rutland's MSS at Belvoir Castle

Mr. D. C. D. Ryder's MSS (Calcraft Papers) at Rempstone

The Marquess of Salisbury's MSS (Chase Price Papers) at Hatfield

The Earl Waldegrave's MSS at Chewton House

Mr. John Wyndham's MSS (Egremont Papers) at Petworth

PREFACE TO FIRST EDITION

IN 1912 I started work on 'The Imperial Problem during the American Revolution'; a year later I had to enter business, but as this carried me across to America, where public libraries are open at night and on Sundays, I was not debarred from continuing my studies. I soon found, as so many have found before me, that the constitutional and political formulas of the problem were exceedingly simple, and the contemporary discussions of it very trite — which usually happens where masses act but are supposed to reason. A restatement of the arguments or an analysis of what is called 'public opinion' would not get us much further; for political problems do not, as a rule, deeply affect the lives and consciousness of ordinary men, and little real thought is given them by these men, whose concerns, none the less, supply the basis of the problems and determine the course of their development.

As the conflict of 1775 was more closely connected with everyday life in the American Colonies than in this country, America has by now entered as a community into the picture of the Revolution, while Great Britain remains more or less the figure on our copper coins; the notion of this country in the conflict needs to be humanized. As happens to most students of the American Revolution, I concentrated at first on the history of the Colonies; but when I went to discuss my work with one of the most distinguished American historians, he, though friendly and helpful, asked me a very pertinent question. 'On this side', he said, 'there are ever so many of us doing the work; why do you not contribute something from your own side?' I saw that his remark was just, but took for the moment no further notice of it; still, it stuck in my mind, and a few months later, when reading the letters in which Edward Gibbon, writing in 1775, described how, while destroying the Roman Empire, he 'supported the British' by voting with the Government, I became interested in the House of

Commons which, in so ill-fated a manner, undertook the work of preserving the First British Empire. In the early summer of 1914 I returned to England for a holiday, and imagined that by the autumn I should be able to produce something on the British Parliament during the American Revolution. Being very young and deficient in sense of time, I did not realize that this would have to be the work of many years.

This first attempt had anyhow to be abandoned in August 1914; Army training and subsequently service under and in the Foreign Office took up the years 1914–20. Next I tried to resume my research work as a lecturer and tutor at Balliol, my old College. But excellent as our tutorial system is for the pupils, it leaves no leisure to the teachers, and I had to go once more into business. Looking back at the time in the Army, the Civil Service, and in business, and at the influence those years have had on my historical work, I am able to appreciate Gibbon's dictum that 'the Captain of the Hampshire grenadiers . . . has not been useless to the historian of the Roman Empire'.

By the time I resumed my work, some four years ago, I had decided to make it a study of the British 'political nation' during the American Revolution, and to pursue it by concentrating on that marvellous microcosmos, the British House of Commons. But next I found that, were I to attempt a narrative, however much of general analysis I put into the introductory chapters, lengthy digressions and appendices could not be avoided — too much in eighteenth-century politics requires explaining. Between them and the politics of the present day there is more resemblance in outer forms and denominations than in underlying realities; so that misconception is very easy. There were no proper party organizations about 1760, though party names and cant were current; the names and the cant have since supplied the materials for an imaginary superstructure. A system of non-Euclidean geometry can be built up by taking a curve for basis instead of the straight line, but it is not easy for our minds to think consistently in unwonted terms; Parliamentary politics not based on parties are to us a non-Euclidean system, and similarly require a fundamental readjustment of ideas and, what is more, of mental habits. A general explanation registering the outstanding differences may be understood but cannot be properly assimilated; one has to steep oneself in the political life of a period before one can safely speak, or be sure of understanding, its language.

With that purpose in view I have written this book: it is, in a way, introductory to my main work. In the first chapter on 'Why Men went into Parliament', I take the reader through the House of Commons as constituted about the time of George III's accession, and I try to analyse it from the angle of purpose. Here is an ant-heap, with the human ants hurrying in long files along their various paths; their joint achievement does not concern us, nor the changes which supervene in their community, only the pathetically intent, seemingly self-conscious running of individuals along beaten tracks. In a future book I propose to deal in detail with the four Parliaments of 1761–84, but here I mainly study types, and I deliberately refrain from discussing so-called parties and political groups, their meaning or lack of meaning; the political life of the period could be fully described without ever using a party denomination. Next, in the essay on 'The Electoral Structure of England', I take the reader through the constituencies, and he must not mind the time spent over details — we distinguish trees by considering their general shape and their characteristic details, for instance, the leaf or the bark; while seemingly more prominent features, such as the circumference, the number of branches, etc., can be safely disregarded, as can so many things which lend themselves best to historical narrative. The short essay on 'The General Election of 1761' serves to show the way in which the political transactions of the time are frequently distorted in accounts based on a few 'classical texts'. The fourth and last essay in the first volume of the book, on 'Secret Service Money under the Duke of Newcastle', deals with that ill-famed, subterranean stream of corruption which, when uncovered and measured, proves to have been after all but a small rivulet, not a river, and not nearly as dirty as generally supposed; it was the last resort of political beggars in distress, and of Opposition leaders in search of a topic.

The second volume supplies further illustrations to the chapters on 'The Electoral Structure' and 'Secret Service Money'. First I take Shropshire, one of the most independent counties at that time, with the appearances of party organization — but even there they prove unreal. Next, I take the notorious Cornish boroughs which, in relation to the Government, stood at the opposite pole to Shropshire. Lastly, I analyse Harwich and Orford, two boroughs under the immediate management of the Treasury. I add at the end a few biographical sketches of Members who drew secret service pensions — they show once more the charitable character of that very humane institution, and the utter unimportance of the acquisitions which the Government made through it.

In an appendix I reproduce the secret service accounts of the Duke of Newcastle; the footnotes will enable the reader to gauge the character of these payments.

When thanking those who have enabled me to do my work, I have to start with two men who have helped hundreds of students of history, the late Mr. A. L. Smith, Master of Balliol, and Walter John, fourth Earl of Chichester. It is difficult for me to speak here about Mr. A. L. Smith who was much more than a teacher to us old Balliol men; he was our friend and guardian to whom we turned for help and advice, and who often helped us without our asking or even knowing. But the particular reason why the first place in the work of his pupils is due to him, perhaps the best history teacher of our time, is that he devoted his life to tutorial work, with the result that he, who had the makings of a very great historian, left no written record — barring a few essays and lectures — by which he would be known and remembered. His work has been merged into that of his pupils.

Lord Chichester, whom I have mentioned together with the late Master, in 1886 presented the British Museum with some 500 volumes of the Newcastle Papers, one of the most valuable collections of political manuscripts in existence. But as he has given them to 'whomever they may concern', the gift and the donor are passed over in silence, or rather appear anonymously in footnotes as Add. MSS. 32679-33201. One needs to

have been a pupil of Mr. A. L. Smith to know how much
we owe him, and one needs to have spent a few years on the
Newcastle Papers to know the value of Lord Chichester's
gift.

I am very grateful to the Marquess of Bute, K.T., and the
Earl of Sandwich, for having in the most liberal way given me
access to their important collections of manuscripts. Comparatively few references to their manuscripts appear in this
book; they will be used more extensively in my work on 'The
Imperial Problem during the American Revolution'.

As I mentioned before, I suffer from a very imperfect sense
of time; the work on these two volumes has taken me much
longer than I had expected, and I could hardly have completed
it without some financial assistance. Two years ago the Rhodes
Trustees made me a grant for my researches, for which my
grateful acknowledgment is due to them, and my friend Mr.
J. W. Wheeler-Bennett offered me a loan, which I gladly
accepted; and last year a friend, who desires to remain anonymous, further endowed my work.

However much I am indebted to those mentioned above,
were I to choose one person to whom to dedicate this book
I should have no doubt to whom that was due. Mrs. Edgar
Dugdale has helped me at almost every step; with her I discussed every chapter before it was written, and she patiently
read through the successive drafts down to the proofs, and
advised me in things big and small. There was many a moment
when without the encouragement and help which she gave me,
I should have had to drop the work altogether. How much I
owe her, only her friends can understand.

I have to thank Mr. C. G. Stone for having systematically
gone through my proofs, line by line, and suggested innumerable corrections, enforced at critical moments by the threat
that if I did not make them, he would not allow me to mention
his having read the proofs. Miss M. Beer and Mrs. Denis
Buxton have done for me the laborious work of checking the
quotations and references in this book, a signal act of friendship.
Miss C. Le Marinel has been my secretary, and I owe much to
her devoted, untiring work.

In transcribing manuscripts I have, on the whole, adhered to the original spelling, but I do not reproduce disturbing graphical signs such as 'y^e', 'y^t', '&', etc., or capitals, of which the eighteenth century was very lavish; nor do I adhere to the original punctuation where it interferes with the sense of the letter or document.

I refrain from adding a bibliography. There can be none for the life of a community; I hardly remember having come across any contemporary materials, or any book reproducing such materials, which did not contribute something to my information.

I wish, however, to mention here works which I have used too often to quote in footnotes on separate occasions: G. E. C.'s *Complete Peerage* and *Complete Baronetage* and especially the new edition of the *Peerage*, one of the best works of the kind ever compiled; the various editions of Burke's *Peerage* and *Landed Gentry*; Joseph Foster's *Alumni Oxonienses* and *Members of Parliament, Scotland*; J. and J. A. Venn's *Alumni Cantabrigienses*; W. R. Williams's *Parliamentary History of Wales* and of Herefordshire, Gloucestershire, Oxfordshire, and Worcestershire, Pink's and Beavan's *Parliamentary Representation of Lancashire*, J. C. Wedgwood's *Parliamentary History of Staffordshire*, H. T. Weyman's essays on Shropshire Members in the *Transactions of the Shropshire Archaeological Society*; Haydn's *Book of Dignities*, and Beatson's *Political Register*; and last but not least, the Blue Book of 1878 giving the lists of Members of Parliament.

L. B. NAMIER

15 GLOUCESTER WALK, LONDON, W.8
27 *June* 1928

CONTENTS

B

I

WHY MEN WENT INTO PARLIAMENT

'You will be of the House of Commons as soon as you are of age', wrote Lord Chesterfield to his son, Philip Stanhope, on 5 December 1749; 'and you must first make a figure there if you would make a figure in your country.' Small boys play at kings and soldiers, or at riders, engine-drivers, chauffeurs, and airmen — the material expression of that fancy varies with methods of locomotion. But for several centuries the dream of English youth and manhood of the nation-forming class has remained unchanged; it has been fixed and focused on the House of Commons, a modified, socialized arena for battle, drive, and dominion. 'To be out of Parliament is to be out of the world', wrote Admiral Sir George Rodney to Lord George Germain from the West Indies in 1780, 'and my heart is set upon my being in.'[1] Democracy, by enlarging the circle of the *citoyens actifs*, has carried this ambition into ever wider circles, and now many a small branch secretary of a trade union or local notable thinks of his own future in Chesterfield's terms: 'You must make a figure there if you would make a figure in your country'.

So many candidates and only some six hundred seats for them to fill — and yet not many men with an enduring will to get there fail to enter the House in which a miracle of seats seems to be performed for every generation. In the eighteenth century it did not perhaps require much of a miracle. About 1760 in Great Britain certainly not more than 70,000 men a year attained majority, and the yearly average of new men entering the House of Commons can be put at about fifty. As the educated classes were even percentually less numerous than they are now, and men in holy orders — deemed ineligible

---

[1] HMC, *Stopford-Sackville MSS.*, vol. ii, p. 173. Rodney had sat previously in the House of Commons, 1751–54 and 1759–74.

to the House — formed a far higher proportion among them, it is hardly astonishing to find (*e.g.* on examining the Newcastle Papers, the biggest mass of election correspondence in existence) how very few among those who desired to enter the House of Commons failed to get a chance. But that it was open to all who could reasonably aspire to it had a wonderfully unifying and stimulating influence on the nation.

Men went there 'to make a figure', and no more dreamt of a seat in the House in order to benefit humanity than a child dreams of a birthday cake that others may eat it ; which is perfectly normal and in no way reprehensible. The figure of their day-dreams differed with their rank and profession, with age, temperament, and circumstances ; so much, however, was common to practically all : the seat in the House was not their ultimate goal but a means to ulterior aims.

PREDESTINATION : THE INEVITABLE PARLIAMENT MEN

Those aims were least distinct and pronounced with a type which might be described as the inevitable or predestined Parliament men, for whom membership of the House was a duty whatever were their individual predilections or ambitions. The eldest sons of politically active peers mostly entered the House of Commons as soon as they were of age ; they owed it to their families and to their own future position, 'M.P.' after their names being a kind of Parliamentary courtesy title preparatory to the peerage. At the general election of 1761 twenty-three eldest sons of English peers were returned to Parliament ; [1] the age of twenty-one among them when first elected to the House was twenty-six or below — they had not

[1] The eldest sons of Scottish and Irish peers are omitted from this calculation even if their fathers sat at Westminster by some English title. For in Scotland the eldest sons of Scottish peers were debarred from standing for Parliament ; while among the Irish peers, one must distinguish between the Irish territorial magnates who frequently had some English title but whose sons would more naturally enter the Dublin Parliament, at least to begin with, and the pseudo-Irish peers, Englishmen who were given Irish titles because they were not considered of sufficient rank for a British peerage. These usually themselves sat in the Commons.

missed a single general election after having come of age ; the remaining two were twenty-nine and thirty.[1]

In leading political families — old aristocratic houses or families which can best be described as the aftermath of great men — the predestination of Parliament extended even to younger sons. The House of Commons of 1761 contained — these are examples, not an enumeration — five Townshends (one of them brilliant) and three Cornwallises, five members of the Manners family (one of them illegitimate) and four Cavendishes (one a Cavendish only by marriage and assumed name) ; and three Walpoles and four Yorkes. The Walpoles in Parliament were a mere aftermath by 1761 ; with the Yorkes the schemings of the great man were still at work, which places their group as an aftermath on the border-line. In 1761, besides four sons, Hardwicke had in the House a son-in-law, Sir Gilbert Heathcote, and two nephews of his wife, Charles Cocks and Sir Wyndham Knatchbull. 'It is . . . a good thing for you and *your fraternity*,' he wrote to his eldest son on Knatchbull's return at a by-election in 1760 ; 'for an extensive alliance in the House of Commons is a thing of figure and weight in the countrey.'[2]

Country gentlemen in possession or control of some borough or single seat, which they never put up for sale but occupied in their own persons, formed another species of 'inevitable Parliament men'. It is impossible precisely to state their number, as the type itself cannot be precisely defined ; one can merely say who were not of it, and give examples of those who were. Clearly, younger sons of peers must not be included, nor men with no real tradition behind them, nor knights of the shire whose tenure of seats was of a very different character ; but families such as the Listers of Clitheroe and the Leghs of Newton [3] (Lancs), the Whitmores of Bridgnorth and the Foresters of Wenlock, the Burrards of Lymington and the Barringtons of Newton (Hants), the Drakes of Agmondesham,

[1] To make it perfectly clear : this was their age at first entering the House, not in 1761 if they had sat in it before.

[2] 35352, f. 139.

[3] These are, of course, the Leghs of Lyme, but here in each case I name the constituency and not the estate of the family.

the A'Courts of Heytesbury, etc. etc. Most of these, though by
no means all, sat for burgage-boroughs, and found themselves
in the House because a seat in it happened to form part of
their inheritance; very roughly their number can be put in
1761 at about twenty-five to thirty.

Still, even men who entered the House without design, once
they were in it and on the side of Administration, had to profit
by it in one way or another, almost as if they had gone there
for the purpose (after a month in the Army there is no difference
between conscripts and volunteers). As the exhilarating Parliamentary game between party teams was not played in 1761,
and men do not go into politics for their health, clearly some
other rational aim had to be provided; and if a man after a
certain term in Parliament had nothing to show for it, one was
forced to conclude that he was an insignificant and neglected
person, 'not an object worthy of consideration'. The only
people who were under no such obligation to profit were the
'Tories' or 'country gentlemen' in the reign of George II,
and the Opposition and 'country gentlemen' in the reign of
George III.

HONOUR WITH EASE: THE COUNTRY GENTLEMEN

Two distinct types are included above under 'predestined
Parliament men': members of political families, born to hunt
with certain Parliamentary packs, and country gentlemen with
seats for heirlooms, who had not as a rule their course mapped
out to the same extent. These, sitting as it were in their own
right, could go whichever way they chose, and some of them
adhered in a more or less disinterested manner to 'the main
Corps of the Whigs', others carefully cultivated their own
interests, while many ranked under George II as 'Tories',
and not by social standing alone but also by their bearing in
Parliament linked up with the group known *par excellence* as
'the country gentlemen'.

What was the exact meaning of that designation? After
all, the vast majority of the House of Commons was composed
of men of that class. The emphasis was on the word *country*

— they were the 'Country Party' as contrasted with that of the Court. To these men alone the House was not as a rule a means to ulterior aims, though it was not their ultimate goal either. They would not have accepted a seat in it at random, merely to be seated. What mattered to them was not so much membership of the House, as the primacy in their own 'country' attested by their being chosen to represent their county or some respectable borough. The Commons were the *communitas communitatum*, originally a quasi-federation of shires and boroughs ; the knights of the shire in the eighteenth century were the consuls of the county republics. This primacy in most cases rested on a tradition, and therefore the seats were in that sense hereditary. Still, any substantial country gentleman who had gained the respect of his neighbours had a chance, while over-emphasis of a hereditary claim was liable to injure a candidate, for he would lay himself open to the accusation of disrespect to his neighbours in treating the county as if it were a pocket borough. Similarly in Parliament county Members had to avoid all appearance that anything counted with them for more than the approval of their constituents.

This type has therefore to be distinguished even from the most independent representatives of hereditary boroughs. It was in men of this type that Pitt found his 'constituency' in the House, and to them he used to pay the greatest attention. 'Mr. Pitt', complained Newcastle to Hardwicke on 15 March 1760, 'by his situation and consequence is at the head of the House of Commons, of which the Tories scarce make a sixth part ; and all *extrajudicial* business is to be agreed and concerted with them, without any notice taken of our friends, who compose the majority of the House of Commons'.[1] A list of the country gentlemen in the eighteenth-century Parliament reads like a register of 'county families'. To give just a few examples taken at random — to that type belonged: the Courtenays, Bamfyldes, and Rolles of Devonshire ; the Cholmondeleys and Egertons of Cheshire ; the Ishams, Knightleys, and Cartwrights of Northamptonshire ; a Lambton or Tempest

[1] 32903, f. 297.

from Durham, or a Sir Walter Blackett from Newcastle-upon-Tyne; also Sir George Savile, of Yorkshire, though in mind and outlook he was far superior to the average of his class and type.

For the distinguishing characteristics of the country gentlemen were as a rule neither political acumen and experience nor Parliamentary eloquence, but an independent character and station in life, and indifference to office. Most of them were accounted Tories under George II, only to find themselves once more in opposition under George III as his reign gradually convinced them that by whatever names courts and administrations go, their essence remains the same. Henry Penruddocke Wyndham, himself a country gentleman, in his introduction to Bubb Dodington's *Diary*, in 1784, addressed to them a few words of warning and spoke of that 'restless aversion to all government, so prevalent amongst them, and against which, the best Minister is no more secure than the worst'. Predominance of their type in the House before discipline was established through party organizations and party electorates would not have proved conducive to the formation of a strong and stable Government. Fortunately their number, though sufficient to supply an independent leaven to the House and a respectable lead in important divisions, was not such as could have disturbed its everyday work. About 1760 their number was something like sixty to eighty, most of them representing counties or considerable boroughs.

Moreover, their attendance on political business was naturally much less regular than that of office-holders and of interested, professional politicians. On 8 September 1741, Chesterfield, writing to Bubb Dodington, pointed out how necessary and how impossible it was to get the Opposition to meet before Parliament assembled: 'I have been these seven years endeavouring to bring it about, and have not been able; fox-hunting, gardening, planting, or indifference having always kept our people in the country, till the very day before the meeting of the Parliament'. Five years later Sir Edward Turner, M.P., wrote about country gentlemen (in a bantering letter to a friend): 'Persons of that denomination seem to have forgot public affairs. Few of their representatives have appeared at the House this session.'[1] Nor did Newcastle when in opposition find it any easier to secure their regular attendance.[2] Critical but 'of little efficiency in public business', these men were no real politicians. As, however, they seldom suffered from ebullitions of wit or spasms of originality, once party organizations had arisen, they were easily absorbed, forming a body both respectable and reliable, in Houses anyhow superior in moral tone to those of a naïvely corrupt and very amusing age.

THE TREASURY BENCH: THE POLITICIANS

Dreams of office and power as motives of action — the Treasury Bench and the 'Marshal's stick' — what is there to be said about them? These dreams are almost universal and usually unavowed; who has not dreamt them? And what a long time it takes before such dreams leave men's fancy! This is matter for biography such as is never written, but hardly for a history of the House of Commons; for these dreams do not change into demands until near realization, which is of course of rare occurrence.

Still, even in eighteenth-century England dreams of attaining the highest positions in the State could be entertained by any member of what may be described as the political nation. A wide class of active citizens was raised above the masses; and though this high plateau had not the even outline of the Athenian political community, it was not overtowered by inaccessible peaks. Undoubtedly a courtesy lord had a marked advantage in obtaining a seat and office, but the difference in the start was not such that others could not overcome it by superior ability and merit. In fact, personality, eloquence, debating power, prestige, counted for more in the eighteenth-century House of Commons (which at all times contained a number of Members whose votes could be turned by the

[1] 6 Dec 1746. See *An Eighteenth-Century Correspondence* (1910), ed. L. Dickins and M. Stanton, p. 124.
[2] See below, pp. 296-7.

debate) than it does now, unless the whips are taken off — an exceedingly rare event. General elections, however big the apparent majorities they yielded, did not settle the event of the sessions — witness Newcastle's worries in September 1754 when he had no first-class leader to put at the head of his enormous majority ; and Lady Yarmouth, voicing the opinion of the Court, told him then that '*they* all' applauded his conduct 'in the choice of Parliament, but that somebody must take the lead in the House of Commons'.[1] A year later, having received little or no support from Pitt, Fox, or Legge, Newcastle wrote to Holdernesse who was with the King at Hanover :

His Majesty has certainly as great a majority in the present House of Commons as ever was known. But the misfortune is that persons in the first stations there, in His Majesty's service, have not supported the King's measures in the manner they ought to have done ; and, if they were to be remov'd, none could be found, whose talents and Parliamentary abilities would enable them to carry on the King's business with ease and success against such an opposition.[2]

'Talents and Parliamentary abilities' were required to conduct the business in the House itself — generalship in the field, not gifts of calculation far behind the front. Newcastle's surrender to Pitt shows what chances the eighteenth-century Parliament offered to personality.

When in January 1766 the Rockingham Administration was tottering, a meeting was held of the 'King's friends', 'of gentlemen who could discourse in confidence with each other on the present state of affairs'. In reviewing the state of parties, they thus described their own group and position :

Those who have always hitherto acted upon the sole principle of attachment to the Crown. This is probably the most numerous body and would on trial be found sufficient to carry on the publick business themselves if there was any person to accept of a ministerial office at the head of them, and this is all they want. This defect, however, makes it necessary that they should be joined if it be possible to some one of the other parties.[3]

---

[1] Newcastle to William Murray, 28 Sept 1754 ; 32736, ff. 591-4.
[2] 11 July 1755 ; 32857, ff. 37-9.
[3] See N. S. Jucker, *The Jenkinson Papers, 1760–1766* (1949), pp. 404-8.

Thus the position of 1754–55 was reproduced in 1766 — the influence of the Crown could secure and command numbers but not leaders. George III had to surrender to Pitt, as his grandfather and Newcastle had done before him.

Yet Newcastle and Pitt (and Burke) are quoted by historians to prove the close oligarchic character of the eighteenth-century Parliament; and so widely accepted is this legend that it cannot be here ignored.

Newcastle's rise to a post to which he was not equal, is ascribed to his vast borough influence, and the fact is overlooked that only a very small part of it was truly his own, while most was derived from his official position under the Crown. Indeed, at the close of his life, after he had sacrificed a large part of his fortune to electioneering, and had for more than forty years used the resources of the Crown to strengthen and extend his own Parliamentary interest, the total number of seats to which he could nominate was about twelve : the Yorkshire boroughs of Aldborough and Boroughbridge alone, Newcastle could describe as 'my own two boroughs'; [1] in each constituency in Nottinghamshire — the county, Nottingham, Newark, and Retford — he could by compromise and arrangement with other people nominate one Member; and similarly in Sussex and the boroughs of Lewes, Seaford, and Rye. [2] Newcastle was a skilful, untiring election manager, prepared to devote his time and sacrifice his ease to work of a most unpleasant character, and to contribute to its expense from his own purse. If his rank and wealth distinguished him among borough-

---

[1] See, e.g., his paper on elections, 19 Dec 1767 ; 32987, ff. 341-2.

[2] This must be treated as merely approximate, but if anything it rather overstates than underestimates Newcastle's command of seats in 1768. Having quarrelled with his nephews, Lord Lincoln and John Shelley, Newcastle in 1768 had to agree to give up Newark, where in 1760 he had transferred his estate to Lincoln, while at Lewes he lost the candidate who could more particularly be described as his own. Had the local manager at Rye, Thomas Lamb, gone the way of Edward Milward at Hastings, Newcastle would have lost Rye also ; and had the Duke of Grafton exerted himself, as Fox or Grenville would have done in his place, Newcastle might possibly have lost even Seaford. On the other hand, he had a certain contributory influence in other Sussex boroughs and some boroughs in the counties adjoining Notts and Sussex, though it nowhere amounted to a 'command'.

mongers, his disinterested, single-minded devotion to tedious
and even dirty business no less distinguished him among
ministers and dukes. It was this (not ducal grandeur as such)
which condemned him to his position.

About Pitt it is often alleged that he was handicapped by
lack of electoral influence ; but, in truth, he did not care to
cultivate it ; and without assiduous application no one could
rise to importance in that species of politics. Had Pitt known
how to work with other men, the materials for an extensive
electoral interest were not lacking even in his own family. His
elder brother, Thomas, commanded three or four seats ; two
at Old Sarum, one at Okehampton, and, together with Hawkins,
one at Grampound ; his cousins, the Pitts of Strathfieldsaye,
usually held two seats in Dorset ; his relatives by marriage, the
Grenvilles and Lytteltons, had several in Buckinghamshire and
Worcestershire. And when Pitt became the idol of the nation,
even strangers offered to accept his nomination to their
boroughs. It was Pitt's intractability and his way of offending
men, including George II, not his being short of Old Sarum,
which hampered his career. In fact, borough influence alone
counted for less in attaining ministerial office than is usually
supposed. Edward Eliot, of Port Eliot, who commanded first
four and subsequently six seats in Cornwall, was eleven years
in Parliament before, by dint of continuous and insistent
solicitation, he managed to obtain from Newcastle a seat at the
lowest Board, that of Trade.

Burke is often quoted to prove that high office, in his time,
was reserved to the well-born. But his party was nearly always
in opposition ; and the office he was given in 1782, of Paymaster
of the Forces, was far from being a small one in the eighteenth
century — Henry Fox had held it at the close of a long and
not unsuccessful career. But if Burke was in a way looked
down upon by his associates, this was due not so much to the
contempt which the nobly born felt for his origin as to the
admiration which he had for theirs : clearly no one can treat
as an equal a man so full of respect and veneration.

That in the eighteenth century a rise from a comparatively
humble position was not impossible for a man even of merely

good average abilities, who was prudent in the choice of party and assiduous in application, is seen by many examples; perhaps best of all in the case of Charles Jenkinson who began his career in no higher position than Burke, and in 1761 thought himself very happy when made a 'commis' (Under-Secretary) by Bute; but he gradually rose to Ministerial rank, and died as first Earl of Liverpool. During a debate in the House of Commons on 12 February 1770, 'Tommy' Townshend, a Rockingham Whig, remarked to him that his pompous manner did not become 'a gentleman risen from the situation he has done'. Jenkinson replied: 'My rise is from as old a family as his own. I have risen by industry, by attention to duty, and by every honourable means I could devise.' Whereupon Sir Walter Blackett, an old Tory, interposed: 'Every man carries his honour in his own hand. Origin is nothing; it shall never have any weight with me.' [1]

This was neither a doctrine nor an empty phrase; it expressed a natural and unavoidable concomitant of English gregarious existence. A House, just as a team, has a joint personality superior to that of the individuals who compose it; and while its purpose dominates them, there can be little regarding of men; neither in the scrum nor in argument can his lordship's pedigree add to his weight. The principle established in France by the Great Revolution — 'a fair field to ability' — was realized, without reasoning, in the eighteenth-century British Parliament; and there was no place where men of minor rank and means could exert their abilities more freely and to better advantage than in the House of Commons. 'The most august of assemblies' was also the fairest of tribunals — which was a cogent reason for men with a good conceit of themselves to wish to bring their case before it; hence the number of those who dreamt of a seat in the House of Commons.

CORONETS : THE SOCIAL CLIMBERS

Social advancement, more easily realized than political ambitions, was, and remains to those who need and desire it,

[1] Sir H. Cavendish, *Debates of the House of Commons*, vol. i, p. 448.

an obvious incentive for entering Parliament. Membership of
the governing body necessarily distinguishes the man, certainly
in his own circle, and opens doors which would otherwise
remain shut against him — 'it occasions for him a more
enlarged sphere to move in'. With what pride did old 'Rio'
Gulston, a mid-eighteenth-century Brazil merchant, refer to
his nephew, Joseph Gulston, M.P., as 'the Member'! And
even the prim, old-spinsterly governess assured Joseph Gulston's
daughter that her father 'was very rich, a Member of Parliament,
and though he was a merchant, a man of great consequence'.[1]
Indeed, the House of Commons has at all times been one of
the great uplifting influences in English social life.[2]

In the eighteenth century the House of Commons was, as
it is now, a convenient stepping-stone to the House of Lords
— though each successive generation thinks that there must
have been once a golden age of the Upper House, when there
were no beginners and all its members were truly patrician
(like the lady who, having seen a new play, remarked that it
was not bad but not good enough for a first night). Then, as
now, peerages were given to tired statesmen and ex-Premiers,
to Lord Chancellors and Chief Justices, to generals and admirals; owners of Parliamentary boroughs (Lords Falmouth,
Edgcumbe, Eliot, etc.) filled the place held in the Lloyd George
era by owners of the popular press; and scores of Members
faithfully served the Government in Parliament and in the
constituencies in hope of a peerage, and solicited it with
importunity, Irish peerages and baronetcies serving as consolation prizes in these climbing competitions.

[1] See John Nichols, *Illustrations of the Literary History of the Eighteenth
Century*, vol. v, pp. 1-60, 'The Gulston Family'.

[2] Still, a rarefied atmosphere tests a man's endurance, and a stout heart
is required for the period of acclimatization. Here is the story of a failure
described by Elizabeth, daughter of Benjamin Heath, town clerk of Exeter,
in a letter to her brother John, on 22 Mar. 1768: 'Mr. Spicer, who was
chose . . . for the remainder of the last session [at Exeter, on 19 Dec. 1767],
declined standing for the General Election after having taken his seat in the
House where, I suppose, he soon found that his consequence was not so
great there as he expected, that his money which was his only qualification
had not weight enough to command respect from the other members, but
that they rather looked down upon him, so that he was not desirous of
purchasing a station for a longer time which he did not find himself fitted
for' (Sir W. R. Drake, *Heathiana* (1882), p. 15).

In 1755 Lord Chetwynd, M.P. (an Irish peer), when asking the King for a British peerage, wrote, after having mentioned his services in 1745 :

The same zeal, Sir, hath been exerted ever since at a constant and considerable expence in supporting the Government interest throughout the county [of Stafford] in opposition to a disafected party and in procureing the return of two of my familly to sit in the present Parliament, and this, without solliciting Your Majesty's Ministers for any employment or other consideration ; it having been my sole ambition to serve Your Majesty in a manner to deserve the honour I now aspire to.[1]

Similarly Sir John Rushout, M.P., wrote to Newcastle on 24 January 1756 :

I have never troubled your Grace for any great, much less, for any lucrative employment . . . for my fortune is sufficient for me, in any station of life, but my whole ambition centers in the hopes of a peerage for my family.[2]

And Thomas Holmes, M.P., though he had a yearly allowance for managing the three boroughs in the Isle of Wight, thus argued (successfully) his case for at least an Irish peerage :

Were I to communicate to your Grace the estates I have in England, Ireland, and Wales, besides money in the stocks and other securitys, you would see my fortune is equal to those honors ; the anual thing I asked as I have no employment was only to repay me the money I am out of pocket in the several services we support, I never meant it should tie me down from receiving some honorable mark of distinction for having brought a factious part of the country over to His Majesty's interest ; every one knows I have a greater weight in the Island of Wight then any Governor or any other person ever had ; my gratitude for the favours my brothers [3] have received from you and your family will oblige me to secure the borroughs for your interest, but shall not chuse to concern my self in any other affairs unless what I have requested is granted, for I think the person that is first in interest and fortune ought not to be the lowest in rank and quality.[4]

---

[1] 32854, f. 152.   [2] 32862, ff. 218-19.
[3] General Henry Holmes, M.P. for Yarmouth (Isle of Wight), and Admiral Charles Holmes, M.P. for Newport (I.o.W.).
[4] 32906, f. 241.

In fact, peerages were an essential commodity for satisfying claims from the House of Commons ; so much so that when in 1760, on the eve of the general election, George II showed himself obdurately German in his 'blue blood' prejudices, Newcastle told him that 'if His Majesty expected that I should be employed in choosing a new Parliament, I could not do it if I had not power to oblige the first gentlemen in the countries'.[1] It was easier to create peers than to find money for places and pensions. When in 1755 Newcastle did not know what to do with Legge, he considered making him a peer, and wrote to Holdernesse : 'something *must be done* for him ; and how can we get off so cheap any other way ?'[2]

By 1784 the House of Commons was universally regarded as the high road to the House of Lords. The announcement at the end of the *Fox's Martyrs* of 1784,[3] and here reproduced on the next page, expresses that view. And when in 1790 Sir Gerard Vanneck, a leading London merchant and M.P. for Dunwich 1768–90, offered himself as candidate for the county of Suffolk, an election squib gauged his ambitions and future :

> For twenty long years I have been independent,
> In the Senate a silent and constant attendant,
> If to me for such service your votes you accord,
> I shall first be your Member, and then be a Lord.[4]

[*cont. on p.* 16

[1] The Duke of Newcastle to Hardwicke, 4 Mar 1760 ; 32903, f. 81. Merchant M.P.'s had as yet to be content with baronetcies, *e.g.* James Colebrooke, Ellis Cunliffe, Samuel Fludyer, and John Major ; and some decades later with Irish peerages, *e.g.* William Mayne (Lord Newhaven), Joshua Vanneck (Lord Huntingfield), John Henniker (Lord Henniker), etc. Smith-Carrington was the first man actually engaged in trade whom George III, with much repugnance, was persuaded to make a British peer. Although George III gloried 'in the name of Britain', he still clung to certain German court prejudices.

[2] 32857, f. 362.

[3] A satire commemorating the followers of Charles James Fox who lost their seats in the general election of 1784.

[4] K. F. Doughty, *The Betts of Wortham in Suffolk, 1480–1905* (1912), p. 249.

In the Prefs and fpeedily will be publifhed,

HUMBLY INSCRIBED TO

THOMAS WILLIAM, fometime EARL OF DOVER,[1]

And now CANDIDATE for the firft Vacancy at the Borough
of KING'S LYNN,

A

COMPANION

TO THE

EXTINCT PEERAGE OF ENGLAND.

CONTAINING

THE MELANCHOLY HISTORY OF THE MANY

DUKES, MARQUISSES, EARLS, VISCOUNTS, AND BARONS,

Who were cruelly ftifled in their Birth

During the late BLOODY PERSECUTIONS.

———————

Quos dulcis vitæ exfortes, et ab ubere raptos
Abftulit atra dies, et funere merfit acerbo !

VIRG.

Snatched from the Sweets of Life's forthcoming Day,
Behold them caft to gloomy Death a Prey ! ! !

---

[1] Undoubtedly meant for Thomas William Coke, of Holkham, who lost
his seat for Norfolk ; he duly finished as a peer.

C

'PRIVATE AND PECUNIARY': PLACEMEN AND PURVEYORS OF FAVOURS [1]

Governor Pitt wrote to his son Robert, the father of Chatham, from Fort St. George on 16 January 1705/6:

If you are in Parliament, show yourself on all occasions a good Englishman, and a faithful servant to your country. If you aspire to fame in the House, you must make yourself master of its precedents and orders. Avoid faction, and never enter the House pre-possessed; but attend diligently to the debate, and vote according to your conscience and not for any sinister end whatever. I had rather see any child of mine want than have him get his bread by voting in the House of Commons.[2]

This was written after a century of Parliamentary contests over causes which had moved the conscience of men and for which they had died on the scaffold and the field of battle. Fifty years later the nation was at one in all fundamental matters, and whenever that happy but uninspiring condition is reached, Parliamentary contests lose reality and unavoidably change into a fierce though bloodless struggle for office. In a House dominated by party organizations such struggles assume the decorous forms of wholesale transactions glorified by the mutual loyalties and the common joys or sorrows of the contending teams. In the eighteenth century the transactions were carried through individually or by small groups, and were therefore as sordid as solitary drinking. Three sets of circumstances tended to aggravate their extent and character. In the first place, the idea that the politically active part of the nation had a claim to maintenance on the State was generally accepted, even if it remained subconscious; [3] secondly, appointments in the Civil Service and even in the fighting services were made at pleasure and not under competitive regulations, and

---

[1] Andrew Mitchell, M.P., Minister to the Court of Prussia, in 1756 marked a letter to Newcastle: 'Private and Pecuniary' (32865, f. 227). The best part of the correspondence addressed to the Duke by Members of Parliament deserves this heading.

[2] See HMC, *Fortescue MSS.*, vol. i, p. 18.

[3] See below, pp. 224-5.

were therefore exposed to Parliamentary influence and patronage, to nepotism [1] and favouritism ; thirdly, a majority of seats
in the House had a quasi-proprietary character — they were a
valuable inheritance or a costly acquisition from which proper
returns were expected. At all times a system of spoils and
benefits necessarily obtains in governing representative bodies
where sharp contrasts of ideas and interests or strong party
organizations do not predetermine the vote of the individual
Member, and do not reduce him to a pawn in the Parliamentary
game. If personal disinterestedness is expected from independent Members, they have at least to secure benefits and advantages for their constituents ; and where the constituents are too
numerous to be benefited individually, it becomes a question
of a commercial treaty, a tariff or bounty favouring some local
industry, of public works in the district, etc. But a system of
Parliamentary spoils, when established, tends to grow worse,
especially if it affects every stratum of the political pyramid,
from the First Minister down to the most insignificant voters.
To destroy it a true political interest is required of sufficient
moment to produce mass movements, to divert the energies and
attention of men to a real political purpose, and seriously to
divide a nation shaken by passions or distress. For Parliament
is not like the ghost in Dickens's *Christmas Carol* which appears
with a crown of flames round his head and a big extinguisher
under his arm; the flames of political passion no longer illumin-
ate the scene when they can be extinguished at pleasure.

With Governor Pitt's exhortation to his son compare the
speech which, half a century later, Edward Gibbon, the historian, put into the mouth of his father, to whom he wrote
some time in 1760 :

When I first returned to England . . . you were so good as to
give me hopes of a seat in Parliament. This seat, according to the

---

[1] A letter from Lord Sandwich to Lieut. Forth, 14 Aug 1764, illustrates
the eighteenth-century view of nepotism in official appointments : '. . . as
to Sir William Burnaby's making his son a Captain, it was very natural for
him to do it ; if he is under age, it rests with the Admiralty board to confirm
him or not, as they think proper ; but I am satisfied in my opinion that no
one has a right to complain that he has given his son the preference over
every recommendation' (Sandwich MSS. at Hinchingbrooke, *Private
Letters*, vol. i, p. 165).

custom of our venal country, was to be bought, and fifteen hundred pounds were mentioned as the price of the purchase. This design flattered my vanity, as it might enable me to shine in so august an assembly. It flattered a nobler passion; I promised myself that by the means of this seat I might be one day the instrument of some good to my country.

Still, he soon perceived that he was not suited to a Parliamentary career, and it was not false modesty, 'the meanest species of pride', which made him think so.

But I hear you say It is not necessary that every man should enter into Parliament with such exalted hopes. It is to acquire a title the most glorious of any in a free country, and to employ the weight and consideration it gives in the service of one's friends. Such motifs, tho' not glorious, yet are not dishonourable; and if we had a borough in our command, if you could bring me in without any great expence, or if our fortune enabled us to dispise that expence, then indeed I should think them of the greatest strength.[1]

As their fortune was not great, he asked that his allowance should much rather be increased to enable him to undertake a journey to Italy.

In 1706 it was 'faithful service to your country'; in 1760 'service of one's friends'. The community had become atomized and individualized, and when another half-century had passed and the idea was proclaimed that the greatest common good is to be reached by every man pursuing his own individual advantage, this was not so much a eulogy of egotism as an apologia for an existing practice. In the eighteenth century that practice had required no justification; now an excuse was provided which in time was bound to change into an acid test. However important the part which economic considerations and theories played in the rise of that doctrine, the moral implications explain why this apparent glorifying of self-interest came largely from the most public-spirited, thoughtful, and moral set of men, the Evangelicals and Dissenters.

---

[1] *Private Letters of Edward Gibbon (1753–94)*, ed. R. E. Prothero (1896), vol. i, pp. 23-4. When fourteen years later Gibbon entered Parliament, he found it 'a very agreeable coffee-house' (*ibid.* p. 248), 'an agreeable improvement in my life . . . just the mixture of business, of study, and of society, which I always imagined I should, and now find I do like' (*ibid.* p. 253).

In eighteenth-century France the Chevalier des Grieux, whenever he found himself without private means or provision from State or Church, could think of nothing better than card-sharping, or else his lady-love, Manon Lescaut, had to sell herself to the highest bidder. In Great Britain the range of employment for gentlefolk was much more extensive. Gentlemen went into trade, to the Colonies, to India, etc. Still, the choice and possibilities were not what they were a hundred years later, and even in regard to non-official appointments political 'interest' was serviceable — an Administration in which everything was done by favour had considerable influence even in business circles. But the most natural thing for 'a pretty young man' of gentle birth and small means was to look for provision directly to the State. If the family was sufficiently great or had borough influence, he would be returned to Parliament and, on the strength of his seat in the House, would seek and obtain some place under the Government — *quelque chose de par le roi* as it was called in pre-Revolutionary France. If his connexions or means were not sufficient for him to start in 'his own bottom', he surely knew someone in Parliament ready to employ his 'weight and consideration . . . in the service of his friends'.

Daniel Finch, second Earl of Nottingham and seventh Earl of Winchilsea, had by his second wife, Anne, daughter of Christopher, first Viscount Hatton, thirty children (the burden on the State was not, however, quite as heavy as on the mother — seven were still-born and ten died young). The fourth son, Henry Finch, educated at Christ's College, Cambridge, became a Fellow of the College, but after ten years at the University, having met with disappointment, had to look out for some other settlement in life. His father seems to have taxed him with idleness, but his eldest brother, Lord Finch, in a letter of 11 February 1723/4, strongly pleaded his case :

I do desire he may be in the way of fortune in some manner or other, for I cannot agree that because he has no profession he therefore will never be able to live. Lett him be tryed as others have been before him and if he fails he cannot be worse than in the way he is.[1]

---

[1] P. Finch, *History of Burley-on-the-Hill*, vol. i, p. 266.

From a previous letter it appears that the question was de-
bated in the family whether Henry should be sent abroad to
'learn languages' and 'rub off the accademical improvements
and habits which in the course of ten years he must have made
and contracted', or whether 'a provision out of Parliament'
would be 'most agreeable to his circumstances'. Ultimately
both expedients were adopted : he was sent for some time to
The Hague, and on a vacancy occurring in May 1724 at
Malton, a pocket borough of his brother-in-law, Thomas
Watson-Wentworth, Henry Finch was chosen for it ; he retained the seat till his death in May 1761. In 1729 he was
made Receiver-General of the Revenues of Minorca ; in 1743
Surveyor-General of His Majesty's Works (£1000 p.a.), and
when in December 1760 'the sudden and positive order' was
given for replacing Henry Finch by Thomas Worsley, a friend
of George III and Bute, due regard was paid to him and to
his nephew and patron, Lord Rockingham [1] — he was given a
secret service pension of £900 p.a.[2] He had, indeed, achieved
' a provision out of Parliament'.

Examples of this kind will be found in almost every essay in
this book. On the higher and more profitable posts or sinecures
in the Civil Service, if compatible with a seat in Parliament, its
Members had a first lien. Newcastle's remark about the office
of Keeper of the Records in the Tower is characteristic : 'All
the earth could not make the King give this place out of the
House of Commons'.[3] There were no party funds from which
to cover election expenses, and secret service money did not
go far in this matter. Offices and sinecures (or contracts in the
case of merchants) were therefore used to compensate faithful
adherents of Government for their electoral expenses and to
reward their services. Thus in 1756 John Frederick, M.P.
for West Looe, when applying to Newcastle for office, pleaded

---

[1] See in the 'Register of Correspondence of the Earl of Bute', 36796,
f. 62, the summary of a letter from Count de Viry to Lord Bute, 23 Dec
1760 : 'Lord Rockingham will resign on his arrival if Mr. H. Finch is not
employed. Recommends a hint to this effect being thrown out to Newcastle
or Hardwicke.'

[2] See below, pp. 217 and 472. As the land tax, normally reckoned at
2s. in the £, was not levied on secret service pensions, £900 was equivalent
to the previous £1000.   [3] See below, p. 250.

'seventeen years implicit obedience to His Majesty's service attended with great expence and attachment to you and your family in every instance'.[1] Similarly Hardwicke, when urging the claim to office of Charles Cocks, M.P. for Reigate, his wife's nephew, wrote on 14 November 1757 : 'He has now been in Parliament ten or eleven years, and allways behav'd there very diligently and very steadily, notwithstanding temptations to the contrary'.[2] And when Philip Stanhope was returned to Parliament on 17 April 1754, Chesterfield, writing to Newcastle on 29 April, plumed himself on his moderation in not asking anything for him : 'I am not fashionable enough to ask for a place for him to-morrow because he came into Parliament yesterday, but should he deserve your Grace's favour I am sure you will show it him at a proper time'.[3]

Lastly, Commissionerships of Customs and Excise, worth £1000 p.a., offered a suitable retreat for Members who for some reason or other had, or wished, to leave Parliament [4] — for men broken in health or disappointed in their bolder hopes and ambitions. Chief Justice Willes, finding that the health of his eldest son 'will not permit him to attend the House of Commons as he ought', asked that he be made Commissioner of Customs.[5] No seat being available for John Frederick in 1761, he was given one of those Commissionerships.[6] When early in 1765 Henry Grenville, M.P. for Thirsk, returned from his Embassy to Constantinople, he too was given a Commissionership of Customs, 'which, as it would oblige him to vacate his seat in Parliament, would exempt him from involving himself in the unhappy differences in his own family'.[7] In short, from a seat in Parliament one could move to the easy-chair of some place or sinecure, snug and genteel, 'and not unworthy any gentleman's acceptance though incompatible with a seat in Parliament'.

---

[1] 31 Mar 1756 ; 32864, f. 113.   [2] 32875, f. 501.   [3] 32735, f. 207.
[4] See W. R. Ward, 'Some Eighteenth Century Civil Servants : The English Revenue Commissioners, 1754–98', *English Historical Review*, Jan 1955.
[5] Willes to Newcastle, 23 Mar 1758 ; 32878, f. 316.
[6] See below, pp. 326-8.
[7] George Grenville's Diary, *Grenville Papers*, vol. iii, p. 117.

There were, however, Members — and a fair number of them — 'in such a way in the world as to have little or no occasion to trouble' Ministers 'with demands'.[1]   But they had relatives, friends, or constituents, whose claims they had to urge. Here is a letter to Newcastle, dated 19 July 1765, from one of the most upright and independent Whigs, James Hewitt, M.P. for Coventry 1761–66 (and subsequently Justice of the King's Bench and Lord Chancellor of Ireland) :

> Serjeant Hewitt who has nothing to ask of Government for himself and who had never received any beneficial mark of public favour, begs leave to recommend his brother, Mr. William Hewitt, for something at home or abroad which may carry some publick mark of respect to the serjeant and therein do him credit. . . .[2]

Here, again, is the description given in Bute's list of the House of Commons of 1761, of Thomas Sergison, M.P. for Lewes, a small man who, after having unsuccessfully contested the seat as an Opposition candidate in 1734 and 1741, took Newcastle's 'livery' in 1747, and represented the borough till his death in 1766 : [3]

> Has two brothers, one in the Navy receiving pay but not serving, the other quartered upon Mr. Shelley, Auditor for South Wales, half the salary, and likewise two sons in law, one of them, Charles Langford, had a private pension till lately, the other is Mr. Tomlinson, Member for Steyning.[4]

There had been no need for Newcastle to buy the vote of Sergison who depended on the Duke for his seat. But it would

---

[1] This phrase is used about himself by James Duff (subsequently second Lord Fife) in a letter to Newcastle, 6 Nov 1754 ; 32737, ff. 292-3.

[2] 32972, f. 300.

[3] Thomas Sergison was the son of Thomas Warden of Cuckfield, Sussex, by Prudence, niece of Charles Sergison, M.P., Commissioner of the Navy ; on succeeding to his estate, Thomas Warden, jun., took the name of Sergison. About Charles Sergison see *D.N.B.* ; about Thomas Sergison and his family, *Transactions of the Sussex Archaeological Society*, vol. xiv, p. 266, and vol. xxv, p. 84.

[4] 38333, f. 100. The list was drawn up about 15 Dec 1761, but this marginal remark was obviously added some time after Newcastle's resignation, for Langford continued in receipt of the secret service pension so long as Newcastle was in office. The list seems to have remained with Charles Jenkinson, and was used till Nov 1763.

have been contrary to the decencies of eighteenth-century politics if the Duke had failed to exercise his power and patronage in favour of the relatives of a faithful follower. As a matter of fact, Sergison remained with Newcastle even when that came to entail the loss of Court favour.

To what an extent providing for the families of Members out of the 'King's money' had become the custom is seen in a letter addressed to Newcastle by Edward Bayntun Rolt, M.P. for Chippenham, to whose election both in 1747 and 1754 the Treasury had contributed £800, and who expected another such contribution in 1761 ; who, in short, was not sufficiently independent to bargain for favours. Still, having a sister who had remained a widow without suitable provision, he asked Newcastle to give her a pension of £300 p.a. ; and when the matter was delayed, as was Newcastle's habit, Bayntun Rolt wrote on 13 August 1760 :

> I have too many obligations to your Grace to presume to take offence ; yet allow me to complain and remind you, that my poor sister Prideaux has continued above a year, in the most miserable situation. As your Grace's sincere friend and humble politician, I have a sort of right to press this matter upon you and flatter myself you will excuse me.[1]

Indeed, so universal was the plaguing of Ministers on behalf of friends and relations that in 1760 a tender mother who wished to see her son in Parliament thought it useful to point out to Newcastle that her son would have no such requests to make :

> Mrs. Boothby Skrymsher's compliments attend upon the Duke of Newcastle.
> She understands the Duke of Rutland has done her son, Mr. Charles Boothby Skrymsher, of Tooly Park in the county of Leicester, the honor to mention him to his Grace as a person desirous at his own expence
> to come into the next parliment under the guidance and protection of the Duke of Newcastle.
> Mr. Boothby Skrymsher is of age and returns from his travells

---

[1] 32910, f. 11. It should, however, be added that Elizabeth Prideaux was the widow of a brigadier-general killed at Niagara on 19 July 1759 (see Maclean, *History of the Deanery of Trigg Minor* (1876), vol. ii, p. 232).

next autumn, by principals and education is zealously attached to
His Majesty's Person and Administration, as is well known to the
Duke of Rutland and Lord Granby.

Mrs. Boothby Skrymsher can with strict truth assure the Duke
of Newcastle that her son has no relations to sollicit favors for, or
any veiws, further than an opinion that parlimentary busness is a
proper employment for the mind of a young man at his first enter-
ance into life.

His Grace, the Duke of Newcastle may depend upon his integrity,
and that he will obey his commands, and with true gratitude,
acknowledge the great obligation confered upon him who will
certainly prove a faithful humble servant to his Grace.[1]

PROFESSIONAL ADVANCEMENT: THE SERVICES AND THE LAW

The Soldiers

On 3 February 1741 Chesterfield, speaking in the House
of Lords against a proposed increase of the Army, descanted
on the dangers that would arise from the larger number of
commissions which — as was said in the protest subsequently

[1] 32902, f. 141; the letter is undated but seems to have been written
in Feb 1760.

Charles Boothby Skrymsher failed to obtain a seat in 1761; came
forward as candidate for Leicestershire in Mar 1762 but withdrew from
the contest (see 32935 and 32936), and committed suicide in 1800, without
ever having improved his mind in Parliament. Later in life his ambitions
were social and not political. The obituary note in the Gentleman's Magazine
(1800, vol. ii, p. 800) states that he was 'a very respectable gentleman
and . . . in the habits of intimacy with the first noblemen in this country'.
'Mr. Boothby was the person supposed to be alluded to by Foote in one of
his farces, as distinguished by his partiality to people of rank, and inclined
to leave one acquaintance to walk with another of superior dignity. Hence
arose his denomination of Prince Boothby.'

His mother, Anne, daughter of Sir Hugh Clopton, Bt., and a cousin of
Horace Walpole's mother, is described by him as 'not . . . the most
amiable person in the world' (to Horace Mann, 10 Apr 1761). She herself
seems to have been aware of the terror she inspired. On 19 July 1761 she
thus prefaced a letter to Charles Jenkinson asking him to procure tickets
for the Coronation: 'Be not terriffied, dear jenkey, with the sight of so
sudden an answer to your obliging letter . . .' (38197, f. 220). And again
on 23 Oct 1762: 'Dear jenky, do not be dismayd at the sight of a letter
from me and fancy I want to ask you questions touching State affairs, no,
wee country country [sic] gentry have not that wicked curiosity . . .' (Jucker,
op. cit., p. 71).

entered by him and others in the Journals of the House —
'may be disposed of with regard to Parliamentary influence
only' : [1] 'What numbers [of officers]', he exclaimed, 'are there
in the other House! and how have they increased within few
years! For it is the known way to military preferment.' [2]

I am not in a position to state how many army officers sat
in the House of Commons in February 1741. A year later,
at the time of Walpole's fall, there were in the House forty-
four army officers actually in the Service.[3] An analysis of
the Parliament of 1754, preserved in the Newcastle Papers,[4]
puts their number at fifty, all classified as 'for' the Government ;
while at the general election of 1761, sixty-four army officers,
actually in the Service, were elected,[5] including the best-known
generals of the time — Field-Marshal Lord Ligonier,[6] Lord
Granby, Sir John Mordaunt, H. S. Conway, Robert Clive,
and George Townshend ; and some who were soon to acquire
prominence — John Burgoyne, William Howe, Charles Cornwallis, etc. One only sat for a Government borough,[7] while
almost all of them belonged to families of social standing, and
nearly half were sons of peers. Still, their professional interests
counted with them for a good deal. When Fox was Secretary of
State in Newcastle's Administration, the Duke of Cumberland,

---

[1] *Journals of the House of Lords*, vol. xxv, p. 586.

[2] Secker MS., 6043, f. 62.

[3] J. B. Owen, *The Rise of the Pelhams*, p. 59.

[4] 33034, f. 173.

[5] In this calculation I do not include officers who had sold out, *e.g.*
Robert Fairfax, Cecil Forester, etc., or Lord George Sackville who had
been dismissed from the Service, or men who had served in their youth or
in times of emergency but were no longer in the Army (*e.g.* Sir James
Carnegie, Bt., who had served at Fontenoy and Culloden, or Edwin Lascelles
who had fought at Minden) ; but only professional soldiers, actually in the
Service.

[6] It was, in fact, considered necessary for the Commander-in-Chief to
be in Parliament. On 1 Dec 1757 Pitt protested to Newcastle against
Ligonier being given only an Irish peerage :

. . . indeed, my Lord, it shou'd have been, on all accounts, an English
peerage, and I trust this will be only a leading step to that proper and
almost necessary dignity . . . his age and value to the Kingdom ought
to put him instantly in a situation, that woud exempt him from the
drudgery of a House of Commons (32876, ff. 197-8).

[7] Henry Holmes, M.P. for Yarmouth, I.o.W., where his brother, Lord
Holmes, was manager of the Government interest.

his patron, acted as whip for the officers in the House. 'I spoke to *the* Duke this morning', wrote Fox to Newcastle on 20 March 1756, 'who most cordially assur'd me that he would have ev'ry officer apply'd to that he could';[1] and two days later: 'the officers attended very well'.[2] Again, when in March and April 1759 the Government to be formed on the death of George II was discussed by Leicester House, Count de Viry reported to Newcastle that the Prince of Wales had declared he would always show due regard to the Duke of Cumberland, but

the Duke was not to expect to have any share in affairs. To which I ask'd, whether that related to the army — my friend seem'd to think, it did; as the army would give great power in the House of Commons.[3]

In November 1745 Pitt, invited by Pelham to join the Government, named among his conditions 'the extension of the Place-Bill, to exclude from seats in Parliament all officers of the Army under the rank of lieutenant-colonel, and of the Navy, under that of captain';[4] and Chesterfield, consulted by Newcastle about Pitt's conditions, replied that he thought this point 'a good one' because of 'the great advantage that will result from it, both to fleet and army, by hindering young subaltern puppys from forcing themselves by their seats in Parliament, into higher posts, than they are . . . fitt for'.[5] But, in fact, their exclusion would not have made much difference — colonels were no less keen on promotion, and could as a rule point to a longer Parliamentary service in support of their claims. Major-General Lord John Murray, fifteen years after having obtained the rank which under the regulations suggested by Pitt would have admitted him to the House, emphasized when asking Newcastle for promotion in the Service that he had 'constantly given his attendance every session of Parliament for these nineteen years' except when ordered to Ireland.[6] When in 1754 William A'Court, M.P.,

---

[1] 32863, f. 398.   [2] *Ibid.* f. 437.
[3] Memorandum of 3 Apr 1759 ; 32889, ff. 348-9.
[4] Newcastle to Chesterfield, 20 Nov 1745 ; 32705, f. 320.
[5] 25 Nov 1745 ; *ibid.* f. 381.   [6] 23 June 1753 ; 32732, ff. 93-5.

Lieutenant-Colonel in the Coldstream Guards, asked to be made a colonel, he pleaded his twenty-eight years in the Service and nine years as lieutenant-colonel, and concluded his Memorial by stating that 'his family and himself have ever been steady supporters of His Majesty's interest in Parliament'.[1] And when Lord Howe was killed at Ticonderoga, and Lord Gage, M.P., asked that Howe's regiment be given to his brother Thomas,[2] Newcastle wrote to him :

I will do my best for Gage if my nephew George Townshend cannot have it, or will not accept it. But as he is so much an older officer than your brother, and may be of great consequence in the House of Commons, I am persuaded that neither your Lordship nor Gage himself can disapprove George Townshend's having it.[3]

Lord Gage replied :

Without entring into a discussion on Mr. Townshend's right to a regiment as an officer ; I think as a Member of Parliament, his abilities and connections give him a claim to favour.[4]

John Calcraft, the army agent, had a younger brother, Thomas, a captain in the Army, and was a close friend of Colonel Sandford, a cousin of Lord Kildare. On 1 November 1760, in view of the approaching general election, he wrote to Kildare about Sandford :

In the present critical juncture I want to know whether in case an opportunity cou'd be found he wou'd choose to be at the expence of coming into the English Parliament ; I wanted also to ask, whether, as my brother is likely to continue on the Irish establishment, it might not be desirable for him to get into that Parliament and if he cou'd put him in the way.[5]

---

[1] 32736, ff. 55-6 ; see also his application for another promotion, 5 Mar 1759 — 'if you think near 33 years unexceptionable service as an officer, and my family Parliamentary connections with your Grace ever since you have been in Administration gives me any title to it' (32888, f. 344).
[2] 23 Aug 1758 ; 32883, f. 64.   [3] 27 Aug ; *ibid.* f. 131.
[4] 29 Aug ; *ibid.* f. 164.
[5] Calcraft's Letterbook, 17495, f. 166. Calcraft, who in 1761 acted as regimental agent for no less than 49 colonels (see *The Court and City Kalendar . . . for the year 1761*), and until Apr 1763 was closely connected with Henry Fox, had extensive political correspondence with Army Members.

Clearly in the choice of Parliament, the regiment and its establishment had to be considered.

Of the 'two golden rules' which governed the Services, 'interest and seniority', the first was infinitely the more important, and men who had no one in Parliament to back their most equitable 'pretensions' were apt to share the fate of the officer in *Tom Jones* [1] who, having for distinguished service been made a lieutenant by Marlborough, continued as such for the next forty years, one reason of 'this ill-success in his profession' being that he had 'no friends among the men in power'.[2] 'What interest has he?' was the foremost question in the eighteenth century.

If you talk to . . . an old stager, either by sea or land, and mention a young fellow who has given proofs of his ability or genius, and being fit for such and such a command, he will tell you, it is *impossible* he should have it. . . . You may as well talk of making me Great Mogul of the Tartars. . . . In the first place, he has no interest; and in the next place, he has no standing in the Service to pretend to such a command. . . .[3]

The one saving circumstance for the Army was that the Hanoverian dynasty, though it adjusted itself to English political conditions, retained a strong German predilection for the parade-ground which it would not unreservedly sacrifice to the Parliamentary arena. It was a standing grief with Newcastle that Army patronage was withheld from him [4] even after Cumberland had fallen into disgrace because of Closterseven; for henceforth appointments were made by George II on recommendations from Ligonier.[5] Similarly George III as a rule refused to subordinate the essential interests of the Army to vote-catching in the House of Commons.

[1] Book vii, chapter xii.

[2] See, *e.g.*, Barré's letter to Pitt, written from New York on 28 Apr 1760, *Chatham Correspondence*, vol. ii, pp. 41-3. 'For want of friends, I had lingered a subaltern officer eleven years, when Mr. Wolfe's opinion of me rescued me from that obscurity.' But now Wolfe was dead — 'By the neglect I have since met with, I am apprehensive that my pretensions are to be buried with my only protector and friend'.

[3] *The London Chronicle*, 12–15 Jan 1760.

[4] This was probably why he 'did not seem . . . to approve of choosing military men [to Parliament]'; Kinnoull to Newcastle, 16 Oct 1758; 32884 ff. 397-8.   [5] See below, pp. 253-4.

The Sailors

In 1753 Henry Pelham, when asking Captain Trelawny, R.N., to defer standing for Parliament, as it would have interfered with some of his arrangements, promised Trelawny to take care in the meantime that by doing so he lost no ground in his profession.[1] No attempt was made to disguise very obvious connexions.

'Most of our flag officers are in the House of Commons',[2] said the Duke of Argyll in a speech, on 3 February 1741. The statement seems amply justified; take the list of admirals as it appears in the *Court and City Kalendar* for 1761 — I add their constituencies and their years in Parliament :

Admirals of the White

George Clinton, M.P. for Saltash 1754–61.

Sir William Rowley, M.P. for Taunton 1750–54, and Portsmouth 1754–61.

Isaac Townsend, M.P. for Rochester 1757–65.

George Anson, M.P. for Hedon 1744–47 (when made a peer).

Admirals of the Blue

Henry Osborn, M.P. for Beds 1758–61.

Thomas Smith.[3]

Thomas Griffin, M.P. for Arundel 1754–61.

Sir Edward Hawke, M.P. for Portsmouth 1747–76.

Charles Knowles, M.P. for Gatton 1749–52.

John Forbes (in the Irish Parliament 1751–63, but declined a seat at Westminster).[4]

Edward Boscawen, M.P. for Truro 1742–61.

---

[1] See below, p. 324.   [2] Secker MS., 6043, f. 67.

[3] Thomas Smith was an illegitimate son of Sir Thomas Lyttelton, fourth Bt., and a step-brother of George, first Lord Lyttelton. At one time he thought of standing for Parliament (see Maud Wyndham, *Chronicles of the Eighteenth Century*, vol. i, pp. 140 and 169, vol. ii, p. 63). He presided at Byng's trial, and in Mar 1757 the King, contrary to the plans of Pitt and the Grenvilles, wished him to succeed Byng as Member for Rochester ; but Smith declined, 'shocked both at succeeding a person he had sentenced, and at being chosen for a stumbling-block to his friends'. (H. Walpole, *Memoirs of the Reign of King George II*, vol. ii, pp. 372-3.)

[4] He consented to enter the Irish Parliament, 'the first time to preserve peace in the county ; and the second, to support family interest ; for he was ever disinclined to be in Parliament, and therefore made it a condition, when he accepted a place at the Admiralty Board, which for some time he declined, that he should not be brought into the British Parliament' ; see J. Forbes, *Memoirs of the Earls of Granard* (1868), p. 175.

Vice-Admirals of the Red

George Pococke, M.P. for Plymouth 1760–68.
George Townshend.[1]
Francis Holburne, M.P. for Stirling Burghs 1761–68, and Plymouth 1768–71.

Vice-Admirals of the White

Thomas Cotes, M.P. for Great Bedwin 1761–67.
Sir Thomas Frankland, M.P. for Thirsk 1747–80 and in 1784.
Lord Harry Powlett, M.P. for Lymington 1755–61, and Winchester 1761–65.
Harry Norris.[2]

Vice-Admirals of the Blue

Thomas Broderick.
Sir Charles Hardy, M.P. for Rochester 1764–68, and Plymouth 1771–80.
The Earl of Northesk (a Scottish peer).
Sir Charles Saunders, M.P. for Hedon 1754–75.

Rear-Admirals of the Red

Thomas Pye, M.P. for Rochester 1771–74.
Charles Stevens.
Philip Durell.

Rear-Admirals of the White

Charles Holmes, M.P. for Newport, I.o.W., 1758–62.
Samuel Cornish, M.P. for New Shoreham 1765–70.
Francis Geary (stood for Rochester in 1768 but was defeated).

Rear-Admirals of the Blue

Smith Callis.
G. B. Rodney, M.P. for various constituencies 1751–54, 1759–74, and 1780–82.

[1] A half-brother of the third Viscount Townshend. It seems incomprehensible how as a Townshend and an admiral he escaped Parliament; but he did.
[2] His father, Admiral Sir John Norris, sat for Rye 1708–22 and 1734–49; his brothers John and Matthew, 1727–33 and 1733–34; his nephew John Norris, 1762–74.

Thus of these thirty officers, twenty at one time or other sat in Parliament, while one was a Scottish peer.

Or again, take the Council of War held on board H.M.S. *Neptune* off the Isle of Aix, on 25 September 1757. There were present :

Admiral Sir Edward Hawke, M.P. for Portsmouth 1747–76.

General Sir John Mordaunt, M.P. for various constituencies 1730–34 and 1735–68.

Vice-Admiral Charles Knowles, M.P. for Gatton 1749–52.

Major-General H. S. Conway, M.P. for various constituencies 1741–74 and 1775–84.

Rear-Admiral Thomas Broderick.

Major-General Edward Cornwallis, M.P. for Westminster 1753–62.

Captain G. B. Rodney, M.P. for various constituencies 1751–54, 1759–74, and 1780–82.

Colonel George Howard, M.P. for Lostwithiel 1761–66, and for Stamford 1768–96.

Thus seven out of eight members of that Council at various times sat in Parliament, and four were actually Members on that day.

Of the famous naval commanders of the Seven Years' War and the American Revolution practically every one sat in Parliament : Anson,[1] the unfortunate Byng, Boscawen, Pococke, Saunders, Hawke, Hardy, Rodney, Howe, Keppel, Palliser, Cornwallis, Alexander and Samuel Hood, Jervis, and Elphinstone, besides such as Rowley, Townsend, Cornish, Pigot, Mulgrave, Shuldham, etc., who held important commands but did not reach the first rank of fame. Seats in the Admiralty boroughs were among the prizes due for distinguished service in the profession : 'I hope my rank and long services will entitle [me] to an Admiralty borough', wrote Rodney in 1780.[2] Of twenty-one naval officers returned in 1761, seven sat on the

---

[1] Also at least five of the officers who had gone with him round the world — Sir Charles Saunders, A. Keppel, Sir Piercy Brett, Peter Denis, and M. Michell ; a sixth, E. Legge, was returned for Portsmouth in 1747 but unseated on petition.

[2] 2 Aug 1780 ; HMC, *Stopford-Sackville MSS.*, vol. ii, p. 172.

D

Government interest,[1] and fourteen received Newcastle's
circular letter requesting their attendance at the opening of
the session — to nine of them it was significantly sent through
Anson, First Lord of the Admiralty ; [2] of the seven who did
not receive the letter, five were away on active service — some
naval Members of the House were absent for years — and two
were Scotsmen who had to be left to Bute (but both had been
on the list of candidates fixed by Newcastle and Argyll in June
1760).[3]

The close connexion between the Navy and Parliament
raised naval debates in the House to a remarkable level, but
when party feeling ran high, introduced political dissensions
into the Service.   In 1782 Lord Rodney declared

that so violent was the spirit of party and faction in his own fleet,
as almost to supersede and extinguish . . . every patriotic sentiment
in the bosoms of many individuals serving under him. . . . There
were . . . officers of high rank and of unquestionable courage, who
nevertheless bore so inveterate an animosity to the Administration
then existing, particularly to the First Lord of the Admiralty, the
Earl of Sandwich, as almost to wish for a defeat if it would produce
the dismission of Ministers.[4]

To these men the House of Commons offered a tribune from
which to vent their griefs, political and professional, against
their chiefs or colleagues.   When on 7 February 1782 Sheridan
attacked North's Government for having driven the most distinguished naval commanders from the Service, he remarked
that

there were several of these officers . . . present in the House, and
he hoped they would now rise . . . and explain fully and clearly,
the reasons which they had for withdrawing. . . . Admiral Pigot,
after some pause, evidently intended for Lord Howe, rose, and stated

-----

[1] Sir Piercy Brett at Queenborough, Sir Edward Hawke at Portsmouth,
Charles Holmes at Newport, Sir George Pococke at Plymouth, and Isaac
Townsend at Rochester.   Lord Howe's tenure of a seat at Dartmouth, and
G. B. Rodney's at Penryn, were not quite in the same category as those of
the senior admirals, personal elements entering into the selection ; still, even
their tenure was of a Service character.
[2] 32929, ff. 303-11.   [3] 32999, ff. 15-17.
[4] Sir Nathaniel Wraxall, *Historical and Posthumous Memoirs*, vol. ii,
p. 324.

in a manly and clear manner the conduct of the First Lord of the Admiralty towards him.[1]

On the whole, in naval appointments political interest was not more than a contributory element, important but not decisive : the Government, the Admiralty, and individual commanders stood to lose too much by wrong appointments, and probably political interest, like noble birth, helped more at the start and in the lower grades than in reaching the top rungs of the ladder. From its very nature the Navy was a comparatively democratic Service.

A man like Anson tried hard to restrict political interference in the Service — 'he withstood recommendations of interest or favor more than any First Lord of the Admiralty was ever known to do', wrote in 1771 Philip, second Earl of Hardwicke.[2] But he had to battle therein both with Newcastle and with his own commanders who, if Members of Parliament or candidates for it, frequently let themselves be guided by election interests in their recommendations.[3]   The following correspondence passed between Newcastle and Anson : [4]

Newcastle to Anson, 15 June, 1759.
My dear Lord,

I beg your Lordship would attend seriously to this letter.

The interest of the borough of Oakhampton (where Mr. Potter is now chose) absolutely depends upon it. The King expects that I should keep up his interest in boroughs : I can't do it without I have the assistance of the several branches of the Government.

Lieutenant Hunt (whom I formerly recommended to your Lordship,) is so strongly insisted upon by the Corporation is lost and with it one, or perhaps two Members.

I state the case as it is. . . .

Anson to Newcastle, Admiralty, 15 June, 1759.
My Lord Duke,

I had the honour of your Grace's letter this morning, and alwayes do attend seriously to whatever your Grace recommends to me, and

---

[1] *Parliamentary Register*, 7 Feb 1782, vol. xxii, p. 419.
[2] 'Memorial of Family Occurrences from 1760 to 1770 inclusive'; 35428, f. 4.
[3] See below, pp. 127-8, 314, and 319.   [4] 32892, ff. 94-6.

shall whenever the borrough of Ockingham [Oakhampton] becomes vacant by the death of Mr. Potter (and I hope you will not wish it sooner) promote Mr. Hunt to a command.—I must now beg your Grace will seriously consider what must be the condition of your Fleet if these borrough recommendations, which must be frequent are to be complyed with ; I wish it did not at this instant bring to my mind the misery poor Pocock that excellent officer suffer'd from the misbehaviour of captains of that cast, which has done more mischeif to the publick (which I know is the most favorite point with you) than the loss of a vote in the House of Commons. My constant method since I have had the honour of serving the King in the station I am in, has been to promote the Lieutenants to command, whose ships have been successfully engaged upon equall terms with the enemy, without having any freind or recommendation ; and in preference to all others, and this I would recommend to my successors if they would have a Fleet to depend on.[1]

I conclude with the case of a worthy, good naval officer who did much hard work and honest service, but in whose career political influence proved, to say the least, opportune. Paul Henry Ourry was the son of Huguenot refugees settled in the Channel Islands ; his father, naturalized in 1713, had held a commission in the British Army since 1707 ; his eldest brother, Lewis, was also an army officer ; another brother, Isaac, was in the service of the East India Company ; a third, George, like Paul Henry, in the Royal Navy.[2] Made a lieutenant in 1742, Paul Henry Ourry subsequently served under George Edgcumbe, with whom he was in the encounter off Mahon, on 20 May 1756, when Byng withdrew before the French fleet. In 1749 Ourry married Charity, daughter of George Treby,

---

[1] About 'Joe' Hunt, see also below, p. 127. He appears to have been a good and gallant officer — but even such had to resort to patronage when everybody was doing so. Having been made a commander on 18 June 1759 (three days after the above correspondence), and a captain on 20 Nov 1760 (on the eve of the general election), Hunt was killed in a successful engagement off the Penmarks, on 11 Jan 1761 ; 'while the surgeon, and his attendants were busily employed in attending, and endeavouring to succour him, one of the seamen, less dangerously wounded than himself, was brought down also, he immediately forbade all farther attention being paid him, saying that he feared his own case was a desperate one, and positively insisted they should proceed to take proper care of the man' (see Charnock, Biographia Navalis, vol. vi, p. 400).

[2] About the Ourry family, see Miscell. Geneal. et Herald., third series, vol. v, pp. 12-16.

M.P.,[1] whose family had electoral influence at Plympton in Devonshire; the chief interest in that borough was, however, with the Edgcumbes who, like the Boscawens, blended Parliamentary interests and naval service into one harmonious whole. Plympton formed henceforth an interesting link between P. H. Ourry and his commanding officer, Commodore George Edgcumbe.

On 24 March 1755 Isaac Ourry wrote to his brother Lewis about the cordial reception he had from Lord Edgcumbe and his brother, the commodore, and the promises they gave him 'of serving the family in anything in their power':

They are very full of business at present to carry some necessary point to strengthen their interest in regard to some boroughs in disputes since the last election [primarily Mitchell in Cornwall] and to optain some favours and places for their familly and borough friends, after which I am very well persuaded they will have a regard to yours when any thing offers they can serve you in. . . . Just after an elextion representatives have many friends to return obligations to, which must have the preference to any other person.[2]

And again from Spithead on 7 April:

The contested elextion of St. Michell is determin'd in favour of the persons they had put up, they are now on the scent to gett a better place for the Sq. and the Comd. [Commodore Edgcumbe] continu'd in his command with a stronger squadron if possible; that and others of the like nature to strengthen their interest in the Government takes up their attention; it would be a pity to trouble them at such time, once they have succeeded they will be better able to serve their friends, but their dependants and such as they have obligations to, must be consider'd first.[3]

Paul Henry Ourry had by now spent three years in the Mediterranean while his wife looked after his professional and political interests; she wrote to Major Lewis Ourry on 6 June 1755:

The death of one of the aldermen at Plympton gives the Edgecumbes an oppertunity of showing their intentions of serveing Mr.

---

[1] About the Treby family, see William Cotton, *Some Account of the Ancient Borough Town of Plympton St. Maurice, or Plympton Earl* (1859).
[2] 21643, f. 3.   [3] *Ibid.* f. 28.

Ourry, if they do not chuse him, I shall be convinced they are not his friends. My brothers' interest Mr. Ourry is sure of; but they have only two voices, I am not a little anxious on this head, nothing like interest in a borough, it carrys every thing; dont mention this to any one, for should Mr. Ourry not succeed I should not care to have it known that we applyed for it. . . .

I am very bussy hay making, my farmering goes on well, the first field of grass cut in the parish, my little girl and myself have had colds but are better.[1]

In 1758 Ourry served in the expedition against Cherbourg, in 1761 against Belleisle, in 1762 against Martinique. In 1763 the Treby family became extinct in the male line, Charity's two brothers, who successively represented Plympton, having died unmarried; and Captain Ourry was now a candidate to their political inheritance, and also to promotion in his profession. Sandwich, at that time Secretary of State, wrote on 20 September 1763 to his friend Captain Augustus Hervey, R.N. :

I am very glad to hear you give so good an account of Captain Ourry's political disposition, in consequence of which if he will apply to Lord Egmont for a guardship at Plymouth I am well assured he will meet with success, and have one of the first ships that is commissioned. . . . You may likewise inform Captain Ourry that his friendly language has saved him from another inconvenience, as there was a candidate ready for Plympton, who will now be stopped.[2]

Ourry very soon got a guardship at Portsmouth,[3] and represented Plympton 1763-75, when he was made Commissioner of the Dockyard at Portsmouth, a place not tenable with a seat in Parliament.

The Civil Servants

It was but slowly that the Civil Service acquired its present corporate structure, independence, and aloofness. About 1760 the 'commis' in the office of the Secretaries of State (who would now be Permanent Under-Secretaries) and the Secre-

---

[1] 21643, ff. 34-5.   [2] Sandwich MSS.
[3] See J. Charnock, *Biographia Navalis*, vol. vi, p. 266.

taries to various Government departments were personal
dependants of the Ministers, but at the same time frequently
Members of Parliament. Both the dignity and inferiority of
the chaplain or curate at a big country house attached to their
persons and position — they had to know a great deal and not
expect too much, to be qualified to sit at the table of their
chief and, in most cases, be satisfied with the lowest places at
it. The question how far their allegiance was due to the person
and how far to the office of the Minister was not solved as yet,
and gave rise to conflicting loyalties and to bitter resentments.
When in July 1765 the Grenville Administration was replaced
by that of Rockingham, Edward Sedgwick, Under-Secretary
in the Southern Department, wrote to Edward Weston, one
of the oldest and most experienced civil servants, now in
retirement :

No Undersecretaries are yet declared, nor I believe, fix'd on in
either Office. But I understand they will all be new ones . . . it is
thought improper and disagreeable to give the entire confidence
which Undersecretaries must enjoy, to men who are known to be
strongly attach'd or greatly obliged to other great personages.[1]

The Secretaries to the Treasury, of whom the senior was
concerned in the management of the House of Commons,
almost always retired with their chiefs. When on the fall of the
Coalition in December 1783, Lord North went into opposition,

of the two former Secretaries of the Treasury, Sir Grey Cooper
continued to support him invariably; but Robinson, conceiving
himself absolved from any obligation to accompany his ancient
principal through all the consequences of his new political alliances,
quitted altogether that party.[2]

He managed for George III the general election of 1784 and
thereby contributed to the political extinction of his former
chief, which North resented so bitterly that when in 1792, on
his death-bed, he wanted to do a last Christian deed he sent
for Robinson and shook hands with him. And yet, thinking

---

[1] 13 July 1765; HMC, 10, i; *Weston MSS.*, p. 391. These and the
Knox Papers, in *Various Collections*, vol. vi, contain most valuable material
for a study of the eighteenth-century Civil Service.

[2] Wraxall, *Historical and Posthumous Memoirs*, vol. iii, p. 236.

in present-day terms, we can hardly condemn Robinson, who considered that he served the Crown and not the individual Minister ; which, in a meaner way, had been also the line taken in 1762 by Philip Carteret Webb, Solicitor to the Treasury. Although Hardwicke had raised Webb to his position, had supported him in his election business at Haslemere (the borough he represented in Parliament), and had always been a friend and patron to him, Webb, at the dinner given in August 1762 by the High Sheriff at the Surrey Assizes, openly declared his allegiance to Lord Bute. Newcastle thus described the scene to Hardwicke on 11 August :

> They then sat down, and every body was to name his toast. The first toast named was Sir John Evelyn ; [1] that went round quietly. Then our friend, Mr. Carteret Webbe named my Lord Bute, upon which the whole company at once got up and would not drink it. . . . This broke up the company. One Mr. Coates, a very considerable wine-merchant, called out, Who gave that toast ? or proposed that health ? Mr. Webbe replied, *He is my master*.[2]

But Hardwicke replied on 21 August :

> I don't wonder at my old friend Webb's proposing the toast, nor blame him for it. 'Twas natural for the Sollicitor to the Treasury to toast the head of it ; and the reason he gave for it — *he is my master*, was a modest one, and took off from any political merit in it.[3]

Seats in Parliament made these civil servants to some extent politicians ; but to some extent only, for again, in judging their actions in the House of Commons, one must remember that they were civil servants. The Secretaries to the Treasury almost invariably sat in Parliament. Of those between 1761 and the fall of Lord North's Government in 1782, James West, Samuel Martin, Jeremiah Dyson, Charles Jenkinson, Thomas Whately, Grey Cooper, Thomas Bradshaw, and John Robinson, sat in Parliament while employed at the Treasury ; two only did not — William Mellish, who held the office for a fortnight in July 1765, and Charles Lowndes, who retained it as long

---

[1] Sir John Evelyn, first Bt., of Wotton, Surrey.
[2] 32941, f. 207.   [3] *Ibid.* f. 326.

as the Rockinghams were in power but did not stand for
Parliament till 1768. The Secretaries to the Admiralty, John
Clevland, sen. (1751–63), and Philip Stephens (1763–95), all
the time combined their tenure of the office with a seat in the
House. Of the twenty-one men who were Under-Secretaries
in the Southern and Northern Departments between 1761 and
1782, when the office was reorganized, eight sat in Parliament
while employed in the Civil Service.[1]

The seat in the House added to the importance and standing
of civil servants, and their presence in Parliament was useful
to their chiefs. In 1758 James West, when refusing to give up
a share of the emoluments of his office, produced the following
version of the precept about the labourer and his hire : ' I hope
it is not arrogant to say, that in my poor opinion, whoever
brings himself into Parliament and honestly discharges the
duty of the office, amply deserves the lawful fees of it.'[2] Here
is a short sketch of the lives of two such civil servants : of
Robert Wood, one of the numerous very intelligent but poor
Irishmen who swarmed in the English political underworld
about 1760 ; and of John Clevland, a hard-working, hungry
Scot who acquired unrivalled knowledge of Admiralty matters,
and thereby rose to a position of considerable importance.

Robert Wood is remembered chiefly as the Under-Secretary
to whom Lord Granville, when signing on his death-bed the
Treaty of Paris, quoted an appropriate passage from the *Iliad*,
and against whom John Wilkes, in December 1763, obtained
a verdict for £1000 over General Warrants. He first came into
prominence as one of the most distinguished Homeric scholars
of his time, and as the explorer of Palmyra and Baalbek. When
in 1753 the young Duke of Bridgwater set out on his grand
tour, Wood was chosen as the most appropriate companion and
guide for him. On their return in 1756, Wood was appointed

---

[1] Robert Wood, Charles Jenkinson, William Burke, Richard Sutton,
William Eden, Thomas Whately, Anthony Chamier, and Benjamin Langlois.
I do not include Lauchlin Macleane, though technically he combined for a
short time membership of the House with an under-secretaryship. But in
fact the House during that time (May 1768) sat less than a fortnight, and he
was *in statu mortis* as an official.

[2] See below, pp. 403-4.

Under-Secretary of State, and in 1761 was returned by Bridgwater for Brackley which he continued to represent till his
death in 1771. Walpole in his *Memoirs of the Reign of King
George III* says that 'his general behaviour was decent as
became his dependent situation', but in 1770 accusations were
raised against him that while Under-Secretary of State he
dabbled in stocks, a thing deprecated even in an age which
was not squeamish about 'finance' in politics; and when it
was rumoured that he was to go out as secretary to the Lord-
Lieutenant of Ireland, the Irish gentlemen objected to his
'mean birth', and 'his public and private character'.[1]

John Clevland, whose father had been a naval officer and
subsequently an Admiralty official,[2] became in 1751 its first
secretary; he sat in Parliament 1741-43, and from 1747 till
his death in 1763. His record is summed up in a Memorial
which, some time in 1762, he addressed to the King; [3] it should
be noted that he nowhere mentions his service in Parliament
and the votes which he naturally gave in favour of the Government — these were taken for granted :

Memorial of Mr. Clevland, Secretary of the Admiralty

That he has been near forty years in the naval service, in the
several stations of a Chief Clerk in the Navy Office, Clerk of the
Cheque and Muster Master at Plymouth, Commissioner of the Navy,
and Secretary of the Admiralty.

That he was the active Commissioner of the Navy in the former
Spanish war, and some time after the commencement of that with
France, Mr. Corbett, then Secretary of the Admiralty being very
infirm, and frequently incapable of his duty, Mr. Clevland was made
Joint Secretary with him, and carried on the business 'till the peace
in 1748.

That the extensive and arduous operations of the present war
have brought such an increase of business on the office of Secretary
of the Admiralty, that Mr. Clevland's health and eyesight is greatly

---

[1] W. G. Hamilton to J. H. Hutchinson, 2 Dec 1769 [should be 1764];
HMC, 8, *Emly Papers*, p. 191. I have used in this sketch W. P. Courtney's
article on Robert Wood in the *D.N.B.*

[2] For the Clevland family see Burke, *Landed Gentry*, under 'Christie of
Glyndebourne'.

[3] 32945, f. 449.

impared by incesant application to the faithful discharge of his
trust, which he flatters himself to have done to the satisfaction of
his superiors, and will not fail in his endeavours to continue the
same whilst his health will permit.

But having a wife and great number of children, is very anxious
to make some better provision for them than his own fortune will
allow of after his death.

Therefore most ardently implores His Majesty, in consideration
of his long and faithful services, to grant to Mrs. Clevland such
pension as shall be thought proper, upon the Irish or any other
establishment, which provision for his family will add greatly to his
happiness, and be the means of prolonging a life entirely devoted
to the publick.[1]

Clevland's Memorial is certainly that of a humble and
hard-working civil servant; but there should be no mistake
about it, he was a man of considerable importance. On the
death of Lord Anson, 6 June 1762, Newcastle, anxious to
retain some channel for soliciting jobs at the Admiralty, courted
Clevland's friendship. 'I beg we may continue the same
friendship', he wrote from Claremont on 7 June; 'and that
you would now and then come and take a dinner with us here;
nobody can be more welcome.'[2] Lord Halifax succeeded
Anson at the Admiralty, and Clevland wrote to Newcastle on
16 June:

[1] Meantime his eldest son, John Clevland, jun. (M.P. for Barnstaple,
1766–1802), had already some provision; in the *Court and City Kalendar*
for 1761 he appears as a clerk at the Admiralty (£100 p.a.), Deputy Judge
Advocate of the Admiralty (£146), Agent for the Marines, and one of
the Commissioners for the Sale of Prizes, but it is not certain that even this
exhausts the list of his employments or sinecures. John Clevland, sen., as
Secretary to the Admiralty, had £800 p.a., but with fees and perquisites over
£2000 net (cf. 3rd Report on Emoluments in Public Offices, 1786, p. 40).
Moreover, he enjoyed the advantage usually derived from being connected
with the Government—his name frequently occurs among underwriters to
Government loans. Thus in a loan anticipating the land tax for 1746,
Sampson Gideon, the famous financier, signed for him for £2000 (P.R.O.,
T. 1/319); in 1760 he was billeted for £10,000 on Amyand's list of sub-
scribers to the war loan (32901, f. 242). In 1762 his eldest son subscribed
£10,000 (33040, f. 290). In all probability, these were 'stagging' operations
rather than *bona fide* subscriptions.

[2] 32939, f. 205. This was not a new attention, born of need; see, *e.g.*,
Clevland's letter to Newcastle, 22 Mar 1759: 'I am very sorry, I cannot
have the honour of waiting upon your Grace at dinner, Mr. Boscawen
dining with me' (32899, f. 37).

Lord Halifax . . . has done me the honor to call upon me, and given me the strongest assurances of his friendship, and desired I would be upon the same footing with him as I was with Lord Anson.[1]

Newcastle replied the same day :

I am heartily glad of it, upon your account, and indeed upon my own ; for, I dare say, he will receive most favorably any applications you shall make to him in behalf of my friends.[2]

And on 17 June Hardwicke wrote to Newcastle about Halifax :

His Lordship has certainly parts and activity, and I wish him success. The most prudent part is that I am told before he accepted, he took care to be assur'd from Clevland that he would continue Secretary during the war.[3]

The Lawyers

The legal profession was the most democratic of all those concerned with matters of State ; for there naturally was no way of rising at the Bar except by ability and hard work, and seldom, if ever, were men raised to the Woolsack or the Bench who had not distinguished themselves at the Bar. And as the path of law was hard walking it was left mostly to the feet of the poor and the steps of the needy, to younger sons or men of small origin. 'There are very few', wrote Addison about the Inns of Court, 'that make themselves considerable proficients in the studies of the place, who know they shall arrive at great estates without them.'

The connexion between the courts of law and the High Court of Parliament is so obvious that it is hardly necessary to enlarge upon it. They are akin in origin, in methods, to some extent even in the business they transact ; and some of the qualities most required are the same in both. Moreover, in the eighteenth century Parliamentary politics were transacted, to a disastrous extent, in terms of jurisprudence. When the repeal of the Stamp Act came before Parliament much attention was paid to abstract rights, and the discussion consequently turned at least as much on legal rules and precedents

---

[1] 32939, f. 367.   [2] *Ibid.* f. 374.   [3] *Ibid.* f. 384.

as on policy — what did the Charters lay down on the point? had Parliament taxed Durham or Calais before they were represented? did the Post Office Act of New York form a precedent for taxing the Colonies, etc.? And on 15 March 1782, in the eighteenth year of the American disputes, when the vote of no-confidence was moved against Lord North's Government, Sir James Marriott, a Judge of the Admiralty, 'defended the American war on the just ground that taxation and representation should go hand in hand; and added, to the diversion of the whole House, that America was represented by the Members of the county of Kent'.[1] Eighteenth-century Anglo-Saxons thought that one could go into the law courts against nations, and in one county of Massachusetts the revolution was started with the grand jury indicting the British Parliament as a public nuisance.

Debates and business in Parliament being of an eminently legal character, 'the gentlemen of the long robe' were welcome in the House, while to them it offered distinct advantages. Most of the highest honours of the profession were usually reached through the House of Commons. But even certain material advantages of an inferior character could best be attained through it: the legal places of profit under the Crown which were open to Members of Parliament were much more numerous than they are now; e.g. the Attorney and Solicitor-General to the Queen, the Solicitor to the Treasury, the Counsels to the Board of Trade, Admiralty, and other Government departments, more frequently than not were Members of Parliament. Moreover, the places of the Master of the Rolls, of the eight Justices of Chester and Wales, and of the Admiralty Judges were tenable with seats in Parliament, and Parliamentary considerations to some extent entered into the appointments. Thus in September 1756, on a vacancy in the office of Second

---

[1] *Gentleman's Magazine*, 1782, p. 164. This of course because all land in America was held in the Manor of East Greenwich. James Marriott, a Fellow and ultimately Master of Trinity Hall, Cambridge, was a prolific writer who composed innumerable and inordinately long letters to Ministers, political tracts, legal discourses, etc. By obsequiousness to the great, he managed to obtain the Fellowship, rather against the inclination of the College, and by twenty years of further endeavours, to get himself into Parliament. He was knighted in 1778.

Justice of Chester, James West (himself a barrister) wrote to Newcastle :

> I hope your Grace will insist on regarding the House of Commons in the Justiceship of Chester. Probably Mr. Bankes would give the nomination for Corfe Castle for it, or Mr. Bond would be effectually secured by it. Moreton would be glad of it from the Oxford Circuit. Or some other Welch Judge's place if removed would serve younger and less aspiring men. I am not clear that Martyn would not quit his old friend and Parliament for it.[1]

And Hardwicke wrote to Newcastle on 10 October that Lord Feversham was pressing for the Justiceship to be given to James Hayes, M.P. for Downton — Feversham claimed to have returned 'more Members at his own expence than almost any private man, without advantage to himself'.[2] It was finally given to Taylor White, a brother of John White, M.P.

Lastly, what tended to increase the number of lawyers in the House was that the Recorders of Parliamentary boroughs, who were usually chosen from among the leading barristers of the circuit, had a considerable influence, especially in corporation boroughs, and often finished by having themselves returned to Parliament.

It is exceedingly difficult to say how many of the barristers who were returned to Parliament in 1761 were at that date 'practising lawyers'. In 1754, Newcastle's Parliamentary lists put their number at thirty-six (Welsh and Admiralty judges are included).[3] My own calculations for 1761 yield a slightly higher figure; about forty will probably be as accurate an estimate as I can attempt.

[1] 32867, f. 41-2. Henry Bankes, K.C., sat for Corfe Castle from 1741 till Nov 1762, when he was made a Commissioner of Customs, and the hereditary seat of his family was put at the disposal of the Government. The Bond family nominated to the other seat at Corfe Castle, and John Bond sat for it himself, 1747-61 and 1764-80. John Morton (this is the correct spelling of the name — he should not be confused with Sir William Moreton, Recorder for the City of London) was Member for Abingdon and was made Chief Justice of Chester in Nov 1762. The 'Martyn' mentioned above is undoubtedly Samuel Martin, subsequently Joint Secretary to the Treasury ; at that time he was attached to H. B. Legge. West seems to have been under the impression that the Justiceship of Chester was not tenable with a seat in the House ; if so, he was wrong ; e.g. John Morton, M.P. 1747-70 and 1775-80, was Chief Justice of Chester, 1762-80.

[2] 32868, ff. 122-3.   [3] 33034, ff. 173-6.

CONTRACTS, REMITTANCES, AND LOANS: THE MERCHANTS AND BANKERS

John Douglas, D.D., the political scribe of Lord Bath, wrote on the eve of the general election of 1761:

> If our House of Commons is to be filled with men who are in trade, and who get themselves elected, only to be in the way of their trade; the contracts, the jobs, the subscriptions, the loans, the remittances &c., &c., with which a Minister can benefit them, are such a temptation to them, to assist in involving the nation in dangerous projects, and ruinous expence, that I know not whether we have most reason to dread a majority of greedy stock-holders, or of indigent placemen, for our representatives.[1]

Professor Werner Sombart, in his studies on the origins of modern capitalism,[2] points to luxury trades and Government contracts as the two factors responsible for its growth before the Industrial Revolution. Although his generalizations seem too sweeping (the brewers were among the earliest capitalists in England, and capitalists would have arisen in the metal trades even without armaments),[3] his thesis is fundamentally correct. By means of taxation and Government loans, agglomerations of capital were effected such as could not easily have arisen in private trade. The Paymasters of the Forces,

---

[1] *Seasonable Hints from an Honest Man on the present important Crisis of a new Reign, and a new Parliament*, p. 46. The pamphlet was published anonymously; a MS. note in the British Museum copy gives the date of publication as 16 Mar 1761, and this seems borne out by extracts from the pamphlet having appeared in the *London Chronicle* between 17 and 26 Mar.

[2] *Luxus und Kapitalismus* and *Krieg und Kapitalismus*.

[3] See, *e.g.*, H. S. Grazebrook, 'The Origin of the Foley Family', in Marshall's *Genealogist*, vol. vi (1882), pp. 117-22; the rise of their fortune is ascribed to Foley (or Brindley) having obtained from the Continent a method 'for slitting iron into rods for the purpose of making nails'. Also, from the account in Hutchinson's *History of Durham* (1787), vol. ii, pp. 441-3, it appears that in Ambrose Crowley's works at Swalwell the objects manufactured were not connected with armaments: they made ship anchors, 'hoes and shovels, and cast pots, kettles, and other domestic utensils'. To some branches of the metal trade war was, in fact, deemed prejudicial; see, *e.g.*, letter from Henry Bowdler to John Douglas, D.D., 2 Apr 1760, inquiring what chance there was of peace as he had several lead mines and a share in two smelt-houses, and trade was bad owing to the war but was expected to improve on conclusion of peace (MS. Top. Salop. c. 3, Bodleian, Oxford).

of the Navy, and the Ordnance, held balances which were of the first importance in the money market; remittances of subsidies to allied countries or of money for the use of troops on foreign or colonial service were among the most coveted plums of finance; even receiverships of the land tax were much sought after by provincial merchants and bankers as providing them with deposits of public money, when private deposits and savings were as yet insignificant.[1] On the other hand, the underwriting of Government loans was the chief financial transaction in an age when joint-stock companies were few and Government stock was the main regular object of speculation in the Alley.

Again, the only vast contracts for ordinary supplies and necessaries of life were those connected with the arming, victualling, and clothing of the Army and Navy. Cloth factors and grain merchants, ironmasters and timber dealers, pulled every possible wire to obtain Government orders. Merchants trading to America and the West Indies would undertake the victualling and payment of British regiments in the Colonies. The Portugal and Spanish merchants,[2] whatever their own particular trade — the export of cloth or fish, the import of wine, etc. — scrambled to get the contracts for the garrisons of Gibraltar and Minorca, for regiments serving in the Peninsula, etc.[3] Subsidies to various German States, the commissariat

[1] See, W. R. Ward, *The English Land Tax in the Eighteenth Century* (1953). See also Martin Dunsford, *Historical Memoirs of Tiverton*, p. 246, about the way in which the receivership of the land tax in the hands of a merchant gave him a financial superiority over his competitors; further, letter from Sir George Smith, Bt., to Newcastle, Nottingham, 20 Nov 1757 (32876, f. 41), written on separating in business from his brother Abel Smith, and asking the Duke to direct that 'the land tax and excise money be returned by me and not by my brother Abel, that so the Government may not have their money made use of against themselves'.

[2] *I.e.* British merchants trading to Portugal or Spain.

[3] Their trade seems to have yielded as a rule considerable balances; *e.g.* some time in 1767 or 1768, Captain Cornwallis was ordered by Commodore Spry to proceed to Cadiz, on account of 'merchants of the British factory at Cadiz requiring a ship to ·convoy the balance of their trade to their correspondents in England', and to take on board of his own ship 'all such remittances of cash and jewels as the merchants of the factory shall desire' (see G. Cornwallis-West, *The Life and Letters of Admiral Cornwallis*, p. 39). But if these merchants could place their surplus cash at the service of the

of the British armies fighting in Germany and remittances of money for their use, opened a rich field for British merchants in the Dutch and Hamburg trade.[1] In short, most merchants trading to foreign parts knew of some convenient sector in the 'far-flung battle line' and eagerly solicited contracts for/under 'palm and pine'. Fortunes were made and the greatness of families founded in army magazines and bread waggons. Defoe remarks in his treatise on *The Complete English Tradesman*, published in 1726, that not so many of the families of the English gentry

have rais'd themselves by the sword as in other nations, though we have not been without men of fame in the field too . . . yet how many more families among the tradesmen have been rais'd to immense estates even during the same time, by the attending circumstances of the war ? Such as cloathing, the paying, victualling, and furnishing, etc., both army and navy.[2]

Government contracts were usually held with a seat in the House of Commons, while baronetcies, the crest over the profits, had to be gained by service in the House ; and a generation or two later, provided the money was preserved, the trade discontinued, and a seat in the House retained, a coronet was within the reach of the children or grandchildren of the successful Government contractors.

Still, the connexion between Government contracts and membership of the House of Commons, close as it was, must not be over-stressed. When in war-time sums had to be raised, enormous for eighteenth-century resources and ideas, those best able to take up or place the loans had to be approached or considered, regardless of the House of Commons. In remittances, where even a small reduction in terms made a very considerable difference, the public interest could not be altogether

Government they made an extra profit on it ; see, *e.g.*, fees charged to the Treasury in 1767 by Messrs. Mayne, Burne, & Mayne for money 'furnished by them for the use of the forces serving in Portugal', 38340, ff. 36-9.

[1] The size of those remittances and the profits on them can be gauged from the following example : the remittances made for the Treasury by John Gore, M.P., to Holland, Germany, Austria, and Piedmont, during the years 1741-51 amounted to a total of £5,046,169 (33038, ff. 243-4) ; and the commission on such remittances in war-time varied from 5 to 15 per cent, much of this, of course, booked against insurance.   [2] Pp. 377-8.

E

subordinated to Parliamentary considerations, especially as Pitt and the country gentlemen were not slow in denouncing flagrant jobberies. In the correspondence which passed between H. B. Legge, Chancellor of the Exchequer, and Newcastle in July 1758 concerning remittances to Germany,[1] the question of the most favourable terms to be obtained for the public and of not disobliging 'the principal money'd men in the City' whose assistance would be required in the raising of loans, was discussed, and Parliamentary considerations were not even mentioned. Similarly in very special lines political calculations had to be sacrificed to efficiency; thus Thornton, the biggest English banker connected with Russia, was able to keep the remittances to that country entirely in his own hands and refuse all share in them to Joseph Mellish, a son-in-law of John Gore, M.P., and to Thomas Walpole, M.P., who both applied to be admitted into these contracts.[2] Even some of the victualling and clothing contracts were held by men who did not sit in the House. But as the biggest merchants and financiers, aiming at social advancement, desired seats in the House and were best able to acquire them, and as only the biggest capitalists could undertake, or be trusted with, contracts of the first magnitude, this alone, apart from Parliamentary considerations, would have resulted in the same business men being Members of Parliament and Government contractors. And where the difference in the terms offered was not excessive, naturally Members of Parliament had by far the better chance, which was one reason why merchants who were out to obtain contracts tried to enter it.[3] In 1761 fifty

[1] 32881, ff. 215-16, 327-8, and 331-2.
[2] 32861, ff. 157, 175-7, and 208.
[3] Even for minor contracts, political recommendations were required. The following letter was addressed to Newcastle by Bridger, his election agent at New Shoreham, on 24 Aug 1756:

I am deeply concern'd in a ship that trades to Jamaica, and have for two year past carry'd Government stores, last year by the interest of Mr. Legg [H. B. Legge, Chancellor of the Exchequer], the year before Lord Delawar wrote to his cousin Mostyn [M.P. for Weobley, Comptroller of the Navy] for us.

It is a matter of indifference to the Navy Board, but they always expect a recommendation, otherwise they will give no attention to an application from the captain or owners (32867, ff. 40-41).

merchants [1] were returned to Parliament, and of these at least thirty-seven can be proved to have had extensive business dealings with the Government. When in 1756, on the death of Peter Burrell, sen., the question arose of the succession to his contracts for some regiments at Gibraltar, Sir Joshua Vanneck asked for them on behalf of his son-in-law Thomas Walpole and his partners, the two Fonnereaus and John Bristow, all four Members of Parliament; he concluded his letter to Newcastle with this warning :

. . . your Grace will no doubt consider the inconvenience that may arise from disobliging, in this critical juncture, four gentlemen Members [of Parliament] of independent fortunes, and with them their relations and friends.[2]

And Newcastle thus explained his view of the matter to Hardwicke : 'As to the equity, my brother [Henry Pelham] thought four regiments were sufficient for four Members of Parliament'.[3]

The Government itself encouraged merchants to undertake constituencies which were too costly for the ordinary run of candidates, and used contracts to indemnify them for their election expenses ; in fact, these men were kept in reserve for such occasions. Thus before the general election of 1754, Henry Pelham, when trying to induce Robert Neale to contest both seats at Wootton Bassett, a difficult and expensive constituency, told him that if he could not get a country gentleman, a merchant would be found to join him.[4] Chauncy Townsend,

---

[1] Merchants in the eighteenth century meant business men, and the term was as wide as trade is even now ; bankers and manufacturers were included. But I do not include among the merchants country gentlemen who owned mines or even iron works but clearly did not belong to the business community, such as Capel Hanbury, M.P. for Monmouthshire, the owner of the Pontypridd works, Herbert Mackworth, M.P. for Cardiff, a mine-owner in South Wales, or Edward Montagu, M.P. for Huntingdon, who developed a coal-mine on his Denton estate in Northumberland.

On the other hand, it is difficult to exclude a man like Matthew Ridley, M.P. for Newcastle-upon-Tyne, who, besides important coal-mines, owned glass-works, salt-pans, a brewery, etc., and was a leading figure in the business life of the town.

[2] See my article, 'Brice Fisher, M.P.', in the *English Historical Review*, Oct 1927, pp. 525-6.   [3] *Ibid.* p. 526.

[4] Robert Neale to Newcastle, 15 Feb 1755 ; 32852, f. 481.

M.P., who had started as a linen-draper [1] but subsequently developed into a general merchant, victualling contractor, mineowner, etc., having in a letter to James West, on 26 June 1754, enumerated the services he had rendered to Administration in elections at a cost to himself of £6000, explained with regard to the reward he expected : 'Mony support I allways declined when hinted — half Gibraltar was my object'.[2] Vanneck, in his letter to Newcastle on 9 August 1756, stated that Thomas Walpole, having been admitted by Henry Pelham to 'the present contract for Gibraltar . . . thought himself obliged to undertake a very costly election' (at Sudbury in Suffolk)[3] and complained of the Duke now introducing new partners (John Bristow and Brice Fisher) into it, when Walpole was 'scarce repaid of his expense by the contract'.[4] And when in December 1762 the Fonnereaus, who held three seats in the House, were on the point of deserting Newcastle for Bute, and Newcastle reminded Zachary Fonnereau of the assurances he had given :

he owned very plainly that it was interest ; that he had a family ; his brother and he had spent thirty thousand pounds in elections ; that he had got but little from my brother and me, and that he must look out to his interest. I suppose, his price is some valuable remittances to Minorca etc. ; when a man knows himself that he is bought, one has nothing to say to him.[5]

Newcastle was mistaken in his supposition concerning Fonnereau's 'price' — the contract for Minorca was given to

[1] See Kent's *London Directory* for 1738.

[2] *I.e.*, half of the contracts for its garrison ; he added that with Pelham 'I had more merrett than all the Gibraltar people together' — meaning the merchants who held the Gibraltar contracts ; 32735, f. 573.

[3] Pelham wrote to the Duke of Grafton on 4 Oct 1753, asking for his support for Thomas Walpole. One candidate he had intended for Sudbury declined as it 'appeared to him a very expensive and . . . troublesome engagement'. 'Upon this I had an immediate conference with young Walpole Vanneck's son. He very roundly engages his person and his purse. . . . I have acquainted our Master [the King] with this scheme who very highly approves of it. He laughd, when I told him a son of Horrace's offerd an unlimited purse ; and would do more so, if he knew, we have nothing promised by our father in law' (Grafton MSS.). Here, incidentally, is an example of how closely George II followed election matters.

[4] See my essay on 'Brice Fisher, M.P.', in the *English Historical Review*, Oct 1927, p. 525.

[5] Newcastle to Thomas Walpole, 17 Dec 1762 ; 32945, ff. 301-2.

George Amyand, M.P. for Barnstaple, and Nicholas Linwood, M.P. for Stockbridge, while the reward of the Fonnereaus, besides being left in their own contracts, was a share of that which Thomas Walpole had held at Gibraltar and from which he was removed in the proscription of Newcastle's friends at the end of 1762. For contracts were the 'places' of merchants : most of them entered Parliament too late in life to aspire to a distinguished political career, and were moreover too profitably employed to undertake a long apprenticeship in administrative places, while even the fattest sinecure could not equal the profits to be derived from contracts.[1]

The following contractors appear in Newcastle's 'Lists of Officers removed in the years 1762 and 1763, whose appointments arise in the Treasury' (the names in the right-hand column denote the men who replaced them) : [2]

Sept. 10, 1762. Joseph Mellish Tho. Walpole	Remitters to Germany	Peregrine Cust.
Nov. 15, 1763. Sir Geo. Cole- brooke. Arnold Nesbitt	Contractors and remitters for North America	Sir Saml. Flud- yer. Adam Drummond.
Sept. 2, 1763. Thomas Walpole	Contractor for Gibraltar with Messrs. Burrell and Fonnereau	Messrs. Burrell and Fonnereau remain in this contract.

A paper in the Liverpool MSS. on the 'State of the several subsisting contracts for supplying His Majesty's forces serving abroad with provisions and for the remittance of their pay', drawn up in 1764, compares the terms of the contracts 'made by the present Treasury Boards' with those of the former.[3] It gives the names of the Government contractors for America,

[1] A few held, however, offices of a business character ; e.g. Abraham Hume was, for a few years during the Seven Years' War, Commissary-General of Stores (£3 a day) ; Peter Burrell, jun., was at one time Deputy-Paymaster of the Forces, etc.

[2] 33001, ff. 23-4. Every man in this table was a Member of Parliament. For Walpole's removal, see also 32946, ff. 17, 19, and 49-50.

[3] 38338, ff. 109-11. This paper naturally does not mention any of the contracts which were in existence in 1761 for the troops and subsidies in Germany, as none of these continued in 1764, and the aim of the paper is a comparison between the terms of existing and previous contracts.

the West Indies, and the western coast of Africa; under Newcastle they were : James and George Colebrooke, Nesbitt & Franks, Chauncy Townsend, M. Woodford, the two elder Fonnereaus, Walpole and Burrell, Bristow, Thomlinson and Hanbury, to whom should be added Baker and Kilby, not mentioned in that paper. Eleven of these fifteen merchants were Members of Parliament. Of the remaining four, Moses Franks and Kilby were Americans working for their partners the American end of the business ; Hanbury was a rich Quaker who had been prominent on the Government side in the Bristol election of 1754 ; and Woodford held one of the smallest of these contracts. In 1764 the contractors were Fludyer, Drummond & Franks, Fonnereau & Burrell, Cumming & Mason, Major & Henniker, Amyand & Linwood, Jones & Cust, Bacon & Lewis, while contracts with Chauncy Townsend, M. Woodford, and Thomlinson, Colebrooke, Nesbitt & Hanbury, concluded by the previous Administration, were still running. Of the twenty-one merchants here mentioned, sixteen were Members of Parliament (only Franks, Cumming, Mason, Woodford, and Hanbury were not).

On the formation of the Rockingham Government, Sir George Colebrooke, who had suffered for remaining faithful to Newcastle, wrote to him on 15 July 1765 :

As you did me the honour, to put the question to me yesterday at Claremont, if there was anything, upon this change of Ministry, which occurred to me to have, permit me, my Lord, in a few words to state to your Grace, how the matter of the contracts stands, in which I was engaged with the Treasury, before Mr. Grenville gave me notice to quit.

There were then two contracts ; one for *the remittance* of money for the use of the troops in North America with Messrs. Thomlinson, Nesbit & Hanbury; the other for *victualling* those troops with Messrs. Nesbit & Franks.

The former expired a few months ago. . . .

The contract for victualling was given by Mr. Grenville to Sir Saml. Fludyer, Mr. Drummond, and Mr. Franks. The two former had signed a contract for Pensicola, but they gave up that to Mr. Henniker, in order to come into the places of Mr. Nesbit and myself.[1]

---

[1] Colebrooke, Thomlinson jun., Nesbitt, Fludyer, Drummond, and Henniker were Members of Parliament.

Now, my Lord, you will be pleased to observe, that Drummond is brother in law to the D. of Bolton and tho' Sir Saml. Fludyer has no pretensions to be well considered by the present Administration, yet Mr. Drummond, I doubt not, will have the protection of the noble Duke above-mentioned, who will expect to see him continued in this thing, or that he shoud be considered in something else.

Thus, my Lord, it stands, as to the contracts, in which I was engaged before the coming in of the late Ministry; and it was for these difficulties, as well as for the consideration of the long warning, which is requisite to make void the present agreements, that induced me to give your Grace the answer I did to your very obliging offer, 'That I did not know what to say as to the business of contracts'.

He concluded by asking for something consistent with his 'walk in life' as a banker, and with the engagements which the Government had to other people.[1]

I take next the Government financiers — who were they? A list of them for 1759–60 can be compiled by taking the names of those whose advice Newcastle, as First Lord of the Treasury, sought in the severe financial crisis of 1759, and from the list of the underwriters to the £8,000,000 loan floated at the end of the year.

A series of papers drawn up by Newcastle and letters written by him between January and April 1759 testify to the intense anxiety he felt at the drain of specie from the Bank and the country, and 'the impossibility of going on in this way'.[2] On 18 April 1759 he wrote from Claremont:

I have order'd Mr. West, and shall do it myself, when I come to town next week, to talk to the most knowing people in the City, vizt. Mr. Gideon, Alderman Baker, Sir Jos. Vanneck, Mr. Bristowe of the S.S. [South Sea] Company, Mr. J. Gore, Mr. Martin, and Mr. Amyand, upon the present state of credit, and the surprising fall of the stocks.[3]

And on 4 August 1759 he complained to his late secretary, Andrew Stone:

[1] 32967, ff. 434-6.
[2] See Newcastle's Memorandum of 28 Feb 1759; 32888, f. 275.
[3] 32890, f. 125.

I saw yesterday the Governor [Merrick Burrell] and Dep.
Governor of the Bank [Bartholomew Burton], Sir Joshua Vanneck,
Mr. Joseph Mellish, Mr. Gore's partner, Amyand, Magens, and
Gashry; and I find we shall have the greatest difficulty to borrow
any considerable sum upon the Vote of Credit.[1]

He directed, therefore, West:

to consider of proper persons, vizt.: Sir J. Vanneck, Mr. Gore,
Mr. Bristowe, Ald[n] Baker, Mr. Thornton, Mr. Gideon, etc., to be
turning their thoughts for raising the money the next year.[2]

The negotiations for the loan were successfully concluded
in December; and, on the 12th, Newcastle wrote in reply to
a request from Lord Bath to be allotted £30,000:

The sum to be raised this year . . . (viz. eight millions) was so
great, that I found it absolutely necessary to agree for it with the
principal and most responsible men in the City. . . . It is not now
in my power to oblige them to lessen the sums they have agreed
for. If your Lordship had sent me your commands last week,
I should have taken care that they should have been complied
with.[3]

The following list [4] gives the names of these 'principal and
most responsible men in the City' and the sums underwritten
by them:

[1] 32893, f. 481.

[2] 'Memorandums for Mr. West', 9 Sep 1759; 32895, f. 295.

[3] Bath to Newcastle, 11 Dec 1759; 32900, f. 5; Newcastle to Bath,
12 Dec, f. 16. Allotments for private people Newcastle secured by billeting
them on the lists of the principal underwriters. Two such lists are preserved
among the Newcastle Papers. 'I send your Grace Sir Joshua Vanneck's
and Mr. Amyand's list . . .', wrote West to Newcastle on 21 Dec 1759.
'I shewed each of those gentlemen the persons your Grace had allotted to
them and they were extreamly pleased' (32900, f. 383). On Amyand's list
(32901, f. 242) there are thirty-seven names for a total of £264,000, leaving
£660,000 to his own firm and its customers. Nineteen of the people
billeted on him were M.P.'s — among them John Wilkes for £5000.
Vanneck's list (f. 240) contains eighteen persons for a total of £200,000,
leaving his firm a clear million. His boarders include the Duke of Devonshire, the Earls of Lincoln, Ashburnham, Hertford, and Verney, Lords
Falmouth, Luxborough, and Anson, Lady Katherine Pelham (widow of
Henry Pelham), John Roberts (Pelham's late secretary), Sir Edward Hawke
(the admiral), and a few Members of Parliament.

[4] 32901, f. 238.

£

The proprietors of Tallies and Orders made out at the Exchequer by virtue of an Act of the last Session of Parliament for enabling His Majesty to raise the sum of one million for the uses and purposes therein mentioned	1,000,000
Mr. Burrell for the Bank of England	466,000
Mr. Bristow for the South Sea Company	330,000
Mr. Godfrey for the East India Company	200,000
Sir Joshua Vanneck & Co.	1,200,000
Mr. Amyand	924,000
Sir James Colebrooke	480,000
Mr. Magens	460,000
Mr. Touchet	420,000
Mr. Nesbitt	350,000
Mr. Muilman	330,000
Mr. Fonnereau	250,000
Mr. Salvadore	250,000
Mr. Martin	250,000
Mr. Honywood	250,000
Mr. Belchier	250,000
Mr. Beckford	100,000
Mr. Hart	100,000
Mr. Fox	80,000
Mr. John Gasper Ringmacher	100,000
Mr. Edwards	50,000
Mr. Gideon	60,000
Mr. Thornton	100,000
	8,000,000

From these sources, checked by other correspondence, I select the names of twenty-two leading City men in close touch with the Treasury and deeply engaged in Government finance ; [1] the constituencies marked against their names without any

---

[1] Henry Fox, M.P., Paymaster-General of the Forces, and Francis Gashry, M.P., Treasurer and Paymaster of the Ordnance, are omitted, as they were not City men and operated with Government money, though, of course, at their own risk and to their own advantage ; further, I omit W. Belchier, M.P., who became bankrupt in 1760 ; William Beckford, M.P., because he was not, strictly speaking, a financier, but merely, as one of the richest men in the British Empire, subscribed a sum which placed him among the chief underwriters ; and Godfrey, Hart, and Ringmacher, whose names do not otherwise appear among the City friends of the Treasury.

dates are those for which they were returned at the general election of 1761 :

George Amyand, M.P. for Barnstaple, Devon.
Sir William Baker, M.P. for Plympton, Devon.
John Bristow, M.P. for Arundel, Sussex.
Merrick Burrell, M.P. for Grampound, Cornwall.
Bartholomew Burton, M.P. for Camelford, Cornwall.
Sir James Colebrooke, Bart., M.P. for Gatton, Surrey.
George Colebrooke, M.P. for Arundel, Sussex.
John Edwards.
Thomas Fonnereau, M.P. for Sudbury, Suffolk.
Z. P. Fonnereau, M.P. for Aldborough, Suffolk.
Sampson Gideon.
John Gore (M.P. for Grimsby, Lincs, 1747–61).
Frazer Honywood, M.P. for Steyning, Sussex.
Nicholas Magens.
John Martin (M.P. for Tewkesbury, Gloucestershire, 1741–47).
Joseph Mellish, M.P. for Grimsby, Lincs.
Henry Muilman.
Arnold Nesbitt, M.P. for Cricklade, Wilts.
Joseph Salvadore.
John Thornton.
Samuel Touchet, M.P. for Shaftesbury, Dorset.
Sir Joshua Vanneck.

Thus fifteen of these twenty-two men at one time or another sat in Parliament, and thirteen were returned to it in 1761. Of the remaining seven, Gideon and Salvadore as Jews, and Vanneck (and probably also Magens) as foreign-born, were debarred from it ; but Vanneck's son-in-law Thomas Walpole, sat in Parliament, while both sons of Vanneck (Joshua and Gerard) and the son of Gideon entered it subsequently. So did Thornton's three sons (one of whom was Henry Thornton, the friend and collaborator of Wilberforce).

On some occasions the Government would go in search of a financial expert for the House of Commons, who could support it in debate with his technical knowledge. Thus in April 1759, when on a vacancy at Camelford, Newcastle instructed James West to consider who would answer the purpose best, West produced six names, seeking among them 'a speaker . . . some bold, spirited man with confidence and volubility', but sadly concluded that it was difficult to find these qualities 'joined to fidelity'.[1] Still, except when forced by circumstances, Government did not willingly encourage 'the moneyed men' to enter Parliament — in Newcastle's words, the 'East Indians, West Indians, citizens and brokers . . . are not very reputable and yet very troublesome Members'.[2]

I conclude with a letter written by James West when, on the death of Frazer Honywood, a banker and Member for Steyning, Newcastle wished a relative of the Duke of Portland to succeed him in the borough. On 31 January 1764 West informed Newcastle that Honywood's partner, Richard Fuller, would have to be the successor, and the reason given — the free postage which this secured for the firm — was in all probability one which to many merchants with an extensive inland correspondence added considerably to the attractions of the House of Commons :

Mr. West presents his respects to the Duke of Newcastle. He is just now informed from Sir W. Baker,[3] that he advised Mr. Fuller [4] last night to apply to Sir John Honeywood [5] for his interest at Steyning, as Sir John declared that neither he or his son would stand, and Mr. Atkins also declining, Sir John has given his interest to Mr. Fuller and an express is gone to Steyning to that purpose. As the correspondence of the shop is very great, having the draughts

---

[1] For the text of the letter, see below, pp. 341-2.

[2] See below, p. 210.

[3] Alderman Sir William Baker, M.P. for Plympton 1747-68, a friend and adherent of Newcastle.

[4] Richard Fuller, M.P. for Steyning 9 Feb 1764-68, and for Stockbridge 1768-74, son of Joseph Fuller, a Baptist minister. His grandfather, a well-known miser, was 'poor Mr. Fuller, who had an estate for each of his [six] sons, but nothing for himself'. Richard's brother William, with whom he was at one time in partnership, died 'a miser worth £400,000'. About them see J. F. Fuller, 'Pedigree of Fuller of Blewbury', *Miscell. Geneal. et Herald.*, fifth series, vol. i, pp. 81-8. They were no relations of the Fullers of Sussex and Jamaica.

[5] Sir John Honywood, third Bt. Frazer Honywood left him his fortune, to the disappointment of poorer relatives who were two degrees nearer to him and had 'expected to inherit considerable property' from him. But as the one had much money and no children, and the other was a baronet, they both thought themselves more closely related than they really were. See article by W. D'Oyly Bayley, 'The Relationship of the Honywoods, Baronets, of Kent, to Mr. Frazer Honywood, the Banker', in J. S. Nichol's *Topographer and Genealogist* (1846), vol. ii, pt. viii, pp. 189-92.

of the Bristol Bank, the very postage of their letters would amount to near £800 pr. ann., and it is otherwise thought to be of great service to the house to have one of the partners in Parliament. Sir Wm. Baker was one of the first promoters and encouragers of the shop, and has a great influence over Mr. Fuller. Mr. West would have rejoiced exceedingly to have been able to have served the Duke of Newcastle or the Duke of Portlands recommendation.[1]

IMMUNITY

Robbers.—'They likewise say that Bacon was obliged to get member, coast what it would, other ways he could not pass his accompts as contractor, he pay'd five guineas a man att Ailsbury.'[2] This was Anthony Bacon, Wilkes's successor as Member for Aylesbury, a Manxman who started his business career in the Maryland trade, subsequently became a Government contractor for the victualling of troops in the West Indies and Africa, a mine-owner and the founder of important iron works in Glamorganshire and one of the greatest manufacturers of munitions during the American Revolution.[3] Whether the reason for his first entry into Parliament is here correctly stated, I cannot say ; but in principle it was plausible. Twenty years later, various nabobs returning 'from India's plundered land', tried to insure against inquiries into the origin of their fortunes by providing themselves with seats in Parliament.

Muddlers.—On the failure of the expedition against Rochefort in the summer of 1757, Hardwicke favoured an inquiry into the conduct of the land officers, though most of them were Members of Parliament : [4]

It is true that the officers concerned are men of great quality, rank and distinction ; but, if that objection should finally prevail, men of quality ought not to be let into the Army, for it will ruin the service. Indeed I have for some time thought that the Army was too full of them.

[1] 32955, f. 320.
[2] Alexander Fall to Charles Jenkinson, 29 Jan 1764 ; Jucker, *op. cit.*, p. 259.
[3] About him see my essay in the Harvard *Journal of Economic and Business History*, vol. ii, no. 1, Nov 1929.
[4] Hardwicke to Newcastle, 16 Oct 1757 ; 32875, f. 144.

And again on 24 October :

> Had Byng's case been enquir'd into by a board of admirals, without the solemnity of a court martial, do you think the opinion would have turn'd out as it did ? I know some of the best of them think it a hardship put upon them ; and how can they deal with Members of Parliament and men of great quality ? I know this was said by some of them, upon occasion of the last reference, in the case of the officers, who concurr'd in the Council of War at Gibraltar.[1]

In extreme cases even Members of Parliament had to suffer — witness the fate of Admiral John Byng, M.P., and General Lord George Sackville, M.P. ; but for minor transgressions the membership of the House was apt to procure immunity.

Bastards.—This essay starts with the reason which in 1749 Lord Chesterfield gave to his son, Philip Stanhope, for wishing to see him in Parliament, the most universal, most obvious of reasons — 'you must first make a figure there if you would make a figure in your country' ; and here is another reason which Chesterfield confided to Newcastle in 1753, when he saw that his son's illegitimate birth counted against him in his career as a diplomat :

> As I shall bring him into the next Parliament at my own (and probably no small) expence, I flatter myself that his seat there will be so far like the cloak of charity as to cover one sin at least, and upon my word I know of no other for which he wants a cover.[2]

Bankrupts.—'I had rather see any child of mine want than have him get his bread by voting in the House of Commons', wrote Governor Pitt to his son on 16 January 1706.[3] But Robert Andrews, the political and financial agent of his grandson Thomas Pitt, the heir to Old Sarum, wrote to Newcastle on 28 February 1761 :

> As to his own burroughs he now tells me, his affairs in regard to his creditors are such that they cannot be finally ended under eight

---

[1] *Ibid.* f. 255.

[2] 30 June 1753 ; 32732, f. 133. Besides Ph. Stanhope, two bastards were returned to Parliament in 1761 : John Manners, M.P. for Newark, son of Lord William Manners ; and Ch. Fitzroy Scudamore, M.P. for Hereford, son of the second Duke of Grafton.

[3] See above, p. 16.

or nine months : and till they are ended, he shall be liable to arrests and vexatious actions from his creditors and therefore he proposes to choose Mr. Coke at Okehampton and one other at Old Sarum, that shall be named, and to fill the other seat at O.S. himself, under an engagement to relinquish it at the time his affairs are setled, which he thinks will be before the House meets next winter, and therefore intends to make no use of his election, but to secure himself from his creditors.[1]

And again on 2 March :

He bids me assure your Grace with the utmost truth and sincerity, that he has fairly and honestly no other motive to desire being chose at O.S. than what I have mentioned . . . and that he will religiously keep his engagement to vacate his seat again, when his perplexities are ended, to whoever he shall be directed to fill it with.[2]

Thomas Pitt, the elder brother of Chatham, had entered Parliament in 1727, directly he came of age ; he managed in Cornwall the general elections of 1741 and 1747 for Frederick, Prince of Wales, and saw himself in future next to the throne ; but in 1751, with the death of his patron, his chances disappeared, while the fortune amassed by his grandfather of diamond fame had been wasted, even his credit exhausted ; he had to give up Parliament, pawn his boroughs, seek obscurity, and flee the country. In 1761, as a man old beyond his years, bare of all hope, full of insane bitterness and wild griefs, he once more had himself returned for that ploughed field of Old Sarum which his grandfather had bought with money acquired in India ('Take care', he had written about a burgage in 1706, 'to plant the piece of new ground with as many trees as it will well take and the improvement of it may in time pay for the vote'). Thomas Pitt took refuge in that miraculous field. He touched it and was safe ; his name was in the writ returned from it on 30 March 1761 ; his creditors could not reach him. Four months later he did not need Parliamentary privilege any more, for the fall of the curtain upon his unnecessary life had signified that all was well with him again.

[1] 32919, f. 340.   [2] *Ibid.* ff. 378-9.

His son, though a better man, promptly repudiated the solemn engagement with regard to the filling of the vacancy.[1]

[1] Thomas Pitt, jun., wrote to Robert Andrews on 21 Aug 1761 : 'I have been often grieved at the scandalous traffick he made of his Parliamentary interest, but cou'd they [the Ministers] suppose me bound in other respects, they wou'd certainly alter their opinion when they come to know, that my father was under a previous engagement to myself to elect me at O.S. when I consented to the raiseing so large a sum for the payment of his debts, and this agreement therefore ought certainly to have taken place of every other consideration' (32927, f. 156).

II

THE ELECTORAL STRUCTURE
OF ENGLAND

THE DISTRIBUTION OF SEATS

THE British House of Commons in the eighteenth century consisted of 558 Members — 489 elected in England, 24 in Wales, and 45 in Scotland. Of the 245 English constituencies, the City of London and Weymouth *cum* Melcombe Regis returned four Members each, 238 two Members, and 5 one Member each; Scotland and Wales had single-member constituencies. Of the 489 English Members at the accession of George III, 80 represented the forty counties, 4 the two Universities, while 405 were returned by 203 cities and boroughs; of the 24 Welsh Members, 12 sat for counties and 12 for boroughs or groups of boroughs; of the 45 Scottish Members, 30 represented counties, one was returned by Edinburgh, and 14 by groups of boroughs.

England elected almost 88 per cent of the House of Commons, and English boroughs almost 73 per cent. Within England the distribution of the Parliamentary boroughs was uneven, as during the formative ages of Parliament population and wealth had been concentrated in the south, even more than they were in 1760. Including the knights of the shires, Cornwall had in the eighteenth century 44 Members in Parliament, Devonshire 26, Dorset 20, Somerset 18, Wiltshire 34 — together, 142; about one-fourth of the House of Commons was thus chosen by the five counties of south-western England. Hampshire returned 26, and Berkshire 9 Members. The three eastern counties south of the Thames, Surrey, Sussex, and Kent, together with the Cinque Ports, returned 60 Members. Thus 237 Members (*i.e.* more than 40 per cent of the House of Commons) were elected in the ten counties south of Bristol and the lower Thames. But the 56 Members for London and

Middlesex and the counties in their neighbourhood — Bucks, Beds, Herts, Essex, and Suffolk — must be added to this 'southern division'. This makes a total of 293 Members — more than half the House of Commons.

Another remarkable feature of the geographical distribution of English Parliamentary boroughs is that almost one-third of them were seaports. This again was a heritage from the times when even inland trade, carried on mainly by river and coastwise, centred in towns on the seaboard. But soon in the sea-borne trade a tendency to concentration set in, and London together with a dozen 'out-ports' swallowed up the trade of the smaller harbours. However much decayed, these still retained their Parliamentary representation, henceforth their most lucrative branch of business.

The obsolete distribution of seats naturally produced electoral absurdities and corruption. But in practice there was a redeeming side to it — as is usual with us, dead forms were made to serve live forces. In counties such as Cheshire, Durham, or Leicestershire, where only the county and the county town returned Members to Parliament, there was no room for outsiders; in fact, hardly enough to satisfy the Parliamentary ambitions of their own 'countrymen'. Nor would a more numerous representation, if based on genuine constituencies, have provided many seats for strangers. But the over-represented southern counties, with their rotten boroughs, offered a substantial surplus for national purposes, and it was there that seats were found for professional politicians, civil servants, and big merchants, *i.e.* for the administrative and commercial classes concentrated in London. At present the national as against the local type of candidate is planted out in the constituencies by the party organizations; in the eighteenth century this was done with the help of rotten or corrupt boroughs. Moreover, about 1760 London was probably the worst under-represented part of England; the area now under the L.C.C. contained more than one-tenth of the population of Great Britain; and even if heads were counted (as now), and not purses weighed (as in the eighteenth century), it ought to have had almost sixty Members. But its statutory representation

F

consisted of only ten : four Members for the City of London, and six for Middlesex, Westminster, and Southwark. The decayed boroughs of the south primarily supplied the corrective for this under - representation of classes which governed in London but could hardly have obtained many seats in independent provincial constituencies. The Government was the chief buyer of, or dealer in, Cornish and Devonshire boroughs, while the London merchants, unless they obtained their seats through the Government, or happened to be connected by origin, family ties, or their trade with some more distant county, cultivated those nearer London.

In 1770 Sir John Molesworth, a knight of the shire for Cornwall, supported a motion for disabling revenue officers from voting in Parliamentary elections. 'Those tools of any Administration', he said, 'have prevailed over the spoils of the East, have prevailed over all family connexions, all the landed interest. If this question is carried, I shall meet more of my countrymen in this House and the boroughs will oftener see their members.' [1] This might indeed have pleased patriotic or ambitious Cornishmen ; but, though something can be said in favour of civil servants and even of mere placemen in the eighteenth-century Parliament, it is hard to see what reason could be adduced for a greater number of Cornishmen than it actually contained ; there was quite a sufficient quota of Boscawens, Bullers, and Bassets, Trevanions, Trelawnys, and Treises.

THE COUNTIES

In all English counties the franchise was the same — ever since 1430 (8 Henry VI) the electorate consisted of forty-shilling freeholders. As the value of money had declined considerably in the intervening 330 years, by 1761 this franchise had become very wide ; especially as a very liberal interpretation was put on the term of freehold, extending it to leaseholds for life, annuities, rent-charges, mortgages, etc., and even to various petty offices.[2] In the smallest county in England,

[1] Sir Henry Cavendish's Debates ; Egerton MS. 220, f. 61.
[2] See E. Porritt, The Unreformed House of Commons, vol. i, pp. 22-3.

Rutland, the number of voters was reckoned in 1760 to be 609 ; [1] in the largest, Yorkshire, 15,054 electors voted in 1741, and 23,007 in 1807. The total electorate in the counties in 1761 cannot be accurately ascertained or calculated. County elections were inordinately expensive, and therefore very few English counties went to the poll — at the general election of 1747 only three contests were fought out to the end (Lancashire, Middlesex, and Staffordshire) ; in 1754, five (Herefordshire, Hertfordshire, Kent, Oxfordshire, and Rutland) ; and in 1761, four (Durham, Hertfordshire, Rutland, and Westmorland). The figures therefore have to be taken from different years and only very rough and approximate estimates are possible ; moreover, these are based on the number of votes actually cast at various polls, and must therefore be short of the potential electorate. Such a calculation yields a probable total of about 160,000 actual voters for all the English counties, *i.e.* an average of about 4000 for each.

This might seem a numerous electorate. But as the voting was open and recorded in poll-books, people in dependent positions could seldom exercise a free choice ; and as the agricultural interest was dominant in the counties, the result of county elections was determined as a rule by the big landowners — the territorial magnates and the country gentlemen. Most counties, in fact, represented this one class only, and the candidates were often fixed upon at the Assizes or local races.

In a few counties only was there any serious influence of a different character. Middlesex was dominated by its London boroughs ; and also in Surrey the London boroughs were gaining in size and importance. 'In some parts of the county, the country gentlemen are said not to like the influence which the borough of Southwark and parts adjacent have in the election for knights of the shire', wrote 'Surriensis' in the *Gentleman's Magazine* in 1788.[2] 'But if, in Queen Anne's

[1] Hardwicke to Sir Gilbert Heathcote, 4 Dec 1760 ; 35596, ff. 197-201.

[2] 'Historical Account of the Elections for Surrey', p. 1053. 'Surriensis' was Sir Joseph Mawbey, a Vauxhall distiller, M.P. for Southwark 1761-74, and for Surrey 1775-90. The identity is disclosed in the obituary note of Sir Joseph Mawbey in the *Gentleman's Magazine*, 1798, vol. i, p. 543 : 'His correspondence with our Magazine may be seen in his history of the Surrey elections, vol. lviii, p. 1052'.

time, that commercial influence was strong enough to bring
in a Member . . . we must not wonder if it should operate
effectually in the present times.' Still, judging by the poll-book
of 1774, even at that date the 'metropolitan' vote in Surrey
could hardly have exceeded 20 per cent.[1] Also in the other
home counties a certain metropolitan influence was felt through
freeholders of these counties settled in London, and through
London merchants owning estates in its neighbourhood. In
certain western counties the clothiers and their employees had
to be reckoned with; Nicolson Calvert, M.P. for Tewkesbury,
when recommending 'the agent for the body of clothiers'
at Gloucester to Newcastle for a Government appointment,
remarked :

It would be needless for me to acquaint your Grace how opulent
and significant a body of men they are in the County of Gloucester,
and as well attach'd to the present Government as any set of men
in this Kingdom.[2]

Even in the vast county of Yorkshire the 'trading places' were
of some importance,[3] and Sir George Savile was described in
1753 by one of his supporters as 'the properest candidate for
this trading county as the situation of his property makes the
prosperity of trade more immediately his concern'.[4]

In Hampshire the Government had an 'interest' through
the Portsmouth and Gosport docks, the Crown tenants in the
New Forest, and through its dependants in the Isle of Wight;
and because of H. B. Legge's case in 1761 and the putting up
of the Court candidate in 1779, it forms part of the regular

[1] There is, in the British Museum, a MS. poll-book of the by-election
for Surrey in 1742 (39291), with a summary of the places of residence of
the 3428 freeholders who voted in that election. 557, i.e. slightly more than
16 per cent, were resident outside the county — 152 of them in London,
31 in Westminster, and 170 in Middlesex, together 353 ; and surely not
the whole of Middlesex can be included in the metropolitan area. 135 were
resident in Southwark and 204 in the Hundred of Brixton, which extended
well into the country. If we put the total metropolitan vote at 500, this is
less than 15 per cent.
[2] 31 May 1760 ; 32906, f. 399.
[3] See letter from Andrew Wilkinson to Newcastle, Boroughbridge,
13 July 1753 ; 32732, ff. 236-7.
[4] Same to same, 19 July 1753 ; ibid. ff. 313-14.

stock-in-trade of text-books. But a careful analysis of the poll-book of 1779 shows that even in Hampshire the direct Government influence can hardly have affected more than one-tenth of the electorate, if so much. Also in Kent the Government had a certain direct influence, especially through the Chatham docks and the Cinque Ports,[1] and in Cornwall through the numerous revenue officers.[2]

Other possible instruments of Government influence in the counties were the bishops and clergy, who formed a network over the whole of England, and as landholders had a certain electoral interest of their own. The help of the episcopate was often invoked. Thus Sir William Maynard, when standing for Essex in 1759, thought it 'of great consequence to him' if Newcastle applied 'to the Bishop of London for his interest

[1] Lord Sondes wrote to Newcastle, 30 Aug 1767 : '. . . the weight of Government, which is more considerable in this county, than any other, having so many churches, docks, hospitals, and custom houses almost in every town from Greenwich to Dover, and I believe no instance of any body loosing the election, that stood upon the Government interest except in 1734, which was owing to the Excise' (32984, f. 368). And Anson to Hardwicke, 31 May 1760 : '. . . upon examining all the votes influenced by Admiralty power (which are many more than I thought them to be) I found . . .' (35359 ff. 427-8). See also letter from Lord Winchilsea to Newcastle, 25 Aug 1767 (*ibid*. ff. 325-6). But on the other hand see the letter which Sir George Oxenden, an old Kentish Whig with a rare knowledge of the county, wrote to Hardwicke on 9 Dec 1760, at a time when the Tories professed hopes of carrying both seats : '. . . the Tories are very uppish . . . possibly they depend upon the Court interest, in the docks, ports &c. Now, my Lord . . . I will venture to prophesy . . . that even supposing that to be the case, we shall be their masters, provided the Whigs are not broke among themselves' (35692, ff. 434-5).

[2] Admiral Boscawen, who intended to stand for Cornwall, wrote to Newcastle, 11 Oct 1760 : 'I . . . intreat your Grace would favour me with the vote and interest of the officers of the Revenue, which are many, in this county and of great weight' (32913, ff. 63-4). While revenue officers were as yet free to vote in elections, those of the Post Office were strictly forbidden to interfere in Parliamentary elections. None the less, the Post Office formed a convenient election agency in the hands of the Government ; its offices in the small towns were places of concourse, conversation, and intelligence, and the postmasters could sometimes be of considerable help by delaying, directing, or misdirecting correspondence at election time, or even by culling useful information from letters opened by them. In spite of all prohibitions the Post Office was used in elections ; thus at a by-election in May 1760, Newcastle asked Lord Bessborough, Joint P.M.G., to 'give the usual directions, that the several post-masters in the county of Kent may know that they are to support Sir Wyndham Knatchbull's interest' (35692, f. 416).

with the clergy'.[1] Similarly, Lord Clanricarde, in the Hampshire election of 1759, asked Newcastle for a letter from the Bishop of Winchester in support of Legge, which would enable him to 'carry many of the clergy'.[2] But the hold which the bishops had on them was limited, and a Whig Government could never rely on the great mass of the lower clergy. Thus Thomas Secker, Bishop of Oxford, wrote to Hardwicke on 8 February 1753 :

> The small property I have in Oxfordshire is either in the hands, or in the neighbourhood, of persons whom I cannot influence. . . . I have no preferments to give the clergy. I cannot promise or threaten to behave to them according as they vote.[3]

In short, the direct influence and power of the Government in county elections was negligible ; if the Crown or Administration interfered at all, they had mainly to work through the big landowners who, if united, were the deciding influence in thirty-nine out of forty English counties.

The regular formula for candidates in the counties was to ask the 'Gentlemen, Clergy, and Freeholders' for their votes and interest — 'interest' denoting the influence which they could bring to bear on dependants. Neither in counties nor in boroughs was the least attempt made to hide or disguise the methods by which votes were secured ; the resultant of social forces was thus obtained without recourse to election stunts. It was taken for granted that the tenants would vote as instructed by their landlord or his agent, and the methods employed were so common that they were seldom named. Here, however, are a few explicit statements : 'I have . . . wrote . . . to my steward to engage my tenants to vote for Mr. Legge', wrote Sir John Miller of Lavant to Newcastle on 7 November 1759.[4] Or again, Lord Monson, on 29 November 1760 : 'Mr. Whichcote begs your Grace will use your best endeavours with Lord Irwin and Mr. Ingram, as no orders as yet are given to their stewards'. Daniel Parker Coke, one of the most upright and independent men of his time and a

---

[1] Lord Rochford to Newcastle, 17 Apr 1759 ; 32890, f. 118.
[2] 3 Nov 1759 ; 32898, ff. 73-4.   [3] 35592, f. 30.
[4] 32898, f. 165.

barrister of very high standing, declared in his nomination
speech at Nottingham in 1803 that he considered it 'quite fair'
that landlords should exercise political influence over their
tenants, and that he would be 'sorry to see the day when men
of property would not use such influence'.[1] Indeed, the idea
that tenants owed political suit to their landlords survived deep
into the nineteenth century.   In the Flintshire election of 1841,
one of the Grosvenor family

complained of Mr. Gladstone for violating the sacred canons of
electioneering etiquette by canvassing Lord Westminster's tenants.
'I did think,' says the wounded patrician, 'that interference between
a landlord with whose opinions you were acquainted and his tenants
was not justifiable according to those laws of delicacy and propriety
which I considered binding in such cases.'[2]

But it was at all times the first article of constitutional cant
to describe the right of freely choosing representatives as 'the
most valuable privilege of every English freeholder'.

   In reality, because of the influence which the landlord had
over his tenants, the political position of a man in his county,
and even to some extent the claim which he could urge for
appearing as candidate, was measured by his rental.   At the
general meeting at York in 1753, Lord Rockingham, when
putting forward Sir George Savile as candidate for the county,
emphasized 'the great property 'which Savile had in it,[3] while
Thornhagh, to give proper weight to his support of Savile,
'talked a great deal of his brother's interest and estate'.[4]   When
Lord Exeter applied to Sir Gilbert Heathcote for his support
in Rutland, Hardwicke was at a loss what advice to give, as
'an absolute submission may exclude him for ever from taking
advantage of the great property which he has in that county'.[5]
In September 1760 the Lincolnshire gentlemen serving in the
militia bethought themselves 'that as they were so considerable
a body together, and had so large a share of property, they

[1] See article about him in the *D.N.B.*
[2] John Morley, *The Life of William Ewart Gladstone* (1905), vol. i, p. 239.
[3] Andrew Wilkinson to Newcastle, York, 16 July 1753 ; 32732, ff. 282-3.
[4] Henry Pelham to Newcastle, Scarborough, 18 July 1753 ; *ibid.*
ff. 301-4.
[5] Hardwicke to Newcastle, 11 June 1760 ; 32907, f. 157.

would do well to consult together about the proper persons to represent the county'.[1] Examples of this kind could easily be multiplied: the conditions which they illustrate were the inevitable result of open voting by people in dependent positions.

When high-sounding phrases were used in an election about the 'independence' of the county and the rights of its freeholders, they did not refer to the right of tenants to make their own choice between candidates, but almost invariably signified a conflict between the rank and file of the country gentlemen and some large aristocratic influence.[2] Broadly speaking, in the south-west and west of England and in many of the midland counties the country gentry were dominant — in Cornwall, Devonshire, Somerset, Dorset, and Wiltshire, practically to the exclusion of aristocratic influence; with one single exception, no son of a peer ever represented any of these five counties between 1707 and 1801.[3] In Somerset the minor gentry are said to have gone so far 'as to pledge themselves not to vote for the brother or son of a peer . . . or for a candidate whom a peer supported'[4] — 'the lords . . . I heate the very name of *themmun*', declared Squire Western.[5] In the eastern counties and in the north the big aristocratic houses had a very considerable say in county elections.

But even where a territorial magnate or a combination 'of the great men of the county' were able to exert a dominant influence in elections, they had to be extremely careful not to

[1] John Green, Dean of Lincoln, to Hardwicke, 27 Sep 1760; 32912, ff. 301-2.

[2] This conflict sometimes coincided with a division between Tories and Whigs, but by no means always, perhaps not even in the majority of cases.

[3] Even this one exception does not run counter to the rule: it occurred because the father of George Pitt, M.P. for Dorset, was in 1776 created Lord Rivers. But the Pitts were one of the most typical West Country gentry families. In Wiltshire on two occasions the Herberts of Wilton, one of the oldest aristocratic families in the county, contested its representation against the Goddards of Swindon, typical country gentlemen. Each time the hue and cry was raised by the country gentry against the Pembroke family, and the Goddard was returned, in 1772 apparently without a poll (about that election see 'The Diary of Thomas Smith', in the *Wilts Archaeol. Mag.*, vol. xi), in 1772 after a battle royal fought out to the bitter end.

[4] See F. Harrison, 'The Great Election Contest in Wiltshire in 1772', *Wiltshire Notes and Queries*, Mar 1906, p. 229.

[5] Henry Fielding, *Tom Jones*, book vi, ch. ii.

excite the jealousy of the country gentlemen. Hardly ever was an attempt made in a county to fill both seats with members of the same family,[1] which, it might have been said, would in appearance have degraded it to the level of a pocket borough. It even seldom happened that both seats were filled by sons of peers ; as a rule, a country gentleman was joined to the aristocratic candidate. Sometimes the aristocratic 'connexion' was able to select the country gentleman, but more often they had to leave the choice to the general meeting of the county. Any appearance of 'dictating' was apt to provoke resentment and opposition.

In 1753, Philip Yorke, having been requested by the Duke of Bedford to propose Lord Upper Ossory for Bedfordshire, asked his father, Lord Hardwicke, whether in his speech he should pay any compliment to the Duke, on whose interest Upper Ossory was standing ; Hardwicke replied that he should not even mention the Duke :

. . . things of that kind are apt not to be well taken by the gentlemen of the countrey. It seems to suppose an influence from such great families, which is not popular to hint to them. The old Lord Onslow (*Stiff Dick*) us'd allways to talk to the Surrey gentlemen as if he was nothing, and it was their interest and support only that he relied upon, which took with them extremely.[2]

During the great Oxfordshire election of 1754 the number of peers on the Whig side (Marlborough, Harcourt, Guilford, and Macclesfield) was a favourite taunt of the Tory country gentlemen against their opponents, and Oxfordshire became a byword in the West Country. ''Tis said, Ld. Weymouth has declared an opposition for this county [Wilts.]', wrote Miss Frances Ernle to her cousin Mrs. Legh on 16 October 1756. 'Mr. Thyn is to be the person so that everybody begins to look about them, these are early days and they do not intend to Oxfordshire us, do they ?'[3]

---

[1] Between 1761 and 1784 there were only two such cases : two Foleys, father and son, represented Herefordshire 1768–74, and two Hills, rather distant cousins, represented Shropshire 1780–84.
[2] 24 July 1753 ; 35351, ff. 239–40.
[3] Money-Kyrle MSS. at Whetham, Wilts.

Rockingham, writing to Newcastle on 24 January 1761 about his success in arranging matters in Yorkshire, was proud of the cry of aristocratic influence having proved ineffective against him :

I have experienced by it that the friendships, which many do me the honour to bear towards me in this county, is *proof* against the clamour that was attempted to be raised personally against me, as desiring to dictate to the county, and which cry tho' your Grace knows the principles and independency of Yorkshire gentlemen, did not affect the decision of any one person, whom I ever reckoned my friend.[1]

In County Durham the Bishop Palatine and the Earl of Darlington, when united, had an exceptionally powerful territorial interest. None the less, to secure one seat to Darlington they had 'as to the other to follow, not to force, the bent of the county';[2] and at the by-election in 1760 the Bishop, to avoid 'the envy and jealousies' that would have attended an early pronouncement on his part, waited to 'feel the pulse' of the county, and therefore refused to declare for any candidate before the general meeting.[3]

The Duke of Northumberland declared in 1774 that if the gentlemen of the county 'would do him the honour to support his son, he would coincide with the sense of the county in the choice of the other member'. No agreement was, however, reached at the general meeting at Morpeth on 26 July, and Lord Algernon Percy and Sir John Hussey Delaval were put up by the Duke of Northumberland, supported by the Duke of Portland and Lords Carlisle, Ravensworth, and Tankerville, while Sir William Middleton and William Fenwick became the candidates of the country gentlemen led by Sir Henry Grey of Howick (but supported also by the Earls of Strathmore and Scarbrough). In the numerous pamphlets and handbills published during that contest,[4] on the very eve of the American

[1] 32918, f. 47.

[2] Lord Mansfield to Newcastle, 29 Sep 1760 ; 32912, ff. 227-8.

[3] Richard Trevor, Bishop of Durham, to Newcastle, 2 Oct 1760 ; *ibid.*, ff. 303-4.

[4] Republished in the *Complete Collection of all the Papers which have appeared from the different Parties in the present Contest for Members for the County of Northumberland* (1774).

Revolution, America is hardly mentioned, and even home politics take second place; the main question before the electorate was whether or not the Duke of Northumberland had kept his promise to accept the 'sense of the county' as to the second member. The result of the election was characteristic: Lord Algernon Percy and Sir William Middleton were returned — the contest was obviously decided by the vote of those who wished to be fair to both sides and were not committed to either, and the compliment of one seat was made to the House of Alnwick, while the right of the country gentlemen to the other was successfully vindicated.

To sum up : the landed gentry were the deciding element in most county elections, though a certain number of seats were conceded by them to the great noble houses — in 1761, 16 out of 80 knights of the shires were sons of British peers and ten of them courtesy lords ; the remaining 64 were country gentlemen. The electorate in the counties formed an independent and fairly large class ; still, it would be ludicrous to talk of any kind of 'democracy' in 39 out of 40 counties. Taking England as a whole, probably not more than one in every twenty voters at county elections could freely exercise his statutory rights, and the county Members, though a valuable element in the House in that most of them were independent of the Government, constituted the purest type of class representation in Great Britain, to a high degree of an hereditary character. Of no less than 32 among the 80 knights of the shires returned in 1761, the fathers had previously represented the same counties, while another 17 had been preceded since the Restoration by more distant ancestors in the direct male line ; together 49 out of 80 can be said to have inherited their seats. Of another 22, ancestors in the direct male line had sat in Parliament since 1660, though for different constituencies, and only 9 were without Parliamentary ancestry in the male line from which a title could have descended to them without special remainder. These nine included the two Members for Middlesex and three Members for Berkshire, Bedfordshire, and Suffolk, whose families had risen through the City or the law.

THE PARLIAMENTARY BOROUGHS

The books on English Parliamentary boroughs published by T. H. B. Oldfield between 1792 and 1820 are a mine worked by generations of historians, with little or no attempt on their part to refine the ore. Oldfield was one of the many West Country attorneys deeply engaged in election business ; [1] his

---

[1] Comparatively little is known about him ; the article in the *D.N.B.* adds the date of his death to the information contained in the British Museum catalogue. In the debate on the disfranchisement of East Retford on 11 June 1827 Charles Tennyson mentioned Oldfield as having been 'employed at Retford by one of the parties in the election of 1812' (*Hansard*, new series, vol. xvii, columns 1209-10). But Porritt's assertion in his *Unreformed House of Commons* (vol. i, p. 358) that Oldfield himself was a dealer in boroughs rests on slender evidence. In the debate on the borough of Penryn, 8 May 1827, Alderman Waithman is thus reported in *Hansard*: 'He himself knew a borough agent who often had fifteen or twenty candidates for boroughs, or their agents at his table. There was one person in the city who must be well known to the leading Members of that House — he meant Mr. Oldfield — who frequently entertained more than twenty attorneys, each of whom introduced some stranger for the representation of a borough in Cornwall' (*ibid.* column 693). Porritt identifies the 'borough agent' mentioned in the first sentence with the Oldfield mentioned in the second, and that Oldfield with T. H. B. Oldfield. The first identification seems uncertain, the second would seem plausible ; still, if Waithman is correctly reported and used the proper tenses, it would appear that the Oldfield he meant was alive in 1827, whereas T. H. B. Oldfield is stated to have died in 1822. But it is not certain what Waithman did say — a very different report of his speech appeared in *The Times* of 9 May 1827 : 'There was what he might call a regular market for borough-seats, at the commencement of every Parliament. This was clearly shown by Mr. Oldfield, the individual who has given the public *The History of Boroughs*. It was well known that at a dinner-party of borough electors, the agent would introduce to them an individual . . . of whom the electors knew nothing.' No connexion is indicated here between Oldfield and the agent who introduced the candidate — in short, the above evidence is not sufficiently clear to conclude that Oldfield the reformer was a professional dealer in boroughs.

A very different piece of biographical information concerning Oldfield is preserved in the Home Office papers at the P.R.O. (H.O. 42/30), in a letter from 'A Prisoner' to Henry Dundas, dated 'Fleet, 14 May 1794' :

Anonymous communications are seldom worth attending to, but this is worth attending to :—

Among the great number of miscreants in this country, who wish to overturn it's happy constitution is one Thomas Oldfield a prisoner here. This gentleman I understand was an Election Agent to Sir Godfrey Webster, and the Pelhams (as he calls them) in Sussex and is as he tells me the author of a book intitled the Boroughs of England exposed, published by a man on Ludgate hill, and from whom he receives pecuniary assistance at this moment, on account of some new matter which he is to bring out respecting the rotten part of the Constitution.

knowledge of the subject was both detailed and extensive, and the record he has left of it is unique. But he was a zealous Parliamentary reformer, and his works had a propagandist bias and purpose. He was out to expose the absurdities of the system and its corruption : it was not for him to show how practice softened and modified them. The picture he gives is at the best an X-ray photograph, and not a portrait.

Porritt's book on the *Unreformed House of Commons* is the outstanding modern piece of comprehensive research into the subject ; it is unbiased and scholarly, and there is no need to do his work once more. Whoever wishes for detailed information concerning the legal and technical aspects of the system, which remained practically unchanged from 1660 to 1832, will find it in his book. But covering centuries, it deals with the constant rather than with the changing elements, and cannot reproduce the colour of any single period.

Although there was a great variety of franchises in the English boroughs, broadly speaking they can be divided into five types. There were boroughs : (1) with what practically amounted to universal franchise ; (2) where the franchise was in those paying scot and lot ; (3) where the vote was in the freemen ; (4) where the franchise was limited to the corporation ; (5) where the franchise was attached to certain houses or plots of ground called burgages. The freemen boroughs were the most numerous — about eighty ; those with an almost universal franchise were few — about a dozen ; the remaining boroughs (about 110) were almost equally divided among the remaining three groups.[1]

He is avowedly closely connected with the parties lately taken up for treasonable proceedings, and has to my knowledge many papers in his possession which would lead to discovery. His Jacobinical doctrines broached here are well known to us all, and evidence in abundance can be produced to fully convict him of treasonable intentions.

[The first edition of Oldfield's *History of the Boroughs of Great Britain* was published by C. Riley, 33 Ludgate Street ; Seaford receives in it at least ten times the space of the average borough ; and Oldfield admits having played an active part in recent Seaford elections, 'Henry Flood, who was introduced to the borough by the author of this work . . .']

[1] I follow here in a general way the account of the franchise given in E. Halévy, *A History of the English People in 1815* (pp. 113-30), though I do not adhere to it in every detail.

The numbers for each category are here but roughly indicated, as no two of the best authorities fully agree in their calculations. There were various mixed forms which lend themselves to different classifications. Moreover the nature of the particular franchises in quite a number of boroughs continued to be contested until they were all swept away by the Reform Act of 1832. To give but one example : Pontefract in 1761 was a burgage borough, and the House of Commons confirmed this franchise by its determinations of 1770 and 1775, but in 1783, 1784, and 1793 reversed those decisions and vested the right of election in the resident householders.

But the franchise alone, though it broadly suggests the character of a borough, did not necessarily determine it ; it is obvious that where votes were attached to certain lands or houses, whoever held a majority of such burgages (which were seldom more than 200, and at Old Sarum as few as seven) had the borough representation in his pocket. The burgage franchise therefore suggests private ownership, and this, in fact, was by 1760 the state of most burgage boroughs but by no means of all (see, e.g., the Chippenham election of 1818). On the other hand, private property in representation could be established even in a borough with a very wide franchise but without inhabitants, where 'a single person . . . keeps a few wretched inhabitants to return whoever he dictates to them'.[1] Oldfield quotes Gatton as an example, where the franchise was wide but the borough consisted 'of only *six houses*' ; and, according to Brayley, in the reign of Henry VIII Sir Roger Copley described himself as its 'burgess and only inhabitant'.[2]

A classification by the size of the electorate gives, perhaps, a better idea of Parliamentary boroughs than any analysis by franchises, though even this must not be made the basis for sweeping generalizations. While burgage boroughs were predestined to become pocket boroughs, narrow corporations offered a favourable field for the operations of the Government and of rich men willing to negotiate and to pay. Still, occasionally a narrow corporation in a flourishing, self-respecting town

[1] Oldfield, *Key to the House of Commons* (1820), p. 63.
[2] *History of Surrey*, vol. iv, p. 92.

acted a very different part. At Bath the Corporation counted 32 members ; but in 1761 it elected William Pitt and Field-Marshal Lord Ligonier, than whom no one was less likely to engage in the usual election practices. The Corporation at Devizes consisted of 38 members, but on a canvass in 1761, 26 electors promised their votes to the old Recorder of the borough, John Garth, a man of small means but high standing in the town, and only eight to Thomas Fludyer, brother and partner of Sir Samuel Fludyer, Bt., M.P., one of the richest men in England.[1] At Bedford, on the other hand, where the right of election was in the freemen and burgesses and in householders not receiving alms, there were in 1774 about 1000 voters, which would make it seem a free and popular borough. But there the Corporation had an unlimited power to create even non-resident freemen, and in 1769 Sir Robert Bernard, a rich Huntingdon-shire squire and a pillar of the ultra-radical Bill of Rights Society, having wrested the control of the Corporation from the Duke of Bedford, made some 500 new freemen, mostly among his Huntingdonshire tenants or neighbours ; and he added another few hundred in the course of the next twenty years. In 1789 the young Duke of Bedford succeeded him as Recorder of the town, and in turn had 350 freemen created mainly from among 'his own tenants or tradesmen, or the tenants and tradesmen of other persons attached to him in politics'.[2]

Nor did even the largest electorates preclude bribery — drink and a few guineas for each voter taking the place of substantial payments and petty offices for a local oligarchy. Gloucester, where 1500 voters went to the poll in 1761, can serve as example. George Selwyn, who represented it from 1754 till 1780, wrote to Lord Holland on 19 March 1761 :

---

[1] See Charles Garth (eldest son of John Garth) to Newcastle, 9 Feb 1762 ; 32934, ff. 243-4.

[2] Thomas A. Blyth, *History of Bedford*, p. 113 ; see also Dodsley's *Annual Register*, 1769, under date of 4 Sep, p. 128 ; and T. W. Pearse, *Observations on the Schedule of the Records and other Documents of the Corporation of Bedford* (1876), p. 11 : 'In 1780, Sir Robert Bernard lent the Corporation £950, and it may be assumed that the loan was not entirely unconnected with this last admission of freemen '.

Two of my voters were murdered yesterday by an experiment which we call shopping, that is, locking them up and keeping them dead drunk to the day of election. Mr. Snell's agents forced two single Selwyns into a post chaise, where, being suffocated with the brandy that was given them and a very fat man that had the custody of them, they were taken out stone dead. Here follows a hanging; in short, it is one roundeau of delights.[1]

And that Selwyn, who was inclined to embroider his stories, did not add much on this occasion, is proved by an account of the incident transmitted to the Duke of Newcastle by Dr. Henry Gally, a famous scholar and Prebendary of Gloucester.[2]

A treatise on the management of freemen in a populous borough is supplied in the beautifully detailed and systematic instructions which John Calcraft issued to his agents at Rochester previous to the general election of 1768 : [3]

[1] See the Earl of Ilchester, *Letters to Henry Fox, Lord Holland*, p. 145. Selwyn's passion for witnessing executions was a standing joke among his friends.

[2] 'The friends of Mr. Barrow and Mr. Selwyn, being informed that Mr. Snell's agents had been decoying several of the freemen of this city into public houses where they were made drunk and then sent out of town in order to prevent their voting at the next election, were obliged to desire yesterday several of the lower class of people to keep together at the New Inn, a public house in this city, but one Matthews, an inn-keeper, having a most enterprizing genius, raised a ladder against one of the windows, got into the house, and took one Pace, a freeman (in the interest of Mr. Barrow and Mr. Selwyn), out of his bed and got him out of the window, and having also by the assistance of one Peyton, a watchmaker in this city, got another freeman, one Clifford, into their custody, they drenched them well with spiritous and strong liquors and put them into a post chaise and last night very late attended them to a house belonging to Mr. Snell's son at Coldthrop about four miles off, but when they opened the chaise door the two persons therein were found to be quite dead. . . . There are now several other persons seized and confined in places unknown which they call shopping . . . so that the agents of Mr. Barrow and Mr. Selwyn are obliged to keep constant guard to prevent these kidnapping attempts which are carried on in defiance of all authority and with the utmost insolence and audacity' (32921, f. 22). For Dr. H. Gally, see the *D.N.B.*, and Nichols's *Literary Anecdotes*, vol. ii, p. 274 ; also in the Newcastle MSS. numerous letters to the Duke begging for Church preferments as reward for his election services. About the above incident, see also *London Chronicle*, 21–4 Mar 1761.

[3] The document, in the possession of Mr. D. C. D. Ryder, of Rempstone Hall, Dorset, is not dated, and the borough which it concerns not named. My reasons for referring it to the Rochester election of 1768 are these : Calcraft was concerned in the boroughs of Rochester, Poole, Wareham, and Corfe Castle. He gave up his attempts at capturing Corfe Castle without ever fighting an election, and amicably carried his claims at Wareham ; while at

These instructions must be thoroughly attended to, the proper persons and places pitch'd and a plan laid accordingly—

To fix the names of half a dozen or more stout freemen, to attend the barr, to make room for our friends to poll easily, and constantly, if possible, to keep the possession of the barr.

To fix on persons who are to attend each house where freemen are, from Sunday evening till the time of polling, and they to keep constantly at those houses, and never stirr out of them till the election is finished; except it be to poll themselves.

To fix on about half a dozen active persons (whether freemen or not) to conduct about 12 or 14 freemen at a time from the houses where they are kept, to the polling place, with directions to see them all polled before they leave them. And let the house managers alwaies deliver out those freemen first, whom they think most doubtfull, and endeavour as much as may be to keep them sober till they have polled.

To endeavour as much as may be alwaies to keep a head of the poll.

By no means to make a parade with the freemen the morning of the election, but to get them as soon as may be, into your private houses, and keep them there till they are polled: to prevent the other side geting away any straglers.

To have some sensible persons, to go about the town, and the poll house, and to the houses of entertainment of the other side, to get away any drunken, or stragling freemen, and to talk with them properly, and poll them immediately, or carry them to our private houses to be conducted from thence to poll.

To every person employed in any office, to have his instructions in writing what part he is to take and desired strictly to adhere to it as a great deal will depend upon conduct and good management.

Towards the close of the poll to spare no expense that may seem necessary.

Between this time and the election get what doubtful persons you can into your private houses and entertain them there till the election comes on.

Poole, where his candidate had to meet an opposition, the total electorate consisted only of about a hundred burgesses — they were too few to require methods such as described in the instructions, and moreover were not freemen. But Rochester was a freemen borough with an electorate of over 500, and Calcraft fought there hotly contested elections in 1765 and 1768. His paper specially mentions the instructions to be given 'to every person employed in any office', which suggests Government support; this he had in 1768, but not in 1765 when he stood in opposition to Grey Cooper, Secretary to the Treasury.

G

Thus neither the franchise nor the size of the electorate gives absolutely reliable indication of its character. Still, one may say with Aristotle, 'the many are more incorruptible than the few'; and with an election agent of Newcastle's, 'it's not in the power of any single person, let his weight be what it will', to determine the mood of 'sixteen or seventeen hundred English electors'.[1] The large constituencies opened a field for mass movements, clean and unclean; the small electorates, for quiet corruption and for loyalties sometimes fine and sometimes of a very peculiar character.

In 1761 only 22 of the 203 English boroughs had an electorate of over 1000. In the 'southern division' there were: Westminster with about 9000, the City of London with about 6000, and Southwark with about 1500 voters; Bristol with 5000, and Exeter, Canterbury, and Colchester with something over 1000 each. Thus of the 261 Members returned by the 129 borough constituencies in the south, 16 only, i.e. about 6 per cent, had an electorate exceeding 1000. In the rest of England, north of the Thames and of the wider London area, the total number of boroughs was much smaller — 74 returning 144 Members — and the corruption both of franchises and electorates was, on the whole, less advanced.[2] Fifteen of its boroughs had an electorate of over 1000,[3] and their Members formed more than 20 per cent of its borough representation. Together, the 46 representatives of English boroughs with an electorate of over 1000 formed almost 11½ per cent of its urban representation.

Next came, in 1761, 22 boroughs with an electorate of 500 to 1000; 13 in the 'northern' division [4] (18 per cent of its

---

[1] J. S. Charlton, M.P., to Newcastle, 1 Aug 1753, in reference to Nottingham; 32732, f. 393.

[2] In Yorkshire there were, however, nine pocket boroughs, and two in Lancashire.

[3] Norwich had nearly 3000 voters, Leicester, Nottingham, York, Newcastle-on-Tyne, Liverpool, Lancaster, and Worcester about 2000 each; Chester, Gloucester, and Coventry about 1500; Durham, Hull, Bridgnorth, and Northampton over 1000 each.

[4] Carlisle, Derby, Cirencester, Hereford, Preston, Grantham, Lincoln, Yarmouth (Norfolk), Newark, Oxford, Lichfield, Evesham, and Beverley.

borough representation), and only 9 in the 'southern' division (7 per cent).[1] Moreover, of the boroughs in the northern group 4 nearly reached the 1000 line (Oxford, Yarmouth, Lincoln, and Beverley), while 3 of the southern boroughs with an electorate of between 500–1000 — Honiton, Reading, and Sudbury — ranked among the most notoriously corrupt in England. Lastly, there were 11 boroughs with about 500 voters, 7 in the southern [2] and 4 in the northern division.[3]

Thus in the whole of England only 112 out of 405 borough representatives, *i.e.* almost 28 per cent, were returned by electorates of 500 or above; in the northern division nearly $44\frac{1}{2}$ per cent, in the southern nearly $18\frac{1}{2}$. Of the remaining 148 urban constituencies the majority consisted of 'close', 'rotten', or pocket boroughs, and these were most conspicuous in the south. None of the 21 Cornish boroughs had an electorate of more than 200; five of the eight Cinque Ports had less than 40 voters each; of the 16 Wiltshire boroughs none had more than 300 voters, and among the 12 Hampshire boroughs Southampton was the largest with about 400 voters; in Surrey and Sussex 28 out of 30 boroughs had less than 200 voters.

Though in most cases I put the number of voters higher than was done by 'the Committee appointed to report upon the State of Representation in England and Wales' (1792), the total figure which I get for the electorate of the 203 Parliamentary cities and boroughs in England in 1761 is about 85,000; 112 of the borough representatives of England were elected by 70,000, and 293 by 15,000 voters. The authors of the 'Report', believing that a sensible electoral system would mean sensible elections, wrote what on their premise is obvious common sense :

If three persons be chosen by 30, and two by 4970, though undoubted the five are chosen by 5000, still it will hardly be contended that such a distribution of the electors does not effectually take away every advantage of popular representation.

[1] Bedford, Reading, Honiton, Maldon, St. Albans, Maidstone, Ipswich, Sudbury, and Dover.
[2] Aylesbury, Wareham, Hertford, Rochester, Taunton, Chichester, and Sandwich.
[3] Stamford, Peterborough, Berwick, and Newcastle-under-Lyme.

It is certain that big popular constituencies had to be dealt with differently from rotten boroughs; it is equally certain that different types of men were attracted by different types of constituencies. A nabob such as Governor Watts of Bengal fame, when offered Ipswich, a middle-sized borough with an electorate of about 700, replied that he was 'quite unfit for a bustle', but always ready with his money 'where no kind of opposition can be'; [1] and James West, a hard-worked civil servant, after the flurry of a contested election at St. Albans (with over 500 voters), remarked to Newcastle in 1761 that 'a Secretary of the Treasury should not stand hereafter for a populous borough, within 20 miles of London'. [2] On the other hand, Edward Bacon in 1756, William Fitzherbert in 1762, and Sir Thomas Clavering in 1760, resigned their seats in rotten boroughs to stand for the populous towns of Norwich and Derby and the county of Durham, with which they were connected.

Still, had none of the boroughs been of the decayed or close type, would the ultimate result have been fundamentally different? Was not the root of the evil in the mentality of the age and the customs of the time, even more than in inherited or distorted franchises? Naturally there must have been interaction; but perhaps what made people endure the system was the fact that at that time there was no vast difference in outlook and morals between the populous cities and the rotten boroughs, and between the Members returned by the two. There is wisdom in Anatole France's favourite thesis that a country at any one time is capable of developing only one type of government; and Soame Jenyns, who had sat in Parliament from 1741 till 1780, in his *Thoughts on a Parliamentary Reform*, published in 1784, forestalled to some extent Anatole France:

Different modes of election may make some difference in the trouble and expence of the candidates, and may differently affect the morals of the people, and the peace of the country, but will make no difference in the representative body when brought together, and it is of little significance by what means they come there: the majority

---

[1] Gov. William Watts to James West, 19 Oct 1759; 32897, f. 263. About him see my article on Brice Fisher in the *English Historical Review*, Oct 1927.

[2] West to Newcastle, 23 Mar 1761; 32921, f. 16.

of any legislative assembly, consisting of 550 members, in the same circumstances and situation, will infallibly act in the same manner.[1]

This statement, though perhaps too sweeping, contains substantial truth.

Boroughs with over 1000 Voters

The first distinctive feature of the larger cities and boroughs was the frequency of election contests in them carried through to the bitter end. Of the 22 towns with over 1000 voters, eleven went to the poll in 1761; of the 22 towns with 500–1000 voters, twelve ; while of the remaining 201 English constituencies only 18 ; *i.e.* more than half of the larger boroughs were contested, and about one in ten of all the other constituencies. Like the counties, the large urban electorates could not be dominated easily and completely by a single interest, but differed from them in having a less homogeneous electorate, which made election calculations and agreements more difficult ; moreover, contests in them, though very expensive, were not quite so ruinous as in the counties.

The second outstanding feature was that none of the 22 largest towns could be converted into a Government borough. Not that the Government interest did not count ; every vote counted — a by-election at Southwark in 1743 was carried by a majority of 41 on a poll of 1655, and at Bristol in 1756 by 71 on a poll of 4765 ; and as the 'natural history' of every voter was known, each received consideration. But the 'interest' of the Government was only one among many in these boroughs, and, as in the counties, it had to add its mite to the fund of one or other powerful candidate.

In the absence of any one absolutely dominant interest, private or official, one never meets the 'yellow dog' among the representatives of these 22 towns. Even where there was a strong territorial interest, it had to be exercised by its holders in their own favour and could hardly ever have been assigned or transferred to outsiders. Among the 46 Members of these towns in 1761 only two could be described as outsiders, Henry

[1] Pp. 15-16.

Crabb Boulton and John Walsh, Members for Worcester, 'East Indians' who captured a very corrupt borough entirely by their own strength and efforts. Another peculiarity of the big boroughs was that, as in the counties, both seats could seldom be filled by members of the same family, though this happened occasionally in the quasi-feudal north, *e.g.* at Chester and Bridgnorth.

But should anyone expect to find in the 46 representatives of the big trading and manufacturing towns typical members of the middle classes, he will be disappointed. In 1761 seven were sons of British peers, and, on the severest scrutiny, excluding amphibious types, at least 25 were country gentlemen. In fact, only seven out of the 46 were actually engaged in trade : three Members for the City of London,[1] the two Members for Southwark, one Member for Liverpool, and one for Newcastle-upon-Tyne. In the City of London it was a time-honoured tradition to elect leading merchants or men who had held City office and distinguished themselves in its municipal life. Besides the City of London, Southwark alone seems by preference to have chosen local business men ; all its Members between 1761 and 1784 come under this description : Alexander Hume (1743–54 and 1761–65), a merchant and Director of the East India Company ; Joseph Mawbey (1761–74), a Vauxhall distiller ; Henry Thrale (1765–80) — the friend of Samuel Johnson — a Southwark brewer ; Nathaniel Polhill (1774–82), an 'eminent tobacco merchant' at Southwark and subsequently a banker ; Sir Richard Hotham (1780–84), a Southwark hatter, subsequently an East India shipper and merchant ; and Henry Thornton (1782–1815), a banker — one of the leaders of the 'Clapham sect'.

The three great out-ports, Bristol, Liverpool, and Newcastle-upon-Tyne, usually returned some of their own merchants to Parliament, but the tradition with them was less strict than in the City of London or in Southwark. In 1761 Sir Ellis Cunliffe at Liverpool, and Matthew Ridley at Newcastle, were their only merchant representatives.

---

[1] The fourth, William Beckford, was a leader of the City business community but not actually engaged in trade.

Outside these five cities one would search in vain in 1761 for big business men returned by populous boroughs (it is only about 1780 that a tendency becomes noticeable in that direction).[1] Whatever traditions there were, worked in favour of the neighbouring nobility and gentry, who also as patrons, customers, and landlords were more important than the local merchants or manufacturers ; while the local bankers, though rising in importance, hardly as yet aspired to seats in the House of Commons. Nor did London merchants go in search of seats to populous, expensive constituencies where they were strangers ; they preferred to buy them outright in pocket boroughs, or to cultivate an interest in some small, manageable corporation. In so far as local candidates were returned by the big provincial towns in 1761 they were mostly lawyers, often closely connected with the trade of their constituencies. There was Jarrit Smith, M.P. for Bristol, a local attorney deeply engaged in the commercial concerns of the city ; James Hewitt, M.P. for Coventry (where his father had been a merchant and mayor of the city), a distinguished barrister ; Charles Gray, M.P. for Colchester and Recorder for Ipswich. If we add two representatives of old town families, John Plumptre, M.P. for Nottingham, and Martin Rebow, M.P. for Colchester (a descendant of Flemish Confessors who had been eminent cloth merchants in the town), we have exhausted the number of those who did not primarily belong to the landed interest.[2] British democracy, unless directed by party or professional organizations, has a preference for the 'well-born', and in the largest,

[1] Both Members returned for Bristol in 1780 are local merchants, Brickdale and Lippincot ; one at Exeter, J. Baring ; one at Canterbury, G. Gipps ; adding the four Members for London and the two for Southwark, ten out of the sixteen in the southern division were local merchants or manufacturers. In the northern division : J. Darker at Leicester ; Robert Smith at Nottingham ; H. Rawlinson at Liverpool ; John Webb at Gloucester ; T. Rogers at Coventry. This makes five out of thirty in the northern division.

[2] This list, which includes 7 merchants, 4 lawyers, and 2 town notables, makes a total of 13 ; adding the 2 'East Indians' at Worcester — 15. But 7 sons of peers and 25 country gentlemen were mentioned above. The apparent discrepancy (there should be only 46) is due to one merchant Member for the City of London, Thomas Harley, son of the third Earl of Oxford, appearing twice.

most democratic, most hotly contested urban constituency, the City of Westminster, after radicalism had arisen, society radicals were pitted against society men. In 1761 Westminster returned without contest Lord Pulteney, son of Lord Bath, and General Edward Cornwallis, son of the fourth Lord Cornwallis; and in 1762, when Cornwallis's seat was vacated by his being appointed Governor of Gibraltar, Newcastle was not certain at first whether the son of Lord Sandys was 'of dignity enough' [1] to represent Westminster. In fact, outside the City of London and Southwark, where self-made men were covered by a corporate or local tradition, and Worcester, which was thoroughly corrupt, there was not one among the 46 representatives returned in 1761 by the 22 English towns with electorates of over 1000, who comes under this description (in saying this I omit lawyers, who had a peculiar status of their own). Rotten boroughs were far kinder and more hospitable to self-made men than the votes and choice of British democracy.

Still, in spite of the predilection which even these large urban constituencies showed for men of rank and birth, heredity in their representation was less marked than either in the counties or in smaller boroughs, the influence of single families being as a rule much weaker, especially in the south. Twenty-one among the 46 Members in 1761 were the first in their families to enter the British Parliament: 3 Members for the City of London, the Members for Southwark, Bristol, and Liverpool, the 2 East Indians at Worcester, the 4 lawyers,[2] and also a few country gentlemen. Of the 25 with Parliamentary ancestry, 11 sat for boroughs which their fathers had represented, and 3 succeeded near relatives. There was a marked difference in the degree of continuity and heredity in representation between the north, the midlands, and the south.[3] In the conservative north the franchise was usually wider and the electorates were less corrupt, but a quasi-feudal tradition prevailed, and the hold of the landed classes even on the big, populous boroughs was remarkable — indeed, in some of them

---

[1] Newcastle to Bedford, 8 Apr 1762; 32936, f. 432.
[2] This includes J. Smith, M.P. for Bristol, once more.
[3] I depart here from my usual classification.

it survived the Reform Act of 1832. The Grosvenors sat for
Chester city without a break from 1715 till 1874, and during
42 of these 159 years held both seats. Similarly, the city of
Durham was represented by the Tempest family from 1742
till 1794, when it became extinct in the male line, and by the
Lambtons from 1734 till 1813, when they transferred themselves to the county. At Newcastle-on-Tyne, Matthew Ridley,
who was the first of his family to represent the borough and
sat for it from 1747 till 1774, was succeeded by his son and
grandson, the three together holding one seat for almost a
century (1747–1836). The case of the Whitmores at Bridgnorth, where they held at least one seat almost without break
from 1661 till 1870, is discussed in the essay on Shropshire.

In the midlands and the south not a single case of long
uninterrupted tenure can be found in any of the large urban
constituencies. The father of John Rolle Walter, who represented Exeter 1754–66, had sat for the city 1713–15 and
1722–27. The uncle and father of George Selwyn had from
1728 to 1751 represented Gloucester, for which he sat 1754–80.
Samuel Milles, the grandfather of Richard Milles, M.P. for
Canterbury 1761–80, had represented the borough 1722–27.
Edward Bacon, M.P. for Norwich 1756–84, occupied the seat
held by his father 1705–10 and 1715–35. Colchester was represented by the Rebow family 1688–1713, 1715–23, 1734–35,
1754–81, and again 1857–59 and 1865–70. At Northampton
five Montagus (of the Halifax branch) represented the town
for thirty-four years between 1707 and 1768, whilst the
Comptons sat for it for about fifty years between 1720 and
1820. These are typical examples. There was heredity, but
no unbroken descent; for there was usually more than one
noble or prominent family to choose from, and there was no
absolute attachment. And in London, Southwark, and Bristol
there was no heredity of any kind.

It seems advisable to analyse the political state of a few of
these twenty-two large city constituencies with a view to
obtaining a picture of English 'urban democracy' about 1760.[1]

[1] I omit the City of London and Westminster, partly because it would
be a task exceeding the limits of short sketches, and partly because conditions

Bristol.—The politics of Bristol, the second largest city in Great Britain, were managed by the 'Union Club' for the Whigs and the 'Steadfast Society' for the Tories. On the eve of the general election of 1754 the Whigs approached the Tories with the suggestion to establish 'that harmoney which becomes fellow citizens, and reciprocally to elect Members who may be willing and capeable of serving us', and thus to concur 'for the peace of the city'.[1] The Tories refused, and put up two candidates; the Whigs, however, to show that they 'did not seek for victory but independence',[2] nominated only one (Robert Nugent) and carried his election; and according to Dean Tucker, 'there was no one thing which contributed to the success of our cause so much as our continual insisting upon the ill behaviour of the Tories in rejecting the compromise'.[3] He thus described the circumstances of Nugent's nomination:

Before Mr. Nugent, now Lord Viscount Clare, was chosen to represent the City of Bristol, it was a general complaint among the citizens, that they had not a friend to whom they could apply for obtaining any favour from the great officers of State:—That a commercial city, such as theirs, stood in continual need of the interposition and assistance sometimes of the Treasury, sometimes of the Board of Trade, and sometimes of the Commissioners of the Customs, and the Excise, &c., &c., to moderate and mitigate the *letter* of the law in contingent cases:—That, more especially during the time of war, they were subject to great distress for want of regular convoys, and of other beneficial protections:—And lastly, that in the disposal of Government-places, belonging to their port and city, it was hard and grating to them to see such numbers of strangers preferred, whilst several of their own tradesmen, reduced by misfortunes, wanted bread.[4]

in them were unique, and no franchise in the eighteenth century could have reproduced them elsewhere.
    [1] Thomas Towgood to the Earl of Berkeley, Bristol, 3 July 1753; 32732, f. 235.
    [2] Josiah Tucker, *Review of Lord Clare's Conduct* (1775), p. 5.
    [3] Tucker to Hardwicke, 13 Mar 1756; 35692, ff. 130-1.
    [4] During the twenty years Nugent represented Bristol he 'was intrusted with the nomination to every place and employment in the disposal of Government within the City of Bristol' (Tucker, *op. cit.*, p. 16).

Here then was the third largest urban constituency [1] in Great Britain no less solicitous of Government favours than some poor, decayed borough. Edmund Burke was yet to learn by experience how much freer an Opposition Member was when sitting for a pocket borough than as a representative of Bristol. On 26 June 1777 he wrote to his friend Richard Champion :

Until I knew it, both by my own particular experience, and by my observation of what happened to others, I could not have believed how very little the local constituents attend to the general public line of conduct observed by their member. They judge of him solely by his merits as their special agent. . . . It is . . . unlucky for the public, that this indifference to the main lines of the duty of a member of parliament should be so prevalent among the electors. For almost all small services to individuals, and even to corporations, depend so much on the pleasure of the crown, that the members are as it were driven headlong into dependence by those whom the constitution, and (one would at first imagine) the very nature of things, had contrived to keep independent of a court influence. This alone is sufficient to show how much a constitution *in fact* differs from a constitution *on paper*.[2]

Even the wider commercial politics of Bristol bore a strongly local imprint. One of the things which had specially recommended Nugent to Bristol in 1754 was that he had proved 'a continual and a successful advocate for the out-ports, when their own members remained silent, never failing to oppose the monopolizing schemes of the City of London' ; and, some twenty years later, Tucker, when defending Nugent's Parliamentary conduct, emphasized that he had been

the sole instrument of rejecting in the last session a bill framed by the bankers of London, and supported by all their interest, for the laudable purpose of bringing to their shops all the deposited money of Great Britain, to the total destruction of the banking business in Bristol, and all other towns except the Metropolis. . . .

During the war he more eminently distinguished himself as our guardian and protector. Not one port in the three Kingdoms was

---

[1] Above I have called Bristol 'the second largest city' : as a city it was larger than Westminster, but it had a smaller electorate.

[2] *Correspondence*, vol. ii, p. 166.

so well, or so constantly provided with convoys and protections, as the port of Bristol.[1]

When the Whigs first invited Nugent to stand for Bristol 'they proposed to stipulate with him for a very large sum of money towards defraying the expenses of a contest'. But when he refused to be at any expense, the Bristol merchants, in the first place the Quakers and Dissenters, raised the necessary funds, which ran into four figures.[2] Here, as in most places, whatever genuine popular party feeling there was, had a religious colouring. Having succeeded in returning one Member in 1754, the Bristol Whigs tried for the second seat at a by-election in 1756, but failed, and after £60,000 had been spent on these two occasions,[3] animosities subsided and 'a reconciliation ensued amongst the citizens'.[4] The Tories, to have 'the opinion on their side that they are not the disturbers of the peace of the city', had announced beforehand 'that in case of a victory . . . they themselves will be the first to propose a compromise for the future'.[5] This was now concluded — 'a solemn agreement between the agents of both parties, that the candidate to be named by one, should be supported by the other, during three successive Parliaments'.[6] In other words, the two competing political organizations took out a joint lease for the two seats, defining beforehand its duration, and Nugent was re-elected as a Whig even after 1762 — on accepting office in 1766 and twice in 1768 — although he adhered to every single Government except that of the Rockinghams, and even voted against the Repeal of the Stamp Act. On 28 June 1768 he wrote to William Knox that he had been re-elected unanimously,

but not without some untoward circumstances arising from a jealousy conceived by the multitude of too much power assumed by the two societies in nominating their candidates ; some grumbled, but all voted for me.[7]

Thus caucus politics, even when successful, were not popu-

---

[1] Tucker, *op. cit.*, pp. 11-12.   [2] See below, p. 252.
[3] *Ibid.*   [4] Tucker, *op. cit.*, p. 6.
[5] Tucker to Hardwicke, 13 Mar 1756 ; 35692, ff. 130-1.
[6] Tucker, *op. cit.*, p. 6.   [7] HMC, *Various Collections*, vol. vi, p. 96.

lar, while party politics on a national scale did not as yet prevail
even in places such as Bristol, which in appearance was politically organized. When the Coalition Government was formed
in 1783, 'the Tory Members for Bristol (Brickdale and
Daubeny) . . . threw in their lot with the Coalition, while
Cruger [1] who . . . was brought forward again at the dissolution of 1784, favoured Pitt'. But a careful comparison of the
poll-books shows that those who supported Cruger, or Brickdale and Daubeny, in 1781 continued to do so in 1784.

A few out-voters, especially from London, transferred their votes,
but in Bristol itself, the only change of any person of standing in
the city was of Edward Brice, alderman (mayor, 1782–83) a member
of an old Whig family, who voted for Cruger in 1781 and for Brickdale in 1784.[2]

Nottingham.—If Bristol serves as illustration for the great
out-ports, Nottingham stands for large county towns dependent
mainly on local trade, and therefore apt to be influenced by
the neighbouring big landowners, who moreover in many cases
owned a considerable amount of house property in these towns.
Its franchise was in freemen and forty-shilling freeholders, and
of its 2000 voters nearly three-fourths were resident in the
borough, the rest mostly in its neighbourhood. The Duke of
Newcastle, one of the chief landowners in the county and
Recorder of the borough, headed the Whigs, Lord Middleton
the Tories, and usually the two parties divided the representation of the town.

'Lord Howe', wrote Newcastle on 21 July 1753 to his chief
agent in Nottinghamshire, J. S. Charlton, M.P. for Newark,

was with me yesterday to ask my interest for Nottingham. I could
give him no positive answer, till I knew the state of the town ;
and the real intentions of those, who have the greatest weight there.

---

[1] Henry Cruger, a New-Yorker by birth, but settled in trade at Bristol,
represented it as an Opposition Whig 1774–80, but was defeated both at
the general election of 1780 and at the by-election in 1781. He was again
returned for Bristol in 1784, though at that time absent in America, but in
1790 moved to New York, where he was elected to the Senate in 1792 (about
him see Henry C. Van Schaack, *Henry Cruger*, New York, 1859).

[2] A. B. Beaven, 'Bristol Men in the Eighteenth Century', in the *Bristol
Times and Mirror*, 15 Feb 1913.

Lord Howe said, the town would neither chuse two Whigs, nor two Tories, but one and one; and thought, he had much the best interest of any Whig.

Newcastle, therefore, wishing to preserve 'the peace of the town', instructed Charlton to ascertain Middleton's attitude.[1] From him Charlton found out that 'the gentlemen in the country' did not think

of proposing two for the town of Nottingham, even should my Lord Howe stand, but as his Lordship was the only gentleman, who subscribed against the burgesses their friends, in favor of the corporation,[2] all attempts to induce them to joine his Lordship would be impracticable. There rather seems a disposition to joine Mr. Plumptre, his family having principally undertook their cause.[3]

Plumptre, a second cousin of Howe, was of a family which sat for Nottingham under Richard II and Elizabeth I, and his father, a faithful adherent of Newcastle, represented it for thirty-two years between 1706 and 1747. But on 9 August 1753 Newcastle desired Plumptre 'to lay aside any thoughts of standing for Nottingham the next election',[4] and considered that Plumptre's election was anyhow doubtful as Abel Smith, the local banker,[5] had declared for Howe.[6] Plumptre, however, was not willing to desist,[7] and subsequently, though hoping to retain Newcastle's 'friendship and goodness', joined interests with the Tory candidate;[8] while on 29 August Charlton thus reported a further visit to Middleton:

I found my Lord in the greatest distress and confusion at the ferment raised in Nottingham on Lord Howe's coming down. The language of the place, that his Lordship had sold the burgesses, and that they would stone both him and his servants, on which his

[1] 32732, ff. 336-7.
[2] Lord Howe had contributed £500 to a lawsuit in which the Corporation was engaged against the burgesses of Nottingham.
[3] 32732, f. 393.   [4] *Ibid.* f. 437.
[5] Before the century was out Smith's bank was one of the first in England, and a grandson of his a peer; and between 1770 and 1910, at least twenty-four of his descendants (not counting those of his brother, Samuel) sat in the House of Commons for a joint term of 364 years.
[6] Newcastle to Charlton, 32732, ff. 439-40.
[7] Letter to Newcastle, 18 Aug; *ibid.* ff. 493-4.
[8] 32733, ff. 122-3 and 166-7.

Lordship sent over that he should be determined by the burgesses. He must otherwise have lost all weight, beside his own ease and quiet, which he will not give up on any consideration whatever.[1]

Still, Newcastle stood by his promise to Howe who, assisted by the most prominent members of the Corporation, 'walk'd the town' (their presence serving at the canvass to exert pressure on their dependants to engage themselves accordingly). Among those who accompanied Howe were Abel Smith and his two sons. But

My Lord Middleton hearing of the extraordinary zeal of the Smith's family (and having constantly a very great sum of money lying dead (as to himself) in their hands which they employ to their own profit) sent his steward . . . to them threatning that unless they imediately chang'd their behaviour . . . he would take all his money out of their hands and perswade all his friends to do the like. This message had such effect upon the mean spirits of the Smith's family (whose idol is money) that one of the sons went next day to Lord Middleton and in the name of his father, his brother and himself, gave up Lord Howe and his interest (as much as in them lay) and promised to do as Lord Middleton should direct them.[2]

This is a typical example of the system of organized bullying which worked from the top downwards. Newcastle's stewards at Nottingham had to secure his dependants, and examine the ways of influencing other voters ; to his estate agents in other parts of the country lists were sent of Nottingham voters in their 'collections' ; the Excisemen were worked with due discretion (as the Commissioners were debarred by law from giving 'directions to their officers about elections') ; the poor burgesses, with whom 'money and the best bidder is become the by-word', received petty bribes ; etc. etc. But two friends of Newcastle who themselves were largely indebted to him for their seats — John White, M.P. for Retford, and John Thorn-

---

[1] 32732, f. 572.
[2] 32733, ff. 174-5. It is obvious from the whole tenor of the letter that its writer, Clay, Newcastle's Nottingham agent, was hostile to the Smith family ; at the end he had, however, to insert the correction that 'George Smith, who married a relation of Lord Howe's', declared that his brother had no right to speak in his name, and that he continued to support Howe.

hagh, knight of the shire — supported Plumptre and secured for him their tenants.[1]

Newcastle and the Corporation proved victorious; Howe received 980 votes (901 of them 'single'), the Tory candidate, Sir Willoughby Aston, 924; Plumptre only 915.

Thus in boroughs, big and small, territorial influences were apt to determine elections. But outside burgage or merely nominal boroughs, those absolutely at one man's command were far fewer than stated in the beautifully clear calculations by reformers. Neither Newcastle nor Middleton could dictate to a borough the size of Nottingham, though both could in various ways exercise very considerable influence.

When in 1758 Howe was killed at Ticonderoga, Middleton declared 'that he was determined to take no part in the Nottingham election that his people might vote as they pleased',[2] while Newcastle thus explained his situation to Charlton on 28 August 1758:

I thought the merit of the Howe family, at this time, was such, that no friend to the Government could be against shewing them a proper mark of respect. For that reason, I have wrote to the present Lord Howe,[3] to propose to him the vacating his seat for Dartmouth, and the chusing him for Nottingham; and, in that case, I would have endeavour'd to get Plumtree chose for Dartmouth to make everything easy. The Mayor and Aldermen of Nottingham have wrote a letter to my Lady Howe, desiring to chuse one of her family. This letter has been shew'd to me, and my Lady Howe desires that her son the lieutenant-colonel,[4] may be chose for the remainder of this Parliament, and the present Lord Howe to come in afterwards. . . . I cannot but think myself extremely ill-used by the Whig Corporation of Nottingham, where I am Recorder, to make all these offers and applications, without taking any *notice* of me, or giving me the least knowledge of them; and it is the more extraordinary and ungrateful, as I serv'd their friend pretty materially the last election against a very good Whig, and the son of the oldest, and one of the best, friends, I ever had in Nottinghamshire.[5]

---

[1] 32733, ff. 242 and 284. White said that Plumptre 'is his old acquaintance'.
[2] J. S. Charlton to Newcastle, 22 Sept 1758; 32883, f. 250.
[3] The admiral in command of the Fleet in America 1776–78.
[4] William Howe, who commanded the British troops in North America 1775–77.
[5] 32883, ff. 141–3.

Finally Newcastle had to accept the arrangement as made between Lady Howe and the Corporation, and so had Plumptre. Before the end of the year Plumptre was returned through Newcastle's mediation for Penryn, and in 1761 and 1768 he and General Howe were elected for Nottingham.

Newcastle-upon-Tyne.—As a third example I take this big, independent trading town in the north. Its electorate exceeded 2000 — 2388 voted in 1741, 2165 in 1774, and 2245 in 1780 [1] — and in 1734 and 1741 two Tories were successful; but in 1747, in view of the heavy expense of the previous contests, the representation was 'compromised'. From that year till 1774, Matthew Ridley, a Whig, shared it with Sir Walter Calverley Blackett, who sat for Newcastle as a Tory from 1734 till his death in 1777. In 1741 Blackett

was at the height of his popularity . . . styled . . . *the Patriot, the Opposer of the Court*, and *the Father of the Poor* ; the latter was, indeed, an appellation he justly merited, for never, perhaps, did the poor of Newcastle and its neighbourhood receive more support or relief from any individual than from Sir Walter Blackett.[2]

Here is a short selection from the 'acts of humanity his generous heart teemed with'. In 1736 he built a public library for Newcastle. When in 1739 the harbour froze, he gave 200 guineas for the relief of the unemployed, and by his personal exertions collected another £1000. In 1751 he gave £200 to the Newcastle Infirmary and £50 to be continued annually for its support; in 1754, £1200 for a Hospital for 'decayed burgesses'; in 1757, £100 for the relief of the poor because of the prevailing scarcity of grain; in 1759, £1000 to the Infirmary; between 1764 and 1774, £2260 to augment seventeen small livings of the clergy, etc. etc. etc.

---

[1] Of these 2245 voters, only about half — 1148 — were resident in the town, 889 were from the country, and 208 from London ; 'every voter at Newcastle upon Tyne, coming from London, is said to cost 30*l*.' (*Report of the Committee . . . upon the State of Representation in England and Wales* (1792), p. 14).

[2] *Memoirs of the Public Life of Sir Walter Blackett of Wallington, Bart.*, Newcastle (1819), p. xv ; by 'J. S.': John Sykes, a Newcastle bookseller and antiquary.

H

By 1774 a new political movement was rising in a constituency which in the reign of George II had been nurtured by Blackett on a combination of private benefactions and Opposition cant. The fact that Ridley and Blackett refused in 1769, during the crisis over the Middlesex election, to present a petition from the burgesses for the dissolution of Parliament, was brought up against them,[1] and radical resolutions for Parliamentary reform were drawn up by the Opposition, whose candidates were Constantine Phipps, subsequently second Lord Mulgrave, a distinguished sailor (after 1775 connected with Lord Sandwich and the Court), and Thomas Delaval,[2] a rich merchant and brother of Sir Francis and Sir John Delaval. Still, non-political considerations had even greater weight. Phipps

on all occasions during his canvass, and upon the hustings, declared his warmest attachment to the best interests of Newcastle, and especially to the improvement of the river Tyne, which he considered as being capable of becoming one of the finest rivers in the world, but which ignorance, inattention and avarice had converted into what he called 'a cursed horse-pond'. That . . . he would exert all his influence with the admiralty, to whom he was personally known, to protect, cherish and aggrandize the important and numerous branches of trade on the river Tyne.[3]

Further, in 1774 Blackett 'was far from being so popular as he was at the preceding contest, having unfortunately engaged in the violent party question relative to the Town Moor, which about this time agitated every breast, and destroyed the peace of many families'.[4] 'Party question' — what was it? In 1772 the Corporation, whose side Blackett espoused, had let out eighty-nine acres of the Town Moor 'for the purpose of being cultivated and improved'. The burgesses who had the right to 'the herbage of the Town Moor, Castle Leazes and

---

[1] See *The Contest* (1774), p. 23.

[2] About Thomas Delaval, an interesting figure, see *The Delaval Papers*, edited by John Robinson; HMC, 13, App. vi, *Delaval Papers*, ed. R. Ward; R. E. G. Cole, *The History of Doddington*.

[3] *Impartial History of the Town and County of Newcastle-upon-Tyne* (1801), p. 181.

[4] *Memoirs of the Public Life*, pp. xxvii-xxviii.

Nun's Moor . . . for two milch cows each',[1] felt injured
thereby and, as their opponents retained '*all* the senior council
on the circuit', turned to a certain George Greive, the son of
an Alnwick solicitor and a prominent radical,[2] 'desiring him to
ask the Bill of Rights influence with Serjeant Glynn to come
and plead their cause : Mr. Greive chearfully undertook the
task.'[3] Thus the Newcastle burgesses pulled political wires
to secure the best counsel, and the radicals in turn tacked their
own political cries on to the milch cows on the Town Moor.
None the less, Blackett and Ridley were re-elected.[4]

On the death of Sir Walter Blackett in 1777, his nephew,
Sir John Trevelyan, came forward as candidate for the borough,
and the following appeal was made on his behalf :

> Though unknown to many of you, yet be assured he inherits the
> same generous principles of his late worthy uncle ; and so much so,
> that the loss of the one can alone be made up by the possession of
> the other.[5]

Neither Mulgrave nor Thomas Delaval was now available,
and George Greive and the radicals put forward as their
candidate A. R. Bowes (originally Stoney), a disreputable Irish
adventurer who, on marrying the Dowager Countess of Strathmore, daughter and heiress of George Bowes, M.P. for County
Durham 1727–60, had assumed her name.[6] The cry was raised
of 'Bowes and Freedom', and the opponents were described
as 'a combination of wealth and power, to suppress the free
elections of the people'[7] — 'O break the *closet-combinations* of

---

[1] On this dispute, see *The Newcastle Freeman's Pocket Companion*, by a
Burgess (1808), and *Report of the Select Committee of Burgesses of Newcastle-
upon-Tyne* (1811).

[2] In 1794 self-styled 'défendeur officieux des braves sans-culottes de
Louvenciennes, ami de Franklin et de Marat, factieux et anarchiste de
premier ordre et désorganisateur du despotisme dans les deux hemisphères
depuis vingt ans'. About him see *D.N.B.*

[3] See *The Contest*, pp. 27–8. Serjeant Glynn was the famous radical,
Recorder of the City of London and Member for Middlesex from Dec 1768
till his death in 1779.

[4] Blackett received 1432 votes, Ridley 1411, Phipps 795, and Delaval 677.

[5] From 'A Free Burgess'; see W. Garret's *Collection of Newspaper
Cuttings, etc.*, 1777–84, in the British Museum, pp. 3 x and 24.

[6] An only child born of that marriage died in infancy.

[7] In Bowes's election address of 19 Feb 1777 ; see W. Garret's *Collection*,
p. 15.

the magistrates and gentry whose glory it seems to be to treat their inferiors as slaves.'¹ But the supporters of Trevelyan wisely pointed out that Bowes, should his wife die, would go 'back to his original insignificancy'; 'would it . . . be proper, would it be decent . . . to entrust our rights and properties with a man who in . . . a few hours may himself be divested of the very appearance of an estate?' Whereas Trevelyan was 'an Englishman of an antient and most respectable family, possessed of a large permanent estate'.² Sir John Trevelyan won the seat by 1163 against 1068 votes for Bowes.³

By 1780 Bowes was deep in debt, and while 'fully engrossed by our patriotic meetings and *their appendages*', was trying to compensate a London creditor by tips for bets; he wrote to him on 29 February:

I am glad to find the opinions of people in London against my election; it will give you an opportunity of making some good bets; and so positive am I, that I have no objection to your standing a third part to nothing, and you may make me liable to pay the whole in case I should not succeed. But you must bet upon a proviso that L[ady] S[trathmore] lives.⁴

This was obviously an indispensable condition for the triumph of 'freedom'. She lived, and Bowes was returned, narrowly defeating Thomas Delaval.⁵ His later adventures, imprisonment and death within the Rules of King's Bench Prison do not enter into this story which can best be concluded with a description of that radical hero, given by his surgeon, Jesse Foot, 'from 39 years professional attendance':

He was a villain to the backbone! . . . He cloathed all his villainies in the dress of virtue. . . . To sum up his character in a

---

¹ From a 'Poor Burgess', *ibid.* p. 20.　　　　² *Ibid.* p. 502.
³ See on that election also *North Country Diaries*, Publications of the Surtees Society, vol. 118 (1910), vol. i, pp. 231-3.
⁴ See *The Lives of Andrew Robinson Bowes, Esq., and the Countess of Strathmore*, by Jesse Foot, p. 70.
⁵ Ridley 1408, Bowes 1135, Delaval 1085. Nicholas Ridley, Matthew's brother, wrote from Blagdon on 25 Sept 1780 to their half-brother Richard that Matthew 'was much sollicited by some of Delaval's friends to turn the scale in his favor . . . but having . . . declared that he stood unconnected with either party, he thought himself bound to act up to his professions' (Ridley MSS. at Blagdon, Northumberland).

few words, he was cowardly, insidious, hypocritical, tyrannic, mean, violent, selfish, deceitful, jealous, revengeful, inhuman and savage, without a single countervailing quality.[1]

Canterbury.—Here was an old cathedral town, opulent and singularly free of any dominant aristocratic influence, in rich agricultural country, an eighteenth-century 'Barchester', ('The great wealth and encrease of the city of Canterbury', wrote Defoe in 1724, 'is from the surprizing encrease of the hop grounds all round the place.'[2]) What were its politics? In what terms were they transacted?

At the dissolution in 1761 its Members were Sir James Creed, a London merchant and Director of the East India Company, a regular follower of Newcastle, and Matthew Robinson Morris, of Mount Morris near Hythe, subsequently second Lord Rokeby.[3] Morris did not stand again, but Thomas Best, another country gentleman[4] who had been returned in 1741 and 1747 but had 'declined the poll' in 1754, came forward, and Newcastle tried, through William Freind, Dean of Canterbury, to arrange a junction between him and Creed.[5] But Best joined Richard Milles, a Tory and country gentleman,[6] and Dean Freind feared that Creed's success would be 'a little doubtful' should he stand alone against their united interests. There was, however, already another candidate in the field, William Mayne, a merchant, about whom Sir Harry Erskine wrote to Lord George Sackville on 11 December 1760 that he 'is attached to Lord Bute, who espouses his interest'. He asked Sackville

to request the Duke of Dorset to recommend him to Sir Thomas Hales, Dr. Curtis, and such gentlemen as have influence in Canter-

---

[1] *Op. cit.*, pp. 185-7.

[2] *A Tour through Great Britain*, vol. i, Letter II, p. 42.

[3] His sister, the tiresome Mrs. Elizabeth Montagu, states that he was re-elected in 1754 without expense; see E. J. Climenson, *Elizabeth Montagu*, vol. ii, pp. 49-50.

[4] Described by Mrs. Montagu as 'a man of fortune' (*ibid.* i, p. 121).

[5] 32915, ff. 71-2.

[6] 32916, ff. 117 and 323. About Milles and his family see Hasted, *Kent*, vol. iii, p. 728; G. A. Carthew, *The Hundred of Launditch*, part 3, pp. 126-7; R. F. Scott, *Admission Register of St. John's College, Cambridge*; Berry, *Kent Genealogies*.

bury, that he may not appear as one totally unknown, which they endeavour to represent him in that city.[1]

On 1 January 1761 Newcastle wrote to Lord Sondes, his nephew by marriage and chief of the Kentish Whigs :

My Lord Bute is a particular friend of this Mr. Mayne ; and is now very desirous, that he should join Sir James Creed ; and I think Sir James can do nothing so well, for his own sake or for the Whig interest, as to join a friend of my Lord Bute's against the Tories.

I have recommended the junction to Sir James Creed ; and I have wrote to the Dean of Canterbury my opinion upon it. I therefore hope you will concur with me in it.[2]

An agreement between Creed and Mayne was concluded on 23 January ; 'the junction formed by Mr. B[est] and Mr. M[illes]', wrote Freind to Newcastle on 3 January 1761, 'has in spite of their endeavours to avoid it, given a *party* complexion to the cause, which will do them no service'.[3]   But Milles, the Tory, came out in support of Sir Wyndham Knatchbull, the Whig Member for the county, and Knatchbull waited with him on Newcastle who was, however, now bound to the other side. 'If Mr. Milles intends to act as he expresses himself now,' wrote Sondes to Newcastle on 21 January, 'tis a pity he had not made his intentions known sooner.'[4]

The campaign which was carried on for Mayne at Canterbury is described in *An Address to the Electors of the City of Canterbury*, by Thomas Roch, citizen.[5]   Stories were circulated

that Mr. Mayne was a man of great merit and fortune ; that he had been preceptor to his Majesty, and that his Majesty was greatly improved in mercantile affairs, and thoroughly a judge of the

---

[1] HMC, *Stopford - Sackville MSS.* vol. i, p. 45.   William Mayne was one of the twenty-one children of William Mayne of Powis, County Clackmannan, had been for many years in the mercantile house of his family established at Lisbon for about a century, but had retired in 1757, and married in 1758 Frances, daughter of Joshua, second Viscount Allen. He sat for Canterbury, 1774–80, and for Gatton, 1780–90, was created a baronet in 1763 and Baron Newhaven [Ir.] in 1776.   There are a few letters from Mayne in the Bute MSS.

[2] 32917, f. 16 ; for Newcastle's letter to Freind, see *ibid.* f. 14.
[3] *Ibid.* f. 112.   [4] *Ibid.* f. 475.
[5] Roch was a cabinet-maker, 'a native of Ireland'. For his obituary notice see *Gent. Mag.*, 1781, p. 46.

ballance of trade, and from his instruction; that Mr. Mayne was a man of great parts, had great interest at court, and was an intimate friend and companion of Mr. Pitt.

. . . If any good woman went to tell her neighbour the good and joyful tidings, she was prevented by, lord! neighbour! I am glad you are come, I have great news to tell you: they say our King's schoolmaster is coming to be our member of parliament, and that the King will do any thing that he asks of him.

In fact, Mayne's position was described as such 'that hopes might be entertained of having a great part of the Court Calendar filled up with the freemen of Canterbury'.

The character and methods of the Tory opposition, on the other hand, can be gathered from letters to Newcastle from Sir George Oxenden, a Kentish baronet and M.P. for Sandwich 1720–54. He wrote on 1 February 1761:

Mayne won't carry it I hear, tho' Creed, it is thought, will; I dined with them; a numerous meeting of shoemakers, broken tradesmen, &c., &c., but few or none of the principal inhabitants of the place.—No Scotch — no foreigner is the cry.[1]

Thus in Kent it was the Tories who worked the cry of 'No Scotch'. Oxenden wrote again on 19 February:

. . . at Canterbury it is certain the principle people in the city are against them [Creed and Mayne], and what is worse the farmers of note round about, and ten miles off, are busy in making votes for Milles and Best, I know their influence very well, by experience at Sandwich in 1741 — where they certainly carried the election for my partner Mr. Pratt — I believe we might stop several of them, but as we stop them in the county where they are inclined, notwithstanding the orders they receive from their landlords, it will be too much to ask them in the city where they have received directions to act as they do.[2]

And on 2 March ·

There will be a hard match at Canterbury, I dare say it will cost them four thousand a man. The other side outmanage them vastly, they certainly have the majority in the town, several Whig tradesmen dead for us in the county, and dead against Creed and Mayne in the town, on account of the near neighbourhood of Milles

---

[1] 32918, f. 179. 'Foreigner' means not a native of Kent.
[2] 32919, ff. 116-17.

particularly. Most of the Prebends in the same way, as the Milles's visit and play at cards always with one or other of them, so that they have got several capital people away from us in the city, and we not one from them. . . . The farmers are all for the neighbors, some of *our* tenants and of the other Whig gentlemen round about, but we do not think it prudent, at least it is my opinion not, to stop them, for they are a stubborn race of men, and as we manage them in other things and they readily follow us, so they like to have their heads sometimes, and it must be done — and Mayne's being called a Scotchman has set them all afire and is, as you may imagine, an indication how much a Scotch interest is cry'd out against in this part of the world.[1]

On 16 March 1761 the Archbishop of Canterbury wrote to Newcastle about Best :

Mr. Best . . . made me a visit this morning : and without asking for my interest, which he appeared sensible ought to be given to the other side, earnestly desired me to assure your Grace in his name, that if he was chosen, he would not enter into opposition, or put himself on a party footing, but concur with the Administration in everything, as far as he honestly could.[2]

On 28 March 1761 Milles and Best, the anti-Scottish 'Tories', were elected by 806 and 788 votes, against 691 for Creed and 686 for Mayne,[3] Bute's 'Whig' candidate. The case is recommended to the consideration of those who discuss the politics of 1761 in terms of 'parties'.

Coventry.—I take this as last illustration of cities with more than 1000 voters — an example of a corrupt borough whose 'politics' were shunned by most of its neighbours. This is the account of it which Taylor White, a younger brother of John White, M.P. for Retford, sent on 22 March 1768 to his daughter Anne :

I dined at Coventry where I found the town had been set into a flame by the accidental coming of a stranger, one Mr. Warren,[4] a Shropshire gentleman, a day or two before the election, the old Members were Mr. Conway, Mr. Archer. The town were displeased

---

[1] 32919, ff. 374-5.   [2] 32920, f. 253.
[3] Of 1339 Canterbury voters in 1790, 832 were resident in the town, 145 from London, and 354 from the country ; see *Report of the Committee*, p. 14.
[4] Walter Waring, not Warren.

at Mr. Archer's not having paid all the demands made on him for his last election, tho' most probably he paid more than was due. They went round the country to the Tory gentlemen, among the rest to Mr. Ludford and Lord Craven's brother, but none of their own country chose to meddle with the Coventry electors. So this Mr. Warren who by the bye has sold all his estate in Shropshire to Lord Clive [1] was invited by the landlord of the Bull Inn at Coventry to stand, which he very wisely accepted of, and stood a poll which he lost by about fifty votes, however he was persuaded to demand a scrutiny and sent for Mr. Newnham to be his council and also to Sergt. Jephson from Shrewsbury. I saw Newnham at Coventry and advised him to take his fees before he went about business for from all accounts of Mr. Warren's finances he would scarce get any if he did not secure them beforehand.[2]

On the poll H. Seymour Conway received 972 votes; Andrew Archer, with whom 'the town were displeased', 633; Walter Waring, 479.[3]

On 30 October 1782 Lady Craven [4] wrote to Lord Shelburne, then at the head of the Treasury, about an imminent vacancy at Coventry : [5]

. . . the people . . . and the City altogether being so worthless have been forsaken by half a dozen *Lords* successively ; my Lord one of them — not knowing, *à quel saint se vouer* — they have tendered the seat to one of Lord Hertford's sons — but the principal interest there is against him. . . . I should suppose that you now may name the member for Coventry — and I hope you will — bid them like base slaves as they are, take whom you please.

But in fact even in 1782 the situation was not nearly as simple as that.

This analysis of a few of the freest and most important boroughs shows that it was not the state of the franchise alone

---

[1] See below, p. 294.

[2] *Memoirs of the House of White of Wallingwells* (1886), pp. 40-1. About Waring and his Coventry elections, see also H. T. Weyman, 'Members of Parliament for Bishop's Castle', *Transactions of the Shropshire Archaeol. Soc.*, second series, vol. x (1898), p. 61.

[3] Of 2525 Coventry voters in 1790, 1891 were resident in the town, 356 were from London, and 278 from the country ; see *Report of the Committee*, p. 14.

[4] For Lady Craven, subsequently Margravine of Anspach, see her *Memoirs*.   [5] Lansdowne MSS. at Bowood.

which about 1760 was responsible for the absence of real politics in elections, and that corruption was not a shower-bath from above, constructed by Walpole, the Pelhams, or George III, but a water-spout springing from the rock of freedom to meet the demands of the People. Political bullying starts usually from above, the demand for benefits from below ; the two between them made eighteenth-century elections.

Boroughs with 500–1000 Voters

None of the twenty-two boroughs with 500–1000 voters was controlled by the Government, and none was absolutely in the power of one family, but most were under a territorial influence. At Bedford in 1761, on a compromise continued from 1754, the Duke of Bedford nominated one Member and the Corporation the other.[1] Derby was under the patronage of the Dukes of Devonshire ; Cirencester, of the Bathursts ; Evesham, of the Rushouts ; Grantham, of the Duke of Rutland and the Custs ; at Yarmouth in Norfolk, between 1722 and 1784, one Member was always a Townshend and the other a Walpole ; during the same time at Newark one Member was always a Manners and the other the nominee of the Duke of Newcastle,[2] but even their united interest had to stand a severe contest in 1754 against that of a local clergyman, Dr. Wilson.[3] At Lichfield

[1] On 8 Aug 1753 Philip Yorke wrote to Hardwicke :
The Duke of Bedford and the Corporation have settled their affairs for the next election. The Duke brings in Mr. Ongley, and the Corporation Mr. Herne, his Grace also to chuse Alderman Dickenson (who is reckoned a moderate Tory) for one of his boroughs (35351, f. 249).
And here is Hardwicke's comment on the deal in a letter to Philip Yorke on 22 Aug :
. . . it is generally thought that his Grace has made an odd bargain with the Tories for the town, and that he has really no Member of his own for that place. It is strongly affirm'd here that your neighbour Mr. Ongley is a determin'd Tory, but I thought you had told me otherwise . . . (*ibid.* ff. 265-6).
In 1761 Ongley was transferred to the county, and Richard Vernon, a regular Bedford Whig, was the Duke's nominee for the borough.
[2] In 1768 the 'Pelham' candidate was chosen by Lord Lincoln, to whom Newcastle had *inter vivos* made over his Newark property.
[3] The Opposition candidate was Edward Delaval, subsequently a distinguished scientist. 'To secure his return', writes R. E. G. Cole in his *History of Doddington*, 'his brothers [F. B. and J. H. Delaval] entered into

the representation was divided between the Ansons and the Leveson-Gowers, and in spite of the apparent size of the electorate, Lichfield, which had a complicated franchise and was swamped by sham-voters, was less of a real constituency than many a smaller borough; at Stafford, with about 320 voters, almost all of them local tradesmen, 'the electorate must have been far more democratic than at Lichfield'.[1] At Honiton the Yonge family had a traditional and very expensive interest,[2] and at Hereford the Scudamores held one seat, 1754–1818 and 1819–26. At Preston, Lord Derby established his influence in 1768 by defeating the Corporation and on petition gaining for the borough the widest male franchise ever known in the British Isles; at that election 'there wasn't a how [whole] winda in t' tawn'.[3] Carlisle was contested between the Howards, Lowthers, and Bentincks, but there was also a strong independent element among the voters.[4] At Beverley there was no one predominant interest. Oxford, Reading, St. Albans, Ipswich, Sudbury, Maldon, Maidstone, and Dover, *i.e.* the medium-sized towns round London, were comparatively free and some of them very expensive; at St. Albans the Spencers [5] and the Grimstons came near being patrons, at Maidstone the Finches

an agreement with Dr. Bernard Wilson, D.D., Vicar of Newark 1719–72, who used all the influence given him by his position there, and the possession of a large fortune obtained by questionable means from Sir George Markham, of Sedgebrooke, to establish a parliamentary influence in the borough.' The text of the agreement is given there in full. For Newcastle's management of that election, see his correspondence, especially with his agent and nominee, J. S. Charlton, in 32733-5.

[1] See J. C. Wedgwood, *Staffordshire Parliamentary History*, vol. ii, p. 278. [2] See below, p. 164.

[3] See W. Dobson, *History of the Parliamentary Representation of Preston* (1856), p. 10. 'Lawless bands of colliers from the neighbourhood of Chorley were here in the interest of the Corporation candidates, while Longridge, Ribchester, and the neighbourhood furnished their quota of armed blackguards (about 2500) for the other side' (*ibid.* p. 11).

[4] See Brian Bonsall, *Cumberland and Westmorland Elections, 1754–1775* (to be published shortly).

[5] Sarah Duchess of Marlborough had an electoral interest at St. Albans which from her passed to the Spencer family. But in 1741, when James West was first returned, it was against her wish: 'The old Dutches told one that since the mayor and aldermen still opposd her intrest, she would find out a way to be even with them before they was aware . . . her Graceless . . . thumpt her cain to the ground in a rage saying they knew not what they did . . .' (G. Neale to J. West, n.d.; 34734, f. 8).

and Marshams, but in neither borough was a firm and exclusive interest established.

But even where there was a well-established territorial influence, the patrons had to be careful and not press their claims too far. If one seat was readily and cheerfully conceded to them in recognition of their pre-eminence and their regular benefactions, they were in most cases well advised to leave the town free to take full advantage of the second seat — a type of compromise frequent even in the smallest corporation boroughs.[1] One of the most prominent territorial influences in the medium-sized boroughs was that of the Cavendishes at Derby, where they held one seat without a break from 1715 till 1835.[2] But they never put up two Cavendishes for the borough, and when in 1748 the Duke's own manager, Thomas Rivett, was returned for the second seat against Lord Chesterfield's candidate, Thomas Stanhope, who was supported by the Duke, the revolt was not visited on the Member and his electors, but smoothed over before the next general election by Rivett receiving a secret service pension, obtained for him by the Cavendishes.[3]

Evesham was represented by the Rushouts (descendants of Flemish Confessors) at the end of the seventeenth century and without a break from 1722 till 1796, and again from 1837 till 1841. In 1761 Sir John Rushout, fourth Baronet, had himself and his son returned for the borough, but he 'had a hard push to get in his son and many that assisted him are sorry that it is so '.[4] Before the next general election James West wrote to Newcastle on 11 October 1767 :

[1] See, e.g., the case of Andover, where the Members were elected by the Corporation consisting of twelve capital burgesses and twelve associates, Lord Portsmouth had considerable influence in the borough, but when. before the general election of 1761, Newcastle applied to him on behalf of Francis Delaval, he replied : 'When I recommended M[ajor] G[eneral] Griffin to my friends at Andover I promissed them that I would not interfere farther in the election' (28 Sept 1760 ; 32912, f. 193). Thus also did the Ryder family act at Tiverton in 1768 (32986, f. 142 and 32987, f. 167) ; etc. etc.

[2] 1742–54, the seat was held by Lord Duncannon, a son-in-law of the third Duke of Devonshire ; 1797–1807, by George Walpole, a grandson of that Duke ; otherwise by Cavendishes.   [3] See below, p. 435.

[4] Thomas Ashfield to James West ; Evesham, 31 Mar 1761 ; 34735, f. 267.

As to Evesham, there will probably be a very warm contest: Sir John Rushout has declined on account of age, and the town where are 900 voters were so angry at his bringing in two last time, that Mr. Rushout has been obliged to declare, he will not join any one and in that light only is his security.[1]

The Monsons represented Lincoln in Parliament in the sixteenth and seventeenth centuries, and for forty-six years between 1722 and 1812, while the Sibthorps held a seat for twenty-five years in the eighteenth century, and, with the exception of only twelve years, from 1800–61. None the less, much more than tradition and influence was required to carry elections in that city. Lord Monson, when applying for a Court appointment, wrote to Newcastle on 22 May 1758:

It is not in my power any longer to support or even maintain the interest I so dearly bought at the last general election at Lincoln (by the desire of Mr. Pelham, more than my own inclination) if your Grace will not think of me; and that the spending £7000 and upwards exclusive of my house being like a fair for two years should not have intitled me to some small favour before this, I own I think hard.[2]

Naturally in constituencies with many poor voters, who could not aspire even to the smallest offices and could profit from *largesse* only, contests were much desired, and, like the landlord of the Bull Inn at Coventry, their managers would go in search of candidates. On 9 May 1741 Lady Cust wrote to her son, Sir John Cust (subsequently Speaker of the House of Commons) about Grantham: 'Monday was our election, which was very peaceable and quiett, the freemen are sadly vex'd, there was no opposition'.[3] At St. Albans, in 1761, 'the third man' was talked about for many months, and became a familiar figure in the town under that significant description — there was no trace of a political element in these discussions. 'The town is very clamorous for a third man', wrote Dr. Handley, a local physician, to James West, one of the two declared candidates, on 5 October 1760.[4] 'Our third man as

---

[1] 32985, f. 443.   [2] 32880, f. 200.
[3] *Records of the Cust Family*, compiled by Lady Elizabeth Cust (1909), vol. ii, p. 245.   [4] 34735, f. 55.

yet is in the clouds', he wrote on 30 November.[1] 'At present no third man appears tho the greatest pains is taken to promote it' (21 December).[2] Another of West's friends, Grindon, on 17 February 1761 : 'Gape . . . has declar'd that if the person sent does not bring a third man', they would start one locally.[3] Iremonger, on 18 February : 'This morning the town was in an uproar. . . . Sherman had received a letter from the 3ᵈ man.'[4] 'Mr. 3' got finally even into the newspapers — the freemen of St. Albans were required not to engage themselves — the following appeared in the *General Evening Post* on 7 March : 'A third person every way qualified for that high trust . . . will be unanimously declared by us, and will very soon make himself publicly known'. A week later he materialized in the person of Thomas Corbett, and on 28 March 1761 received 261 votes against 344 for Lord Nuneham, the Spencer candidate, and 313 for James West. The joint election expenses of the two successful candidates were £3363 : 4 : 9½ [5] — so much immediate profit to St. Albans.

In 1761, of the forty-four representatives of boroughs with an electorate of 500–1000 voters, nine were sons of British peers (three of them courtesy lords and one illegitimate), one an Irish peer, the rest mostly country gentlemen. Not a single one was a local business man, and even of local lawyers there were only two — the old Tories, N. Fazakerley and E. Starkie, Members for Preston. But the radiation of the official and commercial classes of London into the provinces is noticeable in this type of borough. Thomas Fonnereau, of Huguenot parentage, a rich London merchant, and John Henniker, a merchant and shipbuilder, sat for Sudbury ; James West, Secretary to the Treasury, for St. Albans ; and Sir Edward Simpson, at one time King's Advocate-General, and in 1761 Dean of the Arches, Keeper of the Prerogative Court of Canterbury and Judge of the Cinque Ports, represented Dover, with Sir Joseph Yorke, Minister to the Hague, for colleague.[6] Bamber Gas-

---

[1] 34735, f. 94.   [2] *Ibid.* f. 104.   [3] *Ibid.* f. 152.
[4] *Ibid.* f. 160.   [5] *Ibid.* f. 265.
[6] The Yorkes were a Dover family, and Joseph Yorke was not a mere Government candidate planted out on a strange place. Still, their choosing

coyne, whose father had been Lord Mayor of London and whose mother was the daughter of a well-known London physician, was returned for Maldon. Francis Herne, Member for Bedford, was similarly of a London merchant family. Rose Fuller, Member for Maidstone, was a planter in the West Indies and a squire and iron-master in Sussex, at one time Chief Justice of Jamaica, now interested in business ventures in the City, where his brother Stephen, agent for Jamaica, was an eminent merchant. Lastly, there was Thomas Thoroton, Member for Newark, who acted as the 'man of business' to the Manners group (as Rigby did to the Bedfords, Burke to the Rockinghams, Whately to George Grenville, Robert Jones to Lord Sandwich, etc.).

Of the forty-four Members representing medium-sized boroughs, fourteen were the first in the male line of their families to enter the British Parliament ; seven sat for boroughs which their fathers had represented, twelve succeeded near relatives — the corresponding figures for boroughs with over 1000 voters were eleven and three. To some extent this different proportion may be accidental — the figures are too small to yield reliable averages — but it also stands to reason that, given lineal descendants, the more important and dignified a constituency, the more likely was the hereditary principle to work out in a direct succession. The lesser seats would be assigned to collaterals or relatives by marriage ; for although a considerable town might accept a son as successor to his father, it might not agree to extend this hereditary allegiance to more distant relatives.

In this class of boroughs I propose to analyse mainly such as illustrate factors not present in the large towns dealt with in the previous chapter — in the first place, the direct intervention of Government whose influence, though not decisive in any of these boroughs, in a few played a considerable part.

Maldon.—The electorate consisted of some 700 freemen, but as residence was not required and the Corporation could

---

him is significant — it seems doubtful whether any of the large towns would have chosen a Member who, from the nature of his office, could hardly ever attend Parliament.

create honorary freemen, there was a good deal of gerry-mandering.[1] Between 1754 and 1763 there was at Maldon a curious sequence of defeats of Government candidates by men who next tried to win its favour. In 1754 R. S. Lloyd, son of the Solicitor-General, was defeated by John Bullock of Falk-bourn Hall, Essex, son of a late Member for the county, and kinsman of the Duke of Bedford.[2] But having captured the seat, Bullock took thought to connect himself with the Government. In a letter of 14 July 1755 George Townshend recommended him to Newcastle as a man in whom he can 'deposit that confidence and power which every one who proposes to establish an interest in a corporation town is desirous of having on his side'.[3] In 1761 Bullock was joined to Robert Colebrooke as official candidate, but now Colebrooke was defeated by a new interloper, Bamber Gascoyne, and on 31 March complained to Newcastle that 'several Government votes did not support us, notwithstanding your express order they should'.[4] By May 1762 Gascoyne seems to have been on the best terms both with the Government and Colebrooke. Bullock wrote to Newcastle about Maldon on 6 May 1762 :

On my coming there, I found every one of the Corporation in great confusion, occasion'd by Mr. Colebrooke and Mr. Gascoyne's

[1] See, e.g., letter from Sir George Oxenden, of Deane in Kent, to Newcastle, 2 Mar 1761 (32919, ff. 374-5) : '. . . a strange account we lately received from Mr. Colebrooke [M.P. for Maldon] that the town of Malden had, at his desire, made us [Sir George and his son] freemen of that place . . he says "that I may easily guess of the cause I am to serve". I suppose himself is the cause he means.' See also letter from John Bullock to Newcastle asking him to write to Dr. Rutherford at Cambridge 'to come to Maldon to take up his freedom and to vote for Mr. Colebrooke and Mr. Bullock' (32920, f. 351).
[2] He is described as such by Bedford, who supported him, in a letter of 30 Mar 1761 (32921, f. 192). Sir Richard Lloyd himself was defeated at Ipswich. Hardwicke, as Lord Chancellor chief of the lawyer politicians on the Government side, expressed to the King his disappointment at these defeats : 'His Majesty said, so was he, but that he heard he had starved the cause. I told him that the gentleman had himself assured me that he had spent £3000 at both places. That, as to Maldon, I thought his son had been as sure as my own son at Ryegate' (Hardwicke to Newcastle, 24 Apr 1754; 32735, ff. 178-9).   [3] 32857, ff. 103-104.
[4] 32921, f. 242. These were apparently Custom House officials, for in Newcastle's 'Memorandums' of 2 Apr 1761 (ibid. f. 270) appears the entry : 'The account of the custom officers at Malden'.

having been there and Mr. Gascoyne's offering himself for Recorder, every method was tried to induce them to come into it. Your Grace's name in perticuler was used, commanding them to comply and threatening destruction and loss of places should they refuse.[1]

On 9 December 1762 Gascoyne voted against the peace treaty, but four months later accepted a place at the Board of Trade. At the ensuing by-election, at which he was opposed by John Huske, a tough adventurer of American extraction, he naturally had the support of the Treasury; he wrote to Charles Jenkinson, its Secretary, on 21 April 1763:

I have herewith sent you a list of the freemen of Maldon who are in office under the Government, to desire an immediate conveyance to them that they are to assist me; for I am sorry to tell you, that they are to a man almost against me. The opposition to me is carried on with a great violence and open bribery. Ribbons with Liberty, property and no *excise* are the ornaments of my opponent's booths and carriages, and some other devices of this sort which I do not choose to mention. Guineas and scraps of *North Britons* are scattered all over the town and I can assure you that the opposition is founded by that ingenious gentleman Mr. Wilkes and his crew and is more immediately at Government than me.[2]

The same day John Bindley, a Commissioner of the Excise, thus explained to Jenkinson the way of dealing with subordinate officials of his own office, in view of the Act forbidding interference with them in elections:

. . . the affair being of the most delicate nature, I can forsee no way of serving Mr. G. but by his application in person or by letter to those who have votes, in which case leave of absence may be given to the off. who will then understand what is meant. . . .

N.B. The method proposed above is the only one used here in former cases.

P.S. Huske wrote to me yesterday, which I thought very extraordinary, to assist him with the votes here.[3]

---

[1] 32938, ff. 93-4.   [2] Jucker, *op. cit.*, p. 147.
[3] *Ibid.* p. 148. Huske was closely connected with Charles Townshend, to whom he had been deputy in the office of Treasurer of the Chamber 1756–61, and Bindley was a friend of Townshend, which may account for the application. The two, together with Samuel Touchet, were subsequently financial advisers to Townshend when Chancellor of the Exchequer.

I

Two days later, 23 April, Gascoyne wrote to his friend John Strutt : [1]

Dear Jack,

Tis with great cheerfullness that I can inform you all goes surpassingly well in London, and I verily believe I shall shew you a better appearance than the last election, the Treasury hath fully exerted itself which I fancy they must by this time have felt and you heard. . . .
    In high spirits . . .
                              your very affectionate friend and servt.
                                            Bamber Gascoyne.

But Huske reacted energetically to such exertion of the Treasury influence, and wrote to Grenville complaining of Gascoyne having declared to the officers of the revenue who were freemen at Maldon that Grenville had written him a letter which 'commands them to vote for him upon a penalty of losing their places immediately'. Grenville, replying on 25 April, denied having authorized Gascoyne to make such a declaration,[2] and when sending Huske's letter to Gascoyne remarked that he looked upon these 'extraordinary and unjustifiable assertions' as 'mere election artifice'.[3] Gascoyne, in reply, assured Grenville of the 'falsity' of the charge : [4]

I was yesterday to my great surprize sent for by Husk to the Custom house of this place and when I came there among a multitude of people I was charged by Mr. Husk with having used the unwarrantable means alluded in his. I immediately denied the assertion and call'd on him to produce his authority which he refused. Ld. Tylney, Sir Robert Long and Mr. Houblon were present. The wrath of this gentleman and his freinds was very great when they thought they should lose the Government interest, and therefore wrote that letter by way of getting that kind of answer which might induce the placemen to vote for them, which would much injure my election.

Anyhow, Huske's 'election craft' did the work, and Gas-

---

[1] Strutt MSS. at Terling Place, Essex.
[2] Grenville's Letter Book in the Huntington Library. Huske's letter is not extant, but its contents can be gathered from Grenville's reply.
[3] *Ibid.*
[4] Grenville Papers in the possession of Sir John Murray. The letter was written at 2 A.M. — presumably in the morning of 26 Apr.

coyne was defeated by 'the ungenerous behaviour and proceedings of the officers of the Customs and the freemen of that
borough'. The respect due to the 'high station' of the King's
Minister, wrote William Hunter, a Custom House official sent
to Maldon to work for Gascoyne,

and their dependance on his pleasure either to reward or punish
ought to have produced the most chearful complience and concurrence with every request from him to support his election. . . . I
have been upon a visit to the several and respective officers of the
Customs, freemen of the Corporation on behalf of Mr. Gascoyne,
in the course of which . . . nothing has been wanting on my part
to declare how necessary it was to compliment him with their votes
and interest, and I am ready to afirm that not any the least intima-
tions consequent thereon has been delivered to those officers or their
friends from me, but what has been strictly upright and consistent
with the freedom of elections, however warm in His Majesty's
service or the honour of the honourable House of Commons I have
expressed myself.[1]

By June 1763 John Huske seems to have been turning
towards the Government. Edward Richardson, a City agent
of Jenkinson, reported that he had freed Huske's mind from
certain wrong 'surmises' and shown him that it had been 'all
Gasconade'; and yesterday they dined together and 'we toasted
very frankly my Lord Bute's and yours, and next week meet
again for the same good purpose'.[2] Huske did not vote with
the Opposition when on 17-18 February 1764, in the division
on General Warrants, they came very near defeating the
Government.

Maidstone.—The Maidstone election of 1761 completes the
picture of the confusion of parties in the higher political circles
offered by the neighbouring city of Canterbury; shows once
more that in so far as parties existed among the rank and file
of the electorate, they had usually a religious background —
spontaneous Whig action at Maidstone was due to nearly half

---

[1] William Hunter to Charles Jenkinson, 26 Apr 1763; *ibid.* pp. 149-50.
About a fortnight later, Hunter asked, in consideration of his services at
Maldon, to be appointed 'to a small collection in an outport' (38200, f. 331).

[2] Jucker, *op. cit.*, pp. 162-3.

its population being Nonconformist;[1] and exhibits Newcastle handling, or at least professing to handle, Government influence as if it was his personal property.

On 8 February 1761 General Kingsley informed Newcastle that a considerable body of freemen at Maidstone asked him to stand against the two Tory candidates, Gabriel Hanger, supported by Lord Romney, and William Northey, Lord Aylesford's nominee ; but he would not engage against such powerful opponents without Newcastle's assistance.[2] Newcastle answered that, to oblige Lord Granby, he had promised Aylesford 'to be for any person, that he would recommend upon this occasion', and called this 'quite a private family agreement'.[3] Kingsley, in reply, described the Whig interest at Maidstone as 'at its last gasp',[4] and gave up the idea of a contest ; while Oxenden wrote to Newcastle on 19 February :

> People are embarrassed (at least I confess I am), what to say, and how to act . . . when the Court is all Tory at Maidstone and all Whig at Canterbury. They laugh at us and tell us, we make a rout about the Whig interest, when no body above sticks by it.[5]

Newcastle replied in a shuffling manner :

> Before I had enter'd into any engagement to my Lord Ailesford, I asked General Kingsley, whether he would stand at Maidstone, which he then declined. I did not hear of any opposition, and my best friend, my Lord Granby, having earnestly desired me to assist his brother-in-law, my Lord Ailesford at Maidstone . . . I promised . . . so to do. . . . My engagement was merely a private family affair. . . . It had no relation to the Court, or to any one in it; and they knew nothing of it, when it was done. And therefore I am willing to take the whole blame upon myself; and from this instance, the Court can't be called Tory ; for they had nothing to do in it. It is almost the first instance of the kind, in which I ever engaged myself ; and I hope, that, with the reasons I have given for it, will excuse me amongst my Whig friends.[6]

None the less a Whig candidate now took the field, Rose Fuller, a personal friend of Newcastle — he was in search of

---

[1] See Walter Royles's *General History of Maidstone* (1809).
[2] 32918, f. 370.
[3] 10 Feb 1761 ; *ibid.* f. 417.
[4] 12 Feb 1761 ; *ibid.* f. 483.
[5] 32919, ff. 116-17.
[6] *Ibid.* ff. 338-9.

a constituency, as he had no chance of re-election at Romney, where 'several of the governing men are graziers and the Deering and Furnese family have together a very great estate in the neighbouring marsh which is very profitable to and easy for tenants'.[1] He informed Newcastle on 1 March that he was going to Maidstone with the approval of Lord Sondes.[2] Newcastle replied that he could not approve of it and, in spite of his love and esteem for Fuller, would have to oppose him. He also feared that Granby and Aylesford might think he had acted a double part, when his 'most particular friend' Rose Fuller, by the encouragement of his nephew Sondes, opposed Aylesford.[3] Fuller now mounted the high horse of political principle :

> I was . . . invited to offer myself att that town by the Whig interest, which before I was twenty years of age I was convinced was the onely one by which the religion, liberty, property, happiness, power and internal peace of this nation could be preserved. . . . Upon these principles I set out and have continued to act upon and shall persevere into the end of my life.[4]—I attached myself to your Grace because I knew these principles were rivetted in your soul, and not upon account of your birth, riches or power. . . . As the head of that interest . . . your Grace hath a weight in this Kingdom more than you can well conceive, yet I very much doubt your Grace's power in carrying a popular election in any Whig county in favor of one of the other interest.

He found the warmest reception at Maidstone and expected to carry the election, but was alarmed by news from Chatham

> that the Commissioner had . . . sent for all the freemen of Maidstone employed in the dock and acquainted them he had received orders from the Admiralty to direct them to vote for Mr. Northey.

---

[1] Rose Fuller to Newcastle, 23 June 1758 ; 32881, f. 33. Against pasture for the cattle even the amiability of Rose and Stephen Fuller availed nothing. 'Seldom a day', wrote E. Milward to J. Collier in 1756, 'but both the Fullers kiss all the women in the Corporation — 'tis quite in their taste' (W. V. Crake, 'The Correspondence of John Collier', *Sussex Archaeol. Collections*, vol. xlv, p. 94, *n*). The two Members returned in 1761 were Edward Dering and Thomas Knight, both so-called Tories.

[2] 32919, f. 348.   [3] *Ibid.* ff. 410-11.

[4] When he 'totally altered his hue', in 1775, Burke called him the 'old, withered Rose, who in his best was no better than a dog-rose' (*Correspondence*, vol. ii, p. 7).

The letter, which started with principles and proceeded with alarms, concludes with profuse thanks

for what my Lord Kinnoul told me to wit . . . that you had kept a seat in Parlaiment open for me in case I could not carry my election there [at Maidstone].[1]

The same day twelve freemen of Maidstone, for themselves 'and hundreds more', reminded Newcastle, 'the warm and steady patron of liberty', of their past exertions on behalf of 'the illustrious House of Hanover', and expressed their 'real concern' at losing the advantages they 'allways us'd . . . to derive from the assistance of the dockmen at Chatham, and others in His Majesty's service'. Having dealt with the letter read out by the Commissioner at Chatham Yard, they proceeded:

We beg leave farther to inform your Grace, that Mr. Bingle, assistant to the builder at Chatham, came hither yesterday from Mr. Hanway the Commissioner, to desire the vote and interest of Mr. Edward Prentis, and his son, and Mr. Stephen Prentis, timber dealers of the Yard. Your Grace will therefore pardon us for making this our humble request, that those honest men, who had actually promis'd their votes to Mr. Fuller before the above orders arriv'd, may have some assurance, and that too a publick one, given them, that they shall not suffer by fulfilling their engagements.[2]

In a letter of 14 March Fuller harped once more on the Government support for Northey, adding the following comment:

When I consider Mr. Northey walks before His Majesty, as a Gentleman of his Bedchamber,[3] I can conceive, how it happened this letter was sent, and doe not att all wonder att it.—Although I had heard a determination had been taken to permitt the persons in His Majesty's immediate service to vote for those they liked themselves.—I believe this is the first instance of that determination being departed from.[4]

Newcastle replied on 15 March:

[1] 12 Mar 1761 ; 32920, ff. 121-2.   [2] *Ibid.* f. 139.
[3] Northey was one of the five Tories introduced into the Bedchamber in Dec 1760 without the knowledge of Newcastle.
[4] 32920, f. 196.

. . . no consideration can, or shall, induce me to break it [his engagement]. . . . As I am engaged, I will not act one way myself and persuade others to act contrary to it. I have directed Mr. West to let those, who depend upon the Treasury know, that I am for my Lord Aylesford's friend. I have nothing to do with other offices ; and therefore the application of the gentlemen to me about the dock votes was extremely improper. . . . In every other borough in Kent, and I may almost say in every other place in England, any . . . interest which I may have is . . . strenuously employ'd in support of the Whig interest. And this I think should satisfy my Whig friends in Kent.[1]

But however much Newcastle stuck to his engagements, his endeavours to keep in with everybody were apt to cause his being suspected of duplicity. On 23 March Lord Barrington, Chancellor of the Exchequer, reported a conversation with Bute which makes it seem doubtful whether the Court was so uninterested in Northey's candidature as Newcastle tried to make it appear.

He said smilingly that he must complain of the Treasury ; that all the revenue officers to a man who have votes at Maidstone would give them against Mr. Northey ; he thought this would make people suspect you of duplicity, and the more so as Fuller was your friend and a Sussex man. That for his own part he did you justice and did not suspect you. . . . I said I know you had given the usual directions, and had not done any thing to contradict them.[2]

And on 27 March Hardwicke wrote to Newcastle that 'it begins to be talk'd that altho' you give out that it is a sort of family affair . . . yet it was my Lord B. that induced you to support the Tory-Groom of the Bedchamber'.[3]

Rose Fuller carried his election at Maidstone, 'many officers of the Customs and Excise and many employed in the docks and yards' having voted for him ; he now asked Newcastle to

---

[1] *Ibid.* f. 231.

[2] 32921, ff. 6-7. Bute may have been prompted by Northey who wrote that he was 'very apprehensive that the freemen of Maidstone who are employ'd in the docks of Chatham and Deptford will be influenc'd against him . . . unless some hint could be given to the contrary' (Bute MSS.). On 26 Mar Barrington reported a further conversation with Bute reassuring Newcastle that Bute did him most ample justice (32921, ff. 78-9).

[3] *Ibid.* ff. 101-4.

'protect those officers from any censure or discountenance'.[1] Still, now that he no longer required the seat which Newcastle had held for him in reserve, he hinted that the Duke had not wished to see him in Parliament 'in that honorable manner I was in the last, and thank a number of honest independant freemen am in the present'.[2] And in August 1761 Fuller, when soliciting an appointment for Thomas Nightingale, brother of a Maidstone banker, once more reminded Newcastle of his misdeeds :

The Whigs and Dissenters in general, indeed, I might say, all who are any ways connected with this town, stand in need of something to heal their minds of the soreness they felt and have felt, by and since the recommendation of Mr. Northey by the Administration.

The favour to Mr. Nightingale would convince them that 'they are not slighted'.[3]

St. Albans.—Among the papers of James West at the British Museum there are two volumes of his correspondence concerning the management of the borough of St. Albans.[4] From that mass of material I pick a few examples to show the character of its politics. Very seldom — in fact, only three times — are matters of public interest discussed in these papers covering a period of about twenty-seven years, and then they are of a local character. On 2 February 1755 Dr. Handley, a leading man in the Corporation, wrote to West :

Mr. Gore and Mr. Hale [Members for Herts] have sent circulatory letters all over the county of the designed bill to regulate the of carrages desireing the oppinion of their constituents relateing to it, and how they would have them act.—How far something of that kind may be thought proper by you to our worthy gentry here

---

[1] 29 Mar 1761 ; *ibid.* f. 160. The figures were : Fuller 483 votes, Northey 452, Hanger 440.

[2] Fuller to Newcastle, 4 Apr 1761 ; *ibid.* ff. 315-16. Cf. with this a letter which Fuller's nephew by marriage, W. Sotheby, had written to Hardwicke on 18 Sept 1756 when asking for his support with a voter at Romney — he described Fuller as being 'of too much property to desire to be brought in by any interest that should entirely restrain the freedom of his vote' (35692, f. 374).

[3] 32927, ff. 207-8.   [4] 34734 and 34735.

must leave to your superior judgment, but if you will permit to give mine believe it will bee taken well.[1]

West took the hint, for on 17 February the Mayor is seen explaining to him at considerable length how the interests of the borough would be affected by the enforcement of the so-called Broad Wheel Act of 26 George II.[2] The second reference to a public interest is in a letter from West to Handley, 29 September 1759 :

I am glad to tell you that after three years constant application, I have at last fixed the post to come every day to St. Albans whose prosperity and convenience I am always thinking of.[3]

The third is correspondence about the billeting of troops at St. Albans — as John Page, M.P. for Chichester, said in reply to a suggestion of Major Gibbon of the Hampshire Militia (father of Edward Gibbon the historian) for quartering two of its battalions at Chichester : 'One of the tacit obligations upon a Member of Parliament was to keep the place he represented as free as he could from being pesterd and burthend with soldiers'.[4]

Political problems, as now understood, do not appear in the correspondence, which is engrossed with petty local intrigues and jealousies, scrambles for the civic honours of the borough, and endless applications for Government jobs and favours.

When, after eight months out of office (November 1756–July 1757), West returned with Newcastle to his old place at the Treasury, he was thus congratulated by one of his St. Albans constituents :

I beg leave to congratulate you on your return to that place, which has given you so many opportunities, and will still afford you more of indulging two of your most amiable and favourite passions,

---

[1] 34734, f. 92.   [2] Ibid. f. 94.   [3] Ibid. f. 329.
[4] See letter from John Page to Newcastle, 25 Sept 1761 ; 32928, f. 356. See also letter from John Dodd, M.P. for Reading, to Newcastle, 4 Nov 1760 : 'As I find the people of Reading so very desirous of chusing me this next general election, I think it incumbent on me . . . to beg your Grace will speak to Lord Barrington [Secretary at War] to order the regiment that is now quartered at Reading to be immediately removed . . .' (32914, f. 96).

the love of your King and country, and compassion for your distress'd friends.[1]

And here are two typical applications from freemen of
St. Albans :

H. Luck, writing to James West on 12 April 1759, asks
for some small place 'not attended with hurry, fatigue or confinement'. 'I have an interest in the borough of Barnstaple
as well as St. Albans, which I hope will intitle me to your
favour.' [2]

John Stoughton, on 6 May 1759, reminds West of an
occasion when, 'my being a freeman of St. Alban, you was so
kind to promise me, that you would get me to the Board, in
order to be a supervisor in the Excise'.[3]

Army matters play a considerable part in the correspondence
— West had to obtain commissions for gentlemen and discharges for privates. To give one example :

I trouble you now [wrote Handley on 24 March 1759] at the
request of Mr. Franklin the butcher who has a son a soldier in the
Royal Artillery at Bombay in India, he has been gone four years, and
the old man says if you will by any means procure his discharge, he
and his famely will for ever serve you with single votes [4] if requisite
the young fellow has a vote. I should be glad, if it be in your power,
that you will interest yourself in earnest in this affair. . . . The old
man says that last election you promised if he would serve you
that if he ever wanted any service in return you would do every
thing in your power. . . . Our enemies are very bussy, but such
things as these must always frustrate their wicked designs.[5]

I conclude with a letter from a St. Albans alderman to James
West, dated 5 December 1759 :

[1] 34734, f. 122.   [2] *Ibid.* f. 277.   [3] *Ibid.* f. 286.
[4] 'Single votes' means that they would vote for him alone in a two-
member constituency.
[5] 34734, f. 276. The general election of 1761 gave the Franklin family
an opportunity to bring up their request once more ; and the following
information was supplied to West by Robert James from India House
on 30 Apr 1761 :
   William Franklin went to Bombay in the year 1755 as a mattross in
   the King's Train of Artillery, but whether he is living or not cannot
   appear in any of our offices, and if living, as he is in His Majesty's service,
   his discharge cannot depend upon the Company. By the last advice the
   said Train was sent from Bombay to the other side of India to assist in
   the siege of Pondicherry (34935, f. 315).

I heartily congratulate you on your election of High Steward of our borough of St. Albans, I believe we are all extreemly sensible of the benefitts we are likely to enjoy under the influence of a gentle-man whose abilitys and interest are so very extensive, and more especially as you have given us such strong assurances in your polite letter to the Mayor to support the body and be of real benefitt to every member thereof, which hath hastned my intentions of troubling you with the following. . . .[1]

Dover.—There was a castle at Dover, there were forts, ships, trade, and packet boats, which, in terms of patronage, reads : the Lord Warden of the Cinque Ports, the Ordnance, the Admiralty, the Treasury (through the Custom House), and the Post Office. In the sixteenth and seventeenth centuries the Lord Warden nominated to one seat, and this custom so much tended to harden into a regular privilege that in 1689 an Act of Parliament was deemed necessary to declare its illegality.[2] Still, the influence of the Lord Warden survived at Dover (and also at Hythe). There was, however, a strong independent element in the borough, and earlier in the eighteenth century two leading local families, the Papillons and Furneses, appear among its representatives. Later on, Dover was brought into very close connexion with the Government through Lord Hardwicke, its Recorder and Steward 1718–64, who himself

---

[1] 34734, f. 353.

[2] See George Wilks, *The Barons of the Cinque Ports and the Parliamentary Representation of Hythe* (1892). In Feb 1613–14 Lord Northampton, the Lord Warden, claimed it to be 'the ancient usage and privilege that myself and my predecessors have ever had in the nomination of one of the Barons to be elected in the several ports' (*ibid.* p. 66) ; and in 1683 Colonel Strode, by order from the King, reminded the Corporation of Hythe of the privilege 'which the former Lord Wardens have ever enjoy'd . . . "The power or pre-eminence of recommending one of the Barons . . . to be elected for each of the ports"' (p. 88). But the Act of 1689 declared 'that all such nominations or recommendations were and are contrary to the law and constitution of this realm' (pp. 89-90). There were other great Royal officers who in the sixteenth and seventeenth centuries enjoyed similar privileges ; see, *e.g.,* Sir Richard Worsley, *History of the Isle of Wight* (1781), for its Governor's claims in its boroughs ; Pink and Beaven, *The Parliamentary Representation of Lancashire,* for the Chancellor of the Duchy nominating in the sixteenth century to one seat at Liverpool, etc. Lecky's wrong assumption that the Duchy of Cornwall exercised an important influence in Cornish boroughs in 1761 (*England in the Eighteenth Century,* vol. iii, p. 29) is probably based on similar privileges possessed by its officials in an earlier age.

was strongly attached to his native town of Dover, and to the old friends of his family in that place and neighbourhood, such as the Papillons, the Plumptres, the Russells, the Minets, the Wellards, the Gunmans, with whom he kept up an unbroken correspondence. He was constantly visited by them, and many from these families received his invaluable support at their start in life, or during the progress of their careers.[1]

Although Dover naturally benefited by this connexion, sentiment played the chief part in it, and when the Government took to sending the Corporation what one disappointed candidate described as a *congé d'élire*,[2] they were soon reminded of the limitations to their influence.

Philip Minet, of a leading Huguenot family at Dover, wrote to Hardwicke on 22 April 1756 :

> The seat in Parliament which late Mr. Burrell occupied being vacant, I should be glad to know if your Lordship has any person perticularly to recomend . . . any body from your Lordship would meet with success, but as the good people my townsmen have been much disgusted at persons being named, sent downe and recomended, by the Ministry with very little notice or time given them, they and a great number would gladly embrace a person who would opose such. It might be therefore necessary his Grace the Duke of Newcastle should fix on some person agreeable to the towne.[3]

Minet's letter concluded with the suggestion that either Sir Gilbert Heathcote, Hardwicke's son-in-law, or H. V. Jones, Hardwicke's nephew and private secretary to Newcastle, would be a suitable candidate. Similarly John Sauré, Assistant Agent of the Packet Boats, wrote from Dover on 20 April :

> The distiqueshd loyalty of this place has for many years past induced us to pay the greatest regard to the recommendations of

---

[1] Philip C. Yorke, *Life of Lord Chancellor Hardwicke*, vol. ii, p. 563.

[2] Peter Burrell wrote to Newcastle on 16 Apr 1756 :
You may run some risque . . . there are 800 voters, many of whom are ripe for opposition, many more kept steady by the Duke [of Dorset, then Lord Warden of the Cinque Ports] and Lord George Sackville, they expect some connection between them and their candidates and a *congé d'élire* may be a dangerous experiment (32864, ff. 298-9).
See also letter from George Sackville to Newcastle, 17 Apr 1756 (*ibid.* f. 314).

[3] 35692, f. 360.

the Ministry on such occasions, having allway chose such as they recommended, though intirely strangers to us ; by these methods (without any ways consulting the inclinations of the Corporation) I fear the Ministry will in time loose their influence here and indeed I may venture to say, so much of it is allready gone amongst the common freemen (and I am perswaded for no other reasons than above) that if any gentleman of fortune and carractor that is known to this Corporation should offer at this time to oppose a person sent down that we know nothing of, and that has no natural inclination as well as interest to serve us, I realy fear the consequence.

We have above 800 voters and tho many of them are biased by their places and other ways influenced, yet a great majority I beleive are independent ; would it not therefore be prudent in the Ministry at this time to indulge us in their approbation of Mr. Jones . . . when we consider the station Mr. Jones is in, we think it the greatest compliment we can pay to his Grace of Newcastle, and we conceive very agreeable to my Lord Chancellor.[1]

Newcastle at first had asked the 'friends of the Government . . . not to engage themselves',[2] meaning next to recommend to them his candidate ; but when, in a very dutiful letter, his own agent at Dover transmitted the suggestion of Jones's candidature,[3] Newcastle readily accepted it. In 1759, Edward Simpson, Judge of the Cinque Ports, was returned, at Hardwicke's recommendation, in the place of Jones ; and when in 1761 Lord George Sackville, who had sat for Dover since 1741, moved to Hythe, the Town Council 'by general consent' offered his seat to Sir Joseph Yorke.[4] On 17 February 1761 the Duke of Dorset wrote to them 'recommending Sir Edward Simpson to represent this town again in Parliament and expressing his best wishes for the success of General Yorke' :[5] the fine distinction should be noted between the rights which

[1] *Ibid.* f. 343. The letter is not to Hardwicke, for it starts 'Sir', nor does it seem to be to H. V. Jones. It is, however, among the Hardwicke Papers. Jones, too, was a native of Dover.

[2] Newcastle to Barham, Agent of the Dover Packet Boats, 17 Apr 1756 ; 32864, f. 322.

[3] 35692, f. 345. This letter, obviously forwarded by Newcastle to Hardwicke, is in the Hardwicke Papers ; see Newcastle's reply, *ibid.* f. 358 ; further, in the Newcastle Papers, a letter from Barham, 25 Apr 1756 ; 32864, f. 399.

[4] 35692, f. 438.   [5] *Ibid.* f. 394.

obviously the Lord Warden still claimed with regard to one seat, and his concurrence in the choice made by others for the second.

Thus in populous boroughs, even of 'distiqueshd loyalty', Government influence had to be exercised with discretion ; but such niceties are lost in the summaries compiled by reformers from which most of the information concerning the unreformed Parliament is derived.

Boroughs with about 500 Voters

Some of these eleven boroughs did not differ much in social structure from the medium-sized type, others came near that of pocket boroughs, and in all alike election contests were rare — only three went to the poll in 1754 and none in 1761. They formed a very heterogeneous collection. Hertford was a rather dignified constituency with a large Nonconformist vote ; local families of rich business men were practically in control of the borough. In 1761 one Member was a rich brewer, John Calvert, and the other, Timothy Caswall, an officer in the Guards, was the nominee and successor of his uncle, a prominent banker, Nathaniel Brassey. Aylesbury was corrupt and well within the radius of London official and commercial influences ; in 1761 one of its Members was Welbore Ellis, a placeman of Irish extraction and son-in-law of Sir William Stanhope, who had considerable influence in Buckinghamshire, and the other the famous John Wilkes, son of a London distiller, descended on both sides from pious Nonconformists ; on his expulsion he was succeeded by Anthony Bacon, a London merchant. Rochester was considered an Admiralty borough, but there was a strong independent element in it ; Sandwich was under the influence of the Admiralty, the Treasury, and some Kentish neighbours. Berwick-on-Tweed ranked as an open borough, but the Government had considerable influence through the Customs, Excise, and Taxes, the Post Office, and the garrison, Navy, and Ordnance. Peterborough was under the influence of Lord Fitzwilliam and other neighbouring landowners, and of its own town notables ; in 1761 Sir Matthew

Lamb, whose brother Robert was Dean of Peterborough, 1744–64, and its bishop, 1764–69, was one of its Members.[1] At Taunton the local Nonconformists had a considerable influence, and in 1754 applied to Newcastle to provide them with a candidate 'most agreeable to His Majesty and most likily readily to go thro' with the necessary expence of securing his election'.[2] Situated in the cloth-manufacturing district, Taunton, even about the middle of the eighteenth century, occasionally returned local business men, and towards the end of the century became an exclusive preserve of rich bankers and merchants. Of the remaining four boroughs, Stamford was under the influence of Lord Exeter and other neighbouring big landowners; Newcastle-under-Lyme under that of the Leveson-Gowers; Wareham of various local squires (the Pitts, Bankeses, and Draxes, who all finished by selling their Wareham property to J. Calcraft); while at Chichester, although the town was fairly independent, the Duke of Richmond, owner of the neighbouring estate of Goodwood, exercised a considerable influence.

To strengthen it, the young Duke in 1757 asked Newcastle to be allowed to name at Chichester to the places depending on the Treasury and Custom house, and on another occasion extended his claim even to its ecclesiastical preferments. He wrote to Newcastle on 26 August 1757: 'I shall be willing to take the recommendations of any of the gentlemen of the neighbourhood, but lett me have the doing of it'.[3] And on 29 October 1758: '. . . I hope that your Grace will allow all the recommendations to go thro' me. This is what my father allways did. I think I have a right to it, and it is among the very few favours I ask of your Grace.'[4] Finally, in November

---

[1] The father of Sir Matthew Lamb, first Bt. (1755), had been land agent to the family of Coke, of Melbourne, Derbyshire, and Matthew married the heiress of that family. He also inherited 'a large fortune' (according to the *Historical Register*, £100,000) from his uncle, Peniston Lamb, a barrister. He himself was confidential adviser to Lords Salisbury and Egmont and was said to have 'feathered his nest pretty handsomely at their expense' (see A. Hayward, *Sketches of Eminent Statesmen and Writers* (1880), vol. i, p. 332). He is said to have left a million pounds. His son, Sir Peniston Lamb, second Bt., M.P., was in 1770 created Lord Melbourne.

[2] 32736, f. 25.   [3] 32873, f. 293.   [4] 32885, f. 118.

1758, Richmond thus expounded his theory of patronage to John Page, M.P. for Chichester : [1]

That he believed it was the general custom with Ministers to make that compliment to the person of the highest rank in the country and living near to the place in which he cultivated an interest in order to strengthen that interest, which the power of disposing of places would always greatly contribute to, unless the principles of such persons was suspected with respect to the Government.

The counter-claim which Page produced in reply to Richmond's *exposé* was the answer of an old Whig, a Whig by principle and not for profit :

After hearing him with all the patience he himself could think due to his quality, I presumed to tell him ; that I had served near thirty years in Parliament ; that I could prove myself a poorer man by fourteen or fifteen thousand pounds in consequence of it ; that I never had any employment under the Crown, nor any private pecuniary reward from any Minister, though in general a friend to them.

Lastly, he mentioned that before the general election of 1754 Henry Pelham, to induce him to stand again, had promised him a share in recommendations to vacant posts at Chichester.[2]

The Narrow Constituencies

It is extremely difficult to give a coherent account of the remaining 148 boroughs ; but when even the most considerable constituencies, such as Bristol, treated their Members primarily as agents called upon to secure their specific interests, no wonder that in towns with a very restricted electorate the remunerative capacities of the vote were even more marked and were turned even more to the profit of individuals. The ideas of the time closely connected franchise and representation with property, and gradually the vote and seat themselves tended to become realty, like an advowson, sublime in its ultimate significance, beneficial in practice to its owner.

[1] Page to Newcastle, 22 Nov 1758 ; 32885, ff. 507-8.
[2] For other correspondence on this subject see 32873, f. 422 ; 32875, f. 407 ; 32885, ff. 155, 174-6 ; 32886, f. 181.

Patronage benefits being concomitant on the franchise, it was desirable that the professional character of the Members should, if possible, harmonize with that of the borough. Thus towns on the coast showed a preference for naval officers, not only because of the glamour of their exploits at sea. When in 1747 Dr. Ayscough, secretary to Frederick Prince of Wales, encouraged William Lemon, a Cornish mine-owner,[1] to fight the Boscawen interest at Truro, Lemon replied:

> The majority of the electors here are so attached to the Tregothnan family by the behaviour of Captain Boscawen, and his taking some of their sons to sea with him, that the attempt you advise me to make in this place would, I am persuaded, prove fruitless.[2]

On a vacancy at Chichester in 1755, Page, to prepare the ground for Augustus Keppel, a cousin of the young Duke of Richmond, discoursed at the coffee-house that it would be reasonable for the town to accept the recommendation of the Duke's guardians,

> and that the person would, from the reason of things be Commodore Keppel, to whom I would, in that case, give my vote, not only upon account of the recommendation, but because of the Commodore's merits as a good officer, and a rising man in the Navy where he would be able and, if chosen, willing to serve the sons of his friends who should go into the sea service.[3]

And on the eve of the general election of 1761, Luxmore, manager of Okehampton, wrote to Rear-Admiral Rodney:

> I understand that you are now about to have the *Marlborough* as a fix'd ship, and beg leave to remind you of your promise to me, to make Joe Hunt your Captain, so soon as you had one. . . . I have therefore wrote Mr. Hunt's friends that as the *Marlborough* will be soon ready for you, he may depend upon being her captain for that I had your promise long ago.[4]

---

[1] About 'the great Mr. Lemon', who was 'the principal merchant and tin smelter of Cornwall', see *Parochial History of Cornwall*, vol. ii, pp. 67-8. He held from Frederick Prince of Wales 'a grant for a term of years of the dues on all minerals and metals (tin excepted) which he might cause to be discovered within the Duchy lands of Cornwall and Devon'.

[2] HMC, *Fortescue MSS.*, vol. i, p. 109.

[3] 32852, ff. 7-8.   [4] 14 Dec 1760; 32916, f. 257.

K

Rodney thereupon wrote to Robert Andrews, the London manager for Okehampton :

> On my arrival here I received the enclosed letter . . . and as I know Lord Anson will not oblige me in this affair, hope you will lay it before his Grace of N——le that he may insist upon it with his Lordship, in case his Grace should intend that I serve again for Okehampton.[1]

But when Rodney was shifted to Penryn, Captain Peard, a freeman of Penryn 'whose friends have great influence', supplanted Joe Hunt as his candidate for the captaincy in the *Marlborough*.[2]

Almost as welcome as admirals in the naval boroughs were Secretaries to the Admiralty — Clevland, M.P. for Saltash 1741–43 and 1761–63, and Sandwich 1747–61, and Philip Stephens, M.P. for Sandwich 1768–1806 ; or distinguished Admiralty lawyers such as Edward Simpson, M.P. for Dover 1759–64, and George Hay, M.P. for Sandwich 1761–68.[3] In 1792 Oldfield wrote about Sandwich and Stephens :

> The inhabitants of this place are bound to this gentleman by every tie of gratitude, as there is scarcely a single family, some part of which has not been provided for by him, in the admiralty, navy, or marines.[4]

Merchants were a serious competition to sailors in maritime boroughs. About Fowey Lord Edgcumbe remarked, in December 1761, that Captain Walsingham, R.N., would do better in the borough than W. R. Earle (an official of the Ordnance), but that the people 'would rather have a merchant than either':[5] the opponent was one who tried to win the borough by promising to promote its trade. At New Shoreham, a place

---

[1] 19 Dec ; 32916, f. 255. Both these letters were forwarded by Andrews to Newcastle with a covering letter of 22 Dec ; *ibid.* f. 253. For previous correspondence between Newcastle and Anson about Lieut. Hunt and Okehampton, see pp. 33-4.   [2] See p. 314.

[3] James Marriott, of Doctors' Commons, another lawyer practising in the Admiralty courts (in 1764 he succeeded Hay as Advocate-General), asked Newcastle in a letter of 20 Jan 1761 to promote his candidature for Aldborough in Suffolk — 'this borough . . . being maritime, I hope I can always be of use to my constituents in my profession' (32917, f. 447).

[4] *History of the Boroughs*, vol. iii, p. 62.

[5] See below, pp. 318-9.

famous for corruption,[1] the corporate interests of the town also received due consideration in the choice of Members. On 25 September 1766, in a letter to Newcastle signed by eighty out of its 136 voters, they recounted how at his recommendation they had elected Admiral Cornish — 'and we were much delighted with the Admiral's generosity to us since that happened' — but at the forthcoming general election they humbly hoped 'that one of the gentlemen your Grace pleases to name may have it in his power to assist in building merchant vessells, it being the chief manufacture of this borough'.[2]

At Chippenham, in the cloth-manufacturing district of Wiltshire, Sir Samuel Fludyer, a leading clothier, established a strong interest. In the London commercial directories of 1738–63 his firm appeared as 'Samuel and Thomas Fludyer', and in 1769 it became 'Fludyer, Marsh & Hudson': Sir Samuel Fludyer sat for Chippenham from 1754 till his death in 1768; his brother, Sir Thomas, from 1768 till his death in 1769; their brother-in-law, Samuel Marsh, 1774–80, and Giles Hudson from 1780 till his death in 1783 — the borough remained in the firm. Nathaniel Newnham, when trying to establish himself at Ashburton, wrote to Newcastle on 26 May 1760:

I . . . am satisfied that the great services I have already done and may do that borough in promoting the exportation of its manufactores has procured me several staunch friends there.[3]

Most striking of all is the case of Tiverton as related by its historian Martin Dunsford,[4] a local clothier who towards the end of the century became the leader of a movement for extending its franchise. In 1765 the death of Oliver Peard, the political manager of Tiverton and one of its principal merchants

---

[1] New Shoreham was the first borough to be disfranchised for corruption, in 1771 its representation being thrown into the rape of Bramber. For a case of very open bribery at Shoreham (about 100 electors actually received '£20 appiece' with a promise of '20 more'), see letter from William Michell to Newcastle, 8 Nov 1753 (32733, f. 222); 'I never heard of any things being done in so publick a manner'.

[2] 32977, f. 163.   [3] 32906, f. 285.

[4] In his *Historical Memoirs of the Town and Parish of Tiverton* (1790), pp. 245-52. About Dunsford see M. L. Banks, *Blundell's Worthies* (1904), pp. 89-97.

who had conducted an extensive woollen trade, by which a considerable part of the poor inhabitants had been employed many years, occasioned not only a present general stagnation of business, but great fears among the labourers, that the trade itself would be removed elsewhere . . . unless some other merchant, of fortune and capacity, could be influenced to settle in Tiverton. They therefore applied, in a body, to the Mayor and corporation, to request them to elect Mr. Charles Baring,[1] a considerable merchant of Exon, to fill one of three vacancies then in the corporation, as he . . . had offered to reside in the town, and conduct a considerable woollen trade in it.

The majority of the Corporation were at first willing to do so, but subsequently the Mayor and his party changed their minds, giving as a reason that

Mr. Baring had expressed his intention to have his brother and friend also elected to fill the other two vacancies, and to lay the members of the corporation under obligation to him in trade ; and by these means to engross the sole interest and direction of the corporation . . . and get himself or brother chosen one of the representatives in Parliament for the borough.

When the wool-combers, weavers, etc., learnt of the change in the Mayor's attitude, grave disorders ensued which resulted in the sacking of the Mayor's house, much destruction in his works and fulling mills, agreements between combers and weavers never in future to work for any members of the Corporation who did not vote for Baring, etc. To sum up : the chief attraction which Tiverton had for Baring was that it returned Members to Parliament ; the Corporation, in which the franchise was vested, consisted of smaller merchants who would have welcomed him as a leader and friend but feared him as a master ; while the 'labouring poor', who had no vote either in the choice of the Corporation or of Members of Parliament, tried to force the Corporation to deliver the borough to Baring in the hope that he would provide them with employment.

Beside patronage and trade, public works were among the

---

[1] Fourth son of John Baring (who was the first of the family to settle in England, as cloth manufacturer and merchant, at Larkbeer, near Exeter) and younger brother of John Baring, M.P. for Exeter 1776–1800, and of Sir Francis Baring, first Bt., M.P.

most usual corporate interests secured at elections. About
1750 Tewkesbury suffered severely from the deplorable condition of its roads, some 'so narrow that two horses could
scarcely pass each other; others . . . so deep in mud that the
travelling public made tracks in the adjoining fields'.[1] Under
the leadership of 'persons of property in the borough' a club
was therefore formed in 1753 to use the forthcoming general
election for a scheme of public utility. In a letter in *Felix
Farley's Bristol Journal* on 20 January 1753 Lord Gage, who
had represented the borough since 1721 and claimed that he
had neither bought his constituents nor sold them for selfish
purposes, raised the following complaint:

I must own myself greatly mortified to find many of my friends
engaged in a scheme, which, if persisted in, must deprive me of
the honour of representing them; although I flatter myself their
resolution to choose no members but such as will give £1500 each
towards mending their roads, does not proceed from any personal
dislike to me, but from the benefit they conceive the trade of
Tewkesbury will receive by it.[2]

And as Gage refused to accede to these terms, he and his son
Thomas (subsequently Commander-in-Chief in America) were
defeated by John Martin, brother of the well-known London
banker, and Nicolson Calvert, brother of a London brewer,
who 'made their public entry into the town with pickaxes and
shovels carried before them, and flags, with inscriptions thereon,
of "Calvert and Martin" on one side, and "good roads" on
the other'.

Or again, about Newport in the Isle of Wight the following
account was sent by Ralph Jenison to Henry Pelham on 18
February 1754:

The people of that place have taken the opportunity of paving
their town against a general election and Mr. Holmes [the Government manager] says the candidates are to pay for it, that and the
expence at the day of election and some gratuities to particular
people, will amount to six hundred pound for each candidate, which

---

[1] See 'J. T.', 'Tewkesbury Politics in 1753', in the *Gloucestershire Notes
and Queries*, vol. v (1891–93), pp. 509-11.
[2] *Ibid.*

Mr. Holmes desires may be paid into his hands before he leaves London.[1]

On 12 May 1766 the Mayor and Aldermen of Oxford [2] addressed a letter to Robert Lee, one of their Members, describing the distressed condition of the city, which had a debt of £5670, and offering to re-elect him and his colleague if they discharged it. They expressed their indignation at some unauthorised 'person or persons' who had 'taken upon themselves to expose the city to a person in London', but stated that, should their sitting Members refuse to advance the money,

the whole council are determined to apply to some other person or persons in the county to do it, and if possible, by that means, to keep themselves from being sold to foreigners.[3]

The editor of the *Parliamentary History* adds that it was

generally affirmed, and as generally believed, that the gentlemen who signed this letter . . . were not actuated by any motives of self-interest, and that they only meant to benefit the corporation in general by their request.

The methods employed in the management of narrow corporations and the terms in which their politics were transacted will be analysed in the chapters on the Cornish boroughs and on Harwich and Orford, while examples of fairly free boroughs with a strong tradition of heredity in representation will be found in that on Shropshire. Here I merely add an example of a burgage borough and of the terms in which such Parliamentary seats were discussed.

At Clitheroe there were 102 burgages entitled to a vote in elections. In 1717, on the death of Sir Ralph Assheton, whose family had frequently represented the borough in the seventeenth century,[4] his sons-in-law, Thomas Lister and Nathaniel Curzon, 'became possessed of a very considerable joint pro-

[1] 32734, ff. 148-9.

[2] Oxford was not one of the 'narrow constituencies', but the following action of its Corporation is typical of practices adopted by many a corporation borough.

[3] *Parliamentary History*, vol. xvi, p. 398; 'foreigner' here is used in contradistinction to gentlemen of the county.

[4] Another member of the family, Mr. Ralph Assheton, represented Clitheroe in Parliament 1868-80.

perty' and of four burgages at Clitheroe which they continued to hold in common. After the contested election of 1722 they jointly bought the 37 burgages of their defeated opponents,[1] and such purchases were continued until the joint holding comprised 53 burgages, 'a majority of the whole' which converted 'what was before scarcely a reasonable chance of representing the borough sometimes, into an absolute certainty of representing it for ever'.[2] From 1722 till 1780 the two families equally shared its representation, but in 1780 Thomas Lister (subsequently first Lord Ribblesdale), having increased his separate holding from 13 to 30 burgages, played a trick on his partner, Assheton Curzon (subsequently first Viscount Curzon). The total number of burgages being 102, if the joint 53 were annihilated, Lister's separate 30 would be a majority of the remaining 49, and then he could fill both seats, paying no attention to Curzon ; he achieved this by refusing to concur in the conveyances of the joint property which were required for creating nominal voters for the election, *i.e.* after the Curzons had spent their share of money on joint purchases, Lister deprived Curzon 'of the natural advantages of his property for his own benefit'. One can well understand the indignation of the Curzon family, but in neither account of the transaction is it remembered that the object discussed in such purely proprietary terms was the representation of a borough in Parliament. And when the Lister side tried to belittle the solidity of the Curzon interest in the borough, it was pointed out by their opponents, as proof of its real strength, that William Curzon, Member for Clitheroe 1734–47, 'was a stranger in the borough and . . . never paid the compliment of attending at his own election'.

To sum up : power to exercise decisive influence in problems of national importance was vested in an electorate not equal to comprehending them, and in the absence of organized parties that power was used primarily to satisfy local or even

---

[1] The sum paid for 31 of these 37 burgages was only £2950.

[2] The account given above is based on two pamphlets published in 1781, an *Apology for the Conduct of Thomas Lister, Esq., respecting the Borough of Clitheroe*, and *An Answer to the Apology*, etc.

personal needs — one can only wonder that the results were not worse than they were. Naturally the state of the franchise in the majority of boroughs tended to further the proprietary type of politics, while in turn the 'proprietary' politics, prevalent even in most of the big and free borough constituencies, explain why the unreformed franchise was suffered to continue so long. Seeing the purpose for which the unenfranchised population of Tiverton wished to use the Parliamentary representation of the borough, is there anything morally repugnant in the proprietary claim of those who held it ?

Eighteenth-century politics and elections may seem quaint to those who assume that present-day party politics, caucuses, and election stunts are 'normal', and that any other system is curious and extraordinary. But in reality they all are based on the simple fact that the aim in Parliamentary elections is not the mental and moral education of the electorate, but the acquisition of seats ; and once a strictly defined purpose is set to human activities, once they are fixed in definite forms, a ritual develops at the expense of devotion. The forms acquire an independent life of their own, grow and become complex, and the original meaning or purpose is forgotten ; the Thibetans are not the only people to employ praying-wheels. The correlation of human activities to their avowed purposes is in most spheres so dim and uncertain that one wonders how anything is ever achieved. Perhaps this is the answer : if in most tasks humanity scores three marks in a thousand, and learns by experience to consider this a fair average, only with regard to periods widely different from our own are we able to perceive the missing 997 points. The result of any electoral system is a House consisting of individuals representative, not so much because they have passed through a peculiar and possibly altogether irrelevant system of 'election', but because they belong to circles which are primarily concerned with the nation's political business and form therefore the political nation.

Patronage

I feel it incumbent on me, in conclusion of this chapter, to attempt a synopsis of the state of representation and patronage in England at the accession of George III. But the more one knows about the internal condition of boroughs (as about the characters of men) the more difficult it is to classify them. Weather-charts are neatest where there are no proper stations for observation. To this it might be objected that the reformers of 1790–1832 drew up many a clear and exhaustive chart of representation, though they were undoubtedly well-informed. But then their purpose was to show up the absurdities of the system, and they did not therefore mind glossing over difficulties and stating the case in bald, plain, unqualified terms ; a student of history hesitates to proceed in the same rough and ready manner. I therefore wish to restate once more certain difficulties which should be faced before they are passed over.

There were few places, such as Old Sarum, which could in unqualified terms be put down as absolutely and irrevocably under the command of one man, his heirs or assigns. In most cases 'control' meant merely a command so complete that it required exceptional negligence or ill-luck on the part of the owner to be deprived of it. Still, cases of that kind did occur, and there was almost always room for anxiety, even in the case of burgage boroughs over which the hold of the owner was usually most secure. In 1761 anyone would have declared Horsham the outright property of the Ingram family. Their hold on it was shaken and ultimately destroyed when the last male representative of the Ingram family, the ninth Viscount Irvine, died in June 1778, and the eleventh Duke of Norfolk, who had conformed to the Church of England in 1780, developed an interest in boroughs.[1] Boroughbridge was (and remained) the property of the Dukes of Newcastle ; and yet in 1763 Lord Lincoln, Newcastle's heir-apparent, suddenly became hysterical over it :

If you have any regard my dearest Lord, for my *tolerable ease* of mind [he wrote to Newcastle on 19 March 1763] for God's sake ! dont forget what you have promis'd me, if something is not done *now*, depend upon it, the borough is lost to your family for *ever*.[2]

[1] See W. Albery, *A Parliamentary History of Horsham* (1927).
[2] 33067, f. 347. For Newcastle's reassuring reply see 32947, ff. 263-4 : 'I shall not lose sight of the object . . . but it must be done in a gentle

At Bere Alston the majority of burgages were the property of Sir F. H. Drake, fifth Baronet, and of the Earl of Buckinghamshire. But attention was required, and in October 1741, Rowe, Drake's chief agent and a friend of the family, wrote to the young baronet, then at Cambridge, about attempts made to split holdings and propose fresh burgagees :

If they multiply tenants upon you in this manner and a dispute arises, you can have no relief but in St. Stephen's Chapel. It therefore behoves you to look about betimes and to make yourself master as soon as possible at least of election law. . . . Not knowing what may happen, you should always be present at the choosing the Portreeve, to keep your friends together and, though you are not of age, to let them know how soon you shall be. . . . Keep the trust of the parish lands as long in yourself as you can and don't let complaisance draw from you what you have a power to keep.[1]

Although burgage boroughs nearest approached complete control, as the basis for it usually was in property and not in influence over persons, even there the hold was seldom absolute, because in view of the intricacies of electoral law the title itself to the property was seldom perfectly clear and unassailable.

Where human beings were concerned, there never could be absolute certainty. Grampound was talked of in proprietary terms ; but (as shown in the chapter on Cornish boroughs) in 1758 it 'renounced the name' of its patrons, the Edgcumbes, and put itself under different management. Truro was a stronghold of the Boscawens which for a long time no one thought of contesting ; but when in 1780 Basset, one of the richest mine-owners in Cornwall, attacked the Falmouth interest, the Corporation of Truro suddenly discovered that 'the interference of any Peer of Parliament in the election of Members of the

quiet way and not by force'. The question was of burgages belonging to the family of Andrew Wilkinson, Newcastle's manager. For further correspondence about them see 32965, ff. 97 and 189 ; the question of these Boroughbridge burgages was one of the factors which produced the break between Lincoln and Newcastle in 1766.

[1] Lady Eliott-Drake, *The Family and Heirs of Sir Francis Drake*, vol. ii, pp. 244-5.

Lower House is illegal, and subversive of the very essence of our Constitution', and declared that they would elect Bamber Gascoyne and Henry Rosewarne, a local merchant, 'freely, and without expence' to them.[1] Lord Shelburne purchased Calne from Duckett and Northey in 1763–65,[2] and henceforth it was his pocket borough [3] — but a candidate was elected against his choice in 1807. Even Newcastle lost a candidate at Lewes in 1768 — the Duke's illness, the incoherence of his actions at that time, the division in his own family coupled with the imminence of his death and the consequent change of patrons, contributed to that result. Totnes was in 1761 reckoned a Government borough, though the hold on the Corporation was never very strong; [4] in 1780 and 1783, when John Robinson was compiling his charts of boroughs, no trace was left of Government management at Totnes. Portsmouth, a corporation borough, for many years accepted the Admiralty's recommendations for both seats, but about 1774, under the leadership of a prominent local man, John Carter, a revolt was started in the Corporation (largely by the Dissenters) which assumed a

[1] See P. Jennings, 'Notes on the Parliamentary History of Truro', *Journal of the Royal Institution of Cornwall*, vol. xix (1913), p. 232. But lest anyone suspect in this opposition a symptom of political discontent at the close of the American war, the praise should be noted which they gave to Gascoyne for having 'shown himself an able and steady Member in support of his Majesty and his Government (a conduct which, if generally pursued, we incline to think, would be most likely to put a speedy end to the present calamitous war, already lengthened by our unhappy divisions)'.

[2] See my essay on 'Thomas Duckett and Daniel Bull, Members for Calne', *Wilts Archaeol. Mag.*, June 1928.

[3] After the Reform Act of 1832, Calne was represented by the Earl of Kerry, 1832–36, by the Earl of Shelburne, 1847–56, and by Lord Edmond Fitzmaurice, 1868–85, when it was merged in the county.

[4] Charles Frederick, an official of the Ordnance and M.P. for Queenborough, in a letter dated Dartmouth, 30 Aug 1754, wrote about Totnes :

The Government interest is very precarious in that borough, its whole strength depends on one vote among the aldermen, therefore if one of our friends should dye before the chusing of a new mayor or one of the aldermen in the Government interest can be bought off, it is gone out of the Ministry's hands. Lord William Seymour . . . has offered Mr. Vavasor, an alderman of Totnes, £700 for his vote, this Vavasor is very poor, has a large family, and consequently is to be doubted where the temptation is so considerable, however he has promised he will be very firm, provided he is forgiven a debt of £271 which the Navy have against him (32736, ff. 382-3).

real political character and seriously endangered the hold of the Admiralty upon it.[1]

In fact, there was no absolute certainty where there were any real voters, and there was no retaining their allegiance without constant attention, expense, importuning of Ministers on their behalf, entertaining them, currying favour with their wives and daughters,[2] etc.

Another serious difficulty in the classification of boroughs arises from the confusion of private 'interests' with Government influence. Electoral interests as a rule required the support of Government patronage lavished at the recommendation of the borough patrons; while influence in Government boroughs had to be managed through Ministers and local agents, who more often than not tried to get away with them. The condition of Government boroughs and the methods of managing them are described in the chapter on Harwich and Orford, which in 1761 were the two Treasury boroughs *par excellence* (but a year later Newcastle hoped that he would be able to retain influence in them even after he had ceased to be its First Lord). It is more difficult to define the position in boroughs

[1] See Oldfield, *Representative History* (1816), vol. iii, pp. 504-6, R. J. Murrell and R. East, *Extracts from the Records of the Borough of Portsmouth* (1884), and P. A. Taylor, *Some Account of the Taylor Family* (1875). There is also much valuable information about Portsmouth affairs in the Sandwich MSS. at Hinchingbrooke. The true political character of the movement is established by Thomas Binsteed, Lord Sandwich's agent, telling him with reference to a proposed Address to the King concerning America: 'if the Address were to be made to the Deity, and originate from our side, Mr. Carter and his party would oppose it' (letter of 6 Nov 1775). Compare with this the dictum of one of the least partisan among Conservative leaders in the 1920s, who thus explained an unexpected action of his own: 'If the Opposition moved the Ten Commandments as amendment to the Address, the best Christian among the Conservatives would have to vote against them'.

[2] Cf., *e.g.*, election accounts at Grampound in 1754: to each freeman's wife, 'and where no wife to his eldest daughter', one guinea 'to buy a ring'; see below, p. 352. Robert Maxwell, on 8 Aug 1754, after his return to London, thus described his electioneering at Taunton in a letter to Lord G. Sackville: 'I arrived here last night from Taunton after a great deal of smoking, some drinking, and kissing some hundreds of women; but it was to good purpose. . . . I may venture to say that I have now near 150 majority' (HMC, 9, iii, *Stopford-Sackville MSS.*, p. 131). He was elected, but for the cash expenditure on that election from secret service funds see below, pp. 206 and 432-41.

where the Government influence was closely intertwined with some original private interest of a Minister or agent who managed them on behalf of the Government. This was the position of Newcastle in the Sussex boroughs of Seaford, Hastings, and Rye, of the Duke of Dorset at Hythe, and of Lord Holmes in the three Isle of Wight boroughs. It may be seen in the case of the Sussex boroughs how difficult it is to draw a line between the two interests, especially after they had been treated as identical for some forty years. Newcastle's relation to all three was more or less the same, but by 1768 he had lost Hastings, because its manager, Edward Milward, considered himself bound to the Treasury and not to Newcastle; he retained Rye, because its manager, Thomas Lamb, adhered to him; [1] and he was able to save one seat at Seaford by concluding a compromise with an independent candidate, and because Grafton, then First Lord of the Treasury, did not press an opposition against him. With regard to all three boroughs, Newcastle behaved as if they were his allodial possessions, and not fiefs he held *qua* Minister of the Crown; thus in 1761 he felt it necessary to make excuses to Hastings for not recommending a Pelham — 'I should with pleasure now recommend one of my own family to you, had there been any one capable at present of representing you'.[2] Part of his influence in these boroughs still survived in 1768 by force of personal loyalties and regard, but none passed to his heirs on his death, which occurred shortly after that general election.[3]

The Government Interest

It is impossible numerically to express the size of the Government interest in boroughs; it pervaded practically the

[1] For the motives which actuated Lamb and his friends — largely an old feud with Wardroper, the Government manager at Winchelsea, who was close to the Grenvilles — see Miss Margaret Cramp's Manchester University M.A. thesis, 'The Parliamentary Representation of five Sussex Boroughs, 1754–68'.

[2] 32920, f. 369.

[3] Thomas Pelham of Stanmer, who now became Lord Pelham, at first claimed an influence at Seaford (see 33088, ff. 292, 294, 302-4, 310, 319, and 327), but ultimately was unable to maintain it.

entire country — 'that . . . power which every one who proposes to establish an interest in a Corporation town is desirous
of having on his side' [1] — while on the other hand it was hardly
anywhere unalloyed, and, like all electoral interests, was
changing and shifting, receding in one quarter and invading
new ground in another, developing when looked after or decay-
ing rapidly when neglected. Even in the places which most
specifically went by the name of Government boroughs, it can
be fixed by a snapshot only, and then all kinds of accidental
features enter into the picture; and that of 1761 is no longer
true in 1780, nor even in 1768.

Harwich and Orford were in 1761 the two safest Treasury
boroughs; Seaford, Hastings, and Rye were under the Treasury
and the Duke of Newcastle. At Dover the Government (in
this case a very complex entity) can be said to have held one
seat. Five seats in three Isle of Wight boroughs were at the
disposal of the Treasury with a first lien on them for the family
of Lord Holmes, the Government manager; two at Dartmouth,
a borough managed for the Treasury by the Holdsworth
family; into Totnes the Treasury could import one Member,
while the other seat had to be filled by someone with local
connexions. These were nineteen seats managed directly by
the Treasury without the candidates having to 'undertake'
them.

The Cornish boroughs were a chapter in themselves (and
fill one in this book) — a mere enumeration will suffice here of
those under Government management or within the orbit of
its influence. Saltash was an Admiralty borough. The two
Looes and Camelford were managed for the Treasury, but were
practically under the control of the managers. The six seats of
Edward Eliot of Port Eliot, the five of Lord Falmouth, the four
(and usually five) Cornish seats of Lord Edgcumbe (and one
in Devonshire), the four of Humphrey Morice, all in varying
degrees required the help and patronage of the Treasury,[2] and

---

[1] See above, p. 110.

[2] Lord Falmouth, when asking Newcastle to have a friend presented to
the living of Clements, explained that 'the suburbs of my borough of Truro
are in the parish', and asked the Duke to consider 'how low in estimation it

candidates for them were expected to obtain its *placet*. The patron or manager naturally had the first option if he wished to hold a seat himself or fill any with his own relatives or close friends, but if there was a disposable surplus for strangers, the Treasury expected to have its recommendation accepted. Still, its command over these Cornish borough-patrons was far from complete; witness John Buller, Edgcumbe, and Edward Eliot going at various times into opposition.

Lastly, in 1761 the Treasury nominated to Old Sarum and to one seat at Okehampton, which had been pawned with it by Thomas Pitt.

Next, there were in 1761 ten seats in Admiralty boroughs. Saltash, Plymouth, Portsmouth, Rochester, and one seat at Queenborough were considered safe, though several of them were lost subsequently; also at Sandwich the Admiralty recommended to one seat, but this always required much care and attention.[1]

Of the ten Admiralty seats in 1761, four were held by naval

will set my brothers and self in the country if so trifling a favor . . . shou'd be refused us who are in His Majesty's service' (21 Feb 1756; 32863, ff. 53-4).

Lord Edgcumbe wrote to Newcastle on 6 July 1766: 'As your Grace knows how necessary it is for me to obey the commands of all my borough friends, I flatter myself you will easily pardon the trouble I now give you, which is to acquaint your Grace that the living of Landulph . . . is likely to become vacant' (32976, f. 27).

When at the Assizes at Bodmin, two men from Morice's pocket boroughs were condemned to death for wrecking, he wrote to Shelburne, then Secretary of State, asking for a reprieve. Here is a passage from the summary of his letter of 31 Aug 1767, as given in the *Home Office Papers, 1765–69* (pp. 184-5): 'Needs not explain to his Lordship the situation one is in with voters of boroughs just before a general election, and how apt they are to fancy one has not done one's utmost if one fails of success in a point that they have set their hearts upon'. About Morice and his boroughs see also pp. 163 and 300-1.

Thus even in the narrowest Cornish borough it was important for the patron to prove that he had influence with Administration.

[1] John Clevland, Secretary to the Admiralty, wrote to Newcastle on 26 Feb 1761 urging him to declare his candidate for Sandwich or else there was the danger of 'a friend of your Grace's not being chose there' (32919, f. 293); and on 3 Oct 1776 John Robinson, when writing to George III about office for William Hey, M.P. for Sandwich, wished for some delay to 'give time to arrange Sandwich which at present requires attention before the vacancy can be made with safety' (37833, ff. 67-8).

officers,[1] two by officials of the Admiralty, and one by a nephew of its First Lord. For on boroughs controlled by a Government department its leading officers and officials had a first lien [2] — about Queenborough, managed by two departments, Henry Pelham wrote to Newcastle on 24 July 1753 : '. . . the Fleet and the Ordinance have great influence there, and therefore their dependants want to nominate' [3] — which they did : Admiral Sir Piercy Brett represented Queenborough, 1754–74, and Sir Charles Frederick, Surveyor-General of the Ordnance, 1754–84.

Thus in 1761, Administration had thirty seats under its more or less immediate patronage — not all of them very safe — beside the three seats pawned by Thomas Pitt, and a first claim to the marketable surplus of some twenty-five Cornish seats, and also of some in Devonshire, Dorset, Somerset, etc.

Private Patronage.—The authors of the *Report on the State of Representation* wrote in 1792 :

The patronage your Committee have divided under two heads — *Nomination*, and *Influence* ; and attributed it to distinct persons, under the descriptions of *Peers* and *Commoners*.

With respect to this first division, your Committee desire to have it understood, that

[1] The number of naval officers who 'sat on the Government interest' was given, on p. 32, as seven ; but Newport (I.o.W.), Penryn (where Rodney's seat was acquired from Lord Edgcumbe), and Dartmouth, were not Admiralty boroughs.

[2] Under George III the more frequent changes of Ministers and the growth of a bureaucracy tended to strengthen in the Government boroughs the influence of the departments at the expense both of Ministers and of Members. When in Oct 1766 Newcastle applied to Sir Charles Saunders, then First Lord of the Admiralty, on behalf of a friend recommended by Sir Matthew Fetherstonhaugh, M.P. for Portsmouth, Saunders replied that he would gladly oblige him and Sir Matthew,

but your Grace perfectly knows that the interest of Government cannot be supported in the naval boroughs, if favours are bestowed upon them through the medium of any applications that do not come from the Corporations, or the principal people in them, to the person who presides at the Board of Admiralty ; and that consequently how great soever my inclinations are to appoint Captain Hollwall to a guardship at Portsmouth, the giving him one in this mode may subject me to the imputation of not being so attentive as I ought to be to the interest of Government in that borough, as well as to many difficulties and inconveniences (32977, ff. 232-3).

[3] 32732, f. 348. Interesting correspondence about Queenborough in 1774 is preserved in the letter-book of Lord Townshend, Master-General of the Ordnance (P.R.O., W.O. 46/9, pp. 47-9).

By a nomination, they would describe that absolute authority in a borough which enables the patron to command the return. . . . These [boroughs], in general, are the private property of the patrons, or have the right of voting vested in a small corporate body, the majority of whom are his immediate dependents.

By influence, your Committee would describe that degree of weight acquired in a particular county, city or borough, which accustoms the electors on all vacancies to expect the recommendation of a candidate by the patron, and induces them, either from fear, from private interest, or from incapacity to oppose, because he is so recommended, to adopt him.[1]

The same division is adopted here, except that I exclude from patronage 'influence' primarily based on tradition or on good-will : which was conceded voluntarily but could not be enforced.   I therefore do not include any counties, for in none, probably not even in Westmorland, could the most powerful man carry his candidates without the co-operation of other independent landowners.   Nor do I include boroughs such as Chester, Durham, or Newcastle-upon-Tyne, however faithful they were to the hereditary principle.   For to this we have remained faithful even under the widest franchise and a secret ballot without considering ourselves peculiarly unreformed or unredeemed.   The two most revolutionary innovations made in Parliament in our own time were the coming in of Labour men and of women ; and as soon as the sons of three Labour leaders had come of age, they became candidates for Parliament, as the sons of peers in the eighteenth century; while the first three women who took their seats inherited them from their husbands.[2]   In saying that I eliminate seats held mainly through tradition or good-will, I do not mean to imply that there was no such influence in the places which I mention ; in at least four out of five constituencies something of both was required, but their insufficiency could in some degree and in

[1] Pp. 30-1.

[2] Nor is the hereditary principle in elections limited to Great Britain or to Parliament.   In Connecticut the family of Baldwin for over a century supplied a dynasty of Governors to the State, to the distinct advantage of the public.   And on the death of the founder of the Salvation Army, no one was thought of as a possible successor to him on either side of the Atlantic except his son.

L

the last resort be replaced by compulsion, and it is the means of enforcing one's claim which primarily constitutes possession.

I give the result of my investigations, but further research will undoubtedly show that my list requires correction; and as to the classification by 'nomination' and 'influence', probably no two men will from the same data reach identical conclusions.

Borough Patronage of Peers

Names of Patrons	Nomination	Influence
Earl of Abingdon (1)		Westbury (1)
Duke of Ancaster (1)		Boston (1)
Lord Anson (3)	Lichfield (1)	Hedon (2)
Lord Archer (2)	Bramber (2) [1]	
Lord Bathurst (1)		Cirencester (1)
Duke of Beaufort (1)		Monmouth (1)
Duke of Bedford (4)	Tavistock (2)	Bedford (1)
	Okehampton (1)	
Viscount Bolingbroke (1)		Wootton Bassett (1)
Duke of Bolton (1)		Lymington (1)
Lord Boston (1)		Bodmin (1)
Duke of Bridgwater (2)	Brackley (2)	
Earl of Bristol (1)		Bury St. Edmunds (1)
Lord Bruce (4) [2]	Great Bedwin (2)	
	Marlborough (2)	
Earl of Buckinghamshire (2)	Bere Alston (1)	St. Ives (1)
Earl of Carlisle (1)		Morpeth (1)
Earl Cornwallis (2)	Eye (2)	
Duke of Devonshire (3)	Knaresborough (2)	Derby (1)
Duke of Dorset (2)	East Grinstead (2)	
Lord Edgcumbe (5) [3]		Lostwithiel (2)
		Penryn (1)
		Fowey (1)
		Plympton (1)

[1] He had it on lease from Sir Harry Gough, who in 1768 lost the borough to the Rutland family but afterwards regained one seat on a compromise. See Miss Margaret Cramp's Manchester University M.A. thesis, 'The Parliamentary Representation of five Sussex Boroughs, 1754–68'.

[2] His hold on Great Bedwin was not yet complete in 1761.

[3] At Bossiney the Edgcumbes, under an agreement with the Wortleys dated 3 July 1752, returned one Member, and 1761 is the only election in the second half of the eighteenth century when, owing to peculiar circumstances, their interest was in abeyance.

Names of Patrons	Nomination	Influence
Earl of Egremont (2)		Taunton (1)
		Minehead (1)
Earl of Exeter (1)		Stamford (1)
Viscount Falmouth (5)		Truro (2)
		Tregony (1)
		Penryn (1)
		St. Mawes (1)
Lord Feversham (2)	Downton (2)	
Earl Fitzwilliam (1)		Peterborough (1)
Lord Foley (1)		Droitwich (1)
Viscount Folkestone (1)		Salisbury (1)
Earl of Godolphin (2)		Helston (2)
Earl Gower (3)	Lichfield (1)	Newcastle - under - Lyme (2)
Duke of Grafton (3)		Thetford (2)
		Bury St. Edmunds (1)
Earl of Guilford (1)		Banbury (1)
Earl of Hardwicke (1)	Reigate (1)	
Earl of Holdernesse (2)	Richmond (2)	
Earl of Ilchester (1)		Shaftesbury (1)
Duke of Marlborough (2)	Woodstock (2)	
Viscount Montagu (2) [1]		Midhurst (2)
Lord Melcombe (3)		Weymouth and Melcombe Regis (2)
		Bridgwater (1)
Duke of Newcastle (7)	Aldborough (2)	Lewes (1)
	Boroughbridge (2)	Newark (1)
		East Retford (1)
Lord Onslow (2)		Guilford (2)
Earl of Orford (4)	Castle Rising (1)	Ashburton (1)
	Callington (2) [2]	
Earl of Oxford (1)		Droitwich (1)
Earl of Pembroke (2)	Wilton (2)	
Earl of Portsmouth (2)		Andover (1)
		Whitchurch (1)
Earl of Powis (2)		Ludlow (2)
Duke of Richmond (1)		Chichester (1)

[1] The family was Roman Catholic, and therefore could not exercise the patronage in its own favour.

[2] In 1761 Callington and Ashburton were really the property of his mother, the Dowager Lady Orford, who had inherited the influence from the Rolle and Tuckfield families. She recommended at Callington, and he at Ashburton.

Names of Patrons	Nomination	Influence
Marquis of Rockingham (3)	Malton (2) Higham Ferrers (1)	
Duke of Rutland (2)		Newark (1) Grantham (1)
Earl of Sandwich (2)		Huntingdon (2)
Earl of Shaftesbury (1)		Shaftesbury (1)
Earl of Suffolk (1)	Castle Rising (1)	
Earl Temple (2)	Buckingham (2)	
Earl of Thanet (1)	Appleby (1)	
Viscount Weymouth (3)		Weobley (2) Tamworth (1)
Lord Wycombe (Earl of Shelburne) (1)		Chipping Wycombe (1)

Scottish Peers

Earl of Bute (1)		Bossiney (1)
Viscount Irvine (2)	Horsham (2)	

Borough Patronage of Commoners

Names of Patrons	Nomination	Influence
P. A'Court Ashe (2)	Heytesbury (2)	
W. Aislabie (2)	Ripon (2)	
J. Bankes (1)	Corfe Castle (1)	
Sir J. Barrington, Bt. (1)	Newton, Hants (1)	
J. Bond (1)	Corfe Castle (1)	
John Buller (4)	West Looe (2)	East Looe (2)
H. Burrard (1)		Lymington (1)
Sir K. Clayton, Bt. (1)	Bletchingley (1)	
W. Clayton (1)		Great Marlow (1)
C. Cocks (1)	Reigate (1)	
Sir J. Colebrooke, Bt. (1)	Gatton (1)	
A. Curzon (1)	Clitheroe (1)	
Sir J. Cust, Bt. (1)		Grantham (1)
E. Dering (2)		New Romney (2)
Sir J. Downing, Bt. (2)		Dunwich (2)
Sir F. H. Drake, Bt. (1)	Bere Alston (1)	
W. Drake (2)	Agmondesham (2)	
T. E. Drax (1)		Wareham (1)
T. Duckett (2) [1]		Calne (2)

[1] In 1761 Duckett owned the manor of Calne and Calstone, the main electoral influence in the borough, and William Northey the prebend manor

Names of Patrons	Nomination	Influence
E. Eliot (6)	Liskeard (2)	Grampound (2)
	St. Germans (2)	
T. Fane (2)	Lyme Regis (2)	
T. Fonnereau (2)		Aldeburgh (2)
B. Forester (2)		Wenlock (2)
H. Fox (4) [1]		Malmesbury (2)
		Stockbridge (2)
T. Frankland (2)	Thirsk (2)	
Lord Galway (1)	Pontefract (1) [2]	
F. Honywood (1)		Steyning (1)
E. Hooper (2)		Christchurch (2)
G. Hunt (1)		Bodmin (1)
J. Jolliffe (2)	Petersfield (2)	
E. Lascelles (2)	Northallerton (2) [3]	
P. Legh (2)	Newton, Lancs (2)	
T. Lister (1)	Clitheroe (1)	
T. Lockyer (2)		Ilchester (2)
Sir J. Lowther, Bt. (3)	Appleby (1)	
	Cockermouth (2)	
H. F. Luttrell (1)		Minehead (1)
T. Medlycott (1)		Milborne Port (1)
T. M. Molyneux (1)		Haslemere (1)
H. Morice (4)		Launceston (2)
		Newport, Cornwall (2)
R. Nugent (1)		St. Mawes (1)
C. Phillips (2)		Camelford (2)

of Calne, which had previously given him a seat. Shelburne's father already owned Bowood, and he himself, by buying out Duckett and Northey, obtained in 1765 complete control of the borough. But in March 1761 the first Lord Shelburne was dying, and John Bull, steward to Duckett, Northey, and Shelburne, secured the return of Duckett and of his own son Daniel. In Bute's list of 1761 the remark appears against Daniel Bull: 'Inclinable to Lord Shelburne, but elected against his Lordship's will by his father'.

[1] He had in 1761 the management of Stockbridge and Malmesbury, neither on an enduring basis.

[2] Control over the other seat was uncertain in 1761. On the death of George Morton Pitt in 1756 his burgage estate at Pontefract passed to his daughter Harriot with remainder to John Pitt, a first cousin once removed; it was administered by Richard Benyon, G. M. Pitt's executor; but Pitt was disputing Benyon's possession. On Harriot's death in 1763 Pitt succeeded to the burgages, and in 1766 sold them to John Walsh. See Colin Bradley's Manchester University M.A. thesis, 'The Parliamentary Representation of the Boroughs of Pontefract, Newark, and East Retford, 1754–68'.

[3] The Peirse family as a rule held one seat, but while Henry Peirse was under age they left both seats to the Lascelles, 1754–74.

Names of Patrons	Nomination	Influence
J. Pitt (1)		Wareham (1)
T. Pitt (3)	Old Sarum (2)	
	Okehampton (1)	
J. Rashleigh (1)		Fowey (1)
Sir J. Rushout, Bt. (1)		Evesham (1)
N. Ryder (1)		Tiverton (1)
G. A. Selwyn (2)	Ludgershall (2)	
Rev. J. Tattersall (1)	Gatton (1)	
T. Townshend (1)		Whitchurch (1)
G. Treby (1)		Plympton (1)
W. Trevanion (1)		Tregony (1)
J. Tucker (1)		Weymouth and Melcombe Regis (1)
C. Tudway (1)		Wells (1)
Lord Verney (2)		Wendover (2)
R. Waller (1)		ChippingWycombe(1)
W. Whitmore (2)		Bridgnorth (2)

There were in April 1761 166 English peers : 21 dukes,[1] 1 marquis, 78 earls, 11 viscounts, and 55 barons; besides, 2 English dukedoms, 3 earldoms, 1 viscountcy, and 8 baronies — together, 14 peerages — were held by Scottish or Irish peers.

Of the 21 English dukes, 12 had, under both headings of 'nomination' and 'influence', 29 seats at their disposal. The remaining 9 English dukes, Norfolk, Somerset, Cleveland, St. Albans, Leeds, Kingston, Portland, Manchester, and Chandos, had no Parliamentary boroughs. This does not mean that they had no borough influence, but it did not reach the level of 'patronage'; thus, e.g., Somerset had some at Totnes; Kingston at Nottingham; Portland in 1768 captured Wigan; Chandos had an influence in various places in Hampshire, etc. Of the remaining 145 English peers, 40 returned 78 Members of Parliament; and to these have to be added the Earl of Shelburne (Lord Wycombe in England) and two Scottish peers, Lord Bute and Lord Irvine, who together nominated to 4 seats.

This makes a total of 55 peers nominating Members or influencing their elections for 111 seats.

The division between peers and commoners, to which the

---

[1] This figure does not include the Dukes of the Blood Royal.

eighteenth century attached an importance even then no longer justified by the social and economic structure of the country, naturally does not strike us as something fundamental, especially if we rid ourselves of the legend of a close Whig oligarchy. Still, I have kept to it, for the division itself helps to destroy that legend.   Here are 55 peers with an average of only 2 seats each — the whales prove rather common fry; and if we analyse in detail the list of large borough owners there is only the lifelong election agent, the Duke of Newcastle, with 7 seats, and two professional dealers in boroughs, who owed their very peerages to their electoral interests, Lords Falmouth and Edgcumbe, with 5 seats each.

Of commoners I obtain a total of 56 borough patrons determining or influencing the elections for 94 seats.[1]   Six only among them had influence in more than one borough : three Cornish 'professionals' (Eliot, Morice, and Buller) and one ex-professional (Thomas Pitt), Henry Fox, and Sir James Lowther, the Leviathan of Cumberland and Westmorland. Forty-three of the 94 seats controlled by commoners were filled in 1761 by the patrons and 16 by their close relatives ; *i.e.* almost two-thirds were kept for the families, besides 11 for which friends or dependants were returned ; only 24 were sold to strangers.   The list of patrons includes the names of some of the best county families, a good many men who solicited no favours under George II (Lister, Curzon, Legh, John Pitt, Tudway, Hunt, Rashleigh, Dering, etc.) ; and some who were to be of the Opposition under George III (Lord Verney, T. Townshend, the Claytons, the A'Courts, etc.).   These men when self-returned to the House of Commons are certainly not representative in the meaning now attached to the word, but are as representative as any juryman ; and in the absence of an organized party system, the freest and most independent House of Commons would not essentially differ from a jury.

---

[1] I have omitted from this list Lord Holmes (an Irish peer) with his five seats in the Isle of Wight, as his influence in them depended so much on Government support that he has to be treated as a manager rather than a patron ; I have, however, included in it John Buller, though he stands very near the border-line, because on the whole I think his influence at East and West Looe was stronger than that of the Government.

Taking peers and commoners together, I obtain for England a total of 111 borough patrons determining or influencing the election for 205 seats ; adding 30 seats more or less under the immediate management of the Government, I obtain a total of 235 borough seats under patronage. The number is high — almost half of the representation of England — and could be raised still further by adding seats which were not free but merely disputed between patrons. What was the influence which this state of the franchise exercised on divisions in the House ?

DIVISIONS ANALYSED

Let us first examine the vote on General Warrants taken at 4.15 A.M. on 18 February 1764 (but usually referred to as the division of 17 February). From the very beginning it had been realized that the session would be critical for the Government, and every effort had been made to secure a large attendance — 'I never knew a stricter muster and no furloughs allowed', wrote Chesterfield on 17 October 1763 to Philip Stanhope, who held a minor diplomatic appointment in Germany and was summoned to London to attend Parliament.[1] And when on 15 February 1764 the Government majority had shrunk to ten (207 v. 197), frantic activity was displayed on either side to bring up every available Member for the crucial division.[2] George Onslow, M.P. for Surrey, one of Newcastle's reporters from the House of Commons, wrote at the outset of the debate on Friday afternoon, 17 February : 'Everybody almost is down of both sides' ;[3] and this was Horace Walpole's description of the scene : '. . . one would have thought that they had sent a search warrant for Members of Parliament into every hospital. Votes were brought down in flannels and blankets till the floor of the House looked like the pool of Bethesda.'[4] When the vote was taken in the morning of Saturday, 18 February 1764, according to the *Journals* of the

---

[1] See also Chesterfield's letter to him of 19 Oct 1764.

[2] See, *e.g.*, on the Government side the letter from Edward Kynaston, M.P., to Charles Jenkinson, M.P., Secretary to the Treasury (Jucker, *op. cit.*, pp. 265-6) ; and on the Opposition side numerous letters from the Duke of Newcastle to various Members in 32956.

[3] 32956, f. 19.   [4] To Lord Hertford, 19 Feb 1764.

House, 232 voted with the Government and 218 against; that is, including tellers the division was 234 v. 220. Thus even after the most frantic endeavours to secure attendance, the House was 103 short of its full number.

I know of no list of the majority. Of the minority there are several. By an ingenious device, and contrary to the severe rules of Parliamentary privilege, the *London Evening Post* published on 3 March 1764 the names of 220 Members who had come out against General Warrants.[1] It was reprinted with one correction on 8 March, and a list was added of 26 Members absent from the division. There are three manuscript lists of the minority in the Newcastle Papers, dated 22 and 27 February and 2 March [2] — they show doubts and changes but each contains 222 names — two more than there should be. Lastly, there is the list in *The History of the Late Minority*, a work privately printed in 12 copies in 1765, and twice reprinted in large editions in June 1766; it contains 221 names. Both in the Newcastle Papers and in *The History of the Late Minority* lists are added of absent friends (the numbers given vary from 19 to 25). Lastly, in the Liverpool Papers, containing calculations made on the Government side, there is a 'List of Friends Absent February 17, 1764' (46 names),[3] and a 'List of Persons who voted with the Minority on the 17th February, 1764, who are friends or nearly so' (49 names).[4] It is impossible to enter here into the discrepancies between the different lists,[5] but this is the broad basis of my calculations: I take the list of the minority from the *History* with three corrections,[6] and from the

---

[1] It was published under the heading: 'In most societies of this Metropolis the healths of the following gentlemen are drunk as friends to LIBERTY'. There is a cutting of that list in the Newdigate Papers at the Warwickshire Record Office, with some MS. corrections by Sir Roger Newdigate.

[2] 32956, ff. 68-71, 118-21, and 186-9; see also lists of 'Original Tories who voted with us', *ibid.* f. 116.   [3] 38337, f. 192.   [4] *Ibid.* f. 193.

[5] These lists have been carefully examined and collated by two students of Manchester University in their M.A. theses: Alan Hardy on 'The Duke of Newcastle and his Friends, 1762-1765', and John Tomlinson on 'The Grenville Papers, 1763-1765'; and it is with their help that I have revised my lists and calculations.

[6] I have added R. W. Bamfylde (Newcastle's and Jenkinson's lists, and correction by Newdigate) and removed W. Plumer and M. Rebow to the list of Absents, the balance of evidence being for such a classification; this reduces the list to the proper number of 220.

various lists of friends absent I compile one of 71 names. Adding to these the names of 12 Members who can be proved to have been absent [1] (though they are not mentioned in any of the lists which were drawn up for pragmatic and not for statistical purposes or for historical record), and two vacant seats,[2] there remain 18 Members unaccounted for : these need not concern us any further — anyhow the figures are only approximately correct.

I divide the English constituencies into four types : the counties ; the larger boroughs [3] (with over 500 voters) ; the smaller boroughs which include all the remaining English constituencies, barring the two Universities.

	Voted with the Minority		Known to have been Absent	
80 Members for counties .	38	47·5%	17	21%
90 Members for the larger boroughs [4] . . .	44	49%	16 [5]	17·8%
315 Members for the smaller boroughs . . .	126	40%	46	14·5%
4 Members for the Universities	1	25%	1	25%
489	209	43%	80	15·5%

[1] Four diplomats holding important or distant posts who were not summoned home to attend Parliament — Henry Grenville at Constantinople, George Pitt at Turin, Andrew Mitchell at Berlin, and Joseph Yorke at The Hague (there is a letter from him to his brother, Lord Royston, dated The Hague, 17 Feb 1764 : 35367, f. 26) ; Julines Beckford who was in Jamaica ; and five who were travelling abroad : T. C. Cecil, E. Wortley Montagu, Lord Palmerston, Henry St. John, and Lord Tylney ; and two Members who had not taken their seats even in August 1765 when Rockingham was drawing up his Parliamentary lists (now in the Northants Record Office) : William Cartwright and Richard Lyster.

[2] Perthshire, its Member John Murray having succeeded to the Dukedom of Atholl, and Dunwich, on the death of Sir Jacob Downing on 6 Feb.

[3] For statistical purposes these larger divisions have to be adopted or otherwise the results are too easily affected by accidents ; the constituencies with about 500 voters I include among the smaller boroughs.

[4] The word 'borough' stands here for its electorate ; a populous borough may appear among the 'smaller boroughs' if it had a narrow franchise. Thus, e.g., Shrewsbury is included among the 'smaller', while Bridgnorth is counted among the 'larger' boroughs.

[5] Among these I include the Speaker, who did not vote.

Thus of the total of 489 English Members, 209 voted with the Opposition, while 80 were absent, leaving at the utmost 200 to vote with the majority ; and if we assume, on a *pro rata* calculation, that of the 18 unaccounted for, 16 were English Members, we obtain a majority of 25 against the Government. The counties and large urban constituencies gave a decisive vote against the Government, while for the small boroughs, if we add to the 126 voting with the minority the 46 known to have been absent and the 10 Members who are their proportionate share of those unaccounted for, we get 133 as the number of those who voted with the Government — a majority of 7.

It was the Welsh and Scottish Members who saved the Government in this crucial division :

	Voted with the Minority		Known to have been Absent
24 Welsh Members . .	5	21%	1
45 Scottish Members . .	6	13%	5
69	11		6

Adding to the 6 known to have been absent, 3 of the unaccounted for, we still obtain a probable vote of 49 in favour of the Government, which alone would have wiped out completely the majority given to the Opposition by the English counties and larger boroughs. In Wales there was only one borough with a restricted franchise,[1] but the country and its representation had a peculiarly feudal character ; while the voting of the Scottish Members was due not so much to the unreformed character of the Scottish constituencies as to their intense and very natural resentment of the unmeasured abuse which they were subjected to in England at that time from the Opposition, and most of all, from the writer in the *North Briton*, on whose case the vote was taken. In other words, it was not so much the condition of the English franchise which defeated the Opposition on this occasion as the conflict between the two kingdoms.

[1] Beaumaris 'is the only place in Wales where the right of election is confined to the corporation only' (Oldfield, 'History of the Welch Boroughs', in his *History of the Boroughs of Great Britain*, ed. of 1792, vol. ii, p. 397).

Let us next examine the vote on the Repeal of the Stamp Act, usually referred to as of 21 February 1766, but in reality taken on Saturday, 22 February, at 2 A.M. Including tellers, the figures were 276 for and 168 against the Repeal; which, discounting the Speaker, leaves 113 absent. Again I know of no list of the majority. There is *The List of the Minority in the House of Commons who voted against the Bill to Repeal the American Stamp Act*, published in Paris in 1766, and another one sent to Newcastle by Sir William Meredith, M.P. for Liverpool :[1] each contains 168 names but only 153 of them tally, and neither is probably wholly correct; still, of the two the printed list seems more reliable,[2] and I therefore take it for the basis of my calculations. Arranging this new minority in the same divisions as before, we obtain the following results :

	Voted against the Repeal		Assuming a proportionate distribution of those Absent, there would have been Absent
80 Members for counties .	29	36%	16
90 Members for the larger boroughs . . .	19	21%	18
315 Members for the smaller boroughs . . .	85	27%	64
4 Members for Universities	1	25%	1
489 Members for English constituencies . .	134	27%	99
24 Welsh Members . .	7	29%	5
45 Scottish Members .	27	60%	9

[1] 32974, f. 169.

[2] To give a few examples of differences : Meredith's list names as having voted against the Repeal of the Stamp Act Bartholomew Burton, a London merchant, who had been with Newcastle and Rockingham in opposition before 1765, and James Grenville, one of the closest associates of Pitt — two most unlikely cases. On the other hand, it does not include Sir James Douglas and John Eames, who appear in Newcastle's own list of placemen who voted against the Repeal of the Stamp Act (33001, ff. 200-1). Neither list includes G. A. Selwyn, who is mentioned in a note sent to Newcastle by West immediately after the division at 2.15 A.M. (32974, f. 49), nor Sir Charles Hardy mentioned by James Harris in his notes of debates in the Parliament of 1761–68 (Malmesbury MSS.). These discrepancies, important as far as individuals are concerned, do not seriously affect statistical totals.

Thus in England the opposition against concessions to the Colonies was strongest among the representatives of the counties ; it reflected the attitude of the independent country gentlemen. On the other hand, most marked was the majority in favour of the Repeal among the representatives of the larger urban constituencies, obviously under pressure from the trading interests. The representatives of the smaller boroughs stood half-way between those of the counties and of the city electorates, the proportion of those who voted against the Repeal being about the same as in the rest of England taken together. The various conflicting influences on this occasion seem to have neutralized each other, and made the representatives of the smaller boroughs into mere padding to the more independent part of the House. The Scots once more voted to an overwhelming degree on the authoritarian side, to some extent again as a consequence of the baiting which they had suffered during the preceding years from the 'sons of liberty'.[1]

As a third example I take the division over the Middlesex election on 8 May 1769, when 221 voted to confirm Luttrell as the duly elected Member for Middlesex, and 152 against.[2] The division list printed in the *North Briton* for 27 May 1769 gives the names of 219 of the majority (including the tellers) — four short of the total, and 153 of the minority (also including the tellers) — one short of the total.[3] (See p. 156.)

Of the 174 Members returned by the most representative English constituencies — the counties, the larger boroughs, and the Universities — 57 voted for the seating of Luttrell and 57 against, while 60 were absent or unaccounted for. Opinion among the independent Members was divided between adherence to constitutional principles and dislike of the very

[1] I add the corresponding figures obtained from an analysis of Meredith's list — there voted in the minority : Members for English counties, 30 ; for larger boroughs, 17 ; for smaller boroughs, 87 ; for Universities, 1 ; Welsh Members, 8 ; Scottish Members, 25. Thus for our purpose there is very little difference between the two lists ; that of Meredith reduces the number of Scotsmen voting against the Repeal by two, but otherwise emphasizes even more strongly the conclusions given above.

[2] These figures do not include the tellers.

[3] For an analysis of this division list see John Brooke, *The Chatham Administration*, pp. 351-2.

		For Luttrell		Against		Absent or Unaccounted for	
80 Members for counties		24	30%	30	37·5%	26[1]	32·5%
90 Members for the larger boroughs .		32	36%	27	30%	31	34%
315 Members for the smaller boroughs .		125	40%	85	27%	105	33%
4 Members for the Universities . .		1	25%	0	..	3	75%
489 Members for English constituencies .		182	37%	142	29%	165	34%
24 Welsh Members .		9	37·5%	6	25%	9	37·5%
45 Scottish Members .		28	62%	5	11%	12	27%
		219	39%	153	28%	186	33%

dubious character over whom the battle was fought. In these circumstances the representatives of the smaller boroughs, among whom the Government influence was strongest, gave the casting vote. The opponents of Wilkes were, moreover, supported by a large Scottish contingent, again voting on national lines.[2]

What are, then, the conclusions to be drawn from these three divisions? They do no more than confirm what could have been expected from the preceding survey of the personnel of the House and of the electoral structure of the country. The knights of the shires, independent of the Government in their constituencies and, as a rule, not soliciting personal favours, and the representatives of the larger boroughs, similarly independent of the Government for their seats, responded more freely to public opinion than the Members for rotten boroughs and close corporations. Still, the difference was marginal; the bulk of Members in both categories consisted of men

---

[1] This includes Luttrell himself.

[2] William Strahan, M.P. 1774–84, wrote on 26 June 1770 to a fellow-Scot, David Hall, in Philadelphia: 'In Scotland they make a national cause of it, and are quite unanimous in favour of Government: and their union upon this occasion is easily accounted for, as the Jacobite Party, now their old cause is extinguished, from the very nature of their principles, remain firm friends of Monarchy in opposition equally to anarchy and republicanism.' (See *Pennsylvania Magazine of History and Biography*, vol. x, p. 347.

similar in type and character, and even the Members for the worst of the rotten boroughs did not remain impervious to currents of popular feeling ; many of these were, in fact, more independent of the Government, representing their own pocket boroughs or those of patrons belonging to the Opposition, than they would have been as representatives of electorates requiring Government assistance in their concerns. The rotten boroughs supplied the Government with a make-weight of about 5–10 per cent in the House in favour of authority, but also of statesmanship when such was present in the Ministers ; this make-weight being very much less than party discipline supplies at present. As for American problems, had the number of the knights of the shire been doubled at the expense of the rotten boroughs, it seems doubtful whether the result would have been much more favourable to sound Imperial statesmanship. Anyhow, in two out of the three crucial divisions analysed above the result was not fundamentally altered by the rotten boroughs ; the Scottish issue was of greater weight, and while it strengthened the Opposition in the south, it supplied the counter-weight of a more or less solid contingent from 'North Britain' to the other side in the House.

Pitt's remarks during the debate on the Repeal of the Stamp Act about 'the rotten part of the Constitution' are often quoted, but they were made in reply to arguments about virtual representation and not in reference to divisions in the House. He himself represented, from 1735 till 1747, the seven burgages of Old Sarum, 1747–54 an electorate of less than 75 at Seaford (unconstitutionally influenced by the Duke of Newcastle), 1754–56 Newcastle's pocket borough of Aldborough with less than 50 electors, and 1756–66 the 32 members of the Corporation at Bath. At no time during his thirty-one years in the House of Commons did he, the idol of the Empire, represent as many as 100 electors, or experience what it meant to have dealings, say, with 5000 independent voters of Bristol.

III

THE GENERAL ELECTION OF 1761

ON 3 March 1761 Horace Walpole wrote to Horace Mann:

> . . . Parliament . . . now engrosses all conversation and all
> purses; for the expense is incredible. West Indians, conquerors,
> nabobs, and admirals, attack every borough; there are no fewer
> than nine candidates at Andover. The change in a Parliament used
> to be computed at between sixty and seventy; now it is believed
> there will be an hundred and fifty new members . . . venality is
> grosser than ever! The borough of Sudbury has gone so far as to
> advertise for a chapman! We have been as victorious as the
> Romans and are as corrupt.

These were casual remarks and an epigram, not an affidavit to
serve as evidence in the court of history. But so much history
is fancy weaving on the warp of a few common 'texts' that
Walpole's casual remarks and illustrations have gone the round
of the text-books (rightly so called) on English history.[1]

On closer examination only a single one of the more general
statements quoted above is found correct — that which appears
as a mere 'belief'. At the general election of 1761, 126 men
entered the House of Commons who had never sat in it before,
and another 22 who had sat previously, but not at the dissolution; thus the estimate of 'an hundred and fifty new members'

---

[1] See, e.g., W. Hunt's beautifully embroidered version in his *History of
England, 1760–1801*, p. 19: '. . . in this election the Crown itself used its
own means of corrupt influence. Private men followed its example. A
new class of candidates appeared, men without party connexion or local
interest, who had lately become rich, West India merchants, "nabobs"
gorged with the spoils of the East, shareholders of the East India Company,
admirals and others who had reaped a splendid harvest from the destruction
of the commerce and shipping of France. The competition for seats was
extraordinary; at Andover there were nine candidates. Constituencies
which had long obeyed the orders of great landlords were no longer to be
reckoned upon. . . . Bribery was carried to a preposterous height. . . .
The borough of Sudbury went so far as to advertise itself for sale.'

(in a total of 558) was correct.[1] But the further statement on which its value largely depends, that 'the change in a Parliament used to be computed at between sixty and seventy', is a gross inaccuracy. The number of new Members returned at the general elections of 1747 and 1754 was about the same as in 1761.

Nor is there evidence to show that election contests were more numerous than usual. The number of constituencies which in 1761 actually went to the poll was 48 [2] out of a total of 315 ; it was, in fact, smaller than it had been at the general election of 1754, which itself was comparatively quiet, with no opposition on a national scale and no Prince of Wales to back it (as in 1741 and 1747). The number of candidates who stood the poll was, however, invariably only a fraction of those who tentatively offered themselves. In the majority of constituencies the electorates were small, the voting was everywhere open, the keeping of election promises — on whatever basis and by whatever means they were obtained — was considered a matter of honour ; the canvass therefore supplied more or less valid indications of chances, and the man who saw that he had none would, more often than not, 'drop his pretensions and decline the poll'.

Peculiar circumstances at first kept down electioneering activities in 1760, and subsequently compressed them into a short time, producing perhaps thereby an impression of greater intensity. Security of tenure was an important consideration, when a seat in Parliament was a lease paid for in advance on something like 'a house . . . which I had taken for seven years'.[3] The danger of an appeal to the country was negligible ; between 1715 and the dissolution of 1784 the duration of three Parliaments only (in 1747, 1774, and 1780) was slightly shortened by the Government. The main risk lay in the death of the Sovereign, which until 1867 had, within six months, to be

---

[1] To these might be added five men who had not sat in Parliament before, and were elected in Dec 1761 to replace Members returned simultaneously for two constituencies.

[2] This figure covers the whole of Great Britain, whereas the figure of 41, given on p. 83, refers to England only.

[3] Bath to Newcastle, 21 Nov 1759 ; 32899, f. 19.

M

followed by a dissolution of Parliament. In 1760 George II
had reached his seventy-seventh year, and was not expected to
last another Parliament. Hence at first many people were unwilling to become candidates. Lord Kinnoull, when advising
Newcastle to aim at a quiet general election, with the least
possible disturbance of the *status possidendi*, remarked that the
age of the King 'may probably contribute to the more easy
execution of this plan'. 'Nobody, except some extraordinary
genius, or where the future settlement of an interest is materially
concerned, will spend much upon such a tenure.' [1] Newcastle
agreed with Kinnoull: 'I feel every day that private persons
will not risk much money to get into this next Parliament, in
its present circumstance'.[2] Similarly John Calcraft reported
on 14 August 1760 to Colonel Harvey, then on active service in
Germany: 'Elections surprizingly quiet'.[3] By the beginning
of October, Newcastle wrote that 'people begin to stir a little
more of late than they had done, about elections'.[4] But it was
only after the death of George II (25 October 1760) that a more
intense interest awoke in the forthcoming general election. 'It
is imagined there will now be a great contest to get into Parliament', wrote Edward Hooper to James Harris on 8 November
1760.[5] And Newcastle to Granby, on 25 November: 'There
is not much opposition yet declared; tho' some, which would
not have been, had it not been for our late great, and ever to be
lamented loss'.[6]

With the vastly improved prospects of tenure, did corruption reach an unusual height? There is some confusion of
ideas about electoral corruption: no employer of labour, when

[1] 10 July 1760; 32908, ff. 160-77.
[2] Newcastle to Hardwicke, 16 Aug 1760; 32910, ff. 120-35.
[3] 17495, f. 103. Colonel Harvey was of a well-known Essex Parliamentary family, brother of William Harvey, M.P. for the county, and Eliab
Harvey, K.C., M.P. for Dunwich.
[4] Newcastle to Powis, 10 Oct 1760; 32912, f. 295. It is not certain
whether even this statement was not largely an expression of fear, the Duke's
dominant emotion.
[5] *Letters of the First Earl of Malmesbury* (1870), vol. i, p. 83. Edward
Hooper, of an old Dorset family, sat for Christchurch 1734-47, when
appointed Commissioner of Customs; it was on his interest that his cousin,
James Harris, father of the first Earl of Malmesbury, was returned for
Christchurch.   [6] 32915, f. 59.

made to pay higher wages, will call it an increase in output, but corruption is frequently measured by expense; as if the 'purity' of an election was affected by whether the freemen of some borough received £10 or £20 per head, or by the size of the lump sum paid for a seat to its patron.

But what did constitute corruption in eighteenth-century England? For the elector the vote, for the borough its representation, for the Member his seat in Parliament, were valuable assets from which advantages were expected. The Member had to show due regard to his constituents, individually and in the aggregate, to accord to them or obtain for them benefits, and in short be 'indefatigable in serving his friends'; just as he himself expected proper consideration and marks of favour from His Majesty and the Administration, if he was counted among their friends — 'protection is due to attachment, and . . . sentiments of friendship to be reall and lasting must be reciprocall'.[1] By the middle of the eighteenth century these things had come to be considered perfectly legitimate and honourable; and it was merely the manner and the circumstances in which they were received, and the person from whom they were solicited and accepted, that distinguished finding one's legitimate account from taking a bribe. A Member could expect to be provided for by the leader of his party or group, and his not being offered any favours would mark him as an insignificant and neglected person; but an interested change of sides at a critical moment was corrupt. In the same way, every constituency up and down the country, especially every borough constituency, had to be nursed; but such loving care allowed of infinite variations.

There were, among the boroughs, faithful wives — still, even they had not been guided by passion in the choice of their husbands but had paid proper regard to the candidate's family, rank, and financial circumstances. 'You would be flinging yourself away', wrote a prudent father to his daughter, 'had your husband neither birth nor fortune. . . . You would blush for ever to be tied to a low man, and you would starve with a gentleman who could not maintain you.' Then there

[1] Hans Stanley to Newcastle, 26 June 1759; 32892, ff. 245-6.

were kept mistresses, rather expensive, relatively faithful, but not wedded to their elects, and with the money-nexus playing a greater part in their relations than attachment. Lastly, there were prostitutes, 'ready to receive any adventurer whatever who will bring them money', and content to have him introduced by the name of 'General Gold'.[1] Numerical impressions are always unreliable ; but what can be their value where distinctions are of such a delicate nature ? A slow, downward movement was almost unavoidable when financial benefits were an essential part of the electoral system, virtue being more easily lost than recovered. Still, though rare, cases are known of constituencies which to some extent retrieved their character : *e.g.* Bishop's Castle, in Shropshire, after having for a long time been notorious as an 'open', venal borough, from 1768 to 1820 led a much better regulated existence under Clive patronage.

A close examination does not reveal any widespread or rapid downward movement in 1761, and the contemporary outcry about the incredible growth of corruption is merely an inaccurately worded complaint at the 'Immense Expense' of elections (words fraught with such painful meaning as to be accorded capitals even by men who otherwise were sparing of them). But even those complaints, or rather such clamour, cannot be accepted without the evidence of figures, as sentiment discounts past payments no less than future, and, like water at the freezing-point, expense weighs heaviest at the moment of liquefaction.

The so-called 'price of seats' was in reality a payment regulated by certain conventions of the market rather than by the cost of production, and there was, as a rule, a wide difference between the expense and trouble involved in the control of a constituency and the sum paid for a ready-made seat at an election. No average whatsoever can be formulated with regard to the expense of establishing and maintaining an 'interest' in a constituency ; the task was too complex, it varied from place to place, and depended as much on the nature and character of the man who undertook it as on the constituency itself. It was a process which extended over years, and even over generations,

[1] See the Hindon election of 1774.

and involved appeals to tradition, sentiment, interest, fear, etc.
Nor could there possibly be an average price when so often a
pretium affectionis was paid, *e.g.* in contested elections where
two families fought out rival claims to the representation and
control of a constituency long disputed between them —
especially as in such contests more or less permanent possession
and not a septennial lease was frequently in question. No one
ever tried to establish an electoral influence in Parliamentary
boroughs with a view to making money, and whereas scores of
big fortunes were sunk into Parliamentary boroughs,[1] not a
single one, even of moderate size, is known to have been
acquired through them. The price which a candidate paid at
an election for a ready-made seat to the patron or manager of
a borough was usually but a part of the cost involved in its
control, and was seldom expected to reimburse all the expense
which the patron was put to, year after year, in preserving his
'interest' in the constituency. Most of the borough seats sold
by patrons or local managers went to candidates put up by the
Government or approved by it, and such compliance with its
wishes was paid for in titles, ribbons, Court honours, office,
promotions, etc., all adjusted to the rank, standing, and requirements of the person concerned ; and also by support for
the patron's electoral interest — office appointments, jobs,
livings, promotion, etc., had to be provided, on a humbler

---

[1] A good illustration of the economics of pocket boroughs is found in a
paper (Fortescue, vol. v, p. 55) wherein Humphrey Morice, in Apr 1775,
explained to Lord North 'the reason which induced him to part with his
estate and his interest in two boroughs' (Launceston and Newport) — he
had sold them to the Duke of Northumberland :

An estate of twelve hundred pounds p. ann. in a maner given up to
the supporting the boroughs and three thousand pds. besides annually
expended for that purpose and keeping up the house &c.

The trouble of it not to say anything of the expence is more than Mr.
M. can bear with a constitution much impaired by the gout. . . .

He lost a member last year after all the trouble and expence he had
been at and notwithstanding the establishd interest he seems to have he
may be worse off next time. . . .

North's covering letter to the King is dated 'Thursday Ap. 27', to
which Fortescue adds '1780'. The correct date is 27 Apr 1775. See Ian R.
Christie, 'Private Patronage versus Government Influence : John Buller and
the Contest for Control of Parliamentary Elections at Saltash, 1780–1790',
English Historical Review, Apr 1956.

level, for influential men in the constituency at the recommendation of the patron.

It is these imponderables of Government favour which explain why the prices usually quoted for seats were in appearance so low. The net expenditure of the Government at the general election of 1754 was not more than £30,000,[1] in 1774 about £50,000, and in 1780 approximately the same ;[2] and in 1761 no money was spent by the Treasury on the general election. But, to give an example taken at random, Sir George Yonge, fifth and last Baronet, 'is reported to have said in his old age that he had inherited £80,000 from his father, his wife brought him a like amount, the Government paid him £80,000, but Honiton swallowed it all'.[3] Even though this statement must not be treated as statistical evidence, it gives some idea of the difference between the cost of nursing one expensive constituency and the apparent total expenditure of the Government at a general election. Had £50,000 really represented the whole, or even the larger part, of the Government expenditure, any number of subjects of the King could have afforded seriously to compete with him in election activities. For £50,000 was no longer a vast sum in the eighteenth century. Lady Bute, in 1761, is said to have inherited about £800,000 from her father, E. Wortley Montagu ; Lord Bath, at his death in 1764, was reputed to have left £1,200,000 ; the fortune of Sir Samuel Fludyer, M.P., a London merchant, was valued in 1767 at about £900,000 ; William Beckford, M.P., Lord Mayor of London, wrote in a letter to Lady Cathcart, in 1770, that his son's fortune will be £40,000 a year, besides many thousands in cash ;[4] etc.

It was because the price of pocket boroughs was in a way conventional that one can talk about an average ; this, in 1761, was £2000 for a seat. On 3 February 1761 Newcastle wrote to Hardwicke that he had found a place for Sir Gilbert Heathcote, Hardwicke's rich and shy son-in-law. 'But the expence will

---

[1] See below, pp. 202-203.   [2] See Fortescue, vol. v, pp. 477-81.
[3] W. G. Willis Watson, in *Notes and Queries*, 11 s., vol. i, p. 191. Sir George Yonge represented Honiton 1754-61 and 1763-96; he and his ancestors sat for it 101 years in twenty-nine Parliaments.
[4] HMC, Second Report, *Cathcart MSS.*, p. 25.

be very great — the same as the Duke of Newcastle has mention'd upon other occasions, vizt. 2000£, and the Duke of Newcastle is sorry to observe that there are few, or no places where it will be less.'[1] Hardwicke (who was accustomed to have his sons returned by borough-patrons free of charge) replied the same day that Sir Gilbert 'thinks, as every body must, the sum exorbitant', but 'is ready to give it, provided he may be excused from going down to Shaftesbury, and any personal attendance'.[2] At Penryn the two Clive candidates, who stood on the Basset interest, deposited £2000 each, which Hardwicke described to Bute as 'the current price of the times'.[3] John Calcraft reported on 2 December 1760 to Colonel Edward Harvey that everybody was striving to get into Parliament and that it must cost Harvey £2000, if an opportunity was found;[4] similarly to Jenison Shafto, when negotiating a seat for him through Lord Bateman at Leominster: 'You have a sure seat in Parliament and as things go it will be a cheap one for 2000 guineas is offer'd everywhere'.[5] The 'cheapness' in this case seems to have been in pounds being charged (as they usually were), and not guineas; for from Bute's letter to Newcastle, 18 March 1761, it appears that 'Mr. Shaftoe, who comes in for Leominster, will, (to accommodate) relinquish his place to either of the candidates for Midhurst; on paying his expences, amounting to £2000, and on being secur'd by promise in some proper office'[6] — the office being obviously his intended profit on the transaction.

Similarly, £2000 was asked of Sir Thomas Clarke, Master of the Rolls, for a seat at Lostwithiel, and refused by him; Lord Edgcumbe, however, asserted 'that he cannot possibly defray the expence with less'.[7] Again, Chesterfield, in a letter to his son, Philip Stanhope, 19 October 1764, speaks of 'the £2000, which your seat [at St. Germans] cost you in the present Parliament'. When Thomond (the brother of Egremont and brother-in-law of George Grenville) was returned both for Minehead and Winchelsea, £2000 was 'to be paid by the

[1] 35420, f. 177.   [2] 32918, f. 228.   [3] See below, p. 312.
[4] 17495, f. 179.   [5] 3 Dec 1760; 17495, f. 179.
[6] 32920, f. 291.   [7] *Ibid.* ff. 200 and 245.

person that comes in the room of Lord Thomond [at Winchelsea]'.[1] A memorandum by the Duke of Newcastle, dated 11 March 1761, contains the following entries :

> To speak to the Duke of Devonshire and my Lord Hardwicke about Ld. Edgcumbe and his boroughs.
>
> The Master of the Rolls.
> Sir William Baker. } £2000.
> Admiral Rodney.
>
> .   .   .   .
>
> Ld. Falmouth has only £1500.[2]

In short, the ordinary price of safe seats in the disposal of patrons was in 1761 £2000, and only in exceptional cases, where additional advantages were expected,[3] £1500 ; while in 1754 the price of £1500 for a seat, or £3000 for the brace, seems to have been of more frequent occurrence. But then the chances of survival were better in a Parliament coupled with the life of the young King ; and owing to credit-inflation through war-loans, subscribed in excess of actually available means, the general level of prices had in those seven years, if anything, risen even more than the price of seats.

As for an invasion of 'constituencies which had long obeyed the orders of great landlords' by a new class of candidates, 'men without party connexion or local interest', *nouveaux riches* of every description,[4] the complaint is perennial, and yet always brought up as new, both by contemporaries and by historians. Lecky, starting with 1700, writes about 'individual capitalists, and still more the two great corporations' (the Bank of England and the East India Company) which 'descended into the political arena' and 'wrested boroughs, by sheer corruption, from the landlords who had for generations controlled them'.[5] Lord Hervey wrote about the general election of 1734 : 'Notwithstanding the severe Act passed in the year 1729 to prevent bribery and corruption in elections, yet money, though it had been formerly more openly given, was never more plentifully

---

[1] 32920, f. 220.   [2] *Ibid.* f. 103.
[3] *E.g.* in Selwyn's offer to Bute of two seats at Ludgershall, at £1500 each.   [4] See above, p. 158, n. 1.
[5] *History of England in the Eighteenth Century*, vol. i, pp. 200-1.

issued than in these'.[1] Another author [2] speaks about the 'sensible alteration' which in 1747 'was found with regard to many of the boroughs': 'The vast successes of the war, the prodigious prizes taken from the enemy, and the many advantages Britain had acquired in point of trade, enriched the marine and mercantile gentlemen to such a degree that numbers of them were able to aspire to seats in Parliament and were supported with a greater effusion of money than ever had been known to be expended on such occasions'. For 1761, there are Horace Walpole's remarks to embroider upon; for 1768 there is the dictum of Mrs. Sarah Osborn: 'The landed interest is beat out, and merchants, nabobs, and those who have gathered riches from the East and West Indies stand the best chance of governing this country'; [3] for 1774, an entry in Lady Mary Coke's *Journal*, 21 October 1774: [4] '. . . 'tis said there are more odd people return'd to serve in this Parliament than has been known since the Rump Parliament'. But Sir Robert Peel, on the night of his defeat, 25-26 June 1846, still saw 'the Manners, the Somersets, the Lowthers, and the Lennoxes' pass before him; and 'those country gentlemen, "those gentlemen of England" . . . Sir Charles Burrell, Sir William Jolliffe, Sir Charles Knightly, Sir John Trollope, Sir Edward Kerrison, Sir John Tyrrell . . . Sir John Yarde Buller'. 'They trooped on: all the men of metal and large-acred squires. . . . Mr. Bankes with a Parliamentary name of two centuries and Mr. Christopher . . . ; and the Mileses and Henleys were there,

[1] *Memoirs*, ed. by R. R. Sedgwick, vol. i, pp. 291-2.

[2] I quote from an article by Lord Ebrington, *A Bye-Election in 1747*, published in *The Nineteenth Century*, in June 1889 (p. 922). The passage is marked as quoted from Ballantyne's *Life of Lord Carteret*, pp. 323-4, but I have failed to trace it in that book.

[3] *Political and Social Letters of a Lady of the Eighteenth Century, 1721-71*. Edited by E. F. D. Osborn (1890), p. 178. See also entry in Cavendish's notes of debates under 21 Nov 1768 (Egerton MS. 215, f. 195):

> Upon presenting several petitions about elections, the House seemed to set themselves against adventurers: men, who, having no personal interest anywhere, go canvassing from burrough to burrough with their pockets full of money. Though certainly there is good reason to oppose them, yet if even such persons have a legal majority of voters (the bribery not being proved) they ought to be the sitting members. A contrary determination however has too often taken place.

[4] Vol. iv, pp. 415-16.

and the Duncombes, the Liddells, and the Yorkes'; and Walter Long from Wiltshire, and Charles Newdegate from Warwickshire. 'But the list is too long', writes Disraeli; 'or good names remain behind.'[1]

As for social standing, the names of considerably more than half the Commons of 1761 were in the books of the peerage and baronetage. The rest were almost all of gentry origin. There were not more than a dozen men in the House who could be truly described as of obscure origin; and probably not more than forty for whom pedigrees had to be concocted under George III, as they had been for some older families under the Tudors or Stuarts. For even the list of the merchants in the Parliament of 1761 includes names such as Thomas Harley, son of the Earl of Oxford; Thomas Walpole, son of Lord Walpole; Peregrine Cust, son of Sir Richard Cust, second Baronet; Frazer Honywood, descended from the famous Mary Honywood who 'had at her decease [in 1620] lawfully descended from her 367 children', and who on one occasion is recorded to have entertained 200 of her progeny[2] (she could entertain them, but Robert Honywood, 'her onlie husband', could not endow them all with landed estates); Arnold Nesbitt, of the Nesbitts of Lismore; John Bristow, of old gentry, brother-in-law to the Earls of Buckinghamshire and Effingham, etc.

The composition of the Parliament of 1761 can be examined from yet another angle : the family relation of the Members to their constituencies and to Parliament in general. Roughly, 40 per cent of those returned in 1761 sat for constituencies which their ancestors in the *male* line had previously represented, in the majority of cases for generations; another 35 per cent belonged to old-established Parliamentary families, though they did not sit for family constituencies in the narrow sense of the term given it above; and only 25 per cent of the House of Commons had no Parliamentary ancestry.

This figure of 25 per cent might appear high, but it must

---

[1] Benjamin Disraeli, *Lord George Bentinck* (1852), pp. 299-300.
[2] See Nichols, *Topographer and Genealogist*, vol. i, pp. 397-411, 'The Posterity of Mary Honywood'; also Morant, *Essex*, vol. ii, pp. 167-70, and *Notes and Queries*, 12 s., vol. iv, p. 234.

not be brought up as in any way bearing out the contention about 'the new class of candidates . . . without party connexions or local interest'. For there was frequently a 'local interest' without Parliamentary ancestry, and where there was neither, 'party connexions' (if one can speak of 'parties' in 1761) appear strongest. The majority of merchants were men without Parliamentary ancestry, but some of them had a very strong local interest, *e.g.* the Wiltshire clothiers ; then there were men with local connexions arising from their profession, admirals at places such as Portsmouth, Plymouth, or Rochester, recorders at various boroughs, etc. Lastly, the 25 per cent include a number of men strongly rooted in their constituencies, but whose families for some reason or other had not sat before. As for civil servants or professional politicians put up by the Government or some political 'connexion' for pocket boroughs, they did not require, and frequently had not, a local 'interest' of any kind. Had Edmund Burke (to give the best-known example, though he did not enter Parliament till December 1765) a 'local interest' at Wendover or Parliamentary ancestry ? But it was just men like him who had the strongest 'party' connexions ; and he, though exceptional in ability, was not of a rare type.

The number of men in the Parliament of 1761 who were unsupported by family, party, or local connexions, but sat merely because they had money and were prepared to spend it on elections, was exceedingly small ; and of those who thus entered it for the first time in 1761 there were perhaps three, if so many.

One last test shall be applied to the assertion that there was a vast change in the Parliament of 1761 by analysing the various types of interlopers named by those who make it.

To begin with the admirals enriched by prizes : five of those who sat at the dissolution no longer stood at the election of 1761, while only two entered the House for the first time ; on the balance a loss of three, though not a single admiral was among the unsuccessful candidates at the polls (junior naval officers are not taken into account, because those who stood for Parliament did so usually on a family interest, and not in an official capacity, nor on the strength of prizes).

As to East Indian nabobs 'gorged with the spoils of the East', there were only two : the famous Robert Clive, who at Shrewsbury kept out Lord Pulteney, the son of Lord Bath, a young man burdened with difficult parents, an unhappy youth, little character, and no merit ; and Clive's cousin, faithful friend, and secretary, John Walsh, a man of good character and a scientist of mark. Besides these, a cousin of Clive stood at Penryn but was defeated, and Laurence Sulivan unsuccessfully attacked Thomas Walpole (and the family interest of the Dowager Lady Orford) at Ashburton — which attack, in spite of rather strained family relations, may have impressed his cousin Horace. But one would indeed be sorry for a British House of Commons which had no place for a Clive ; as John Bennett, Mayor of Shrewsbury, explained to the irate and overbearing Earl of Bath in a letter dated 27 June 1759 : 'The Colonel, being of a family of great antiquity and meritt amongst us, and having so remarkably distinguished himself in the service of his country, was agreed by all to be a proper candidate'.[1] Besides Clive and Walsh only some nine or ten merchants could be (remotely) classed as 'East Indians', because, together with much other big business, they had prominent interests in the East India trade and at one time or other were Directors of the East India Company (H. Crabb Boulton was the only one among these who had ever been out to India). In short, the nabobs in 1761 are a mare's nest. It was only in the Parliament of 1768 that they for the first time became a more definite and more numerous body, provoking a scaremongering indictment from Chatham, the grandson of Governor Pitt of Madras, and 1735–47 M.P. for Old Sarum, where the political foundations of his own branch of the Pitt family had been laid with money sent over from India. And it was not until about 1780 that the so-called 'Bengal Squad' made its appearance, with adventurers of doubtful character, such as Richard Barwell, Paul Benfield, or General Richard Smith.

As for the 'West Indians' and 'West India merchants', there were comparatively few big merchants in Great Britain in 1761 who, in one connexion or other, did not trade with the

[1] See below, p. 322.

West Indies, and a considerable number of gentry families had interests in the Sugar Islands, just as numbers of Englishmen now hold shares in Asiatic rubber or tea plantations or oil-fields without thereby becoming Asiatics. Classifying as West Indians those only who were born in the West Indies, had spent there part of their lives, had been members of the Assembly or Council or had held office in one of the islands, the number of West Indians returned at the general election of 1761 amounts to thirteen, marking an increase of only three on their number at the dissolution.

Lastly, the 'merchants' — a term as wide as 'trade' is even now. Of these some are already included among the East and West Indians, but taking them all their total number in the new Parliament is found to have been fifty, marking an increase of six on their number at the dissolution. There was a very severe financial crisis in 1759 and another early in 1761. On 28 May 1761 Joseph Watkins, a London merchant, reported to Newcastle: 'Private credit is at an entire stand in the City, and the great houses are tumbling down one after the other, poor Touchet [M.P. for Shaftesbury, 1761–68] stop'd yesterday and God knows where this will end, for private paper has now no subsistance, every one is afraid of his neighbour'.[1] Touchet managed soon to reopen, but at least two other merchant M.P.'s (Bristow and Shiffner) were in similar difficulties, while William Belchier the banker, who had sat for Southwark in the previous Parliament, had refrained from standing at the general election of 1761, being bankrupt. Again the story of a mass attack from this quarter in 1761 is found to be a legend.

To sum up: the number of changes in the new Parliament was by no means greater than usual. The number of contests which were carried to the poll was, if anything, smaller. As to widespread corruption, there was a rise in the price of seats, fully justified by circumstances, but which anyhow can merely indicate the cost, not the extent, of corruption. Nor did the character of the House change to any appreciable extent: the number of admirals diminished; the East India Lobby (if one

[1] 32923, f. 282.

can speak of such a thing in 1761), the West Indians and merchants, increased very little. There was a time when writers dealing with the accession of George III would have prefaced their remarks with the Latin tag : *novus nascitur ordo rerum.* Consciously or subconsciously this idea still lingers at the back of people's minds ; they forget that even an age pregnant with great events takes some time to give them birth. The Parliament elected in 1761 was remarkably normal.

IV

SECRET SERVICE MONEY UNDER THE DUKE OF NEWCASTLE

ACCOUNTS AND LEGENDS

WHEN leaving the Treasury in July 1766, Lord Rockingham inquired of the old, experienced Duke of Newcastle how to close the secret service accounts and what to do with the money remaining in his hands. Newcastle thereupon sent him accounts covering part of the time he himself had been at the head of the Treasury.

I have sent the two last books of the present King [he wrote to Rockingham on 25 July 1766, in a letter marked 'Very Secret'], signed as usual by the initial letters of His Majesty's name; which is the method always used. I believe the late King used to burn them in the presence of the person, who was concerned; but I chose rather to bring the books away, and keep them for my own justification.

The arrear always went over to the next account; and, I suppose, I paid it to my Lord Bute who succeeded me; I am sure, I did not retain it myself. But I will enquire of Jones how that was.

You will see all the private money which pass'd thro' my hands in this reign; that it was much more than in the former reign: but I am afraid, your Lordship has found *that* very much increased, since.[1]

Hugh Valence Jones, Newcastle's late private secretary, replied to his inquiry on 26 July:

In answer to your Grace's question, whether I remember what was done with the money, which remain'd unpaid upon closing the present King's *private account* in 1762; — I have the honour to acquaint your Grace, that, to the best of my recollection . . . the balance . . . was carried by your Grace to His Majesty, at the same time with the *book* which was signed by the King. If, after this, any doubt should remain, I am sure, I shall be able, in one

[1] 32976, f. 243.

173

minute, to clear it up, when I have the honor to see your Grace, and can have an opportunity of explaining the accounts, which were constantly attended to with the utmost care.[1]

At the time of Newcastle's resignation the closing of these accounts was actually mentioned by him in a letter to Rockingham :

I was this day at Court [he wrote on 14 May 1762]. His Majesty was barely civil. . . . I desired the King's leave to attend His Majesty some day next week, to settle my *private account* ; and that I hoped His Majesty would allow me to retire from my employment a day or two after the Parliament rose. His Majesty ask'd me whether I should go to Claremont ? I said, yes ; I might afterwards go to other places.[2]

That this was all the King had to say to him, 'after near fifty years spent in the service and in undoubted zeal' for the Royal family, was to Newcastle a subject for bitter reflections,[3] though the King's question, which seemed specially offensive to him, was of the kind frequently asked by George III when embarrassed ; and that he was, is shown by the fanciful account of the conversation given by him to Bute : [4]

The D. of N. has been here and said he is preparing his accounts, that he may retire, I did not say anything more than that I hop'd they would be full, he is to bring them next week.

He apparently thought that this would have been the proper 'spirited' remark to make to the oldest servant of the Crown ; but as no mention of it occurs in any letter from Newcastle, who revelled in complaints, it probably never was made. Anyhow, the secret service accounts, which had always been 'attended to with the utmost care', were full ; and Rockingham, in accordance with the promise in his letter of 26 July 1766,[5] did return them safe. They are now among the Newcastle Papers at the British Museum.

---

[1] 32976, f. 279.　　　　　　　　　　　　　　　　[2] 32938, f. 264.
[3] See, *e.g.*, his letter to the Duke of Cumberland, 17 May 1762 ; *ibid.* f. 306.
[4] *Letters from George III to Lord Bute*, ed. R. Sedgwick, no. 142 ; 14 May 1762.
[5] 32976, f. 254.

Volume 33044 of the Additional Manuscripts contains three 'books'; of the first there is one copy, of the second three copies, and of the third two. The first is in the handwriting of John Roberts, who, as 'the very faithfull secretary' [1] of Henry Pelham, had been entrusted with the secret service accounts, and who continued to keep them during Newcastle's first term at the Treasury, March 1754–November 1756. The book consists of rough notes with the names originally indicated by initials, though a good many were filled in afterwards; it closes on 9 November 1756 with an entry of £1359 : 14 : 6, the balance in hand, paid over to H. V. Jones. A fair copy was probably made from these notes for George II, [2] but by 1766 Newcastle's overburdened memory and anxious mind no longer retained any record of what the King had done with it — in the letter to Rockingham he speaks of George II's way of dealing with secret service accounts as if he had never had any personal experience of it.

The next book starts in July 1757, after Newcastle's return to the Treasury, and closes with the death of George II in October 1760. The first three entries, in what appears to be the original copy, are in the Duke's own handwriting, the rest in that of H. V. Jones, who continued to keep the accounts so long as Newcastle had the disposal of the money. At the death of George II they stop for almost five months; during these George III aspired to virtue and Bute to office, and no money was paid into, or disbursed from, the secret service fund; not even the late King's arrears were cleared. But when the rule of 'religion and virtue' in the new reign had been secured by Bute's assumption of a Secretaryship of State, Administration was allowed to revert to its ordinary methods and Newcastle to resume the management of the secret service money. On 6 March 1761, the day on which he 'recommended' the appointment of Bute to the King, the 'private pensions' appear at the

[1] Thus described on the tablet put up to him by his sisters in Westminster Abbey; see my note on 'Three Eighteenth-Century Politicians', in the *English Historical Review*, July 1927.

[2] Newcastle, in Nov 1756, at the end of one of his last papers on secret service disbursements (32997, f. 72), puts the query : 'What I shall do with the Book ?' — but there is no reply.

N

head of his 'Mem^{ds} for Lord Bute'.[1] The subject of secret service money was thus opened up between them.

Five days later, Newcastle 'receiv'd the King's orders to pay the arrears . . . up to Michaelmas last ', and these accounts are incorporated in the 'old book'; while the 'new book', now opened, continues till 25 May 1762. The two together contain the 'private account' mentioned on 14 May ; they were submitted to the King at the parting interview on 26 May, and were initialed by him. Always afraid of prosecution and impeachment, Newcastle preserved them for his own 'justification'; and they serve this purpose, but in a way which was hardly in his mind — they dispose of legends which have grown up about secret service money and the use to which it was put.

Legends naturally surround all 'secret service'; its very name inspires fear and distrust and stimulates men's imagination — it is believed to be wise and wicked, efficient and powerful. In reality the most common characteristic of political secret service at all times is its stupidity and the unconscionable waste of money which it entails. Where its task is to obtain 'intelligence', it most frequently produces tales which could not stand five minutes' cross-examination in a law court, but which, by the presumed nature of the service, are secured against effective criticism, and are made credible by being framed to suit the bias of the employers. Where the task of a secret service is corruption, it buys men whose services are not worth having, and, more often than not, changes into a mutual benefit society for pseudo-political parasites. Bribery, to be really effective, has to be widespread and open ; it has to be the custom of the land and cease to dishonour the recipients, so that its prizes may attract the average self-respecting man. Such were political emoluments in Great Britain about the middle of the eighteenth century, and the real mystery about the secret service fund of that time is why it should have existed at all, when, to say the very least, nine-tenths of the subsidizing of politicians was done in the full light of the day. But it did exist, supplying a subject for speculation to contemporaries,

[1] 32919, f. 475.

and a wide field for fanciful anecdote to later generations. The legend about the secret service has become deeply embedded in the history of the period ; here are a few examples.

According to Sir Nathaniel Wraxall, John Roberts had avowed to a common friend of theirs 'that while he remained at the Treasury, there were a number of members who regularly received from him their payment or stipend at the end of every session, in bank notes', and that the sums varied from £500 to £800. One would hardly guess that 'a number of members' stands for an average of about 15 individuals in a House of 558; nor, when reading W. R. Williams's note on John Roberts in the *Dictionary of National Biography* — 'it is said that he paid each ministerial Member from 500*l.* to 800*l.* per annum' — would one guess (had not Williams indicated the source) that 'each ministerial Member' — there were nearly 400 — is his rendering of Wraxall's words 'a number of Members'. But that is how historical legends grow. The further stories in Wraxall — how Roberts used to squeeze the money into the hands of Members as they passed him, how Newcastle, Fox, etc., tried to get hold of the book of pensioners after Henry Pelham's death, and he (Roberts) delivered it to George II who burnt it in the presence of Pelham's disconcerted successors — are too obviously embroidered to be accepted by any but the most uncritical readers. After Pelham's death, Fox refused the post of Secretary of State and Leader of the House of Commons because Newcastle denied him its 'management', *i.e.* the political patronage of which secret service money formed only a very small part ; and it seems probable that Roberts submitted to George II Pelham's secret service book — the King's 'private account', as it was called — and that the King burnt it as, according to Newcastle, was his habit. But Roberts continued for more than two years and a half in charge of the secret service funds under Newcastle ; and the late recipients of the 'King's bounty' from those funds, so far from wishing the fact to remain hidden from Newcastle, are more likely to have clamoured that, as successor to his everlamented brother, he should continue the favours bestowed on them by Henry Pelham. Certain lists preserved in the

Newcastle Papers [1] seem to confirm (what one would have any-how expected) that Newcastle was accurately informed of the secret service pensions paid at the time of Pelham's death.

W. J. Smith, the usually careful and well-informed editor of the *Grenville Papers*, found among them a letter from Lord Saye and Sele to George Grenville, dated 26 November 1763, wherein he returned a bill for £300 which Grenville had favoured him with that morning — 'as good manners would not permit my refusal of it, when tendered by you'; he added that no spur was required to make him support Administration.[2] This letter Smith printed 'as an interesting illustration of the mode in which some part at least of the Secret Service Money was disposed of'; and the reader is left to picture to himself the noble lord much taken aback by the sudden offer of a bribe but sufficiently self-possessed to postpone its return till he had reached his own house. G. E. C., in his *Complete Peerage*, in a footnote about Richard, sixth Viscount Saye and Sele, mis-quotes the letter as returning 'a bill sent him for having supported the Administration', and remarks that he 'shows himself neither insulted nor surprised at the offer'. But why should he, on being paid the half-yearly instalment of a pension which, to begin with, he himself had urgently solicited and, next, had enjoyed for ten years, and which, though explained as help to enable him to attend the House of Lords, had been given as royal charity to a man of high rank and no means rather than as a bribe? What needs to be explained is not why Grenville tendered him the bank bill but why Saye and Sele returned it. Did he wish to exchange it for a place both of honour and profit, or perhaps would he have preferred a step up in the peerage? for by that time his financial position had changed considerably. Whatever his motives may have been, he still drew the same pension eighteen years later.[3] It is dangerous to quote a single letter relating to business of that

---

[1] *E.g.* 33038, f. 352, 'Diminution of Pensions since April 1754'; and f. 415, containing a comparison of pensions in Mar 1754 and Mar 1755.

[2] Vol. iii, pp. 145-6, footnote.

[3] See Secret Service Accounts of John Robinson, 1779–82, 37836, ff. 61-114.

description without a thorough knowledge of the circumstances and of the habits and methods of the time.[1]

When in 1756 the sum spent on 'secret and special service' suddenly rose to the unprecedented height of over £140,000,

[1] Richard Fiennes, great-grandson of the first Viscount Saye and Sele, was the son of a country clergyman, and succeeded in 1742 to the title, but apparently to very little besides. On 3 Apr 1750 he wrote to Lord Brooke (32720, f. 212):

It has given me much concern that I have not had the oportunity of paying my respects to you to have acknowledg'd the great honour you did me by introducing me to his Grace the Duke of Newcastle who was extreamly obliging and promised to recommend me to His Majesty's favour would I continue to attend the House of Lords till the latter end of last session of Parliament: which I accordingly did and should likewise have attended it this session . . . had suitable or even necessary means been ready for such an attendance, but as they were not then, so neither now are they: permit me therefore to renew my sollicitations to your Lordship to speak to his Grace in my behalf; and to acquaint him my neglecting Parliament was through necessity. . . .

P.S. If your Lordship thinks proper, communicate this letter with my duty to his Grace.

Lord Brooke forwarded this letter to Newcastle (13 Apr 1750; 32720, f. 209):

Your Grace will there see the true reason of his absence and likewise joined to that very little knowledge of the world and busyness renders his situation the more unhappy. I hope your Grace's goodness will . . . make this easy to him by soon procuring him such a settlement from the King's bounty that he may be enabled to attend his commands in a manner suitable to his rank.

There are two more letters from Brooke to Newcastle, who had gone to Hanover with the King, pressing for a settlement for Saye and Sele and assuring the Duke that he would be 'found worthy of His Majesty's favour' (32721, ff. 287 and 495). The matter reappears in a paper on 'Requests from several Lords' (undated but apparently drawn up in 1753): 'Lord Say and Sele — a small pension — £600 p.a.' (32995, f. 52). It was now granted, and can be traced throughout the secret service accounts of 1754–56 and 1757–62 (33044); in Jenkinson's 'List of Peers who receive private salaries or pensions', 1763 (Windsor Archives); in Rockingham's secret service accounts, 1765–66 (at Sheffield); and in Robinson's, 1779–81 (37836, ff. 61–114) — Saye and Sele died on 29 July 1781. Presumably it was paid also during the intervening years.

Solicited and obtained to succour real need, the pension was continued even after Saye and Sele had in 1754 more effectively provided for himself by marrying at the age of thirty-seven a widow of fifty-nine. 'His Lordship was the last of his line', wrote *The Gentleman's Magazine* in the obituary note of the Viscountess in 1789 (vol. ii, p. 764), 'and though he knew his title of viscount must become extinct if this sprig of evergreen should survive him, yet he thought it better to get possession of a good buxom widow of nearly threescore, with an excellent fortune, that would furnish him with all the comforts and elegancies of life, than to pass his days in straitened

Leicester House alleged and, which is more surprising, seems to have believed that this addition was for buying votes in the House of Commons.[1]   In reality the expenditure of secret service money, in the strict sense of the term, was very moderate in 1756, and the true facts of the case can be learnt from a letter which Newcastle wrote to Hardwicke on 16 August 1760.[2]   That year (Midsummer 1759 to Midsummer 1760) the income of the Civil List produced £1,080,000, '£280,000 more than it was given for', and Newcastle submitted certain suggestions to George II as to presents to be made out of this surplus, among others one to the Hereditary Prince of Brunswick.   When on 15 August Newcastle brought the King a warrant for £5000 to the Hereditary Prince, the King 'flew in a passion' and demanded that a warrant be made out

payable to himself; (as secret service). He would send it to Hanover, and that they should send it from Hanover to the Hereditary Prince; and make the most of it for him. I replied only, It is Your Majesty's own money; you may do with it what you please.

Still, Newcastle highly disapproved of the method:

Could ever any thing be so cruel to me, as preventing me of all opportunity of shewing my regard to this great and deserving young Prince? Or could any thing be so cruel to the nation, as to let the German Ministers only have the merit? And this money, sent from hence to Hanover, have the appearance and merit of coming out of the revenue of the Electorate.

Though he said nothing to the King that day, he proposed to speak to him about the matter when bringing 'the warrant for the £5000 secret service' and to represent to him that 'the

---

circumstances, merely for the purpose of transmitting splendid poverty to a son.' 'She was supposed to be the viscountess delineated in Hogarth's print of the Five Orders of Perriwigs, Coronets, etc.'

Lastly, the style of Saye and Sele's letter to Grenville, beginning with 'Honoured Sir', is peculiar, well according with a bizarre character.

[1] Samuel Martin, having put down the sums spent on secret and special service 1747–56, placed the following note against £90,000 of 'special service' money: 'N.B. This was the year wherein the Duke of Newcastle then at the head of the Treasury was much opposed in the House of Commons as to the grant of the subsidy stipulated by a Treaty of that year with the Empress of Russia' (41356, f. 8).

[2] 32910, ff. 122–7.

immense sum in the Exchequer, on the account of the Civil List, is known to every clerk there' and may easily produce an inquiry in Parliament next session, and while a present to the Hereditary Prince would be popular, an addition to the secret service fund 'will have the very contrary effect'.

I will then instance the year, that I went out [1756]. The King had for special service, which was sent to Hanover for the payment of troops etc., 90,000*l.*, which we did not think advisable to lay before Parliament. I know the Princess of Wales said, that those great sums drawn that year on account of the Civil List, were employed for bribing the House of Commons, to approve the Russian treaty. The King does not know, what hurt he does to his own affairs.

The allegations made by Leicester House in 1756 took root in contemporary opinion and continue to be reflected in historical text-books. It was implied that votes in the House of Commons were bought for particular divisions. There is no indication of this having ever been done under Newcastle; neither in the secret service accounts, nor in the mass of contemporary correspondence, have I found a single line which would supply any ground even for a suspicion of that kind. Nor is the allegation inherently probable. The buying of votes for single divisions would naturally have occurred when the Government was in distress, and not the individual Member; but when votes were eagerly sought for, Members certainly did not need to prostitute themselves politically by accepting casual payments in lieu of the customary rewards for adherence to Administration, which were places, contracts, or pensions. The divisions on the Peace Preliminaries in December 1762 will perhaps be urged against this contention, and although there is not the same amount of evidence about them as about transactions during Newcastle's term of office, I shall take them as my last example of the growth of historical legends about the 'secret service'.

Horace Walpole in his *Memoirs of the Reign of King George III* recounts how Henry Fox,

leaving the grandees to their ill humour . . . directly attacked the separate members of the House of Commons; and with so little

decorum on the part of either buyer or seller, that a shop was
publicly opened at the Pay-Office, whither the members flocked,
and received the wages of their venality in bank-bills, even to so
low a sum as two hundred pounds for their votes on the Treaty.
Twenty-five thousand pounds, as Martin, Secretary of the Treasury,
afterwards owned, were issued in one morning and in a single
fortnight a vast majority was purchased to approve the peace ! [1]

This account has become common property of history books
and is reproduced and embellished, not quoted,[2] the writers
apparently not feeling the need to name their authority or to
adhere to the exact terms of the statement any more than they
would in saying that George II died in 1760.

What evidence is there for the story ?   None in Horace
Walpole's contemporary letters, but then very few are extant
for that period ; nor even in the vast correspondence of Newcastle where a great deal is said about blandishments, intimida-
tion, and defections.   Some evidence that partly supports but
also circumscribes Walpole's story is in British Museum MSS.
which none of the historians who so glibly repeated it can have
known.   In the Liverpool Papers there is a computation of
'Money issued for Secret and Special Service, from the year
1751 to the year 1763',[3] which shows that on 9 December 1762,
i.e. the day of the first vote on the treaty, £25,000 was drawn by
Samuel Martin for 'secret service' ; and in the Martin Papers
there is a copy of the receipt for this money which was paid
over by him to the King.[4]   This obviously is the £25,000 which

---

[1] Edited by G. F. Russell Barker (1894), vol. i, p. 157.
[2] See, *e.g.*, Lecky, *History of England in the Eighteenth Century* (1892
edition), vol. iii, p. 225, and William Hunt, *History of England 1760–1801*,
p. 40.   [3] 38335, ff. 214-15.
[4] 41354, f. 66. It runs as follows :

GEORGE R.

We acknowledge to have received of our trusty and well beloved S.
M[artin] Esq. the sum of 25,000 : which sum in pursuance of an order
dated the 9th day of December 1762 was issued to him at the receipt of
our Exchequer for our special service. Given at our Court at St. James's
this 10th day of December in the 3rd year of our reign.

Examined   G. R.
BUTE

The memory of the £25,000 seems still to have haunted Bute seven
years later ; for on 4 Nov 1769, as he was about to leave England 'to try

according to Walpole Martin owned to have been 'issued in one morning', and according to Lecky (who often treats statements as if they were cipher wires which must be paraphrased for publication), 'were expended, in a single morning in purchasing votes'. It is immaterial whether George II is said to have died, expired, or been no more on 25 October 1760 ; but there is a difference between money being 'issued' and 'spent'. Martin's alleged statement means that this unusually large sum was issued to him in a lump (which is correct), while Lecky's embellished version seems to suggest that more money was spent in the afternoon, or at least on other days. Now the facts are these : for years it had been usual for the Secretary to the Treasury to draw the sum of £10,000 about four times a year for the secret service ; two instalments of that amount were drawn by James West, Newcastle's senior Secretary to the Treasury, on 10 February and 26 May 1762, and one by Samuel Martin on 6 July ; none at Michaelmas when Fox was about to take over ; but on 9 December the sum drawn by Martin was £25,000 ; and the next issue to him for secret service was £10,000 on 21 January 1763. In other words, the sum drawn on the morning of 9 December was unusually large, but it was the only one paid into the secret service fund while Fox was securing a majority for the treaty. Had all this ammunition been spent in one morning, nothing would have been left for the afternoon and the following six weeks. The rise by £15,000 above the normal requires an explanation ; but conversely, the amount to be explained is only £15,000, which is

once more the effect of a warm climate during the winter months', he wrote to George III concerning the accounts of the Civil List expenditure which were about to be submitted to Parliament :

. . . of the summs issued during the year I had the honor to serve in the Treasury ; some were for Secret Service, others for Special Services ; which last were regularly delivr'd into Your Majesty's hands ; and were dispos'd of by your self ; there was besides a sum of £25,000 issued on the tenth of December under the name of Secret Service, that I had the honor to carry to Your Majesty, in the same manner that I had done those before, that were issued for your Special Service (Fortescue, vol. ii, pp. 109-10).

As a matter of fact, in the accounts that sum was booked against Samuel Martin and Bute's name was not mentioned ; but his letter shows the way in which this money was handled.

very much less than current allegations would make one expect.[1] And for the expenditure of secret service money or the methods of corruption better evidence is required than a 'confession' such as that of John Ross Mackye, recorded (or alleged) by Wraxall [2] — a picturesque statement made under the influence of liquor, many years after the event.

PUBLIC PENSIONS AND SPECIAL SERVICE

The first thing to be ascertained with regard to secret service money as an instrument of Parliamentary corruption is what sums were available for the purpose. This necessitates a careful examination of all entries in the Civil List accounts which might possibly have covered disbursements of that nature. Material for such an inquiry abounds in the Civil List accounts for the years October 1752 to February 1769, called for when George III asked the House of Commons to pay his debts, and submitted in January 1770; [3] in the Treasury Papers at the P.R.O.; in the Newcastle Papers at the British Museum; and in those of several Secretaries to the Treasury:

[1] The explanation which I would tentatively suggest is this : Fox was securing a following for the new Administration ; some resignations of office by opponents had been received, the dismissal of others was imminent ; but the redistribution of places required time. The candidates on the waiting-list received pensions in lieu of office until provided for. But the difference between securing a regular following and buying votes in the market is not unimportant.

[2] John Ross Mackye is reported by Wraxall (*Historical Memoirs* (1836), vol. iv, p. 671) to have claimed, in 1790, at a dinner at Lord Bessborough's, that it was through him that votes had been secured for the peace of 1763. 'With my own hand I secured above one hundred and twenty votes, on that most important question to Ministers. Eighty thousand pounds were set apart for the purpose. Forty Members of the House of Commons received from me, a thousand pounds each. To eighty others, I paid five hundred pounds apiece.' The figures are as beautifully even as at a sixpenny store. One would, however, like to know from what funds this money was taken and under what heading it was booked. The public accounts of that time are certainly not remarkable for their perspicuity ; still, I have searched carefully and have failed to find any loophole through which a sum of that size could have been drawn. But Wraxall says that Mackye made the statement under the influence of 'excellent champagne' to which he 'was partial'.

[3] *Journals of the House of Commons*, vol. xxxii (1768–70), pp. 467–603. The original MS. accounts are in the P.R.O., T. 38/226.

James West, who, with a short interval in 1756–57, held the office from 1746 to 1762, Charles Jenkinson (1763–65), and John Robinson (1770–82). Certain difficulties arise from the year in various computations being calculated as from different days — Midsummer (5 July), Old Christmas (5 January), Old Lady Day (5 April); still in others as from 25 October, the day of George II's death [1] — and from the same items not being always classified in the same way; still, even though the figures supplied in the various papers do not invariably tally, and the way in which matters are mixed up causes confusion, results sufficiently reliable can be obtained from them without entering into a minute examination of the Treasury accounts.

A notebook of James West contains 'An Account of the Income and Expence of His Majesty's Civil Government', 1752–60.[2] The table attached gives all the entries which might be suspected of having supplied money for secret service; I propose to examine them one by one.

A detailed account for each year of the 'Pensions and Annuities' payable at the Exchequer can be seen in the Civil List accounts at the P.R.O.[3] They start with the first dukes of the Kingdom; for some of these, pensions (most of which were presumably treated as additional salaries to Court offices) were merely a welcome and useful recognition of their importance, for others a necessary help to keep up the appearances of strength and splendour required from men placed so near the Throne. In 1754–55 the second on the list is the Duke of Grafton with £3000, followed by the Dukes of St. Albans and Somerset, and further down by the Dukes of Marlborough and Bolton; the next year the Duke of Rutland appears in the list, in 1757–58 the Dukes of Devonshire and Dorset, etc. Beside English noblemen, there is every year a long list of Scottish peers;[4] some widows and orphans, the Fellows of Eton College, the Fellows and Master of Emmanuel College, Cambridge, readers of 'physick' and modern history at Oxford and

---

[1] Thus in the accounts submitted to the House of Commons in 1770.
[2] 30205, ff. 10–13.
[3] For 1754–59, T. 38/163, and for 1759–67, T. 38/164.
[4] £5800, in a total of £8700, of these Scottish pensions is, however, marked in 38338, f. 22 as 'police, not pension'.

Cambridge, etc. etc., various deans, vicars, corporations, the poor of St. John the Baptist, and the churchwardens of St. Michael's, Cornhill, etc. etc. Not a single Member of Parliament appears in these lists; obviously it was not customary for Members of Parliament to figure in them (but one has only to turn over a few pages to find them drawing salaries as Grooms of the Bedchamber, as Keepers of the Records in the Tower or of His Majesty's Tennis Courts, Rangers of Windsor Forest or of some London park, as Tellers of the Exchequer, as Clerks of the Pells, or of Foreign Estreats, etc. etc.).

Next come the pensions 'per Paymaster'; 'by Compton' is merely a different description of the same thing — he was Paymaster at that time,[1] and, in 1755, was succeeded in the office by Lord Gage. In a speech which Alderman Beckford delivered in the House of Commons on 28 February 1769, during the debate on the arrears of the Civil List, he is reported to have said :

Are we to have no account of this £800,000 [to be granted to the King], disposed of, perhaps, to influence the freedom of this country, to influence the freedom of this House ? a man who receives alms : a pensioner is an alms-man. Why is not P.P., for public pensioner, as well upon his shoulders, as the shoulders of a poor man ? . . . An alms-man cannot vote, ought a pensioner ? . . . I want to see the pensions paid by Lord Gage, Paymaster of the Pensions. . . .[2]

If he had, how many Members of Parliament would he have found in Gage's lists.

In the accounts at the P.R.O. more than half the money spent on such pensions appears under the summary heading 'To clear Pensions and Annuities payable in this Office', but a detailed list for the year 1754 is preserved among the Newcastle Papers,[3] and full accounts covering nineteen out of the twenty-five years during which Gage held the office (1755–63 and 1765–83) are preserved among his papers at Firle — in fact, for his second term the accounts of only one year, 1780–81,

---

[1] Charles Compton, fourth son of the fourth Earl of Northampton and father of the seventh Earl. He was consul at Lisbon 1727–41, and envoy extraordinary 1741–45. In 1745 he was appointed Paymaster of Pensions, was returned to Parliament for Northampton on 9 Dec 1754, and died on 20 Nov 1755.   [2] Egerton MS. 218, pp. 182–4.   [3] 33044, ff. 1–17.

are missing. The lists are as varied as those of the 'Pensions and Annuities' payable at the Exchequer, but on the whole are of a less dignified character. About three-fifths of the recipients are women, and about a quarter foreigners, male and female: people who as a rule could not have received the King's bounty through office sinecures. There are again some great but needy peers, *e.g.* the Dukes of Somerset and Chandos; some men who had spent their lives in the service of the nation, such as Field-Marshal Lord Ligonier or Edward Weston; many smaller retired officials or servants; Lady Katherine, widow of Henry Pelham, and Lady Albemarle, widow of the Ambassador, left at his death in distressed financial circumstances; many widows and daughters of less eminent men; and a great many parasites, big and small, such as abound in every pensions list during the period. Lastly there are stipends, pensions, and charities to clergymen, professors, schoolmasters, to the poor of certain parishes, and to French Protestants. But in all the lists covering twenty years there appear only two names of Members of Parliament: Thomas Pelham, £800 p.a., in the lists of 1754–63, and Charles Vernon, £300, 1756–82. So far I have found nothing to explain Thomas Pelham's pension, or definitely to identify its recipient with the Member for Rye 1749–54, and for Sussex from 1754 till 1768 when he succeeded Newcastle as Lord Pelham; except that I can find no one else to whom it could refer. If indeed Thomas Pelham, M.P., was its recipient, he certainly did not require being bribed to adhere to Newcastle. Charles Vernon can be identified as the Member for Tamworth, 1768–74. Here is the story of that pension. James Vernon, Secretary of State in the reign of William III, in 1710 managed to provide for his son James in a Commissionership of the Excise; and after forty-six years in that office James Vernon struck an excellent bargain with the Treasury: he gave up the Commissionership on 6 April 1756 (and died nine days later) while his son Charles received the pension [1] which he retained at least till 1803,[2] and possibly

[1] The grant of a pension to Charles Vernon directly follows in the Treasury books on James Vernon's replacement at the Excise (P.R.O., T. 52/47, pp. 538-9).   [2] T. 28/330.

till his death in 1810 — a good example of family provision at the expense of the State. But even this pension, given when there was no prospect of the recipient entering the House, would not have been found in Gage's list while Vernon sat in Parliament: it was stopped on 7 December 1768, and restarted on 5 July 1774, while in the meantime it was 'made payable to Thomas Coutts, Esq.'.[1] The placing of Members on that list was obviously avoided, and although in a few cases Members may possibly have been the beneficiaries, pensions through the Paymaster can be dismissed as a source of Parliamentary corruption.

As for the 'Privy Purse', under George II no money from it is known to have been used for elections or for pensions to Members of Parliament; at least there is no hint to that effect in Newcastle's domestic correspondence, of which elections, places, and pensions are the main topics. Nor do the Privy Purse accounts of Bute as its Keeper during the first two-and-a-half years of George III's reign, preserved among his papers, show any trace of money used for Parliamentary purposes; nor again does his correspondence yield any hints to that effect. It was only beginning with November 1777 that George III set aside £1000 a month from his Privy Purse for financing elections.

To take the last item not directly described as 'secret service' but which might be suspected of having covered money for Parliamentary corruption — 'Contingencies'. Their ordinary purposes are clearly shown in the Civil List accounts and are enumerated in James West's notebooks:

Contingencies are under divers heads, vizt. law charges, rewards for services, liberates at the Exchequer, surplus on sheriffs' accounts, and rewards for apprehending highwaymen, disbursements, printers of their bills, riding charges to messengers, post fines, City impost, rents payable by the Crown.[2]

It is stated in an analysis made in 1763 and preserved among the papers of Charles Jenkinson that 'the necessary expenses under this head do not amount to more than £57,729 : 6 : 2½

---

[1] T. 52/59, p. 455; 52/66, p. 15; and 38/229.
[2] 30219, f. 11 and 30216, f. 120.

a year'; and this is the sum at which the contingencies approximately stood during the years 1751–55.[1] But also expenditure of a different and more mysterious kind, described as a rule as for 'special service', was included under 'contingencies', causing their sum total to vary considerably during the concluding years of George II's reign. A digest in the

	In the Year ending 5 July										
	1756			1757			1758			1759	1760
	£	s.	d.	£	s.	d.	£	s.	d.	£	£ s. d.
'o the Secretaries of the Treasury for special services .	90,000	0	0*	10,000	0	0	..			30,000	20,520 14 0
'o John Thornton, Esq., for special services . . .	16,933	6	6	10,520	11	6	..			..	..
'o James Wallace, Esq., for special services . .	..			..			18,000	0	0	..	..
'o Andrew Drummond, Esq., for special services .	..			..			20,665	18	0	..	..
'o Richard Stratton, Esq., for special services . . .	..			..			5,254	10	0	..	..
'o Baron Münchhausen . . .	..			..			1,585	0	0	..	..

* £50,000 of this sum was issued in weekly instalments of £10,000 between 23 Sept and 21 Oct 1755; see 33038, ff. 450 and 472.

Liverpool Papers — 'Particulars of the Sums paid for Contingencies in the Civil List Accompt for ten years ended the 5th day of July, 1760'[2] — supplies a convenient survey of the principal items of 'special service' money issued during the years 1756–60; the list is not complete, but as it is not here a question of a minute and exhaustive analysis, it will serve the purpose (see table above).

Although I am not able fully to explain every single position, it can be shown that this money was used for service abroad,

[1] See 'An enquiry into the extraordinary expences of His Majesty's Civil Government . . . in . . . 1763 . . .', 38338, f. 104.

[2] 38332, f. 223.

not at home.[1] Thus the £90,000 drawn by James West and Nicholas Hardinge in 1755–56 are obviously those transmitted by George II to Hanover and mentioned by Newcastle in the letter to Hardwicke on 16 August 1760.[2] Similarly the £20,520 : 14s. in 1759–60 booked against the Secretaries to the Treasury seem to have been sent to Germany.[3] The payments to John Thornton, the London banker, one may confidently assume, because of their date, his person, and the fees charged on them,[4] to have been for presents at the Russian Court — he had the remittance of Government money to Russia.[5] When in 1759 Robert Keith was charged with certain negotiations at St. Petersburg, he was authorized to make 'private presents to proper persons', and 'to give as far as twenty thousand pounds sterling to such person or persons as can bring His Majesty's wishes to bear. The money to be paid upon the exchange of the ratifications'.[6] A similar authorization, up to £100,000,

---

[1] I have not read the papers in the Newcastle MSS. dealing with diplomatic affairs ; in these, presumably, detailed explanations could be found for the above disbursements. The only one among them of which I cannot define even the character is that of £10,000 in 1757 ; possibly the entry of £10,000 paid 'to the innholders which will be repaid' — whatever this may mean — refers to it ; see paper signed by James West, 33039, f. 13.

[2] See above, pp. 180-81.

[3] There is a note among the Newcastle Papers (32894, f. 209), docketed 15 Aug 1759, which seems to refer to this transaction : 'Nicholas Magens, Esq., proposes to send the neat value of 20,000£ sterling to Messrs. Hanbury & Halsey merchants at Hamburgh with directions that they shall dispose of the money in such manner as Prince Ferdinand shall be pleased to order.' £20,520 : 14s. would be 'the neat value of 20,000£' plus charges for transmission.

[4] It appears from the Treasury accounts at the P.R.O. (T. 38/163) that £16,000 in 1756 and £10,000 in 1757 were paid to John Thornton 'to reimburse the like sum expended by him for His Majesty's service', while £933 : 6 : 6 and £520 : 11 : 6 was for 'fees attending the same' ; the percentage is that of rather costly foreign remittances. A further confirmation of this money having been used for Russia is supplied by a paper of James West drawn up in 1757 (33039, f. 13) containing the entry 'for Russia £26,933 : 6 : 6', which is obviously the sum total of the first remittance with fees charged on it, and the second, without the fees.

[5] See, e.g., 32861, ff. 175 and 208.

[6] Holdernesse to R. M. Keith, 13 Feb 1759 ; 30999, f. 11. Holdernesse, however, forgot to inform Keith 'in whose hands the money was lodged', which did not matter much as Keith had no occasion for it at that time ; see letter from Sir R. M. Keith, Memoirs and Correspondence (1849), vol. i, p. 34. Curiously enough, the letter from Keith, which is obviously a reply to the preceding, is dated in this collection, 'St. Petersburg 2/13 May 1760'.

was again given to Keith by Bute on 6 February 1762,[1] and a letter of credit for that amount was issued to him from Messrs. Thornton & Cornwall in London on Messrs. Ritter, Thornton & Cayley at St. Petersburg.[2] Payments made in these circumstances had naturally to appear as for 'special service', and in order to provide some cover for them in public accounts, they were booked against the banker through whom they were made. Similar transactions were covered by the entries which appear against two other London bankers, Andrew Drummond and Richard Stratton.[3] As for James Wallace, he was at that time Under-Secretary of State in the Northern Department, and his name once more suggests foreign service.

Lastly, the exceedingly high sum of £112,641 : 13 : 9 entered for 'contingencies' between 5 July and 25 October 1760 is shown by the Treasury accounts [4] to have covered £79,490 : 15 : 5¾ to Philip Adolph, Baron von Münchhausen (the Hanoverian Resident in London) 'for his late Majesty's special service'; [5] and 'to Nicholas Magens, Esq.,[6] to be remitted to the Marquis of Granby, to be paid by his Lordship into the hands of the Hereditary Prince of Brunswick £5000',

---

[1] 30999, f. 14. [2] 32934, f. 193.

[3] These two sums are thus analysed in the Civil Service accounts for 1757–58 (T. 38/163, p. 48): 'To Andrew Drummond & Co. to answer the following bills of exchange drawn on them by Joseph Yorke, Esq., at the Hague [British Ambassador to the States-General] for His Majesty's service, viz. :

	£	s.	d.
A bill from abroad	3,207	0	0
Fees attending the same	172	11	6
Sundry bills from abroad and fees attending the same .	17,286	6	6
	20,665	18	0
Richard Stratton to reimburse expences for His Majesty's special service	5,000	0	0
To defray fees and charges attending the receipt thereof	254	10	0
	5,254	10	0

[4] T. 38/164.

[5] This money was to be repaid into the Exchequer (see Newcastle's paper on the money remaining in the Exchequer at the death of George II ; 33045, f. 141), and was in fact repaid (see T. 38/200).

[6] A London banker who, together with George Amyand, had frequently the remittance of Government money to Germany; see, e.g., 32878, ff. 214-15, 32881, ff. 331-2, and 32889, f. 96.

O

with £364 : 2 : 6 in 'fees attending the receipt thereof'; [1] etc.

Thus contingencies also do not seem to have yielded money for Parliamentary corruption. But the mystery which surrounded the 'special service', and the fact that so much of its money was drawn through the Secretaries to the Treasury who were in charge of the domestic secret service funds, have given rise to legends, and continue to confuse the accounts in various summaries of the expenditure of that period.

Secret Service Accounts

Under secret service disbursements labelled as such there is a standing payment of £6000 a year to the two Secretaries of State, £3000 to each. Its nature was set forth by George Grenville in the House of Commons on 2 March 1769, during the debate on the arrears and debts due upon the Civil List: he described these secret service payments as 'an annual salary added to the . . . Secretaries of State'.[2] This explains the very considerable discrepancy between the salary of the Secretaries of State as entered in the Civil List accounts — £1850 each — and the average of £5780 p.a., 'the clear profits of the office of Secretary of State' during the seven years 1747–53 as given in the paper drawn up for Newcastle on the subject; [3] the rest being derived from fees, e.g. on commissions issued from the office. This item of 'secret service' again had therefore nothing to do with Parliamentary corruption.

Next, there is a regular payment of secret service money to the Secretary of the Post Office.[4] A list of disbursements from

---

[1] See also Newcastle's Memorandum of 19 Aug 1760 (33040, f. 5): 'Mr. Magens. His proposal about the £5000 present, whereby no mortal can know any thing of it, 'till the money is certainly given by my Lord Granby, from the King, to the Hereditary Prince.' This is the present discussed above, pp. 180-81.

[2] Sir Henry Cavendish, Debates of the House of Commons, vol. i, p. 294. See also the remark in a letter from George Grenville to Thomas Whately, 20 July 1766 (Grenville Papers, vol. iii, p. 276), about 'half England' really believing 'that the three thousand pounds a-year which was payable to Mr. Pitt as Secretary of State now lie unapplied' [in the Treasury].

[3] See below, p. 227.

[4] In redrafting the following paragraphs on the secret service in the Post Office, I have had the help of Dr. K. L. Ellis of Durham University, whose forthcoming book, The British Post Office in the Eighteenth Century, deals with this subject in a most thorough and illuminating manner.

this fund for the year ended on 5 April 1763, sent to George Grenville by the Secretary, Anthony Todd, is published in the *Grenville Papers* : [1]

The Bishop of Bath and Wells . . .	£500	Brought forward .	£3375
		Peter Hemet . .	300
Thomas Ramsden . .	500	Stephen Dupuy . .	300
Edward Willes . .	500	John French . .	300
Francis Willes . .	300	John Ernest Bode, jun. .	300
James Wallace . .	400	William Augustus Bode .	200
James Rivers . .	200	John Ulrick Selshop .	100
Peter Morin . . .	250	John Calcott . .	60
Cuchet Juvencel . .	150	James Holcome . .	40
John Ernest Bode, senr.,		James Sanders . .	60
£400 ; extra allowance,		Anthony Todd . .	750
£100 . . .	500	The same person for dis-	
The same person for seals,		tributing these allow-	
&c.	75	ances . . .	25
Carried forward .	£3375		£5810

Not a single Member of Parliament appears in this list. Edward Willes, Bishop of Bath and Wells (1743–73), was engaged since 1716 in deciphering intercepted correspondence for the Secretaries of State, and was also rewarded by ecclesiastical preferments. His sons, Francis and Edward (not to be confused with the Member of Parliament of the same name, son of Chief Justice Willes and a nephew of the Bishop) assisted him as decipherers, and the family continued to work for the Secretaries of State till 1844. Similarly the Bode family were a regular Post Office dynasty connected with it till 1844 ; one of their functions in 1763 was, as Todd mentions in the covering letter to Grenville, 'engraving the many seals we are obliged to make use of' (counterfeit seals for letters opened in the Post Office). Peter Hemet was a superannuated Post Office official, Thomas Ramsden ('Latin secretary to the King'), James Wallace, James Rivers, and

---

[1] Vol. iii, p. 311 ; corrected above from the original in the possession of Sir John Murray.

Peter Morin were past or present Under-Secretaries of State of the humbler kind — none of them ever sat in Parliament, and they were clerks rather than politicians ; similarly, Cuchet Juvencel [1] belonged to the minor official fry. These men, who would now be Foreign Office officials, seem to have been attached to the secret service of the Post Office for the double purpose of reading intercepted foreign correspondence and of drawing additional emoluments. 'I am informed', wrote James Wallace to Bute on 11 May 1761, 'that the payments of the secret service branch of the Post Office, which have been suspended ever since His Majesty's accession by reason of the alteration made in the Hereditary Revenue of the Crown, are now about to be put in course again from the time of suspension.' The post he had held in that office since 1749 was 'the German clerkship, the functions of which consist in translating the intercepted letters that are in the German or Dutch languages'.[2] The remaining recipients of salaries named in the list were employed in the Post Office.

Other lists of recipients from the Post Office secret service are available for the years 1742,[3] 1745,[4] 1761,[5] 1765,[6] and 1801,[7] and none includes any Member of Parliament.

Thus for Parliamentary corruption we are left with no other secret service money than that paid to the Secretaries to the Treasury, which (with one single discrepancy of £2000 in 1756) [8] will be found to correspond exactly to the sums accounted for in Newcastle's secret service books. The table

---

[1] At one time he was provincial agent for North Carolina. Between 1761 and 1767, he was a clerk in the office of the Secretaries of State, and in July 1765 he was appointed private secretary to Grafton, then Secretary of State (see *Gentleman's Magazine*, 1765, p. 348). On 6 Apr 1767 he was made one of the Clerks of the Privy Seal (*H.O. Papers*, 1766–69, p. 265), and there became attached to Chatham. He lived in a house on Chatham's estate at Hayes, cashed his annuity for him at the Exchequer, and even incurred debts on his behalf (see Chatham MSS. at the P.R.O., G.D. 8/47). He died in 1786. [2] Bute MSS.

[3] *Further report from the Committee of Secrecy appointed to enquire into the conduct of Robert, Earl of Orford*, 1742, app. 16.

[4] T. 53/41, f. 466.

[5] P.R.O. 30/8/83, Todd to Newcastle, 6 Jan 1761, enclosure.

[6] 38339, f. 143. [7] 38357, f. 36.

[8] See table opposite p. 185, footnote (2).

below from the Liverpool Papers [1] covers almost the whole of George II's reign, and gives the money received and disbursed for secret service free of all 'special service' accessories, which are lumped with it in many other tables; each year is calculated till Midsummer (5 July).

To complete the table of the secret service money of the Treasury under George II we have to add £10,000, issued to West on 29 September 1760.

	£	s.	d.		£	s.	d.
1728.	45,743	14	0	1745.	24,000	0	0
1729.	57,880	0	0	1746.	22,000	0	0
1730.	53,391	0	0	1747.	41,000	0	0
1731.	63,918	0	0	1748.	33,000	0	0
1732.	73,781	8	0	1749.	38,000	0	0
1733.	87,470	0	0	1750.	29,000	0	0
1734.	117,145	19	0	1751.	32,000	0	0
1735.	66,630	1	10	1752.	40,000	0	0
1736.	95,312	10	4	1753.	35,000	0	0
1737.	61,999	10	0	1754.	50,000	0	0
1738.	72,827	19	0	1755.	40,000	0	0
1739.	74,249	16	0	1756.	38,000	0	0
1740.	80,116	8	5	1757.	50,000	0	0
1741.	80,976	15	2	1758.	40,000	0	0
1742.	64,949	5	5	1759.	30,000	0	0
1743.	54,300	0	0	1760.	40,000	0	0
1744.	34,970	0	0				

Expenditure of secret service money through the Secretaries to the Treasury thus regularly increased about the time of general elections (1734, 1741, 1747, and 1754); was especially high during the last years of Sir Robert Walpole's administration, while he fought desperately for his political existence; and was lowest during Henry Pelham's time at the Treasury (August 1743–March 1754), which explodes the story of the numerous secret service pensions paid at that time to Members

[1] See 'An Accompt shewing the Monies issued for . . . secret service . . . from Midsummer 1727 to Midsummer 1760 . . .' (38337, f. 44). The same figures appear in a paper in the Newcastle MSS. covering the years 1730–57: 'An Accompt of all Monies issued for Secret Service since the year 1730 distinguishing each year' (33039, f. 37).

of Parliament by John Roberts. The secret service fund of the Treasury was used for various purposes, and never more than one-third of it, and often considerably less, went in pensions to Members of the House of Commons ; the average total under Pelham, including years of general elections, amounted to something over £30,000 — how many pensions of £500-800 a year could be carved out of, say, even £10,000 ? A comparison of the totals during the years when Henry Pelham was at the Treasury with those of Newcastle suggests that Pelham's mysterious books — according to Wraxall, 'too sacred and confidential to be thus transferred over to the new Ministers' — did not differ widely from those preserved in the Newcastle Papers.

The General Elections of 1754 and 1761, and the Nursing of Constituencies

The accounts which John Roberts kept under Newcastle as First Lord of the Treasury open on 21 March 1754, on the eve of the general election, and during the next two or three months election expenses naturally rank foremost. James West, having on 13 March received Newcastle's commands through Lord Dupplin 'to know what engagements Mr. Pelham had mentioned to me relative to the next election', sent him the following paper — 'all that I know from himself' ; [1] the paper [2] is annotated in the margin by Roberts, while further information can be obtained from a series of papers in Roberts's handwriting preserved in 32995.

Shoreham. Agreed to defray all expences exceeding £1000 for Mr. Bristowe.[3]

Barnstaple. Agreed to defray all expences exceeding £1500 to Mr. Amyand. £1000 has been already advanced.

---

[1] 32734, f. 237.　　　　　　　　　　　　　[2] Ibid. ff. 239-40.

[3] In the paper of 16 Mar 1754 (32995, f. 96) this engagement is differently stated : 'Mr. Philipson — Shoreham. His son Mr. Bristowe to come in by agreement with Mr. Stratton. To be paid £1000 to assist him, and to expend another 1000 by himself.' About Phillipson see below, essay on Harwich, pp. 359-67.

Evesham.   Agreed to defray all expences exceeding £1500 to
Mr. Alderman Porter.

Totness.   Agreed to be at the whole expence for the Master of
the Rolls in case he had stood, but as he has declined and (by
me) acquainted Mr. P[elham] it was very indifferent to him,
whether he was in Parliament now, or on any future vacancy,
that engagement is at an end ; tho' there is an old claim of the
Corporation for discharge of a debt of 800£.   Mr. P. was to
have seen the D. of Somerset, for his son, to join Mr. Trist.

Worcester.   Mr. P. feared this would cost 4 or 5000£ and
advanced some money to Mr. Tra[cy] and his agent Mr.
Lilly.[1]

[Marginal remark in Roberts's handwriting :   'Mr. P. seemed
desirous to break off all engagements here, if he had known how to
extricate himself.'][2]

Honiton.   Agreed to advance a certain sum in support of Mr.
Yonge.

[Roberts : 'This measure was not agreable to Mr. P.']

Saltash.   The candidates[3] were to be at the whole expence as
settled with Mr. Clevland.

Old Sarum.   The sum uncertain, complained greatly of its being
too excessive.

[Roberts : 'A sum has been advanced.'[4]]

[1] In the paper of 18 Mar 1754, *ibid.* f. 98 : 'Mr. Tracey — has had
1000£ for his election, demands 3500 more — offers to desist for 2000 — to
be chosen at another place — and if not chosen will return 1000£'.   Newcastle's remark against it : 'will lay it before the King'.

[2] Several letters from Tracy to Pelham and Newcastle dealing with the
Worcester election are among the Newcastle Papers.   The last (32734,
f. 332), dated 24 Mar 1754, reads :

My Lord Duke,

I beg your immediate answer whether the £2500 will be paid, £1000
tomorrow, and the remaining £1500 when I go down ; if these terms are
not agreed to, and you will be pleased to determine tonight whether you
will or will not make them good, I shall trouble neither the King nor
your Grace any further, nor shall I be with you on Thursday morning,
but will stand the poll for Worcester unassisted by your Grace, and
free, I thank God, from all obligations.   Your Grace must be peremptory
tonight, or you will see me no more.

P.S.   Tomorrow I shall begin executing the plan necessary to secure
my election, and will be put off no longer.

Newcastle managed 'to extricate himself' (see 32995, ff. 104 and 115) and
Tracy was not elected ; but this was not the last Newcastle saw of him.

[3] Lord Duncannon and Lord Barrington who, a few days later, was
replaced by Admiral George Clinton.

[4] £1000 (see 32995, f. 120) ; but this was reimbursed by Lord Bath
(see p. 444).

<u>Reading.</u> Mr. D[odd] has already received £1000 and the
engagement stands for 5 or 600£ more.[1]

<u>Glocester.</u> Mr. P. had agreed to be at some part of the expence,
the quantum not known.
[Roberts: 'As far as I was informed, expressions were very
loose and general here.']

Wallingford. Agreed to be at some part of the expence.
[Roberts: 'Some assistance has been given which is best known
to a certain person.'[2]]

Lord Edgcumbe and Lord Falmouth were to have received
largely out of the last money.[3]

<u>Kent.</u> 2000£ advanced on a bad security by Mr. Galfridus
Mann to Mr. Fairfax which Mr. West has obliged himself
to pay Mr. Mann and Mr. Pelham has obliged himself to pay
to Mr. West.[4]
[Roberts: 'This sum was £2233 : 3 : 2.']

A few more engagements have to be added to the above.
In a paper on arrangements made between Pelham and
Dupplin in January 1754,[5] it is mentioned that 'incidental
expences of £170' at Camelford were 'to be defrayed by the
Government'; and that about Shaftesbury 'Mr. Fox told the
Duke of Newcastle, that Sir Thomas Clavering had already
paid £2000 and that Mr. Pelham had promised to pay what
was wanting above that sum'. In the paper of 21 March [6] it

[1] In the paper of 16 Mar 1754 (*ibid.* f. 99): 'Mr. Dodd — Reading —
has received 1000£ — was promised 500£ more and that it should not be
lost for 3 or 400 more.'

[2] In the paper of 16 Mar 1754 (*ibid.* f. 97): 'That Mr. Sewel was
promised to have the expences for Wallingford born, after he had expended
1000£ of his own money — That in consequence of that promise he had
received already 1200£ — and that more will be wanting — [remark by
Newcastle: "NB. Mr. Roberts says some money has been already advanced
— That I can give no answer, till I have laid it before the King."]. And
if Mr. Sewell did not succeed there, he should be brought in somewhere else,
at a convenient time' [remark against it: 'To that I can say nothing.'].
In the paper of 21 Mar (*ibid.* f. 112) Sewell is stated to have 'had already
1250£', and the remark is added that he 'desires nothing further at present;
that he has now 300£ in cash, but will let me know, when further expence
will be necessary'.

[3] 'The last money' presumably means the last payment into the secret
service fund.

[4] About the transactions concerning Kent see below, essay on Fairfax,
pp. 413-4.

[5] 32995, ff. 63-5 and 69-71.   [6] *Ibid.* f. 112.

is noted that Hitch Young at Steyning 'was promised to have 1000£ given to defray his expences'. On 18 July 1754 Roberts, in a letter on the Westminster election, explained to Newcastle that Sir John Crosse had declared he would not put up more than £500,[1] and, as this was insufficient, Pelham tried to find someone who would go the length of £2000 but, having failed, accepted Crosse's offer. Edward Cornwallis, the other candidate for Westminster, claimed to be let off all expense, and his reasons 'seem indeed to be well founded as Mr. Hardinge is elected at Eye in his room by Lord Cornwallis'.[2] The opposition at Westminster was hopeless and was put up solely 'to occasion money to be spent'.

I do not wonder [wrote Roberts] that, after the care your Grace has taken to keep down the expences and claims from every quarter, this large demand [£1800] should give you some uneasiness ; at the same time it will not escape your Grace's judgment, how necessary it is that it should be satisfied.[3]

Further, on 25 March 1755, the Duke of Marlborough reminded Newcastle of the engagement with regard to the Oxfordshire election of 1754.

. . . when Lord Macclesfield sett up Lord Parker to support the Whig cause, poor Mr. Pelham promiss'd with the King's consent and knowledge, he should receive to support the necessary expences four thousand, and afterwards three, in all seven thousand, of which Lord Macclesfield has I believe as yett receiv'd but two.[4]

Let us now extract from Roberts's accounts the disbursements made on the general election of 1754 ; they can be easily distinguished, and an additional check is supplied by a paper compiled for Newcastle on the eve of the general election of 1761 and marked 'Disbursements for Parliament from March 21st, 1753 [i.e. 1753/4] to September 19th, 1760'.[5] Where there is more than one payment, the sum total is given of the various entries referring to the constituency.

---

[1] See also ibid. f. 98.
[2] Nicholas Hardinge was Joint Secretary to the Treasury, and Eye was a pocket borough of Lord Cornwallis.
[3] 32736, ff. 53-4.   [4] 32853, f. 460.   [5] 32999, ff. 34-5.

£

J. Dodd for Reading [1]	1000
J. Talbot for Ilchester [2]	1000
E. Bayntun Rolt for Chippenham [3] . . .	800
Sir William Yonge for Honiton [4]	500
J. Clevland for Barnstaple [5]	1000
Thomas Leslie for Forfar Burghs [6] . . .	800
B. Trist for Totnes [7]	200
Lord Macclesfield for Oxfordshire [8] . . .	3000
Hitch Young for Steyning	1000
C. Whitworth for Minehead [9]	1000
S. Martin for Camelford [10]	740
T. Sewell for Wallingford	780
Lord Archer for Bramber [11]	1000
Lord Falmouth for Tregony [12]	1455
Lord Edgcumbe and Mr. Andrews [13] . . .	700
The Duke of Argyle for Scotland	1000
Sir Jacob Downing for Dunwich [14] . . .	500
Lord Ilchester for Shaftesbury [15]	330
J. Philipson for R. Bristowe for Shoreham . .	1000
J. Porter for Evesham [16]	1000
R. Jenison [17]	700
J. S. Charlton for Newark [18]	1000
E. Cornwallis and Sir John Crosse for Westminster [19] .	1800

£22,305

(For footnotes 1 to 19 see below and following pages.)

[1] £100 paid to Dodd in Jan 1755, presumably for expenses connected with his election petition, is included.

[2] Ilchester was an expensive constituency managed by a local man, who was a merchant in London, Thomas Lockyer, M.P. for Ilchester 1747–61. 'It was the genius, the ruling passion, of Thomas Lockyer, to make the utmost of whatever money came to his hands — so well known in the country, for heaping up and accumulating, as to acquire the name of *Snowball* — justly representing his character, and, it is presumed, his fate'; see *The Case of Maria Perry* (1789).

John Talbot (1712–56), third son of Charles, first Lord Talbot, sat for Brecon 1734–54, and for Ilchester from 1754 till his death in 1756. The following note on him appears in the paper of 15 Mar 1754 (32995, f. 67): 'Mr. Legge has acquainted the D. of N., that, as Mr. Talbot cannot come in where [he] is now chosen, he is desirous to represent some other borough.' From Roberts's notes of 20 Mar it appears that Talbot was expected to contribute £1000 of his own to the purchase of the seat (*ibid*. f. 105).

[3] In the paper of 21 Mar (*ibid*. f. 114): 'Mr. Bayntun Rolt, Chippenham, says that the expence of the election will amount to 1500 — that Ald[n] Fludyer pays as much — that he Bayntun was offered 800£ [marginal remarks by Newcastle: 'to receive the King's order upon it' '800 granted']

Adding the £4250 mentioned by James West and in the papers of March 1754 as paid to Amyand, Dodd, Tracy, and Sewell, before Henry Pelham's death, a total expenditure of

---

and afterwards that there should be no difference — appeals to his conduct in his office for saving the King money' [Surveyor-General of the Dutchy of Cornwall].

Chippenham was a borough rendered expensive by the competition of rich clothiers. Edward Bayntun Rolt (1710–1800), of Spye Park, was a neighbouring squire, apparently of small means. He sat for Chippenham 1737–80, and originally belonged to the Opposition — it was over the election petition brought against his return that Walpole was defeated in 1742; but in 1747 Bayntun Rolt received £800 from the Government towards his election expenses (see *ibid.* f. 120), and in 1751 was appointed Surveyor-General of the Duchy of Cornwall. On the accession of George III he was one of the first to detach himself from Newcastle.

4 Sir William Yonge, fourth Bt., had sat for Honiton 1714–54, when he moved to Tiverton. At Honiton he was succeeded by his son George, for whose election this money was paid; possibly Sir William, feeling near death — he died in 1755 — preferred to settle his son in that expensive borough. About George Yonge and Honiton see above, p. 164.

5 This money was paid for George Amyand but is booked against John Clevland, Secretary to the Admiralty, who, having personal connexions with Barnstaple, acted there for the Government. His son, John Clevland, jun., sat for Barnstaple 1766–1802. George Amyand (1720–66) was a London merchant-banker and a Director of the East India Company, and is said to have left at his death a fortune of 'clear 160,000*l.* stg. and perhaps more' (see HMC, 10, i, p. 401). He surely did not require financial help — but why not take it if obtainable ? For the accounts of the Barnstaple election of 1754 see 32995, ff. 106-7.

6 This total is made up of £300 given to him on 1 Apr 1754, and a further £500 added on 15 Apr 1756, in reply to his pathetic appeals to Newcastle: 'if your Grace don't do for me, I shall be undone . . . my creditors wont have no longer patience with me' (30 Mar, 32864, f. 97; see also letter of 8 Apr 1756, *ibid.* f. 182).

7 See accounts under 2 Apr 1754; also 32995, f. 180.

8 This includes the £1000 paid through the Duke of Marlborough in July 1754.   9 About Whitworth see below, pp. 418-25.

10 This includes £570 paid to him on 6 Dec 1754, in response to the undated paper, 32737, f. 237. About Camelford see below, p. 339. Originally only the 'incidental expences of £170' were to have been defrayed by the Government; see Roberts's paper of 15 Mar 1754 (32995, f. 63), and payment made on 5 Apr 1754; see below, p. 428.

11 This seat was bought from Lord Archer for Lord Malpas (about him see below, p. 440, n. 3) to make him desist from opposing Lord Milton at Dorchester; see MSS. 32734, ff. 19, 69, 361-3, and 32735, ff. 34 and 52-6. Archer wrote to Roberts on 8 Apr 1754 that his agent was going down to Steyning and Bramber and that he 'has always carried the cash with him, which he proposes to do now, having a guard come up from those two places to escort him. I therefore desire the £1500 which must be in cash, may be paid this evening or early to-morrow morning' (32734, f. 64).

12 See 32995, ff. 64, 70, 188, 199.

13 This was for Grampound; see below, p. 349. In a paper dated

only £26,555 is obtained for the general election of 1754. It was stated at the end of Roberts's paper of 15 March 1754 that he and Dupplin were to peruse Pelham's letters relating to

9 Apr 1754 (*ibid.* f. 205) the sum of £2000 is named as paid to Edgcumbe for Cornish elections ; but part of this was returned by the candidates.

[14] In Roberts's paper of 15 Mar 1754 (*ibid.* f. 67) : 'Dunwich . . . Sir Jacob Downing [to be one Member] and offers the other Member to the D. of N. for £1000'. The seat was bought for Soame Jenyns, a friend of the Yorkes, on his being shifted from Cambridgeshire in order to accommodate Lords Royston and Granby in the county.

[15] On behalf of Sir Thomas Clavering ; see above, p. 198, and also 32995, f. 126.

[16] This payment was made on 8 May 1754 ; at the end of Mar, Porter was prepared for a compromise with his opponents, who offered to buy him off with £1200 — he claimed by then to have spent £1750 ; he left the matter to Newcastle to decide, and it was stated afterwards that the compromise was broken off by the Duke's command ; see 32734, f. 305, 32735, f. 201, and 32995, f. 104. See, however, paper of 21 Mar 1754 (32995, f. 114) — it appears that Porter stood on James West's interest, and the remark is added : 'Mr. Ald^n Porter desires not to give it up' ; see also ff. 195 and 203.

[17] There is no positive evidence of this payment having been made for election purposes. But Ralph Jenison, M.P. for Northumberland 1723–41, and for Newport (I.o.W.) 1749–58, held no private pension in 1754, while extra payments which he received as Master of the Buckhounds appear in the ordinary Civil List accounts. Moreover his letter to Henry Pelham of 18 Feb 1754 seems to suggest that this payment was for his election ; see above, pp. 131-2.

[18] Job Staunton Charlton was Newcastle's manager in Nottinghamshire, and in this election Newcastle was really financing his own borough interest. The opponent was a merchant, Thomas Delaval, a brother of Francis Blake and John Hussey Delaval ; he was no Tory, merely an intruder, and was supported by Dr. Wilson, a Newark clergyman who at other times worked for Newcastle but who had a personal quarrel with Charlton. About this election see 32733, ff. 204, 206, 253, 569, 598, and 621 ; 32734, ff. 102, 104, 109, 111, 371-5, and 389-91 ; 32735, ff. 42, 470, and 575. On 27 Mar 1754 Charlton sent Newcastle a paper (32734, f. 375) showing that there were 537 good votes at Newark, that he and his fellow candidate, John Manners, had 307 certain votes each, that each had already spent about £650, and that 'if no money be given' the further expense for each would amount to another £350.

'If money be given, will be added to the above expence to preserve our majority — if £5 per man to 120, half £300

> if £10 per man be given, then 150 is supposed must be purchased, the one half is £750.'

Charlton and Manners won the election, and on 15 June 1754 Charlton reported to Newcastle : 'election charges . . . daily increase by fresh demands, they are come up to almost 1700' (32735, f. 470). See also Dupplin's paper about Newark, 32995, f. 128.

[19] For a detailed account of the expenditure on this election, amounting to a total of £2281 : 1 : 6, see 32995, ff. 174-5 ; £500 was borne by Sir John Crosse. The heaviest items were tavern bills.

elections 'and extract from them whatever can be found therein'.[1] With the help of such information further lists were compiled, and it seems improbable that any large sums paid out by Henry Pelham for the general election escaped them or would not, in the further course of election business, have been brought to Newcastle's notice; nor does the sum of £35,000 for secret service in 1753 suggest any marked expenditure on the forthcoming general election. But what was £26,555? On the Oxfordshire election of 1754 the Tories alone spent £20,068 : 1 : 2,[2] and the Whigs hardly less :[3] expenditure in one single constituency thus exceeded the total spent by the Government in the whole of Great Britain. Again : at Bristol, according to Dean Tucker, £60,000 was spent on the two contests of 1754 and 1755.[4]

Barring the lump payment of £1000 to the Duke of Argyll for Scotland, the expenditure of secret service money at the general election of 1754 was made for 24 candidates; and of this money almost one-third was practically of no avail. The Whig candidates were defeated in Oxfordshire and were only seated on petition by a party vote in the House of Commons; Dodd lost his election at Reading by one vote; Tracy was given up, and lost his seat at Worcester; and the Government candidates were defeated at Wallingford by Richard Neville Aldworth, a Bedford Whig, and John Hervey, a Welsh judge.[5]

---

[1] *Ibid.* f. 67.

[2] See James Townsend, *The Oxfordshire Dashwoods* (1922), p. 28.

[3] See, *e.g.*, paper of 25 Mar 1754 (32995, ff. 126-36).

[4] See his letter to Hardwicke, 3 Jan 1761; 35596, f. 207. Other evidence seems to confirm the statement; thus, Newcastle wrote to the King on 6 Apr 1754 that Nugent and Hanbury, 'the great Quaker', had informed him of an express 'from the Whigs at Bristol, who had directed Mr. Hanbury to engage to indemnifie Mr. Nugent against all expences of his election . . . to the sum of £10,000 . . .'; 'one single man, a considerable Quaker in Bristol, has subscribed £500' (32735 ff. 48-9).

[5] The case of Hervey supplies a curious illustration of the politics of the time. Hervey, who had risen under Hardwicke's wing, wrote to him on 10 Jan 1754 :

I declared to Mr. Aldworth that in case I was returned for Wallingford I should vote in Parliament on the side of the Administration. . . . Indeed . . . it would have prejudiced my interest, if I had publicly declared my attachment to the Ministry, but it was so understood, which

In short, the ideas about the importance of secret service money in elections, certainly in so far as the general election of 1754 was concerned, are greatly exaggerated. George II loved 'always . . . to have as great majorities as possible' in Parliament,[1] and Newcastle's anxious nature never allowed him to feel even comparatively safe unless he paid everybody and for everything. Actually by 1754 there was no real opposition, the number of 'Whigs' was growing continually, and the difficulty of Administration was 'to find pasture enough for the beasts that they must feed'.[2] Had all the 24 elections financed from secret service funds gone against the Government, which, on Newcastle's own findings, had a majority of 213,[3] some places or pensions might have been saved but the Government would have suffered no harm.

Of the regular Government boroughs practically none appears in the list of special disbursements made at the general election — they had to be nursed year by year and mainly by means other than secret service money. Neither Harwich nor Orford is mentioned, nor Queenborough, nor any of the Admiralty boroughs or of the Cinque Ports ; nor the numerous west country boroughs in which the Government arranged the purchase of seats for its supporters, cash being provided by the candidates, and patronage and favours by the Government ; nor the still more numerous boroughs in which the interest of patrons and candidates required the countenance of Adminis-

---

made some not so zealous in my interest as otherwise they would have been (35592, ff. 6-7).

And again on 20 Jan :

This morning I saw Mr. Pelham. We talked over the affair of Wallingford and I made him all the assurances I could, and sincerely, of my steady attachment to the Administration. He said he was perswaded it was so, but that I was so unhappily linked he must oppose me. At parting he called to me in this manner, Hearken, Hervey, we'l fight it out in the countrey, and be good friends in town (35592, f. 23).

The election was fought out 'in the countrey', and Hervey was one of the 'opponents' whom secret service money did not succeed in keeping out of the House.—For some of the reasons of the Government defeat at Wallingford, see letter from Robert Nedham to Mrs. Hucks, 9 Jan 1755 (32852, f. 128).

[1] Newcastle to Devonshire, 17 Jan 1756 ; 32862, f. 122.
[2] Chesterfield to S. Dayrolles, 16 Nov 1753.
[3] See his 'Memds. for the King', 20 May 1754 ; 32735, f. 298.

tration, giving it therefore an influence in the choice of representatives. The price of this system of indirect subsidies was enormous but incalculable, for it is obviously impossible to estimate how much of the salary paid to a placeman was remuneration for work done, and how much was a political sinecure; or how much the public interest suffered by men being preferred for political reasons where personal qualifications and merit should have decided.

To this indirect expenditure the annual payments made from secret service funds in some boroughs under Government management, or under patrons favoured by the Government, formed an insignificant addition : there was a yearly bounty of £100 at Harwich; at Orford £200 for the rent of houses to provide the necessary qualification for out-voters in the Government interest, and £100 for other expenses; £200 a year was spent on Okehampton, and £70 a year was paid to Manly, the manager at Taunton; £120 a year was paid for two years by Clevland to an unnamed clergyman for an unnamed election; £100 was paid by Gashry to Lady Trelawny;[1] £550 a year was given for Cambridge through Montfort, Dupplin, or C. S. Cadogan[2] — presumably because Newcastle, as Chancellor of Cambridge University, took a particular interest even in the town. Beginning with July 1756 a subsidy of £600 a year was paid to Thomas Holmes for nursing five seats in three Isle of Wight boroughs (Newport, Newton, and Yarmouth). Thomas Pitt, the prodigal brother of William Pitt, had a pension of £1000 p.a. for having ceded to the Government the patronage of two seats at Old Sarum and one at Okehampton, and whatever interest he possessed at Grampound or Camelford; but as

[1] The character of this payment is not quite clear. In a memorandum of 26 Apr 1755 (32996, f. 91), the entry appears : 'Mr. Gashry. Cornish borough. Sir John Trelawney, £200.' No such payment was made at the time, and Trelawny died early in 1756 (about him see p. 321). In Nov 1756, just before Newcastle resigned, the entry occurs : 'Mr. Gashry has advanced Lady Trelawney £100' (32997, f. 68 ; also ff. 70 and 74), and the money was repaid to him on 6 Nov 1756. I suppose the payment was connected with the Trelawny interest at Looe, and I therefore include it here.

[2] Thomas, second Lord Montfort, sat for Cambridge 1754–55, when he succeeded to the peerage, Lord Dupplin from 1741 till be succeeded his father as Lord Kinnoull in 1758, and Montfort's brother-in-law, C. S. Cadogan, 1749–54 and 1755–76.

his pension was on the Irish Establishment, it does not enter into these accounts. From 1757 onwards, £100 was paid to Henry Fane in support of his family interest at Lyme Regis, and was much appreciated by him — he wrote to Newcastle on 29 May 1762, three days after the Duke had resigned the Treasury :

Mr. Henry Fane presents his most respectful compliments to His Grace the Duke of Newcastle, with many thanks for the 75l. for his freinds at Lyme. As he is not well versed in the political system of this country, he cannot tell what to say on the late changes he hears of amongst the Great ; but wishes his Lyme friends may meet with so good a paymaster as his Grace has been to them.[1]

The total of disbursements made on elections and the nursing of boroughs from secret service funds during Newcastle's first term at the Treasury, March 1754 to November 1756, was as follows :

On the general election of 1754 [2]	.	£22,305 0 0
On seven by-elections [3]	.	8,901 11 0
On the nursing of constituencies [4]	.	5,010 0 0
		£36,216 11 0

[1] 32939, f. 93. The £75 covered three quarters till Lady Day.

[2] The payments made in the lifetime of Henry Pelham are not included.

[3] £2000 was spent on the by-election at Bristol in Feb 1756, which the Whig lost by 71 votes on a poll of almost 5000. £4675 was spent on the by-election of Dec 1754 at Taunton, where Robert Webb, a local man who had represented the borough 1747–54, withdrew, foreseeing that the expense would amount to £5000, and the leading Dissenters turned to Newcastle for a candidate 'most agreable to His Majesty and likily readily to go thro' with the necessary expence' (32736, f. 25). £173 was spent on Radnorshire (see pp. 254-55), £500 on Dodd's election at Reading, £100 at Old Sarum, and £1000 had to be reimbursed on this occasion to Sir William Irby under a complicated arrangement, £313 : 11s. at Hindon ('If no help is to be had in a venal borough, venal boroughs must go to your enemies', wrote Henry Fox, at that time Secretary of State, to Newcastle on 11 Jan 1756 ; see 32862, ff. 79-80, and also ff. 61-3 and ff. 81-2), and £140 at Totnes.

[4] Harwich £300 ; Orford £800 ; Isle of Wight boroughs £600 ; Cambridge Town £1650 ; Okehampton £380 ; Manly of Taunton £140 ; Bryer of Weymouth £200 ; Cleveland's clergyman £240 ; Lady Trelawny £100 ; Thomas Rivett £600. Manly was Newcastle's election agent at Taunton. Less clear is the case of Bryer of Weymouth. Various Members had friends for whom they managed to obtain pensions from secret service funds, but this does not prove their having been election agents for their patrons (thus there is nothing to show that Mr. Cooke, 'Mr. Gybbon's

A total of £115,365 : 1s. of secret service money was spent through Roberts from March 1754 to November 1756 ; and although this period includes the best part of a general election, only 31·5 per cent of the money was used for elections and the nursing of boroughs.

The expenditure on by-elections, the nursing of boroughs, etc., during the time from Newcastle's return to the Treasury in July 1757, to the death of George II on 25 October 1760, was naturally even less ; adding the arrears paid off under George III, it amounted to £14,747 : 10s. out of a total of about £127,000 spent during this period. There were the payments to boroughs under regular Government management (Harwich, Orford, Cambridge, and Okehampton) and subsidies for the management of the Isle of Wight boroughs, of Lyme, Taunton, Derby, Yarmouth, Retford, Weymouth, and Rye, making a total of £9847 : 10s. Duckett [1] was paid £1500 (a pension of £500 p.a.) for vacating his seat at Calne when Pitt required one for Dr. Hay. Thomas Pitt extorted £1000 from the Treasury over Pulteney's re-election at Old Sarum in December 1759, [2] £300 was spent in law charges at Rye, £300 on a by-election at Camelford, [3] £500 was given to Colonel Leslie for Perth Burghs, and £300 to Baikie for the Orkneys with a view to the approaching general election of 1761. Lastly, £500 was paid on 25 July 1760 'to the Earl of Lincoln, as High Steward of Westminster, for the expences of the Deputy Steward and Court of Burgesses in order to secure the election without any further expence',

---

friend', either lived at Rye or ever acted for him). Similarly, there are a number of local people in receipt of secret service pensions about which I have no evidence that they were given with a view to cultivating the Parliamentary interest (Mr. Till of Chichester, Dr. Thorpe of Hastings, etc.). But where a man obtained a secret service pension through a Member representing the borough, the presumption is that it was for election services. Bryer's pension was obtained for him through Welbore Ellis, Member for Weymouth, and is included in expenditure on nursing con-stituencies. Lastly there is Thomas Rivett, the Duke of Devonshire's 'chief friend and manager' at Derby, who at a by-election in 1748 had himself returned against the Duke's candidate, but stood down in 1754 and received a pension of £300 p.a. which by Nov 1756 accounted for £600.

[1] See my essay on 'Thomas Duckett and Daniel Bull, Members for Calne', in the *Wiltshire Archaeol. Magazine*, vol. xliv, June 1928.

[2] See 32899, ff. 19, 53, and 325-6.   [3] See below, p. 343.

P

and another £500 on 12 January 1762 to cover his expenses up to Christmas 1760 [1] (besides £625 on 25 May 1762 to cover them up to Lady Day of that year).

Deducting the seven and a half months of the Devonshire-Pitt Administration in 1756–57, Newcastle was, between the death of Henry Pelham and that of George II, nearly six years at the head of the Treasury. During that period, in round figures, £243,000 was spent in 'secret service', of which £51,000, *i.e.* slightly more than one-fifth, was used for elections and expenditure directly connected with them.

A month after the accession of George III the new Court, to advertise its virtue, announced that none of the 'King's money' would be employed in the forthcoming general election; Newcastle broke out into his usual lamentations, and a few writers of letters and memoirs made malicious remarks on the subject: materials for an historical legend. Thus Hunt writes in his *History of England, 1760–1801* : [2]

> The court spread the idea that it was for purity of election; it was known that Newcastle's hands were tied, and it was expected that no money would be issued from the treasury. Nothing was less true. Corruption was rampant and the treasury issued large sums.

Neither statement is correct. It was Newcastle who managed the general election of 1761, and no money for it was issued from the Treasury; none was available for secret service between 25 October 1760 and 19 March 1761 — at least there is no entry in the Civil List accounts which could cover payments of that character, nor any disbursement in Newcastle's books; nor, after the secret service fund had been set to work once more, are there any entries, other than those connected with the regular nursing of certain constituencies, which might bear retrospectively on that general election. Those who assert that Bute 'secretly made full use of the coffers' of the Treasury [3] should explain how he managed it, through whom, and on what warrant.

---

[1] This payment, though part of the arrears, is entered in the 'new book'.
[2] P. 19.
[3] See, *e.g.*, the Earl of Ilchester, *Henry Fox, First Lord Holland*, vol. ii, p. 129.

In reality, the money expended by the Government in general elections constituted only a small addition to official patronage, and to the vast sums spent openly year after year on voters and Members through offices, sinecures, and contracts employed for advancing the Parliamentary 'interest'. This, of course, everyone knew at the time ; 'those powers of office and influence arising from thence', wrote Newcastle to Hardwicke on 7 December 1760, 'which my good friend Mr. Pitt says will be sufficient to carry a Parliament with some perhaps *immaterial* alterations, without giving one farthing of the King's money'.[1] And John Douglas, D.D. (subsequently Bishop of Salisbury), the political scribe of Lord Bath, thus argued the matter in his *Seasonable Hints from an Honest Man on the present important crisis of a new Reign and a new Parliament* :

I am very sensible, that there are many well-meaning persons who seem to think, that without corruption, there might be danger apprehended from democratical encroachments on prerogative.— But . . . when we consider, in how many boroughs the Government has the voters at its command ; when we consider the vast body of persons employed in the collection of the revenue in every part of the kingdom ; the inconceivable number of placemen, and candidates for places in the customs, in the excise, in the post office, in the dock yards, in the ordnance, in the salt office, in the stamps, in the navy and victualing offices, and in a variety of other departments ; when we consider again the extensive influence of the money corporations, subscription jobbers, and contractors ; the endless dependence created by the obligations conferred on the bulk of the gentlemen's families throughout the kingdom, who have relatives preferred, or waiting to be preferred, in our navy, and numerous standing army ; when, I say, we consider how wide, how binding a dependence on the crown is created by the above enumerated particulars, no lover of monarchy need fear any bad consequences from shutting up the Exchequer at elections ; especially when to the endless means the crown has of influencing the votes of the electors, we add the vast number of employments, which the fashion of the times makes the elected desirous of, and for the obtaining which, they must depend upon the crown.[2]

Newcastle at times suspected in the refusal of secret service money a wish on the part of Pitt for a radical Parliament —

[1] 32915, f. 334.   [2] Pp. 37-8.

'as like the Common Council of London as possible' — and a scheme of Bute's to swamp it with Tories, as had been done in 1710; but even he, in calmer moments, put the matter on much narrower ground. In 'Heads for my Conference with my Lord Bute', dated 14 December 1760, he wrote:

> The expence of several places I know already will be so very great, that it will be difficult to find private persons, able to be at it; and therefore we shall not have great choice.[1]

And again in a letter to Lord Mansfield, dated 26 December:

> The thing that embarrasses me most is the choice of the Parliament. The expence is become very great (in many places 3000£ is the price or near it) that it will be very difficult to get private persons to support it; and yet that must be done. But it will fling the boroughs into East Indians, West Indians, citizens and brokers, who are not very reputable, and yet very troublesome Members.[2]

In other words, secret service money was required to enable some country gentlemen to fight elections in expensive boroughs; or else the Government had to adopt candidates with longer purses of their own.

What was the result? Of the twenty-four candidates subsidized in 1754, eight were re-elected in 1761 for the same constituencies without financial help,[3] four were returned for other constituencies,[4] four had died,[5] and four did not seek re-election;[6] Thomas Leslie (who had received £500 before George II's death) was defeated; Sir Thomas Clavering, by his own choice, changed his constituency, but lost his seat;[7]

---

[1] 32916, f. 56.

[2] *Ibid.* ff. 337-8.—Later on, George III showed a similar dislike for these types of Members; in a letter to North, 24 Aug 1774, he gave it as a reason in favour of an early dissolution of Parliament, that 'it will fill the House with more gentlemen of landed property, as the nabobs, planters, and other volunteers are not ready for the battle' (Fortescue, vol. iii, pp. 125-6).

[3] Dodd, Bayntun-Rolt, Amyand, Trist, S. Martin, Fanshawe, M. Burrell, and E. Cornwallis.

[4] Lord Parker, Whitworth, Lord Malpas, and Jenyns.

[5] Talbot, H. Young, Porter, and Jenison.

[6] John Fuller, R. Bristow, Charlton, and Sir John Crosse.

[7] Sir Thomas Clavering vacated his seat at Shaftesbury in Dec 1760 to contest co. Durham, where he was defeated both in 1760 and 1761.

Sewell, defeated in 1754 at Wallingford, now met with the same fate at Exeter ; and possibly Sir George Yonge at Honiton did not stand because of the threatened expense — though even this is doubtful. There was neither an inrush of East Indians or West Indians, of citizens or brokers. In fact, the only West Indian who came in for any of these seats in 1761 was Sir John Gibbons at Wallingford, where the Government money was of no avail in 1754. And the number of merchants in these seats remained the same.[1] Nor, as is shown in the chapter on 'The General Election of 1761', was any such change noticeable in the general complexion of the House of Commons. William Pitt and John Douglas were right. The means for influencing elections were sufficient without the use of secret service money.

When payments from secret service funds were resumed in March 1761, the usual expenditure on the nursing of constituencies was continued and payments were made as from October 1760 ; the sum thus spent up to Newcastle's resignation on 26 May 1762 amounted to £4592 : 10s.[2] in a total of £48,981 : 9 : 2¾. Rounding off the figures, Newcastle as First Lord of the Treasury spent £291,000 on secret service, of which £55,500 went for constituencies and elections.

PENSIONS IN THE HOUSE OF COMMONS

Cognate to expenditure on constituencies and elections was that on pensions to Members of Parliament. These were but a small supplement to the eighteenth-century type of 'payment of Members', and that system itself must not be judged by standards alien to the age.

According to eighteenth-century theory, the executive, which had to carry on the business of the nation, consisted of

---

[1] The place of Alderman Porter at Evesham was taken by John Rushout, jun., but at Shaftesbury Samuel Touchet, a merchant, replaced Clavering.

[2] Isle of Wight £900, Cambridge £825, Okehampton £300, Orford £350, Harwich £150, the Orkneys £300, Lyme £125, Taunton £105, Westminster £625, Retford £62 : 10s., Yarmouth £300, Derby £450.

the King and his Ministers ; and the task of the legislature was to advise the King and to control his servants. The proper attitude for right-minded Members was one of considered support to the Government in the due performance of its task. What other grounds could there be for a 'formed opposition' than disloyalty to the established order (*e.g.* Jacobitism) or a selfish, factious conspiracy of politicians to force their way into offices higher than they could obtain by loyal co-operation with their Sovereign and his Ministers ? But if it was proper for the well-affected Member to co-operate with the Government, so long as his conscience permitted, attendance on the business of the nation was work worthy of its hire, and the unavoidable expenditure in securing a seat deserved sympathetic consideration. 'I have ever apprehended it to be reasonable', wrote in 1757 a Whig who, after seventeen years in Parliament, held neither place nor pension, 'that those who dedicate their time and fortune to the service of the Government should be entitled to a share of the rewards that are in its disposal'.[1] Nor did such a share necessarily deprive them of their independence — about 1750 even Cabinet Ministers could speak and vote against Government measures ; the one thing which place or office precluded, 'formed opposition', was anyhow considered reprehensible. Even in 1764, after the heat of Parliamentary contests had risen very high, George Grenville still argued, in the case of H. S. Conway, that he meant to leave every Member, whether in civil or military employment, free to vote according to his conscience, and that he drew the line only at systematic opposition. At the present day a Member may accept from his party organization payment of expenses incurred in his constituency ; when faced by financial disaster, some have applied, not unsuccessfully, to their Whips ; but a Member must not change sides from patently interested motives ; and he must, as a rule, vote with his party — discordant votes at the behest of a tender conscience have to be extremely rare or otherwise prove him unfit to be a party Member, which is the only type now in existence. The party intervenes between the individual Member and the State, and also between the

[1] J. Garth to Newcastle, 10 Sept 1757 ; 32873, f. 558.

Member and his constituency; it has created new loyalties, a new morality, and a new type of dishonesty.

'Every set of men are honest' was, according to Shelburne, Henry Fox's doctrine; 'it's only necessary to define their sense of it to know where to look for it.' This is even more true as between different generations; each age opens to men certain permissible ways for pursuing their own interest in politics, and provided they keep within these limits they are deemed honest. To quote Fox once more — he wrote to Shelburne on 29 December 1761:

> A man who follows his own interest, if he makes no undue sacrifices, either private or public, to the worship of it, is not dishonest or even dirty. I wish your Lordship . . . would not be so free of thinking or calling them such. Whoever goes on with what I have left off — ambition — must wish for such supporters, and it would be an additional curse of that cursed trade to have a constant bad opinion of one's most useful friends and most assiduous attendants.[1]

The peculiarity of our own time is that the individual Member can best pursue his interest by strictly adhering to his party, and that this is the only way in which he is entitled to pursue it. But about 1750 there were no parties in our sense of the term, certainly no party organizations, and His Majesty's Government and the State as such were in theory the party which embraced all well-affected Members. To adhere to them in spite of changes of Ministers did not necessarily mean changing sides, and to accept rewards from them was not necessarily synonymous with being bribed. Considering the matter from the other end, eighteenth-century Administrations, not being able to control individual Members through a party machine and a party-trained electorate, had to bind their following by honours, places of profit, contracts, and pensions; in these, Ministers had to find the attractive and constraining force to satisfy the self-interest, to tame the exuberance, and restrain the consciences of individual Members, which otherwise would have produced a condition of permanent instability and uncertainty. In 1784, after a Parliamentary

[1] Lord Fitzmaurice, *The Life of William, Earl of Shelburne*, vol. i, p. 101.

experience of almost forty years, Soame Jenyns, when writing on Parliamentary reform, declared that an independent Parliament consisting of Members 'unawed and uninfluenced, and guided only by the dictates of their own judgment and conscience', never existed and never could exist.

Take away self-interest, and all these will have no star to steer by . . .; a Minister . . . must be possessed of some attractive influence, to enable him to draw together these discordant particles, and unite them in a firm and solid majority, without which he can pursue no measures of public utility with steadiness or success. An independent House of Commons is no part of the English constitution. . . .

A numerous assembly uninfluenced is as much a creature of imagination, as a griffin or a dragon. . . . Parliaments have ever been influenced, and by that means our constitution has so long subsisted; but the end and nature of that influence is perpetually misrepresented and misunderstood. They are seldom, very seldom, bribed to injure their country, because it is seldom the interest of Ministers to injure it; but the great source of corruption is, that they will not serve it for nothing. Men get into Parliament in pursuit of power, honors, and preferments, and until they obtain them, determine to obstruct all business, and to distress Government; but happily for their country, they are no sooner gratified, than they are equally zealous to promote the one, and support the other.[1]

What was the approximate number of Members in the House of Commons thus rendered zealous by employments under the Government? It is very difficult to form an estimate, infinitely more so than appears to writers who hawk about a figure because it was once named by a contemporary. There is a list in the Newcastle Papers of 'Employments in the House of Commons'[2] compiled when the Rockingham Government was about to be formed, and dated 2 July 1765. It contains 163 names, and the selection, which is not invariably convincing, illustrates the inherent difficulties of making it. The Governor of the Bank of England is named as if that had been an official post, but nothing is said about Government contractors; even the Speaker of the House of Commons appears

---

[1] *Thoughts on a Parliamentary Reform* (1784), pp. 20-4.
[2] 32967, ff. 200-3.

in it, while others holding regular places of profit are forgotten. It was hard to remember everybody, and still harder to know where to draw the line; it would be difficult to say how to class those who had their places for life, and were therefore independent of the Government in power, but who often held another smaller place during pleasure; etc.[1] In short, the figure of 163 in 1765 should not be made into an Apocalyptic name for the Beast of Parliamentary corruption; it is given here merely as an approximate estimate whereby to measure the relative importance, or rather unimportance, of the secret service pensions in the House of Commons.

The number of Members in receipt of these was between 1754 and 1760 thirteen to fifteen,[2] and at the time of Newcastle's resignation, in May 1762, there were sixteen.[3] The number of Members of the House who received pensions or gratuities from secret service funds during Newcastle's time at the Treasury in the reign of George II was twenty-eight,

[1] A computation which I have made for June 1761 yields a figure of about 170 as the total of 'placemen'; this includes all Members holding civil appointments of any description — in the Government or Civil Service, the Diplomatic Service or Judiciary, posts at Court or in the household of other members of the Royal family, or mere sinecures; further, colonels of regiments, governors of castles, etc. It does not include the Speaker, the Governor of the Bank, Lord Lieutenants of counties, or officers in the Army and Navy holding nothing besides their commands; nor does it include contractors.

[2] The 'List of Members of Parliament who received private pensions with the arrears due to Michaelmas last, 1760' (33040, f. 23), contains eighteen names; but it includes Lord Holmes because of the payment of £600 p.a. 'for the Isle of Wight', which cannot be treated as a private pension and is in this essay included in expenditure on constituencies; and the Chairman of Committees whose pension of £500 p.a. is here counted among salaries; lastly, there is the name of Jeffreys with a justified query against it — so far he had no regular pension and had merely received a gratuity of £500 in 1758.

[3] In the 'General List of Persons who receive Additional Salaries and Pensions privately', dated 18 May 1762 (33040, ff. 358-60), the Members of Parliament are grouped together, and eighteen names are given. The payment to Lord Holmes is no longer placed among pensions to Members, but the Chairman of Committees appears among them; moreover, Lord Malpas is included, though there is no record of his having received any payment from secret service funds later than 21 Apr 1761, and Dugall Campbell, who had none under George III, not even the arrear of £200 due to him at Michaelmas 1760. This leaves fifteen, to whom Richard Bull must be added: he had been in receipt of a pension as from Lady Day 1761.

and the total paid to them (including arrears) was £49,900. When payments were resumed in March 1761 the pensions were continued as from October 1760, and a total of twenty-one Members of Parliament received pensions from Newcastle under George III. All but six were men whose names had appeared in the secret service books under George II (and of these six, four, if not five, were given their pensions at Newcastle's recommendation).[1] The sum received by them for the period October 1760 till May 1762 was £14,775, making a total of £64,675 for the seven and a half years of Newcastle's term at the Treasury and an average of £8600 p.a. In fact, the pay roll of Members of Parliament as it stood in April 1756 (excluding the Chairman of Committees) was £6700 a year; £8200 in October 1760, and £10,400 in May 1762,[2] sums much smaller than the talk about secret service pensions and 'bribes' would make one expect. If to this £64,675 £4000 is added, representing pensions continued to ex-Members,[3] we obtain a total of £68,675.

On the opposite page are the names of all the men who were given by Newcastle pensions and gratuities from secret service funds while in the House of Commons, the rate at which they were paid, the period during which they drew their pensions, and the sum total received by them (for biographical notes about them see footnotes to the 'Secret Service Accounts' at the end of volume).

[1] The doubtful case is Richard Bull, the friend and nominee of Humphrey Morice, M.P., who had been offered a pension by Newcastle in Mar 1761 but refused it both on its own merits and because of an alleged 'disgrace' put on Morice by Newcastle. In Oct 1761 he informed Newcastle, on instructions from Morice (then at Naples), that Morice had desired the King to nominate to a vacancy which was expected at his borough of Newport (Cornwall), and would not accept Newcastle's directions (see secret service accounts under 18 Nov 1761). Considering, however, Newcastle's nature, he may again have suggested to the King that Bull should be given a pension.

[2] The marked increase was due to a pension of £2000 p.a. given by George III to James Stuart Mackenzie, M.P., brother of Lord Bute, on his relinquishing the Turin Embassy in 1761. It no longer appears in the two Windsor lists of 1763 and 1764, and presumably ceased when Mackenzie was appointed in Apr 1763 Keeper of the Privy Seal of Scotland.

[3] This sum consists of £2100 paid to Sir Duncan Campbell, R. Neale, and J. Carmichael after they had left Parliament in 1754, and £1900 paid to J. Mordaunt, J. Pelham, and R. Colebrooke, after 1761.

A more motley crowd than the thirty-five Members in this list can hardly be imagined, and the variety in type is only equalled by the variety of reasons for which these pensions

	Period during which Received [1]	Annual Pension	Total Received
		£	£
Thomas Medlycott . .	1754–62	600	4700
George Mackay [2] . .	1754–56	300	900
Colonel John Mordaunt [3] .	1754–61	800	5100
S. Jenyns [4] . . .	1754–55	600	1200
Sir C. Powlett [5] . .	1754	1000	1000
Colonel James Pelham [6] .	1754–61	500	4125
Sir William Middleton, Bt. [7]	1754–55	800	2400
Sir Francis Poole [8] . .	1754–62	300	2675
Brereton Salusbury [9] .	1754–55	500	1000
G. Harrison . . .	1754–55	500	1000
A. Acourt [10] . . .	1754–62	500	4625
John Buller [11] . . .	1755–56	200	400
Dugall Campbell . .	1755–60	400	2000
Thomas Fane [12] . .	1755	200	200
Charles Whitworth .	1755–60	400 (From 1785, £200)	1700
James Vere [13] . . .	1756–59	400	1200
George Brudenell . .	1756–62	500	3625
Robert Colvile . . .	1756–58	300	600
Lord Malpas . . .	1756–60	600	3000
Robert Colebrooke [14] .	1756–61	600	3000
John Offley . . .	1758–62	400	1900
Thomas Watson . .	1758–62	800	3400
Ralph Jenison [15] . .	1758	1800	1350
John Dodd . . .	1758–62	500	2500
Robert Fairfax [16] . .	1759–62	500	2000
Lord Parker . . .	1760–62	600	1650
A. T. Keck . . .	1760–62	600	1350
John Jeffreys [17] . .	1761–62	500	1250
Richard Cavendish . .	1761–62	800	800
Sir Thomas Hales . .	1761–62	600	600
Henry Finch [18] . .	1761	900	225
Richard Bull . . .	1761–62	600	600
James Stuart Mackenzie .	1761–62	2000	2000
James Brudenell . .	1761–62	600	600

(*For footnotes 1 to 18 see below and following page*)

[1] Payments received between Nov 1756 and July 1757 are not included, and there is no certainty that all these pensions were continued during that break in Newcastle's tenure of office.

[2] Appointed in 1756 Master of the Mint in Scotland.

[3] He did not stand at the general election of 1761, but his pension was continued. He must not be confused with his cousin General Sir John

were given. Two general principles can, however, be laid down with regard to them : that as a rule they were given in lieu of places, and that there was more jobbery and charity about them than bribery.

Secret service pensions were on the whole unpopular with Members of Parliament, except with those in acute financial distress, and were treated in most cases as a temporary arrangement pending something better. They offered neither the security nor the chances of advancement inherent in office, and certainly conferred no honour on their holders. When in 1757, on a rearrangement of offices necessitated by the Coalition, Ralph Jenison gave up the Mastership of the Buckhounds, which he had held for eighteen years, and was offered as com-

Mordaunt, M.P., who commanded the expedition against the French coast in 1757.

[4] Appointed in 1755 Commissioner for Trade and Plantations, which office he retained till 1780.

[5] His father succeeded in 1754 to the dukedom of Bolton, and Lord Winchester, as he now was, was appointed Lieutenant of the Tower of London ; on this appointment the pension was discontinued.

[6] He did not stand again at the general election, and died on 27 Dec 1761 ; £250 received by him for that last half-year, when he was no longer in Parliament, is not included in the sum.

[7] He died on 28 Sept 1757. The last yearly payment was made to him by Newcastle on 21 May 1756. Whether he received one in 1757, before Newcastle's return to the Treasury, is uncertain.

[8] An extra £200 was given him in Nov 1756.

[9] He died on 9 Mar 1756.

[10] He seems to have been so indifferent to the money that sometimes for two years he did not trouble to draw it.

[11] John Buller was Government manager for the boroughs of East and West Looe in Cornwall, and this payment was to make up his salary as Comptroller of the Mint to £500 p.a., but was not continued after 1756. See below, pp. 321-23

[12] He was given the pension on his brother Francis relinquishing a Commissionership of the Board of Trade, in Dec 1755. He waived it in 1758. See accounts under 2 Nov 1756 and 1 July 1758.

[13] Identification confirmed by 32997, f. 237.

[14] He was defeated at the general election of 1761, but the pension was continued to him till he was appointed Minister to the Swiss Cantons ; during that time he received another £450, not included above.

[15] He died before the year was out.

[16] At first these payments were treated as 'gratuities', but subsequently were converted into a pension. About him see below, pp. 413-17.

[17] This includes a gratuity of £500 in 1758 ; about him see below, pp. 402-6.

[18] He died after one quarter only had been paid.

pensation a secret service pension of £1500, he replied by asking
that £1000 of it be placed on the Irish Establishment, as secret
service pensions depended upon the life of the King.[1] Also
Medlycott begged in 1755 to be 'settled upon the Irish Establishment'.[2] Richard Bull, the friend and nominee of Humphrey
Morice, M.P., instructed by him 'to accept of nothing from
the Duke [of Newcastle], except what will give me an honourable reason for saying I am contented', refused a secret service
pension : 'Now, my Lord, your kind offer to me, being of an
uncertain duration, and of rather too private a nature, I cannot
consistent with my own and my friend's honor, accept it'. [3]
Charles Whitworth, who had for years solicited employment,
when given a secret service pension of £400 p.a., did not desist
from his endeavours to secure office, and when the Deputy-
Governorship of Tilbury was secured for him, Newcastle
thought that he would accept a place of half the value of his
pension as a sufficient equivalent.[4] John Buller silently dropped
his pension in 1756, and merely used this fact subsequently to
reinforce his claim to office. Thomas Fane, who was given a
pension of £200 on his brother relinquishing a place at the
Board of Trade, drew it once and then gave it up for half the
sum to be paid to his brother Henry as a subsidy for their

[1] 32872, ff. 55-7.
[2] See below, p. 407. In view of these requests it might be supposed
that pensions on the Irish Establishment were used extensively for bribing
Members of the British Parliament. A 'List of Pensioners on the Irish
Establishment laid before the Irish House of Commons, pursuant to their
order of November 3, 1769' was published in The London Museum in 1770
(pp. 17-27). It contains the names of four men only who at any time sat
in the British Parliament ; and all four were given their pensions for life,
and for work done. A pension of £800 a year was given to John Roberts
on 3 June 1754, i.e. after the death of Henry Pelham, whose private
secretary he had been for twenty years (moreover at that time Roberts was
not yet in Parliament) ; a pension of £2000 p.a. was given to Sir Thomas
Robinson (subsequently Lord Grantham) in 1755, on his relinquishing the
Secretaryship of State to Henry Fox ; in 1758, £500 p.a. to J. S. Charlton,
in exchange for a place which he had held in the Ordnance, 1751-8 ; and in
Mar 1760, after the victory in Quiberon Bay, Admiral Sir Edward Hawke
was given a pension of £2000 a year.
[3] 17 Mar 1761, 32920, f. 308 ; see below, p. 476, under 18 Nov 1761.
[4] See 'State of Private Pensions', drawn up early in 1758 (33039, f. 77).
To those under 'Decrease' is added Whitworth's pension of £400, though
with a query before his name.

family borough of Lyme Regis. At least eighteen out of the thirty-four pensions can be proved to have been given either as compensation for places relinquished (Salusbury, Jenison, Offley, Fane, Cavendish, and Finch), or to make up the value of a place to a certain sum (Pelham, Buller, Jeffreys, and Whitworth after 1758), or until their holders could be provided for in office (Mackay, Jenyns, Colebrooke, Keck, Hales, James Brudenell, Bull, Stuart Mackenzie, and Whitworth until 1758).

Nor were most of the recipients of secret service pensions men who would otherwise have gone into opposition. Colonel Pelham and Sir Francis Poole were cousins of Newcastle, returned by his influence, and their pensions were sheer family jobbery on his part; and when he resigned in November 1756, to them alone their pensions for the current year were paid before they were due. Whitworth was by marriage distantly connected with the Pelham family. Jeffreys, Offley, Dodd, and George Brudenell belonged to the intimate circle of Lord Lincoln, Newcastle's nephew and heir, and son-in-law to Henry Pelham. Soame Jenyns was a protégé of the Hardwicke family, and Robert Colebrooke was a brother of James and George Colebrooke, both Members of Parliament and big merchants bound by numerous interests and contracts to the Treasury and Newcastle. Keck was returned to Parliament by the Duke of Marlborough, and received his pension because, wrote Newcastle, 'His Majesty was very glad of an opportunity to oblige your Grace',[1] but the Duke's attitude certainly was not determined by that pension; Richard Cavendish was given his pension because the Duke of Devonshire asked it as a favour to himself, but no one can suppose that without it the Cavendishes would have gone into opposition to Newcastle; nor was there any need for George III and Bute to bribe his brother, James Stuart Mackenzie. Nor were Medlycott, Jeffreys, or Fairfax of the stuff of which oppositions are made.[2]

The charitable character of the secret service pensions is further shown by the fact that in many cases they were continued after their recipients had left Parliament. In 1760 the

---

[1] See below, p. 464.
[2] About them see chapter on 'Parliamentary Beggars', pp. 402-25.

death of the King, from whose 'bounty' these pensions had
been given, and the break in payments for almost half a year,
would have offered a particularly good opportunity for stopping
them to those who did not stand for Parliament at the forthcoming general election. None the less, they were continued
both to Colonel Mordaunt (whose pension was even raised by
£400 p.a.) and to James Pelham ; and also to Robert Colebrooke
who lost his seat. But while offices, places, and even pensions,
when publicly avowed, had to bear some proportion to the rank,
standing, and merit of their holders (for whatever was given in
excess to any man was certain to be made into a precedent, a
claim, or a grievance by all his equals), secret service pensions
could be readjusted to needs. Two entries in Newcastle's
'Memorandums for the King' about a pension for Sir Thomas
Hales, Vice-Warden of the Cinque Ports and Clerk of the
Green Cloth, well illustrate this principle.

March 11, 1761.

Sir Thomas Hales.   Two sons and four daughters. Hopes to
                     have £800 per ann. amongst them till some
                     thing may fall to provide for some of them.[1]

March 19, 1761.

Pension for Sir Thomas Hales's children.
£600 for his son.[2]

THE ARISTOCRATIC DOLE

Even more clearly apparent was the benevolent character
of secret service pensions 'in the Lords' : a bounty given by the
King to men of rank in distress. On page 222 is a list of peers
who received such pensions from Newcastle, indicating the
years during which they drew these pensions, their annual
rate, and the total received ; the list includes at the end a few
Scottish and Irish peers but does not include those who received
their pensions as 'additional salaries'. For biographical notes
see again footnotes to the 'Accounts'.

Who were these peers in receipt of secret service pensions ?
Were they broad-acred noblemen who through their tenants

<hr>

[1] 32920, ff. 102-3.   [2] *Ibid.* f. 315.

could sway county elections, or owners of rotten boroughs who from the Upper House packed the Commons ? Neither ; in most cases they were men who had inherited titles without estates, and possessed little land and no boroughs. John

	Period during which Received [1]	Annual Pension	Total Received
		£	£
The Earl of Warrington .	1754–58	1,500	6,000
The Earl of Radnor . .	1754–56	800	2,000
The Earl of Peterborough .	1754–62	400	3,100
The Earl of Warwick [2] .	1754–62	500	4,500
The Earl of Tankerville .	1756–62	800	4,700
Viscount Saye and Sele .	1754–62	600	4,200
Lord Raymond. . .	1754–56	800	2,400
Lord Dudley . . .	1754–56	600	1,800
Lord Willoughby of Parham [3]	1755–62	400	2,800
Lord Montfort . .	1758–62	800	4,200
Lord Delamer . . .	1761–62	800	800
The Earl of Kinnoull [4] .	1754–58	800	3,200
The Earl of Home . .	1754–58	200	800
The Earl of Leven . .	1754	500	500
Lord Morton's Lords [5] .	1754–62	250 (after 1759 £150)	1,700
The Earl of Cork . .	1756–62	800	4,400
			47,100

Robartes, fourth and last Earl of Radnor of that creation, had succeeded his cousin in the title, while most of the estates and the Parliamentary influence in Cornwall went to a nephew of the third Earl, George Hunt, M.P. for Bodmin. Edward Rich, eighth and last Earl of Warwick, did not receive with his title any of the family estates. The similar case of Lord Saye

[1] Payments made between Nov 1756 and July 1757 are not included in these accounts.

[2] He died in 1758, but the pension was continued at the same rate to his widow and to his daughter, Lady Charlotte Rich, and is here included.

[3] He held, besides, a pension of £200 a year 'payable per Paymaster'. See 33044, f. 9.

[4] He had, besides, a hereditary pension of £1000 p.a. which had been granted to the fourth Earl and his heirs by Charles II on the surrender of their 'fee' of Barbadoes and the Carribee Islands.

[5] Lords Rutherfurd (£150), Kirkcudbright, and Borthwick (£50 each) ; Lord Rutherfurd died in 1759, but one-third of his pension was continued to his widow.

and Sele has been mentioned.[1] Ferdinando, eleventh and last Lord Dudley, succeeded his uncle in that title, while the barony of Ward and the castle and lands of Dudley devolved on the Ward family. Lord Cork succeeded his distant cousin Richard, fourth Earl of Cork and third Earl of Burlington, in his Irish honours, while the barony of Clifford and the large estates of the Clifford and Boyle families descended to his cousin's daughter, Charlotte, Duchess of Devonshire. Thomas, second Lord Montfort, inherited his estate 'in a very ruinous condition', and 'incumbered with debts to the amount of above £30,000'.[2] Lord Delamer was heir to a barony and to the poverty of the Earl of Warrington. The Earl of Kinnoull was so poor that when his son, Lord Dupplin, married Miss Ernle, the heiress to Whetham in Wiltshire, 'with £3000 p.a.',[3] this was considered a sad *mésalliance* for her;[4] but Dupplin was a close friend and faithful drudge of the Pelhams, which may have helped his father to the pension. As for 'Lord Morton's Lords', so far none of them had been able to establish his claim to the title, to say nothing of estates; William Maclellan, Lord Kirkcudbright, 'was in poor circumstances, and followed the occupation of a glover in Edinburgh';[5] Henry, Lord Borthwick, claimed a dignity which some of his predecessors had refrained from assuming, considering that 'a title without a suitable fortune was not eligible';[6] while the position of George Durie, Lord Rutherford, can be gauged by the letter he wrote to Newcastle on 12 October 1757: 'I have for these three years past payed a hundred pounds yearly to my creditors in London which put it out of my power to doe any thing to purpose for my creditors in Scotland with whom I'm just now teased out of my life'.[7] In short, most of the men in this list can be described as noblemen living on the dole or on old age pensions; for these were not invented by modern Radicals, only their wide application is a sign of democracy and a concomitant of universal suffrage.

[1] See above, pp. 178-80. [2] 32864, f. 524.
[3] *Gentleman's Magazine*, 1741, p. 331.
[4] It is described as such in a letter from her cousin, Miss Frances Ernle, to Mrs. Legh of Caveley, in Cheshire (Money-Kyrle MSS.).
[5] See Douglas-Paul, *Scots Peerage*. [6] *Ibid.* [7] 32875, f. 64.

Q

The theory of the 'State paupers' is probably as old as the State itself : those who form the political nation have, when in need, a claim to public support to be given them as their due, without loss of rank or citizen rights. Tacitus wrote of the Germanic warriors that they expected to be supported by their leader; and in France, during the 'Guerre du Bien Public', in 1466, the Duc de Nemours demanded from Louis XI that he should have justice done to the people and relieve them, and besides, that he should entertain the nobles *et leur donner grosses pensions*.[1] The same principle still prevailed in eighteenth-century England and was stated by Hardwicke, in 1762, in the case of Lord Willoughby of Parham, for whom he had originally obtained the secret service pension. On 28 July 1762 — two months after Newcastle had been driven from office — Bute mentioned to Hardwicke that he had neither seen Willoughby 'nor knew where to send to him'. Hardwicke, having acquainted Willoughby with what Bute had said, received the reply that he had determined not to apply to Bute for this favour, thinking that it might be displeasing to Newcastle and Hardwicke; but that if Hardwicke did not forbid him, he would now write to Bute. Hardwicke thereupon asked Newcastle's opinion about the matter, adding:

I look upon such pensions as a kind of obligation upon the Crown for the support of ancient noble families, whose peerages happen to continue after their estates are worn out; and that they ought not to be stopp'd upon any change of Ministry or measures; and I have so good an opinion of our friend that I don't believe he would suffer his conduct to be influenc'd by it in any material point.[2]

Newcastle replied on 19 August: 'You have done very right about Lord Willoughby of Parham'.[3]

A similar plea was put forward by Lord Powis in favour of a pension for Lord Hereford; he wrote to Newcastle on 14 June 1760,[4] that he knew 'how necessary in that respect is the

---

[1] Lavisse, *Histoire de France*, vol. iv, part ii, p. 344.
[2] Hardwicke to Newcastle, 12 Aug. 1762; 32941, ff. 210-11.
[3] *Ibid*. f. 304.
[4] 32907, f. 231. For a previous entry on this subject see Newcastle's 'Mem⁸ for the King' of 12 Sept 1756 (32867, ff. 290-91):
[5] Lord Powis. Ld. Visct. Hereford's sons education £600 p.a.

aid of the Crown — not only in support of the dignity of the peerage, but of his Lordship, his two sons and two daughters. They are all, from 14 to 20 years of age.' And he added in a postscript : 'I have omitted to observe that Lord Hereford's younger children are unprovided for : nor is it . . . in his power to do anything for them'; implying obviously that it was for the King to provide for them in these circumstances. A pension was granted to Hereford, but not out of secret service money.

The rule that noblemen in distress should be provided for by the Crown without any regard to politics signally appears in the case of Lord Aston, who, in the first place, was only a Scottish peer ; secondly, was a Roman Catholic, and therefore excluded from active politics ; and thirdly, never succeeded in definitely establishing his claim to the title. Lady Temple wrote to her husband on 6 January 1761 : [1]

You have heard a story of a cook who is become Lord Aston, and the Roman Catholics allow him a hundred a year. My Lord Bute went from the King to the Duchess of Norfolk, to say that His Majesty could not hear of a peer in that distress, though of a different religion, without contributing to his maintenance ; therefore had sent by Lord Bute two hundred pounds, to be disposed of to Lord Aston in the manner she thought proper. . . . I should add, that Lord Bute told her Grace this was to be continued every year out of his Privy Purse, which she told the cook Lord.[2]

Another example of such undenominational charity to men who were gentle but poor, was the pension of £500 p.a. from secret service funds to Sir Henry Bedingfeld, third Baronet, who too was a Roman Catholic.

Adding his pension (which during the years 1754–60 makes a total of £3000) to the aristocratic dole, we find that around £50,000 was spent on it by Newcastle from secret service funds.

---

[1] *Grenville Papers*, vol. i, p. 358.

[2] He died on 25 Mar. 1763, and an obituary notice in the *Gentleman's Magazine* (p. 146) stated :

Lord Aston, Baron Forfar of Scotland . . . was a few years ago cook to Sir [Charles] Mordaunt, bart., when the title descended to him ; he is succeeded by Mr. Walter Aston, a watchmaker.

This Walter Aston, whose title to the peerage was established in 1769 through the death of his kinsman William Aston, was granted by George III a pension of £300 a year on the Scottish Establishment.

PAYMENTS FOR SERVICES

A curious feature of the secret service list is what may be called service pensions or 'additional salaries'. In the first place, there is in Roberts's accounts a quarterly blank with £1050 against it. In the alphabetical register of secret service pensions drawn up in April 1756 [1] this blank appears under the letter 'N', with a yearly total of £4200 marked against it. In another computation of 'the total annual amount of private pensions' [2] the same sum appears against a discreet 'N.B.', but in Newcastle's accounts, 1757–62, the matter is stated every time in plain, though apologetic terms : 'Retain'd to myself by Your Majesty's special command — one quarter, £1050'. The origin of this additional salary paid to Newcastle while at the head of the Treasury is shown in a paper which, judging by internal evidence, must have been drawn up in 1760 or early in 1761 to explain the matter to George III : [3] the pension was given to Newcastle to make up for the financial loss which he suffered by exchanging the Secretaryship of State for the Treasury, and, seeing that Newcastle anyhow spent vast sums of his own money on what he considered the service of the King, this supplementary salary cannot be viewed in an invidious light.

Comparison between the profits arising from the offices of Secretary of State and First Commiss[r] of the Treasury.[4]

At a medium, for seven *ordinary* years, (vizt. from 1747 to 1753 inclusive) the clear profits of the office of Secretary of State, appear to have amounted to . . . £5780
The neat income of the office of First Commissioner of the Treasury, in the year 1754, with the Land Tax at 2s. in the pound, appears to have been 1480
The private addition to the Duke of Newcastle was . 4200

———
£5680

---

[1] 33038, ff. 497-8.   [2] 33040, f. 31.
[3] In Newcastle's 'Memorandums for my Lord Hardwicke', 23 Dec 1760 (32999, f. 133) appears the following entry :
'To consider in what manner I should acquaint the King with my £4200 a year. To look out the paper from whence Mr. Jones made the average.'
[4] 33039, ff. 309-10. The paper is in H. V. Jones's handwriting.

N.B.—The two last sums added together, do not make the neat income so much as it was, at a medium, for seven *ordinary* years, in the Secretary of State's office, by one hundred pounds pr. an. :—and the Land Tax, being now, and having been for several years, *four* shillings in the pound, makes a further deduction of £120 pr. an., which, if added to the abovementioned £100 pr. an., would make the deficiency 220£ pr. an.

N.B.—The year of an accession to the Crown, has always encreas'd the profits of a Secretary of State very considerably. The present year will do so in a *more* than *ordinary* manner, on account of the *extraordinary* number of military commissions.

To this paper is appended another drawn up by James West and explaining the way in which the income of the First Lord of the Treasury was calculated.[1]

Net income of the Office of First Commiss^r of the Treasury, July 2, 1754.

The Salary, as first Commissioner of the Treasury .	£1600	0	0
New-Years-Gifts, as a Lord of the Treasury .	40	19	0
	£1640	19	0
Deduction of 6[d] pr. £ . . . £40			
Land Tax at 2s. pr. £ . . . 120			
—	£160	0	0
	£1480	19	0

As the Land Tax encreases, the net income is less—J. WEST.

Newcastle's additional salary, which was paid for all his time at the Treasury barring one month before his resignation in November 1756, makes in his secret service accounts a total of £30,538 : 19 : 2¾.

Similarly, an additional salary of £1500 p.a. was paid to Lord Halifax, President of the Board of Trade, 1748–61. 'A great deal was done at different times to gain and soothe my Lord Halifax', wrote the second Lord Hardwicke in a note on a draft of a letter from his father to Newcastle.[2] The pension was obviously a *douceur* of this kind, but it started before Newcastle came to the Treasury, and stopped on Halifax going

---

[1] *Ibid.* f. 311. The document is marked 'Copy', and is in Jones's hand.
[2] 35417, f. 80.

as Lord Lieutenant to Ireland — the entry on 7 May 1761 is marked 'This is to be the last payment'. Halifax's additional salary stands for a total of £10,125 in Newcastle's secret service accounts. Whatever view one may take of Halifax as a politician, he did good and honest work at the Board of Trade, and there was more justification for this payment than for nine out of ten openly avowed pensions; but it was presumably given in that form in order not to make it a precedent for his successors or provoke similar demands from his colleagues.

Two other well-earned pensions were, that of £400 p.a., paid, with a short interval in 1755, to Sir John Fielding, the magistrate who made London a safe place to live in; and £200 p.a. to Thomas Lane, Chairman of the Quarter Sessions of Middlesex. The total paid to them by Newcastle, 1754–62, was £3950.

Another pension which, although paid to a Member of Parliament, must be treated as a salary, for it was given to the office independent of its holder, was £500 paid every year about Lady Day to the Chairman of Committees in the House of Commons. As such, J. S. Charlton received from Newcastle, 1754–61 (both years included but not the spring of 1757, when Newcastle was not in office) £3500, and his successor, Alderman Marsh Dickenson, £500; together, £4000.

Lastly, there were two pensions classified by Newcastle as 'additional salaries', £400 p.a. to Lord Ilchester and £1000 p.a. to Baron von Münchhausen. It is not clear what real work was ever done by Ilchester, Joint Comptroller of the Army Accounts 1747–76, and his pension looks more like part of the spoils which his brother, Henry Fox, the most rapacious of eighteenth-century statesmen, succeeded in obtaining for his family at the expense of the King and the nation. It may also have been a retaining fee for his borough interest at Shaftesbury — there is an entry about it in connexion with the general election of 1754.[1] Still, as it is of such a mixed character, I follow Newcastle's classification and include it among the salaries — it makes a total of £3300 during Newcastle's tenure of office. As for Münchhausen, he was a

[1] Memorandum of 25 Mar 1754; 32995, f. 126.

Hanoverian, and the work he did was for the Electorate rather than for Great Britain; I therefore include his pension among the King's gifts and payments to Germans.

The additional salaries to Newcastle, Halifax, Ilchester, the magistrates, and the Chairman of Committees, make a total of almost £52,000.

At the other end of the scale stand the salaries paid out to the *canaille*, to hired journalists and pamphleteers, and to secret agents and spies. William Guthrie, James Ralph, and David Mallet, whose lives and works are recorded in the *Dictionary of National Biography*, are in the first category, the 'propaganda department'; their hire during Newcastle's term of office amounted to a joint £4000.[1] To this the £500 should perhaps be added of a pension paid to Archibald Bower, ex-Jesuit, who, while resuming relations with the Jesuits, wrote an anti-Romanist *History of the Popes.* The anti-Jacobite spies were John Gordon of Sempill, an old driveller who remained active throughout the period and had a half-illiterate transcriber paid to copy his nonsense; Alexander 'Pickle' (1754–55), one of the most prominent dealers in Jacobite romances; Allan Macdonald, another spy, on 'the Highland service'; and possibly also Fitzgerald, whose funeral was paid for out of secret service money in March 1755. Their joint takings were £1940 : 10s. Next come the foreign agents: Springer, 'the Swedish merchant who has suffer'd so much' — he had acted as British agent, had been imprisoned a few years by the French party in Sweden, in 1756 found a refuge in England, and was given a pension of £100 p.a. ; it makes a total of £600 in Newcastle's accounts. Mr. Tyrell, *recte* Pichon, 'the French officer who was employed in matters of secrecy by Colonel Lawrence in Nova Scotia', had a pension of £200, and received a total of £1050. Thierry (misspelled Querré), the French pilot who directed the British attack against Rochefort in 1757, received during the following four years £750.[2] £100 was

---

[1] Guthrie had £200 p.a. (about him see footnote in the secret service accounts under 20 June 1754); Ralph had £300 p.a. (see under 24 Oct 1754); Mallet had no regular pension but was given £300 for his attack on Admiral Byng (see under 9 Nov 1756).

[2] The pensions to Springer, Tyrrel, and Querré were still paid at the

issued on 13 April 1759 'to the person who sends the intelligence to the Duke of Devonshire', and £50, in 1759–60, 'to Mr. Reiche, for the French commissary who gave intelligence to Prince Ferdinand'. Thus £2550 can be traced as spent on foreign agents.

THE FRIENDS OF FRIENDS, AND OTHERS

If Members of the two Houses could expect, when in need, to be supported from the 'bounty' of the King, next came their friends for whom they themselves could not provide, or found it more convenient to provide at the expense of the State.

The Duke of Hamilton had a poor cousin, James Hamilton,[1] and asked Henry Pelham to give him a consulship in the Mediterranean, or a place in the Customs or the Excise; Pelham promised to do so, and in the meantime, as an earnest of his good-will, gave him an annuity of £200 from secret service funds. When Pelham died, the Duke of Hamilton, in his letter of condolence to Newcastle, asked that the pension be continued — 'this is all the young gentleman has at present to subsist upon'. The 'young gentleman' occasionally raised again the question of a place, but meantime subsisted on this retaining fee, which was still paid when Newcastle left the Treasury in 1762, and in his secret service accounts is responsible for a total of £1400.

Thomas Burrowes was esquire-beadle to the University of Cambridge, of which the Duke of Newcastle was Chancellor. This, of course, was a sufficient reason for Burrowes to be given a pension of £100 a year from secret service money; it makes a total of £800 during Newcastle's term at the Treasury.

'Count' Hewett was a protégé of the Duke of Devonshire, Dr. Hepburn had been physician to Sir Robert Walpole, and G. L. Scott tutor to the Prince of Wales, Mr. Allen was a nephew of Speaker Onslow, Mr. Cooke was a friend of Gybbon, the oldest Member in Parliament, Mr. Langford was son-in-law

time of the fall of the North Administration in 1782 ; see below, pp. 444, 448, and 450.

[1] See accounts under 26 Apr 1754.

to Thomas Sergison, Newcastle's nominee for the borough of Lewes, etc. etc., and so they were all in receipt of pensions from secret service funds. The persons of these distant friends to the Government are so unimportant that in many cases their names never appear — one merely reads about 'Lord Rockingham's two friends', 'Sir Jacob Downing's man', or 'Mr. W. Leveson-Gower's friend'. Moreover, there is a regular 'Speaker's List' of £360 a year, a compliment to the distinguished Speaker Onslow, continued to him even after he had retired from the Chair and the House.[1]

Further, there were some special cases calling for sympathy and help, e.g. of men who had been deprived of their jobs, sinecures, and their livelihood through the loss of Minorca. Charles Hamilton, ninth son of the sixth Earl of Abercorn, had been Receiver-General of the island, and as a compensation for his loss was given a secret service pension of £1200 p.a.[2] Dr. Molesworth, sixth son of the first Viscount Molesworth, had been made in 1735 'physician to [the garrison of] Minorca, by the late Queen', and was now 'starving'; he was therefore given a pension of £200 per annum.[3] Henry Poole, son of Sir Francis Poole, Bart., M.P., by his wife, Frances, née Pelham, had been Deputy-Paymaster and the family were 'starving by the loss of their place in Minorca' — he was given £500 p.a.[4]

Lastly, gifts and pensions appear in the secret service

---

[1] The list is of a non-political character; this was its composition in 1754 (33038, f. 354):

	£		
Sir More Molyneux . . .	£100	0	0
Mrs. Goode	100	0	0
Mr. Glover	20	0	0
Mrs. Forbes	25	0	0
Mr. Hill	17	10	0
Mr. Wattleton . . .	17	10	0
Mr. Camber	17	10	0
Mrs. Denyer	17	10	0
Mrs. Benbrick . . .	15	0	0
Mrs. Hayman . . .	10	0	0
Mrs. Smith	10	0	0
Catherine Martin . . .	10	0	0
	£360	0	0

[2] See accounts under 5 Aug 1757.
[3] Ibid. under 21 Dec 1758.   [4] Ibid. under 19 Dec 1758.

accounts of which the payment from that money would seem incomprehensible had it really been treated as a fund for political corruption, and not primarily as the King's private money which he could use according to his pleasure. There was a 'Lutheran clergyman', and subsequently his widow, in receipt of £20 p.a., and Capel Hanbury, M.P. for Monmouth-shire, was paid every year £100 for the dissenting ministers of his county. Colonel Clavering, 'who brought the news from Guadeloupe', was given by the King's order £500, Major Wedderburn the same for bringing the account of the battle of Fillinghausen, and Garstin, 'the messenger', £50 for bringing the news of a victory of the King of Prussia. Sir Francis Eyles Stiles, Commissioner of the Victualling Board, received £300 by the King's order 'to enable him to go abroad for the benefit of his health'. Finally, there are two mysterious ladies in receipt of pensions, a Mrs. Krahé and a Mrs. Cannon, who, on investigation, turn out to have been, the first 'an old servant of the late Queen Caroline', and the other 'midwife to the royal family'.

The total of secret service money thus spent on distant friends, humble relations, and what might be called inmates of the casual wards, amounted during Newcastle's term at the Treasury to about £40,000.[1]

---

[1] The following case, though it did not enter into the secret service budget, may serve as an illustration of the degree which 'providing' at the expense of the State assumed in the eighteenth century.

John Twells, 'the Duke of Newcastle's domestic apothecary', held a sinecure in the Customs — he was Accountant of Petty Receipts, and had in 'net sallary and allowances' £531 : 18 : 6 p.a. (see 38334, f. 211). In the massacre of the Pelhamite innocents, which Bute and Fox perpetrated about the New Year of 1763, Twells was marked down for dismissal. His merits and sufferings are best related in the words of his patrons.
Newcastle to Hardwicke :
    Claremont. Jan^ry 5th, 1763 [32946, f. 67].
. . . these barbarous men intend to turn out poor Mr. Twells, of a place I gave him . . . in consideration of seventeen years constant attendance upon the Dutchess of Newcastle in all her illnesses ; and who is perfectly well acquainted with them, and apprized of all, that Sir Edward Wilmot, and Dr. Shaw did, whenever she had them. . . .
The Duchess of Newcastle to Lord Halifax (at that time Secretary of State) :
    Claremont. Jan. the 5th, 1763 [32946, f. 70].
Mr. Twells, is a physical person, and was in a very good way, but left

The Hanoverians

'I replied only, it is Your Majesty's own money ; you may
do with it what you please.' [1] This was the mid-eighteenth-
century view about the Civil List money in general ; and
secret service money was in an even more special sense the
King's own 'private account'. George II had his Hanoverian
friends ; they were not popular in England ; still, when Members of either House could billet friends on the 'King's bounty',
surely the Elector of Hanover was fully justified in providing
for some of his own men from that source. Thus Philip
Adolph, Baron von Münchhausen, Hanoverian resident in
England, had a secret service pension of £1000 a year which

his proffession singly to attend me, when I had a very tedious illness ;
and as my state of health has been more uncertain, ever since that time,
than it was before, he has been constantly with me. Yr. Lordship will
easyly see how incumbent it was upon me, to get something done, for a
person so very necessary to me, and who had given up ev'ry other prospect
in life, upon my account.

Halifax to the Duchess of Newcastle :

Bushey Park. Sunday night. Jan^ry 9th, 1763 [*Ibid.* f. 81].
I lost no time after the receipt of your Grace's letter, but found strong
reason to think it a desperate one. . . .

Meantime 'the unheard-of cruelties' which Newcastle received from
Bute, brought his blood into an 'extreme bad state', and on 12 Jan it was
the Duchess who had to write to Hardwicke about Twells (*ibid.* ff. 95-7).
She informed him that the Duke had 'already order'd an annuity, equal to
the value of Mr. Twells's employment to be settled on him for his life',
and inquired in her own and the Duke's name what Hardwicke would
think of their applying to Bute to save the poor man. Hardwicke, in his
letter of 13 Jan, advised them not to do so (*ibid.* ff. 100-101) but added :

. . . this last instant of Mr. Twells is not only the most cruel, but the
most ungentlemanlike and lowest of all ; — in case it shall take place,
which I can hardly force myself to believe. For this reason I hope that
any other provision, which my Lord Duke shall make for Mr. Twells,
will be penn'd conditionally and eventually in case his present place shall
be taken from him, and no other of a proper value given to him.

In 1765 the advent of the Rockinghams restored 'truly constitutional
government' to a harassed country, and Mr. Twells to his place in the
Customs.

[1] Newcastle in an interview with the King, 15 Aug 1760; see above,
p. 180. Such was the old theory ; for the more modern view, see George
Grenville's speech in Parliament on 28 Feb 1769 : 'the civil list is the
money of the public' (Cavendish, *Debates*, vol. i, p. 273).

was continued to him even under George III [1]; and George Schutz, son of George II's great favourite, Augustus Schutz, had £400 a year. Their two pensions together made a total of almost £12,000 under Newcastle. In December 1757, £2000 was given to the Hereditary Prince of Wolfenbüttel, and various presents, similar to those mentioned before as given to English officers, were made to Germans who brought the news of victories, etc. In 1758, £1500 was spent on a sword, and in 1759 another £1500 on a 'George', for Prince Ferdinand; and under date of 12 February 1756 appears a *douceur* of £500 to Michel, the Prussian Minister in London.

The payments from secret service funds to Germans during Newcastle's term of office make about £21,000.

SUMMARY AND CONCLUSIONS

The total of secret service money spent by Newcastle from the Treasury during his two terms of office March 1754–November 1756 and July 1757 – May 1762 amounted to £290,848 : 17 : 2¾, or in round figures, £291,000. Of this, £55,500 was spent on elections and constituencies, and £68,675 in pensions to Members of Parliament — thus £124,000, *i.e.* 43 per cent, was spent on the House of Commons; £50,000 was doled out to the aristocracy, £61,000 went in additional salaries and to secret agents, almost £40,000 to friends of friends of the Government, and £21,000 to Germans. The vast fund of Parliamentary corruption called 'secret service money' has proved surprisingly small, a mere supplement to places and other open favours; and on further inquiry it is found that there was more jobbery, stupidity, and human charity about it than bribery. 'For the wicked are more naive than we think; and so are we ourselves.' But the Duke of Newcastle was not even wicked, nor were Sir Robert Walpole and Henry Pelham, George III and Lord North.

---

[1] This was probably obtained through Bute; the following entry occurs in the 'Register of Correspondence of the Earl of Bute' (36796, f. 61): 16 Dec 1760. 'Munchhausen to the Earl of Bute. Thanks for assurances of friendship, and for his kind representations to the King on his behalf.'

V

SHROPSHIRE POLITICS AND MEN AT THE ACCESSION OF GEORGE III

FOR several reasons Shropshire politics about 1760 deserve attention. Here was a county which returned twelve Members to Parliament, but among its five boroughs there was only one that, by the standards of the time, could be described as corrupt. In none of them had the right of returning Members passed into the hands of a narrow, self-recruiting Corporation ; in none was it attached to burgages which, if bought up in sufficient numbers, would have secured its representation to their owner ; in none had the Government much electoral influence ; and in none were the resident burgesses swamped by out-voters. In all the Shropshire boroughs the franchise was fairly wide ; and since the death of Henry, third Earl of Bradford, in 1734, the county was singularly free of an overtowering territorial influence. Still, the representation of the Shropshire constituencies was practically hereditary in about a dozen families, and in three of its boroughs remained so even after 1867.

Another remarkable feature of Shropshire politics towards the end of George II's reign was that this county, though free of Government influence and aristocratic predominance, and situated in what then was the Tory belt of the north-west of England, returned as a rule a solid corps of at least eight Whigs — solid especially by its following one leader in a manner unknown at that time in any other English county. 'The Shropshire Whigs' were treated as a group, and most dealings between them and Administration passed through their acknowledged chief, Henry Arthur Herbert, Earl of Powis, Lord Lieutenant of Shropshire. It was he who would solicit and negotiate for them favours and places from the Government, who would arrange Shropshire election affairs with Newcastle, and to whom the Duke would apply for the attendance and votes of its 'old corps of Whigs'. Still, no one would ever have thought of describing them as the 'Powis Whigs'. It was not he who returned them; a Forester at Wenlock or a Whitmore at Bridgnorth did not depend on him for his seat; nor did even a Hill or a More at Shrewsbury, although Powis was Recorder of the town. There was voluntary interdependence between them, faintly reproducing 'livery', modestly anticipating party organization.

That peculiar Shropshire formation helps by contrast to bring out certain features in the Parliamentary structure of other counties. Take Cambridgeshire, whose solid Whig representation at the dissolution in 1761 was continued at the general election in its three constituencies (the County, the Borough, and the University). Lord Granby, the famous general and son of the Duke of Rutland, and Lord Royston, son of Lord Hardwicke, the Hon. Charles Sloane Cadogan and Soame Jenyns, a Commissioner of the Board of Trade, the Hon. Thomas Townshend and the Hon. Edward Finch naturally did not require the mediation of a territorial manager with the Government; each of them belonged to an important political connexion, and the territorial element counted for very little with them. Or again in Yorkshire, where in 1761 Lord Rockingham was the leader of the Whigs, a Whig Member returned for a pocket borough of the Duke of Newcastle or the Duke of Devonshire had obligations which cut across territorial alignments; nor did a son of the Duke of Rutland, when sitting for a Yorkshire constituency, owe suit to the territorial manager. The Shropshire Whigs, on the other hand, were almost all independent country gentlemen, unconnected either with Administration or with any great territorial houses; which helped to produce that curious group formation.

During the comparatively short term of its existence the Shropshire group showed singular vitality; Powis's electoral interests and political activities extended into North and Mid Wales; and the group grew also through personal connexions — *e.g.* John Walsh, M.P. for Worcester, connected with Clive, adhered to it. At the head of such a group, Powis carried

political weight out of proportion to his own territorial influence
and standing, but he had also to shoulder political obligations
such as, *e.g.*, the Duke of Bedford did not bear to his immediate
followers, most of whom owed their seats to his electoral influence. In the last years of George II's reign, Powis, as leader
of his group, came into conflict with two great (and very petty)
men, William Pulteney, Earl of Bath, and Lord Carnarvon,
son and heir to the second Duke of Chandos. To their intense
surprise, dismay, and indignation, Powis, whom they considered
their inferior, got the better of them. For it was a fight
between essentially different political formations, in which
Newcastle, however anxious to please everybody and make
everyone 'easy', could not disavow the leader of such a respectable corps of Whigs. Administration had to stand by its
own steady adherents. This gave new offence to Bath and
Carnarvon, who had never been on close terms with Newcastle
and the main body of the Whigs, and made them turn once
more to the reversionary resource of the Prince of Wales; on
whose accession they both resumed, under more auspicious
circumstances, their old quarrels in Shropshire and Radnorshire.

On 19 December 1760 Newcastle, in one of his habitual
fits of panic and despair, complained to Richard Rigby of 'the
very little weight he had in the closet' and of the Whigs being
'given up in many parts of England', and named three in-
stances to prove his assertion: the first was that of Legge in
Hampshire (which, too, was a petty Leicester House conflict
engineered and managed by Carnarvon);

the second was the turning out Lord Powis from his Lieutenancy
of Shropshire to make way for Lord Bath; and the third was the
removing certain persons in South Wales, who have long had the
management of elections in that part of the world: I conjecture
his Grace meant Mr. Gwynne, who is now Member for Radnor,
where Lord Carnarvon is sent down with pretty large powers; and
Sir Jn. Phillips's support in Pembrokeshire against Sir William Owen.[1]

---

[1] Rigby to Bedford, 19 Dec 1760; *Bedford Correspondence*, vol. ii, pp.
423-4. The following remark appears against the name of Sir William
Owen, Bt., in Bute's list of M.P.'s returned in 1761: 'Join'd with Sr John
Philips to turn out Campbell of Calder, afterwards was turn'd out of the
county by Sr John Philips, and compromised for the borough' (38333, f.

Indeed, Powis and the political affairs of Shropshire and Radnorshire loomed large in the early conflicts of the new reign. These opening incidents have to be reduced to their proper dimensions and to be freed from the legend which has grown up about them — a legend which has its roots in the ever-recurring neurotic fears of the Duke of Newcastle ; in the high political cant of Lord Bath, a brilliant, eloquent, vindictive, mean man, whose arguments were always grand and 'whose head went perpetually wrong' ; and in the literary afterthoughts of Edmund Burke and the latter-day Whigs.

A last, accidental, circumstance which imparts a peculiar interest to the Shropshire politics of that time is that, beginning with about 1761, a powerful East Indian interest arose in the county. It happened that Lord Clive and Lord Pigot were both connected with Shropshire which became the political base of the Clive family. Clive, his brother William, his cousin George, his sons Edward and Robert, and his secretary, Henry Strachey, all at various times sat for Shropshire boroughs ; so did Pigot and his brother Hugh ; while Clive's father sat for Montgomery, and John Walsh, Clive's relative, secretary, and faithful friend, for the town of Worcester. Subsequently, through the marriage of Clive's son and heir to a daughter, and ultimately heiress, of Powis, the political 'interests' of the Clives and the Shropshire Herberts became merged, and in 1804 the title of Powis was re-created in the descendants of Lord Clive.

THE SHROPSHIRE CONSTITUENCIES

The County

About the middle of the eighteenth century Shropshire was a thoroughly independent county — the choice of its knights

106). By the time Newcastle preferred his complaint, full harmony seems to have been restored in Pembrokeshire. At the county meeting, on 4 Dec, Sir John Phillips was proposed by W. Edwardes, M.P. for Haverfordwest, and seconded by Sir Thomas Stepney, 'upon which Sir William Owen, bart. (the present Member), thanked the gentlemen for their former services, and joined in the unanimous resolution of the gentlemen at the meeting . . . we hear Sir William Owen will be elected for the town of Pembroke' (*The Public Ledger*, 11 Dec 1760, p. 1146).

of the shire was left to the rank and file of the country gentry. These, in turn, hardly ever interfered in the boroughs which were, with the exception of Bishop's Castle, controlled by the Powis group. When, before the general election of 1754, a 'Tory' opposition was apprehended at Shrewsbury, Powis sent word that he could not be persuaded 'but the leading gentlemen of the party' would be able to stop it [1] — which they did : the candidates approved by him were returned unopposed with the two Tory knights of the shire attending in support. Again, before the general election of 1761 Lord Bath met with 'little encouragement' from the Tories in his attempts to get his son, Lord Pulteney, returned for Shrewsbury,

the greatest part of them choosing rather to give no support to Lord Bath, in a point he could not carry against us at Shrewsbury, than by interposing there, give offence to the Whigs ; and provoke them, by way of reprisal, to engage in a contest for the County ; of which, two gentlemen on the Tory interest, have long been representatives.[2]

These two, in 1760 both about seventy years old, had tried in their youth to battle against the Whig corporation at Shrewsbury and against the Whig majority in a House of Commons which decided election cases on party lines ; and both finished by abandoning the hopeless contest. Sir John Astley, second Baronet, born in 1687, sat for Shrewsbury 1727–34 and for Shropshire from 1734 till his death in 1772. His colleague, Richard Lyster, considered a Jacobite, was born c. 1691, and belonged to a family settled at Rowton Castle since the fifteenth century, well known and popular in the county ; he was returned for Shrewsbury in 1722, but unseated the next year on a petition which claimed 'that the Abbey Foregate, in which his interest greatly preponderated, was not included within the voting liberties, though it had enjoyed that privilege for many years'.[3] When the House

---

[1] Thomas Hill to Edward Kynaston, 30 Aug 1753 ; Hill's Letter Books, in the Attingham MSS., at the Salop R.O. There is, among these papers, a series of letters from Powis to Hill on the subject, and his answers are in the Letter Books.

[2] Powis to Newcastle, 17 Oct 1760 ; 32913, ff. 171-2.

[3] J. B. Blakeway, *The Sheriffs of Shropshire* (1831), p. 145.

R

decided against him, he put on his hat, turning his back on the
Speaker ; and when Members called him to order 'he, looking
round, with a firm and indignant tone said, "When you learn
justice, I will learn manners"'. In 1727 Lyster, together with
Astley, was returned for Shrewsbury by an undisputed majority,
but in 1734 was defeated by the partiality of the returning
officer who, like the whole Corporation, adhered to the Whigs.
Returned for the county at a by-election in 1740, he continued
to represent it till his death in 1766.

The following description which J. B. Blakeway gives of
Richard Lyster [1] may be taken as the picture of a typical old
Tory knight of the shire :

The establishment of Mr. Lyster was administered upon the
most ample scale of ancient English hospitality : one day in the week
his table was open to every class of his constituents, from the very
highest to the lowest of those who could with propriety appear at
it. . . . His progress to London to attend the duties of parliament,
in which he is described to have been very assiduous, had somewhat
of the feudal cast. . . . He travelled in his coach and six, and was a
week upon the road : his principal tenants and tradesmen accom-
panying him as far as Watling Street, where they were entertained
at his expense. At Highgate he was met by a select body of his
London tradesmen, and thus ushered to his town house, in Bow
Street, Covent Garden : and the same ceremonies were repeated
on his return into Shropshire. All this cost was maintained by a
rental of £1800 a-year.

Shrewsbury

Shrewsbury was an independent borough which acknowledged no patron but chose its Members usually from among
old Shropshire families — the Myttons, Kynastons, Corbets,
Leightons, etc. The right of election was in resident burgesses
paying scot and lot, and the number of voters in 1722 exceeded
1300 ; it was, however, on the trial of that election severely
cut down by the determination of the House of Commons,
which excluded certain parts of the town from the limits of the
Parliamentary borough : less than 500 voted in 1734, and only
about 300 in 1747. Even so the borough remained independent.

[1] J. B. Blakeway, *The Sheriffs of Shropshire* (1831), p. 145. About him
see also H. L. L. Denny, *Memorials of an Ancient House*, pp. 303-4.

The two Members returned in 1754 were Thomas Hill of Tern, and Robert More of Linley.

Thomas Hill, born in 1693, was the son of Thomas Harwood, a Shrewsbury draper, by Margaret, daughter of Rowland Hill of Hawkstone, Shropshire, and nephew and heir of Sir Richard Hill, financier and diplomatist, whose name he assumed.[1] Sent by him to the Continent to 'be bred a merchant', he spent the first three years in Germany, and the next seven, 1714–21, in Holland apprenticed to Clifford, the Amsterdam banker. 'I hope', wrote Richard Hill to his nephew on 10 May 1715, 'you will come home to London with the character of an honest and understanding man.' It seems doubtful whether on his return to England he ever set up in a 'counting house' of his own, but his letter-books for 1740–59, preserved among the Attingham MSS. (now at the Salop Record Office) bear witness to his wide financial interests and dealings. In 1727 he inherited the bulk of Richard Hill's fortune, and in 1749 was returned to Parliament for Shrewsbury, with the support both of Powis and the Tories. He retained the seat till 1768, when succeeded by his son Noel Hill, subsequently first Lord Berwick (between 1748 and 1814 there were only ten years during which Shrewsbury was not represented by a Hill of this or of the Hawkstone branch). Thomas Hill was a regular member of the Powis group, in receipt of Newcastle's Parliamentary Whip so long as Powis adhered to him. None the less he is classed as 'Tory' in Bute's list of 1761, in Rockingham's of December 1766, and in Newcastle's of March 1767 — which only shows once more how little contents there was in such denominations.

Robert More, born in 1703, was a grandson of Samuel More who during the Civil War held Hopton Castle for over a month with thirty-one men against 500 Royalists, and represented Shropshire in the Parliament of 1656. Robert More was 'an inflexible Whig . . . proud of his grandfather, the defender of Hopton Castle'.[2] From 1727 till 1741 he sat for

---

[1] He is usually stated to have taken the name of Hill in 1727, but letters to him from his uncle as early as 1710 are addressed to 'Thomas Hill'.

[2] J. B. Blakeway, *The Sheriffs of Shropshire*, pp. 220-1.

Bishop's Castle (which his great-grandfather had represented both in the Short and the Long Parliament, and his uncle in 1681, 1688, and 1695), and for Shrewsbury 1754–61, when he declined standing again. More was a great traveller,[1] a botanist of mark, and a friend of Linnaeus ; and it was he who brought the musk-rose to England. His great-grandson and heir, Robert Jasper More, of Linley Hall, represented Shropshire in Parliament, 1865–68, and its Ludlow division from 1885 till his death in 1903 — an example of the hereditary character of Parliamentary representation in Shropshire.

Bridgnorth, Wenlock, and Ludlow

The Parliamentary history of these three Shropshire boroughs is best summed up in the pedigrees of three families : the Whitmores at Bridgnorth, the Foresters at Wenlock, and the Herbert-Clive family at Ludlow. Their quasi-hereditary tenure of seats survived the first two Reform Acts (the three boroughs were merged in the county in 1885) : the Whitmores continued to hold one seat at Bridgnorth from 1832 till 1870, when Henry Whitmore accepted the Chiltern Hundreds ; the Foresters retained one seat at Wenlock without a break, 1832–1885 ; and the Herbert-Clive family held one seat at Ludlow, 1832–39 and 1847–85. In short, social structure and political tradition proved much stronger than legislative enactments and franchises. It did not matter much whether the electorate numbered a few hundred or a few thousand, whether it was enlarged or reduced, whether the voting was open or secret — the same families continued to represent these boroughs.

Bridgnorth had one of the widest franchises in England ; the right of election was 'in the burgesses and freemen within and without the borough'.[2] In the contested elections of 1727, 1734, and 1741 the number of voters each time exceeded 1000 ;

---

[1] A few of his journeys can be traced in papers preserved at Linley Hall : thus in 1749 he started out for Portugal, in October was in Madrid, spent most of 1750 in Italy, returning home about the end of the year by way of Vienna and Leipzig ; and the best part of 1751 he spent in Scandinavia, Russia, and Germany.

[2] Oldfield, *Key to the House of Commons* (1820), p. 119.

in fact, it was considerably higher than after 1832. None the less, during the 209 years 1661–1870, for 191 years one Member for Bridgnorth at least, and sometimes the other as well, was a Whitmore.

BRIDGNORTH

[The dates denote tenure of a seat at Bridgnorth]

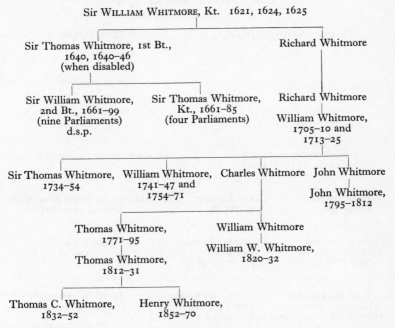

Sir WILLIAM WHITMORE, Kt. 1621, 1624, 1625

Sir Thomas Whitmore, 1st Bt.,
1640, 1640–46
(when disabled)

Richard Whitmore

Sir William Whitmore,
2nd Bt., 1661–99
(nine Parliaments)
d.s.p.

Sir Thomas Whitmore,
Kt., 1661–85
(four Parliaments)

Richard Whitmore

William Whitmore,
1705–10 and
1713–25

Sir Thomas Whitmore,
1734–54

William Whitmore,
1741–47 and
1754–71

Charles Whitmore

John Whitmore

John Whitmore,
1795–1812

Thomas Whitmore,
1771–95

Thomas Whitmore,
1812–31

William Whitmore

William W. Whitmore,
1820–32

Thomas C. Whitmore,
1832–52

Henry Whitmore,
1852–70

At *Wenlock* the right of election was in the burgesses at large. 285 voted in the election of 1820, the first since 1722 to be carried to a poll. The registered electorate in 1832 numbered 691, and by 1874 it exceeded 3000. Seven members of the Lawley family represented the borough in the seventeenth century; two Foresters represented it in the sixteenth century, and ten between 1678 and 1885 (besides two strangers who had married into the family); and the election of 1874 was contested between a Forester on the Conservative, and a Lawley on the Liberal side. Between 1734 and 1885 there were only three months in 1780 and something over a year in

1784–85 when no Forester represented Wenlock. The second
seat was filled from 1768 till 1820 by two Bridgemans, father
and son.

WENLOCK

[The dates denote tenure of a seat at Wenlock]

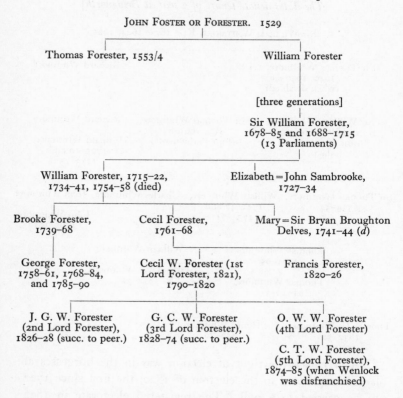

JOHN FOSTER OR FORESTER. 1529

Thomas Forester, 1553/4   William Forester

[three generations]

Sir William Forester,
1678–85 and 1688–1715
(13 Parliaments)

William Forester, 1715–22,   Elizabeth=John Sambrooke,
1734–41, 1754–58 (died)   1727–34

Brooke Forester,   Cecil Forester,   Mary=Sir Bryan Broughton
1739–68   1761–68   Delves, 1741–44 (d)

George Forester,   Cecil W. Forester (1st   Francis Forester,
1758–61, 1768–84,   Lord Forester, 1821),   1820–26
and 1785–90   1790–1820

J. G. W. Forester   G. C. W. Forester   O. W. W. Forester
(2nd Lord Forester),   (3rd Lord Forester),   (4th Lord Forester)
1826–28 (succ. to peer.) 1828–74 (succ. to peer.)
                                                  C. T. W. Forester
                                                  (5th Lord Forester),
                                                  1874–85 (when Wenlock
                                                  was disfranchised)

At *Ludlow* the right of election was in the resident common
burgesses. 710 actually voted in 1727 ; after that no election
contest was carried to the poll till 1812, by which time the
electorate had been reduced below 100 ; the Reform Act of
1832 raised it to 300-400. Between 1689 and 1719 Francis
Herbert represented Ludlow in five Parliaments. Between
1727 and 1832 the Herberts and the Clives always held one
seat at Ludlow, and (if we include two relatives by marriage)

even both seats during forty-nine out of 105 years. Between 1832 and 1885, except for eight years, 1839–47, Ludlow was never without a Herbert-Clive representative. Moreover, members of that family sat for the southern division of Shropshire 1832–59 and 1865–76, and for the northern division 1843–48 ; and the son of the last Member who sat for Ludlow before it was merged in the county represented the Ludlow Division of Shropshire 1923–45.

Bishop's Castle

Bishop's Castle was the one notoriously corrupt borough in Shropshire where the voters took money even from strangers in disregard of inherited ties of allegiance ; and before 1761 it was the only Shropshire borough of which the representation was not confined to honest (and usually inarticulate) country gentlemen, but frequently included distinguished outsiders, in the first place London barristers and merchants and bankers : Sir Matthew Decker, first Baronet, the financier and writer on trade, born at Amsterdam and naturalized before the date as from which naturalization no longer admitted foreign-born subjects to the House of Commons ; William Peere Williams, a barrister, well known as a law reporter ; Samuel and Francis Child, bankers at 'the Marygold by Temple Bar' ; Barnaby Backwell, a nephew of Samuel Child and a partner in the bank ; Peregrine Cust, a merchant ; and George Clive, Alexander Wedderburn, and Henry Strachey, after the borough had come under Clive patronage.

Some incidents from the earlier record of Bishop's Castle indicate its character. In 1726, Charles Mason, a local squire, alleged on petition that of the 52 voters who had carried the election against his own 16, 47 had received between them £667 : 16s., and that 'most of the voters thus bribed were tenants to the petitioner, and always in his interest, and that in general they declared they would have voted for the petitioner but for the sitting member's money'.[1]

---

[1] Oldfield, *Key to the House of Commons*, pp. 105-6. Mason carried his petition ; he represented Bishop's Castle 1708–10, 1715–22, and 1726–27.

On 26 July 1739, James, first Duke of Chandos, whose son, Lord Carnarvon, was to stand for Bishop's Castle at the forthcoming general election, wrote to his nephew John Walcot, the owner of an estate which adjoined the borough :

As I am wholly a stranger at Bishop's Castle I must leave the management of that election to your devotion, and the person you tell me you have engaged for the agent. . . . Whatever the expence shall be I will readily bear, but I must trust to him to steer clear of the Act of Parliament, so as that no proof may be capable of being brought to the contrary.[1]

When elected, Carnarvon rejoiced at his 'good fortune at honest Bishop's Castle'; [2] but he received from his father 'nothing towards it but £70'; and even after having succeeded as second Duke of Chandos, was still unable to discharge his election accounts, and wrote to Walcot on 17 February 1746 : 'I cannot but wish I had never seen Bishop's Castle. . . .'

In 1755, Walter Waring, of Owlbury, Salop,[3] whose estate gave him considerable influence in the borough, was elected for Bishop's Castle, but being in need of money seems to have treated his seat as a marketable commodity. In 1759 he vacated it in favour of a complete stranger, Henry Grenville, brother of Lord Temple and George Grenville, and brother-in-law of William Pitt.

Every thing was conducted there with great unanimity, decency, and good order, in spite of all the carousing and festivity which prevailed there [wrote Henry Grenville on 22 February 1759] ; Mr.

---

[1] See Rev. J. R. Burton, 'Two Elections for Bishop's Castle in the Eighteenth Century', *Transactions of the Shropshire Archaeological Society*, third series, vol. ix (1909), pp. 259-66 ; from Walcot MSS. now at the Salop R.O.

[2] J. R. Burton, *op. cit.*, in the *Transactions of the Shropshire Archaeological Society* ; letter to John Walcot, 12 May 1741.

[3] Walter Waring was a grandson of Edmund Waring, M.P. for Bishop's Castle 1660–81 and 1685. He was educated at Shrewsbury school and St. John's, Cambridge ; married, 1758, Hannah, daughter of John Ranby, Serjeant-Surgeon to the King. (See on him, 'Suffolk Genealogies', 19154, ff. 206-7 ; *Gentleman's Magazine*, 1809, vol. ii, p. 1191 ; R. F. Scott, *Admissions to St. John's, Cambridge.*) In 1768 Walter Waring unsuccessfully contested Coventry (see above, pp. 102-3), but was returned at a by-election on 25 Jan 1773, and continued its representative till his death in 1780.

Waring's interest and Mr. Pitt's popularity, united, seemed to me quite invincible there.[1]

The two men returned unopposed for Bishop's Castle in 1761, Francis Child and Peregrine Cust, though they cannot be described as absolute strangers (for they both had some family antecedents in the borough), had no real connexion with Shropshire ; and while Child was usually classed as a Tory, he had no more in common with the two Tory knights of the shire than with Powis's group of Shropshire Whigs.

Francis Child, although only twenty-five, was the head of the famous bank [2] established by his grandfather, Sir Francis Child, a self-made man. The son of a Wiltshire clothier, Sir Francis in 1698 was returned to Parliament by the Wiltshire borough of Devizes, and, in the usual style of the *nouveaux riches*, founded a regular Parliamentary dynasty. Three of his sons sat in the House of Commons : the youngest, Samuel, from 1747 till his death in 1752 for Bishop's Castle, where his eldest son, Francis, succeeded him in 1761 — not for long, for he died on 23 September 1763.[3]

Peregrine Cust was the fourth son of Sir Richard Cust, Baronet, by Anne, daughter of Sir William Brownlow, Baronet, and granddaughter of Sir Richard Mason, of the Masons of Bishop's Castle, from whom she inherited estates in its neighbourhood. The eldest brother was Sir John Cust, third Baronet, Speaker of the House of Commons 1761–70 ; the second, William, a sailor, had been killed in action in 1747 ;

---

[1] *An Eighteenth-Century Correspondence*, ed. Lilian Dickins and Mary Stanton (1910), p. 402.

[2] About the bank and the Child family see F. G. Hilton Price, *The Marygold by Temple Bar* (1902).

[3] Shortly before his death, Francis Child became engaged to Maria Constantia, daughter of Robert Hampden, subsequently fourth Lord Trevor and first Viscount Hampden. 'Mr. Child's wealth', wrote Hampden to Lady Suffolk (widow of the tenth Earl) on 21 Sept 1763, 'has been one of his least recommendations with me ; as I can assure you I have not met with any young man of fortune so much, in all respects, after my own heart as himself' (*Letters to and from Henrietta, Countess of Suffolk* (1824), vol. ii, p. 280). A week later follows a letter about his sudden death ; 'with his last breath', as a mark of his affection, he left his fiancée £50,000, 'to which his surviving brother has been so genteel as to add all the family jewels that were making up for her' (*ibid.* p. 281). She married Henry, twelfth Earl of Suffolk, on 25 May 1764.

the third, Francis, was a barrister; and 'little Perry', the fourth, born in 1723, was apprenticed to a firm of linen-drapers, in which, in 1744, he became a partner. By 1761 he was a prosperous merchant, well able to defray election expenses at Bishop's Castle; still, it was to his mother that he chose to ascribe his success.

> My first frank and my first thanks [he wrote to her on 31 March 1761] are due to your Ladyship for your assistance in procuring me the greatest honour which can be conferr'd upon a British commoner, not only without opposition but with the united hearts of the whole town.[1]

LORD POWIS AND HIS SHROPSHIRE MEN

The story how George Whitmore, of the Whitmores who sat for Bridgnorth, became Commissioner of the Stamp Office, illustrates the relations between Lord Powis and the men 'under his care' and also the working of the patronage system as practised in the eighteenth century. Powis carefully watched vacancies in offices [2] which he thought would suit his friends or their relatives — their fitness for the posts he took for granted. Newcastle (who as First Lord of the Treasury had to provide for many besides the Shropshire Whigs) fended, shuffled, and arranged matters as well as he could, receiving rebuffs from the King, Lord Anson, etc., when he tried to subordinate the interests even of the fighting services to the securing of votes in the House of Commons, and earning re-proaches from those who felt disgusted whenever their candi-dates were not promptly provided for or promoted. The correspondence quoted below is typical of letters which reached Newcastle from hundreds of people and from every part of the country.

On 5 October 1754, Powis wrote to Newcastle that he had read in the newspapers about the death of 'old Mr. McSwinney, who held a good post at the Customhouse in London'; and

---

[1] *Records of the Cust Family*, compiled by Lady Elizabeth Cust (1909), vol. ii, p. 290.

[2] Shipping intelligence and obituary notices of placemen were great features in eighteenth-century newspapers.

reminded the Duke of his friends, George Whitmore [1] and John Shrympster.

The former is brother to Sir Thomas Whitmore ; and the other is recommended by the Messrs. Forester (the father and son), who serve in Parliament for Wenlock. I mention'd to your Grace t'other day how much they were all alarm'd with the disposal of the place of Housekeeper at the Customhouse, without any notice taken of the former applications. . . . Your Grace must be sensible, I have no reason to give myself any trouble in affairs of this kind, but to serve those whom I wish well to, in the Administration. To enable me to do so, they must support my credit with those gentlemen, that I have under my care.

Another disappointment, he concluded, would be attended with much uneasiness.[2]

Newcastle replied, on 6 October,[3] that the place of house-keeper at the Custom House was only £170 p.a. : 'I should have never thought of it for a gentleman of Mr. Whitmore's familly and rank. I have given it to an old servant of my own.' [4] Similarly he did not think of offering Mr. Whitmore the place of McSwinney, which was £100 p.a. He intended to give him a Commissionership of £400-£500 a year, but there were two previous engagements for these places :

I did and do repeat my intention to serve Mr. Whitmore, when-ever it is in my power, but I cannot think that lays me under any engagement not to dispose of any employment, though indeed in my opinion not at all proper for Mr. Whitmore, without first knowing his thoughts about it.

Powis took note of what was said about George Whitmore and Commissionerships, and on 15 February 1755, Anson, First Lord of the Admiralty, had occasion to acknowledge receipt of a letter from Newcastle with one inclosed from Powis recom-mending Whitmore for a vacant Commissionership of the Victualling Office :

[1] In 1748 George Whitmore had been a candidate for the Governorship of North Carolina ; see Powis to Newcastle, 7 June 1748 ; 32715, f. 174.

[2] 32737, ff. 33-4.   [3] *Ibid.* f. 55.

[4] Cf. list in the Liverpool Papers prepared in Dec 1762 with a view to proscriptions (38334, f. 216) : 'John Greening — Housekeeper of the Customhouse, was the Duke of Newcastle's House Steward. Worth 300£ per ann. net.'

. . . his Lordship might as properly have asked to have had him made a Capt. of a Man of War, that branch having always been filled with a seaman [was Anson's comment] . . . instead of adding to the useless people that are already in that office (if we should have a war with France) more people of business must be brought into it.[1]

The next day Powis suggested George Whitmore for a place at the Green Cloth, which he thought vacant,[2] and in June 1755 for the office of Keeper of the Records in the Tower, which had become vacant through the death of William Hay, M.P.[3] Newcastle replied on 25 June 1755 :

All the earth could not make the King give this place out of the House of Commons ; and, as it is for life necessarily, I have recommended my own nephew, Jack Shelley, for it.[4] This has been my answer to several Members of the House of Commons ; and, I hope, will be a satisfactory one to Mr. Whitmore. These places for life . . . are always dispos'd of in this manner.[5]

The hint that George Whitmore, not being a Member of Parliament, should not compete for places open to Members, was duly taken ; and on 2 November 1755 William Whitmore, M.P., wrote to Newcastle 'that Mr. Shelly,[6] Commissioner of the Stamp Dutys, is dyeing and cannot recover'; and as this office was not tenable with a seat in Parliament, he solicited it for his brother.[7]

Meantime, as Parliament was to meet on 13 November, Newcastle, on 1 November, sent Powis the customary reminder for those 'under his care', coupled with appropriate promises :

My dear Lord,—You will forgive my putting you in mind to write to Mr. Harris,[8] and to all our Shropshire friends, to be in

---

[1] 32852, f. 485.

[2] *Ibid.* f. 511. Its holder, Sir Thomas Hales, Bt., did not die till 1762.

[3] About him see John Nichols, *Literary Anecdotes*, vol. vi, pp. 346-58 ; he is best known as the author of the *Essay on Deformity*.

[4] Sir John Shelley, fifth Bt. (1730–83), M.P. for East Retford 1751–68, Newark 1768–74, and New Shoreham 1774–80.

[5] 32856, f. 205.

[6] Richard Shelley, a brother of Sir John Shelley, fourth Bt.

[7] 32860, f. 317.

[8] John Harris, of Pickwell, Devon, M.P. for Barnstaple 1741–47 and 1754–61. He was married to a sister of Lord Powis.

Town the first day of the session, and if possible, at the meeting
at the Cockpit the night before. We are in great hopes of getting
something for Sir T. Whitmore's brother; Mr. West has informed
you how the matter stands. Mr. Bridgeman of the Guards, would
have had a company, if we had applied in time, as soon as Barrington
comes in, he shall take care of it.[1]

Powis replied on 4 November, from Darsham in Suffolk : [2]

I am honoured with your Grace's letter, which mentions your
commands in relation to my Shropshire friends. Had I receiv'd
them sooner, I wou'd have endeavour'd punctually to have obey'd
them : but as your Grace's letter bears date on the first of this
month, and I am in Suffolk, it will not be possible for me to get
my friends to London in time for the meeting at the Cockpit on
Wednesday next, but at the meeting of the Parliament the next day,
I doubt not the appearance of them all. I will do what I can to
serve your Grace. . . .
I know not yet what has pass'd between your Grace and Coll.
Whitmore, in consequence of the letter I receiv'd from Mr. West,
by your Grace's order, in relation to Mr. George Whitmore; but I
understand (and I think proper to apprize your Grace of it) that he
is greatly disgusted with you, and that I shall hear from him, in a
day or two, what has done it.

Next day Powis reported a letter from Colonel Whitmore
'full of sentiments of disgust,' because he had been told that
the place of Richard Shelley was already 'engaged'.[3]

I assure your Grace that if the abovementioned employment
should be vacant and not disposed of in favour of Mr. George
Whitmore, such a clamour and uneasiness will certainly attend the
disappointment, as will really disable me from answering your
Grace's expectations in respect to my Shropshire friends.

This threat obviously had the desired effect, for the next
letter from Powis to Newcastle, dated 'Wednesday night,
8 o'clock' [12 November 1755] showed renewed zeal and
confidence :

My dear Lord,—I was not out of my bed till six o'clock, Mr. Hill,
one of the Members for Shrewsbury (and of whom your Grace

[1] 32860, f. 279. Barrington was about to succeed Fox as Secretary at
War.
[2] *Ibid*. f. 342.   [3] *Ibid*. ff. 369-70

enquired of me particularly) letting me know that he wou'd call upon me this evening, ill as I have been I saw him and have the pleasure to tell you he is this moment gone down to the Cockpit. The rest of my countrymen are in town or will be tomorrow. I think all goes well with them all.[1]

And on 15 November Powis assured the Duke once more of 'the good services' of his Shropshire friends, and added that Colonel Whitmore was 'full of spirits and confidence in your Grace's kind disposition to serve his brother in the affair of the Stamp Office . . . your favour to him will be a matter of éclat, that will enable me the better to support your Grace's measures for His Majesty's service'.[2]

On 5 December 1755, George Whitmore was appointed Commissioner of Stamp Duties in succession to Richard Shelley, deceased.[3]

Less successful were the endeavours of Powis and Newcastle in the matter of Cecil Forester, of the Foresters who sat for Wenlock. The story starts with an entry in Newcastle's 'Memorandums for the King' (notes for conversations, not memoranda presented to him), under date of 6 March 1759: 'Lord Powis — Mr. Forrester — Lieut.-Colonel Cecil Forrester';[4] and on 15 March 1759 the Duke received a direct application from Brooke Forester, M.P. [the 'Mr. Forrester' mentioned above], asking that his brother be made aide-de-camp to the King.

The long steaddy attachment my family has always show'd, and the few favours we have solicited, I think makes my request far from

[1] 32860, f. 461. Note the use of the word 'countrymen'; in the eighteenth century the county was often described as one's 'country'.

[2] *Ibid.* f. 490.

[3] In Jan 1763, during the proscription of Newcastle's followers, the remark appears about George Whitmore in the list of 'Officers of Stamp Duties', drawn up for the Treasury: 'George Whitmore, a brother of Genl Whitmore, appointed about five years ago by the interest of Lord Powis. A good Commissioner' (38335, f. 58). He was none the less dismissed in Feb 1763, but reinstated by the Rockingham Government in 1765. He retained the post till his death in 1775.

[4] 32888, f. 373. Cecil Forester (1721–74), Major in Colonel Murray's Regiment of Foot 1748; Lieutenant-Colonel 1752–60, when he left the Service; M.P. for Wenlock 1761–68.

unreasonable. . . . As my brother has been ill us'd, if he is not prefer'd he is determined to give up immediately.[1]

The Duke, as usual, was anxious to oblige, but had any number of requests for military promotions from Members, and, fortunately for the Army, it was not Newcastle who placed military recommendations before the King.

The affairs of the Army are totally out of my department, [wrote Newcastle on 24 March 1759 to Viscount Fitzwilliam, who had applied to him on behalf of his brother, John Fitzwilliam, M.P.] and if I ever mention them to the King, I must own His Majesty is not pleased with it. My Lord Ligonier is the proper, and indeed the only person, to lay applications of this sort before the King.[2]

But the fact that such an important branch of patronage was not under his charge was a standing grievance with Newcastle. The entry in the 'Memorandums' of 19 March 1759 — 'Military recommendations from the House of Commons'[3] — is thus amplified on 20 March :[4]

Military paper.
To know the King's pleasure what I must do in it.
All Members of the House of Commons.
If the King expects that I should keep up an interest there, I must be supported ; and military commissions, when asked for proper persons, when there are ninety thousand men, it will furnish many opportunities of doing it.

In the next few months further entries about Forester continue to appear in the Duke's memoranda ; 'Colonel Forester, Aide-de-Camp', 'Lord Powis and the Shropshire Members — Lieut.-Colonel Forester', etc. Later on, Powis tried to link up the case of Colonel Forester with the, for Newcastle highly embarrassing, affair of Shrewsbury,[5] asserting that no accommodation could be reached in it unless Forester was made aide-de-camp to the King or given a regiment. On 12 August 1759, Newcastle replied in despair :

[1] 32889, f. 86. In Bute's list of the House of Commons the remarks are placed against the name of Brooke Forester : 'Old Whig'. 'By Whiggism attach'd to Lord Powis as the head of that party in Shropshire, but solliciting very few favours of Government' (38333, f. 93).
[2] 32889, f. 223.   [3] Ibid. f. 140.
[4] Ibid. f. 155.   [5] See below, pp. 257-68.

Your Lordship knows my zealous wishes for Colonel Forester's service ; the King knows them ; my Lord Ligonier knows them. It is not in my power to make any absolute promise of any military preferment ; and therefore I should be extremely to blame to promise what it may not be in my power to perform.[1]

He failed, and consequently Cecil Forester seems to have left the Army in disgust. Returned to Parliament for Wenlock at the general election in March 1761, he entered the House apparently bearing no ill-will to the universal scapegoat, the Duke of Newcastle.

LORD POWIS AND RADNORSHIRE

When in February 1755 a vacancy occurred in the representation of Radnorshire, George Rice, M.P. for Carmarthenshire and one of Newcastle's political managers in Wales, informed him that two years earlier, in expectation of the event, Pelham had consulted Powis, and 'Mr. Howell Gwynne was fixt upon as a proper candidate' ;[2] and that he (Rice), Lord Carnarvon, Mr. Lewis,[3] and Lord Bateman,[4] would wait on the Duke about it. Carnarvon failed to attend, but was apprised by Newcastle of the others being agreed that Gwynne, 'a gentleman of known zeal for His Majesty and his Royal Family, and of very considerable property in the county of Radnor, will be the most proper person to be candidate upon the present vacancy'.[5]

'My Lord Powis and the gentlemen your Grace mentions in your letter, by residing in that part of the country, must know Mr. Howell Gwynne much better than myself', wrote Carnarvon on 9 February, in reply to Newcastle's request that

[1] 32894, f. 103.   [2] 7 Feb 1755 ; 32852, f. 388.
[3] Thomas Lewis of Harpton (1690–1777), M.P. for Radnor Borough from 1715 till 1761, when returned again, but unseated on petition.
[4] John Bateman, second Viscount Bateman of Ireland (1721–1802), M.P. for Orford 1746–47, Woodstock 1747–68, and Leominster 1768–84. A grandson of Charles, third Earl of Sunderland, and great-grandson of John, first Duke of Marlborough, he was politically connected with the third Duke of Marlborough and also with Henry Fox ; after the accession of George III he became a 'King's friend'.
[5] 32852, f. 404.

he should support Gwynne; but he declared himself bound by a previous promise.

When I offered myself a candidate for that county, Mr. Howell Gwynne opposed me very strongly; when Lord Oxford gave me his interest, and thro' his means I got the better of his opposition, and upon declining the county of Radnor, to offer myself for Winchester [1754] I promised then, my interest in the county to Lord Oxford's friend at the next vacancy. By this your Grace will see, it is not in my power this time to assist your Grace's nomination, but at another election, your Grace may command.[1]

However, Oxford's candidate, Sir Richard Chase, declined 'standing the poll',[2] and Howell Gwynne was returned unopposed; and only £173 of secret service money was required for the election, 'a moderate expense in an affair of so great consequence to the Whig interest in the county of Radnor'.[3]

Although the promise to Oxford, a prominent Tory, shows that Carnarvon was ready to deal with either side, at this time Newcastle seems to have considered him a friend,[4] and Carnarvon tried to regain the Government favour enjoyed by his grandfather, the first Duke of Chandos, but forfeited by his father, who, as first Gentleman of the Bedchamber to the Prince of Wales, was 'unfortunately oblig'd to obey the late Prince's commands', though previously he had 'always voted with the Administration'.

That the late Duke, your petitioner's grandfather, [wrote Carnarvon to the King][5] from the time of the accession of the Crown to your Royal and Illustrious House, had spent sixty thousand pounds in elections; and never brought in a person who gave a vote against the Ministry; and when he had impair'd his estate by this, and his generosity to mankind, etc., Your Majesty was graciously pleased to give him a pension; nevertheless he died considerably in debt.

---

[1] *Ibid.* f. 404; for other correspondence relating to this election see 32853: Thomas Johnes to Powis, 14 Feb 1755 (f. 460); H. Gwynne to Newcastle, 15 Feb (f. 483); Powis to Newcastle, 18 Feb (f. 536); Thomas Villiers to Newcastle, 22 Feb (f. 581).

[2] Thomas Villiers to Newcastle, 10 Mar 1755; 32853, f. 170.

[3] George Rice to Newcastle, 15 Mar 1755; 32853, f. 301. In the secret service accounts the sum appears under date of 16 Apr 1755.

[4] He was, *e.g.*, sent for during the critical divisions over the Mitchell election; see 32853, f. 313.

[5] 33055, f. 88; undated; presented about 1754.

S

Carnarvon now asked for 'a mark of favour' for his father —
obviously a renewal of the pension.[1] And when in June 1755
a vacancy seemed imminent in the Lord Lieutenancy of
Radnorshire, Carnarvon wrote to Newcastle :

> I may venture to say, I have as large property in that county
> as any one man, in consideration of which His Majesty was pleas'd
> formerly to confer it on my grandfather. This office would greatly
> strengthen my interest in the county, and I flatter myself, your
> Grace knows my attachments too well, to think me capable of making
> a bad use of the power lodged in my hands.[2]

Gwynne meantime faithfully discharged his duties in
Parliament.

> Your Grace was pleasd to tell me, [wrote Powis to Newcastle on
> 15 December 1755 [3]] that I must take care of Mr. Howell Gwynne,
> who serves for the county of Radnor.—And I have the pleasure to
> assure your Grace that his conduct in Parliament has hitherto been
> agreeable to your wishes.—I am under a necessity now of putting
> him into your Grace's hands, recommending to your Grace in my
> turn, that *you will take care of him.*

Gwynne wished his brother to be made Customer of the Port
of Milford [4] — 'on easier terms, your Grace could scarce desire
it : and it will oblige him', was Powis's comment. 'What your
Grace thinks proper to trust to my management, I venture to
give my opinion upon.'

Carnarvon's conduct was less steady ; on 13 November
1755, in the division on support for Hanover, he voted against
the Government,[5] which must have offended George II. When
on 23 December he none the less repeated his application for
the Lord Lieutenancy of Radnor, now actually vacant, Newcastle replied :

> Mr. Gwynne, who is chose for the county, was so strongly recom-
> mended to the King by the gentlemen who are friends to the

---

[1] Chandos renewed the request for the pension on 19 Feb 1761, himself
applying for it to Newcastle : he deplored the 'shyness' which for some time
past had arisen between them, and of which he professed not to know the
cause, 'as I am an entire stranger to my son's affairs' (32919, f. 108).

[2] 32856, f. 571.

[3] 32861, ff. 312-13. Powis dated the letter 'Monday November 15th,
1755', but it is docketed 'December 15', which was a Monday.

[4] *Ibid.*, ff. 316-17.   [5] See James West to Newcastle ; 32860, ff. 471-2.

Government in that county; and it was represented to be so much for His Majesty's service to have the Lord Lieutenant residing there, that His Majesty did think proper to appoint him.[1]

This produced a breach between Carnarvon and Newcastle and a renewal of his feud with Gwynne:

If it is more for his Majesty's honour and service, to have Mr. Gwynne at the head of that county than myself: I am very well content: but I may be able in a future election to shew that that gentleman is not unanimously supported by the gentlemen of the county; any more than the gentleman who now serves for the borough of Radnor [Thomas Lewis].

I will make no apology for troubling your Grace with this second letter; but will promise that your Grace shall never be troubled with any other application from etc.[2]

In November 1759, on a vacancy in the representation of Hampshire, Carnarvon, whose father was a considerable land-owner in the county, proposed Simeon Stuart in opposition to Legge, Newcastle's candidate, and secured for him the support of Bute and Leicester House.[3] Nevertheless, Stuart had to give up the contest; but the aftermath was to prove fatal to Legge, who incurred the displeasure, indeed the hatred, of the Prince of Wales and Bute.[4] Carnarvon remained with Leicester House, and, like all who joined it because of some real or imaginary grievance against Newcastle, did his best to set the Prince and Bute against him.

LORD BATH, LORD POWIS, AND SHREWSBURY

Some time in June 1759 Bath addressed the following letter to Robert More, M.P. for Shrewsbury:

I doubt not but you remember the letters you wrote to me, when you desired my interest for the town of Shrewsbury, and

---

[1] 27 Dec 1755; 32861, f. 481.

[2] Carnarvon to Newcastle, 1 Jan 1756; 32862, f. 3.

[3] For Carnarvon's letter to Bute, 3 Nov 1759, see 'Register of Correspondence of the Earl of Bute, 1739–62'; 36796, f. 43.

[4] For the correspondence which arose over this election see *Some Account of the Character of the late Rt. Hon. Henry Bilson Legge* (1764). The pamphlet was by Dr. John Butler, Bishop of Oxford (1777–88) and Hereford (1788–1802).

therefore I do not question but you will readily give your assistance
to my son, whom I have declared, shall be a candidate at the next
election.   It is true, it will be a considerable time, before a new
Parliament.   But some people having mentioned Mr. Clive, without
his knowledge or authority, as I am informd, makes it necessary
for me, to apply thus early to you, as well as to the rest of my
friends ; Mr. Clive is a very worthy man, as well as a very dangerous
antagonist, but yet I must support my son, because I think I am at
the same time doing my duty to the Bradford interest, which he will
in time (by being the possessor of their property) ¹ represent ; and
therefore should apprehend, it may be injudicious in those, who
may mean the same thing, to create divisions in the county by
opposing him.   Your vote and interest for my son, will greatly
oblige, Sir, etc.

Robert More replied from Linley, Shropshire, on 19 June :

I did not receive the honour of your Lordship's letter, till since
the return of the last post, having been at my house at Linley near
Bishop's Castle.—As the civil and religious liberties have been
driven to a party for their support in the Parliament of 1641, when
the great conflict began (and when the Newport family supplied the
TYRANT with money for a title) ² my ancestor, a Member, then
had and all his posterity to this day have, uniformly and very
zealously attached themselves to that party in the cause of liberty ;
with them I have always voted in elections and will vote, — with
them I live and dye ; they chose me into the present Parliament
without any interest of my own, without sollicitation, without influence of Minister of State or Lord, indeed, I believe, they chose
the meanest among themselves to show their contempt for the

¹ These estates comprised the castle of Shrewsbury, the hundreds of
Bradford North and Bradford South, and of Condover, and fourteen manors
in Shropshire, and in 1805 produced a rental of about £45,000 p.a. Henry,
third Earl of Bradford, by his will, dated 8 May 1730, 'devised the said
property to the use of John Newport, Esq., then called John Harrison (who
by act of parliament assumed the surname of Newport only) and his heirs
in tail male. This John Newport afterwards became a lunatic and continued
so until his death . . . in 1783' (*Antiquities of Shropshire*, by Edward Lloyd,
revised by T. F. Dukes, Shrewsbury, 1844, p. 243). John Harrison was a
natural son of Lord Bradford by Mrs. Ann Smith, and after his death,
'there being no direct heir', the estates passed 'partly to the Crown and
partly to the representatives of his mother [the heirs of Lord Bath], she
having disposed of the reversion during her lifetime . . .' (H. E. Forrest,
'Some Old Shropshire Houses and their Owners', *Transactions of the
Shropshire Archaeological Society*, 4 s., vol. vii, part ii, 1920, p. 139).

² Newport in 1642 paid Charles I £6000 for being created a baron. See
Clarendon, *The History of the Rebellion*, Bk. vi, § 66.

influence of the greatest, and one least capable of corrupting to show how much they scorned corruption.

I have declared my inability to continue in the station I am in ; but have had no hand in proposing Colonel Clive ; and that your Lordship's proposal may be acceptable to the town, will give you the most friendly advise. It is that in your applications you should not mention your own interest, or any family's except the King's, but make to them those noble professions of disinterested patriotism, which I've heard from you when a Commoner, and particularly when we carried by one vote the Bill against Bribery. If this fails, there is a borough hard by which chose the Earl of Bradford [1] (I do not recollect that Shrewsbury ever did this), has lately chosen a Granville,[2] and would rejoyce to see any one backed by your Lordship pitted there with Colonel Clive.[3]

About the same time Lord Bath turned to John Bennett, Mayor of Shrewsbury, who, on 27 June 1759, replied that a member of the Corporation had written from London recommending Colonel Clive to succeed Mr. More,

and signifying that Lord Powis, our Recorder, approved of him ; — this letter I immediately communicated to severall gentlemen, who met and consulted together on the subject of it, and the Colonel

[1] Bishop's Castle. [2] Henry Grenville ; see above, pp. 246-7.
[3] Copies of these letters are in the Bodleian, at Oxford, among the papers of Henry Bowdler, a Shrewsbury attorney (MS. Top. Salop. c. 3, f. 100). I am not aware of their having ever been published, but copies probably circulated in Shropshire, and it is undoubtedly to these letters that Blakeway alludes when writing about More's 'correspondence with a celebrated orator of the last age' (*The Sheriffs of Shropshire*, p. 221). There is among the Attingham MSS. an undated paper with a damaged yet perfectly intelligible superscription : 'LD BATHS answ . . . RE who had acquainted him by letter on his being . . . SHREWSBURY'. It obviously refers to More's candidature in 1754, and is Bath's reply to the application referred to in the opening sentence of his letter of June 1759 : presumably circulated by Bath himself as counterblast to the correspondence quoted above. After some flattering remarks about More's conduct in the House when they were both Members, and wishes for his success, Bath informs More that he had thought of offering his son as candidate for Shrewsbury, and might have done so had he known that his kinsman Sir Richard Corbett would not stand again ; expresses surprise at a bargain having been made 'for the more easy conducting the election' for the county 'without ever consulting the people of the chiefest property in it' ; and reserves his claim on behalf of the Bradford interest—

I shd be sorry to see that intrest declining in my hands and diminishing under my management. I am determined to support it to the utmost . . . and this I will do as an honest guardian to Mr. Newport shd he recover his sences . . . or for my own benefit who am heir to him if he shd die.

being of a family of great antiquity and meritt amongst us, and having so remarkably distinguished himself in the service of his country, was agreed by all to be a proper candidate. Mr. Hill allways since we chose him has served us very worthily. . . .

They therefore intended to re-elect him. Subsequently they received letters from Clive's father recommending his son and Bath's letter to Bolas putting up Pulteney. It was then proposed in the Corporation that, as all three candidates were 'unexceptionable', they should be asked to confer and agree together 'which two of the three should stand'. But in the course of the debate, some 'shewing a zeal (a little too warm) for their respective friends . . . caused the opinion of the House to be taken as to their own choice'. This being done, Clive obtained a considerable majority, and it was decided that he should stand in conjunction with Hill.

At the same time I can venture to assure your Lordship, the Corporation retains the greatest respect and regard for you and Lord Pulteney, and would gladly have accepted your Lordship's offer could they by any means have done it with honour and a sure prospect of success.[1]

Bath replied on 30 June criticizing the 'hasty resolution which a majority of the Corporation meeting hath come to so long before the next election', and expostulating that, though he had not taken any steps on behalf of Pulteney so far in advance, his intention to put him up for the borough had been known. He tried to discover whether Clive himself had come forward as candidate, or whether the idea had been suggested by Powis, and next broke out into virtuous indignation, waxing enthusiastic over the rights and privileges of the town :

. . . to suffer Lord Powis to pretend to have a right of nominating to you who shall be your Member, is what I never can submitt to, nor can I think his having obtained, in a precipitate and hasty manner, about 23 of the Corporation which consists of upwards of 70, is sufficient to carry an election, where there are 400 votes. No ; I would have it understood by all the burgesses and inhabitants that I am determined to support their rights and priviledges against this arbitrary nomination of any one at the pleasure of any one

[1] 32892, f. 333.

man's; nor will I suffer the voters of so considerable a town as Shrewsbury, to be transferred at the pleasure of any lord, like a poor Cornish borough, that he might vainly flatter himself was his own property.

Lastly, while acknowledging Clive's great services, Bath tried to suggest that the attempt to put him up as a candidate was untimely 'just after his accepting the Government of Bengal which makes his return to England very uncertain'. He concluded:

I should be very sorry to be the means of destroying the harmony of the town; or of introducing divisions amongst you; but you see, Sir, it is they who thus attacked me, who have begun. Had my son been suffered to come in quietly on Mr. More's resignation, it would have been a much greater honour for him, to have had the unanimous suffrages of so respectable a borough.[1]

The next move on the part of Bath was to apply to Newcastle, complaining of Powis having put up Clive in opposition to his son:

All I can say is, that it is extremely hard, when I desire no favours from the Court, that those who are supposed to have the direction of the interest of the Court, should be sufferd to oppress me: I imagine Mr. Clive, from what happend lately in Parliament, will not be any warm friend to your Grace's. . . .[2]

I must beg leave to assure you, that if I do not meet with protection against Lord Powis in this affair, I shall resent it with that warmth that will become me on the occasion, and never be easy whilst he remains in the Lieutenancy of that county, which he never could pretend to, til the Bradford family failed, by the management of whose interest, he first made himself considerable in Shropshire, and whose property and the power attending it, being all to center in my son, give me the best claim to that honour which his Lordship hath so long enjoyd, and to which he hath so little pretence, from any considerable share of his own possessions in that county.[3]

Newcastle replied, he had been told by Powis only a few days ago that More declined re-election, and that it was intended to set up Clive in his room. But then he did not know

---

[1] *Ibid.* f. 332.

[2] In Feb-Mar 1755 Newcastle most strenuously supported the election petition against the return of Robert Clive and John Stephenson at Mitchell, and succeeded in having them unseated.   [3] 32892, f. 272.

about Bath's intentions, and as he himself had no interest at
Shrewsbury, and the Government very little, he made no
objection to Powis's suggestion. Now, however, he will try
to prevent a dispute between Powis and Bath and will 'offer
to find out some other place for Colonel Clive ; which, I should
hope, might make things easy'.[1]

Indeed, three letters which passed between Powis and
Newcastle the next day [2] testify to the Duke's endeavours to
bring about a compromise, though its terms are not disclosed.
Meantime Bath, on 29 June, addressed another letter to Newcastle full of abuse of the 'little, busy, warm medlers' and of
'this little mortal' Powis, who should be hindered from using
the interest 'he derives from His Majesty from oppressing me ;
as for his own interest and power in Shropshire, I despise it' ;
of Clive, 'a *nabob* worth half a million', etc.[3]

Most extraordinary of all was the next move by Bath, one
of the richest men and most notorious misers of the age, who
at his death in 1764 is said to have left £1,200,000 in 'land and
money' but practically no legacies. On 20 July 1759, his son,
Lord Pulteney (M.P. for Old Sarum), went to Pitt and offered
to raise at his own expense a regiment of one thousand men
for service in the war.[4] 'His Majesty approved it cordially',[5]
and gave the regiment the name of Royal Volunteers. Its
headquarters were fixed at Shrewsbury, and officers were
selected for it whose recruiting (and presumably also electioneering) influence in Shropshire could be made serviceable to
the regiment (and Pulteney). John Calcraft, Henry Fox's

---

[1] 32892, f. 274.   [2] *Ibid.* ff. 314, 318, and 320.
[3] *Ibid.* f. 316.   [4] 17494, f. 136.
[5] *Ibid.* f. 133. The transaction with the King is reported at length
in a letter written to Lord Bath by John Douglas, his chaplain, at Lord
Pulteney's request (Eg. 2186, ff. 154-5) ; it is marked merely 'Saturday
afternoon', but was obviously written on 21 July 1759. It had originally
been intended to make Lord Pulteney colonel of the regiment, but the King,
while highly approving of the scheme, 'said, if it proceeded from a right
and disinterested motive, this would not be insisted upon, and the second
command satisfy his Lordship'. Lord Pulteney is ready to accept this —
he 'believes the more disinterested a part he acts, the more honour and
credit he will acquire, which is his chief object' ; and he proposes to 'lose
no time in setting out for Shrewsbury ; where he will arrive with some éclat,
if he can carry a few blank commissions to be filled up with the names of
persons, whom his friends there may recommend to him'.

right-hand man, was made agent to the regiment,[1] Pulteney was Lieutenant-Colonel, and John Craufurd,[2] brother of Patrick, a favourite of Bute's, was its Colonel; the list of officers [3] included Lord Brome, M.P. (subsequently second Earl Cornwallis), Lord Warkworth, Edmund Nugent, M.P., son and heir of the famous political wire-puller, Robert Nugent, M.P., Charles Cooper, a natural son of Henry Fox, William Forester, son of Brooke Forester, M.P., Peter Bathurst, Temple West 'Mr. Pitt's kinsman',[4] etc.[5] It was to be one of the most fashionable regiments in the British Army.[6] The Prince of Wales was asked to stand godfather to it (his acceptance was signified in a letter to Bute, 24 July 1759).[7] Indeed, the most was made of the patriotic offer. Newcastle explained to Powis: 'His Lordship [Bath] has absolutely refused to put the Government to any expence for levy money, but takes *that* wholly upon himself, which is a very heavy article'.[8] It is true, when it came to disbursing money, his Lordship's patriotic zeal was not quite equal to the occasion.

The connection with Lord Bath is an unpleasant one [wrote Calcraft to Craufurd on 28 August]; . . . a certain sum from Lord Bath, if it could be got, would be best, but I don't think it will.[9]

For the time being, the only money they saw was £1000 given

---

[1] 17494, ff. 136-7.

[2] Having combined recruiting for the regiment with some judicious borough electioneering, John Craufurd secured for himself a seat at Berwick-on-Tweed at the forthcoming general election.

[3] 17494, f. 141. In 'A List of Officers belonging to the Royal Volunteers', sent by Calcraft to Sir Jeffrey Amherst, Commander-in-Chief in North America, it is stated that four of the captains, St. J. Jeffreys, T. West, C. Egerton, and W. Forester, were to 'pay their own levy money' (R.O., W.O., 34/99, f. 33).

[4] Dr. West, grandfather of Temple West, married Maria, eldest sister of Lord Cobham.   [5] 17494, f. 140.

[6] On the eve of an expedition which was soon countermanded, *The London Chronicle* of 25-7 Nov 1760 published the following 'Extract of a letter from Portsmouth, November 25':

It is remarkable that in the Royal Volunteers, commanded by Brigadier Craufurd, who are going and now on board for the expedition, there are two lords, one baronet, three Members of Parliament; and officers whose landed estates are to the amount of 180,000*l.* per ann.

[7] Sedgwick, no. 32.   [8] 32893, ff. 436-7.

[9] 17494, ff. 166-7.

by General Pulteney (Bath's brother) to his nephew 'to fit himself out', but not to be used for levy money.

When, a year later, the accounts had to be settled, Bath would have nothing to do with them. Calcraft wrote to Captain Bathurst on 10 August 1760 :

> There is curious doings about the levy money of the Royal Volunteers. Lord Bath has taken to his bed at sight of the account and says he is too ill to enter upon such business, that he will have nothing more to do with the Regiment, and Crawfurd and his son may pay it out of their profits.[1]

He returned the letter which Calcraft wrote him, 'and absolutely forbid further correspondence on the subject'.[2]   In the end he had to foot the bill, but deducted £1000, his brother's present to Pulteney.[3]   However, in July 1759, Newcastle was still congratulating Bath on his 'generous and most uncommon zeal'.[4]

On 28 July 1759, Powis reported to Newcastle that Bath's letter to the Mayor of Shrewsbury had 'raised a spirit among the old Whigs in Shropshire' to exert themselves in Powis's favour, 'and has given offence to all people'.[5]   And he proceeded to quote the following example :

> As to Sir Richard Corbet and his brother, they (as relations) will each of them give one vote to Lord Pulteney and one to Mr. Hill : — but all the interest they can make, will by them be firmly secur'd to Mr. Hill and Mr. Clive.

On 1 August, Newcastle explained his position at great length to Andrew Stone, who had been his secretary and the Prince's tutor, blaming both Powis and Bath for the line they had taken. 'I have endeavour'd to frighten him [Powis] with the P. of Wales, etc. and have constantly told him that I could not oppose my Lord Bath.' Powis complained of the way in which he had been treated, but was prepared to let Pulteney be

---

[1] 17495, f. 88.   [2] *Ibid.* f. 105, and also f. 94.
[3] *Ibid.* f. 154. 'The family paid near five thousand pounds for the Regiment', wrote John Douglas on 10 Mar 1763, in a letter trying to defend Bath's treatment of his son in money matters (Chase Price MSS. at Hatfield). The reference to what 'the family paid' seems to confirm Calcraft's account of the brother's present having been deducted by Bath.
[4] 27 July 1759 ; 32893, f. 321.   [5] *Ibid.* ff. 335-6.

chosen, provided Newcastle arranged matters with Hill; whom the Duke proposed to have returned in some other place or made an Irish peer, or both. Newcastle's position was very difficult, as the Whigs, to a man, were opposed to Pulteney, and he was not prepared to break with Powis and 'the Shropshire Whigs, which is a most steddy, valuable corps'; still, he wished also to help Bath and Pulteney.[1] The next day he wrote to Powis expressing his concern for all parties in the dispute. It was not an easy thing to fight against such wealth as that of Bath, 'which upon this occasion he will not fail to employ', and against the 'other assistance which Lord Pulteney will not fail of having'. He then proceeded to expatiate on the offer of the regiment in view of which no opposition must be given to him by anyone 'immediately in the King's service'. The regiment, suggested Newcastle, might be 'a good handle' for putting 'an honourable end to the opposition'.[2]

Stone replied that Bath understood

that your Grace neither can, nor will, nor ought, to give up the Whigs at Shrewsbury, or any where else; and should himself be sorry to be too much obliged by the Tories; but they say, they can carry the election for Lord Pulteney; and that is what must be done if possible. . . . He shew'd me a letter he received this day from Dr. Douglas, who is now at Shrewsbury with Lord Pulteney, who entertained the town on the occasion of the victory in Germany, and meets with great encouragement; though they seem sensible that the Corporation are (very near, if not to a man) unanimous in the interest of their antagonist.[3]

On 12 September 1759, Henry Bowdler, a Shrewsbury attorney whom Douglas had left in charge of Pulteney and his affairs, wrote to Douglas:

I have the pleasure to inform you that Lord Pulteney is in perfect health and that he gains ground in the esteem of the town people. But tho' this is what may be reasonably expected from his Lordship's

[1] *Ibid*. ff. 410-11.
[2] *Ibid*. ff. 436-7. Douglas wrote to Bath on 14 July 1759: 'If after what your Lordship has so generously done towards assisting his Majesty's service, an opposition should still be carry'd on by Lord Powis, it will be shameful' (Eg. 2186, f. 157).
[3] 15 Aug 1759; 32894, ff. 199-205.

good sense and behaviour, that only must not be relyed on in the affairs of electioneering.

His antagonists, you know, have appointed agents here (viz. Oliver, Cross, Devereux etc.) with discretionary power to act for them in strengthening their interest, and it will in my opinion be necessary for Lord Bath to have some friends among us arm'd with like power to act for his interest. Though we are not by any means a mercenary people, but on the contrary have always shew'd our contempt of venality, yet there are among the lower class several burgesses who will have their interest in veiw at the same time that they go along with their party or serve their friend, and even at present, tho' so long before the expected time of an election, there are necessary things to be done which will require management and some expense. For instance — by the last resolution of the House of Commons the right of voting here is fixt in the burgesses inhabiting in Shrewsbury [who] pay scot and lot; the same resolution fixes what parts of the town were the antient borough and what not — all the Abbey Foregate to the middle of the stone bridge, part of Coleham and all Cotton Hill are not in the voting part of the town. There are many burgesses live in these excluded parts who would be glad to serve Lord Pulteney. It may be necessary therefore as well as practicable, to bring some of these people into the voting part of the town.

There are likewise some burgesses who do not live in their own parishes but belong to other parishes in town, those not being assest for fear of making them settlement, will not be entitled to vote. But it may be so managed as they may be situated in their own parishes, where they must be assest and entitled to vote. . . .[1]

Meantime the negotiations for a compromise, carried on by Newcastle with Powis, dragged on their weary course; on 3 October 1759, Powis formulated the following terms which, he insisted, should be put forward by Newcastle as his own,[2] as they had not the concurrence of the Corporation of Shrewsbury :

That Lord Pulteney will stand on the Whig interest for that borough, with the consent and approbation of the Corporation — joyntly with one of the candidates nominated by them ; in case the other should be prevailed upon to desist : and that Lord Pulteney will engage to assist and support the Corporation interest, not only

[1] Bodleian, MS. Top. Salop. c. 3, f. 94.
[2] See his subsequent letters of 4 Oct, 32896, f. 272, and 7 Oct, *ibid.* f. 336.

upon any future vacancy, but also upon any event which may happen to prevent him from being a candidate.[1]

No agreement was reached, and in December 1759 Bath was instrumental in the publication of the pamphlet *A Letter to Two Great Men*, written by John Douglas under his direction. Newcastle heard that it was by Bath himself and was 'much in the stile that my Lord Bath talked to your Lordship [Hardwicke] upon the subject of peace'. He asked Hardwicke to read it and let him know his thoughts about it.[2] Hardwicke feared that it was 'of pernicious effect'. 'It is so writ as to be readily swallowed by the people and to create difficulties to the Administration in the terms of peace'; and it is like Bath's 'former manner of debating in the House of Commons; haranging with spirit upon his own topicks, without stating, or attempting to answer, manifest objections'.[3]

Further negotiations for a compromise, in the spring and summer of 1760, availed nothing, and in July Clive's return from India settled the question. On 31 August, Powis reported that things at Shrewsbury stood 'on the part of Mr. Hill and Colonel Clive as well as their own hearts can desire',[4] and on 25 September, that Bath had given up 'his point'. 'After the arrival of Colonel Clive from the East Indies, Lord Pulteney had really no chance of success'.[5] Bath observed that 'it was in vain to contend with the power of the Corporation and the wealth of the Indies'; another circumstance which made him desist, wrote Powis on 17 October, was 'the little encouragement he met with from the Tories', who did not wish, by opposing the Whigs at Shrewsbury, to provoke retaliatory measures on their part in the county.

It is extreamly remarkable, that at the late races, that were given at Shrewsbury by Mr. Hill and Coll. Clive (some days before Lord Bath's letters appear'd there, as above), the Tories attended with great civility and good humour; — a compliment to us, on their part, never before known in Shropshire; where an election was depending![6]

[1] *Ibid.* f. 252.   [2] 24 Dec 1759; 32900, f. 276.
[3] 27 Dec 1759; *ibid.* ff. 355-6.   [4] 32910, f. 450.
[5] 32912, ff. 106-7.   [6] 32913, f. 171.

Powis rejoiced — eight days before the accession of George III was to give Bath his chance to settle accounts between them. Clive and Hill were, however, returned without opposition on 27 March 1761, while Pulteney was elected for Westminster in his absence, for he had started with the Royal Volunteers on the expedition to Portugal from which he was never to return ; on his way home he died of a fever at Madrid on 11 February 1763.

RADNORSHIRE AT THE GENERAL ELECTION OF 1761

On the accession of George III, Carnarvon proceeded with his threatened opposition to Gwynne, knowing that the influence of the Court would now be exerted in his own favour. He wrote to Bute on 22 November :

I caught the Duke of Newcastle yesterday before he had left St. James's. I acquainted him that His Majesty had given me leave to offer myself as a candidate for the county of Radnor, and had permitted me to acquaint his Grace therewith and to beg his countenance and assistance. The Duke told me that Lord Bateman, Mr. Rice, and Mr. Gwynne had been with him that morning,[1] and . . . they assured him, that the county was engaged in favour of Mr. Gwynne, and that I cou'd not possibly have any chance to be chose. . . . I told his Grace . . . that Mr. Gwynne must have a very extraordinary opinion of me, to imagine that I shou'd give up my pretensions to the county, on his assuring me that I cou'd not carry my point.

Newcastle next inquired of Carnarvon 'what interest the Government had in that county', and finally remarked

that as he had supported Mr. Gwynne at the former election, he did not know what to say to it, but desired I wou'd press him no further 'til he had seen them [his Radnorshire friends] again. This my Lord was my answer, and such a one that I fear leaves me little room to hope for his Graces assistance.[2]

On 26 November, Carnarvon wrote to Newcastle :

When I had the honour of talking with your Grace on Fryday last [21 November] . . . your Grace seemed persuaded . . . that I cou'd have no chance of being chose for that county, even if supported

---

[1] See Newcastle's minute of 21 Nov 1760 ; 32999, f. 96.

[2] Fortescue, vol. i, no. 8.

by your Grace, Mr. Gwynne having secured a large majority. I must therefore beg leave to inform your Grace that letters I recieved from Lord Oxford and other friends of mine in that quarter, by yesterdays post, give me the strongest assurances of success, so much that I have very few apprehensions from Mr. Gwynne. Under these circumstances, my Lord, I repeat the request I made to your Grace last Fryday (by His Majesty's permission) and flatter myself your determination will be in my favour.[1]

'I hope to settle things to your Lordship's satisfaction, and . . . I think you may venture to declare', wrote Oxford to Carnarvon on 15 November; and the next day, that Gwynne had set out for London, presumably with a view to securing a sheriff, which should be prevented.[2] These two letters Carnarvon forwarded to Bute, adding with a delicacy perhaps prompted by the prospect of replacing Gwynne as Lord Lieutenant :

. . . if . . . it shou'd be customary for the Lord Lieutenant to recommend, I am very far from even wishing to alter the common course of any business for any private interest of my own, particularly as (however Mr. Gwynne's interest and mine may clash in the county) I believe he is perfectly well attach'd to His Majesty and his Familly.[3]

Meantime Rice, having failed to dissuade Carnarvon from standing, and seeing the Court influence exerted on his side, guessed the line Newcastle would take ; he assured the Duke, on 26 November, that he would 'endeavour to satisfy Mr. Gwynne, should his Grace take a part in favour of Lord Carnarvon, that it is not from want of regard to Mr. Gwynne'.[4] Indeed, on 28 November Newcastle promised Carnarvon 'to do all he cou'd' for him in Radnorshire ; but Powis remained obdurate — 'he looks upon Mr. Gwynne as his nomination', wrote Carnarvon to Bute on 30 November, 'and will support him to the utmost of his power'.

[1] 32915, f. 90.   [2] Bute MSS.
[3] Bute MSS. This letter is undated except 'Wednesday evening'. 19 Nov might have seemed the most likely Wednesday for Oxford's letters to reach Carnarvon, but as in the letter to Newcastle, on Wednesday, 26 Nov, he states that he received them 'by yesterday's post', probably the letter to Bute was written on the same Wednesday — unless there was an amount of finessing which one cannot assume without positive evidence.
[4] 32915, f. 92.

However, if the Duke of Newcastle is in earnest, and will prevail with Mr. Lewis, the Bp. of St. David's and Coll. Hodges to give me their assistance, Ld. Powys can do me very little hurt. . . .

Mr. Lewis is Steward of the King's Lordships of Cantimellioneth in Radnorshire, and entirely under the direction of the Duke ; Mr. Lewis from his office can influence many freeholders. . . .

Mr. Gwynne went back to day for Radnorshire with a thorough resolution of standing.[1]

On 2 December, Carnarvon reported progress to Bute :

Lord Oxford is arrived and brings accounts from Radnorshire very pleasing : he has secured the whole Hundred of Payns Castle for me, which consists of 200 votes, besides most of the gentlemen in the other hundreds of the county. If I can secure Mr. Lewis, and the sheriff, Mr. Gwynne can have no chance.[2]

And on 10 December, Carnarvon wrote to Newcastle :

I must beg of your Grace to speak to Mr. Lewis (who *must* go as you bid him) . . . besides . . . it is his interest to go with me while espoused by your Grace, for there is a man (and a very rich one) ready to give him much trouble in his borough,[3] and I should be sorry to be drove to avail myself of that means of preventing Mr. Lewis hurting me.[4]

The same day, in a letter to Bute, Carnarvon expressed the fear that Newcastle was playing double and could not be trusted.[5] But in reality Newcastle was honestly trying to settle things to the satisfaction of both sides.[6] Gwynne was sent for,[7]

---

[1] Bute MSS.

[2] Bute MSS. The letter is undated except 'Tuesday morning', but it mentions two letters 'received from Hampshire last night', which are probably the letters from Thomas Worsley (27 Nov) and from Simeon Stuart (30 Nov), extant among the Bute MSS. ; this letter was therefore probably written on Tuesday, 2 Dec. Moreover, in the letter of 30 Nov Carnarvon wrote : 'I expect Lord Oxford in town this evening', and this letter starts : 'Lord Oxford is arrived. . . .'

[3] Edward Lewis, a London merchant, no relation of Thomas Lewis ; he was Oxford's candidate.

[4] 32915, f. 382.

[5] The letter was not among the Bute MSS. which I have seen, but is summarized in the 'Register', 36796, f. 59.

[6] See Newcastle's 'Memorandums' of 3 Dec : 'Ld. Carnarvon — Radnorshire election. Endeavour to get Mr. Gwyn to decline it by chusing him elsewhere' (32999, f. 108) ; 5 Dec : 'Radnorshire election. To try to accomodate it . . .' (32915, f. 315).

[7] See letter from Bateman to Newcastle, 14 Dec 1760 ; 32916, f. 251.

and on 18 December the following minute was drawn up at Newcastle House by Powis, Gwynne, and Thomas Lewis :

If Mr. Gwynne can be brought into Parliament without expence at some other place, and my Lord Carnarvon and his friends will give no opposition to Mr. Lewis for the town of Radnor, and the Lieutenantcy and Custos Rotulorum shall remain in Mr. Gwynne's hands ; and Mr. Lewis continues steward of the King's Courts, Mr. Gwynne is ready (with the approbation of his friends which is not at all doubted) to desist for this election and give his interest and that of his friends to the Marquis of Carnarvon ; by which his Lordship will come in for the county of Radnor without any opposition.[1]

'. . . the election in Wales for my Lord Carnarvon. . . . I have accommodated for him if he pleases', wrote the Duke of Newcastle next day to the Duke of Devonshire ;[2] and Gwynne started out for Radnorshire 'in order to engage his friends in the compromise with Lord Carnarvon'.[3] The work of securing the county representation for Carnarvon, initiated by Oxford and the Tories, was thus to be completed by Gwynne, under sanction from the Whig leaders ; for no real political principles were involved in these personal reshufflings at the accession of George III. Nor was there much feeling about it even locally — witness the following note of 25 December :

Lord Bateman presents his compliments to Lord Bute. He has the pleasure to inform his Lordship that Mr. Gwynne has by express sent an account this morning that he has had a meeting of the principal gentlemen of the county of Radnor and that they agree to his declining on the terms offered by the Duke of Newcastle to Mr. Gwynne.[4]

A fuller account of the meeting was sent to Carnarvon by Powis on 27 December ; he reminded Carnarvon of the promise he had been authorized to give to Gwynne of a seat

---

[1] 32918, f. 200 ; another copy in 32999, f. 127.
[2] 32916, ff. 207-13.
[3] Powis to Newcastle, 22 Dec 1760 ; 32916, f. 67.
[4] This letter is in the Musgrave Papers ; as Sir William Musgrave used these letters for his collection of autographs, he cut off the top of the letter and pasted it into another book, so that the first line, 'Lord Bateman presents his compliments to', is in 5726 B, f. 5 ; the rest in C, f. 18.

T

in the next Parliament, which assurance had been confirmed by Newcastle :

But Mr. Gwynne's friends, not caring to rest the certainty of his seat in Parliament, on the chance of his Grace's life or continuance at the head of the Ministry, require me to inform your Lordship 'that it is their unanimous opinion and advice to Mr. Gwynne, that your Lordship should now engage, to interpose (in either of the cases above mention'd) with his Grace's successor in power ; and secure to Mr. Gwynne in like manner, a seat in Parliament, without expense '.[1]

After this for a month there is nothing about Radnorshire either in George III's *Correspondence* or in any of the collections of manuscripts I have examined. But from letters written about the end of January,[2] it appears that the compromise had not been concluded, Carnarvon demanding the Lord Lieutenancy of Radnorshire and Gwynne refusing to give it up, wherein he was warmly supported by Powis, himself similarly placed with regard to Shropshire. On 2 February, Powis declared to Newcastle that no compromise was possible

without Mr. Gwynne's continuance in the Lieutenantcy &c. . . . Giving up the Lieutenantcy &c. wou'd be giving up the power of the county out of his hands ! His friends wou'd never forgive it ! — were he disposd to do so ![3]

Newcastle, in his embarrassment, advised Powis to try Bute, who in turn preferred to throw the burden on Newcastle :

Lord Bute's compliments attend Lord Powis ; the present situation of his family will not permit him to see his Lordship on business this week, but in relation to Lord Carnarvon, the Duke of Newcastle alone can speak to his Lordship, he having, as Lord Bute immagines, receiv'd His Majesty's directions originally upon that affair.[4]

[1] See Fortescue, vol. i, no. 11, and L. B. Namier, *Additions and Corrections*, pp. 9-10.
[2] The following entry occurs in the 'Register', 26 Jan 1761 : 'Lord Carnarvon to the Earl of Bute. Enclosing two letters from Lord Powis and soliciting advice thereon.—Lord Powis to Lord Carnarvon. As to election affairs for the borough of Radnor.' (36796, f. 71.)
[3] 32918, f. 196.
[4] 29 Jan 1761 ; *ibid.* f. 198. Bute's father-in-law, Edward Wortley Montagu, had died on 22 Jan, and Bute went into mourning and a decorous

On 3 February, Carnarvon informed Bute that he had refused to accept the conditions,[1] and next day wrote to Newcastle [2] asking him to secure Thomas Lewis's support.

If he will join me heartilly in the county, I will support him as
strongly in his borough, and use my endeavours towards keeping
every thing quiet there ; but if he rejects my offer, I will take care
to find him employment enough between this and the election — I
know how strong an influence your Grace has over him.

Thomas Lewis, again, appealed to Newcastle in terms not
of parties and politics but of seats and safety, of no superfluous
expense and 'the peace of the county' :

. . . my joining Mr. Gwyne must inevitably bring an opposition
against me and throw both town and county in a flame and great
confusion. As you are so good to bring in Mr. Gwyne elswhere,
why then can't we be at peace ? Your Grace can easily settle this,
which is now come to a crisis.[3]

A further series of conferences between Newcastle, Bute,
Powis, and Carnarvon produced no result ; and on 20 February
1761 Powis wrote to Bute :

I saw Lord Carnarvon this day at St. James's and after we had
talk'd over the affair of Radnorshire . . . found this to be his final
determination (viz[t].) 'That his Lordship chose rather to give up
the certainty of a seat in Parliament for that county, than his pretensions to the Lieutenancy and office of Custos Rotulorum'. I
have nothing therefore to do further, than to leave Mr. Gwynne
and Mr. Lewis at liberty to pursue their own measures, in respect
to a contest.[4]

The same day Carnarvon reported to Bute :

According to your Lordship's directions, I waited upon the Duke
of Newcastle and Lord Powys, to both of whom, I declared, the
never having seen the minute, or understood by the verbal conversation I had with Lord Powis, that I was to preclude myself from an

confinement, especially strict with regard to people he did not find it convenient to see. But on 9 Feb, Powis wrote to Newcastle : 'I have had a
conference with Lord Bute about the Radnorshire compromise ; and have
something very material to mention to your Grace' (*ibid.* f. 382).
    [1] 'Register of Correspondence', 36796, f. 73.
    [2] 32918, f. 259.   [3] 15 Feb 1761 ; 32919, f. 21.
    [4] Bute MSS.

application for the Lieutenantcy etc., after the expiration of the six months.[1]

This morning Lord Powis came up to me at St. James's . . . he represented to me . . . the many difficulties that I must meet with, . . . concluding all by saying, that out of friendship to me, and for the peace of the county, he hoped (or rather advised) I wou'd confirm the treaty, as before offer'd, and added that your Lordship wou'd speak to me upon it.

I answer'd him, that no one wou'd do more to preserve the peace of the county, than myself, but as to the affair of the Lieutenantcy I had already given him my answer, therefore unless Mr. Gwynne wou'd give up that point, it was impossible for me to enter into any compromise. Here ended the conversation.

Mr. Gwynne is gone down to renew his canvass, and Mr. Lewis has declared for him ; therefore I am now at liberty as to the borough (and unless I receive any directions to the contrary from your Lordship) I shall write Mr. Lewis Jun[r] word . . . that I will support him with all my interest, as will Lord Oxford, and I have no doubts but he will drive his enemy, so supported.[2]

But as for giving the Stewardship of the King's Lordships to Edward Lewis, Carnarvon thought that in view of his being a stranger in the country, it should preferably be given to himself together with the Lord Lieutenancy — 'as the whole interest the Crown has in Radnorshire consists in these offices, the splitting them in a degree must weaken it'.

At the last moment an agreement was reached after all. Howell Gwynne and Thomas Lewis signed the proposal for a compromise sent to them by Powis,[3] and on 2 March 1761, Powis transmitted the paper for Carnarvon's signature, reminding him that he would have to give peremptory orders to his friends in favour of Thomas Lewis. 'You will then be rid of all trouble, and the county will be restor'd to its former quiet.' [4] Here is the full text of the agreement : [5]

---

[1] This statement, two months after the minute for the compromise had been drawn up at Newcastle House, is, to say the least, amazing. The six months he mentioned were the period after the King's death for which commissions were extended pending definite appointments.

[2] Bute MSS.

[3] H. Gwynne to Carnarvon, 28 Feb 1761 ; 5726, D, f. 75, and B, f. 37.

[4] Bute MSS.

[5] Townshend MSS. at Dalkeith House. No copy of the agreement seems to have been sent to Newcastle or Bute, possibly because of the

Lord Carnarvan [1] engages that Mr. Gwynn shall be brought into Parliament for some borough without expence at the next General Election and agrees that the offices of Lieutenancy and Custos Rotulorum for the county of Radnor be continued to him for five years.

Upon the above terms Mr. Gwynne (with the approbation of his friends) agrees to desist from being a candidate at the ensuing General Election for the county of Radnor and with his interest and that of his friends to support Lord Carnarvan's interest there.

Lord Carnarvan likewise engages to support Mr. Lewis (the present Member) for the borough of Radnor at the ensuing Election with his interest and that of his friends, and agrees that the Stewardship of the Kings courts remains in his hands.

Upon the above terms Mr. Lewis likewise agrees to support Lord Carnarvan's Election for the county of Radnor.

Carnarvan

March 1761

Secret Article

Mr. Lewis agrees to hold the courts as long and to resign them to the Earl of Oxford at the same time and upon the same terms as Mr. Gwynne continues and parts with the Lieutenancy.

Some mystery attaches to this secret article : its not being mentioned at the time is understandable, but there is no reference to it even in certain later correspondence in which one would expect to see it quoted — was it considered void because Carnarvon had been unable to secure Lewis's unopposed election ? Though even this would not justify Lewis's asserting in 1765 that according to the terms of that agreement the Stewardship was to continue in his hands ' without any limitation '.[2]

We have two great difficulties to surmount [wrote Carnarvon to Bute on 2 March], the one to stop the opposition in the borough ; and the other to pacify our own friends in the county, who are very angry with me for the compromise.

secret article. Carnarvon sent a copy to Grenville, 2 Feb 1764 (Grenville MSS., J.M.), but the enclosure is missing — did it include the secret article ? How and when Charles Townshend obtained his copy is not known — possibly Oxford communicated the text of the agreement to the Treasury when in the autumn of 1766 he applied for the Stewardship of the King's manors.

[1] It is thus that he signed his name.   [2] See below, p. 278.

I saw Mr. Lewis junior last night, and shall see him again this evening ; but as the canvass has begun absolutely against my advice, doubt much being able to stop it.

P.S.—I want much to explain to your Lordship, what Mr. Lewis mentions as to my having promised him my interest.[1]

And in a further letter marked 'Saturday evening' :

By the treaty I enter'd into with Lord Powis, I shall hope to meet with no opposition for the county, from Mr. Gwynne ; yet as some of his agents have been endeavouring to raise a flame in the county, and to persuade some of my friends that I had deserted them, by acquiescing to his continuing five years in his office of Lieut^{cy} and Custos Rot. (if approved of by the King) I am not altogether without suspicion that I may meet with some foul play.

He therefore asked that the Lieutenancy be not filled till after the election ; though, if the other side adhered to the compromise, he would agree to Gwynne's continuing in office for five years :

I have done all I can towards stopping the opposition in the borough of Radnor but find it impracticable ; but I shall act in it consistant to the treaty.

The Duke of Newcastle has given me authority to inform Mr. Gwynne that Old Sarum is the borough designed for him.

Lord Powis has promised me that I may recommend Justices, when the Commission of Peace passes for that county.

On 11 April 1761, Carnarvon was returned unopposed for Radnorshire,[2] while Howell Gwynne had been returned for Old Sarum on 30 March ; and from now onwards Gwynne, on whose behalf Newcastle had so strenuously exerted himself, was one of the most faithful followers of Bute and a regular 'King's friend'. For Radnor borough a double return was made of the two candidates on 3 April. Newcastle continued to support Thomas Lewis, with which Powis was well pleased :

---

[1] Bute MSS. The letter is merely dated 'Monday, 4 o'clock' ; presumably 2 Mar.

[2] The next day he wrote to inform Bute about it ; see 5726, C, f. 120. In a previous letter, of 2 Apr, mentioned in the 'Register' (36796, f. 85), he had complained of delay in the Radnorshire election 'caused by the writ being secreted', and declared that neither Thomas Lewis nor Gwynne could be trusted.

Otherwise, indeed [he wrote to Newcastle on 13 April 1761], the peace, as well as the power, of the country wou'd be left on such a footing (by means of what has been done lately, by a sett of low, turbulent people, the remains of the old Tories who, to revive that interest, have absolutely made this contest to be a party-dispute in Radnorshire) that there will be no living there for any friends of your Grace.—Their insolence is the more extraordinary as their aim and endeavours were to oppose and defeat that compromise, which was concluded under your Grace's protection, for the service of Lord Carnarvon, with the approbation of Lord Bute.—They regarded his Lordship's success no further, than to make use of him as their instrument, to destroy that interest of the Whigs in Radnorshire, which for these forty years has been so well established, as to withstand all their efforts to shake it.[1]

Probably none of these Radnorshire politicians could have named any marked difference between 'Whigs' and 'Tories', except that in the county they were the two sides in an organized quarrel. For even while there were still real differences between the two parties, animosities in the counties were always more bitter than at the centre. In 1712 Addison wrote in his *Sir Roger de Coverley* :

I observe that the spirit of party reigns more in the country than in the town. . . . At the same time that the heads of parties . . . keep up a perpetual intercourse of civilities, their tools . . . in these out-lying parts will not so much as mingle together at a cock match.

And Sir Roger himself was

a much stronger Tory in the country than in town, which, as he told me in my ear, is absolutely necessary for the keeping up his interest.

No parties or politics were mentioned in the letter which Edward Lewis, the 'Tory' candidate, wrote to Bute on 12 June :

Inclination when in prosperity attach'd me to your Lordship, permit me now, in the adverse situation of my affairs . . . to entreat your Lordship's advice in regard to my election at New Radnor. . . . I am sensible, a man's being merely unfortunate, is not with a person of your Lordship's way of thinking, reason sufficient to deprive me of your protection.[2]

[1] 32921, f. 454.   [2] 5726, D, f. 205, and B, f. 56.

When in November 1761 the Radnor election came before the House of Commons, Thomas Lewis withdrew and Edward Lewis was seated. The 'Whig cause', considered primarily in terms of quasi-proprietary claims of the 'Whig' incumbents of seats and places, was satisfied, for the time being, by the Stewardship of the King's Manors in Radnorshire being left to Henry, brother of Thomas Lewis.

To secure the peace and quiet of the country allready too much harassed with vexatious law suits to the ruin of many [Thomas Lewis wrote to Newcastle on 16 December 1761] and to prevent any trouble or difficulty upon my account, I chose to decline a tedious contest in the House at this juncture. . . .

Having, my Lord, a considerable independent landed property in my country, I will not omitt the earliest opportunity of a place where I have so long sate, to continue with the usual zeal the service of my King and country.[1]

And again, on 20 September 1765, when Oxford, considered a Tory, applied to Rockingham for the Stewardship of the Radnorshire Manors, Thomas Lewis wrote to Newcastle :

Your Grace will, I hope, pardon my acquainting you that Mr. Pelham put the Steward[p] of the King's Lordships in Radnorshire, into my hands in the year 1746 : which has an influence in the burrough, and uninterruptedly possessed by me till His Majesty's accession when Lord Carnarvon, finding my interest in the county absolutely necessary for him, with very high authority rather demanded than intreated it, this coming from the person he made no scruple of mentioning induced my compliance upon the terms of the Stewardships continuing in my hands without any limitation.

Should he be deprived of it, this would hurt 'the Whig interest' in the county and be

a very sensible mark upon me likewise who for 47 years served in Parliament upon my own expence and interest . . . never varying but constant in the support of His Majesty's and the Whig interest.[2]

Thomas Lewis, though he lived till 1777, did not stand again for Radnor, but his nephew and heir, John Lewis, contested it against Edward Lewis in 1768, 1774, and 1780, and was returned each time, only to be unseated on petition. The

---

[1] 32932, f. 208.   [2] 32969, f. 450.

son of John Lewis, Sir Thomas Frankland Lewis, first Baronet, regained the borough for the Harpton family in 1847, and in 1855 was succeeded in its representation by his son, the well-known statesman, Sir George Cornewall Lewis, who retained the seat till his death in 1863.

LORD POWIS AND THE NEW COURT

Henry Arthur Herbert, son of Francis Herbert, M.P. for Ludlow, was not heir to any title, but as other branches of the family became extinct he managed to have their titles re-created in his person. Thus that of Lord Herbert of Chirbury, which had become extinct in 1738, was given him in 1743 ; and when his exceedingly distant cousin, the third and last Marquis of Powis (a Roman Catholic and Duke of Jacobite creation), died in 1748, leaving his estates to Lord Herbert, he promptly turned to Newcastle with a request for the titles :

As the late Marquis of Powis [wrote Herbert on 7 April 1748] by giving me his estate, has done so much for a Protestant family, I should be very sorry to find that His Majesty with the interposition of my friends, shou'd not be prevail'd upon, to honour me with his approbation of it by granting me his titles. . . .

P.S.—Let me add further that my disappointment in the point abovemention'd, wou'd make a very unfavourable impression upon the minds of those in the country that are the friends of the Government and are my friends ; and have express'd very greatly their joy and satisfaction with my good fortune ; to which they hope for the addition of the title.[1]

On 27 May 1748, Lord Herbert was created Earl of Powis, and three years later married Barbara, posthumous daughter and sole heiress of Lord Edward Herbert, only brother of the last Marquis.

In 1734, on the death of Henry, third Earl of Bradford, Herbert was appointed Lord Lieutenant of Shropshire. In 1745 he was chosen Recorder of Ludlow, which he had represented in Parliament 1727–43. He was, moreover, Recorder of Shrewsbury and Deputy Lieutenant of Montgomeryshire. In short, he captured whatever office of influence he could within the sphere of his election activities.

[1] 32714, f. 442.

But on the accession of George III, Bath proceeded to carry out his threat concerning the Lord Lieutenancy of Shropshire. The following entry appears in a 'Memorandum of Conversation with Lord Bute and Mr. Pitt', drawn up by Newcastle on 15 December 1760 :

Lord Bute is acquainting me with what had pass'd with Lord Powis. His desire that his Lordship should be of the Bedchamber ; and that that might be an expedient for the Lieutenancies.

That my Lord Bath had told Mr. Pitt that the King had promised him both the Lieutenancies of Shropshire and Montgomery — that the King had made him no promise ; but that Lord Bute wish'd it could be accommodated by making him Lord of the Bedchamber, giving the Lieutenancy of Shropshire to Lord Bath, and that of Montgomery to Lord Powis. I begg'd nothing might be done hastily in it ; and stated the ill consequences it might have in Shropshire.

. . . . .

Mr. Pitt . . . gave me the history of my Lord Bath's application — seem'd rather inclined to him ; but hoped that the Bedchamber might be an expedient.[1]

A memorandum, drawn up by Newcastle on 16 December, gives the substance of a conversation with Lord Powis :

Lord Powis.—Thinks he cannot take the Bedchamber on condition of his resigning the Lieutenancy to my Lord Bath. To acquaint my Lord Bute and Mr. Pitt that this seems to be my Lord Powis's resolution ; but that I think it should be postponed till the Duke of Devonshire comes to town, who is Lord Powis's great friend.[2]

The same day Powis wrote to Newcastle :

I shall not depart from the sentiments your Grace found me in . . . as I have liv'd on very good terms many years with my Whig friends in the country (and on a late occasion particularly experienc'd their regard and attachment to me) no personal considerations shall tempt me to give them up ; or warrant them to say —

vendidit hic auro patriam, dominumque superbum
imposuit.[3]

On 17 December, the Duke of Devonshire begged Newcastle to prevent such a disgrace from falling on Powis, and authorized

---

[1] 32916, f. 81.   [2] *Ibid.* f. 83.   [3] *Ibid.* f. 96.

him, if necessary, to use his own name in the strongest manner —

the consequence his Lordship is of in that part of the world; the influence he has over several Members of Parliament, and the attachment to him of all those who have been in that country the true friends and steady supporters to this Royal Family, are considerations that will I hope plead in his favour.[1]

Newcastle certainly did not require any urging in this matter; he was warm, indignant, exasperated about it. 'The turning out Lord Powis from his Lieutenancy of Shropshire to make way for Lord Bath' was cited by him to Rigby, on 19 December 1760, as evidence of the Whigs being 'given up in many parts of England',[2] and in a conversation he had the same day with Bute it produced so much heat as to result in a temporary suspension of negotiations between them. Bute, wrote Newcastle to Devonshire on 19 December,

took it very high and said, Is the King to do nothing? Is a possession for twenty-five years to prevent the King in a new reign from giving a Lieutenancy to a man of my Lord Bath's great consideration and estate in Shropshire?[3]

On 24 December, Lord Mansfield, when trying to bring the two together once more, assured Newcastle that there was no bad will on the part of Bute and that Powis's affair embarrassed him, 'it having been rashly promised'. 'It is thought you mean to be absolute and to force, etc., and to hallow the Whigs upon the incident of Lord Powys.' Thus to Newcastle the promise to remove Powis from the Lieutenancy of Shropshire, which Bath had obtained to satisfy his petty vanity and mean vengeance, was part of a scheme to overthrow the Whigs; while to the new Court, Newcastle's defence of an old friend and political dependant was a sign that he meant to establish his superiority in the new reign. And these exaggerations have become embedded in the history of the time.

But in February 1761 Powis got into direct touch with

[1] *Ibid.* f. 152. On 16 Jan 1761, Lady Grey wrote to her husband, Lord Royston, that two days ago Newcastle 'had all the Shropshire gentlemen with him in a body to remonstrate against the intended change of their Lord Lieutenant. This was a sort of triumph for Lord Powis, but it is said Lord Bath has obtained the promise' (35376, ff. 45-6).

[2] See above, p. 237. [3] 32916, ff. 207-13.

Bute over the Radnorshire elections, and the affair of his Lieutenancy, which had loomed so large, was soon accommodated between them. On 3 March, the day after Powis had completed the Radnorshire agreement for Carnarvon, he wrote to Bute :

> I should be extremely glad of the honour of an audience of His Majesty. Before I attempt it, I beg leave to state matters to your Lordship : and at the same time, when I wish to be inform'd of your sentiments, let me ask pardon for giving you this trouble.
>
> Being now removed from the office of Lieutenant and Custos Rotulorum of Shropshire, I am desirous to assure His Majesty, not only of my submission to his will and pleasure, on that occasion, but of my duty and attention, on every other, to His Majesty's service : — and since reports have been spread abroad 'that it is my misfortune to be under His Majesty's displeasure' (which indeed, your Lordship has been so good as to leave me no room to be under apprehensions of) I wish likewise to lay before His Majesty in the most respectful manner the great satisfaction I should have in receiving (when ever it shall be judg'd proper) some mark of His Majesty's favour.[1]

Bath was appointed Lord Lieutenant of Shropshire on 9 March 1761, but an appropriate 'mark of his Majesty's favour' for Powis was soon found. Newcastle wrote to Hardwicke on 14 May 1761 : 'Lord Powis will have the Comptroller's Staff. That will do well. Considering what has passed with Lord Bath.'[2] On 22 May, Powis was appointed Comptroller of the Household, and in June, Lord Lieutenant of Montgomery and a Privy Councillor. He was now fully satisfied, and the 'Whig cause', as he conceived it, was safely established (moreover, on the death of Bath in July 1764, Powis was reappointed Lord Lieutenant of Shropshire). He continued to manage Shropshire affairs, happy to be able, for the present, to serve two masters — or rather to serve Bute and make Newcastle take care of the jobs which he wished to have done for his friends.

On 15 October, after Pitt's resignation and on the eve of the first session of the new Parliament, Newcastle wrote to Powis :

> There is one earnest request, which I have to make of . . . all my Shropshire friends ; and that is, that they would all be in town,

---

[1] Bute MSS.   [2] 32923, f. 70.

the first day of the session, and at the Cockpit the night before, on Monday November 2. It highly imports us, and all our friends, to have a great appearance at our first meeting; if ever the Whigs intend to show their strength in support of the King and the present Administration, now is the time; and the whole depends upon the appearance and attendance at first: pray, speak yourself personally to every one of your friends, and let me know their answer. I think, I have a right to ask this favor of you, and them; especially when I can have no view in it, but our common interest. Having thus lodged this request with your Lordship, I shall not make any other application to them.[1]

With this letter Powis received a list of the friends he had to summon. It included the two Members for Shrewsbury (Hill and Clive), the two Members for Ludlow (Herbert and Bridgeman), General Whitmore, and the two Foresters; the name of Peregrine Cust was added with a query against it.

Powis replied on 18 October:

I can already assure you, that all my friends (I shou'd say your Grace's friends under my care) will certainly appear, — except Coll. Forester and Mr. Hill. The former now lies ill of the gout: — and Mr. Hill's eldest daughter . . . is now given over by her physicians: yet if he and Coll. Forester can possibly get up to town, I am sure they will do it.[2]

When Newcastle was forced to resign, on 26 May 1762, he encouraged his friends to retain office (hoping that this would pave the way for his own return). Powis was only too glad to do so, but henceforth, while attending Bute's levees,[3] kept away from Claremont, where Newcastle tried to outshine his successor by arranging for the greatest possible concourse of friends. Newcastle wrote to Devonshire on 15 July:

I have my house full every day. . . . I will only observe, by the by, that I have seen your friend my Lord Powis but *once*; and that at eight o'clock in the morning, two days after I came hither.[4]

The decisive test for Powis came when Devonshire was dismissed from office and struck off the roll of Privy Councillors

---

[1] 32929, f. 281.   [2] *Ibid.* f. 361.
[3] See, *e.g.*, list of people present at Bute's levee, sent to Newcastle by H. V. Jones, 12 June 1762; 32939, ff. 309-10.
[4] 32940, ff. 343-4.

by George III. On 31 October 1762, Newcastle wrote to Lord George Cavendish :

My Lord Powis came to me yesterday morning from Devonshire House ; he was in extreme good humour, seem'd enraged at what had passed ; and I gave him gently to understand, or at least he might perceive what, I thought, he should do, considering his long attachment to, and connection with, the Duke of Devonshire, and his family.[1]

Powis, however, though 'enraged', was slow to take the hint, and was finding excuses for not resigning. Hardwicke wrote to Newcastle on 15 November :

My Lord Powis will, in my opinion, not quit, and I look upon his postponing his *determination* till the Duke of Devonshire comes to town as a sign of it ; for his meaning seems to me to be, then to put it to the Duke of Devonshire whether he absolutely insists upon his resigning, which I suspect his Grace will not say plainly he does. The fear of my Lord Bath is a mere frivolous pretence.[2]

The next day, in a letter marked 'Very secret', Newcastle appealed to Devonshire to make Powis resign :

As to my Lord Powis, your Grace must exert yourself, both for your own sake, his Lordship's sake, and that of us all. His quitting perhaps would have more effect with the Whig country gentlemen (and they are the persons upon whom we must depend) than any body's. His Lordship is certainly in great doubt, and undetermined what to do. He sees his figure concern'd on one side, to act a part becoming him towards your Grace, and your family : and what is really for the support of the Whig interest. On the other hand, he loves Court, is used to it ; and thinks, that his interest in the country has been greatly supported by his interest at Court. Hitherto, to be sure, that has been greatly the case ; but that was, when the Court had their interest (the Whigs) infinitely more at heart, than, I am afraid, the Court at present has ; that Court acted according to their principle and inclination, in supporting my Lord Powis ; this Court will certainly act contrary to their rule and inclination, if they do it. And I wonder, his Lordship don't see my Lord Bath in a different light from what my Lady Powis represents him to do.

But, my Lord, my Lord Powis will certainly ask your Grace,

whether you wish that he should resign; he may go farther, and ask you whether you insist upon it; I really think you owe it to the Whig cause, without any delicacy about yourself (for allow me to say it, you are above that), to give my Lord Powis plainly to understand, that you do think that, in the present formation of the Administration, he ought not to make a part of it; and that, I am persuaded, will do.[1]

Another letter, again marked 'Very secret', followed on 20 November:

My Lord Powis has declared to me his intention not to resign his Staff; and that, in a manner, that does not do him honor; tho' I beg, your Grace would take no notice of that. His Lordship denies his having ever told me, *that he would determine nothing, 'till he saw your Grace*, asserts, that I had never done him any one favor; (that is pretty extraordinary indeed); and to sum up all, that the King solely gave him his employment; that he can't resign without offending the King; that, in that, he follows my example, who, he says, told him, that in the affair of my Lord Bath, I could not offend the King; altho' I represented against it, in the strongest manner, as your Grace knows, to the King himself. And I believe, your Grace and I contributed something to his having the Staff.[2]

A week later Newcastle was already counting his Shropshire votes apart from Powis. He wrote to Rockingham on 27 November:

. . . of Lord Powis's party, I think, we are sure of two Clives, two Forresters, Gen[l] Whitmore, and, I hope, Bridgeman.[3]

In the list of the House of Commons which Newcastle had compiled on 13 November 1762, seven Shropshire Members were placed among his friends (Whitmore, Bridgeman, Herbert, Hill, Clive, and the two Foresters) and five among his opponents (the three Tories — Lyster, Astley, and Child — and John Grey, M.P. for Bridgnorth and brother of Lord Stamford, and Cust). On Powis's defection, Herbert was naturally given up, and also Hill. In the division on the preliminaries of peace, on 9 December 1762, only Lord Clive, the two Foresters, and Whitmore voted with the Opposition; the absence of Bridgeman must not, however, be taken as a proof of a change in

---

[1] *Ibid*. f. 52.   [2] *Ibid*. f. 89.   [3] *Ibid*. f. 162.

attitude, as there was extreme mismanagement of the division on the Opposition side.

LORD CLIVE, HOME POLITICS, AND BISHOP'S CASTLE [1]

Lord Sandwich was for many years closely connected with India House,[2] and Robert Jones, M.P., his friend, 'man of business', and nominee at Huntingdon, was a Director of the East India Company.   In home politics Sandwich still followed in 1761 the Duke of Cumberland who, as the dynastic opposition in the new reign, was drawing closer to Newcastle; therefore also Sandwich, for the time being, co-operated with him. On 24 April 1761, he wrote to Newcastle that this was a favourable moment to secure the friendship of Colonel Clive, 'as he is dissatisfied with the person to whom he seem'd most inclin'd to attach himself [Pitt], which I did not fail to make the proper advantages of'.   He proposed to send Jones to Clive,

to go from me to him, to give him an account by word of mouth of your Grace's inclination to serve him. This will be a means of preventing a necessity of putting anything into writing . . . and as I can entirely depend on Jones's discretion and address, it will be a means of preventing a relation of his who is allways at his elbow . . . from making impressions on him in favour of his former friend.

Sandwich added that Clive 'will carry at least two Members besides himself; and will never have anything to ask beyond the present favour'.[3]

  [1] In the first edition of this book I wrote in a footnote that Clive's biographers 'seem shy of plunging into the maze of the extremely complex home politics of the time'; and I added: 'Still, the history of India House and of its connexions will have to be written some day'. This has now been done by Miss Lucy S. Sutherland in her masterly work on *The East India Company in Eighteenth-Century Politics*, published in 1952.   Here I am only concerned with Clive's Parliamentary and electoral affairs 1760–63, and his capture of the borough of Bishop's Castle.
  [2] The origin and nature of this connexion I have not been able to trace — they are probably recorded in some very obvious place, only I do not happen to have come across it.
  [3] 32922, ff. 181-2. The two Members were his father, Richard Clive, returned for Montgomery by Powis, and John Walsh, M.P. for Worcester. The 'favour' may have been a K.B. or an Irish peerage; he shortly received both.

On 3 May, Clive wrote to Sandwich from Bath :

I am more obligd than words can express for the part your Lordship has taken in my behalf, any notice taken of me, as the reward of my successes (rather than merits) cannot but be very acceptable, I should have been sav'd from much anxiety, if when so many others were thought of, I had not been forgotten, not that I pretend to plead any other merit than the notice which was taken of me by the Duke of Newcastle and the public. If less had been said, I should have been less ambitious and consequently less unhappy.[1]

'The enclosed letter', wrote Sandwich to Newcastle when forwarding the above, '. . . seems to shew that we have fully succeeded in our negociation at Bath.'[2] On 13 July 1761, an entry appears in Newcastle's Memorandums that the 'first Red Ribbon' is to be given to Clive :[3] and during the next months entries occur about the Irish peerage solicited for him by Powis and Devonshire.[4] Clive, on receiving it, thanked Newcastle on 1 December 1761 as its 'first cause and principal promoter' ;[5] and Newcastle continued to be harassed by Powis with requests on behalf of Clive[6] and Walsh, 'a very sensible man, and not unworthy of your attention . . . who has your Grace's service very much at heart'.[7] Three days before Newcastle left the Treasury, he was still asked by Powis to help Maskelyne, Clive's brother-in-law, to a Commissionership of Taxes.

I resign, as your Lordship knows, my employment on Wensday [replied Newcastle on Sunday, 23 May] ; and I wonder, after the usage, you know I meet with every day from the King, you can imagine H.M. would let me recommend a Commissioner of Taxes on any account. . . . I beg you would shew my Lord Clive that it is impossible for me to do it.[8]

By November 1762 Cumberland was very nearly in declared opposition to the Government, while Fox, previously his chief political agent, had gone over to the Court and persuaded

---

[1] *Ibid*. f. 348. [2] *Ibid*. f. 346. [3] 32925, f. 42.
[4] 5 Aug 1761, 32926, f. 181 ; 15 Sept, 32928, f. 187 ; 22 Oct, 32929 f. 436 ; 24 Nov, 32931, f. 244.
[5] *Ibid*. f. 368. [6] 32934, ff. 33, 223-5, 312 ; 32935, f. 370.
[7] *Ibid*. f. 20 ; about the petition against his election at Worcester, see 32931, ff. 9, 11, 17, and 31.
[8] 32938, f. 417 ; see also *ibid*. ff. 401-3 and 415.

U

Sandwich, who was in financial difficulties, to do likewise and accept the Embassy to Spain.

> . . . it is with the greatest heart breaking [wrote Sandwich to Cumberland on 10 November] I am obliged to say, that my affairs being in the most confused condition . . . I could never have any peace of mind if I was to throw away the means of making some reparation to my family, for the damage they will have suffered from my indiscretions.[1]

On 12 November, Fox, engaged on forming a Court party, wrote to Sandwich :

> Pray, my Lord, send Mr. Major, Mr. Henniker, Mr. Stephenson [2] and, if you can, Lord Clive, to me next Tuesday. I am told Lord Clive's great love to the D[uke] of D[evonshire] is new and not fix'd. To your Excellency it is neither new nor weak. And I hear the whole family were, not long ago, vastly pleased with a letter Lord Bute wrote to his Lordship. Let him come, if you can, and ask *one* thing, not *two*. Adieu.[3]

The scheme to gain Clive failed. He wrote to Major Carnac on 23 November 1762 :

> I still continue to be one of those unfashionable kind of people who think very highly of independency, and to bless my stars, indulgent fortune has enabled me to act according to my conscience. Being very lately asked, by authority, if I had any honours to ask from my sovereign, my answer was, that I thought it dishonourable to take advantage of the times ; but that when these Parliamentary disputes were at an end, if his Majesty should then approve of my conduct by rewarding it, I should think myself highly honoured in receiving any marks of the royal favour.[4]

Although on 24 November 1762 Clive's father attended the meeting at the Cockpit preparatory to the opening of the

---

[1] Sandwich MSS. There is a draft and a copy of this letter at Hinchingbrooke, both in Sandwich's hand.

[2] All three were merchants and Members of Parliament. Major was Henniker's father-in-law, and Stephenson was politically connected with Lord Sandwich. These three were got over to the Court.

[3] Sandwich MSS. In 1754 Clive was allied to Sandwich's candidate Stephenson in the Mitchell election and over the subsequent petition. The letter from Lord Bute mentioned above is possibly that of 1 Sept 1762, from which an excerpt appears in Sir John Malcolm's *Life of Robert, Lord Clive* (1836), vol. ii, pp. 207-8. Bute thanked him therein for his 'Memorial as to the East Indies'.   [4] Sir John Malcolm, *op. cit.* vol. ii, p. 205.

session, it is not certain whether Clive himself was present; [1] and in the division of 1 December 1762 the Clives voted with the Opposition,[2] and on the 9th Clive and John Walsh were of the minority of sixty-five who voted against the preliminaries of the peace treaty.

In April 1763 Clive, engaged in a bitter contest with Sulivan at India House, turned to Newcastle, the greatest of eighteenth-century electioneers. On the 8th he received the following note :

> The Duke of Newcastle sends his compliments to my Lord Clive ; and returns him many thanks for the printed list; and is very glad to see that by that list we have so great a majority ; which the Duke of Newcastle hopes will increase.
>
> The Duke of Newcastle has gone through the whole list very carefully ; and has taken out the few names which he has any means of gaining, who are not engaged on either side ; and will send to them immediately ; nothing has been or shall be wanting on his part.[3]

But James West reported on 14 April :

> I am sorry to tell your Grace Mr. Sullivan and his list have carried the ballot. Lord Clive was 81 lower than the lowest in Mr. Sullivan's list and the highest in Lord Clive's list was 20 below the lowest in Sullivan's list. Lord Clive must have been strangely misled in his calculations.[4]

'We have been cheated out of the election by the Clerks of the India House',[5] was Thomas Walpole's comment.

Clive had returned home determined to cut a great figure in the country ; and his *jagir* of £27,000 a year, the fee of a purely nominal office under the Mogul, became his dominant concern. 'My future power, my future grandeur,' he wrote to a friend, 'all depend on the receipt of the jaghire money';[6] and again : 'Believe me there is no other interest in this kingdom but what arises from great possessions'.[7] That *jagir*

---

[1] 33000, ff. 169-71 and 175. [2] *Ibid*. ff. 195-6.
[3] 32948, f. 69. For the lists of names of proprietors of East India stock and selections of those to whom Newcastle applied see 33031, ff. 69-73.
[4] 32948, f. 130.
[5] *Ibid*. f. 128. The letter, unsigned, is in his hand.
[6] To John Pybus, 27 Feb 1762 ; Malcolm, *op. cit.* vol. ii, p. 195.
[7] R. Clive to H. Vansittart, 3 Feb 1762 ; Clive MSS.

the East India Company, after Clive's defeat at India House, was calling in question. As Hardwicke was told by Clive and his father, who came to him 'to discourse about it', the Company 'sent an order to their Governor and Council of Bengal to remit no more money to his Lordship on that account; but to retain it in the Company's cash, and to keep a distinct account of it'.[1] The next day Newcastle received a message about it through Lord Bessborough, a brother-in-law of Devonshire, to whom Clive complained of the very bad turn done to him by those he had saved from perdition; Bessborough advised Clive to go to Hayes 'and acquaint his friend Mr. Pitt of it', which Clive seems to have done.[2]

On 19 May, Clive again applied for Newcastle's help at India House,[3] and Newcastle 'immediately set about engaging all those' whom he could 'possibly get at'.[4] He also invited Clive, his father, and Walsh to dine with him at Claremont, and wrote to Clive on 30 June: 'I hope your affairs at Shrewsbury go well; I heartily wish you success there and everywhere else'.[5]

In August 1763 Newcastle's return to office, together with Pitt, was generally expected, and Clive, at Condover near Shrewsbury, had not received the news of the failure of the negotiations when he wrote to Newcastle on 5 September:

All our friends in Shropshire are as firm and steady as your Grace can wish, and by a late purchase I entertain the most sanguine hopes of making the burrough of Bishop's Castle more useful than it has hitherto been, at least I think the present Members can have no expectation of being rechosen for that place. . . .
I never shall desire to know anything of ministerial secrets, but if a much wish'd for event either happens or is likely to happen, a line from your Grace will be very acceptable, that I may come to town to congratulate you upon the occasion, for no one can be more steadily attach'd to your Grace's interest than etc.[6]

---

[1] 32948, f. 189.
[2] Clive to George Grenville, 21 Dec 1763; *Grenville Papers*, vol. ii, pp. 183-4.
[3] 32948, f. 338; ff. 333-5 contain the lists sent by Clive on this occasion.
[4] Newcastle to Clive, 22 May 1763; *ibid.* f. 359.
[5] 32949, f. 244.
[6] 32950, ff. 331-2.

Francis Child, M.P. for Bishop's Castle, died on 23 September 1763, and on 10 October Newcastle wrote to Clive :

I long to hear something about Bishop's Castle ; upon the present vacancy they say you can do what you will there. I am sure you will do what is right. . . .

P.S. . . . I hear everything is settled to your satisfaction at Bishop's Castle ; I rejoice at it.

Clive replied on 14 October :

Your Grace may remember that I inform'd you the purchase of the Walcot estate would in the end secure to me the Borrough of Bishop's Castle, the death of Mr. Child happen'd rather sooner than I could have wish'd as I did not take possession of the estate till last Michaelmass and was almost an utter stranger to the borrough. Mr. Waring who has an interest here also receiv'd an express from his father-in-law, Mr. Ranby a surgeon of Chelsea Hospital by which means he got the start of us, 24 hours, and began to canvass for himself immediately, fortunately for us young Mr. Walcot who had promis'd me all his interest was upon the spot and hearing of Mr. Waring's proceedings came immediately in person to give me the intelligence. Mr. Walcot's short absence lost us some votes who upon a supposition that there would have been no opposition gave their promise to Mr. Waring, notwithstanding all these disadvantages we have a very clear and considerable majority, all the gentlemen both of town and country have join'd me to a man and every friend Mr. Waring has, endeavord to prevail upon him to desist but to no manner of purpose hitherto, Mr. George Clive is nominated the candidate, supported by all mine and the Walcot interest.

As Mr. Waring is a friend to our cause as well as myself and pays great defference to Mr. Pitt, your Grace and Mr. Pitt cannot do Mr. Waring a greater piece of service than persuading Mr. Ranby to prevail upon Mr. Waring to drop this contest, which must end in his utter ruin and destruction without a possibility of succeeding, his fortune being by no means equal to such an undertaking.

Your Grace I am persuaded knows enough of me to be convinced, that I will spend the utmost farthing sooner than give up my interest in this borrough, which I have great pretensions to from my late purchase.[1]

He added at the bottom of the letter :

[1] 32951, ff. 424-5.

For Mr. George Clive :

> 57 Burgesses.
> 11 Aldermen or Capital Burgesses.
> —
> 68.

For Mr. Waring :

> 41 Burgesses.
> 4 Aldermen or Capital Burgesses.
> —
> 45   M[ajority] 23.

Newcastle replied on 18 October : he doubted whether he could influence Waring and Ranby, but Pitt could — 'I dare say, he will be very glad to do everything, that may be agreable to your Lordship'; and (deserted by Powis) Newcastle now asked Clive to act for him in Shropshire.

> I hear, all our Shropshire friends are just as you and I wish them; I wish, your Lordship could contrive to speak to them, to be in town, at the opening of the session. I beg my compliments to Mr. George Clive, with my best wishes for his success, and to all your family, and friends.[1]

Clive answered on 31 October :

> Since I had the honor of paying my respects to your Grace at Claremont I have seen Harry Bridgman and upon discoursing together we both are of the opinion that if your Grace would write a line to Mr. Brooke Forrester of Dothill desiring his and his brother's attendance at the first opening of Parliament, it would have very good effect, and we shall be ready to support your Grace's letter with all our interest.[2]

Meantime Clive did not hesitate to accept George Grenville's help at India House —

> as our friendship has induced you to be a mediator between me and the Court of Directors [he wrote to Grenville on 7 November 1763], in compliance with your desire I now send you the terms on which I am ready to make an absolute cession of . . . my jaggeer, in favour of the East India Company.[3]

---

[1] 32952, f. 38.
[2] *Ibid.* f. 154. For Newcastle's letter to Brooke Forester see *ibid.* f. 174.
[3] *Grenville Papers*, vol. ii, pp. 160-1.

But two days later he is found writing again to Newcastle about Shropshire affairs, and soliciting his help at Bishop's Castle :

I suppose your Grace has receiv'd an answer from Forrester before this ; enclosed is the one I have just receiv'd, by which your Grace will perceive we may depend more upon Forrester than he thinks we can depend upon Harry Bridgman.[1]
Ranby is gone down and some say Cust with him. I have just now received advice that £500 have been offerd for ten of our voters, but to very little purpose, nothing can hurt us provided the returning officer be steady which I have reason to think he will be, the only thing which gives me uneasiness is that I have not yet got his son discharged altho Col. Reynolds has made a promise to General Mostyn. I wish your Grace would press this matter to the Duke of Devonshire and Lord Rockingham.[2]

Waring, whose father-in-law, John Ranby, was Serjeant-Surgeon to the King, had apparently the assistance of Government promised to him, even though Clive described him to Newcastle as 'a friend to our cause'; but as Clive was now drawing nearer to the Government, Sandwich, at that time Secretary of State, inclined to help him at Bishop's Castle in so far as previous engagements permitted. On 17 November he wrote to Ranby that he was working the excisemen at Bishop's Castle in favour of Waring, but also transmitted a proposal from Clive to pay Waring £1000 'for the expenses already incurred', if he declined the contest.

I will farther add that it will not be unpleasing to Government, but otherwise, if this offer is accepted ; yet I would not have you suppose that there is any alteration in the disposition of Government towards you, which is the same in every respect as when you left London.[3]

Waring declined the offer, and on 24 November 1763 was defeated by George Clive, who secured eighty votes against Waring's fifty-three.

[1] For Forester's letter to Clive, 7 Nov, see 32952, f. 282 : 'I hope by Tuesday to have the pleasure of meeting you and Mr. Bridgeman, and that by this time he has fix'd whether he votes with us or not'.
[2] *Ibid*. f. 308.
[3] Sandwich MSS., 'Private Letters', vol. i, pp. 35-6 ; the letter is marked 'Thursday', which appears to have been 7 Nov 1763. There is a copy of another letter, of the same day, to Powis informing him of the offer to Ranby (p. 33).

On 13 December, Clive, who by that time seems to have definitely dissociated himself from Newcastle, is found writing to George Grenville about the anxiety he laboured under concerning his compromise with the East India Company, 'more essentially necessary towards establishing my peace of mind than the improvement of my fortune':

Discountenanced and hated by the party I have abandoned, as much as I was before respected and esteemed, if I should, through the obstinate injustice of the Directors (notwithstanding your powerful mediation) be disappointed, I must confess to you, Sir, that I have so much sensibility inherent in my nature, that my mind will be too much affected to recover so severe a shock for some time; but be the event what it will, I have taken my part, and you may be assured that my poor services, such as they are, shall be dedicated for the rest of my days to the King, and my obligations to you always acknowledged, whether in or out of power.[1]

The compromise, patched up by Sandwich between Clive and Sulivan, was unanimously rejected by the Court of Directors.[2] But this is a matter which need not be pursued here any further.

To conclude the story of Bishop's Castle. At first both Waring and Walcot retained a certain influence in the borough where voters were not averse to election contests. 'There is not the least doubt of your Lordship's nomination of *one*', wrote George Clive to Lord Clive on 6 October 1767, 'but a quarrel with Walcot would risk both.'[3] In the end, Waring, when applied to by the opposition, thought a contest too expensive, and by an agreement dated 26 December 1767 sold his Shropshire estates to Clive for £30,500;[4] he also promised to give Clive 'his entire interest *bona fide* at all times with respect to Bishop's Castle'.[5] With 1768 starts the era of Clive domination at Bishop's Castle, which continued unbroken till 1818, and even unchallenged except for one contest in 1802.

---

[1] *Grenville Papers*, vol. ii, pp. 180-3. In 1765, after the fall of the Grenville Administration, the Clives attached themselves once more to Newcastle.

[2] George Onslow to Newcastle, 18 Dec 1763; 32954, f. 36.

[3] Clive MSS.

[4] See Private Act 8 George III c. 62, confirming the agreement.

[5] John Walsh to Lord Clive, 17 Dec 1767; Clive MSS.

'The day I staid at Shrewsbury', wrote Taylor White on 22 March 1768, 'Mr. George Clive and Captain Clive, *i.e.* Lord Clive's brother, came from their election at Bishop's Castle where they had no opposition. My friend More [1] was with them and advised them, if they intended to do any good in Parliament to be as unlike the persons they represented as possible.' [2]

THE SHROPSHIRE GENTLEMEN

Before the division of 17-18 February 1764 on General Warrants was taken in the House of Commons, the Clives had thus gone over to the Government; and Hill had likewise been gained. In a letter dated 23 January 1764, Lord Holland informed Lord Sandwich of a call which 'Mr. Hill of Shropshire' paid him that morning (the first meeting he ever had with him), and during which Holland told Hill that Sandwich had supported his son. 'He will come to wait on you, pray if not at home, send and appoint him; for he seems to me to be fix'd very reasonably.' [3] When, on 16 February, Hill's nephew, Edward Kynaston, M.P. for Montgomeryshire, a Tory who acted as one of Grenville's Parliamentary managers, in a letter to Jenkinson reviewed the forces the Government could muster for the critical division, he remarked about Hill that he seldom stayed out 'a long day' [4] — hardly surprising in a man of seventy-one; and indeed Hill's name appears in the list 'of friends absent, 17th February, 1764', [5] or rather at the division taken on the 18th at 4.15 A.M. Great efforts were made by Powis to muster his Shropshire friends on the Government side, [6] but Bridgeman, Brooke Forester, and Whitmore voted

---

[1] Robert More: about him see above, pp. 241-2 and 257-9.

[2] *Memoirs of the House of White of Wallingwells*, p. 40.

[3] Sandwich MSS.

[4] N. S. Jucker, *The Jenkinson Papers*, pp. 265-6. The letter is dated by Kynaston Thursday, and docketed by Jenkinson 15 Feb, which was, however, a Wednesday.

[5] 38337, f. 192.

[6] There is a letter from Bridgeman among the Powis MSS., undated and endorsed 'March 1764', but clearly written on 17 Feb. Bridgeman tells Powis that 'on the most mature and deliberate thinking and conversing

with the Opposition ; also Cecil Forester, who was absent, was counted among the Opposition Members. Lyster, too, must have been absent — as late as the autumn of 1765 the remark appears against his name in Rockingham's 'List of Members' :[1] 'not taken his seat'. Astley, John Grey, Edward Herbert, Peregrine Cust, and two Clives (Lord Clive and his cousin George) presumably voted with the Government, as they do not appear either in the Opposition lists or in the Government list of absent friends. In a division in which the Government was saved by an insignificant majority, of 234 against 220, Shropshire gave six votes to the Government and only three to the Opposition.[2]

Thus the two Foresters, Whitmore, and Bridgeman alone remained with Newcastle. Indeed, the Whitmores had for a long time been to the old Duke an outstanding example of loyalty — in anticipation of his retirement he had written to the Duke of Devonshire on 10 January 1762 : '*Whitmores* and some few will stand by me, in spite of every body ; not as one of the King's Ministers, but from their private regard to me'.[3] So they did ; still, the name of none of the Shropshire Members appears in the list of the Opposition club in Albemarle Street — they kept to their own county and did not move about much in the political circles of London. A good description of their attitude and moods is given in a letter which Newcastle wrote to George Onslow, M.P. for Surrey, from Bath on 21 March 1765 :

I am sorry to tell you, that your opposition is in very low esteem here at Bath. I have had a great deal of discourse with two old, and very honest friends, Sir Thos. Whitmore, and Sir Wm. St. Quintin ; they are what they have always been ; and just as I could wish

on the subject his Lordship alludes to in his note, he thinks himself indispensably oblig'd to give his vote today as he did on Tuesday [14 Feb, when Bridgeman voted with the Opposition]. If it was a matter relative to any private affairs of his Lordship, Mr. Bridgeman would think himself not only guilty of a great breach of friendship, but of the highest ingratitude ; this being an affair of national concern, he thinks, as he has already shewn his opinion upon it, his character might be justly call'd in question if he did not pursue it with steadiness and resolution.'

[1] Fitzwilliam MSS. at the Northants. R.O.

[2] Richard Clive and Walsh are not included in this calculation as they did not sit for Shropshire constituencies.

[3] 32933, f. 177.

them: But I don't see any reason to think, that my friend General Whitmore will attend any more this session.

I have also had a great deal of discourse with the two Forresters. The Stag,[1] and his brother, the Coll:; I believe, neither of them will come up. The Stag is very zealous, as he always was, and ever will be; I think, he has still some correspondence with his old friend, my Lord Powis; tho' he resents extremely the part he takes; and has a good deal of partiality for my Lord Granby. But, when he came to the point, he said, (what all the world say, except a very, very narrow clique) 'that we have no *Head*; nobody to lead them, etc.'. I puffed your friends Sir Geo: Saville and Sir Wm. Meredith, and particularly Sir George, and our young friends as much as could be. The Stag said, it was true; but they were young men, and *had no experience*. In short I see, we shall have no assistance from the very best set of men, I ever knew, in Parliament, what we used to call *the Shropshire Gang*.

The Stag told me, he had had a letter from honest Sir H. Bridgeman; wherein he said, they had had a division, and the minority had had but one Shropshire man in it, Sir Harry himself.[2]

When in July 1765 the Rockingham Whigs, who now claimed a monopoly in Whiggism, were about to assume office, Newcastle was determined that Powis should be made to pay for his defection. On 4 July he wrote to Lord Albemarle, the political agent of Cumberland:

His Royal Highness seem'd disposed, not to remove my Ld. Powis, imagining, he was of great importance in Shropshire. I know the contrary, having had very free discourses upon his subject

---

[1] Brooke Forester. He wrote in a letter to Clive on 7 Nov 1763, when asked to attend Parliament: 'Your Lordship seems to expect good diversion in town, but had you been at our last hind chace, of near five hours, you likely would not have dispized that amusement of the country' (32952, f. 282). Perhaps Brooke Forester's predilection for this kind of chase earned him his nickname.

[2] 32966, ff. 79-80. Even 'Stag' Forester's zeal and complaints somewhat change complexion in the light of a letter he wrote about that time to Lord Gower, asking for assistance in obtaining Army promotion for his youngest son (27 Feb 1765; Grenville Papers in the possession of Sir John Murray). At the beginning of the last session, he wrote, he had refused to support Administration thinking himself 'under the strictest obligations to the Duke of Devonshire' with whom he had been connected for upwards of twenty-five years. 'But since his death, I think myself now as free from all politicall connections both private and publick, as if I came but yesterday into Parliament, exclusive of the principles I ever have, and ever will support as a Whig.'

with my friends Sir H. Bridgeman, Sir Thomas Whitmore, and Forester *the Stag*.[1]

And again to Rockingham on 12 July :

I hope nobody will keep in my Lord Powis ; there, I am sure, the Devonshire family ought to be concerned.[2]

But Powis understood so much ; Rockingham reported to Newcastle on 14 July, 7 P.M. :

Lord Powis — stole a march and resigned.[3]

With the flight of Lord Powis before his returning friends we may close the story of the 'Old Corps of Whigs' of Shropshire and their chief.

---

[1] 32967, ff. 220-1.   [2] *Ibid.* f. 351.   [3] *Ibid.* f. 393.

VI

THE CORNISH BOROUGHS

THERE was a peculiar excellence in the Cornish boroughs, an elaborate and quaint machinery for making Members of Parliament, in which irrelevancy reached its acme. Twenty-one boroughs returned 42 Members; their total electorate was less than 1400; and those enfranchised did not think of politics while engaged in election business. As an archaic ritual and a pursuit of pleasure and profit, Cornish borough elections have the charm inherent in human actions when sincere; and there was no humbug about the way in which Cornish boroughs chose their representatives. Thomas Pitt, an old experienced hand, wrote in October 1740: '. . . there are few [Cornish] boroughs where the common sort of people do not think they have as much right to sell themselves and their votes, as they have to sell their corn and their cattle'.[1]

The Cornish borough Members were, on the whole, more closely connected with Government than those in most counties. Still, six of the 42 returned in 1761 at other times represented counties, an honour never attained by any of the 10 Members elected by Norfolk boroughs in 1761, or of the 28 elected by Yorkshire boroughs, while in Wiltshire it fell to only one among the 32, and he sat in 1761 for Old Sarum. But it is natural that this should have been so; with election business so beautifully simplified, the Cornish boroughs were fit to serve as a waiting-room for rising men and as a refuge for those on the downward path; for men as respectable as John Parker, M.P. for Bodmin 1761–62, and for Devonshire 1762–84 (when created Lord Boringdon), and for a scamp as amusing as Edward Wortley Montagu, jun., who, while there was hope of redemption, represented the county of Huntingdon, but subsequently Bossiney — during the Parliament of 1761–68 he

---

[1] 'The Present State of the Boroughs in the County of Cornwall'; P.R.O., Chatham Papers.

travelled in Turkey, Egypt, Asia Minor, etc., and never took his seat.

For 1760 we have an electoral survey of the Cornish boroughs by one of the best local experts. Lord Edgcumbe [1] wrote to Newcastle on 20 May 1760 :

In obedience to your Grace's commands I have the honour to lay before you the state of those boroughs in Cornwall wherein I have any concern ; but as your Grace, if I understand right, is desirous to know that of Cornwall in general, I write by this post to my steward and manager there, who, being an intelligent man, will . . . make a just representation. . . .[2]

We need not enter here into Edgcumbe's own statement,[3] but can turn at once to the much fuller account given by his agent,[4] which is preserved among the Newcastle Papers and docketed 'State of Cornish Burroughs from Lord Edgcumbe ; received June   ,[5] 1760 '.

Launceston. Mr. Morice's [6] interest seems at present the prevailing one in the burrough for both members.

---

[1] Richard Edgcumbe (1716–61), M.P. for Plympton 1742–47, Lostwithiel 1747–54, and for Penryn 1754–58, when he succeeded his father as second Lord Edgcumbe.

[2] 32906, ff. 184-5.   [3] *Ibid.* f. 186.

[4] The name of the steward was Thomas Jones (see below, p. 432). On 27 Aug 1775, the Rev. B. Foster wrote to Richard Gough about Restormel, 'the property of the Duchy of Cornwall' : 'Thomas Jones, an attorney who died a month ago, held it . . . under a lease for lives. Mr. Masterman, a solicitor in London, and my esquire of Bradoc now has the lease ; he married a niece of the late Mr. Jones' (Nichols, *Literary Illustrations*, vol. v, pp. 861-2). Masterman was associated with Jones in the management of the Edgcumbe interest in Cornish boroughs ; in 1764 he was elected Mayor of Lostwithiel (see HMC, *MSS. of Lostwithiel Corporation, Various Collections*, vol. v, p. 337) ; in 1771 he became deputy town clerk and in 1781 town clerk of Tintagel, *alias* Bossiney (see Maclean, *Trigg Minor*, vol. iii, p. 211). In 1774 he appears in the correspondence between Lord North and John Robinson negotiating on behalf of Lord Edgcumbe the sale of seats to the Treasury (see Laprade, *Parliamentary Papers of John Robinson*, p. 26), and, as it so often happened in the second generation of borough managers, he finished by being himself returned to Parliament — for Bodmin in 1780. HMC, *Lansdowne MSS.* (p. 257), mention 'Mr. W. Masterman's compendium of the rights and privileges or mode of election of Members to serve in Parliament, drawn alphabetically in tabular form with an abstract of the gradual alterations in representation'.

[5] 32907, ff. 461-2. The day has been erased.

[6] Humphrey Morice (1723–85), M.P. for Launceston 1750–80 ; inherited the Werrington estate and the two boroughs of Launceston and

Sir John St. Aubyn [1] hath many friends in the town but in appearance he declines being further concern'd. The Duke of Bedford hath also some friends there. A junction of those gentlemen might give Mr. Morice's interest a great shock if not entirely overturn it.

Newport. This burrough elects by owners of burgage tenures and scot and lot men. Mr. Morice is lord of the burrough, has the nomination of the Returning Officer and the greatest part of the houses are his. So that his interest is certainly very strong. The Duke of Bedford is a considerable landholder in the town and can always poll a great many votes but probably not enough to carry an election against Mr. Morice assisted by the Returning Officer.

Camelford. Mr. Martyn,[2] one of the present Members, seems to have acquired some personal interest in the burrough. But Mr. Phillipps [3] has the principal influence over the votes, who are generally a low set of people and depute him to make terms for them. The Duke of Bedford has the largest property in the town and of course if he attacks the burrough will be supported by many of his tenants, but 'tis much to be doubted whether his Grace cou'd make himself strong enough to carry his point against Mr. Phillipps and almost the whole Bench.

Tintagell [*Bossiney*]. Mr. Wortley [4] is promised his man by a great majority of electors. The other is intended to be put up to the best bidder. But with proper means used, there is a good chance of securing this burrough in the interest of Lord Edgcumbe and Mr. Wortley. Tho' in any event, an adventurer will find encouragement.

Newport from his second cousin, Sir William Morice, third and last Bt. Catherine, sister of Sir William Morice, married Sir John St. Aubyn, third Bt. Sir John St. Aubyn, fourth Bt., mentioned below, was their son.

[1] Sir John St. Aubyn, fourth Bt. (1726–72), M.P. for Launceston 1747–54 and 1758–59 (when unseated on petition), and for Cornwall from 1761 till his death in 1772. Of his sisters, one married John Buller, M.P. for East Looe 1747–86 ; another, F. Basset, M.P. for Penryn 1766–69 ; and a third, Sir John Molesworth, M.P. for Cornwall 1765–75.

[2] Samuel Martin (1714–88), a West Indian and brother of Joseph Martin, Governor of North Carolina ; Joint Secretary to the Treasury 1758–63 ; M.P. for Camelford 1747–68, and for Hastings 1768–74.

[3] Charles Phillips (1720–74), M.P. for Camelford 1768–74 ; about him see below, pp. 336–44.

[4] Edward Wortley Montagu, sen., M.P. for Westminster 1715–22 ; Huntingdon 1722–34 ; and for Peterborough from 1734 till his death in Jan 1761. He was the father of Edward Wortley Montagu, jun., M.P. for Hunts 1747–54 and for Bossiney 1754–68, and of Lady Bute, to whom he bequeathed his enormous fortune.

Saltash. Mr. Cleveland [1] has in appearance this burrough very secure in the Admiralty or Navy interest.

Callington. Lady Orford [2] has this burrough without any opposition. There have been several attempts to elect a Member here against her Ladyship's family interest, but without success.

St. Germans. Mr. Eliot.[3]

Liskeard. Mr. Eliot rules there at present tho' probably his interest is not so firmly established as to be impregnable from every quarter.

East Looe. ⎰Mr. John Buller [4] manages these burroughs for the
West Looe. ⎱Administration and himself and the interest seems well settled in that channell.

Lostwithiel. Lord Edgcumbe.

Fowey. Lord Edgcumbe and Mr. Rashleigh.[5]

Bodmyn. Mr. Hunt [6] and Sir William Irby.[7]
Mr. Hunt hath met with great difficulties of late and 'tis still a question whether his interest is well established. The town in general seems better disposed toward Sir William Irby than Mr. Hunt, but I think no adventurer cou'd prevail unless Sir William joined him, or at least stood newter.

Tregony. Lord Falmouth [8] and Mr. Trevanion [9] have a very strong interest in this burrough. But my Lord's interest singly is

[1] John Clevland (1706-63), Secretary to the Admiralty; on him see above, pp. 40-41.

[2] Margaret, daughter and heiress of Samuel Rolle, M.P. for Callington from 1702 till his death in 1719; her maternal grandfather was Roger Tuckfield, M.P. for Ashburton 1708-9 and 1713-39. From them she inherited Parliamentary influence in the two boroughs. She married in 1727 Robert Walpole, subsequently second Earl of Orford; he died in 1751.

[3] Edward Eliot, of Port Eliot (1727-1804), M.P. for St. Germans 1748-68 and 1774-75; for Liskeard 1768-74; for Cornwall 1775-84, when created Lord Eliot.

[4] John Buller (1721-86), M.P. for East Looe 1747-86; on him see below, pp. 321-34.

[5] Jonathan Rashleigh (1693-1764), M.P. for Fowey 1727-64; about his family see below, pp. 316-18.

[6] George Hunt (1720-98), M.P. for Bodmin 1753-84; his mother was Lady Mary Robartes, sister and heiress of Henry, third Earl of Radnor; from the Robartes family Hunt inherited the electoral interest at Bodmin.

[7] Sir William Irby, second Bt. (1707-75), M.P. for Launceston 1735-47, and for Bodmin 1747-61, when created Lord Boston.

[8] Hugh Boscawen, second Viscount Falmouth (1707-82), M.P. for Truro 1727-34, when he succeeded to the peerage.

[9] William Trevanion (1728-67), M.P. for Tregony 1747-67.

by much the best. There are always a large number of votes (who are pot boilers) ready to receive any adventurer whatever who will bring them money.

Grampound. In its present situation is very open to an attack but as the Bench have (at the law courts held within a month of Michaelmas and Easter) a power of increasing the number of freemen and as the Bench have very perfidiously left Lord Edgcumbe and attached themselves to Mr. Eliot and Mr. Trevanion — there is no doubt but that they will at the next Michaelmas court, endeavour to make themselves strong enough to carry their point at the general election tho' they can in no event be secure against candidates with heavy purses.

St. Maws. Lord Falmouth and Mr. Nugent,[1] but the latter is Lord of the Burrough and makes the Returning Officer and thereby has the strongest and most secure interest.

Penryn. Lord Falmouth and Lord Edgcumbe joined have the burrough very secure. But disunited Lord Edgcumbe would be sure of his man and Lord Falmouth as sure of being disappointed.

Mr. Basset,[2] a neighbouring gentleman and a considerable landowner in the town, has been talked of for a candidate, but at present there is not much probability that he will meddle — and this is a burrough where a foreign adventurer would meet with very little encouragement of chance or success.

Helston. Lord Godolphin.[3]

St. Ives. By the late junction of Lord Buckingham [4] and Mr. Stephens,[5] their interest seems pretty well secured, tho' Mr. Praed [6]

[1] Robert Nugent (1702–88), of Irish extraction, inherited this borough from his first wife, daughter and co-heiress of James Craggs, M.P., P.M.G.; sat for St. Mawes 1741–54 and 1774–84, and for Bristol 1754–74; created Viscount Clare [I.] in 1767, and Earl Nugent [I.] in 1776.

[2] Francis Basset (1715–69), M.P. for Penryn 1766–69; about him see below, pp. 306–15.

[3] Francis, second Earl of Godolphin (1678–1766), M.P. for Helston 1701–8; for other constituencies 1708–12, when, on the death of his father, the famous statesman, he succeeded to the peerage.

[4] John Hobart, second Earl of Buckinghamshire (1723–93), M.P. for Norwich 1747–56, when he succeeded to the peerage.

[5] John Stephens 'for many years was agent for the Duke [should be Earl] of Buckingham in managing the political affairs of the borough of St. Ives, but at last broke off the connexion by obtaining the return of his own son in 1751' (G. C. Boase, *Collectanea Cornubiensia* (1890), p. 927). Samuel Stephens sat for St. Ives 1751–54, and contested it unsuccessfully in 1774 and 1775.

[6] Humphrey Mackworth Praed (1719–1803), M.P. for St. Ives 1761–68; for Cornwall 1772–74.

X

has a strong party in the town and pushes his interest. The Duke
of Bolton [1] has also some pretentions. But it does not seem probable that his Grace and Mr. Praed joined to any other interest
which can be made wou'd be a match for Lord Buckingham and
Mr. Stephens.

Truro. Lord Falmouth.

Mitchell. The Superior Lord on whose favor the interest of
this borough will always depend is Lord Arundell of Wardour.[2]
The five under Lords are Lord Edgcumbe, Admiral Boscawen,[3] Sir
Richard Vyvyan,[4] Mr. Courteney,[5] and Mr. Scawen,[6] one of whom
must at Lord Arundell's Court be chosen Portreive and Returning
Officer for the burrough. The Members are chosen by the inhabitants paying scot and lot — who being in general low, indigent
people, will join such of the under Lords from whom they have
reason to expect most money and favours. Admiral Boscawen either
has purchased or is in treaty for Sir Richard Vyvyan's Lordship,
and by purchasing several other lands and tenements which make
votes, by supplying some of the voters with money and conferring
favours on others, seems to be adding very considerably to the
strength of his interest. Mr. Courteney's interest is supported by
his kinsman's, Mr. Williams,[7] a gentleman who lives near the town
and hath a considerable influence over many of the voters.

Of these boroughs I now propose to take six (Penryn,
Fowey, East and West Looe, Camelford, and Grampound) as
examples, and deal with their electoral structure, their repre-

---

[1] Charles Powlett, fifth Duke of Bolton (1718–65), M.P. for Lymington
1741–54, and for Hants 1754–59, when he succeeded to the peerage.

[2] Henry, eighth Baron Arundell of Wardour (1740–1808); a Roman
Catholic; took no part in politics.

[3] Edward Boscawen (1711–61), brother of Hugh, second Viscount
Falmouth; Admiral of the Blue; M.P. for Truro 1742–61.

[4] Sir Richard Vyvyan, fifth Bt. (1731–81).

[5] Captain Charles Courtenay (killed in Germany in 1761) was the only
son of Kelland Courtenay (M.P. for Huntingdon from 1747 till his death
in 1748), by Elizabeth, sister of John, fourth Earl of Sandwich. His father
is often described as 'second son of Sir William Courtenay, of Powderham
castle in Devonshire', which is wrong; he was of the Courtenays of Tremere.

[6] Thomas Scawen; his son James Scawen (1734–1801), was M.P. for
Mitchell 1761–74, and for Surrey 1774–80.

[7] Probably Courtenay Williams of Trewithan, 'who is said to have
dissipated a handsome fortune by indulging himself in low pursuits and
in low company, and especially by maintaining a set of people to accompany
him from parish to parish, for (what seems quite ludicrous in present times)
the purpose of ringing bells' (D. Gilbert, *op. cit.*, vol. iii, p. 367).

sentatives, and their politics. But one general point should first be noted: that in Cornwall, as in some other counties, there was at that time a tacit understanding of mutual forbearance between the 'Tory' Members and electorate in the county, and the 'Whig' managers in the boroughs.[1] When in September 1760 Admiral Boscawen thought of offering himself as candidate for the county, Edgcumbe reminded Newcastle of the line Sir Robert Walpole and Pelham had taken on similar occasions, and warned against 'setting up a new party interest (as lately in Oxfordshire)';[2] but as Admiral Boscawen insisted on standing (he died, however, before the general election) and Newcastle saw no way of refusing support to a man of his rank, merit, and family,[3] Edgcumbe acknowledged that he too would have to give his interest to the admiral, though he was sorry to be 'call'd upon for it', as such a contest, by provoking the Tories, 'must draw on many disagreable consequences to us who live in the county, and who are concern'd in boroughs'.[4]

PENRYN

Penryn had a wide franchise — inhabitants paying scot and lot; and, as Cornish boroughs went, a large electorate — in the eighteenth century 130-200 voters, and by 1831, over 500.

[1] For such a tacit understanding in Shropshire, see above, p. 238-9. In Oxfordshire during the general election of 1754, Lord Guilford (the father of Lord North), though a Whig, refused to embark wholeheartedly in the Whig cause, for fear of the Tory gentlemen, and especially Sir James Dashwood, one of the Tory candidates, retaliating in his own borough of Banbury. In Nov 1752, in a letter to Sanderson Miller (a friend of the Whig candidate, Sir E. Turner), Lord Guilford declared that he had little 'interest' in the county — 'I never wished for it nor endeavoured to cultivate it, lest it should occasion me any embarassment in my Banbury affairs' (see Dickins and Stanton, *An Eighteenth-Century Correspondence* (1910), p. 206). And on 8 Nov: 'My principal attention must always be to the Corporation of Banbury. Those Sir Edward has greatly disgusted . . . and many of them have a personal regard, and some, great obligations to Sir James Dashwood who has an estate in and near the town, and has not attempted to do me any ill office there' (*ibid.* pp. 207-8). It was not, however, Turner's politics which had disgusted the townspeople of Banbury but his closing their markets and slaughtering cattle because of an outbreak of foot-and-mouth disease.   [2] 28 Sept 1760; 32912, f. 195.
[3] Newcastle to Edgcumbe, 2 Oct 1760; *ibid.* f. 297.
[4] Edgcumbe to Newcastle, 12 Oct 1760; 32913, ff. 75-6.

During the thirty years preceding the first Reform Act it became notorious for its corruption, because this came to be practised without the intervention of titled borough-brokers and the Treasury; but in the reign of George II the borough was still eminently genteel.

The two most prominent election managers in Cornwall, Lord Edgcumbe and Lord Falmouth, were its established patrons, and Richard Edgcumbe and George Boscawen were returned for Penryn in 1754. The borough valued itself 'upon having had representatives of name and note', and when in 1758 Richard Edgcumbe succeeded to the peerage, he suggested to Newcastle a candidate for Penryn connected by marriage 'both to Lord Falmouth's family and to ours'; 'our interest in that borough is joint, and I hope will ever continue so'. As to an opposition, it 'has been threaten'd openly by a very potent man, Mr. Basset, at the next general election, tho' by what I am assur'd, he has no intention of stirring now'.[1] Newcastle replied on 25 November: 'The King order'd me . . . to thank your Lordship for your intention to recommend to Penryn such person as His Majesty should desire';[2] and as the candidate suggested by Edgcumbe had already been elected elsewhere, Newcastle, 'with the King's approbation',[3] recommended John Plumptre, a perfect stranger to Penryn, who was, however, duly returned through the influence of the two patrons.

In 1760 Edgcumbe's steward thought that there was 'not much probability' of Basset meddling this time in the election — but he did, putting up George Clive, a cousin of the famous Clive, and Edmund Maskelyne, Clive's brother-in-law, against Admiral Rodney and Sir Edward Turner, Baronet, the candidates on the Edgcumbe-Falmouth interest, who had made for Penryn, as in a game of musical chairs, and just escaped being left without seats.

---

[1] Edgcumbe to Newcastle, 22 Nov 1758; 32885, ff. 500-1.

[2] 32886, f. 13. The use of the King's name was not a mere form; George II took a personal interest in elections, which it is important to note in view of all that is written about the 'great change' which supervened on the accession of George III.

[3] Newcastle to John Plumptre, 25 Nov 1758; 32886, f. 17.

George Brydges Rodney first entered Parliament in 1751, at a by-election for the Admiralty borough of Saltash. At the general election of 1754 he was left out in the cold by the Government and unsuccessfully contested Camelford against its candidates ; [1] but at a by-election in 1758 was returned by Newcastle for Okehampton. On 2 December 1759, Rodney wrote to him from Spithead :

> I beg your Grace will permit me to return you my most sincere thanks for the honour you have bestow'd on me in chusing me a Member of Parliament for Oakhampton ; a steady adherence to your Grace's commands shall ever distinguish me while I have a seat in the House.[2]

At a by-election in December 1756, during a short break in Anson's eleven years at the head of the Admiralty, Charles Townshend was returned for Saltash. But in 1761 both its seats were filled with regular Anson candidates, and Townshend had to go in search of another constituency. After peregrinations, amusing and turbulent like most of his life, he was finally, at George III's express demand, accommodated by Newcastle at Harwich.[3] Wenman Coke, displaced from Harwich, was transferred by Newcastle to Okehampton ; and Rodney wrote to James West, Secretary to the Treasury, on 27 February 1761 :

> A letter I received by last night's post has given me inexpressible concern. Mr. Andrews [4] acquaints me therein that he had received the Duke of N—e's commands, that Mr. Wenman Coke was to be chose at Okehampton on Mr. Thomas Pitt's interest. For God's sake Sir what have I done to gain his Grace's displeasure, you know full well, Sir, that it was to serve him that I came into Parliament, and was desirous to continue on no other foundation.
>
> I must entreat you Sir, to represent my case in the humblest manner to his Grace and beg of him not to let me suffer in the eye

---

[1] 'As to Captain Rodney,' wrote Hardwicke to Newcastle on 19 Apr 1754, 'Lord Anson desires me to acquaint your Grace, that he never heard of his intention to stand at Camelford, and is much surprised at it. It is true he is a captain in half pay, but has a very good fortune of his own ; and having formerly offered to come in at one of the Court boroughs at his own expence, may possibly be a little piqued' (32735, f. 104). See also below, p. 339.   [2] 32899, ff. 266-7.   [3] See below, pp. 372-3.

[4] Robert Andrews, Government manager of Thomas Pitt's Parliamentary interest ; about him see below, pp. 348-9.

of the publick, as a person obnoxious to him, and unworthy his protection, which I shall infallably do, unless his Grace vouchsafes to let me have a seat in Parliament, by his influence.

Your mind, Sir, must dictate what I at present feel, better than my words can express it.[1]

But it had never been Newcastle's intention to drop Rodney, and in his list of candidates, on 17 February, Rodney's name had been tentatively put against Portsmouth ; on 28 February, against Penryn, with Portsmouth as possible alternative ; finally, he was nominated for Penryn on Edgcumbe's interest. He may possibly have had also some support from the late Leicester House set gathered round Bute ; for Lord Carnarvon, son of the Duke of Chandos, was one of their most active wire-pullers in elections, and Rodney was a distant kinsman and a godson of Chandos.[2]

Edward Turner was the son and heir of Sir Edward Turner, first Baronet, a merchant [3] and Chairman of the East India Company, by Mary, daughter and sole heiress of Sir Gregory Page, Baronet, M.P., one of its Directors. Consequently he was a country gentleman of recent date and very considerable wealth.[4] In 1754 he and Lord Parker, son of the Earl of Macclesfield, were the Whig candidates in the famous Oxfordshire election ; their Tory opponents, Lord Wenman and Sir James Dashwood, Baronet, were returned by a majority of about 100 votes on a poll of nearly 4000, but on petition were unseated by a party vote in the House of Commons. The expense of the election and of the subsequent petition was indeed prodigious. Henry Pelham, 'with the King's consent and knowledge', had promised Macclesfield £7000 'to support the necessary expenses'.[5] On the Tory side the total expendi-

---

[1] 32919, f. 324.

[2] Rodney's father had through Chandos's interest the command of the royal yacht under George I, and the King and Chandos stood sponsors to the future admiral, named after them George Brydges ; see Mundy, *Life and Correspondence of Admiral Lord Rodney* (1830), p. 36.

[3] According to Dickins and Stanton, *An Eighteenth-Century Correspondence*, p. 201, Turner's father was originally a brewer.

[4] In a list of shareholders of the East India Company (32948, f. 335), whom in May 1763 Clive asked Newcastle to canvass on his behalf, Turner appears as holder of £28,500 of stock. He is, in fact, the largest holder in that list.　　　　　[5] See above, pp. 199-200.

ture amounted to £20,068 : 1 : 2,[1] and a public subscription was opened to defend the rights of the freeholders and 'the freedom of election in the county of Oxford'. Independent country gentlemen from all over England contributed to the fund, and the first list, preserved in the Newcastle Papers,[2] yields a sum of £4235 : 10s. ; the total subscribed was ultimately £8595 : 10s.[3] Francis Basset, in 1761 the opposition patron at Penryn, was one of the trustees of this Tory fund, and himself subscribed £300.

A contest of this kind was hardly ever repeated at consecutive elections, financial exhaustion rendering both sides favourable to a compromise. Charles Godwyn, Fellow of Balliol, wrote to Charles Gray, a Tory Member, on 28 November 1760 :[4]

> The most remarkable occurrence which has lately happened here is the compromise, which is very much approved of. After a long debate it was agreed to join Lord Charles Spencer with Sir James Dashwood. . . . Lord Litchfield, Sir James Dashwood, and almost all the gentlemen on that side of the country were very strenuous for the compromise. This was the worst event that could befall the New Interest [the Whigs]. It has destroyed their expectations entirely.

And Lord Talbot wrote to Bute that Lichfield had told him about Bute's intention 'to prevail upon Ld. Abingdon to agree to the Oxfordshire compromise'; and he added : 'possibly you may not know, that the chief Whigs in that county are so incensed by the unconcerted conduct of the Marlbro family relatively to election affairs, that it is probable they would prefer a Tory to Ld. C. Spencer'.[5] The terms of the compromise can be gathered from subsequent events. Sir James Dashwood, Tory candidate in 1754 (and second cousin of Sir Francis Dashwood, one of Bute's chief followers), and Lord Charles Spencer, brother of the Duke of Marlborough, were returned unopposed, while the two Whig members who had represented

---

[1] James Townsend, *The Oxfordshire Dashwoods* (1922), p. 28.
[2] 33055, f. 81.   [3] Townsend, *op. cit.*, p. 28.
[4] HMC, *Round MSS.*, p. 296.
[5] Bute MSS. ; dated 'Wednesday morning' and docketed 'November 1760'.

the county at the dissolution were taken care of by George III.
On 19 January 1761, Bute informed Newcastle that 'Lord
Falmouth had offered the King three members',[1] but did not
tell him the King's answer. Falmouth, in 1761, returned his
brothers, John and George Boscawen, for the family borough
of Truro; and for the other three seats, at Tregony, St.
Mawes, and Penryn, was obviously prepared to accept the
King's nominees. Still, Richard Hussey, his Member for
Tregony, looks like Falmouth's own choice (he was the son of
the town clerk of Truro and had been the Falmouth candidate
at Mitchell in 1754), and Abraham Hume, his Member for St.
Mawes, a big London merchant, looks very much like a paying
guest. At Penryn, however, Sir Edward Turner was put up
by the wish of the King, who similarly provided for Lord
Parker at the Admiralty borough of Rochester.[2] George III
and Bute are usually described as inclined to the Tories, though
in reality they indiscriminately favoured men whom they expected to adhere to them independently of, or even against,
Newcastle and Pitt; but they certainly had no predilection for
Members chosen by George II. Still, the two Whigs of
Oxfordshire fame, financed in 1754 'with the King's consent
and knowledge', now stood and succeeded under their auspices.
Turner henceforth seems to have been considered as belonging
to Bute, and is marked as such in his list of the House of
Commons compiled December in 1761,[3] and even at that time
Newcastle, though still co-operating with Bute, did not send
Turner his circular letter at the opening of the session; nor
was it sent to Rodney, but then he was absent on active
service. After Newcastle's break with Bute, Turner was always
classed by Newcastle as doubtful or as an opponent; and in

---

[1] Newcastle to Hardwicke, 19 Jan 1761; 35420, ff. 166-7.
[2] See letter from Newcastle to Hardwicke, 19 Jan 1761: 'His Lordship
[Bute] told my Lord Anson that my Lord Parker had been with him and
he thought my Lord Parker should be brought into Parliament and asked
whether that could not be in some Admiralty borough' (35420, ff. 166-7);
also Dodington's 'Diary' under 2 Feb 1761: 'Lord Bute . . . had told
Anson, that room must be made for Lord Parker'. Parker was one of the
three candidates of the King whose names were given to Newcastle by Bute
on 4 Feb (32918, ff. 310-11 and 362).
[3] 38333, f. 77. In the same list Rodney is marked 'Admiralty and Bute'.

none of the important divisions is he found voting any more with Newcastle's friends.

The personnel on the opposition side at Penryn completes the picture of the confusion, or rather of the absence, of party lines. Francis Basset, of Tehidy, was a Tory by tradition, estate, and connexions. He was, through his mother, a great-nephew and the heir of Alexander Pendarves (the first husband of the tiresome [1] Mrs. Delany), who had represented Penryn in nine Parliaments between the Revolution and the accession of George I. In 1756 Francis Basset married Margaret, a sister of Sir John St. Aubyn, fourth Baronet, who in 1761 was returned as a Tory for Cornwall. For some unknown reason, in 1761 Basset did not stand for Penryn himself but put up two candidates nominated by Robert Clive.[2]

Bute and his friends were obviously anxious about Turner's chances against the Basset-Clive combination, and on 26 February 1761 Bute received the following note from Sir Harry Erskine, one of his election managers :

Lord Powis is the person who has the most influence with Mr. Clive. Perhaps Mr. Clive might drop his attack upon the Falmouth family, if he knew that his Lordship had made a present of his borough interest to His Majesty. Mr. Clive is Lord Powis's election bull-dog ; and the master can certainly call him off.[3]

Nothing apparently was effected by this means, and the help was next invoked of Lord Hardwicke, who over the Mitchell election of 1754 had favoured Clive, although Newcastle supported the other side. Hardwicke wrote to Bute on 4 March 1761 :

. . . Col. Clive call'd upon me this morning to give me his answer. He acquainted me that his two friends, who stand at

[1] I use this adjective as *epitheton ornans* whenever Mrs. Delany or Mrs. Elizabeth Montagu is mentioned.

[2] The Clive family seems to have had some connexion with Penzance. Davies Gilbert mentions it in his *Parochial History of Cornwall* (vol. iii, p. 94) without stating its nature.

[3] Bute MSS.—There is among them a letter from Turner to Bute dated 2 Mar 1761, and asking for an opportunity to thank Bute 'for the message he was pleased to send him by Lord Carnarvon'. The nature of the message is not indicated, and there is nothing more about it in the extant correspondence.

Penryn, are his brother in law, Mr. Maskelyne, and Mr. Clive, a cosin of his.[1] That they stand merely upon the interest of Mr. Basset, a gentleman of a very great estate in that County, and that the sum, which each of them has deposited, is £2,000, the current price of the times. He read me part of a letter from Mr. Basset, wherein he says, that he is ready to accept Sir Edward Turner in the room of one of those gentlemen, provided he will stand upon his, Mr Basset's interest, and agree to the same terms. Col. Clive, who had some obligations to me at the election of this Parliament [*i.e.* of 1754], assur'd me that he is ready to facilitate this scheme by inducing one of his two friends to withdraw, which he believes must be Mr. Maskeline, his wife's brother, provided Sir Edward will come into the terms, and reimburse him the deposit, which he has made. This is the whole of what Col. Clive communicated to me.[2]

Bute replied the same night :

I have the honor of your Lordship's letter, and cant go to bed without returning a thousand thanks for the very friendly part you have taken in the business of Penryn, and making my excuse for the trouble I have given ; Ld. Falmouth told me to day, that it was a false allarm, but I see plainly his Lordship will find it a very serious one ; and I begin to be in great pain for Sir Edward Turner ; who was to have come in at Penryn on the Falmouth interest.[3]

The next morning, at 10.30, Hardwicke wrote again to Bute :

I this moment receiv'd the inclosed from Col: Clive, which I think it my duty to communicate to you. If Sir Edward Turner is to be declar'd one of the candidates, I suppose it will be necessary for him to comply with *this request* at the proper time ; but that this intention of the candidates going down to the Borough ought not, in point of honour, to be disclosed to the adverse party. From your Lordship's letter, I apprehend the difficulty will be in Sir Edward's quitting Lord Falmouth's interest to stand upon Mr. Basset's ; which, according to their proposition, I presume he must do. I happen to know that Mr. Basset has a great estate, and is full of money, from copper-mines, discover'd and work'd upon his estate, not many years ago. Under these circumstances, I doubt he will not be induc'd to let in a candidate upon Lord Falmouth's interest,

---

[1] George Clive, a London banker, paid his own expenses, but in a letter of 13 Dec 1765 mentions that he still owed Lord Clive '2000 guineas advanced for Penryn' (Clive MSS.).
[2] Bute MSS.   [3] 35423, f. 260.

which may occasion an expensive and troublesome contest; but of this I cannot pretend to judge. Your Lordship observes that Colonel Clive presses for an answer.[1]

The following letter, which does not name the person to whom it was addressed, but is dated 'Berkeley Square, March 5, 1761', is obviously the enclosure mentioned above:

Last night I receivd an express desiring the candidates might set out for Penryn as soon as possible, if your Lordship will be so kind as to inform me what hath been done,
    you will oblige him who has the honor to be &c.[2]

No compromise was reached and the struggle continued. On 25 March, Lord Falmouth and George Edgcumbe, brother of Lord Edgcumbe, wrote a joint letter from Penryn to the Duke of Newcastle:

Notwithstanding Mr. West's letter signifying your Grace's great desire for our success, on our arrival here we find our opponents have given out and even read a forged letter to poison the minds of the people, making them believe they have your favor, by which means they have drawn aside several Customhouse officers. We must therefore request your Grace to make an example of one, by name, Charles Robins, tidesman etc., in the Port of Falmouth, and that his dismission may be sent here express to arrive before the election which may have a proper effect on the others, and contribute to our success. We must again desire this may be imediately done. . . .[3]

To support this request, Rodney himself wrote to Newcastle on the same day from Penryn:

I must beg leave to lay before your Grace the present situation of affairs at this place where I arrived on Sunday last [22 March] and have in company with Lord Falmouth and Mr. Edgcumbe canvassed the town.
    We find at presant but a small majority owing to the defection of several officers in the Customs and Salt Office, both here and at Falmouth, as likewise two men belonging to the packquetts, who are

all obstinate in the opposition, the agents of the other party having had the presumption to read a letter as from your Grace, which has deluded these people so much, that Mr. West's letter signifying your Grace's pleasure, had not the least effect. I must therefore joyn with Lord Falmouth and Mr. Edgcumbe for the dismission of one Charles Robbins, a tydesman etc., at Falmouth, which may have the desired effect on the other officers.

I must now take the liberty to point out to your Grace a measure which I am sure will infallibly secure the election, and which I most earnestly intreat may take place immediately, as it will convince the people in general (whose minds have been poison'd with different notions) that I have the honour to be nominated by your Grace as a candidate.

Capt. Peard of the Savage sloop of war, a freeman of this town, whose friends have great influence, has been offer'd by the adversarys a bond of one thousand pound, and that they will procure him a post ship ; he has resisted the temptation and continues firm.

If your Grace will make it a point, that it may appear here, before the election that Captain Peard has post, I am sure all difficultys will be removed ; my ship the Marlborough has no captain appointed as yet.[1]

The poll was taken on 4 April, and the result announced to Bute by Falmouth in the following letter :[2]

I have the satisfaction to acquaint you, all is over where I have been concerned with success here unanimously by the Magistrately and the Commonalty.

Turner and Rodney . .	68.
Clive	63.
Masculine . . .	61.

I have the honor to be My Lord
Yr. Lordship's etc.
This place has been expensive.

It was the last time that a Falmouth candidate succeeded at Penryn ; on the death of Edward Turner, in 1766, Francis Basset was returned in his place, and until 1802 the Basset influence remained predominant in the borough.

The Penryn election of 1761, with all that lies behind it, well illustrates the purely personal character of politics at that

---

[1] 32921, ff. 51-2.　　　　[2] Bute MSS.

time, parties, if ever mentioned, appearing merely as combinations of men with no definite principles to bind or divide them. The Oxfordshire election of 1754 was still fought, in appearance, on strict party lines, in a county where, under the influence of the University, high Toryism had continued an ideological existence longer than in most parts of the country. But in 1760 the traditional leader of the Whigs in Oxfordshire, the Duke of Marlborough, concluded a compromise with the Tories, apparently without consulting the party, which incensed them so much that they would now, it was reported, have preferred even a second Tory to the Duke's brother. Next, the late Whig champion, Sir Edward Turner, was put up by directions from the King and Lord Bute, supposed to favour the Tories, for a seat which Lord Falmouth, an election manager who had served Sir Robert Walpole and the Pelhams, had offered to the new Court in his eagerness, as Lord Hardwicke put it, to worship the rising sun. Francis Basset, a Tory who, according to the usual story in the text-books, ought to have thrown himself with joy at the feet of George III, paid no regard to the change in the person of the sovereign, but quietly went on with the contest against the Falmouth interest, as he had planned before George II's death. For his candidates he chose men connected with one of the strongest Whig groups in England, whose leader, Lord Powis, was already busy getting favour with the new Court. During the negotiations for a compromise, carried on through Lord Hardwicke, naturally not a word was said about practically non-existent parties and principles, and the only banners were those of Falmouth and Basset — if Turner had been prepared to stand as a Basset candidate, he would have been accepted without a thought of this implying anything as to connexions or action at Westminster. And before the year was out, Robert Clive, who had given all this trouble both to Newcastle and Bute, was made an Irish peer, probably not so much because of his great achievements in India, as for fear that otherwise he, together with his father, who sat for Montgomery, and his relative John Walsh, M.P. for Worcester, might be induced to join Pitt.

FOWEY

Against Fowey Lord Edgcumbe's steward briefly put the names of 'Lord Edgcumbe and Mr. Rashleigh', and refrained from entering into details. Indeed, the election law of that borough was such that even then it required a Cornish attorney to understand it and numerous Parliamentary committees to declare it. Suffice it therefore to state that according to the last determination of 5 May 1701 the right of election at Fowey was 'in the Prince's tenants . . . capable of being portreves of the said borough, and in such inhabitants . . . only as pay scot and lot'; 'the Prince's tenants' being defined 'as to be such as have been duly admitted upon the court-rolls of the manor, and have done their fealty'.[1] The size of this electorate, because of differences in interpretation which resulted in the creating or disfranchising of voters, varied in the eighteenth century between 40 and 100.

The 'Prince's tenants' resembled 'burgagees', and even in 1571, when after an interval of 230 years the Parliamentary representation of Fowey was revived, 12 out of 31 holdings which carried votes belonged to the Rashleigh family; in 1650, 15. 'From 1728 to 1817', writes E. W. Rashleigh, 'the borough was completely a pocket borough of the Rashleigh family',[2] which statement is more or less correct in so far as one seat was concerned. For during that period Fowey was really under the management of the Rashleighs and the Edgcumbes, a combination specially interesting before 1761, when the Rashleighs were Tories and the Edgcumbes the most faithful borough managers of Robert Walpole and the Pelhams.

The Rashleigh family, who had settled at Fowey in the reign of Henry VIII and had first represented it in Parliament in 1588, did not go to market with the seat under their control, and in Parliament were independent and did not hunt for places and pensions. Jonathan Rashleigh, M.P. for Fowey

[1] Oldfield, *The Representative History of Great Britain and Ireland* (1816), vol. iii, p. 206.
[2] *A Short History of the Town and Borough of Fowey* (1887), p. 30.

from 1727 till his death in 1764, was the sixth of the family to
represent it ; he was succeeded by his son Philip Rashleigh, a
famous mineralogist and antiquary, who sat for it till 1802 —
father and son making up between them seventy-five years of
continuous representation. The other seat was held from 1746
till May 1761 by Captain George Edgcumbe, R.N., a younger
son of the first Lord Edgcumbe, who, on the death of his
brother in 1761, succeeded to the peerage and the management
of the Parliamentary interest of his family in Cornwall. From
now onwards the Edgcumbe seat at Fowey was in the market.
I have no certain information concerning the sum paid for it
at the by-election in December 1761, when Captain R. Boyle
Walsingham, R.N., was returned by Lord Edgcumbe at the
recommendation of the Duke of Newcastle ; [1] or in 1768, when
James Modyford Heywood (descended from the Modyfords
and Heywoods of Jamaica) was elected. In 1774, £3000 was
demanded by Edgcumbe and probably paid by the Government.[2] In 1780 and 1784 the Government paid for its nominees the price of £3000, by that time customary.[3]

The marketing of Fowey was no more distinctive than its
price. But its hybrid franchise resulted in some interesting
attempts to establish electoral control in the constituency, at
one time by reducing, and at another by building up the
borough. When, under William and Mary, a new Corporation
was established at Fowey, consisting of fourteen burgesses,
these, according to Oldfield,

[1] Newcastle first meant to put up for it Rawlinson Earle, an official of
the Ordnance, who had contested Cricklade at the general election, and,
after having 'spent near £5000', was defeated by Arnold Nesbitt, a London
merchant and an insubordinate dependant of Newcastle's (32935, f. 402).
Newcastle was now determined that Earle should have the first vacant seat
in Parliament (see his memorandum for Bute of 17 Apr 1761 ; 32922, f. 14).
But on 12 June Newcastle wrote to the Duke of Devonshire : '. . . *singly*
out of regard to you, I have agreed with my Lord Edgcombe that he should
chuse Captain Boyle at Fowey. . . . Poor Erle, I am afraid, will suffer by
it. . . . Captain Boyle must take Mr. Erle's expence upon him as if he was
the person himself to be chose ; however, that will be the same thing to
them both' (32924, f. 54). It is not clear what expense of Earle's Boyle
Walsingham was to bear, nor is it clear where Edgcumbe came in.

[2] See W. T. Laprade, *The Parliamentary Papers of John Robinson*, p. 26.

[3] Laprade, *op. cit.* ; for 1780 see p. 58, 'His Majesty's private account' ;
for 1784, p. 108.

with their patron, Mr. Rashleigh, used every exertion to reduce the inhabitants of this once populous and trading town, to a number inferior to the freeholders, in order to assume the control of their political rights, by which means this place became nearly de-populated ; as it is proved by the parish registers, that in a few years after the charter began to operate, the population of the town decreased more than two-thirds.[1]

When in 1747 Thomas Pitt, on behalf of the Prince of Wales, became deeply engaged in Cornish elections, he wrote about Fowey on 12 June : 'As to Foy and Lostwithiel, I am sifting and enquiring'.[2] On 13 June : 'I am in hopes of both Lostwithiel and Fowey ; but I must be enabled to make the deposit in case my scheme takes . . . £1000 for each Member'.[3] On 19 June : 'If I can do it, shall I engage for two at Fowey ? May Rashly be turned out ? Won't it disoblige the Tories too much ?'[4] He failed at Fowey,[5] but on 2 August 1747 wrote in a survey of Cornish boroughs :

I have gained a good footing at Fowey, which, by bringing some kind of trade, may be established to be a prevailing interest. I understand there is a Club of West India merchants who make it a rule to promote the trade of any borough where a friend may be chosen. Could they not be prevailed on to order some of their ships to be victualled at Fowey ?[6]

Fourteen years later this method was to be pursued by others ; on 26 June 1761, Edgcumbe wrote to Newcastle :

I am like to meet with more trouble at Fowey than I imagined, for two of the agents that were employed at Penryn by Clive are there makeing interest for Crocket, a merchant of London, who (they say) engages to bring a number of Carolina ships there every year, and offers a bond of ten thousand pound for the performance of it ; how farr these people are realy authorised by Crocket I know not, or if it is a spirit of revenge for their disappointment at Penryn, but . . . the opposition is become serious, and I have but a small majority, though I think enough to insure the election, for the whole bench and every gentleman of the town are with me, but notwith-standing that, it will cause an expence never known in that borough before.

---

[1] *A Key to the House of Commons* (1820), p. 183.
[2] HMC, *Fortescue MSS.*, vol. i, p. 110.   [3] *Ibid.* p. 111.
[4] *Ibid.* p. 114.   [5] *Ibid.* p. 122.   *Ibid.* p. 127.

There will be less difficulty, he thought, with Captain Walsingham than there would have been with Mr. Earle, though the people at Fowey 'had rather have a merchant than either'. The letter closes with a recommendation that the son of one of the Fowey electors, who was on board Edgcumbe's own ship, should be made a lieutenant, to secure his father's vote.[1]

The 'Crocket' mentioned in this letter was Charles Crockatt, a big London merchant who traded with America, and especially with South Carolina, and is described by Oldfield as 'largely concerned in the rice trade'[2] (rice was one of the staple products of the Carolinas). His father, James Crockatt,[3] had been for many years a leading merchant at Charleston, S.C., and in 1736 was prominent in organizing the first insurance company in America; appointed to the Council of the Province in 1738, a year later 'he closed out his Charleston business and returned to London', where he continued in the American trade; and in 1741 he was replaced on the Council by Charles Pinckney, as his own 'affairs do not permit him to return from England'.[4] From 1749 till 1757, James Crockatt acted as agent for South Carolina in Great Britain,[5] while John Nutt, his son-in-law, appears occasionally as its banker.[6] In 1764 Charles and James Crockatt and John Nutt are among the signatories to a Memorial of the London merchants trading to the American plantations in favour of a bounty to be given in the Colonies on the growing of hemp;[7] and on 4 December 1765, at a meeting of the merchants, Charles Crockatt was

[1] 32924, ff. 265-6. Newcastle replied on 4 July (*ibid.* f. 412) — he has spoken to Lord Anson and the thing shall be done.

[2] *A Key to the House of Commons* (1820), p. 183.

[3] The name is spelled in various ways: Crockett, Crockatt, Crokatt, etc.

[4] See *Acts of the Privy Council (Colonial)*, 1720-45, pp. 837-8.

[5] About James Crockatt see W. Roy Smith, *South Carolina as a Royal Province* (1903), and D. D. Wallace, *The Life of Henry Laurens*; Laurens was apprenticed to him 1744-47, and was to have been entered into partnership with him, which scheme was frustrated by an intrigue.

[6] On him see Hunter, *Familiae Minorum Gentium*, p. 745: 'John Nutt of London, merchant, mar. a daughter of James Crockett of London, merchant'. He appears as a banker for S.C. in a letter from Charles Garth to the S.C. Committee of Correspondence, 30 July 1763 (in the copies of Garth's letter-books at Haines Hill, Berks).

[7] *Acts of the Privy Council (Colonial)*, 1745-66, p. 648.

Y

elected a member of the committee formed to obtain the Repeal of the Stamp Act.[1]

There is no record of the contest between the Edgcumbe interest and Crockatt having been carried to a poll in December 1761, but after Jonathan Rashleigh's death, on 24 November 1764, Charles Crockatt once more came forward as a candidate for the borough.   John Henniker, a big London merchant, who in 1761 had been returned for Sudbury 'supported in his election by a very considerable sum and the Duke of Newcastle, £5,500',[2] and in the autumn of 1762 had promptly deserted Newcastle for Bute and Fox, on 19 December 1764, wrote about Crockatt to Charles Jenkinson, then Secretary to the Treasury :

A friend of mine, a merchant and a man of fortune and character, and a friend to Government — is desirous to represent Fowey — but if any other gentleman has already the favour of Government he will decline seeking further after it — or if not — he will wait on Mr. Grenville. . . .[3]

Charles Jenkinson submitted this letter to Grenville who, having examined how far he was at liberty to assist Crockatt at Fowey,[4] wrote to him on 25 December wishing him success.[5]

I flatter myself . . . that every friend of mine will concur with me in these sentiments, and endeavour to contribute to an event so agreeable to me as that of your being elected at Fowey.

Consequently on 1 January 1765 Jenkinson wrote to J. R. Webb, Member for Bossiney :

Mr. Jenkinson sends Mr. Webb inclosed a list of votes at Fowey and desires that his friend would mark those he can influence in favour of Mr. Crockatt, and that he would not fail to secure them. Mr. Jenkinson desires to have the list returned with his friend's observations.[6]

---

[1] 38339, f. 166.
[2] See Bute's list of the House of Commons of 1761, 38333, f. 97.
[3] 38458, f. 56.   [4] 38304, f. 102.
[5] Grenville's letter-book, in the Stowe MSS. at the Henry H. Huntington Library, San Marino, California.
[6] 38304, f. 109.   The list is not in the Liverpool Papers.

Crockatt, an 'American' merchant who a year later was actively to oppose the Stamp Act, had thus the support of the Grenville Administration against Philip Rashleigh, a member and heir of an old Tory family; and on the day of election, 21 January 1765, Crockatt 'had a majority of legal votes', but the returning officer, while rejecting nine 'Prince's tenants' made by Rashleigh for this occasion, 'rejected a greater number of legal votes among the inhabitant householders paying scot and lot, who tendered for Mr. Crockatt, and gave the return to Mr. Rashleigh',[1] putting his vote at twenty-seven and Crockatt's at twenty-four;[2] against which decision a petition was presented by Mr. Crockatt, but never tried. Charles Crockatt did not stand again in 1768,[3] and died on 27 April 1769.

EAST AND WEST LOOE

About East and West Looe Edgcumbe's steward wrote in 1760: 'Mr. John Buller manages these burroughs for the Administration and himself and the interest seems well settled in that channell'. And Buller himself wrote in a memorandum for Newcastle on the eve of the general election of 1761 :[4]

Sir R[obert] W[alpole] made Mr. Trelawny Commissioner of the Customs, and then Governor of Jamaica;[5] he also regimented the Independent Companies there, and made him the Colonel: Sir John Trelawny[6] had also an allowance of £500 a year, and a present of £1000 the year of the general election; and sometimes four friends were chosen and sometimes three.

Upon the death of Governor Trelawny, Mr. Pelham thought Mr. John Buller a proper person to manage the interest at Looe,

---

[1] A Key to the House of Commons (1820), p. 183.

[2] MS. poll-book in the Rashleigh Papers at the Royal Institution of Cornwall, Truro.

[3] The figures for that election as given in the MS. poll-book were :

Philip Rashleigh	.	.	69
Js. Modyford Heywood	.	.	61
John Williams	.	.	29
Tho. Arthington	.	.	26

[4] 33055, f. 336.

[5] Edward Trelawny, Commissioner of Customs 1732–36, Governor of Jamaica 1736–52; died 6 Jan 1754.

[6] Sir John Trelawny, fourth Bt. (died 1756), was a brother of Governor Trelawny.

and promis'd he should be Comptroller of the Mint, and that the salary should be made up £500 a year, and order'd Gashry to assure him of some farther mark of the King's favour.

My Lord Duke of Newcastle, succeeding to the Treasury, made good Mr. Pelham's engagement, by giving Lord Aylmer a pension of £500 a year; [1] and Mr. Buller, Mr. Noel,[2] Mr. Frederick,[3] and Mr. Gashry [4] were chosen at the last general election, agreable to his Grace's recommendation.

The salary of the Mint has never been worth more than £240 in any one year : the deficiency never paid but for one or two years.[5]

What Mr. John Buller now desires is to receive some mark of the Duke of Newcastle's favour and confidence, in being made a Commissioner of the Excise or Customs, by which his Grace may put in another Member at Looe, and Mr. Buller will have the satisfaction of knowing that his Grace has some regard for him. Mr.

[1] For vacating the post of Comptroller of the Mint.

[2] William Noel, M.P. for West Looe 1747–57, when he was appointed a Judge in the Court of Common Pleas.

[3] On him see below, pp. 326-8.

[4] Francis Gashry, M.P. for East Looe 1741–62, is a somewhat mysterious person. He seems to have been of foreign parentage, and to have had connexions with America and the West Indies. His monument in the churchyard of All Saints at Fulham (which seems to have suffered considerable damage since I first saw it in 1926) bears a coat of arms, but I have not found his family in any English genealogical work. The name is occasionally spelt 'Gachery'; possibly he was descended from Stephen Gascherie, a Huguenot naturalized in 1687 (see Agnew, *Protestant Exiles from France* (1886), vol. ii, p. 55). On 7 July 1737, £300 was paid to Francis Gashery for a 'Royal present to the Mohegan Indians of Connecticut' (see *Calendar of Treasury Books and Papers*, 1735–38, p. 426); and in 1702 there was a family of Gacherie, or Gasherie, settled in the Province of New York (see *Documents relating to the Colonial History of New York*, vol. iv, p. 1010; also *Registers of Births, Marriages and Deaths of the 'Église Françoise à la Nouvelle York'*, 1688–1804, ed. by the Rev. A. V. Wittmeyer, *Collections of the Huguenot Society of America*, vol. i, pp. 95, 113, and 117). In 19038 there is a series of letters from Gashry to Governor Trelawny in Jamaica, whose agent he seems to have been in England ; this correspondence continued with Trelawny's successor, Admiral Knowles. 1740–43 Gashry was an Extra Commissioner of the Navy, and 1744–47 Comptroller of the Victualling Accounts of the Navy. These appointments he owed to Admiral Sir Charles Wager, M.P. ; on the monument which Gashry raised to him in Westminster Abbey in 1747, Wager is described as his 'Great Patron'. 1751–62 Gashry was Treasurer of the Ordnance and the intermediary between the Treasury and the local managers of the two Looes. As Treasurer of the Ordnance, Gashry dabbled in finance and was summoned by Newcastle to some of the conferences with City financiers. He was also a Director of the South Sea Company. According to the inscription on his tomb, he died aged sixty-one.

[5] Two payments to Buller, of £200 each, appear in the secret service accounts on 28 Apr 1755 and 10 June 1756 ; see below pp. 437 and 441.

Buller promises the most zealous attachment to his Grace's interest, in this election, and in every future one.

My Lord Duke will please to consider, that six votes in the House depend on gratifying Mr. Buller in this request. Captain Trelawny,[1] Mr. Gashry and the person to be chosen in the room of Buller, will undoubtedly be his Grace's freinds. Whereas should Mr. Buller continue a Member and chuse a freind of his owne, these two and Captain Trelawny, who will be aw'd and influenced by Buller, will most certainly not be his Grace's freinds.

The Trelawnys were one of the oldest Parliamentary families in Cornwall ; between the time of Edward II and the Reform Act of 1832, twenty-three of their name represented Cornish constituencies in Parliament. But about the middle of the eighteenth century the male representatives of the family rapidly died off ; Sir John Trelawny, fourth Baronet, was the last of four brothers, none of whom left any descendants. Similarly his cousin and heir, Harry Trelawny of Butshead, had no children, and was succeeded by his nephew, Captain William Trelawny, R.N., the Member for West Looe mentioned above ; while John Buller who, according to his own statement, was thought by Henry Pelham 'a proper person to manage the interest at Looe', was through his mother a nephew of the Governor and of Sir John Trelawny.[2]

The Bullers, younger as a Parliamentary family than the Trelawnys, had come to the fore in the seventeenth century, and continued to gain ground on the electoral map of Cornwall ; between 1620 and 1832, twenty-two of them sat in Parliament for Cornish constituencies. They seem to have had some interest of their own at West Looe, which they contested against the Trelawnys in 1660, but predominance at the Looes

---

[1] William Trelawny, M.P. for West Looe 1757–67 ; Captain R.N. ; Governor of Jamaica from 1767 till his death in 1772. In 1762 he succeeded to the baronetcy as its sixth holder. His father was a first cousin of Sir John Trelawny, fourth Bt., and of Rebecca Buller, the mother of John Buller, M.P.

[2] The Trelawnys were Recorders of East Looe 1677–1754 ; John Buller 1754–86 ; his brother William, Dean, and later on Bishop of Exeter 1786–97 ; etc. (see Thomas Bond, *History of East and West Looe*, 1823). The same Rev. William Buller was elected four times Mayor of East Looe, 1760, 1767, 1774, and 1780, obviously each time in anticipation of a general election ; John Buller in 1746, 1754, and 1772 ; James Buller 1752 ; Francis Buller 1762 (see *ibid.* pp. 234-5).

came to them with the management of the Government interest ; and as in numerous boroughs all over England, the private interest of the influential local manager gradually absorbed that of the Government.

Before the general election of 1754, William Trelawny applied to Henry Pelham by order of his uncle, Harry Trelawny of Butshead — 'as a person who from the natural interest of my family and the good will that is born to it at the two burroughs of East and West Looe, had very good pretensions to offer myself as candidate for a seat in one of those burroughs at the ensuing election'. Pelham admitted his claim, but the candidates had already been settled with Governor Trelawny — if he now acceded to that arrangement, Pelham would support him on the next vacancy ; and 'in the mean time he said he would take care that I lost no ground in my profession by making him that concession'. William Trelawny agreed, and received the command of the *Peregrine* sloop with the promise of a post ship.[1]

Pelham dying on 6 March 1754, the management of the general election devolved on Newcastle. Informed by Gashry of his brother's engagements to William Trelawny, Newcastle renewed the promise to recommend him 'that he may be made a captain', and tried 'to find out something that may be agreable to Mr. John Buller'.[2] The four Government candidates were duly returned at the Looes, and on 30 April the Duke wrote to Harry Trelawny : '. . . the disinterested manner in which they [the Corporations of East and West Looe] have resisted the solicitations and temptations that were thrown in their way, . . . entitle them deservedly to my regard for their interests'.[3] It does not appear from this correspondence that at that time John Buller was considered the exclusive manager of the Government interest which he claimed to be in his own memorandum.

---

[1] William Trelawny to Newcastle, 26 May 1755 ; 32855, ff. 227-8.
[2] Newcastle to Harry Trelawny, 23 Mar and reply 25 Mar 1754 ; 32734, ff. 314-15, and f. 385. See also address from the Corporations of East and West Looe to Newcastle, *ibid.* f. 392. There are forty-one signatories to the address, including William Trelawny as High Steward of West Looe, and John Buller as Recorder of East Looe.   [3] 32735, f. 215.

A year later William Trelawny reminded Newcastle of his promise,[1] and, on receiving fresh assurances through Gashry, wrote another letter [2] which throws light on the relations between the Trelawnys, the Bullers, and the Government :

I have a request to make of your Grace . . . founded in a caution I received from Mr. Pelham . . . who asked me whether there was not some danger to be apprehended from Mr. James Buller, one of the Members for the county. I answered that I thought not, because the attachment of the people in both burroughs was so very firm that it cou'd hardly be got the better of. Mr. Pelham replied that he was glad to hear it was so, but added that I must keep a good look out towards that quarter, for that Mr. Buller had a pretence to call himself one of the family, and very great property to support any pretence he pleased to advance, and if he shou'd get the burroughs into his hands the consequence would be that neither he nor any friend of his could expect any support from the representatives of them.

Mr. Buller has already tried the ground without success, but I am apprehensive that he may attempt it again, and in case I should be out of the way at a critical time may have a chance of carrying his point. My request therefore to your Grace is . . . that you would be pleased to intimate to the Lords of the Admiralty that I should be employed (when I have the honour to command a post ship) in a station that may not be too much out of reach when I am wanted to attend at either of the Looes.

Not a word is said about John Buller, who, as Member for East Looe and its Recorder, was more immediately concerned in the boroughs. James Buller, his elder brother, was obviously the better peg for the fears and the story, because as a knight of the shire he was a 'Tory', which at that time hardly meant anything but that he was independent; while John, being more closely concerned in boroughs, by their patronage and traffic was connected with the Government, and was therefore a 'Whig'. Still, both brothers were concerned in establishing the family interest in the boroughs, and by 1759 had therein even the help of the Trelawnys.

At West Looe the Corporation consisted of twelve burgesses, one of whom was Mayor; they constituted the entire Parlia-

---

[1] 26 May 1755 ; 32855, ff. 227-8.
[2] 27 July 1755 ; 32857, ff. 392-3.

mentary electorate of the borough, and as they were recruited
by co-optation, circumstances favoured its conversion into a
family preserve. In 1820 Oldfield wrote about West Looe:
'John Buller, of Morval, Esq. [grandson of James Buller] is
proprietor of this borough'.[1]

At East Looe the Corporation consisted of a Mayor, recorder, eight aldermen, 'and an indefinite number of freemen,
or burgesses, who possess the right of election'.[2] Neither the
Trelawnys nor the Bullers ever obtained quite the same hold
on this borough as on West Looe. John Buller stated in his
memorandum for Newcastle that 'sometimes four friends were
chosen and sometimes three', and in depicting the future consequences of his displeasure, again spoke of three seats only.
The uncertain seat was at East Looe.

One of the Members returned for West Looe in 1754,
John Frederick, was descended from Sir John Frederick, 'a
merchant of great opulence and Lord Mayor of London in
1662', and his family was prominent in the City of London
and the East India House, as Government contractors and in
the Civil Service. He had sat for West Looe since 1743, and,
as was usual in the eighteenth century, by establishing an
interest of his own in the borough tried to render himself
independent of those to whom, at least in part, he owed his
seat. Here are a few letters written to him by some of his
twelve electors, illustrative of 'politics' in a close Cornish
Corporation :

Richard Puddicombe to John Frederick.

WEST LOOE. *September* 11, 1759.

Honourable Sir,

I am sorry to find you are so very ill, I hope by this time you are
quite recovered. As to the Salt Office place for my Brother John,
I hope you have obtaind as it is our borough's property, and my
brother John is an alderman as well as the person that had it last.
We who signed the last letter to your Honour are the persons that
the interest of this borough depends on, and I say farther your
interest as well, and I assure you, Sir, if you obtain this place, it

---

[1] *Key to the Houses of Parliament*, p. 80.   [2] *Ibid.* p. 81.

will be a great mains in promoting your interest. I have no time
to write any more as I am now on Corporation business of great
importance.[1]

*Robert Hearle, Richard Puddicombe, and Stephen and John
Puddicombe to John Frederick.*

September 29, 1759.

. . . Unluckily for us Mr. Nath[l] Hearle, who was a father to two
of us, died about a fortnight since, and this day by the influence of
Mr. James Buller, a Member for this county, Mr. Samuel Bowden,
sen. was chosen mayor for the year ensuing in the room of Stephen
Puddicombe in order, as 'tis supposed, to fill up the vacancy on
the Bench with one Mr. Dido, a clergyman and schoolmaster of
Tiverton, Devon, a remarkable Anticourtier, which we strenuously
opposed. The mayoralty has gone on for many many years by
agreement, by rotation. And it was Rich[d] Puddicombe's turn to
be mayor this year, Bowden is elected entirely as a tool, but what
is more extraordinary is that Mr. John Buller, a Member for East
Looe should join those who are directly opposite to his Grace the
Duke of Newcastle's interest. We are sorry to say this, but you may
depend on the truth of it, and we have reason to fear gentlemen of
a different way of thinking from you and his Grace of Newcastle
intend to divide the borough at the next election, but give us leave
to say you may depend upon our utmost efforts in the support of
your interest and at all events are determined to join you. . . .[2]

On 4 October these same aldermen again reported to John
Frederick that the new Mayor had summoned a court of
aldermen the previous day, but that none of the signatories
had attended, 'well knowing that the mayor could not get more
than four aldermen (and those all non-resident, viz. James
Buller, John Buller, Francis Buller, and Charles Trelawny,
Esqs.) besides himself and son to sit on the Bench'. Without
a quorum they proceeded, however, to transact business,
elected Dido an alderman, had the son of James Buller, though
a minor, sworn a freeman, and Henry Trelawny nominated for
a freeman. 'You may see, Sir, by this that our fears and
apprehensions were not groundless, and that those gentlemen
are aiming at you equally with us.'[3] Still, not at West Looe
alone, but with the Government itself, the Buller influence was

---

[1] 32895, f. 357.   [2] 32896, f. 174.   [3] *Ibid.* f. 274.

superior to that of Frederick. On 21 December 1759, Richard
Puddicombe reported to him a rumour that the Salt Office had
been obtained for James Dyer, a freeman of East Looe. 'We
did realy think that my brother John Puddicombe woud have
succeeded as the place belongs to our borough.' [1] On 5 February 1761, Richard Puddicombe wrote again :

Honourable Sir,
    As the dessolution of this Parliament is very near, and my self,
brothers and brother-in-law have had several gentlemen to desire
our vots, and interest, for them to be our representatives in Parliament at the next election — we have denied every gentleman as yet
that have asked our vots on your account ; therefore I humbly beg
the favour of your Honour to inform me whether you'l be pleased
to offer your self a candidate for our borough, and at the same
time be pleased if you can to informe me whether his Grace the
Duke of Newcastle doth intend to recommend any person.—I assure
you we have kept our self entirely to oblige you and his Grace, and
I have waited every post thinking to hear from you, but I think I
have received no answer from you since Michaelmas last.[2]

    The Puddicombes and Hearles ultimately regained their
position in the borough,[3] but John Frederick had to abandon
his seat to Francis Buller, younger brother of John Buller.[4]

---

[1] 32900, f. 379.   [2] 32918, ff. 289-90.
[3] After some seven stormy years, during which several times no mayor
was elected 'owing to equal votes', a compromise seems to have been
concluded, a new rotation established, and the Puddicombes and Hearles
reinstated.   Richard Puddicombe was Mayor of West Looe six times
between 1768 and 1787 ; Stephen Puddicombe eleven times between 1769
and 1802 ; Nathaniel Hearle eleven times between 1782 and 1807 ; his
son, bearing the same names, every second year from 1808 onwards.   The
circle was obviously getting more and more restricted.   See Thomas Bond,
History of East and West Looe (1823), pp. 242-3.
[4] Newcastle tried at first to find another constituency for John Frederick,
whose name appears in lists of candidates (see, *e.g.*, that of 17 Feb 1761 ;
32919, f. 62) ; and in another undated list of 'Persons who have applied
to be brought into Parliament' (32999, f. 222), the following remark is put
against his name : 'Turn'd out of Parliament by Mr. Buller.—Has had long
expectations and constant disappointments'.   Finally, his name is crossed
out from the list of candidates and the significant word 'Customs' is put
against it.   For years John Frederick had been pressing unsuccessfully for
a place at one of the Government Boards (see letters of 20 May 1756,
32865, f. 69 ; 27 May 1757, 32871, f. 149 ; 1 May 1759, 32890, f. 436 ;
7 May 1759, 32891, f. 23 ; 23 Dec 1759, 32900, f. 266) ; now he received
his consolation prize as Commissioner of Customs (salary £1000 a year), a
place not tenable with a seat in Parliament.

Judging from the style and contents of John Buller's memorandum for Newcastle and the fact that the office he claimed was not given to him, one might have expected him to desert Newcastle as soon as power and patronage passed out of the Duke's hands. It happened otherwise; he was closely connected with H. B. Legge, to whom, as Chancellor of the Exchequer, he had been secretary, and who in March 1761 was driven from office by the new Court, the first victim of Leicester House rancours; Buller remained faithful to him and Newcastle. Early in 1762, Gashry, who had 'long been in a declining state', was not expected to 'hold long' any more; and Legge reported to Newcastle: 'Buller is ready to receive any friend of your nomination into the borough upon very easy terms and your Grace will not be sorry to settle your measures a little beforehand against Gachery's death'.[1] The terms were '1000l. only' from the Member to be elected, and the succession to Gashry as Treasurer of the Ordnance (£500 p.a.) for John Buller.[2]

By 19 April, Gashry was on the point of death, and Legge again pressed Newcastle concerning the borough and the place at the Ordnance.[3] Newcastle, no longer the 'disposing Minister', had to speak to Bute about it, and received an ambiguous reply. By the middle of May Newcastle was on his political deathbed. 'I can . . . assure your Grace', wrote Legge on 14 May, 'that Buller is not more desirous of obtaining the office himself than of bringing a person into Parliament of your nomination.'[4] Gashry died on 19 May, and on the 20th, at 9 P.M., Bute inquired of Grenville how the borough stood — 'don't let us be jockeyed . . . if it can be avoided'.[5] Grenville replied 'near 12 at night';[6]

I entirely agree with you in wishing to secure the vacancy made by Mr. Gashery's death, if it is possible. . . . Mr. Buller, I imagine, will at this time be easily engaged, and there will not be the least difficulty of finding a proper person, if he will accept the recommendation.

[1] 32934, f. 490.
[2] Newcastle's 'Memorandums for Lord Bute', 7 Apr 1762; 32936, f. 412.   [3] 32937, f. 225.   [4] 32938, f. 270.
[5] Grenville Papers, vol. ii, p. 443.   [6] Ibid. p. 444.

On the 21st, 'near 11 o'clock' [A.M.], Samuel Martin wrote to Grenville : ¹

. . . Mr. John Buller left London last night, with a design to travel all night, and proceed to East Looe in Cornwall with all possible haste : alarmed . . . with the rumour of an opposition at the ensuing election for that borough, by Sir William Trelawny.

Martin proposed to see Buller's brother, presumably Francis, the next morning.

Bute wrote to Grenville the same night, 'past 10' : ²

What do you think of the inclos'd ? ³ We must not be affronted at first setting out, and yet Buller has no demands on us. If any thing is determin'd, no time is to be lost.

Grenville replied an hour later.⁴ He knew nothing about the borough except what he learnt from Martin's letter that morning ; feared it might be too late to make the necessary applications on behalf of Trelawny ; but saw no reason to dissuade him 'from trying his interest if he thinks he can make anything of it'.

Meantime Legge, on 19 May, once more urged Newcastle to do his utmost for Buller, and added : 'I have seen Lord Palmerston who takes the approbation of him very kindly'⁵ (they thus had picked the successor to Gashry's seat without reference to the King and Bute — which may have been the affront mentioned by Bute). Newcastle replied the next day, sadly describing how everything was done 'to mortifie me at my going out'.⁶ Still, he tried, and on 21 May wrote again to Legge :

I this day . . . acquainted the King with the vacancy of the Treasurer of the Ordnance ; and that I had, some time ago, recommended to my Lord Bute Mr. Buller to succeed him. I set both Mr. Buller's pretensions, both as to his consequence and merit, in the best manner I could ; particularly his credit and influence in

---

¹ Grenville Papers, vol. ii, pp. 445-6.   ² Grenville MSS. (J. M.).
³ Missing ; presumably a letter from Trelawny.
⁴ Grenville MSS. (J. M.).   ⁵ 32938, f. 344.
⁶ 20 May 1762 ; 32938, f. 365.

the two boroughs of East Low and West Low. His Majesty said nothing, as I knew, he would not give me any promise or encouragement; but as I have now prepared them, I should think, if Mr. Buller has any way of applying, it would do; but in my present situation, I can do nothing. . . .[1]

Legge replied the same day :

If without further application the thing is done, very well, but if fresh solicitation is to be made, he [Buller] will never get it. I cant take some means of asking, and if I could, Buller is not a man to take even what he wants by all means; tho' I believe the place might be had if nothing but the mere obtaining it were to be consider'd. He has been examin'd about the borough and has declared himself engaged to Lord Palmerston a gentleman of my recommending approv'd by you, and is gone down to Loo without asking any further questions to make good his engagement.[2]

It shows character and independence in Buller to have quoted Legge and Newcastle as the men whose recommendation he had accepted; Lord Palmerston was returned for East Looe, but naturally the place of Gashry as Treasurer of the Ordnance was not given to Buller — it went to Charles Jenkinson, at that time Bute's secretary.

During the next three years John Buller is found in all the main divisions voting with the Opposition. He was one of the minority against the Preliminaries of the Peace of Paris on 10 December 1762; he voted with the Opposition over General Warrants on 17-18 February 1764; and as the only one of the Buller family, was a member of the Opposition club at Wildman's in Albemarle Street in 1764. As Newcastle put it in a letter to the Duke of Devonshire on 21 December 1763 James Buller, the Member for Cornwall, had always been 'a most staunch, determined Tory; which his brother John has never, or at least for many years, been'; [3] while Francis, in December 1763, accepted the place of Groom-Porter from the Grenville Administration. But as to John Buller, Legge wrote to Newcastle on 22 December: '. . . whenever he falls off I shall have no further confidence in myself and you may expect to hear I am turn'd into a Commissioner of Hackney

[1] 32948, f. 349.   [2] 32938, f. 386.   [3] 32954, f. 121.

Coaches'.[1] When in February 1764 a Government crisis seemed imminent, Legge named John Buller among the few friends whom he asked Newcastle to take care of;[2] and in his last will he appointed his wife (Lady Stawell), John Buller, and 'Spanish' Charles Townshend[3] (a cousin of his more famous namesake) his executors and guardians of his son. 'He could not have chose properer persons', wrote Newcastle to Lord Ashburnham on 4 September 1764.[4] 'There never lived a man of a sounder understanding, or a better heart', wrote 'Spanish' Townshend about John Buller.[5]

When the Rockingham Government was being formed, Lady Stawell wrote to Newcastle on 5 July 1765 :

Mr. Buller's steady and warm attachment to the Whigs added to his great influence in the borroughs of Looe are all to well known to your Grace to need my repeating ; I shall therefore only recommend him to you as Mr. Legge's friend . . . and I hope I shall not see Mr. Legge's memory so little regarded as to be left in doubt of Mr. Buller's being of the Treasury or Admiralty board.[6]

Newcastle thereupon wrote in a memorandum for Lord Albemarle, secretary and political representative of the Duke of Cumberland :

The Duke of Newcastle has a letter, from my Lady Stawell, recommending, in the strongest manner, Mr. John Buller, who is now Comptroller of the Mint (400£ pr. an.) to a better employment.

She lays it very strong upon the Duke of Newcastle, as due to the memory of poor Mr. Legge ; and, as Mr. Buller had been so strongly recommended to him by Mr. Legge.

Paymaster of the Marines, if Mr. Offley is otherwise provided for, Mr. John Buller.

There are other political reasons, which make the Duke of Newcastle wish, that Mr. Buller may be provided for, which the Duke of Newcastle was ignorant of, 'till yesterday morning.

---

[1] 32954, f. 142.   [2] Letter of 16 Feb 1764 ; 32956, f. 6.

[3] Charles Townshend (1728–1810) of Honingham Hall, Norfolk (son of William Townshend and grandson of the second Viscount Townshend), M.P. for Yarmouth 1756–84 and 1790–96 ; created in 1797 Baron Bayning. Before entering Parliament he was Secretary to the Embassy at Madrid, which supplied the adjective 'Spanish', to distinguish him from the more famous Charles Townshend who was a son of the third Viscount Townshend.

[4] 32962, f. 17.   [5] 13 Sept 1764 ; ibid. f. 107.

[6] 32967, f. 255.

Mr. Buller, upon the death of his two brothers,[1] both friends
of the last, or present Ministers, has settled his affairs of the two
Lowes, that Mr. Buller can bring in *three Members*, without the
least opposition.

As to his merit, he is a very honest man ; has a family, with a
small fortune ; and has been a most firm friend ; and refused the
Treasurer of Ordnance, offer'd to him, when it was given to Mr.
Mackye. . . .[2]

The same day Newcastle wrote to Lady Stawell assuring
her that he would not be capable 'of being wanting in any
mark of respect or attention' to the wishes of a friend whom
he had loved so sincerely, but added that the Treasury and the
Admiralty, which 'are the two first Boards', are likely to be
settled by now and that he would have to find something else
for Buller.

I have had very few opportunities of seeing Mr. Buller since [the
death of Legge] ; and indeed, 'till yesterday morning, I had not seen
him, since there had been any report of a change in the Administration ; or, did I ever know, 'till yesterday, that since the death of
his two brothers, he had settled the two boroughs so, that he (Mr.
Buller) will chuse three Members, without any opposition.[3]

Lady Stawell replied in an indignant letter that Buller had
asked Townshend (the 'Spaniard') to tell Newcastle 'how little
satisfied he was with what had past' in his conversation with the
Duke, and how 'determin'd he was never to trouble you more'.

As to myself I am hurt tho' not at all *surprized* that in the
arrangement no care should have been taken of one so warmly
recomended by Mr. Legge as you know Mr. Buller was, and that
after it having been Mr. Legges dyeing request to your Grace, you
should have thought it necessary to know *exactly* how many members
Mr. Buller could bring into Parliament.[4]

But Townshend took a saner view of the situation :

Mr. Townshend will see Mr. Buller, will endeavour to soften his
Cornish spirit, and to prevent him from injuring himself, and from

[1] Francis Buller died on 31 Oct 1764, and James Buller on 30 Apr 1765.
[2] 7 July 1765 ; 32967, f. 273-4. John Ross Mackye had succeeded
Charles Jenkinson at the Ordnance in 1763.
[3] 32967, f. 282.   [4] 7 July 1765 ; *ibid.* f. 284.

giving pain to those, whose inclination Mr. T. knows it is to give
all due weight to Mr. Buller's merit and pretentions.[1]

Newcastle meantime most vigorously pressed on Rockingham the claims of three friends, James West, John Offley, and
John Buller, and wrote to him on 12 July :

> I think my honour so much concerned in the three following
> persons, that, if something is not done, or proposed, for them, I
> don't see, that I can have any share in the Administration. . . .
> As to Mr. Buller, the Admiralty is what he wants ; and, I hope,
> in regard to Mr. Legge's memory, in consideration of Mr. Buller's
> own merit, and the three Members of Parliament, that he can chuse,
> that no one will be prefer'd to him ; if I find, there was, I must
> take the liberty to speak to the King upon it. I hope therefore,
> your Lordship, and the other Ministers will make it unnecessary,
> to trouble His Majesty upon these occasions. . . .
> I shall take the liberty to send an extract of this part of my letter,
> relating to my three friends, to the Duke [of Cumberland] ; and I
> hope, His Royal Highness will not think it unreasonable.[2]

On 13 July, Rockingham offered to make Buller a Commissioner of the Board of Trade, but finally he was appointed
to the seat at the Admiralty which he desired, and this he
retained under successive Administrations till 1779. In 1780
he was advanced to the post of a Lord of the Treasury, and he
went out with Lord North in 1782. His was the story of so
many who in the early years of George III had adhered to the
Opposition, but having lost their bearings during the subsequent
changes, returned to the safe Government fold. John Robinson, Secretary to the Treasury, in his 'State of English Constituencies', prepared in December 1783, when George III
wanted to know what chances Pitt would have on a dissolution
of Parliament, put down against East Looe : 'Mr. Buller's
senior, who most likely will come in himself and may by civility
be made steady'.[3] Meantime, the direction of West Looe, by
a family arrangement, had passed to John Buller, jun.,[4] son of
James Buller and nephew of John Buller, sen. The two seats

[1] To the Duke of Newcastle, 11 July 1765 ; *ibid.* f. 325.
[2] 32967, ff. 347-8.   [3] See Laprade, *op. cit.*, p. 83.
[4] At the time of his father's death in 1765, John Buller jun., born in
1745, was still under age. He was returned for Exeter in 1768.

at West Looe were bought from him for the Pitt Government in 1784 for £6000.[1]

CAMELFORD

The right of election at Camelford was disputed between the 'capital burgesses' and the freemen resident in the borough and paying scot and lot ; either way, the number of voters did not exceed fifty and was more often less than twenty-five. The Duke of Bedford, as stated by the steward of Lord Edgcumbe, had 'the largest property in the town', and many tenants to support him ; but the 'principal influence' was with the Phillips family, who, during the greater part of the eighteenth century, managed Camelford. They themselves rose but slowly to the height of Parliamentary ambitions, and became extinct before they had time to proceed any further. Thus there was no initial mortgage on the representation of Camelford, and, except for a few relatives of the Pitt family, its Members during the eighteenth century present a long succession of strangers, mostly unconnected by family ties.

John Phillips of Treveanes in St. Teath, the founder of the family, was a Cornish attorney who, as so many attorneys in the West of England, dabbled in boroughs and elections. Early in the eighteenth century he 'settled in Camelford and availing himself of the political advantages of the town, obtained much influence in the borough and acquired a considerable fortune'.[2] About 1720 he became connected with Governor Thomas Pitt, immortalized by the size of his diamond, the violence of his passions, and the fame of his grandson, Lord Chatham. On 10 August 1721, Governor Pitt wrote to his eldest son Robert :

> I have been thinking that if we should have a new Parliament
> . . I would have you and Phillips lay your heads together where

---

[1] Laprade, *op. cit.*, p. 108.
[2] See Gilbert, *Parochial History of Cornwall*, vol. i, p. 380.— I stated on p. 163 that not a single fortune, even of moderate size, is known to have been acquired in Parliamentary boroughs ; but this applies to patrons, not to election agents.

z

the interest of my estate lies strongest for electing three or four Parliament men for that I hear the borough hunters of Cornwall are willing to commute with me, and if they do not, and that there is a new Parliament, I will give them all the trouble I can imagine.[1]

Under Phillips's management Robert Pitt was elected for Okehampton in Devonshire, but when Phillips's account came in for '2549 l. 14s. besides 150 l. he said he had paid otherwise', the Governor wrote again in no less a characteristic strain :

. . . you have been such a son to me as he has been a steward who I will very suddenly discharge as a cursed and unfaithful steward.[2]

And a friend who happened to be present, thus reported to Robert Pitt the Governor's comments on the bill :

He swore most heartely, and said he would send for Phillips to towne, and he must certainly suffer death, besides his being turned out of his stewardship.[3]

The cursing of Phillips, 'that most notorious villain as ever was heard of', continued for some time,[4] and of Robert Pitt so long as the Governor lived (he died in 1726, Robert in 1727). But the connexion between John Phillips, and after his death c. 1740, between his sons and the Governor's family was not broken ; in 1727 John Pitt, the Governor's youngest son, was elected at Camelford, in 1734 Sir Thomas Lyttelton and James Cholmondeley, both connected with the Pitt family, and in 1741 the candidates of the Prince of Wales, for whom Thomas Pitt, son and heir of Robert, managed Cornish elections. Similarly in 1747 two candidates approved by the Prince, Ridgway third Earl of Londonderry, a grandson of Governor Pitt, and Samuel Martin were returned for Camelford.[5]

A year later Pitt had fallen out with Charles Phillips, John's eldest son, and was, moreover, threatened by a new, formidable opponent. On 12 October 1748 he wrote to his

---

[1] HMC, *Fortescue MSS.*, vol. i, p. 66.
[2] Governor Pitt to Robert Pitt, 16 June 1722 ; *ibid.* p. 67.
[3] Sir Thomas Hardy to Robert Pitt, 16 June 1722 ; *ibid.* p. 67.
[4] *Ibid.* pp. 68 and 69.
[5] *Ibid.* pp. 109, 110, 113, and 120.

brother-in-law, the Rev. Dr. Ayscough, Clerk of the Closet to the Prince : [1]

His Grace of Bedford is become the terrour of the West. Having purchased Mr. Manatten's estates at Newport and Camelford,[2] he has, under the management of Charles Phillips, attacked Sir William Morris [Morice] and intends under the same agent, to do me the same favour at Camelford. Phillipps' behaviour since I have been in the country, has been very suspicious. . . . I am at work to defeat him . . . but the ungratefull villain has worked underground something too long. My situation here with regard to matters of a publick concern, added to my situation in private, is enough to make a man mad.

Pitt's financial straits were indeed desperate.[3] Then, on 20 March 1751, the Prince died. 'Deprived of his patron, mark'd and turn'd out by the Ministry', and attacked by Bedford at Camelford and Okehampton, Pitt felt 'that a private gentleman's fortune could not withstand such united efforts, and therefore he was obliged to look about him ' : [4] he leased his borough interests to the Government. But as most of the Prince's party now made their terms with the Pelhams, candidates of the old Leicester House set were continued at Camelford in 1754 — Samuel Martin and John Lade, distantly related to the Grenvilles through his wife, a sister of Henry Thrale. The only opposition now came from Bedford, who, however, started by negotiating with the Government. Henry Pelham wrote to Martin on 1 September 1753 that the Duke had offered to name a candidate in the King's service :

First I think his Grace should name the gentleman in the King's service he proposes to chuse, otherways you being named on our side we are not upon equal terms, secondly is it in the Duke's power and ours jointly to prevent an opposition, will not the Phillips's

---

[1] *Ibid.* pp. 132-3.

[2] Between 1688 and 1710 the family of Manaton, who owned a considerable part of Camelford, had a strong hold on the borough ; they also owned estates near Tavistock, for which borough they 'waged deadly war' with the Russells (W. P. Courtney, *op. cit.*, pp. 347-9). They finished by selling their estates to the Duke of Bedford.

[3] See *Fortescue MSS.*, vol. i, pp. 133-5.

[4] Account given by Pitt to R. N. Aldworth, in Dec 1753 ; see Aldworth to Bedford, 20 Dec ; Bedford MS., 29, f. 128.

secure a contest on one side or the other, to shew their own influence ? As to advancing more money as yet to Phillips, you are
the best judge, does he give you an account what he has done with
that you gave him before ; I should look after him a little nicely,
tho' not shew any suspicion of him, for upon that family undoubtedly
depends the election, compromised or not.[1]

On 9 September 1753, R. N. Aldworth, a political dependant
of the Duke of Bedford, informed Martin that the Duke's
intended candidate was Captain Bateman,[2] a brother of Lord
Bateman and nephew of the Duke of Marlborough. Pelham's
reply is mentioned in a letter from Bedford's agent, John
Butcher, to Martin, on 30 September [3] (but so far has not been
traced in any of the extant collections) : it seems to have been
non-committal.

Bedford's next move, in the letter from Butcher, was an
offer to Thomas Pitt that they should jointly return Bateman
and Martin, and hereafter share the borough to the exclusion
of the Phillips family, whom, wrote Butcher, Pitt 'has as contemptible opinion of, as they deserve'. Whatever assurances
they may have given him, 'there have been the like . . .
assurances given to his Grace'; but nothing less will satisfy
the ambition of Charles Phillips and of 'his insatiable family
. . . than the sole and absolute controul and dominion, which
their father exercised to the enriching his own family, at a vast
expence of every one he had to do with . . .' Should Pitt
set up a second candidate, or suffer Phillips to do so, the Duke
is determined to contest the borough.

Except for a formal acknowledgment, Martin did not reply
till 26 October.[4] Pitt, he then wrote, could not have been
expected 'to take any resolution without first knowing Mr.
Pelham's sentiments', who, in turn, suspended his final determination till Martin had examined the state of the borough.
He is now 'of opinion that he may easily carry both the
Members, and besides that a compromise is impracticable'.

In December, Pitt met Aldworth,[5] and possibly also Bedford
(though 'circumstanced as he is at present', wrote Aldworth

---

[1] 41354, f. 14.   [2] *Ibid.* f. 16.   [3] Bedford MSS. (unbound).
[4] *Ibid.*   [5] Bedford MS., 29, f. 128.

to the Duke on 20 December, 'he could wish the meeting should be private'). Still, he was no longer a principal, and the contest between the Duke of Bedford and the Administration proceeded, at high cost to either side. On 11 April 1754 the following entry appears in Newcastle's 'Minutes': [1]

Camelford .	. Mr. Lade.
	Mr. Martin.
Commodore Rodney }	3000 each.
Captain Vernon [2] }	

The same day, Legge, now Chancellor of the Exchequer, wrote to Martin :

I suppose that Mr. Andrews will have acquainted you already by express how much your friends here are alarmed with the apprehension of an opposition at Camelford. There is great confidence here in your discretion and good conduct but in order to strengthen your hands and add to your stock of ammunition I am to acquaint you that Sir William Ashburnham, aged 76, was said to be very ill a few days ago. In case of his death Mr. Phillips may depend upon one of his places, that is either Commissioner of the Alienation Office or Treasurer which is better. This near [. . .] prospect of performance may strengthen the faith which Mr. Phillips carried away with him in promise. As it is said your antagonists go well arm'd, it is desired that you will not lose your election on that account, and any reasonable sum necessarily expended will be made good.[3]

Lade and Martin spent £740 from secret service funds on the election, and even if £2000 is added which they seem to have contributed of their own money,[4] this is much less than was offered by the opposition, which shows the value of constant nursing and of the other advantages expected from Government favour by the manager and voters of Camelford. In

[1] 32995, f. 217.

[2] Richard Vernon, brother-in-law of Lord Gower, returned by Bedford for Tavistock in Dec 1754 ; a regular 'Bedford man'. About Rodney's candidature at Camelford, see also above, p. 306-7.

[3] 41354, f. 18. There is among the Newcastle Papers (32737, f. 237) one marked 'Mr. Martin's Paper about Camelford', undated, but placed at the end of the volume covering Oct 1754. In this Martin states that the Bedford candidates 'offered no less than 4000£ to be chosen', and repeats that he was informed 'he should be allowed any reasonable expence that the opposition might render necessary'.

[4] 32995, f. 63.

December 1755, Charles Phillips having been given the promised place in the Alienation Office,[1] gratefully assured Newcastle that he and his family would support the friends of the Government 'in any part of Cornwall', promptly put up fresh demands for his brother, etc.,[2] but, on the whole, seems to have been satisfied, as at the by-election at Newport in June 1756 he readily placed his vote and interest at Newcastle's service.[3]

It was a fairly common occurrence for voters in neighbouring boroughs to dispute certain local Government appointments, not clearly connected with either borough, but claimed by each as its 'property' — the electors of such and such town would claim a prescriptive right to a Receivership of the Land Tax, or a post of Surveyor of Window Lights, or to a place in a decayed harbour which by exceptional ill-luck happened not to be a Parliamentary borough. Such a conflict occurred in 1758 between Camelford and Bossiney (*alias* Tintagel), where Edward Wortley Montagu, the father-in-law of Lord Bute, and Lord Edgcumbe had the principal interest. The Duke of Newcastle, who at that time obsequiously courted Lord Bute, hastened to assure him that the vacancies 'in dispute between the towns of Camelford and Bossiney' would be filled in accordance with his wishes ; but as they were in the appointment of the Commissioners of the Customs, Lord Edgcumbe and Mr. Martin had to arrange the matter with them.[4] To this Bute replied with the haughtiness of a Scottish lord unaccustomed to have a small man cross his path, and ignorant of the regard due to any one in charge of a Parliamentary borough :

When L^d. Edgcumbe and Mr. Wortley first mentioned their pretensions to the little office in Bossiney, I own I was so astonish'd at Mr. Philips's presuming to enter into competition with men of their rank and fortune, about a second office after an agreement made on his obtaining the first, that I resolv'd to state the whole matter to your Grace, not in the least doubting but you would think it for the common interest necessary to interpose on the behalf of persons of such consequence.[5]

---

[1] Sir William Ashburnham, 2nd Bt., died on 7 Nov 1755.
[2] 32861, f. 192.   [3] 32865, f. 371.
[4] 8 Feb 1758 ; 32877, ff. 382-3.   [5] *Ibid.* ff. 408-9.

The contest was renewed in 1760.[1] Edgcumbe demanded 'the dismission of two Customhouse officers' and the grant of a place in the Custom House at Padstow to a Bossiney man; [2] Martin claimed the place for a Camelford man, and, himself since 1758 Joint Secretary to the Treasury, shielded the obnoxious officers, who were apparently Camelford men. 'The intention was to have it done immediately to strike a kind of terror, and to make appear that I had an interest with Government', wrote Edgcumbe on 24 January 1761, but now it is delayed

till Mr. Martin can hear from Mr. Philips whether it be agreable to him, or not. What makes this the harder is, all this court of Mr. Martin to his Camelford friends adds not a grain to his security, whereas had the blow been struck in time, it would have restored me a place at Tintagel ; for my agents both in town and country are convinced that, if we fail, it is purely for want of this support.

Edgcumbe's further reasoning about the matter throws light on the conventions then observed in patronage matters : Martin does not assert that these officers had been appointed through Camelford influence, whereas he himself, had he not been told that they had both been put in by his father, 'would not have consented to ask to have them turn'd out'.[3]

Through Martin's position in the Treasury, Camelford was brought into specially close touch with it. When Sir John Lade (created a baronet in 1758) died in 1759, this being a time of acute financial crisis (caused by the excessive drain of money for the campaigns in Germany and America), Newcastle felt that someone should be chosen in his place, from whom the Treasury could obtain expert support in the House of Commons. On 21 April 1759, James West, the senior Secretary to the Treasury, wrote him the following letter reviewing possible City candidates for Camelford :

I have the honour of your Grace's commands this moment, and can only return my faithfull thoughts for your Grace's goodness.

---

[1] See letters from Edgcumbe to Newcastle, 12 and 21 Oct 1760; 32913, ff. 75-6 and 255.
[2] 32916, f. 90.   [3] 32918, ff. 51-2.

Mr. Thrale has so close connections with the Grenville family,[1] that
I should doubt whether his new relation [2] can answer sufficiently
for him; Mr. Savage [3] I beleive has no inclination to come into
Parliament, and tho' a good Whig and very rich, has peevishness
and singularity in many things to a high degree; Mr. Burton [4] is
a very good sensible man, but I do not think of any great weight
in the City; . . . Mr. Thornton [5] is very rich, in great credit and
esteem, and of as much weight in the City as any one man I know,
has been generally esteemed by Sir J. Barnard,[6] the Martins,[7] and
the whole Clapham Club, and, I am sure . . . as unexceptionable
a person as your Grace can chuse. I have a value for Mr. Touchit,[8]
but considering the late reflections, however ill-grounded, and
which have made him very unpopular, I cannot think his coming
into Parliament at this time, upon your Grace's interest, would be
right. I ought to add Mr. Thornton will never be a speaker, I
wish your Grace to have some bold, spirited man with confidence
and volubility, such a one is much wanted, but difficult to find
joined to fidelity. I have sent to Mr. Martin [9] to know the state
of Camelford. . . . Your Grace will see if there is much difficulty or
expence, it will not be easy to engage a proper person for so short a
term as the duration of the present Parliament to undertake it.[10]

The next day (22 April) the following entry occurs in Newcastle's 'Memorandums for the King':

> D. Bedford   The Camelford Election
>   Mr. Burton. Mr. Thornton.

The choice fell on Bartholomew Burton, for many years a
Director of the Bank of England and in 1759 its Deputy

[1] Lord Cobham, uncle of Lord Temple and George, James, and Henry
Grenville, had been married to a first cousin of Henry Thrale's father.
According to Mrs. Piozzi (Hester Thrale), old Thrale 'lent them [the
Grenvilles] money, and they furnished assistance of every other kind'.

[2] Arnold Nesbitt, M.P., married in 1758 a sister of Henry Thrale.

[3] In 1758 Governor of the Bank of England.

[4] Bartholomew Burton, a merchant and Director of the Bank of England.

[5] A big banker, father of Henry Thornton, M.P., the friend of Wilberforce.

[6] Sir John Barnard (1685–1764), one of the most prominent City
financiers, M.P. for the City of London, 1722–61; see on him D.N.B.

[7] The family of bankers at the sign of the 'Grasshopper'; not related
to Samuel Martin.

[8] Samuel Touchet, returned for Shaftesbury in 1761; a Government
contractor; connected with Henry Fox, and, later on, with Charles Townshend.

[9] Samuel Martin.   [10] 32890, ff. 231-2.

Governor; and Bedford, at that time on friendly terms with Newcastle, was requested to support him. 'There was not the least hesitation', wrote Richard Rigby, his political agent, to Newcastle, 'as soon as your Grace's inclination was known.' [1]

On 27 April 1759, Charles Phillips sent the following report to Samuel Martin concerning his election preparations at Camelford:

I . . . got our friends toegether who all were unanimous in electing any person his Grace the Duke of Newcastle should think proper to represent the burro' — most of the opposite party were also present and agreed to the same proposal. This must necessaryly enhance the expences of the present but may be the means of saving a great deal of trouble and expences at the general election.

His Grace may be assured we will use our utmost endeavours to make the affair become as little chargeable as possable but imagine the freemen cannot have less than 10 or 12*l*. each, so desire you will send 500*l*. and what ever can be saved shall be regularly accounted for.

At a late re-election at Tintagel the freemen of that burro' had that summe wil probably make ours expect the same. . . .[2]

Ten or twelve pounds a man and a total of £500 was not a high price, even though the Parliament had only two more years to run; by the beginning of the nineteenth century the price at Camelford was £300 a vote in an electorate of about twenty-five, and in 1818 more than double that amount was paid.[3] But not even £500 were spent by the Treasury in 1759. On 3 May, Newcastle wrote in a 'Memorandum' for the King:

Given to Mr. Martin towards Camelford election, 300*l*. Mr. Burton pay a part.[4]

On 25 May 1759, Bartholomew Burton was duly returned for the borough, and at the general election of 1761 he and Samuel Martin were re-elected. In 1768 Charles Phillips himself was returned for Camelford; on his death in 1774 his brother Jonathan, a surgeon in the Royal Navy, succeeded him

[1] 27 Apr 1759; 32890, f. 372. [2] *Ibid*. f. 374.
[3] Oldfield, *A Key to the House of Commons* (1820), p. 145.
[4] 32890, f. 449. See also secret service accounts, under 2 May 1759, p. 457: 'To Mr. Martin towards Camelford election £300'. This is the only disbursement from those funds on that by-election.

in the Recordership of Camelford and as manager of the borough in the Government interest; but (except for a few months in 1784) he himself did not sit in Parliament. In 1780 the two seats were sold through Government mediation to 'East Indians', James Macpherson, of Ossian fame, and John Pardoe, the son of a Director of the East India Company, each paying £4000 for his seat.[1] Prices were rising, the freemen showing greater independence, but the nature of Camelford 'politics' remained the same.

GRAMPOUND

Edgcumbe, in his letter to Newcastle on 20 May 1760, uses the curious phrase: 'Grampound, which renounced my name upon the death of my father'; and his steward writes in June: 'the Bench have very perfidiously left Lord Edgcumbe and attached themselves to Mr. Eliot and Mr. Trevanion'. The transaction thus described illustrates the system of infeudation for electoral purposes practised in many Cornish boroughs, an act in which the small group of insignificant voters enjoyed more independence than is usually supposed.

The Corporation of Grampound consisted of a mayor, eight aldermen, a recorder, and a town clerk; 'and as soon as the mayor was chosen from among the aldermen he selected two of his aldermanic colleagues, called *eligers*, to join with him in nominating eleven freemen. These fourteen worthies formed a jury, made presentments and created freemen, whose only qualification was the payment of scot and lot.'[2] As was stated

---

[1] See W. T. Laprade, *The Parliamentary Papers of John Robinson*, p. 34. For the election of 1774 see *ibid.* p. 23. On the fall of the North Administration in 1782, Robinson drew up an 'Account of Payments made by Lord North, submitted to His Majesty for his Orders which of them he will be pleased to have continued and delivered over' (37836, ff. 137-9). In it there appears among annual 'Payments for Parliamentary Purposes' (f. 138) the following entry:

Camelford. Mr. Phillips   .   .   £100 0 0⎫
           Mr. Carpenter .   .   50 0 0⎭ £150 0 0

John Carpenter, of Mount Tavy, near Tavistock, married to Christian, only daughter of John Phillips, and sister of Charles and Jonathan Phillips, eventually inherited the Phillips interest in the borough.

[2] W. P. Courtney, *op. cit.*, p. 184. See also Oldfield, *op. cit.*, p. 70.

by Edgcumbe's steward, the Bench had 'a power of increasing the number of freemen'. When there were no contests in the borough its managers naturally tried to avoid any such increase, but whenever a struggle arose each side endeavoured to create new freemen in its own interest.

In 1741 Grampound was contested between the Government and the Prince of Wales, whose agents, Thomas Pitt, elder brother of William Pitt, and Christopher Hawkins (a Cornish gentleman of Trewithan, in the neighbourhood of Grampound, originally connected with the Edgcumbes), had their candidates returned against those of the Government manager, Richard Edgcumbe. In 1747 Pitt and Hawkins again acted for the Prince, who 'intended' them 'the honour of being considered a coprincipall as well in the last as in future engagements'.[1] The game was not easy, as the Mayor was against them and there was the danger of his admitting new freemen and rejecting some of theirs.[2] Still, with the support of a few other Cornish gentlemen and a disregard of expense, they hoped to succeed. The story is told in letters from Pitt to Ayscough, one of the chief political agents of the Prince of Wales :

June 12, 1747.—On Wednesday we went round the town and found the people, as one must expect, in such a venal place, some open in promising us, and others hanging off to see what they can make of it ; but none said they had promised against us, not even those who we know are determined against us. . . . As you tell me, I am not to give up on any appearance of difficulties, I have issued forth the insidious arguement plentifully. . . . I have likewise bid high for the Mayor.[3]

June 13, 1747.—As for Grampound I think we can carry it, but it must cost damnably dear. The villains have got a-head to that degree, and rise in their demands so extravagantly, that I have been very near damning them, and kicking them to the devil at once. The dirty rascals dispise 20 guineas as much as a King's Sergeant does a half-guinea fee. If it had not been for the orders by your letter, spare neither pains nor money, I would not have gone on at such a rate.[4]

---

[1] Christopher Hawkins to Thomas Pitt, 4 Jan 1747, HMC, *Fortescue MSS.*, vol. i, p. 107.

[2] T. Pitt to C. Hawkins, 5 Dec 1746 and 17 Jan 1747, *ibid.* p. 107, and T. Pitt to Dr. Ayscough, 12 June 1747, p. 110.

[3] *Ibid.* p. 110.   [4] *Ibid.* p. 111.

By 19 June Pitt hoped for only one seat at Grampound;
'and perhaps Hawkins may give up to me, for he is sweated
at the expence'.[1] On 1 July he reported that at Grampound
'the affair is compounded one and one',[2] *i.e.* that they and
Edgcumbe were to return one Member each; and Pitt and
Hawkins agreed to nominate alternately to their common seat,
each paying the expenses whenever he had the nomination.[3]
'I have . . . thought proper to give Mr. Hawkins his option
to be elected and take the whole expence upon him, or leave it
to me. I believe the expence will make him chuse the latter.'[4]
But Hawkins chose to have his son Thomas elected, and Pitt
consoled himself with the thought that Hawkins had it 'upon
a very dear footing', and that 'the money will come like drops
of blood from him'.[5] In August, Pitt presented Hawkins with
his bill, in September insisted on payment, and in October
desired to know whether he was to look 'upon the office of
Vice-Warden as actually resigned'[6] — Pitt was Warden of the
Stanneries, and Hawkins his Vice-Warden. By November a
critical stage was reached in the electoral history of Grampound,
steps having been taken by Edgcumbe and Hawkins 'to get rid
of forty or fifty disreputable and very troublesome fellows on
both sides and to render matters as easy and quiet for the future
as things of this nature will admit of'. But before perfecting
these arrangements, Hawkins, in view of his quarrel with Pitt,
desired Ayscough to let him know 'on what footing he was to
be for the future, as well as for the time past'.[7] To placate
Hawkins, the Prince of Wales ordered the charges of the
previous election to be reduced, and annexed a salary to the
office of Vice-Warden which it did not carry before; whereupon Hawkins promised faithfully to do the Prince's election
work and to settle the borough in so frugal a manner that in

---

[1] HMC, *Fortescue MSS.*, vol. i, p. 114.
[2] *Ibid.* p. 119.
[3] For the text of the agreement dated 30 June 1747, see *Fortescue Papers*, vol. i, p. 121.
[4] T. Pitt to Dr. Ayscough, 1 July 1747, *ibid.* p. 119.
[5] Same to same, 2 Aug 1747, *ibid.* p. 127.
[6] *Ibid.* p. 128.
[7] 8 Nov 1747, *ibid.* p. 129; cf. also about it letter from Robert Andrews to John Roberts, 20 Mar 1754; 32862, ff. 351-2.

future a Parliamentary election should not cost more than
'7 or 800l. at the most'.[1]

But when the election of the Mayor came on at Grampound,
in September 1748, Pitt, mad and quarrelsome, openly attacked
Hawkins and Edgcumbe,[2] and on 27 September wrote to
Ayscough :

> Mr. Hawkins' behaviour I found was treacherous and base
> towards me, and the interest he pretended to engage in [of the
> Prince], and for which he had a salary appointed last winter, in
> joining with Lord Edgcumbe to turn me absolutely out of the
> burrough, that I have thought it necessary to make use of a favour-
> able opportunity of turning the tables upon them, which I hope
> I have done, and think it is in my power to turn them both out. I
> have elected the Mayor, and have at least 3 parts in 4 of the people
> most zealously with me.[3]

Hawkins in turn described to Ayscough how Pitt appeared
at Grampound 'full of passion and resentment', and added the
following conjectures :

> The reasons which have occurred to me for this attempt are
> these. By the death of Moor, the magistrates (held indisputable)
> are now reduced to four, White, Pomeroy, Nance, and Pearce ;
> (Hoyt illegal). Nance a man poor, but of a bold and turbulent
> spirit, not being able to bear seeing the burrough likely to be re-
> duced to some order and peace, prevailed on Pearce to go with him
> to Boconnock [Pitt's Cornish seat] with a tender of their services,
> and with assurances that if Hoyt could have his debts paid to Mr.
> Hawkins, be established a magistrate, and some of the disclaimers
> restored, the next election should be as Mr. Pitt pleased.[4]

But as the scheme for disfranchising fifty voters at Grampound turned on Hoyt 'being no *legall magistrate*', Pitt's action
threatened to endanger the work undertaken by Edgcumbe and
Hawkins. Pitt triumphantly announced to Ayscough :

> They have no chance of keeping their heads above water, but dis-
> qualifying Hoyte from being a magistrate or capital burgess. . . .
> This must be defended. . . . It has already cost me upwards of

---

[1] C. Hawkins to Dr. Ayscough, 12 Dec 1747, p. 129.
[2] Same to same, 14 Sept 1748, p. 130.
[3] *Ibid.* p. 130.   [4] *Ibid.* p. 131.

200*l.* and must cost more ; yet I think it worth while, as the entire interest of the burrough depends upon it.

I wish James Nance had his patent of tinblower.[1]

Hawkins was ready to accept the challenge, and politely refused Ayscough's mediation ; but Pitt's financial ruin, to which the Cornish elections had contributed their share, now compelled him to desist. Here ends the part of the history of Grampound contained in the Fortescue Papers, and henceforth it is continued from the Newcastle MSS. at the British Museum.

When it was agreed that Pitt should transfer his interest to some other person, recounts Robert Andrews, 'I having then the honour to be in his R-l H-h-s's service as Auditor of the Dutchy, and on that account going every year into Cornwal, his Royal Highness pitched upon me for that duty'.[2] An agreement was concluded between Hawkins and Andrews whereby Andrews stepped into Pitt's shoes.[3] By the time of the Prince's death (20 March 1751), *i.e.* in less than two years, their half of the expenditure on Grampound amounted to about £1500, two-thirds of which had been spent on the lawsuits for reducing the electorate.[4] But the Princess Dowager refusing to concern herself in elections, Hawkins and Andrews now offered their services to Henry Pelham, and were accepted by him [5] — an act of infeudation on the part of managers.

At the general election of 1754, Simon Fanshawe, a friend

---

[1] 12 Oct 1748 ; *op. cit.*, p. 132.

[2] R. Andrews to John Roberts, 20 Mar 1754 ; 32862, ff. 351-2.

[3] For its text see *ibid.* ff. 343-4.

[4] In the Newcastle MSS. there is a paper giving 'Totalls of Lord Edgcumbe's disbursements on several following Burroughs, since the last Generall Election in July 1747' (33038, f. 236) ; it is not dated, but the sum spent on Grampound seems to indicate that it was compiled at the time of the Prince's death. Grampound appears in it as the most expensive of the boroughs in which Edgcumbe was concerned :

Grampound .	. . £1445	4 2
Lostwithiel .	. . 1271	19 1
Bossiney .	. . 126	18 2
Fowey .	. . 110	9 2½
Mitchell .	. . 199	10 5

£3154   1   11½ [*sic*]

[5] See note from C. Hawkins to Robert Andrews, 24 Nov 1751, with a marginal remark in Andrews's handwriting ; 32862, f. 345. Also letter from Andrews to Roberts, 20 Mar 1754 ; *ibid.* 351-2.

of Henry Pelham's nephew and son-in-law, Lord Lincoln, and a Court parasite, was named by the Treasury to Andrews, whose turn it was to nominate one Member, while Merrick Burrell, a London merchant and a Director of the Bank of England, was returned on the Edgcumbe interest.[1]

But two years later, on 31 January 1756, Andrews is still found applying to Newcastle 'for the £1500 due to me in respect of the Grampound election'. This claim he reinforced by an appeal truly of an eighteenth-century character :

I am, my Lord, by Dr. Shaw's advice, going in a short time to Bath, to aid a very worn-out constitution, the event is very uncertain, and it is my dernier resort, and as this sum will greatly affect my family in case I miscarry in recovering my health, the having it paid before I go, will much contribute to my ease of mind, and consequently benefit the re-establishing my health.[2]

Newcastle turned to Roberts, who was most likely to know the arrangements made between Pelham and Andrews ; and Roberts, in reply, sent whatever papers he had concerning Grampound, adding :

What passed between Mr. Pelham, Lord Edgcumbe, and Mr. Hawkins of Grampound . . . I never heard . . .; but when the agreement between Mr. Hawkins and Mr. Andrews . . . was delivered to Mr. Pelham, he then was pleased to say to me thereupon, that the King would certainly not bear to hear of an application to him for the reimbursement of expenses incurred in direct opposition to his Government.

Roberts had thought that Andrews's employment of Comptroller of the Cash in the Excise had been given him in compensation for these disbursements, but Andrews denied this ; and the joint expenses of Andrews and Lord Edgcumbe were about £6000 — 'an expense much greater surely than the object'.[3]

---

[1] There were at first some difficulties as to how much either should pay (see Newcastle's Memoranda of 16 and 18 Mar 1754 ; 32995, ff. 96-9) ; finally it was settled that 'Mr. Fanshaw pays 1000*l.* to Mr. Andrews. Mr. Burrell will pay 1600 to Mr. Roberts' ('Minutes', 21 Mar 1754 ; *ibid.* f. 111 ; see also f. 116).

[2] Andrews to Newcastle, 31 Jan 1756 ; 32862, ff. 313-14.

[3] Roberts to Newcastle, 4 Feb 1756 ; 32862, ff. 341-2.

Among the papers sent by Roberts was 'An Account of Disbursements made in Respect of the Interest at the Burrough of Grampound' (January 1748 to March 1754), four long sheets of paper, telling the story of how such a Cornish borough had to be managed. The most striking feature is the individual character of the treatment accorded to the voters. At the time of a Parliamentary election there was a certain measure of uniformity in payments, coupled here and there with attempts to equalize the benefits received during the preceding years. But, even so, there remained considerable differences for which the reasons do not appear in the accounts. In some cases the managers perhaps let themselves in for more than they had expected — here is the story of one Grampound freeman :

	£	s.	d.
January 7, 1748. To John Hodge, a freeman, to discharge him from his several creditors for an horse to go about his business on	13	14	1
Sept. 26. To paid and advanced to and for John Hodge £51 : 11 : 8 for which he hath given bond for £25 : 15 : 10 to my Lord [Edgcumbe] and £25 : 15 : 10 to Messrs. Hawkins and Andrews .	25	15	10
January 7, 1750. Paid Mr. Walker rent due to him from John Hodge, freeman	6	0	0
January 19. Given to the said John Hodge . .	0	13	6
January 26. To ditto	0	10	6
February 1. Given to John Hodge . . .	0	5	3
October 10, 1753. To cash advanced since Michaelmas, 1753, to John Hodge . . . who being considerably more indebted than the 50 guineas amounted to [the total received before the general election by each freeman from both the patrons of the borough], was not paid the sum, but had some small sums given him to keep him easy	5	15	6
——. To paid for a laced hat for John Hodge . .	0	5	3

And then, presumably on 8 April 1754, a last payment was made to save the money previously invested in his vote.

	£	s.	d.
. . . advanced to discharge John Hodge from an arrest made on him, by Mr. Bonython, the day before the election	5	16	6

The payments to him on account of one party in the borough management, make a total of £58 : 16 : 5 ; thus his vote cost the two patrons during the six years preceding the general election of 1754 nearly £120 !

Every year, at least once before Michaelmas, when the Mayor was elected, a largess was distributed to all the freemen ; it took the form of advances 'against their notes', which naturally were never brought up so long as the recipients kept to their electoral engagements. The amounts paid to them ranged from 10s. 6d. to £3 : 10s. from each of the two parties in the borough management. Some freemen had their own special terms, receiving payments, e.g., of 3s. a week from each patron ; some others were on yearly allowances at a higher rate. Further, there were special benefits in case of sickness, payments for funerals, schooling, etc. In short, the franchise served as a general free insurance. And even more — here is one of the most interesting entries in the accounts :

	£	s.	d.
October 28, 1752. Paid for fitting out Mr. Walker,[1] a freeman's son, to the East Indies . . .	50	0	0

Lastly, there was general expenditure for the benefit of the whole town, repairs to the Town Hall, the chapel, to the town clock, etc. ; and on special occasions 'a bullock' was distributed among 'the Grampound poor'.

The Mayor received every year from each of the two partners 10 guineas 'kitchen money' ; while Edgcumbe's steward, Thomas Jones, who acted as 'principal agent for the whole interest', received from Andrews 'for one year's trouble and expenses in managing the affairs of the burrough', £25. But in the year of the general election all charges swelled prodigiously. The Mayor and five capital burgesses received 50 guineas each, from each of the two patrons ; twenty freemen, 25 guineas each ; and a few other freemen, who were on regular allowances or badly overdrawn, received small consolation prizes. Thomas Jones, 'for his extraordinary trouble to the

---

[1] But his father was a notable in the borough — in the Grampound accounts among the Hawkins MSS., in the Royal Institution of Cornwall at Truro, he is described as Dr. Walker.

2 A

day of the election', was given £50. The Mayor, 'by way of gratuity for his extra trouble', 25 guineas, and his wife, 'for extraordinary expenses at her house for the last half-year', 10 guineas. To each freeman's wife, 'and where no wife, to his eldest daughter', 1 guinea was given 'to buy a ring'. 'Digory Tresize, a freeman', had a 'suit of cloaths' paid for (£1 : 12 : 2), etc. (those interested in prices should, however, remember that these entries stand for half the amount only).

The other side of life in the electoral nursery also appears in the accounts — punishments meted out to the dishonest :

	£	s.	d.
January 7, 1748. Paid Mr. Webber, an attorney, for prosecuting John Pearce, a freeman who had acted contrary to his engagements	6	14	0
February 1, 1750. To costs paid Richard Sandys, attorney-at-law, costs in prosecuting three freemen . . . for not performing their engagements .	19	16	5
[1754.] To cash advanced to John Watts, another freeman, on his solemn engagement to stand by the interest which he deserted, hath been arrested, and is now in Bodmyn prison for the same money .	24	18	0
To paid charges of the arrest and law charges already incurred, and which will be incurred to keep him in prison and charge him in execution .	7	15	0

The ordinary expenditure on Grampound during the six years preceding the general election of 1754 amounted to about £2100 for each of the two partners in the borough ; to this a further £800 was added for legal expenses incurred in 1748–49 in connexion with reducing the electorate to such 'frugall' dimensions. The total bill as presented by Andrews amounted to £2931 : 4 : 8, i.e. half of the £6000, which, as Roberts remarked, was 'an expense much greater surely than the object'.

But even so, the Grampound electors do not seem to have been satisfied with the management. There had long been opposition to Edgcumbe in the borough, and on 28 August 1755, Hawkins, then his ally, thus summed up his 'private thoughts' on the matter : [1]

---

[1] Hawkins MSS.

The united interest in this burrough has of late been much annoyed by two small batteries lately erected in its neighbourhood, namely the Leskeard [Eliot] and the Tregony [Trevanion], wch are played and directed by the skilful hand of an Irish engineer from St. Mawes Castle.[1] The erection of these batteries has lately occasioned within the town much mutiny and desertion from the united interest. . . . It's not to be doubted that if the Newcastle would but appear and lye long side of these batteries, she might with a very few cannon shot, silence both, and shake even the Castle of St. Mawes. If this be done the mutiny within may, with proper management be quieted, and the people restored to peace and unity.

And on 16 September Thomas Jones wrote to Hawkins, by Edgcumbe's order, on the 'odd situation' at Grampound where the discontented found themselves in a majority on the alder-manic bench, and consequently, so far as its power went, had now the borough in their hands. 'I think we are at present strong enough among the freemen, but you know 'tis very much in the power of the Bench to increase the number of freemen.'[2]

The final revolt did not, however, occur till 1758, on the death of Richard, first Lord Edgcumbe — which is character-istic: it shows the quasi-feudal sense of personal allegiance terminated by the death of the man to whom they had infeoffed themselves. On 28 November Richard, second Lord Edg-cumbe, wrote to Newcastle: 'Messrs. Eliot and Trevanion have set up their standard at Grampond [sic]. I am little acquainted with the state of my father's interest there, or whether 'tis worth endeavouring to preserve or not.' Still, he asked the Duke to refrain for the time being from entering into engagements with 'this new alliance'. 'These are two stirring young gentlemen, and, may be, think to take advantage of me, as one of an opposite character. But the world shall see that if I have been idle, it was only because I had nothing to do.'[3]

On the same day (28 November 1758) Edward Eliot wrote to Newcastle:

The Mayor and Magistrates of Grampound have prevailed upon Mr. Trevanion and myself to accept of the Parliamentary interest of that borough.

[1] Robert Nugent, uncle by marriage to Eliot.
[2] Hawkins MSS.   [3] 32886, f. 76.

When they first proposed it, after having thanked them, I added — that I should always endeavour to support and to defend the interest which I had already in my country,[1] but did not propose to attack Lord Edgcumbe. They answered me by saying, that I might lay it down as *an ulterable* [sic] *principle with them* to have no further connexions with the family of Edgcumbe after the late Lord's death : that having a higher opinion and a greater friendship and respect for Mr. Trevanion and for me than for anybody else whatsoever, they made us the first offer of the borough ; that if we refused it, they should be extremely grieved but would in that case most certainly make an offer elsewhere.

They proceeded to tell me, that they were friends to Government, and should be very unwilling to throw the town into any hands which were not so likewise, but that however they were resolved to do anything or suffer any extremity rather than engage afresh in the Edgcumbe interest.

Knowing them to be 'men most particularly firm in their resolutions', Eliot and Trevanion thought that they would not be doing their duty to Government and to themselves if they rejected this offer.

We therefore (after the late Lord Edgcumbe's agent had by letter notified his Lordship's death) appeared at Grampound last Saturday where we were received by the body of the freemen with the greatest joy and had the strongest assurances of their support.

Their number is small, we have nine out of ten. The mayor and magistrates are with us most zealously and unanimously. They can make what freemen they please, and are determined, upon the least occasion, to exert that power.

In short, my Lord Duke, with a little attention on our parts, all the security and certainty that borough affairs ever can admit of, we have at Grampound.

Lastly, Eliot pointed out to Newcastle that 'by a written agreement' the Edgcumbe interest named one member only, the other being chosen alternately by Hawkins and Andrews ; Hawkins, 'one of those gentlemen commonly called Tories', was to have been returned at the next election. Thus the change meant 'a gain' to Government.[2]

---

[1] Eliot had already four seats at his disposal, at Liskeard and St. Germans ; and in the partnership with Trevanion, his closest friend, now played the predominant role.

[2] 32886, ff. 78-9.

Here was a complete change in patrons, but at the general election of 1761 the same two candidates favoured by the Government were re-elected, Merrick Burrell and Simon Fanshawe. Cornish boroughs and elections and the management of both had nothing to do with 'politics'.

PERSONNEL AND VOTES

The representation of Cornwall was much less aristocratic than that of the rest of Great Britain : 93 sons of British peers were returned in 1761, and Cornwall's proportionate share would have been at least 7 — but there were only 3,[1] 2 Boscawens and one Edgcumbe, whose families owed their peerages to their borough interests; while of 34 courtesy lords, none sat for a Cornish constituency. Seventy-one baronets were returned in 1761, but only 2 in Cornwall.

Classified by professions, the representation of Cornwall in 1761 included 6 merchants,[2] forming a higher proportion than in the rest of Great Britain, 5 Army[3] and 3 naval officers,[4] again more than the average ; 4 (out of a total of 8) regular officials,[5] and one diplomat ;[6] and 4 barristers.[7] In short, more than half of the representation of Cornwall consisted of merchants, officers, civil servants, and lawyers, while in the rest of Great Britain they formed hardly one-third of the representation.

The proportion of strangers among the Cornish Members was naturally considerable, though not greater than in Devonshire, Dorset, or Wiltshire. Of the 44 Cornish Members in 1761, 15 were Cornishmen (all but 2 with a long Parliamentary ancestry), 4 were connected with the county through female ancestors, while 25 were strangers, the majority of them with

---

[1] I do not count Ph. Stanhope, as he was illegitimate.

[2] Merrick and Peter Burrell, Bartholomew Burton, Abraham Hume, Jonathan Rashleigh, and John Stephenson.

[3] John and George Boscawen, Charles Hotham, G. Howard, and E. Nugent.

[4] G. Edgcumbe, G. B. Rodney, and W. Trelawny.

[5] S. Martin, John Clevland, Ph. Stephens, and F. Gashry.

[6] Ph. Stanhope.

[7] R. Hussey, J. R. Webb, F. Buller, and A. Champion.

no Parliamentary ancestry anywhere. But in Devonshire, in 1761, 14 out of 26 Members had no previous connexion with the county, in Wiltshire 18 in 34, in Dorset 12 in 20. If one seeks a real contrast to the representation of Cornwall, one has to turn to counties such as Norfolk and Lincolnshire, or even Yorkshire, in spite of its numerous pocket boroughs. In 1761, of the 12 Members representing Norfolk constituencies, 6 were sons of British peers and 2 were baronets; not one was a merchant, an official, or a practising lawyer; and only one was a stranger to the county. Of the 12 Members representing Lincolnshire, 4 were sons of British peers (3 courtesy lords), one the son of an Irish peer, and one a baronet; and only one Member was a merchant and a stranger to the county. Yorkshire was represented by 30 Members; 5 were sons of peers (3 courtesy lords) and 6 baronets; one was a merchant, and none a regular civil servant; 11 were strangers, mainly put in for pocket boroughs.

In 1761, of the 44 Cornish Members, 19 were 'placemen' in the sense given to the term in my computation on p. 215 (footnote (1)), as against 151 in the rest of Great Britain — making 43 as against 30 per cent. Moreover, the proportion of Members who depended for their seats on Government support or mediation was very much higher in Cornwall than in any other county. This fact naturally tended to affect Parliamentary divisions. That on General Warrants, 17-18 February 1764, forms an exception: 19 (including the 2 Members for the county) voted in the minority and 7 were absent; therefore at the utmost 18 could have voted with the Government. On 21-22 February 1766 only 7 Cornish Members voted against the Repeal of the Stamp Act,[1] i.e. 16 per cent of the representation, which is even less than among the

---

[1] These were: Lord Mountstuart, the eldest son of Lord Bute; S. Martin, Bute's Secretary to the Treasury; S. Fanshawe, a courtier; J. E. Colleton and E. Nugent, both connected through Robert Nugent with George Grenville; John Stephenson, an adherent of Lord Sandwich; and F. W. Sharpe, a nephew of the Governor of Maryland, Horatio Sharpe. Two of these seven were born in the West Indies (Martin and Colleton, who, moreover, was closely connected with South Carolina), and one, F. W. Sharpe, had connexions both with the American Colonies and the West Indies. I follow here the printed list; see pp. 187-8.

representatives of the larger boroughs, and much below the
average for the whole of England (27 per cent). In the division
of 8 May 1769, over the seating of Luttrell for Middlesex, 22
Cornish Members voted with the Government, 14 were absent,
and only 8 voted with the Opposition. The proportion of those
absent was about the same among the Cornish Members as in
the whole House. But while 27 per cent of the House voted
with the Opposition, of Cornish Members only 16 per cent.
Similarly in the crucial divisions of 1780–82, the Cornish
Members voted overwhelmingly on the side of Government.

VII

TWO TREASURY BOROUGHS

HARWICH

AT Harwich the Parliamentary franchise was in the Corporation which consisted of eight aldermen and twenty-four capital burgesses recruited by co-optation; and as most of them were in some way or other provided for by the Government, the borough was under its control. Even so, its history was variegated. The Government influence was in two departments which did not always work together harmoniously — the Treasury whose influence was exercised through the Custom House, and the Post Office in control of the four Harwich Packet Boats whose captains were 'generally elected into the corporation'.[1] Moreover, at various times Ministers and managers tried to convert the official interest at Harwich into private domain — as was the custom in the eighteenth century with regard to public property.

Boroughs could be literally owned where the vote was attached to certain holdings or houses and the voters were created for the day of the election. But the Crown did not, and could not, own burgage boroughs; while in Corporation boroughs, such as Harwich, capital burgesses had to be chosen whenever vacancies occurred, and could not be removed if duly elected. Their allegiance in Government boroughs was secured by choosing into the Corporations men who held (or aspired to) places under the Government, and who therefore were likely to be determined by a threat of dismissal. Such control though fairly secure was not absolute, and close acquaintance with the men and their circumstances and much attention were required: the management had to be local and personal.

In the eighteenth century each Minister treated Parliamentary seats controlled by his department as perquisites of

[1] John Roberts to Newcastle, 5 Aug 1755; 32857, ff. 590-1.

his office, and, nepotism being an acknowledged principle in administration, it was taken for granted that his relatives had a first claim to them. Similarly the local Government manager would pack the Corporation under his care as far as possible with his own relatives, and thus provide for them financially and for himself politically. In theory selections of this kind were justified as offering additional security for the behaviour of the nominees, bound as they were by personal ties to a man ever zealous for 'His Majesty's service'. But in practice wherever this system was allowed to prevail the manager tended to become a partner in the borough; indeed in some Government boroughs the management of the Corporation came to be hereditary in local families (*e.g.* the Holdsworths at Dartmouth, the Milwards at Hastings, etc.), and occasionally even a small manager finished by claiming and obtaining Government nomination to Parliament for himself or a son brought up as a gentleman. In the case of Ministers and Governors, with whom the management of Government boroughs was an incident and not a profession, the matter was more complex; but if their own estates were anywhere near the Government borough — which was often the case with territorial officers, such as the Warden of the Cinque Ports or the Governor of the Isle of Wight — they usually employed the official influence to strengthen their private interest, and sometimes succeeded in changing office perquisites into heirlooms.

Harwich escaped being converted from an electoral fief into an allodial possession, but not for lack of attempts in that direction.

The Members returned for Harwich in 1754 were Wenman Coke, nephew and heir of Thomas Earl of Leicester, then Postmaster-General; and John Phillipson, a typical representative of a local official dynasty, which after a process of incubation in minor Government offices, pecked its way into the first division of English public life.

The father of the Member, Captain John Phillipson, starting as an ordinary seaman, rose to be Agent of the Harwich Packet

Boats, and married the daughter of a previous Agent. In 1730 he addressed the following Memorial to Sir Robert Walpole :

He has been fifty years in the service of the Post Office, did command one of the packet boats the two Wars with France, during which he distinguished himself by his diligence and behaviour, particularly in two actions, when attack'd by Dunkirk privateers, he got clear of one, and boarded the other, took her, and brought her into Harwich.

He has been many years one of the capital burgesses, and alderman of the Corporation of Harwich, and several times Mayor. This town sends two Members to Parliament, and that it might be properly represented, he has always endeavoured to get the majority of electors in the interest of the Government and on every vacancy of a capital burgess, has espoused such as had any dependance on it.

At his late Majesty's happy accession to the Throne, Mr. Mildmay (a Tory), Sir Philip Parker and Mr. Heath (Whiggs) were candidates for Members of Parliament, he gave his vote and interest for the two latter. The next election Mr. Parsons (a Tory), Sir Philip Parker and Mr. Heath were candidates, he gave his vote and interest for the two latter, and as a strong proof of his regard to your Honour, at the last election, notwithstanding his son was a candidate and had the best interest of any body, yet he declined standing by command from his father, to whom it had been intimated that you desired Lord Percival and Sir Philip Parker might be chosen, and they were unanimously.

It is indeed his peculiar happyness that on every election, throughout his life, either in the Town of Harwich, or County of Essex, he has voted agreable to the Post-Master Generall and inclined others so to do. He therefore most humbly begs your protection, and that he may not be dismiss'd a Service in which he has had the honour to serve so many years, and, as he hopes, without blemish.[1]

John Phillipson, jun., began as clerk in the Navy Office, and next married the daughter of a Commissioner of the Navy.[2] In 1727 he was in fact considered a possible candidate for Harwich,[3] and in 1734, so 'that he might not try to get in at Harwich',[4] was encouraged by the Government to stand for New Shoreham, in Sussex, a borough where the Treasury

---

[1] 19038, f. 18. The Memorial can be dated by reference to HMC, *Egmont Diary*, vol. i, p. 78, 11 Mar 1729/30.

[2] *Ibid.* vol. iii, p. 325.

[3] *Ibid.* vol. i, p. 78.

[4] *Ibid.* vol. i, p. 420.

and the Pelhams had some influence, but even their candidates needed long City purses ; and where shipbuilders were specially welcome, this being the chief trade of the town. Presumably, therefore, by 1734 John Phillipson, jun., was a wealthy man, and certain incidental remarks about later orders given by him to shipbuilders,[1] suggest that he was concerned in shipbuilding, probably on Government account. Duly returned at New Shoreham, he is next found in the financial departments of the Navy : in May 1739 he was appointed Comptroller of the (Naval) Storekeeper's Accounts, and in 1740 Comptroller of the Treasurer's Accounts. Moreover, about that time he became a Director of the South Sea Company, which included many Government financiers. In 1741 he was at last returned to Parliament for Harwich, where, until checked by Pelham, he continued to improve his family interest. Thus in 1745 Leicester complained to Bedford of Phillipson's views 'to get the borough absolutely to himself, independent of the government', and of his 'having got such people into places as he could depend upon'. 'He works so well with those under me, that they not only refused my orders in the choice of a burgess, but, even while in place under me, and in my chief trust . . . brought in his creatures upon the floor [of the Corporation] . . . if Mr. Pelham, who now supports him, does not immediately take care, he will . . . become absolute master of the borough. . . .'[2] And Lord Egmont wrote about Harwich in an electoral survey which he made for the Prince of Wales c. 1750 :[3]

[1] See below on p. 366 letter from G. Davies to Roberts, 15 July 1755.

[2] *Bedford Correspondence*, vol. i, pp. 30-3. On 4 May 1750 Robert Page, a member of the Harwich Corporation, addressed the following letter of warning to Henry Pelham :

Right Hon[ble]
it is whispered about town that your Honour is inclined to oblige Mr. Phillipson to give countenance to the election of his kinsman Mr. Holden, if your Honour would be pleased to calculate the number of his relations now Cappetal Burgeiceis, your Honour I believe would be rady to think as I doe, that it would be dangerious to leat him have any more, for wee are pritty well acquainted with his constitution and tirony, that reaally it is my opinion the way to keep him a friend is to keep it out of his power to be an ennimi. . . . (32735, f. 314).

[3] Egmont MSS. at the British Museum (unbound).

Philipson has now got so great a footing in this borough that he can carry two Members. But for a good employment he must allways bring in one for the Court, tho he is a bold kind of man, and gives himself great airs to the Ministers about this borough on all occasions — yet he cannot afford to lose an employment, or to contend at great expence against power. . . .

But to return to Phillipson's official career — for one year, December 1743 till December 1744, he held a seat at the Board of the Admiralty, an advance remarkable for the son of the Agent of the Harwich Packet Boats, perhaps even excessive, as he had neither family connexions [1] nor any marked achievements to his credit; and when he had to leave the Admiralty he was compensated with the place of Surveyor of Woods and Parks on this side of the Trent. This he retained till his death in 1756, by which time he had risen to be Deputy-Governor of the South Sea Company.[2]

When in March 1754 Newcastle succeeded Henry Pelham at the Treasury, Charles Hanbury-Williams wrote to Henry Fox: 'To whom are the Members of the House of Commons to address themselves? To the D. of Newcastle? Alas! he wont know their names in two years, and will forget them in two days.' [3] The repetition necessitated by the Duke's incapacity to remember was annoying to contemporaries but has provided plentiful material for the historian: thus the state of Harwich had to be repeatedly explained to him by Roberts, Pelham's assistant in the management of Government boroughs.

The most concise account is in a memorandum,[4] apparently drawn up when Newcastle took over his brother's official legacy:

[1] When on one occasion it was suggested to Phillipson that he did not behave altogether like a gentleman, 'he answer'd angrily . . . he could trace his pedigree further back than somebody else, but did not name whom he means' (32735, f. 312). It would seem from the context that he meant Wenman Coke.

[2] Phillipson's only daughter married Robert Bristow, a London merchant and nephew of John Bristow, a famous Government contractor and Director of the South Sea Company, of which he was Deputy-Governor, 1733-56, and Sub-Governor, 1756-62 (i.e. chief, as the King was its nominal Governor). To him Phillipson may have partly owed his rise in the Company. Robert Bristow sat from 1747 till 1761 for Phillipson's first constituency, New Shoreham.

[3] Letters to Henry Fox, edited by the Earl of Ilchester (1915), p. 60.

[4] 32735, ff. 308-9.

The borough of Harwich is at present so well disposed to the Government, that they readily accept of any two persons to represent them, who are recommended by it.

This was not the case some years ago : the Post-Master General claimed the right of recommending, and a private interest [Phillipson's] had likewise great weight : but Mr. Pelham was determined to alter that situation, and by proper resolution effected it. He consulted and depended entirely upon the reports of Mr. Davies, Collector of the Customs, whom he found, from the experience of many years, to be a zealous Whig, an honest and a dextrous man. The Post-Master General often tried his interest to remove him, and Mr. Philipson did the same : but each of them gave up any further expectations of succeeding, finding Mr. Pelham resolved to carry on the Government's interest thro' the Officer of the Customs, and convinced of Mr. Davies's fidelity.

Mr. Pelham had many eclaircissemens with Mr. Philipson upon this subject : the latter of whom, in the end, promised solemnly never to interfere in any matters relating to the Corporation : and the Treasury had brought the Post-Office not to disallow, that the recommendations of Members belonged to the former.

The interest there is maintained by the Officers of the Customs, the Masters of the Pacquets nominated by the Post-Master General, and by the lands and houses in the town.

Mr. Philipson applied for a lease of these lands : but Mr. Pelham would by no means consent to it ; on the contrary, thought proper to grant a lease of them to Mr. Roberts, not only in order to keep that part of the interest in his own hands, but to shew Mr. Philipson that he would not suffer him to meddle in the Corporation : and Mr. Philipson has often appealed to Mr. Roberts how strictly he had kept the promise he had made to be quiet.

If Mr. Davies should be removed from his office, the interest of the Treasury will suffer considerably, and perhaps can never be recovered.

Griffith Davies was in 1754 Mayor of Harwich, and as such had to get Wenman Coke and John Phillipson re-elected for the borough. But although, obeying orders from the Treasury, he laboured in the service of these candidates, he was requited by them with slights and attacks — which, with much picturesque detail, he recounted to Roberts in a lengthy memorandum.[1]

At a dinner with the Corporation Davies sat next to Phillipson, who thus

[1] May 1754 ; *ibid.* ff. 310-13.

had an opertunity of insulting without being heard by the whole company. He said amongst other things that the Duke of New-castle had sent for him some time ago, and after *kissing* and *hugging* him, and that sort of stuff, *as he term'd it*, he beg'd he would take Shoreham in hand, which to oblige him he had undertaken, and had cost him near £5000 [1] . . . in consideration of which the Duke bid him do what he would at Harwich, by puting in or out as he pleased.

After this significant introduction, Phillipson proceeded to tell Davies in a sneering manner :

Your friend Roberts is not to continue with the Duke as he was with Mr. Pelham ; . . . he told me so himself, and that he was only with him to communicate what he could recollect of Mr. Pelham's intentions concerning the elections.—And then said, your friend Mr. Pelham (as you call him) . . . whenever I mentioned any thing about Harwich to him, he often said Damn Harwich, I wish it was under water, it was you brought that fellow Davies to me first. And your friend Roberts told me t'other day that it was very absurd to set one public office to govern the whole town. . . . And that he had no notion of one man's acting as a little Minister and tyranizeing over all the rest, and that he believed it would not be so in future.

As for Leicester, according to Phillipson, it was his

desire that the officers of the Customs and Post Office should agree and live neighbourly, and that in future they whose fault it was that they did not, let them take care &c.—To which I reply'd that I had taken a great deal of pains to bring that about ; but had never been able to effect it : nor never could be effectually done as long as the Post Office attempted to keep up a separate interest from that of the Government.

Hines, the postmaster, and his brother contributed their share to inter-departmental amenities in the Government borough of Harwich ; they opened and stopped letters of the Custom House officials and spread rumours that Davies would soon be dismissed, or at least removed from Harwich.

Neither my brother or me can pass the street without hearing something of this sort from them ; sometimes, he has outlived his

---

[1] This election of Phillipson's son-in-law at Shoreham anyhow cost the Treasury £1000. The following entry appears in Roberts's accounts of secret service money on 2 May 1754 : 'Mr. P[hillipson] for Mr. B[ristow] for Shoreham £1000.0.0' ; see below, p. 430.

friends . . . now it is the turn of the Post Office to have power;
at other times they cry out in my hearing as I pass, his Pelham is
gone to the D——l, and he will soon follow him.

And Mr. Coke's 'chief servant' said that Harwich was 'a pretty
little town', and his master was going to have a house in it and
be elected a capital burgess; which

convinces me that they design if possible to throw the borrough into
the hands of Lord Leicester and Mr. Phillipson, who will be as ready
as any two men in England to attempt to bully the Ministry out of
it, and this I believe will be the case, except it be nip'd in the bud.

In short, as Davies put it in a letter of 29 August 1754, he now
saw his little bark drawn 'into a sea of the mercyless waves of
insolence and arbitrary power of Toryizm'.[1]

When the campaign against Davies was at its height,
Roberts, on 21 November 1754, explained to Newcastle once
more how Pelham had found Harwich 'divided into many little
parties, which had gone near to destroy the Government's interest there', and how, in order to put an end to 'squabbles
and jealousies', he had taken its management 'into his own
hands'; he concluded:

Mr. Pelham's regard to Mr. Philipson had made him determine
to prefer him to any other representative that might offer himself for
that borough; and he pas'd the same compliment to the Earl of
Leicester, by introducing his son Lord Coke there, and afterwards
Mr. Coke the present member. But, if it was determined to recommend his Lordship's near relation there, because he had an interest
as Post-Master General, I can take upon me to say, that Mr.
Pelham would never have consented to any step, which would have
given Mr. Coke an interest in that borough hereafter, whenever
Lord Leicester shall cease to be His Majesty's Post-Master General.
Nor can I conceive with what other view it can be so much desired,
but to extend his claim beyond that contingency; if I recollect
right, the late Lord Coke was not a capital burgess there: nor would
Mr. Coke have been (I verily beleive) if Mr. Pelham had lived. . . .
I should likewise add that the King is not ignorant of the manner
in which it [Harwich] has been conducted for several years past;
and, if your Grace should think proper to know his pleasure thereupon, it will appear to be, that the same conduct (unless you should

---

[1] 32736, ff. 378-80. Neither the Cokes nor Phillipson had any inclination
toward 'Toryism'; but this was the word with which to brand one's
opponents.

see cause to recommend a contrary one to His Majesty) should be complied with.[1]

Davies remained Collector of Customs at Harwich and continued to manage the Government interest in the borough under Roberts, while Roberts, as a devoted follower of Newcastle, began to wonder whether (for the Duke's sake) he himself should not acquire a proper foothold in the borough. Accordingly, on 15 July 1755, Davies addressed to him the following letter,[2] which he duly transmitted to Newcastle : [3]

I am very glad you have thought of fitting up a house for yourself [at Harwich] ; I have been inclined to mention it, for some time past, as it will in some measure facilitate and take off some objections to an affair which I hope will happen on the next occasion [obviously Roberts's election to the Corporation]. The borough is now in as much danger to be lost to the Government, as it was at first, every method is used by fair and foul means to make a defection among the Ministers friends.

I look on John Turner as lost to the Duke, Mr. Phillipson having got him a 20 gun ship to build here. And he, Mr. Phillipson, has order'd Mr. Slade the builder at Deptford, not to suffer young Pulham to be promoted in the Yard, unless his father will ask it as a favour of Mr. Phillipson. The Post Office is also at work, they have brought 24 actions against the collectors of the Land Tax, and threaten ruin to all that oppose, some of our friends are frightened and others discouraged from acting with spirit, so that unless his Grace will encourage them a little, the borough will be stole out of his hands. This situation makes it necessary for you to be one of our number, as all the arts they are masters of is used to take off my weight at this place. . . .

On 5 August, Davies informed Roberts of the death of a capital burgess, and expressed the hope that Roberts would succeed him ; [4] but in spite of earnest warnings given to Newcastle about the danger which otherwise threatened Harwich,[5] it was only on the next vacancy that Roberts and Davies had

---

[1] 32737, ff. 369-72.   [2] 32857, f. 121.

[3] In a letter of 20 July 1755 ; *ibid.* f. 276.

[4] *Ibid.* f. 592. About this time Treasury debts were cleared at Harwich, but, curiously enough, this was done through the Secretary to the Post Office ; in the secret service accounts the entry appears under 20 Aug 1755 : 'Mr. Shelvoke for Harwich £300.0.0' ; see below, p. 439.

[5] In a new 'State of the Corporation of Harwich' ; *ibid.* ff. 590-1.

their way — 'in consequence of your Grace's recommendation', wrote Roberts to Newcastle on 27 September 1755, 'I was yesterday elected a capital burgess of this Corporation, without any opposition'.[1]

Newcastle resigned the Treasury on 11 November 1756; John Phillipson died on the 27th; and Leicester, visibly rejoiced at having a chance to bring Harwich business before a First Lord uninfluenced by Roberts, inquired of the Duke of Devonshire [2] for whom the Post Office should vote —

for as yet (though there has been great endeavours to get it into private hands) the Treasury may command there. . . . Give me leave to hint to you that that puppy Roberts who waited on Mr. Pelham's children, and was afterwards his secretary, imposed his reports about that burrough on Mr. Pelham and the Duke of Newcastle,[3] in order to get the burrough into his management, and bring himself in, so I hope you won't fix on him, if you do you give away in time the burrough from the Government.

And in a postscript:

Davis the present mayor on Mr. Roberts recommendation to the Duke of Newcastle is a lying and sad dog, and joins with Roberts to give him the burrough.

Next, in a letter of 30 November, Davies, elected that day Mayor of Harwich for the ensuing year, introduced himself to the Duke: in elections both to Parliament and the Corporation he has for many years acted for Pelham and Newcastle

whose commands were convey'd to me upon all occasions through the hands of John Roberts Esq., by which means this Corporation that heretofore was look'd on as almost private property, has with great care and trouble been for some years past at the devotion of the First Lord of the Treasury, and in this state your Grace now receives it.

Phillipson's place as capital burgess had to be filled immediately, before a Mayor could be elected; and

[1] 32859, f. 250.
[2] 29 Nov 1756; among the Devonshire MSS. at Chatsworth, as are all other letters to the Duke of Devonshire quoted below.
[3] In another letter, of 10 Dec, Leicester speaks of Davies and Roberts 'grossly imposing' on Newcastle 'whose hurry would hear no body else'.

2 B

they pitch'd on Mr. William Deane, a very honest man, and zealously affected to His Majesty and his Government.[1]

And as it may be soon necessary for your Grace's most dutyful servants to know your pleasure with regard to a new representative in Parliament for this borough : I should think myself wanting in duty to your Grace, if I did not signify that the wishes of a great number of your faithfull friends and servants are, that your Grace would please to recommend to them to be elected the said Mr. Roberts ; who has a property amongst us, and has behaved so as to deserve no enemies.

Devonshire replied with a nomination so patently proper that neither side could object : of his own brother-in-law, Lord Duncannon, whose seat at Saltash had been vacated by his promotion in office. Duncannon was duly returned on 13 December, but about this time a new crisis occured in the Corporation : a capital burgess, Coleman, wrote Carteret Leathes [2] to Leicester on 10 December, 'lay speechless, . . . in strong convulsions, with all symptoms of death upon him' should he die, his place would have to be filled before they could proceed to elect a Member —

we begg leave to offer your Lordship your old servant Mr. John Hynes the Post Master of this place . . . if we have not that favor, Davies the Collector, will certainly bring in some creature of his own. . . . He has already by such surreptitious methods of proceeding, got in so many of his own friends, and most of them independent people, that . . . if he is not disappointed in this instance, he is very near master of the burrough.

Leicester forwarded the letter by express to Devonshire asking him to nominate Hines, and admitting that he himself had done so already, but not that in so doing he had said he could answer for the Duke's approval.[3]

---

[1] But Leicester wrote to Devonshire, 27 Dec 1756 : '. . . they chose one Deane a carpenter dependent as I hear on Roberts . . . instead of one in office under the Government'.

[2] A landowner in the neighbourhood of Harwich ; M.P. for Harwich, 1734–41 ; connected with the Post Office group in the borough, and an enemy of Roberts (see Roberts's remarks about him in Table B, facing p. 379).

[3] See James Clement, Agent of the Packet Boats at Harwich, to Lord Leicester, 14 Dec 1756, Devonshire MSS. ; also Leicester's letter to Devonshire, 27 Dec, quoted below.

But Devonshire once more nonplussed both sides by recommending Duncannon also for the vacancy in the Corporation. In an embarrassed letter, on 27 December, Leicester tried to exculpate himself and indict his opponents.

Suspecting (as it happen'd) that Davies would be hurrying on an election for his or Roberts' dependent, I indeed wrote that I could answer your Grace would approve of Hines, which I thought I might venture to do, because my nephew sent me word, you desired such as were dependent on the Government might be chose, and the Post Master being dependent, Roberts . . . always kept him out. . . I am much more pleased you have chose Lord Duncannon on the floor than any body else for that may give him an opportunity of being thoroughly inform'd of the state of the burrough, and your Grace may by him send your directions what you would have done in it, for I beg you will put so much trust in me as to be assured if you employ Roberts in the management of it, you will certainly throw the burrough out of the Government into his hands, and that ink shiting prig will at last outwit us all.

And on 16 January 1757:

I am very happy to find you don't disapprove of the liberty I took in troubling you so much about Harwich, and that when we meet at London you will be so good to hear me farther about . . .

Even after Devonshire had left the Treasury, Leicester continued to ply him with letters about 'that prig Roberts and rascal Davies', 'the most impudent lying fellows breathing', who 'will get Harwich in the end'.[1] Apparently Devonshire, while still in office, bid Leicester's candidate Crowe to be chosen capital burgess, and on leaving obtained Newcastle's promise to see it done. But Davies and Roberts claimed that the burgesses would not elect him — 'is not that then proof that they have betrayed the burrough and taken it out of the hands of the ministry?' The burgesses being so low and poor that 'they must be dependent on some body, which undoubtedly is on Roberts or Davies. . . .' Indeed, the only way of saving the borough to 'His Majesty (who seems to have it so much at heart as to call it his own)' is by dismissing Davies and forbidding Roberts to interfere at Harwich.

[1] In letters from Holkham dated 3 Aug, 16 Oct, and 11 Dec 1757.

Davies, on the other hand, assured Devonshire, in a letter of 4 February 1758, that if his life had depended on Crowe's election, he could not have done more.

This was the hardest task I have ever had, since I had any thing to do with the Corporation, and the only thing I have fail'd in. . . . But . . . I really believe I should have got him elected, if Crowe himself had not counter acted me, by an impudent message he sent the electors : viz. 'Damn the *Clan*' (a name with which they honour the friends of the Treasury) 'they shall elect me in spite of their teeth's ; and I desire youl tell them so.'—This message was delivered to them, the night before the election when they had met together, as usual ; this treatment, they have since inform'd me, put them into a great rage, when they made a resolution never to vote for that man ; and to prevent their being importuned, bound themselves to secrecy till the election should be over.

On 4 July 1758, Duncannon succeeded his father as Earl of Bessborough, and on the 9th, Henry Pelham's widow, Lady Katherine, asked Newcastle to return Roberts for Harwich : 'you can't take my doing it amis ; nor wonder that I wish him to fill up the vacancy. . . .'[1]

The same day Roberts submitted to the Duke a scheme for rearranging his sinecures so as to render him eligible for Parliament :

Mr. Roberts humbly entreats to be permitted to exchange his post of Deputy Paymaster of Gibraltar with Mr. Sloper, one of the Commissioners of the Board of Trade ; and also to resign his office in the Customs to Mr. John Hughson.[2]

These disqualifications being removed, if his Grace the Duke of Newcastle would be pleased to do Mr. Roberts the honour to bring him into Parliament, he would use his best endeavours to make himself useful to his Grace upon all occasions.[3]

This time Devonshire, prompted by Leicester, tried to influence Newcastle's choice of a successor to Bessborough

---

[1] 32881, f. 319. The question of returning Roberts to Parliament had been raised in Apr 1754 : it was stated that such had been Pelham's intention (see 32735, f. 184). Roberts himself told Newcastle that 'when the King ordered me to let him know if I had a mind to be in it, I answered, that I was very indifferent about it' (Roberts to Newcastle, 27 Apr 1754; *ibid.* ff. 201-2.

[2] John Hughson was a cousin of Roberts ; see 32854, f. 489; 32895, f. 35 ; and 32946, ff. 349-50.   [3] 32881, f. 320.

and foil the ambitious plans of Roberts;[1] and on 16 July
Leicester wrote to Newcastle from Chatsworth

to receive your directions, who you would have our people vote for
as Member of Parliament that I may send them your orders. If
Duncannons being a Peer vacates his being on the floor at Harwich,
I hope your Grace will send orders to Davis and Roberts to chuse
Crow in his room . . . and by that you'll see whither those gentlemen will obey your orders with as little hesitation as I shall always
do, but that I much doubt.[2]

On 15 October 1758, Leicester again pressed for Crowe to
be chosen a capital burgess :

Your Grace may remember I told you that your orders on that
affair would be slighted . . . you will . . . be convinced that all I
have told you of the contrivances of Roberts to get that burrough
into his own hands from the Governments is true. . . . I know
they won't chuse Crow . . . they did exclude the people dependent
on the Government to bring in independent or such as only depended on themselves. What I do is for the Governments service, I
have no private views. . . . Roberts I know has apply'd to others,
whither to your Grace I know not, to be chose for Harwich, you are
the best judge whither he is a proper person . . . or if you please
to give the burrough into private hands, would have you do it with
your eyes open.[3]

Thomas Sewell, a son-in-law of Thomas Heath, M.P. for
Harwich 1715–22, himself a distinguished barrister and a great
favourite of the Dissenters whose cases he fought in the law
courts, was returned for Harwich on this vacancy. But in
1759, in connexion with a by-election at Orford, Newcastle
definitely promised Roberts to bring him into Parliament,[4] and
in the list of new Members to be chosen at the general election
of 1761, which was submitted to Newcastle by Roberts on
14 December 1760, his own name appears against Harwich.[5]

[1] See letters from Leicester to Devonshire, 12 July (Devonshire MSS.) ;
from Bessborough to Newcastle, 16 July (32881, f. 359) ; and to Devonshire,
20 July (Devonshire MSS.).
[2] 32881, f. 361. The peerage did not vacate Bessborough's 'being on
the floor at Harwich' (see list of May 1763, Table B, facing p. 379).
[3] 32884, ff. 382-3.
[4] Roberts wrote to Newcastle on 7 Dec 1759 : 'Since your Grace is
pleased to assure me of your kind intentions to bring me in to Parliament...'
(32899, f. 366).   [5] 32916, f. 65.

George III had, however, some candidates of his own to provide for, and although his claim (which at one time Newcastle
feared would prove very extensive) was raised on behalf of very
few men, it included the nomination of Charles Townshend to
Harwich. Newcastle now found himself between the upper
and nether millstone, the King and Lady Katherine Pelham,
and he hardly knew which was the more formidable.

In answer to Lady Katherine's expostulations, Newcastle
wrote on 5 February 1761 :

I had a long conference yesterday with my Lord Bute ; which,
almost in every point, pass'd entirely to my satisfaction. The chief
disagreable thing was this point of Mr. Roberts'. Lord Bute said
that the King had promis'd to bring Mr. Charles Townshend into
Harwich. I disputed it, combated it, and oppos'd it, as much as I
could. I did not prevail ; but yet I don't despair, but I shall at
last be able to get Mr. Roberts in at Harwich.[1]

Meantime Roberts for the tenth time had to transmit to him
'the state of the boroughs of Orford and Harwich'. Having
described Orford as financed and directed by the Treasury
alone, Roberts gave an account of Harwich [2] rather different
from that which he had given while he was not a claimant to
its representation :

At Harwich the case is far from being the same [as at Orford] ;
indeed the First Lord of the Treasury has likewise there the principal
influence ; but the expence to the Crown has been very small ; and
there has always been an independent interest, which was formerly
in Mr. Philipson and since his death has been in other hands ; so
that the Crown itself has not an equal claim for nomination there
as in the borough of Orford ; yet still, whenever the First Lord of
the Treasury thinks proper to acquaint them with his inclinations,
he will hardly fail of due attention from the constituents, provided
the Members proposed be not very disagreable to them.[3]

Newcastle accordingly noted down in his 'Memorandums'
on 6 February :

The state of the boroughs of Harwich [and] Orford.
Absolutely dependent on the Treasury.

---

[1] 32918, ff. 279-80.   [2] *Ibid.* ff. 281-2.
[3] Presumably the 'private interest' hinted at above but not named was
now in Roberts's own hands, and he and his friends were the constituents to
whom the Members proposed were not to be excessively disagreeable.

Conducted by Mr. Roberts.
Mr. Roberts could chuse himself at Harwich.
The great stress my Lady Katherine and my Lord Lincoln lay upon
it.[1]

Prodded by Roberts — 'the constituents, most of them,
have been consulted, and have actually promised to make me
their representative'[2] — and, in vigorous terms, by Lady
Katherine (who, besides a seat at Harwich, demanded for
Roberts a place at the Board of Trade),[3] Newcastle finally
accommodated both Townshend and Roberts at Harwich,
transferring its sitting Members to other places.

The storm had passed, and when on 27 February Roberts
had again to give 'a particular account' of the borough, it was
both cheerful and dutiful.[4]

At Harwich, there is a zealous disposition in the majority to
serve the Duke of Newcastle, out of particular regard to his Grace,
as well as on account of his being at the head of the Treasury.

As First Lord, he advances one hundred pounds yearly for some
private benefactions; and the manager is out of pocket generally
as much.

There is an independent interest always here, but this is well
inclined at present; and the Duke of Newcastle has the nomination
of both the Members.

On 30 March 1761, Charles Townshend and John Roberts
were returned for Harwich unopposed. But when in 1763
Townshend had to be re-elected on having been appointed to
office, Egmont, then Joint P.M.G., wrote to Bute on 27 February: 'Mr. Townshend has been imprudent . . . in not
going thither himself for it was (as I am informed) difficult to
chuse him there the last time on account of the like slight

---

[1] 32918, f. 311. Lincoln was a nephew of the Pelhams, a son-in-law of
Henry Pelham, and heir to Newcastle.
[2] Roberts to Newcastle, 10 Feb 1761; *ibid*. ff. 407-8.
[3] Lady Katherine Pelham to Newcastle, 12 Feb 1761: 'Mr. Roberts
tells me that you have been so good (have been so good are Mr. Roberts
words, and not mine I assure you) . . .' '. . . let me advise you to apply
. . . immediately, least you should be disappointed in this, as you have
been on other occasions by your delay. I am really sorry for the distress
you are in . . . but you must give me leave to say, that you bring them
chiefly on your self' (*ibid*. ff. 471-2).   [4] 32919, f. 323.

shewn to the borough then'. And in a postscript: 'I know the agent of the Post Office of Harwich to be disinclined to Townshend and that he will endeavour to defeat him if he can have any plausible excuse'.[1]

In December 1761 Roberts was made a Commissioner for Trade and Plantations. He continued manager of Harwich,[2] but was not a favourite with Newcastle. His attachment was primarily to Lady Katherine and Lord Lincoln, and the relations between Lincoln and Newcastle were not satisfactory. On Newcastle's side there was sincere affection for Lincoln, mixed with suspicion and grievances (such as he harboured against everybody), and with annoyance at getting no help from that indolent hypochondriac. For Lincoln preferred to lead an easy life and mind his diseases, and was equally sick of Newcastle's cordiality, jealousy, claims, and promptings, and altogether bored with his uncle for whom he had neither love nor loyalty. But for the crises which periodically occurred in the family, Newcastle chose to blame Roberts whom he accused of intriguing between them — 'in what an odious light your Grace has view'd and represented me for above a twelvemonth past', complained Roberts on 22 February 1762.

I think I never said or did what might tend in any degree to widen the breach. . . . My interest, if I had ever looked for any, must depend upon the union and harmony of those, from whom alone I ever sought, or can hope for protection and patronage ; . . . but I have attached myself to your Grace and all your family from inclination more than from self-interested views.[3]

On 26 May 1762, Newcastle resigned the Treasury but desired his followers to retain office, a wish with which Lincoln and his friends readily complied. Still, when Newcastle in August 1762 had refused to resume office under Bute, and Henry Fox had been called in to manage the House of Com-

---

[1] Bute MSS.

[2] See, *e.g.*, his letter to Newcastle, 26 Sept 1761, concerning a vacancy among its capital burgesses : 'There is no person who has any post under the Government in that town, proper to be elected upon this vacancy'. He suggests therefore a local fisherman who 'promises strongly to support the Government interest' (32928, f. 375).

[3] 32935, ff. 14-16.

mons, when Devonshire had been dismissed and Newcastle had started urging his 'considerable friends' to resign office, Lincoln had to go, though very much against his own wish and choice (in secret, he complained to the King of his uncle, who meantime informed all the world that Lincoln behaved 'like an angel' [1]). Roberts had to follow Lincoln — 'Roberts's resignation', wrote George III to Bute, 'I look on as certain, Lord Lincoln having set him the example'.[2] When in December the proscription was started of Newcastle's friends in minor offices — whom Bute and Fox quite reasonably refused to support for Newcastle and the Opposition — Roberts, too, was deprived of the sinecure of Inspector of the Accounts of the Collectors of the Out-Ports (worth about £400 p.a.), which was held in trust for him by his cousin, John Hughson.[3] He became a martyr who secretly fawned on his presumed executioners. 'Roberts's letter is very handsome', wrote George III to Bute on 23 December. 'I know him to be an honest and honourable man, but feel the situation of things made it necessary to make his vacancy, otherwise he never was a creature of the Duke of Newcastle, on the contrary that Duke never would have any connection with him.' [4] But when invited to Claremont, in recognition of his faithful sufferings, Roberts assured Newcastle how much he enjoyed 'having acted honorably and honestly'. 'We are both [Roberts and his friend Mellish] consoled for our disgraces, or rather repent not of our incurring a resentment, which proves how much we are attached to you.' [5]

At Harwich itself no changes were made in the crisis of December 1762–February 1763, though some had been planned by Fox. The following entry occurs in a 'Supplemental List of Customhouse Offices with Observations',[6] dated 18 December 1762 and obviously drawn up with a view to dismissals :

[1] *E.g.* in a letter to Lord Granby, 5 Nov 1762 ; 32944, f. 275. The same phrase occurs in several other letters.

[2] Sedgwick, no. 227.

[3] See in the Liverpool Papers the 'List of several Persons holding Offices in the Customs by Patent during Pleasure', 18 Dec 1762 ; 38334, ff. 211-12.

[4] Sedgwick, no. 248.

[5] Roberts to Newcastle, 27 Jan 1763 ; 32946, f. 224.

[6] 38334, f. 216.

Davis. Collector at Harwich. Worth near 300£ a year. Mayor of Ditto — employed by Mr. Roberts to manage the borough.

Davies appealed for help, among others, to Lord Egmont who on 1 January 1763 wrote to Bute : [1]

As I think the state of the Borough of Harwich has not been rightly represented to yr. Lordship, I should wish some day or other to explain it better. No man can know it much better than myself. As the Parker estate from the Conquest lay and still lies within two miles of it, and had such influence upon it, that from Queen Anne's time till the year 1733, my uncle,[2] or my uncle and father jointly were absolute masters there and served for it. In the year 1734 by great art and management I lost my election there, by one vote only, since which time it has been a Government Borough and we never have, or mean again to be concerned with it.

But as many of his former friends still continue at Harwich, he is able to prevent Bute 'from being led into some errors in regard to that place' ; and communicates to him two letters 'from the suspected person who is intended as I hear to be dismissed' — obviously Davies.

He is now Mayor and Relieving Officer, and a very able man of great personal interest, and I believe never has been so utterly attached to any man as to my father and myself, though we have left him to take the course best suited to his own interest from 1733 to this day. From hence your Lordship will presently judge, whether better methods than those of rigour may not be used to accomplish what you wish.

And the King, who since Leicester House days never ceased to loathe and distrust Fox, wrote to Bute 18 January 1763 : [3]

Lord Egmont's intelligence from Harwich is a small example of the many harsh things Mr. Fox will attempt to drive my Dear Friend into ; but his sense and good heart will make him see what steps are necessary to ruin the Newcastle faction, and those that would be only ruining individuals who are not attached to that party ; this ought to serve as a lesson that no man should be dismissed unless others besides the Foxes declare them to be of that denomination.

---

[1] Bute MSS.
[2] Sir Philip Parker, third Bt. (1682–1741), M.P. for Harwich 1715–34 ; his sister Catherine married in 1710 John, first Earl of Egmont.
[3] Sedgwick, no. 263.

Davies made his submission to Bute, and immediately started building bridges for Roberts. On 18 January he wrote to Charles Jenkinson, then Bute's secretary, with whom he had entered into official correspondence about Harwich : [1]

> I called at your house on Saturday . . . to intimate to you, that I had seen Mr. Roberts, who inform'd me that he had wrote to my Lord Bute concerning the Borough of Orford ; and that if his Lordship pleased, he would wait on him after the holydays to explain something relating to it . . . without some intimation that his Lordship would see him he could not with any propriety go to his Lordship. . . .

The intimation was presumably received, for on 5 February Roberts wrote to Newcastle with obvious embarrassment :

> I entreated Lord Lincoln to acquaint your Grace, that I had been with Lord Bute on Friday last, by his order ; the subject was principally the borough of Orford. In the conversation I introduced some particular circumstances relating to myself, which he heard patiently enough, but said little ; except general expressions of the honourable manner, in which he was pleased to say, I had behaved with relation to Harwich and Orford, and a declaration that he would do me the justice to represent them in an higher place. I can relate viva voce, much better than write the whole of what passed, when I shall have the honour next to see your Grace.[2]

This drew a very angry reply from Newcastle who had hoped, though in opposition, to retain the borough influence he had gained as First Lord of the Treasury :

> I have, this moment, received your letter, which, I own, has extremely surprized me ; I never heard one word of it from my Lord Lincoln ; he would not own to me having given any such advice ; and I did not imagine, that any advice, or consideration, could have carried you to my Lord Bute, after the injuries, and indignities, which his Lordship has put upon *me*, all *my brother's friends*, and indeed personally *upon yourself*. He had a great mind, to turn you out of Harwich, this Parliament, if I would have permitted it ; and I cannot think, any friend of mine, after this treatment, in any ways obliged to fling Orford or Harwich into his Lordship's hands.[3]

---

[1] Bute MSS.   [2] 32946, f. 319.
[3] 6 Feb 1763 ; *ibid.* f. 333.

Roberts replied on 7 February :

A letter, in the stile of that, which I had the honour to receive from your Grace this morning, I must confess I little thought of receiving from your Grace, at this time. It cannot but be matter of surprize to me, that, after having stood with firmness the late fiery tryal, I should be now suspected of having taken any step that derogates from the attachment I have long professed, and so invariably shewn to you. In the present instance your Grace expresses your displeasure before you are acquainted with the facts.

Mr. Rigby [1] (whom your Grace formerly permitted to interfere rudely with me in the corporation of Harwich) had, it seems, obtained from Lord Bute a sort of promise that he should by degrees get footing in that borough. Mr. Davies the Collector was on the point of being dismissed, and one Mr. Lucas, brother in law to Mr. Calcraft,[2] who has now another place, was to succeed him. All those in the Customs, who should adhere to me, were to be turned out. Intelligence of these intentions reaching Mr. Davies, he came up to London, and by the assistance of Lord Egmont, Lord Harcourt, Mr. Schreider, and others, was just in time to save himself. Could I perswade a poor man to do otherwise, who must have starved, with his wife, and five children, if I had insisted upon his sharing my fate ?

Having further described the position at Orford, he concluded :

The interests are actually in the First Lord of the Treasury, and, if I had been so enclined (which in honour I ought not be), I could not, as those boroughs are now constituted, have made any material opposition in them ; so that your Grace, upon a cooler reflection, will not charge me with having flung them into the hands of Lord Bute, but do me the justice to allow, that they were there, in spite of me.[3]

No reply to this letter appears in the Newcastle Papers, but soon correspondence on other subjects passed between them, and when Newcastle returned to power, in the Rockingham

[1] M.P. for Tavistock and political manager of the Bedford group ; a this time a close personal friend of Henry Fox. He owned Mistley Hall near Harwich.
[2] John Calcraft, the regimental agent and right-hand man of Henry Fox. Anthony Lucas, of Ancaster, Lincs., married Calcraft's sister, Christian (see Maddison, *Lincolnshire Pedigrees*).
[3] 32946, ff. 349-50.

Administration of 1765, Roberts was restored to his seat at the Board of Trade and to his lost sinecures (that of Receiver of the Quit-Rents of Virginia, had remained to him throughout, being for life, as was his pension of £800 p.a. on the Irish Establishment).

In May 1763, presumably at Jenkinson's request, Davies rendered to him a detailed account of the state of Harwich, which is reproduced as Table B, opposite. This list of the Harwich electorate reminds one somehow of a theatrical programme ; here are the persons of the play, and added to them a few 'citizens' to represent the people. The central figure is Griffith Davies, 'determined to support the interest of his Majesty and his Ministry against all opponents whatsoever' ; lower down (No. 19) appears John Roberts, M.P., who had given proper assurances that 'he would concur in supporting the Crowns interest here' ; and his cousin and puppet, John Hughson (No. 27). The Parliamentary past of Harwich is represented by Nos. 28-30, Lord Bessborough, Wenman Coke, and Carteret Leathes, late Members for the borough, still retaining their places 'on the floor' of the Corporation ; and by No. 31, Henry Pelham, a cousin put in by the great Pelhams. Then there are the two antagonistic groups of dependants of the Post Office and the Treasury ; the agent of the Packets (No. 3) and their four captains (Nos. 4, 5, 7, and 18), and nine men connected with the Custom House, who, under various designations, were supposed to watch the land and the sea, the waters and the tides (Nos. 9-17). Nos. 2 and 20, men living on their 'fortunes' (and on Treasury pensions), No. 6, a shipwright (for whom Phillipson had got 'a 20-gun ship to build here'), and No. 8, the local 'surgeon and apothecary', must be added to the list of notables in the Corporation. The play-bill is completed by two innkeepers, at whose houses civic celebrations and election entertainments were presumably held, a house carpenter, a farmer, and three master fishermen.

Of the thirty-two mentioned in the list, seventeen were in minor Government offices. Of those not in Government posts, some were relatives of officials, while two or three were on the waiting-list, comforted in the meantime by pensions out of

the £100 which was the direct yearly contribution paid by the
Treasury in support of the Government interest at Harwich ;
and they were 'in great distress' if any serious delay occurred in
payments, as was usually the case.[1] In this respect Ministerial
changes had no material effect on relations between Harwich
and the Treasury. The letter from Davies to Jenkinson, on
7 May 1763, enclosed a receipt for £50, the half-yearly payment
to the borough ;[2] and the next instalment was late as usual :
'As Michaelmas is now past, be so good, as to send me £50 to
give the three persons whom you know, as usual'.[3]

In London, political alliances and rivalries were no longer
a subject for a picture — a film would have been required ; but
at Harwich the battle between Griffith Davies, of the Customs,
and Hines, of the Post Office, continued as of old. When in
1764 it was proposed that George Grenville should become
Recorder of Harwich[4] with Mr. Rant, a barrister,[5] for deputy,
Davies pressed for a decision —

[1] See papers submitted by Roberts to Newcastle, 17 July 1758 ; for ten
years past £60 a year had been paid to Phillips, and £40 to Richman,
who had nothing for the last five quarters and were 'in great distress on
that account' ; 32881, ff. 371-3. On 7 Jan 1764, Griffith Davies, on the
death of his brother Daniel who had been Tide Surveyor in the port of
Harwich, suggested to Jenkinson that Andrew Smith, 'the oldest burgess
unprovided for', should succeed him. 'You know he has now £35 per
annum, and in case he be appointed, that money may be given either to one
of two others, which will strengthen the Government's interest greatly'
(38202, f. 10). Andrew Smith was appointed, and on his death in May
1765, 'Mr. John Deane, the oldest capital burgess unprovided for', was
recommended in his place. 'You know he has now £35 per annum, and if
he has this office, that sum may be given to one other of the capital burgesses
farther to secure the Government's interest' (Davies to Jenkinson, 1 June
1765 ; 38204, f. 258).   [2] 38200, f. 329.
[3] Davies to Jenkinson, 8 Oct 1763 ; 38201, f. 170. The three recipients
of pensions at Harwich were at that time Andrew Smith, £35 ; John Deane,
£35 ; and Henry Stevens, £30 p.a. ; see 38202, f. 10, and 38477, ff. 35-6.
[4] See correspondence between Davies and Jenkinson, Oct-Dec 1764,
passim ; Davies's letters are in 38203 ; Jenkinson's replies in his letter-book,
38304.
[5] Sir Richard Lloyd, who died in 1761, had been Recorder of Harwich,
Orford, and Ipswich ; in all three boroughs he was, in time, succeeded by
Humphrey Rant (see 'Collections for the History of Ipswich', by W. Batley ;
25335, f. 65), who as Recorder played a considerable part in their politics.
The history of such Recorders running groups of neighbouring boroughs
would deserve closer investigation. Rant was a Norfolk man, educated at
Caius, Cambridge, and the Middle Temple ; he died in 1779, at the age
of seventy.

as we have several traverses to try that I am not well acquainted with, vizt. two for sodomitical practices, and two for threatening letters to extort money, besides ordinary business : and what makes it more necessary to have a lawyer of the court is, that Hines the Deputy Post-Master, and the fishermen, have contributed money to pay counsell to appear in behalf of some of the delinquents. . . .

This fellow Hines gives more trouble to the friends of the Government, than all the rest of the malcontents in the town.[1]

The correspondence between Davies and Jenkinson during the two years of the Grenville Administration (1763–65) deals with Harwich affairs even in greater detail than Roberts's letters to Newcastle ; for however passionately fond the Duke was of doing the work of subordinate officials, they too had their jealousies, and Roberts did not allow every detail of Harwich patronage to reach the First Lord of the Treasury. Still, in this mass of correspondence two cases only seem to deserve special mention : one, of a mild revolt among the Harwich dependants of the Treasury who, seeing its ascendancy in the central Government, wished to share in victory and spoils ; the other, of endeavours among the rank and file of Harwich burgesses to create family groups in the Corporation such as the great political families formed in the House of Commons.

The story of the revolt is told in a letter from Davies to Jenkinson, on 7 July 1764 :

. . . for the people whom I was to pay the £50,[2] but it happened none of them were at home ; after the return of Mr. Stevens from a journey, and Mr. John Deane from Norway, I paid them their stipends ; but observed an unusual coolness and shyness in their behaviour, as well as in the rest of our friends, which I could not account for, and for the present did not care to ask the reason of.

Mr. Nathl Saunders, whom I thought the properest to recommend to you, to have the £35 pr. an. instead of Mr. Smith, being then in Norway, at his return I sent for him and told him that as he had been a steady friend to the Government, I believed I could get him a small stipend of £35, if he would accept of it. He thank'd me, but said that, although he had a large family, he could make a

---

[1] Davies to Jenkinson, 15 Dec 1764 ; 38203, ff. 305-6.
[2] The top and bottom of the paper have rotted away, and the extant text starts as above.

shift to maintain them without such a triffle . . . that the other friends of the Government . . . as well as himself, thought it a very aggravating mortification to see Phillip Baggott *a boy and no voter*, made a Captain of a Pacquet over their heads, some of whom were qualified for it, and were voters here, for the Government interest, before he (Baggott) was born ; and what still more mortifies them is, that this young fellow is no seaman, and consequently not qualified for the lucrative employment he undeservedly enjoys, having never been at sea, but by going now, and then, a voyage with his father, nearly like a passenger. . . . That it was another provoking circumstance, that this man, who had always opposed the Treasury interest, during the life of Lord Leicester, who many years endeavoured to steal this borough from the Crown, to make it a family borough ; should now have interest enough to perpetuate an employment of £1500 p. annum, in war time, and above £1000 in peaceable times, in his family, to the prejudice of those voters that have always been zealous in supporting the interest of the Crown here. . . .

I . . . assured them that I was . . . far from assisting or even being privy to any part of this business. . . . They clamoured pretty loudly, and said they had but small encouragement to be zealous in supporting the Government's interest . . . when the Pacquet Boats which are as good as a Vice-Admiral's place, are given to those who have opposed it . . . and all they had to expect . . . after many years zeal for the Crown's interest, was some little Custom-house place which was scarcely bread ; when one of the Captains of the Pacquets income annually, was more than that of all the officers of the Customs, in the whole port, put together. That those Captains put in by Lord Leicester, to assist him in opposing the Treasury have acquired large estates ; that Capt. Cockerill has been Capt. about twenty years, has raised a fortune of £30,000 besides bringing up his family. Capt. Hunt have been in about fourteen years, and have rais'd about £18,000. Capt. Hearn in five years has raised about £6000. . . .

That as Lord Leicester did in his time oblige these Captains to pay certain sums to other voters to keep up an interest to oppose the Treasury ; they should be glad to know if it would not be full as just for them, now, to pay something out of their great profits, to support the interest of the Crown under the direction of the Treasury. That these Captains could very well afford £200 per annum each, but if they were to pay £100 each, it would be better than nothing ; to be distributed as Mr. Grenville should direct, by a person by him appointed.[1]

[1] 38203, f. 23.

Jenkinson replied on 27 July :

You may very safely assure the gentlemen of Harwich, that neither I, nor even Mr. Grenville, knew anything of the appointment of young Baggot, so that if 'tis a disobligation to them, we at least have no concern in it. . . . I hope that when you have sufficiently explained it to your friends, they will become again satisfied, and I am sure that if at any time, it is proper for Mr. Grenville to interfere in their favor, he will readily give them his assistance. . . .

. . . As to the other proposition you make, it is of a nature which Mr. Grenville has always disapproved of, and never practises, even with respect to offices that are immediately under himself ; he cannot think therefore of proposing this practice to others, and I know that what Lord Leicester did of this kind, tho' at the time it might answer his purposes, met with general disapprobation. . . .[1]

The question of family groups in the Corporation arose in May 1765, when Charles Townshend, on becoming Paymaster General, had to seek re-election ; 'we cannot go to election for Member of Parliament untill the Corporation is filled up', wrote Davies on 27 May, asking for instructions concerning the choice of two capital burgesses.[2] 'It is left to your discretion to do it with such persons as you and the Corporation shall approve of', replied Jenkinson on 28 May.[3] But the same day Davies put forward the following request :

. . . in your answer, I beg you will add words to this effect. Vizt. 'that Mr. Grenville desires that I will take care that not above two of one family, may be elected into the Corporation'. My Lord Egmont in the year 1734 had very disagreable experience of the want of this caution, as he then lost his election, by a defection of four in one family.

The reason of the necessity of this caution at present is, that there are no less than three familys, that have each of them already two in the Corporation, and are now pressing for a third.[4]

Jenkinson willingly complied.

I am directed now by Mr. Grenville to give you one caution, which is, that for the future not above two of any one family be elected into the Corporation.[5]

[1] 38304, ff. 37-8.   [2] 38458, f. 64.   [3] 38305, f. 5.
[4] 38458, f. 66.   [5] 29 May 1765 ; 38305, f. 5.

2 C

But, while anxious to check the rise of other family interests in the Corporation, Davies, as every manager of every Government borough, seems to have been at work to build up his own position independent of the Government and his office. He was spending money of his own on the borough, of course 'for His Majesty's service'. In one of the many letters asking for a Government post for his son, he wrote to Jenkinson : [1]

I doubt not bu[t you] will wonder when I tell you that every shilling that I s[aved . . .] good husbandry, from my office, I have spent in supporti[ng the] Government's interest at this place ; and therefore am [. . .] nothing but what fell to me by my relations, and what I recei[ved . . .] my wife. . . . Mr. Pelham in his life-time was [. . .] of the expence I was continually at, and did intend to give [me] something in addition to reimburse me, but his death [. . .] by all my hopes ; for the Duke of Newcastle who succ[eeded] him, I believe hated me, as he took every oppertu[nity] to browbeat me ; and for no other reason that I ever [. . .] learn, but because he knew his brother had a friends[hip for] me ; and I learn't from my good Lord Harcourt th[at my] case was not singular.

Were Davies's endeavours and expenditure at Harwich altogether disinterested ? Jenkinson wrote to him on 11 June 1765 :

I cannot help mentioning to you that we have received complaints here that the two persons you recommended to fill up the Corporation have no offices under Government and consequently not bound to it by that obligation, while others who have offices and were in other respects very proper persons, were neglected : as Government trusts wholly to you in this affair I cannot help earnestly desiring that in your future recommendations you would name such as are held to Government by the strongest ties and not to let any private disagreements among yourselves too far interfere so as to prevent your availing yourself of the assistance of those who are in the service of Government and well disposed to it, and Mr. Grenville recommends to you in particular that Mr. Charles Lloyd his private secretary may be elected one of your number the

---

[1] 2 Feb 1764 ; 38202, f. 75. The blanks in the text marked by square brackets are caused by the edges of the paper having rotted away. Davies seems to have played the benefactor even to the town as such ; see, e.g., Morant, *Essex* (1768), vol. i, p. 500, for a description of the sea-front at Harwich, where 'Griffith Davies, Esq., hath made two very convenient baths ; one cold, and the other hot'.

first opportunity that offers. I wish also to receive from you a state of the borough as it now stands setting against each mans name the office he holds.[1]

Charles Lloyd was obviously to have been Grenville's Roberts; he was already a capital burgess at Orford,[2] and had Grenville continued in office much longer, would undoubtedly have been brought in for a Treasury borough. But the Rockingham Administration was in sight; and on 16 July 1765 Davies wrote to Jenkinson 'greatly amazed at the very sudden changes especially at the Treasury, which I all along flatter'd my self could not, or would not happen'.[3] He concluded: 'I am now set a drift again in a turbulent sea'. But he soon reached port, or perhaps never left it.

The question of the packet boats continued to cause trouble. In May 1766, under the Rockingham Administration, members of the Harwich Corporation complained of their having been 'injured and slighted by having two of the most lucrative employments in the gift of the Crown at this Borough given to strangers who had neither vote nor interest here, in preference to many worthy, able and experienced persons who had for a number of years voted in conformity to the will of Government and for forty years past returned such representatives as were recommended by the first Minister': [4] James Clement, Agent of the packet boats, eighty-four years old, had been permitted to resign his employment to his nephew, and Bossom, though a stranger to Harwich, had been appointed to command one of its packet boats. This so much enraged 'the greater part of the Corporation' that Roberts had to ask Newcastle to testify that Roberts had made representations against the appointment.[5]

On 13 October 1766, a formal letter was sent to Charles Townshend, now Chancellor of the Exchequer, signed by

---

[1] 38305, f. 8.   [2] See below, p. 395.   [3] 38204, f. 310.

[4] A copy of their letter to Rockingham was apparently sent by them to Charles Townshend, and is quoted in a further letter to him, 13 Oct. 1766 (Townshend MSS. in the possession of the Duke of Buccleuch).

[5] 32977, f. 242; the letter is misdated by Roberts 12 Oct 1766, but is docketed 12 Aug; and Newcastle's reply to it, 21 Aug 1766, is in 32976, f. 443.

H. Stevens, mayor of Harwich, Griffith Davies, and 16 members
of the Corporation (all in Davies's interest) asking that these
two appointments be set aside in favour of some properly
qualified voters, undoubtedly supporters of Davies. But meantime a rift seems to have occurred between him and Roberts
who, on 22 October, forwarded to Townshend a letter about
Davies received, presumably by arrangement, from Nathaniel
Saunders, a leading fisherman at Harwich. 'I find by Mr.
Davies's scheme', wrote Saunders, 'that he even wants to be
above the Lord of the Treasury as well as the Post Masters
General.' He tells the Corporation that they need not 'mind
great men either the Postmaster or Treasury . . . it seems very
plain to me that unless the Post Office's interest is kept up the
very Ministry will loose this Corporation', and neither they
nor the King will be able to call Harwich 'their borough':
Davies should therefore not be allowed to fill with his own
nominee a vacancy shortly expected in the Corporation. To
this letter Roberts joined an extract from Davies's letter to the
Duke of Devonshire, 30 November 1756,[1] stating that orders
to Harwich used to be sent through Roberts; and he added in
the covering letter:

The only way to put an end to these cabals, I think, will be to
bring him back to the same degree of subordination. If this be not
done upon the present vacancy, the Collector at the head of the
Custom house officers, and the independents he has lately very
irregularly made, will have it in his power to bully his masters,
whenever he shall be disappointed in his expectations.[2]

Roberts, Townshend's colleague in the representation of
Harwich, was now fighting the battle against the local manager
which Leicester had unsuccessfully waged ten years earlier;
and on 1 November he asked Townshend to communicate
through him the decision about filling the vacancy: 'indeed

---

[1] See above, p. 367.

[2] There is among the Townshend Papers an undated list of Harwich
Corporation which shows that of its 32 members 10 were officers of the
Customs and 14 were independents. It was probably drawn up about this
time: Andrew Smith, who died in 1765, no longer appears in the list, but
John Mathews, whose death in October 1766 caused the expected vacancy,
is still in it.

not to receive such a mark of your confidence and countenance would be no small mortification to me, as it would confirm the insinuation, which has been most industriously propagated of late amongst our constituents, that I am so unhappy as to have a less share of your good graces than Mr. Davies'. Davies on his part wrote to Townshend, on 22 October, that next time he was in London he would 'make it appear as clear as the sun, that the whole of the allegations [against him] are founded on nothing but falsehood and malice'.

The further story of Harwich does not appear in the collections of manuscripts on which the above account is based. But obviously Davies continued in charge of the borough,[1] assisted by his son,[2] Henry Pelham Davies, who on his father's death in 1778 succeeded to his office and functions.[3] H. P. Davies died in 1782, at the age of only thirty-eight;[4] but for this untimely death, he or a son of his might some day have entered the House of Commons as Member for Harwich, and a descendant, no doubt, the House of Lords.

Harwich meantime continued a Parliamentary stronghold of the Treasury, receiving, besides other benefits, its regular £100 a year;[5] on the death of Charles Townshend, in 1767,

---

[1] He was undoubtedly treated as the first man in the town, and presumably lived in a good house and in comfortable circumstances. When on 2 Oct 1766, George III's sister, who married King Christian VII of Denmark, set out for Rotterdam by way of Harwich, 'Her Majesty rested the night at Mr. Davis's the Collector of Customs' (see 'A Short Journal, &c.'; Fortescue, vol. i, p. 404). In his last will, proved on 13 Oct 1778, and preserved at Somerset House, Griffith Davies gives to his son 'my books, my mathematical and optical instruments, my swords, guns, pistols, and the watch with the seal of the arms of my family'.

[2] See letter from H. P. Davies to C. Jenkinson, 7 Aug 1772; 38458, f. 89.

[3] In the *Gentleman's Magazine*, 1782, p. 94, Henry Pelham Davies is described as 'Collector of Customs at Harwich'; and there is a letter in the Rainsford Papers, dated 4 July 1781 (23654, f. 56), signed by him as such.

[4] See Thomas Wright, *Essex* (1835), vol. ii, p. 818, for monumental inscription in St. Nicholas Church at Harwich.

[5] The secret service accounts of John Robinson, Secretary to the Treasury, for the period Jan 1779 till Mar 1782 are in 37836. In these Harwich still appears with its £100 a year. Also, in the 'Accounts of payments made by Lord North submitted to His Majesty for his orders, which of them he will be pleased to have continued and delivered over' (*ibid.* ff. 137-9), drawn up on the fall of the North Government in 1782, there occurs the entry: 'Harwich — yearly towards expenses of the Cor-

Thomas Bradshaw, Secretary to the Treasury, was returned for Harwich ; in 1772, on the death of John Roberts (who was left in possession of his seat at the general election of 1768), Charles Jenkinson, at that time one of the Lords of the Treasury ; John Robinson, Secretary to the Treasury, sat for Harwich from 1774 till his death in 1802, with G. A. North, the eldest son of Lord North, for colleague 1778–84 ; etc. The Crewe Act of 1782 for a moment seemed to endanger the Treasury influence — Robinson, in his notes of December 1783, wrote against Harwich : 'By the disfranchisement of the revenue officers rendered hazardous, but probably Mr. R[obinson] and another friend of government may be elected'.[1] His expectations were fulfilled, and soon, by roundabout ways, things returned to their normal condition. Even attempts by managers to pack the borough with their own dependants, or allegations that they did, continued. Thus on 28 May 1796, J. E. Urquhart (a son-in-law of Samuel Cockerell, captain of a packet boat at Harwich [2]) wrote to William Pitt : [3]

My connection by marriage and a residence in Harwich for some time, gave me an opportunity of knowing the electors of the borough of Harwich, and finding Mr. Robinson was taking every means he could to bring in his own relations and connections as electors in that borough, I had the honour of transmitting in 1792 a state of the interest in the borough of Harwich as it then stood to the Right Honble Mr. Secretary Dundas for the information of administration.

Urquhart was offering himself 'as a candidate for the borough in the event of Mr. Robinson's declining or a vacancy happening by his death'.

'It would be a great saving to the country', wrote Oldfield in 1820, in connexion with Harwich, 'if the clerks of the Treasury were authorised to perform the ceremonies necessary

---

poration at Lady Day, £100'. Moreover, in the expenditure on the general election of 1780, £350 was booked against Harwich (£100 under 6 Sept and £250 under 26 Oct 1779) ; see W. T. Laprade, *Parliamentary Papers of John Robinson*, pp. 57-8.

[1] W. T. Laprade, *op. cit.* p. 73.
[2] See Table B, facing p. 379.
[3] P.R.O., Chatham MSS., 185.

at these elections, instead of pensioning so many corporations, at such a distance from London, to act the farce of choosing members of parliament.'[1]   Inherited historic forms are seldom cheap or simple, but either have some valid justification or are doomed — as the Corporation of Harwich was in 1820, though not in 1760.

ORFORD

Orford was a Corporation borough on which the Crown managed to gain a hold perhaps more complete than it had on any other place, only to make a present of it, in 1766, to a nobleman who, for the preceding ten or twelve years, had unsuccessfully urged a claim to it — a measure so extraordinary as to evoke amazement and criticism at the time.   Incidentally the case of Orford helps to disprove the anyhow untenable story that George II took no interest in boroughs and elections, and shows George III, in the early years of his reign, less intent on them than his grandfather.

Of Orford, as of so many other boroughs, Oldfield gives an excessively simplified account, and he omits what is perhaps the most interesting chapter in its history.   Having stated that it had been bought by the Earl of Hertford from the executors of Price Devereux, Viscount Hereford, he thus describes its constitution :

> The right of election in this nominal borough is vested in the corporation, consisting of a mayor, who is the returning officer, recorder, eight portmen, and twelve capital burgesses ; but this number, we understand, is never complete, and mostly composed of non-residents, who are the brothers and relations of the proprietor.   The constituent and representative body being generally made up of this nobleman's family, the usual mode of canvassing is dispensed with. . . .[2]

Lord Hertford himself, in a letter to Newcastle, on 1 August 1758, claimed that he had bought 'the late Lord Hereford's estate' with a view to the borough ; that he was encouraged therein by Henry Pelham and Newcastle, and paid a price

---

[1] *Key to the House of Commons*, p. 146.
[2] *Ibid.* (1820), p. 158.

which would otherwise have been excessive ; that at that time he asked Pelham for his brother to have 'the preference given him of being returned for Orford' ; but Mr. Pelham's 'answer to me was that he was for the present so farr engaged to Mr. Offley [that] he could not, but desired me not to be discouraged from thence, for that he would use his endeavors to throw the borough into my hands'.[1]

As votes at Orford were not attached to particular holdings or houses, the influence which the estate gave its owner in the borough was probably due to some voters being his tenants, and others local tradesmen, labourers, etc., on whom he could exert pressure, both directly and through his tenants.[2] Possibly with a view to countering this territorial influence, the Treasury started packing the Corporation with outsiders, which could not have been pleasing to the Orford citizens, and which had to be accompanied by at least a formal denization of these strangers — members of the Corporation had apparently to be ratepayers, and therefore householders, in the borough.

Here, as at Harwich, Roberts acted as manager for the Pelhams. On 18 September 1757, having received Newcastle's directions concerning the choice of an outsider as a capital burgess, he remarked :

We want upon this occasion a person, who will be ready upon all our elections, either of Mayors or Members of Parliament to go down upon a short warning, and transact such business, not only to the satisfaction of the gentlemen concerned but also of the inhabitants of the place, who are not managed without a great deal of attention and difficulty.[3]

On another vacancy, in July 1758, he pressed Newcastle for an immediate decision whom to nominate, as otherwise 'we

---

[1] 32882, ff. 190-1. Hertford bought the Orford estate in 1753 (see W. A. Copinger, *The Manors of Suffolk*, vol. v, p. 150), and the election mentioned above is that of 1754, when Offley was first put up for the borough.

[2] A letter from Hertford to George III, 31 Aug 1778 (Fortescue, vol. iv, pp. 190-2), gives an account of Orford and of his own position with regard to it : 'the town of Orford is so near and so much connected with me in all respects that it is in a manner my own house'. 'The town, small as it is, is composed of houses belonging to very poor laborers, or to the burgesses of the place who occasionally reside in them and they belong almost entirely to me.'   [3] 32874, ff. 134-5.

shall be reduced to the necessity of chusing a townsman, the number of which it would be better not to encrease'.[1] As for Hertford's claim to the borough, Roberts, a typical official, naturally disliked the idea of power passing out of Government hands (unless into his own), and explained that such a transfer would hardly work as Hertford imagined :

As to the borough in general, I can scarce think Lord Hertford knows the complex state of it : if he did, he would see many difficulties and discouragements in his way at present ; besides no inconsiderable annual expence (which probably his Lordship has not been acquainted with) independent of the great trouble and charge, which many gentlemen undergo for the sake of the Government chearfully, but which they might not chuse to continue for the service of a particular person.

Hertford, with equally tender concern for other people's convenience, argued that Pelham had obviously thought such a transfer advantageous to the Government — 'if he had not thought it agreable to the interest of the Crown he would not in any shape have thought of recommending it to the King'. His view presumably arose 'from the expence it annually puts the Crown to and the greater it might have been attended with if this estate had fallen into the hands of an enemy'. Hertford concluded : 'if upon a view of the borough you shall think it right to interest yourself in it and to obtain an influence for me at Orford, I shall esteem the obligation great'.[2]

Newcastle replied on 11 August 1758 :

I had obey'd your Lordship's orders in speaking to the King before I receiv'd your letter. I laid before His Majesty the state of the borough of Orford, and your Lordship's request relating to it. The King . . . made no sort of objection to your Lordship's having it, if anybody had it but himself ; but His Majesty said, as I told your Lordship I was apprehensive he would, that he could not part with *his boroughs* to anybody.

None the less, the rumour of an intended transfer to Hertford did not die down, and when on a vacancy, in December

---

[1] 17 July 1758 ; 32881, ff. 369-70. This seems to indicate that, at that time at least, capital burgesses had to be elected whenever a vacancy occurred, and the Corporation could not be left incomplete, as Oldfield understood it to have been about 1820.   [2] 1 Aug 1758 ; 32882, ff. 190-1.

1759, Newcastle had Colonel Fitzroy, a brother of the third Duke of Grafton and nephew of Lady Hertford, returned for the borough, Roberts wrote to him on 24 December :

> I ought not to conceal from your Grace, that an opinion prevailed universally in the town, that a compromise had been made between your Grace and the Earl of Hertford for the borough in future ; which, if it is not to be removed, by contrary assurances, will, in a short time, put the greatest part of the Government interest there into his Lordship's hands.[1]

The nature of some at least of these necessary assurances can be gathered from a letter which Roberts had addressed to Newcastle on 7 December :

> Since your Grace is pleased to assure me of your kind intentions of bringing me in to Parliament, may I entreat you to apprize Colonel Fitzroy now, that, if you do not place me elsewhere, you have destined me for a seat at Orford at the general election ?[2]

Indeed, Roberts's nomination for the borough would have been an expression of Government predominance in it.

Orford remained a Treasury borough under Roberts's management, with its expenses paid out of the secret service funds, but paid irregularly, as was the habit. Its annual allowance consisted of £100 for 'expences' and £200 for the rent of houses. By the time of George II's death, one year's expenses and five quarters of rent were unpaid.[3] This was awkward, as the general election was approaching and George III refused to allow any expenditure from secret service funds. Roberts was receiving sharp reminders from Orford and transmitting them to Newcastle. Thus on 11 January 1761 :

> . . . the landlord of the houses at Orford [John Whittingham] grows very obstreperous for his rent. There is one year and a half's rent due last Christmas, amounting to three hundred pounds ; and

---

[1] 32900, f. 290.   [2] 32899, f. 366.
[3] In the secret service accounts, Mar 1754–Nov 1756, £800 was booked against Orford ; in those covering the disbursements from July 1757 till the death of George II on 25 Oct 1760, £900, the arrears at the latter date amounting to £350 (see 33040, ff. 15-16). It seems to have been pretty well customary to be behindhand with payments : the rent for the Orford houses due at Midsummer 1754 was paid on 24 Apr 1755, the rent due at Midsummer 1759 on 27 Mar 1760, etc.

one hundred pounds besides, which latter sum His late Majesty constantly allowed, under Mr. Pelham's and your Grace's approbation, for the accidental yearly expences in that borough; for the payment of both which sums. . . . His late Majesty was pleased to engage himself to me, when I had the honour to receive his commands in his closet.

If this money is not sent, 'I cannot pretend to appear at Orford at the general election; and for want of it I am daily pestered with impertinent and abusive letters'.[1]

And again, on 13 January 1761:

Having received this day another letter from Orford concerning the rents due for the houses there, I take the liberty to lay them before your Grace for your perusal. I have tried all means in my power to pacify the landlord, without telling him (what I imagine was improper to trust him with) that the death of the King was the cause of the delay of the payment. I must now receive your Grace's directions, what answer to give him to his last importunity. Is there any objection to the laying my letter to your Grace of yesterday before the King?[2]

When in February 1761 Roberts was asked by Newcastle for a 'state of the boroughs of Orford and Harwich', he informed the Duke that Orford was more particularly under the direction of the Treasury:

. . . the Crown has been at a considerable expence; and care has been taken by the manager to make most of the constituents such, as were likely to be under the influence of the First Lord of the Treasury; tho' it costs always much trouble to keep them zealous and united.[3]

And at the end of the month, when asked for a 'more particular' report on the two boroughs, he thus described Orford:

At Orford, the First Lord of the Treasury pays two hundred pounds yearly, for a lease of some houses there; and one hundred pounds besides for the disbursements of the repairs, taxes, and the expences of the Mayor's Feast.

The majority of this Corporation are gentlemen residing chiefly in, or near London, most of whom have some employment under

---

[1] 32917, ff. 244-5.   [2] *Ibid.* f. 298.
[3] 5 Feb 1761; 32918, f. 281.

the Government. All these, in their turns, as many of them as are necessary, go to Orford, which is a journey of near an hundred miles, at their own expence, every Michaelmas, to elect their Mayor ; and upon other occasions accidentally when required.

Notwithstanding the sum which is thus furnished, the person who has had the management of this Corporation for many years past,[1] has expended between three and four hundred pounds out of his pocket in the course of seven years, which sum is more than the two Members usually incur for their election ; and, if he had not continued to direct it, the borough had not now been under the influence of the Treasury ; but as it is constituted at this point of time, the recommendation of the First Lord of that Board for the Members, and of him only, will be prevailing.[2]

The candidates now put up for Orford were John Offley, who had sat for it since 1754 and was a particular friend of the Pelhams, and Thomas Worsley of Hovingham, an old friend of Bute and George III ; and as soon as the secret service funds were made available once more, the arrears of Orford were paid on 14 April 1761.

When in February 1763 Roberts surrendered Harwich and Orford to Bute, in the correspondence which ensued between him and Newcastle,[3] he thus excused his action with regard to Orford :

The gentlemen of Orford will, no doubt, behave like most other gentlemen nowadays ; there is not one of them for whom I ever could obtain a favour from your Grace except Mr. Powell ; they will bow before the new First Lord of the Treasury, rather than part with their employments ; and this being the case in my little concerns, as well as in the great ones respecting your Grace, it was in vain for me to think of retaining an interest, where few, except my cousin Hughson, would have sacrificed themselves, to stand by me.[4]

A full list of 'the gentlemen of Orford', with their employments noted against their names, is preserved in the papers of Charles Jenkinson, who under Bute and Grenville managed the Treasury boroughs. The list is marked 'The Corporation of Orford, September 19th, 1764' : [5]

[1] Obviously himself. [2] 32919, ff. 322-3.
[3] For this correspondence see above, pp. 377-8.
[4] 7 Feb 1763 ; 32946, ff. 349-50. [5] 38477, f. 37.

PORTMEN.

1. Samuel Tufnell ✓ 1   .   Not able to attend.
2. Abraham Farley   .   .   A Deputy-Chamberlain in the Exchequer.
3. Richard Hammond   .   A clerk in the Pell Office and a man of fortune.
4. Richard Morley   .   .   Keeper of the Records at Westminster.
5. John Roberts. ✓
6. Charles Desborough   .   A Deputy-Auditor of Land Revenue.
7. George Mingay   .   .   Resident at Orford and a place in the Customs there.
8. Thomas Brady   .   .   Do.
9. Milward Rowe   .   .   Treasury.

CAPITAL BURGESSES.

1. Sir Joseph Ayliffe Holding, Bart.2   .   .   .   A Keeper of Records.
2. John Kirby   .   .   .   Collector of Customs at Colchester.
3. Thos. Brady   .   .   .   Resident at Orford and a place in the Customs there.
4. Wm. Bird   .   .   .   Do.
5. Saml. Randall   .   .   Do.
6. Edward Ellis   .   .   .   A place under the Lessee of the Light Houses at Orford.
7. John Hughson ✓   .   .   Mr. Roberts's nephew 3 and a clerk under Lord Lincoln in the Auditors Office.
8. James Powell   .   .   A clerk in the Custom House, London.
9. Robert Laughton. ✓
10. John Shackleton   .   .   Limner to His Majesty.
11. Edmund Barham   .   .   Agent for the Packets at Dover.
12. Charles Lloyd   .   .   Treasury.

Thus of the twenty-one members of the Corporation, six only were resident at Orford, all of them in employment under

---

1 This mark probably denotes supposed adherents of the Duke of Newcastle.

2 Obviously Sir Joseph Ayliffe, sixth Bt.; b. 1709, d. 1781; educ. Westminster School and Lincoln's Inn, F.S.A., F.R.S.; a prominent member of the Spalding Society; appointed, 1763, 'one of the three Keepers of the State Paper Office'.   3 Should be 'cousin'.

the Government; and the list as a whole can hardly be said to bear even a distant resemblance to what one usually understands by a Parliamentary electorate. Even in the eighteenth century Orford was almost unique, and there was no reason why the Treasury should not have continued working it as a contrivance for returning 'official Members' to the House of Commons so long as this remained unreformed. None the less, Hertford did not give up hope. Under George Grenville, a Prime Minister with the mind and instincts of a permanent official, he obviously had no chance, but things assumed a more favourable aspect when in 1765 the Rockingham Administration was formed with Hertford's brother, General H. S. Conway, as Secretary of State for the Southern Department. Hertford now approached Newcastle once more on the matter, and the correspondence which ensued between them fully explains the situation and what passed upon it.

Hertford to Newcastle.[1] *London. 29 September 1765.*

As your Grace has been so good to assure me of your good offices in the affair of Orford which I have so much at heart, you will give me leave to acquaint you that the King before he decides upon the fate of it, has ordered Lord Rockingham to bring him an account of the present state and circumstances of the borough :

This account will of course be drawn at the Treasury and probably determine whether I shall at present succeed or not ;

The King is well disposed, but if it is unfavourably represented I must take it for granted he will still decide against my wishes ; I am farr from desiring His Majesty to be deceived in order to serve me. I wish him to know the true state of it, but as there are two ways of representing even truth itself it is natural I should desire the most favorable method to be pursued in this case, and that all the expences and inconveniences which do at present or may in a future day affect the borough be fully stated.

Mr. Roberts or more probably Mr. Mellish,[2] will be emploied in drawing this case. Let me therefore beg your Grace to lose no time in informing these two gentlemen that you are pleased to interest

---

[1] 32970, ff. 97-8.

[2] William Mellish (1711–91), M.P. for East Retford 1741–51, Commissioner of the Excise (£1000 p.a.) 1751–60, Receiver-General of the Customs (£1500 p.a.) 1760–Jan 1763, when he was removed in the pro-

yourself for me ; Mr. Rowe [1] has likewise been often emploied there, he owes his future to your Grace's family, and therefore by notice from you may not be so much disposed to prejudice me on this occasion as he seems to have been very lately at Orford in conjunction with Mr. Loyd.[2]

I shall feel sincerely obliged by any services you shall think proper to do me upon this occasion as I cannot I will confess freely, give up my views upon this borough after all that has passed about it.

The present time seems favorable to my wishes but if I should not succeed I must comfort myself in his Majesty's favorable disposition towards me, and wait with patience for a more favorable minute.

Newcastle to Hertford.[3] *Newcastle House.* 30 *September* 1765.

I have sent to Mr. Roberts to come to me ; he is a difficult gentleman ; and I can't pretend to say, what he will do. Mr. Mellish will be absolutely governed by My Ld. Rockingham ; but I will speak to him, when I see him. I will also send to Mr. Rowe, with whom I fancy, I have some credit. . . .

Hertford to Newcastle.[4] *Pall Mall.* 2 *October* 1765.

By a letter I have received from Orford since I had the honor of seeing your Grace this morning, I find the foreign portmen and burgesses have been acting very unwarrantably at their last meeting there : Mr. Loyd whom I mentioned to your Grace this day as a person who had himself particular views on the borough, seems to have been the cheif actor in it, supported by Mr. Rowe.

I have the honor of giving your Grace this account to prove the difficulties to which the present sistem will be exposed if every step was disputed with them, and to furnish you with another argument in my favor if you are so good to use your endeavors with Lord Rockingham to remove the scruples he has adopted.

---

scription of Newcastle's friends ; Joint Secretary to the Treasury under Rockingham in July 1765 ; and again Receiver-General of the Customs 1765–86, when he resigned. About him see *Gentleman's Magazine*, 1791, vol. ii, p. 1166.

[1] Milward Rowe (1716–92), chief clerk of the Treasury ; an Orford portman — see above, p. 395.

[2] Charles Lloyd, late private secretary to George Grenville ; about him see above, pp. 384-5 and 395.

[3] 32970, f. 116.
                                    [4] *Ibid.* f. 141.

Perhaps Mr. Roberts or Mr. Mellish from his ideas may have contributed to place them there.

. . . . .

Newcastle to Hertford.[1] *Newcastle House.* 3 *October* 1765.

I have had my friend Mr. Rowe with me this morning. He has explained the whole matter to me. I find, they proceed upon Mr. Grenville's plan; Mr. Rowe has receiv'd no orders from my Lord Rockingham; but he was sent down to Orford by Mr. Roberts, who, Rowe says, has again the management of Orford in his hands, from which he was removed by the late Treasury.

Mr. Roberts was still so ill, that he sent me word, he could not come to me, this morning. But, my dear Lord, it all depends upon the Treasury. I will talk it over fully to my Lord Rockingham : but your Lordship and *your brother* will have more weight with his Lordship, than I shall have.

I will explain the great difference of the case from what it was the last reign, and is at present. The late King absolutely refused it; this King is willing to do it. I shall give my Lord Rockingham some private reasons, which are not fit to be put in writing.[2]

I will continue to see Roberts, as soon as possibly I can ; but he is not the man to do the business. We must go higher.

. . . . .

Hertford to Newcastle.[3] *Pall Mall.* 3 *October* 1765.

I return your Grace my sincerest thanks for your very obliging letter :

As I am going so soon to Ireland,[4] I shall not be upon the spot to sollicit the continuance of your good offices, but I shall beg the exertion of them with Lord Rockingham, where they may be very material for my service : my brother shall be instructed to talk with your Grace upon it if you will allow him to take that liberty, and I shall beg the matter may be laid before the King and its fate decided one way or other by the opinion of the present Ministry as soon as possible.

. . . . .

The following letter explains how Hertford conceived the 'transfer' of the borough — some of the officials in the Corpora-

---

[1] 32970, f. 153.

[2] Was it perhaps that from their point of view it was better to have boroughs placed in the hands of well-affected Whig aristocrats than in those of the Treasury which might again pass to their opponents ?

[3] 32970, f. 163.

[4] *I.e.* as Lord Lieutenant.

tion were to resign and their places were to be filled by nominees of his own :

Hertford to Newcastle.[1] *London. 7 October* 1765.

. . . if His Majesty should give his free and unreserved consent to transfer his interests at Orford with the expences of the borough over to me I must then beg your Grace's influence with some of the portmen and burgesses, to make it secure to me by putting into their place some of my own freinds : your Grace knows that many of those persons have undertaken it because they were ordered by the Crown so to do without any inclination for the place and it is only attended with trouble to them : some measures of this sort may be more necessary as Mr. Loyd whom I mentioned before to your Grace seems now to have taken the mask entirely off, and to set up for a personal interest in the borough ; Mr. Row is supposed to be connected with him but perhaps without foundation : Mr. Loyd has built a fine house and assembly room at Orford and without the least pretence except his being brought into the Corporation by Mr. Grenville is gone down there when there is no business to do except to prosecute his own views upon the borough and has declared his intention as I am informed of residing there six weeks. . . .

Hertford's hopes were to be disappointed once more, as is shown by the following letter :

Hertford to Newcastle.[2] *Dublin Castle. 20 November* 1765.

. . . Lord Rockingham has not behaved kindly to me about Orford, and I will confess I am much hurt ; it is the object of my wishes, your Grace knows my pretensions to it, I do not ask it against the King's inclination, and I have some hopes that my undertaking a very troublesome office to serve the present Ministry might have been an argument in my favor.

· · · · ·

Same to same. Woodford. 4 January 1766.

I am very grateful to your Grace for mentioning Orford, and whatever reason I may have to complain of Lord Rockingham's very unfriendly behaviour towards me, I am pretty sensible of your good wishes. . . .[3]

In July 1766, Rockingham resigned and the Chatham Administration was formed with H. S. Conway at his old post ;

---

[1] 32970, ff. 222-3.   [2] 32972, f. 3.   [3] 32973, ff. 43-4.

2 D

and now at last Hertford carried his point. It was conceded to him as part of the compensation for the Lord Lieutenancy of Ireland in which he was replaced by Lord Bristol. On 15 September 1766, George Selwyn wrote to Lord Holland :

> Ld Hert^d will return two Members for Orford ; he has been soliciting that affair these 15 years, I hear, but it was not to interfere with any other pretensions of his Lordship's.[1]

Indeed, it did not. Alexander Wedderburn reported to George Grenville on 25 September 1766 :

> I have heard no other news except that Lord Beauchamp has got the place of Constable of Dublin Castle, with an additional salary of 1000*l.* to the old 500*l.*, and for life : this with Orford, and the Mastership of the Horse, is a very reasonable compensation, methinks, for a troublesome office.[2]

The same day, Richard Rigby, having enumerated Hertford's acquisitions, concluded :

> . . . in short, what with sons and daughters, and boroughs and employments of all kinds, I never heard of such a trading voyage as his Lordship's has proved.[3]

Equally incomprehensible was the matter to Newcastle, who wrote to Rockingham on 17 September 1766 :

> The whole transaction with my Lord Bristol and my Lord Hertford, I don't understand. It is said that the King makes over to Lord Hertford all His Majesty's interest and property in the borough of Orford for three lives or thirty-one years.[4]

And the Duke of Portland wrote to Newcastle on 1 October :

> . . . the chief object of conversation, general astonishment and as general censure is the giving the borough of Orford to Lord Hertford for 30 years.[5]

No one was misled by the apparent limitation put on the grant of the borough. Mrs. Sarah Osborn, a woman of con-

---

[1] Ilchester, *Letters to Henry Fox*, p. 271 ; where Orford is misspelt into Oxford.
[2] *Grenville Papers*, vol. iii, p. 325. Lord Beauchamp was the eldest son of Lord Hertford.
[3] *Bedford Correspondence* vol. iii, pp. 345-6.
[4] 32977, ff. 94-5.   [5] *Ibid.* f. 186.

siderable political experience and much worldly wisdom, wrote
to her grandson, John Osborn, on 7 October 1766 : [1]

> The borough of Orford [2] is given to Lord Hertford for his
> services in London. This is an unprecedented note above a pention,
> for it is for ever.

And indeed Orford now remained a Hertford pocket borough so long as it retained its representation at Westminster.
In Robinson's list of December 1783 the following entry
appears against it : [3]

> Lord Hertford's borough ; will not be altered probably,[4] but yet
> only classed doubtful, as the family like to support.

The representatives of Orford from 1768 till 1832 were
all either members or friends of the Hertford family ; Lord
Beauchamp represented it from 1768 till 1794, when he succeeded to the peerage as second Marquis of Hertford ; Robert
Seymour Conway, 1771–84 and 1794–1807 ; George Seymour
Conway, 1780–90 ; William Seymour Conway, 1790–94 ; and
Horace Seymour was returned for it in 1820 and 1826, but
elected to serve for other boroughs, Orford being merely used
for purposes of hedging.

[1] *Political and Social Letters of a Lady of the Eighteenth Century*, ed.
Emily F. D. Osborn (1890), p. 153.
[2] Again misprinted into Oxford.
[3] See W. T. Laprade, *Parliamentary Papers of John Robinson*, p. 91.
[4] *I.e.* its representatives, Viscount Beauchamp and Robert Seymour
Conway, who had supported the Coalition Government, will be returned
once more.

VIII

PARLIAMENTARY BEGGARS

JOHN JEFFREYS

SIR JEFFREY JEFFREYS of the Priory, Brecon, and St. Mary
Axe, London, M.P. for Brecknock 1690–95 and 1701–9, was
a merchant 'of great fortune, rank and quality'.[1] His brother,
John Jeffreys, M.P. for Brecknockshire 1702–5, also a London
merchant, married a daughter of Sir Anthony Sturt, M.P., and
John Jeffreys, the subject of this essay, was their son. He was
a well-known 'club-man' and a member of fashionable London
society, described by Horace Walpole as a product of 'the
Opera-House and White's'.[2] He soon ran through most of
his patrimony, and in 1749 had to sell some of his Welsh
estates. After unsuccessfully contesting Brecknockshire in
1727, he sat for it 1734–47, and for Dartmouth from 1747 till
his death in January 1766. His official career, which he seems
to have started under the auspices of Lord Bath,[3] and continued
under those of Lord Lincoln, a nephew and son-in-law of
Henry Pelham, resembled that of Lord Lundy in Belloc's
Cautionary Tales (who after a brilliant start was dropped from
office to office, and finished as Curator of Big Ben). In December
1742 John Jeffreys was appointed Joint Secretary to the
Treasury, and removed from it in May 1746; in May 1752
he was made Secretary to the Chancellor of the Exchequer
and removed in April 1754; and he finished as Warden of the
Mint and Deputy-Ranger of St. James's and Hyde Parks.

On 26 October 1757, he wrote to Newcastle:

---

[1] About him see W. R. Williams, *The Parliamentary History of Wales*
(1895), pp. 18-19; also about John Jeffreys, sen., and John Jeffreys, jun.
(p. 19).

[2] To Horace Mann, 26 Dec 1743.

[3] See Ode to Lord Bath, by Charles Hanbury-Williams, *Works* (1822),
vol. i, p. 196; also 'Letter to Mr. Dodsley', *ibid.* vol. ii, p. 107; both
written in 1743.

My Lord,

Your Grace, I hope, will forgive my taking the liberty of troubling you with this letter which is occasion'd by my not being able to acquaint your Grace with my unfortunate circumstances by word of mouth so well as by letter.

Upon the death of Mr. Pelham, your Grace was so good as to assure me I should remain in the same situation [at the Exchequer], till something should happen to provide for me in a more certain manner.—Mr. Legge would not retain me as his secretary; I was displaced; but soon after, on the death of Mr. Herbert,[1] your Grace was pleased to appoint me Warden of the Mint, an employment the income of which at present don't produce near so much as the former, and cost me above £200 for the Patent and re-election [9 December 1754], besides paying for the first election the same year £400. . . .

Upon Mr. Schutz's[2] death, Lord Lincoln told me, that your Grace was very desirous I should succeed him at Richmond Gardens, for which I am greatly obliged, but that could not be obtain'd.

Merit I don't pretend to, all I plead is pity and compassion, which shine in the highest light among your Grace's other great qualities.—Though I have committed many folly's with regard to my private fortune, I flatter myself I cannot be accused of any misconduct to my patrons, acquaintance, or the publick: if I have, I am not conscious of it.

Had I been so happy as to have succeeded as Customer of Milford Haven, I should have had £300 per ann. certain to have supported me in my old age.—Indeed I don't mean to complain, but must beg leave to assure your Grace upon the word of an honest man, that no one is more faithfully attach'd to your person and family, nor any one whose poverty stands more in need of your Grace's kind assistance and protection.

My utmost wish is some provision for life, it would be impertinent in me to chalk out any method to your Grace, but should any unfortunate accident happen to your Grace's life, your poor, unhappy, humble servant must either beg or starve; my good and gracious Lord, remove me from this very disagreeable situation.[3]

Newcastle thereupon tried to quarter Jeffreys on James West, M.P., Secretary to the Treasury, an honest and hardworking civil servant.   But West rightly protested, and even threatened to resign:

[1] Richard Herbert, M.P. for Ludlow, brother of Lord Powis, died 16 May 1754.
[2] Augustus Schutz died 26 May 1757.   [3] 32875, ff. 275-6.

I hope it is not arrogant to say, that in my poor opinion, whoever brings himself into Parliament and honestly discharges the duty of the office, amply deserves the lawful fees of it. . . .

Your Grace asks, Is Mr. Jeffreys to starve? God forbid! I love him, have frequently sollicited for and done him services. May I humbly ask, am I to work for him?[1]

Newcastle thought next of a pension for Jeffreys — witness entries in the Memoranda for the King; on 10 October 1758: 'Mr. Jeffreys — £500';[2] and on 17 December: 'Mr. Jeffreys — starving';[3] but although on 19 December he was given £500 from the secret service funds,[4] nothing seems to have been done to render his position secure, and Jeffreys continued to beg for 'some additional certainty for life'. 'I shou'd then be enabled to pass the remainder of my days with my much honor'd friends in ease and quiet.'[5] And again on 3 December 1760:

Your Grace will, I hope, permit me to mention my very distress'd circumstances, and how uneasy and precarious my present situation is; therefore hope your Grace will be so good as to compassionate my case: what I now receive from your Grace's favor, may, I hope, be settled in some certain manner. . . .[6]

In the same letter of 3 December 1760 Jeffreys wrote about his candidature at Dartmouth, at the impending general election. Mr. Holdsworth, Governor of Dartmouth Castle, he informed Newcastle, 'has the entire interest in the borough', and will choose him to the next Parliament — 'provided he receives a letter in my favour from your Grace'. Holdsworth was written to,[7] and replied on 24 March 1761:

I had the honour to receive your Grace's recommendation of Lord Howe and Mr. Jeffreys and have the pleasure to assure your Grace that all my friends are unanimous in their behalf.[8]

In the new reign, when payments of secret service money were resumed, Jeffreys received a regular pension of £500 a

---

[1] To Newcastle, 17 Jan 1758; 32877, ff. 168-9.
[2] 32884, f. 308.   [3] 32886, f. 356.
[4] See below, p. 457.
[5] John Jeffreys to the Duke of Newcastle, 12 July 1760; 32908, f. 225. See also his previous letter of 21 Aug 1759; 32894, f. 360.
[6] 32915, f. 286.
[7] Newcastle to Arthur Holdsworth, 6 Mar 1761; 32919, f. 491.
[8] 32921, f. 43.

year.[1] On 29 May 1762, three days after Newcastle was forced to resign office, John Jeffreys wrote to his successor, Lord Bute:

My Lord,

I saw the Duke of Bedford this evening, who was so good as to tell me, that his Grace has represented my situation in a kind and compassionate manner to your Lordship: any day and hour that will be most agreeable to your Lordship, I will do myself the honour of attending your Lordship.[2]

Naturally, then, in the lists which, on 13 November 1762, Newcastle drew up of the House of Commons, he had to class his 'poor, unhappy, humble servant' Jeffreys among his opponents.[3] The same story is told by Bute's list of 1761. First the word 'Newcastle' was written against the name of Jeffreys; this was subsequently crossed through, and 'Government' substituted for it.[4]

Newcastle's resignation had not immediately produced an open break between him and the Court; that came after he had gone into opposition to the Preliminaries of the Peace of Paris. When consequently, in December 1762, a proscription was started of his friends and dependants, some of them, who might have been spared, felt in honour bound to resign. George III, in a letter to Bute, having mentioned a few of the resignations, added: '. . . little Jeffries, I found from Lord Egremont, was to be ordered by the D[uke] of N[ewcastle] to retire, he must then starve, being these many years a bankrupt; thus two or three base, designing men, to distress Government, ruin their dependents'.[5] Still, Jeffreys did not retire and Newcastle did not take it amiss — for what could one expect from a pauper? He voted with his masters and kept in with his friends.[6]

---

[1] See accounts, 22 Apr and 29 Oct 1761, and 27 Apr 1762.
[2] 5726, D. f. 169.   [3] 33000, f. 153.
[4] 38333, f. 80.   [5] Sedgwick, no. 228.
[6] Jeffreys continued to be received at Claremont — Lord Ashburnham wrote to Newcastle on 2 Aug 1763: 'I have had the satisfaction to hear by Mr. Jeffrys . . . that he left you and the Duchess of Newcastle yesterday iu perfect health . . .' (32950, f. 27). And when Newcastle, on 29 Aug 1763, anticipating a return to office, drew up a list of those 'to be considered', Jeffreys was in it (*ibid.* f. 278).

When on 10 July 1765 the Rockingham Administration was formed, with Newcastle for Lord Privy Seal, John Jeffreys wrote to him, from Bath, in a hand grown shaky with age and illness :

My Lord,

Give me leave to congratulate your Grace, and the publick, on this most agreeable and happy change in the Administration.

Permit me, my Lord, to beg the favor of your Grace to recommend me to Lord Rockingham's protection. I now receive 1,100*l.* per ann., in your Grace's Administration it was 200*l.* more.

I shou'd have done myself the honor of waiting on your Grace immediately, but my medical director insists on my staying at least a fortnight longer : — indeed, I was in a very dangerous state of health when I first came to this place, but have received so great and constant a benefit from drinking these waters, that I hope your Grace will excuse my not paying my respects in person so soon as I could wish.[1]

He did not live to congratulate yet another Government (and the publick) on a further 'agreeable and happy change'; for he died in January 1766.

Thomas Medlycott

The first of the family to enter Parliament was Thomas Medlycott, a distinguished barrister who sat for Abingdon, 1689–90. His eldest son, James, represented Milborne Port from 1710 till 1722 ; another, Thomas, 1727–34 (member also of the Irish Parliament from 1727 till his death in 1760, and Chief Commissioner of Revenue in Ireland). He is occasionally confused with the subject of this essay, Thomas, son of James Medlycott, born in 1697, who succeeded his uncle Thomas at Milborne Port, and with a break of five years, 1742–47, sat for it from 1734 till his death in 1763. There is no record of his having spoken in Parliament, and his name is hardly ever mentioned in contemporary political correspondence. When Newcastle became First Lord of the Treasury in March 1754, Medlycott was in receipt of a secret service pension of £600 a year, which he still enjoyed when Newcastle resigned in May

[1] 13 July 1765 ; 32967, f. 385.

1762. He tried to obtain some office, and the only place he is known to have held was curiously appropriate — in 1742 he was appointed Commissioner of Hawkers and Pedlars. To none of his letters in the Newcastle Papers is there a reply ; in fact, no one of those here classed as 'Parliamentary beggars' seems ever to have been honoured with a written answer from the Duke. Still, wretched as he seems in his appeals to Newcastle, there is reason to believe that he remained faithful to the Duke after his removal from office ; or at least he preserved appearances, which many others dispensed with. His letters to Newcastle can be left to tell the story.

31 December 1755.

Your Grace knows my present situation well, which if it could be settled upon the Irish Establishment [1] would fix me yours for ever. If you have any mistrust, I will quitt my seat in Parliament now to any friend of yours or when your Grace shall think proper to call upon me so to do, for all I mean upon my honor is to free my self from any influence but yours in whose cause I am embarked and will at all events continue so to my dying day.[2]

On 9 June 1756 he thus leads up to a request to be received by the Duke : 'As I have been very little troublesome to you this year. . . .'[3] And he writes again on 11 December 1756 : 'For tho I see great things done for many people I will not even ask what you have done for your Grace's real friend and obedient servant. . . .'[4] And during the Cabinet crisis in the spring of 1757 :

Give me leave, my Lord Duke, to assure you that interest had no part in my consideration when I offerd my service to you at the beginning of this sessions, nor is it any motive towards my persevering in it but I hope it will be no offence to tell your Grace that I am in my body politick what the cripple at the pool of Bethesday was in his body naturall, when the waters are troubled I have no body to putt me. . . .[5]

On 9 May 1758 he asks the Duke

---

[1] *I.e.* he asked that his pension be settled on the Irish Establishment, which would have rendered it more secure.

[2] 32861, f. 512.   [3] 32865, f. 243.   [4] 32869, f. 345.

[5] 3 Apr 1757 ; 32870, f. 360.

to extend your bounty a little further for this year only because I have strained every point to gett rid of an obligation that I was under to my collegue,[1] but am I thank God now independent of him.[2]

20 *January* 1761.

I am just come from Milborn Port where I had an opposition allmost too mighty to withstand. But I used my utmost efforts and have succeeded in order to be of service to you if you should ever want it which I hope will induce you to give me some extraordinary aid this year. I shall be very moderate in my desires which if you comply with cannot make me more your friend but will enable me to resist all opposition that may happen at the next election. In short, I shall be miserable without your assistance but happy with it.[3]

As no money was issued from the Treasury for the general election of 1761, it is to be feared that Medlycott remained 'miserable'.

25 *February* 1761.

I don't know that I have been admitted to a few minutes conversation with you in your dressing room these severall years, the reason of which I cannott tell except it is that I am waining in your favour; if so, I am sorry for it, but my heart is as warm towards you as ever. I wanted yesterday to tell you something that nearly concerns you. If you know it allready, my good will is not the less, if you dont know it, 'tis proper you should. I shall wait on you next Tuesday.[4]

4 *May* 1762.

A favour well bestowed is allmost as great an honor to him who confers it as to him who receives it, for which reason I should be highly obliged to your Grace if you would inable me to take leave of you next Thursday for the summer having been allready six months in town and every day I stay here is prejudiciall to the health as well as to the affairs of etc.

P.S.—I shall not quit the town if anything materiall wants me.[5]

---

[1] Medlycott's colleague at Milborne Port was Edward Walter, son of Paget and grandson of Peter Walter, 'the usurer', depicted as 'Peter Pounce' by Fielding. He sat for Milborne Port 1754–74, when he was returned but unseated. About the family see Hutchins, *History of Dorset*, vol. iii, pp. 671-2 ; and E. C. Waters, 'The Walters of Surrey, temp. George II' in *The Herald and Genealogist*, vol. viii, pp. 1-5.

[2] 32879, f. 467.   [3] 32917, f. 443.   [4] 32919, f. 283.

[5] 32938, f. 57 ; this was a request for an earlier payment of his secret service pension.

12 *May* 1762.

I have now conform'd to your Grace's desire of staying till allmost the end of the session of Parliament and hope therefore that you will oblige me to-morrow. If you condescend I give you my word and honour that I will not go out of town till the Sunday sevenight after, but I have an affair to transact that cant be done but by your Grace's assistance. . . .[1]

An instalment of his secret service pension was due but was not paid to him till 25 May, Newcastle's last day in office, and acknowledged by Medlycott on the 29th :

This waites on you to return you my most humble thanks for this last as well as all former favours. I hope God has given me a gratefull heart and that I shall show upon all occasions how sincerely I am etc.[2]

In the list of the House of Commons of 13 November 1762, Newcastle still classed Medlycott among his friends; but there were so many about whom he was mistaken that this proves little. The last letter Medlycott wrote to Newcastle, though no evidence for the part he took in Parliament, shows at least that he retained some regard for the fallen Minister :

8 *April* 1763.

I did myself the honour to call at your house as soon as I was able to crawle and indeed before I could well gett up your steps to your house. The reason of my waiting on you was to enquire after your Grace's health and to assure you of the fidelity of etc.[3]

Thomas Medlycott died on 24 July 1763.

ROBERT FAIRFAX

The case of Robert Fairfax illustrates the charitable character of the secret service funds and the benevolence of those who administered them. 'Gratuities' were obtained for him by Newcastle because he was 'starving'; his defection to Bute and Grenville was excused — what else could be expected from one so situated? . And his pension was continued by George III after he had left Parliament.

[1] *Ibid.* f. 196.   [2] 32939, f. 97.   [3] 32948, f. 75.

Robert Fairfax was the third son of Thomas, fifth Baron Fairfax, a cousin once removed of the famous Commander-in-Chief of the Parliamentary Army. His mother was the daughter and heiress of Thomas, second Baron Colepeper, Governor of Virginia 1680–82,[1] and, through her, Leeds Castle in Kent, the 'Northern Neck' in Virginia comprising 5,282,000 acres, and Lord Colepeper's debts, came into the Fairfax family. Andrew Burnaby, in the account of the family appended to his *Travels through the Middle Settlements in North America*,[2] relates how Robert Fairfax's eldest brother, Thomas, sixth Lord Fairfax, was

persuaded, upon his brother Henry's arriving at the age of twenty-one years, or rather compelled by the ladies Culpepper and Fairfax under a menace, in case of refusal, of never inheriting the Northern Neck, to cut off the intail and to sell Denton Hall and the Yorkshire estates . . . in order to redeem those of the late Lord Culpepper, that had descended to his heiress, exceedingly encumbered and deeply mortgaged. This circumstance happened while Lord Fairfax was at Oxford. . . . He conceived a violent disgust against the ladies who, as he used to say, had treated him with such unparalleled cruelty; and ever afterwards expressed the keenest sense of the injury that had been done, as he thought, to the Fairfax family.[3]

The story is touching, but hardly credible in all its detail. Thomas, fifth Lord Fairfax, died on 10 January 1709/10, and his mother-in-law, Lady Colepeper,[4] on 10 May of the same year. Thomas, sixth Lord Fairfax, was born in 1692. He matriculated at Oxford in January 1709/10, and his brother Henry in March 1713/14, aged 16; and by 1717, when the estate was sold to the Ibbetsons,[5] Thomas is not likely to have been at Oxford any longer, while Henry, if the entry is correct, was not yet of age.

A man who played a considerable part in the lives of that

---

[1] His appointment was dated 1675, but he did not go out till 1680.

[2] Third edition (1798), Appendix No. 4, pp. 159-72.

[3] *Op. cit.* p. 159.

[4] Burnaby describes her as 'a princess of the House of Hesse-Cassel'; but in reality she was the daughter of Jan van Hesse, Heer van Piershil, in Zealand.

[5] See Indentures in the West Riding Registry of Deeds, County Hall, Wakefield.

generation of Fairfaxes was a first cousin of their father, Bryan Fairfax, from 1723 till his death in 1749 a Commissioner of Customs. He was known to his contemporaries as an antiquary of distinction, an expert collector of coins, medals, marbles, and books, Vice-President of the Society for the Encouragement of Learning.[1] To the young Fairfaxes he was a kind friend and quasi-guardian to whom they turned in their troubles. Mary complained to him when she suffered from an excess of 'imployment' in the house and of 'fategue';[2] Robert had to be consoled and advised by him when a vacant majority in the Life Guards was given to another captain;[3] Lord Fairfax had to be instructed how to supply a qualification for Parliament to Robert when he stood for Maidstone.[4] Among this correspondence is also an undated letter from Bryan Fairfax to Lord Fairfax opposing the sale of Denton. Bryan computed the value of his cousin's estates at £44,000; 'your debts I cannot possibly imagine to be more than £27,000, including my Lady's[5] joynture'.

I dont find [he wrote] that by any way you can make £100 p. ann. more by parting with Denton then by keeping it, which with humble submission I dont think equivalent to more valuable considerations. It is a great disgrace (if possible to be avoided) to have sold one's whole estate, and in the eye of the world I think a lord with his paternall seat and by the name of which he has been allways distinguish'd may make a better figure in England then one with much more money in his pockett, like a merchant, that has not a foot of land and consequently no more interest.[6] And if you think the help of great men may be of use to you, by keeping this estate you may sometime or other expect to find it from your countrymen such as the Dukes of Somersett, Devonshire, Newcastle, the Earl of Burlington, and besides the generality of the gentry who have all

---

[1] About him see *D.N.B.* and Nichols, *Literary Anecdotes*, vol. v, pp. 326-7.

[2] 'I had a letter this week from the Cornet [presumably Robert], who tells me he is mighty well but dont like Coventry. I hope he on't have occasion to stay longer than a month, for I am left in care of so large a family which is full imployment for me, without stiring out of the house, and a fategue I should be glad to be rid off' (Leeds Castle, 5 Oct 1726, *Correspondence of the Family of Fairfax*, vol. ii; 30306, f. 63).

[3] *Ibid.* f. 106. [4] *Ibid.* f. 108.

[5] *I.e.* of his mother, who died on 1 June 1719.

[6] That is, Parliamentary interest through his tenants.

sometime or other, courted the family, and perhaps may have occasion again, which should you part with they respect no more than a Scotch or Irish lord being able to do them no service here. I shall not mention those imaginary arguments of a family, of the place where your ancestors were born and bury'd and which name your successors must go by.[1]

Denton was sold after all, and in 1735 Lord Fairfax went out to Virginia to survey his American inheritance, and was sorely disappointed by 'the irregularity of the books' and the confusion into which his coming over put the family of his manager.[2] In 1740 he was back in England, but a few years later, having made over Leeds Castle to his brother Robert, returned to America for good, to continue there, under radically different conditions, the life of an English country gentleman.

He was Lord Lieutenant and Custos Rotulorum of the county of Frederic, presided at the county courts held at Winchester, where during the sessions he always kept an open table, and acted as surveyor and overseer of the highways and public roads. His chief if not sole amusement was hunting; . . . so unexceptionable and disinterested was his behaviour, both public and private, and so generally was he beloved and respected, that during the contest between Great Britain and America he never met with the least insult or molestation from either party, but was suffered to go on in his improvement and cultivation of the Northern Neck. . . .

His motive in settling in America was of the most noble and heroic kind. It was, as he always himself declared, to settle and cultivate that beautiful and immense tract of country of which he was proprietor; and he succeeded beyond his most sanguine expectations, for the Northern Neck was better peopled, better cultivated, and more improved than any other part of the dominion of Virginia.[3]

A connexion was established between the families of Fairfax and Washington. In 1743, Ann, eldest daughter of Colonel William Fairfax (and half-sister of Bryan eighth Baron Fairfax), married Laurence, elder brother of George Washington; and in 1748–49 Lord Fairfax employed George Washington to

[1] 30306, f. 110.
[2] See his letter to Bryan Fairfax, South Potowmack, 14 July 1735; 30306, f. 144. It contains an interesting description of the style of Virginia country houses.
[3] Burnaby, *op. cit.* pp. 163-6.

survey his lands west of the Blue Ridge mountains. Lord Fairfax died on 12 March 1782.

To return to Robert Fairfax : he was born in 1707, served in the Royal Regiment of Horse Guards, and next in the 1st Life Guards, but resigned his commission in 1746. In 1741 he married Martha, daughter and co-heiress of Anthony Collins, and after her death in 1749, Dorothy, sister of Thomas Best, M.P. In 1740–41, and again from 1747 to 1754, he represented Maidstone in Parliament, and in 1754, with the support of the Duke of Dorset, was returned for Kent. Bryan Fairfax, dying in 1749, bequeathed to him 'a very considerable fortune', besides his collections. None the less, Robert Fairfax continued short of money : in April 1751 he sold by auction the coins and medals which Bryan had prized so much, and in 1756 was about to deal likewise with his library — it was saved from dispersal by Francis Child of Osterley (the banker, and a kinsman of Fairfax's first wife) buying it from him privately for £2000.[1] But all this was not sufficient to cover his requirements, increased as they were by election expenses. When he had to borrow money for the general election of 1754, he could supply only 'bad security',[2] and at the approach of that of 1761, he makes his appearance in Newcastle's agony columns.

Thus in Newcastle's Memorandums for the King, on 12 April 1759, there is the following entry :

> Mr. Fairfax — The D^e Dorset.
> The Whig cause in Kent.
> £500 end of the session.
> £500 the beginning of the next.

And on 26 July 1759, Robert Fairfax gave to Newcastle this account of 'the unhappy situation' of his affairs :

---

[1] See Nichols, *op. cit.* vol. v, p. 327.

[2] See above, p. 198. Some rearrangements seem to have been made to enable Fairfax to raise the money he required for the election. The following note appears in Newcastle's 'Memoranda' of 16 Mar 1754 (32995, f. 97) : 'Mr. West represents that if the security is not delivered up to Mr. Fairfax to get more money upon, Mr. Fairfax will not be able to go on with the election'. And on 30 Mar (*ibid.* f. 132) : 'Lord George Sackville — Mr. Fairfax to give up the mortgage on condition of his raising money upon it for the election'.

I have been near eighteen years in Parliament, have stood two contested elections, one for Maidstone, the other for the county of Kent, which has run me into such difficultys and distress that I shall have an execution next week in my house at Leeds Castle, which will be my absolute ruin and distruction, and oblige me to leave the county for ever. My estate, which is small, is all entail'd, so that I can't raise one shilling to help myself. I therefore most humbly intreat your Grace, if you think proper to recommend me to His Majesty's favour and protection for some assistance. I hope my conduct both in Parliament and private life will in some degree induce your Grace to think me worthy of being named to His Majesty, as I have never been troublesome or ask'd any thing for my self but on this occasion.[1]

The appeal produced an immediate return, a thing almost unknown in Newcastle's practice ; in the secret service accounts, under date of 27 July 1759, appears the following entry :

> To Mr. Fairfax as a gratuity by Your Majesty's
> particular order £500

Still, this was not a regular pension, only a gratuity ; and on 23 May 1760, the name of Fairfax appears again in the Memorandums for the King with £500 against it.[2] The proposal was repeated on 26 May,[3] and once more met with immediate success ; for on 27 May another £500 was paid to Mr. Fairfax 'by Your Majesty's particular order'.

When, early in 1761, Lord Middlesex, eldest son of the Duke of Dorset, thought of standing for Kent, Fairfax seems to have been prepared to make way for him. 'Lord S[ondes] tells me Fairfax has declared himself unqualified', wrote Sir George Oxenden, a Kentish squire, to Newcastle on 1 February 1761, 'and that Lord Middlesex is to stand in his room. I hope in God not, for I do not know a man so improper in the world as he is.'[4] Such was the unpopularity of Middlesex that he had to give up his intention, and Sir Wyndham Knatchbull and Fairfax were returned unopposed. It may seem surprising that a man in Robert Fairfax's circumstances should have been elected by one of the proudest and most independent counties

---

[1] 32893, f. 293. [2] 32906, f. 235.
[3] *Ibid.* f. 277. [4] 32918, f. 178.

of England, when his constituents must have known that he could not afford to be either. But this was probably the easiest way of preserving the peace of the county, and there always has been considerable reluctance in Englishmen to deprive anyone of his job.

Very soon the tale of Fairfax's financial difficulties restarted. Payments from secret service funds had been resumed in March 1761, and on 1 May Newcastle put down in his Memorandums :

> Mr. Fairfax £500 now — another next year — his great distress — had £1000 of the late King.[1]

And again on 8 June 1761 :

> Mr. Fairfax — £500 — charity.

But this time the success was not immediate, and on 11 July Sondes wrote to Newcastle :

> I have receiv'd a letter from Mr. Fairfax, who begs your Grace to think of him before it is too late, as his affair presses very hard upon him at this time.[2]

On 22 October Newcastle again noted : 'Mr. Fairfax — 500l. now and 500l. more on the rising of Parliament' ; and in four further Memoranda : 'Mr. Fairfax starving — £500',[3] the last two entries being prompted by a letter from Fairfax, dated 8 December.

> Your Grace [he wrote] has long been acquainted with the unhappy situation of my affairs. Permitt me therefore to tell you that they are now come to a crisis, and unless your Grace will please to give me your immediate assistance, I must sink under the weight of my misfortunes, I am neither able to stay here nor go home to my house in the country.
>
> I hope your Grace will consider my distress'd condition, and not suffer me to be torn in pieces and forc'd to leave my country and friends. I beg pardon for troubling you so often, but hope your Grace will forgive me.[4]

The request was granted once more — witness entry in the secret service accounts on 10 December 1761 :

---

[1] 32922, f. 290.   [2] 32925, f. 18.
[3] 13 and 24 Nov 1761, 32931, ff. 17 and 245 ; 8 and 9 Dec, 32932, ff. 34 and 72.   [4] *Ibid.* f. 56.

2 E

> To Mr. Fairfax as a gratuity by Your Majesty's
> particular order £500

These gratuities were now assuming such a regular character as very nearly to constitute a pension. They were treated as such in a 'List of Members of Parliament who receive private pensions' drawn up some time in 1761,[1] though its character of a pension was queried in the list of 18 May 1762.[2] Anyhow Newcastle on the very last day of his official life still thought of the starving, distressed Fairfax, and the penultimate entry in his secret service accounts (the last is the final payment to himself) was another £500 'as a gratuity' to Fairfax.

Newcastle was afraid that this would not be continued to Fairfax by his successors.[3] But things took a different turn. In the list of the House of Commons compiled on 13 November 1762, Newcastle still classed Robert Fairfax as one of his friends, but Henry Fox had already started his operations to win votes for the Treaty of Paris, and on 27 November Sondes wrote to Newcastle :

> I have seen Mr. F——x this morning, who says he will call on your Grace next week. I dont much like his discourse.[4]

The pension was continued to him, and he followed the Government through thick and thin. When in the summer of 1763 the Grenville Administration tried to obtain addresses from the counties approving of the Treaty of Paris, Fairfax had to move one in Kent. With unfeigned compassion Newcastle wrote to Rockingham on 30 July 1763 :

> In Kent the address, proposed by poor Fairfax, was rejected, by Sir Wyndham Knatchbul (the other Member for the county) and 14 more of the Grand Jury against Fairfax and 5, viz. 15 against 6. This was owing to the spirit and zeal of my friend Rose Fuller.[5]

And similarly to Hardwicke on 2 August :

---

[1] 33040, f. 274. [2] *Ibid.* ff. 358-60.
[3] See list of pensions '*after* and *before* Wednesday, May 26, 1762', *ibid.* f. 390.
[4] 32945, f. 170. 'F—x' stands obviously for Fairfax ; Sondes, a nephew of Newcastle by marriage, was his manager for Kent.
[5] 32949, ff. 438-9. See also letter from Wyndham Knatchbull to Hardwicke, 24 July 1763 (35692, f. 487) ; he puts the numbers as 16 *v.* 5.

I am heartily sorry for poor Fairfax; I doubt, not only his circumstances, but also that our old friend the Duke of Dorset or my Lord George [Sackville] had a considerable share in it.[1]

Hardwicke replied on 6 August :

As to poor Mr. Fairfax your Grace may be in the right as to the persons who swayed him ; but nobody can wonder at what he did.[2]

Naturally Fairfax was not one of the 220 who very nearly defeated the Grenville Administration over General Warrants on 17–18 February 1764 ; nor was he one of those who defied the Rockingham Administration over the repeal of the Stamp Act. And when in 1766 the Chatham Administration was formed, he was again with the Government.

He withdrew from Parliament in 1768, but the pension was charitably continued to him — witness the following letter addressed to him by George Onslow on 2 May 1772 :

Several days ago I spoke to Mr. Robinson [Secretary to the Treasury] desiring him to remind Lord North that your money was due at Lady Day, and wish'd him to let me have it for you. He has been particularly busy of late which I suppose is the reason of my not having heard from him on the subject. I imagine and hope that nothing can prevent its being ready for you next week.[3]

In the autumn of 1778 Fairfax entertained the King and Queen at Leeds Castle ; [4] and in 1782 he succeeded his brother as seventh Baron Fairfax, only to see whatever he inherited of the American estates confiscated by the Legislature of South Carolina. The compensation he claimed was £98,000, but only £13,758 was awarded to him by the Commission of Enquiry.[5] He died in 1793, and the title passed to his American cousins.

---

[1] 32950, ff. 16-17. [2] *Ibid.* f. 45.

[3] 'Original Letters and Papers addressed or relating to Members of the Fairfax Family, 1635–1790', 11325, f. 37. See also the secret service accounts of John Robinson for the years 1779–82, 37836, ff. 61-138 ; Fairfax appears in them in receipt of a regular pension of £500 p.a. ; moreover, there is an entry under date of 19 June 1779, 'Robert Fairfax by order £1000'.

[4] Two letters from Lord Amherst to the King, dealing with the preparations for this visit, are published in Fortescue, vol. iv, pp. 209 and 212.

[5] P.R.O., A.O. 12/109.

CHARLES WHITWORTH

Charles Whitworth, son of Francis Whitworth who represented Minehead from 1723 till his death in 1742, was a nephew of the well-known diplomat Lord Whitworth, and the father of the even better known British Ambassador to Russia, Charles, first Earl Whitworth. He was born about 1721, and as a child of six suffered his first disappointment in the matter of official promotion. George I had intended to give him the reversion of his father's sinecure of Secretary and Clerk of the Courts in the Island of Barbadoes, but died before the patent was completed ;[1] thus Charles Whitworth started life with a well-founded grievance. On the death of his father he meant to apply for his West Indian sinecure, but was persuaded to desist, having received a promise from Newcastle to provide for him ;[2] this added a well-founded hope to his political equipment. In 1747 he was returned to Parliament for Minehead (the Whitworth family owned the adjoining manor of Blackford), having since his father's death 'both by publick and private benefits . . . maintained that interest as entirely as he enjoyed it, with a view to offer myself the first opportunity'.[3] In 1749 Whitworth married Martha, daughter of Richard Shelley, Commissioner of the Stamp Office, and niece of Sir John Shelley, fourth Baronet, the husband of Newcastle's sister Margaret. As even the most distant connexion with the Pelham tribe counted with the Duke, who had intense family feeling and no children, this marriage seemed to improve Charles Whitworth's chances, and during the next years he became remarkable for application of the kind best known to eighteenth-century politicians. (W. R. Williams remarks about him in the *D.N.B.* — where Whitworth's numerous compilations on trade and Parliament have earned him a place — that he was 'a great student of Parliamentary customs'.)

---

[1] See an undated memorial from Francis Whitworth asking that the reversion be none the less given to his son Charles ; 33057, f. 501.

[2] See letter from Whitworth to Newcastle, 10 Nov 1755, reminding him of the promise and the circumstances in which it was given ; 32860, f. 436.

[3] C. Whitworth to Henry Fownes Luttrell, 19 Mar 1747 ; H. C. Maxwell Lyte, *History of Dunster*, vol. i, pp. 230-1.

As your Grace [he wrote to Newcastle on 10 April 1750] has frequently done me the honour to testify your readiness to serve me, I have taken all opportunities of waiting upon your Grace, but have never troubled your Grace for anything, being sensible your Grace would have confirmed your assurances, if an opportunity had offered, therefore take the liberty to trouble your Grace, as your Grace. . . .[1]

The letter is humble in tone, and 'your Grace' occurs almost in every line.

The next year he applied for a place in the establishment of the Prince of Wales ; he was ambitious, was looking forward to a long and distinguished career, and thought it best to connect himself, if possible, with the King under whom it was most likely to develop.

I intreat your Grace [he wrote on 19 April 1751] that you will not suffer an old friend to whom you have made such kind professions to be left out on such an occasion, as the honour of being in this young Prince's family is what as a young man I should covet preferable to anything.[2]

As the years went by, his hopes and claims sank but his manner became more aggressive. On 13 September 1753, he once more reminded Newcastle of the frequent promises, and asked to succeed Sir Andrew Fountain as Warden of the Mint ; [3] and the next letter of 17 October starts with an inimitable sentence blending anxiety with presumption :

I flatter myself I am not out of your Grace's thoughts, so am persuaded though not apprised, of your Grace's good services to procure me the honour of the employment I took the liberty to apply for.[4]

His first term of seven years in Parliament ended in disappointment, and now he had to face a contest at the forthcoming general election, the other two candidates being Daniel Boone, a late adherent of Leicester House supported by Lord Egremont, and Henry Shiffner, a London merchant. The strongest 'natural interest' in the borough was that of H. F. Luttrell, through his wife owner of Dunster Castle and of

---

[1] 32720, f. 201.
[3] 32732, f. 626.
[2] 32724, f. 240.
[4] 32733, f. 87.

Minehead Manor, which, however, in 1753 he was trying to sell in order to clear off the debts encumbering the estate. The Parliamentary interest naturally counted for a great deal with would-be purchasers, but its worth had still to be proved after its eclipse through neglect in 1747. 'I wish', wrote an agent of Luttrell's to him on 13 August 1753, 'you had or would soon make a personal experiment of your strength in the borough.'[1] Then, on 26 February 1754, Shiffner, though a complete stranger to Minehead and Luttrell, applied for his interest.[2] Luttrell hesitated at first to give it to any but 'a purchaser or a particular friend'.[3] But meantime the other claimants were warming up to the contest.

My Lord [Egremont] says he'll spend ten thousand pounds; and Whitworth says he'll sell his estate in this part of the world to supply his friends if they'll stand by him this once. He writes prodigiously in favour of Mr. Shiffner and I believe would be glad to join him.[4]

Perhaps not to be cut out a second time, Luttrell now agreed to support Shiffner provided he stood on 'the country interest', and joined neither of the other two (also provided 'no purchaser for the Manor interferes').[5]

Egremont, hard pressed, applied to Newcastle, who on 21 March noted in his election memoranda: 'To speak to Mr. Whitworth to espouse Mr. Boone at Minehead to the utmost'; [6] and the next day assured Egremont that these two interests 'shall be most heartily and zealously supported by the Government'.[7] And then in the memoranda of 31 March: [8]

Mr. Whitworth. An unexpected opposition against him, and Mr. Boone, the Tories give 10£ a man — he desires the King's consideration, that H. Mty would be graciously pleased to give them 1000£ towards his expences, which will amount to 2500, and he is willing to give 1500£.

[1] Conand Prowse to H. F. Luttrell; Luttrell MSS. at Dunster Castle.
[2] *Ibid.*
[3] Draft of letter from Luttrell to Cholwich, 5 Mar 1754; *ibid.*
[4] James Gould to Luttrell, 5 Mar; *ibid.*
[5] Copy of letter to Shiffner, 8 Mar; *ibid.*   [6] 32995, f. 114.
[7] Wyndham MSS at Petworth.   [8] 32995, f. 134.

But news of Whitworth having written 'prodigiously in favour of Mr Shiffner', the alleged Tory (who by now was precluded by Luttrell's conditions from joining Whitworth), must have reached Newcastle; for Whitworth wrote to the Duke on 4 April:

My Lord,

That your Grace might not think I came away with any intention of throwing myself into measures or with people I have opposed from principles, I trouble your Grace with this to assure you to the contrary, and that I write down to my friends at the borough upon the same Whig principles as I have allways profest. My farther conduct I leave to your Grace's answer as you mentioned to-morrow, being desirous of still continuing, my Lord, your etc.[1]

It is not clear what those 'Whig principles' were, but the nature of Newcastle's answer expected for 'to-morrow' appears on 5 April in the secret service accounts:

Mr. Whitworth for Minehead . . . . £1000.[2]

But Egremont was still pressing Newcastle, who wrote to him on 9 April how extremely concerned he was for anything which might be disagreeable to Egremont at Minehead; that he had never intended or imagined that any assistance given to Whitworth should prejudice Boone; and that he would never countenance any such design.

I have this morning spoken to Mr. Whitworth's father in law Mr. Shelley very plainly upon the subject, and . . . I now write to Mr. Whitworth to desire, that he would not in any event do any thing to prejudice Mr. Boone, but prefer his interest to his own. . . .

He hoped that the result would be agreeable to Egremont's wishes, but added that should Whitworth withdraw, 'he should be consider'd by the other candidates with regard to his expences'.[3]

In the end Whitworth was returned with Boone after a hotly contested election, and having been brought into Parliament with the help of Government money, he had, as was so often the case, to be further supported while in it. Beginning

[1] 32735, f. 38.　　[2] 33044, f. 18; see pp. 200 and 428.
[3] Wyndham MSS.

with February 1755, he received a secret service pension of £400 a year.[1] He would, however, have preferred a place, as more honorific and more promising for the future. On the death of William Hay, M.P., Whitworth was among the many who aspired to succeed him as Keeper of the Records in the Tower (net annual value £420). It was given to his wife's cousin, John Shelley, M.P.

Richard Shelley, Whitworth's father-in-law, died in November 1755, and although his place of Commissioner of the Stamp Office was incompatible with a seat in Parliament, Whitworth was anxious to secure it; and everything now seemed to plead in his favour. But the place was given to George Whitmore.[2] Embittered by this disappointment, Whitworth felt even more severely the death of his father-in-law and reproached Newcastle with insensibility to a mourner.

As I intended myself the honour of applying to your Grace in part to repair the loss sustained by the death of so valuable a friend as poor Mr. Shelley, your Grace is sensible it must add to my concern, to find myself not likely to succeed.

I shall from this, my Lord, despair of being favour'd with any preferment, since there will never be wanting variety of sollicitations to your Grace for whatever should fall.[3]

In 1756 a new household was formed for the Prince of Wales, who had now reached the age of eighteen, and on 31 October Whitworth wrote to Newcastle:

I was in hopes your Grace would have done me the honour of recommending me to one of the employments lately establisht in the Prince of Wales' household, as I flatter myself your Grace intends fulfilling the promise you have so frequently given me.[4]

A fortnight later Newcastle resigned office, and he had not yet resumed it when, on 6 May 1757, Whitworth, in anticipation of the event, was again soliciting his favour:

---

[1] See 33038, f. 352, among 'Pensions added since April 1754', 'Mr. Whitworth—£400'; also f. 415, 'Pensions in March 1755', and ff. 497-8, for Apr 1756. In the secret service accounts (see Appendix), entries of £200 each, paid to Whitworth, appear on 25 Feb, 18 June, and 12 Dec 1755, and on 6 Apr 1756; on 3 Sept 1756, £100 'to Midsummer'.

[2] See above, pp. 250-2.   [3] 10 Nov 1755; 32860, f. 436.

[4] 32868, f. 515.

I cannot help begging your Grace's recommendation to some employment which I dare say your Grace will shortly have opportunity of doing. The uneasiness I am under at seeing so many gentlemen fixed in places, makes me so frequently troublesome to your Grace upon the occasion.[1]

He returned to the charge with the approach of the Parliamentary session :

I flatter myself [he wrote on 24 August 1757] your Grace will before the meeting of Parliament honour me with your recommendation to some employment, as nobody has been a more constant supporter of Government, and your Grace has promised me so frequently your assistance.[2]

Instead of a place, his pension of £400 p.a. was continued.[3] But Whitworth persisted, and on 14 February 1758, applied to Newcastle for the Deputy-Governorship of Gravesend and Tilbury, which had fallen vacant. 'As it is in my neighbourhood [he owned Leybourne in Kent] will be more agreable than a place that may require a more constant attendance in London', and as he had been in the army, it would not vacate his seat in Parliament.[4] On 18 February he added : 'I know it will be agreable to the principal people of our county'.[5] But should Newcastle not choose to solicit that for him, he had another scheme to submit which would have involved his withdrawal from Parliament :

That if Mr. Vaughan or any other elderly and infirm gentleman in the Customs or Excise would be induced to let my name be put into the Commission, I would . . . allow the gentleman a proportion for his retirement; at the same time, I could give my interest to any person your Grace would approve of, who might be chose at Minehead and secure a permanent interest.[6]

On this occasion, however, Newcastle obtained for him the post at Tilbury, but it took some time before the matter was settled.

[1] 32871, f. 29.   [2] 32873, f. 273.
[3] On 19 Oct 1757, there is an entry in the secret service accounts 'To Mr. C. Whitworth, half a year, £200'. On 25 Jan 1758, 'one quarter to Christmas, £100'; on 20 Apr 1758, 'one quarter to Lady Day, £100'; and on 7 July, 'one quarter to Midsummer, £100'. See Appendix.
[4] 32877, f. 462.   [5] Ibid. f. 486.
[6] 1 Mar 1758; 32878, ff. 81.

As your Grace [Whitworth wrote on 24 July] must naturally conceive the uneasy situation of uncertainty, I intreat your Grace to relieve me out of the anxiety and put it out of the power of common accidents to prevent my succeeding.[1]

A fortnight later Whitworth effusively thanked Newcastle.[2] But soon he recommenced his solicitations, as the new office was worth only half the pension he had previously enjoyed, and therefore required supplementing.

It is great concern to me [he wrote to Newcastle on 11 June 1759 to think that your Grace has not yet honoured me with my request, as it is above a month ago since your Grace flattered me it would be done the next day.

If I do not hear from Mr. Shelley this week I take for granted, I must conclude that your Grace is not willing to be troubled any more on my account; having done me the honour to raise my expectation I laid great stress and reliance upon it, which makes the disappointment more than otherwise it would be.[3]

A fortnight later he wrote again : 'I take the liberty of mentioning that my banker is Mr. Campbell in the Strand.'[4] And once more on 5 September, in anticipation of the reassembling of Parliament — 'this is the time it will be of the greatest service to me'.[5]

It was not till 25 January 1760, as a result of a further reminder,[6] that Whitworth received £150, 'three quarters at the rate of 200£ pr. ann., in order to make up his Government 400£ pr. ann.',[7] this payment covering the time from Midsummer 1758 till Lady Day 1759; and on 21 March 1760, £150 was remitted to him through Shelley, covering the time up to the end of 1759.[8] Thus at the death of George II the arrears on his pension amounted to another £150.[9] Curiously

---

[1] 32882, f. 56.   [2] *Ibid.* f. 239.   [3] 32892, f. 3.
[4] *Ibid.* f. 221.   [5] 32898, f. 114.

[6] Whitworth wrote to Newcastle on 21 Jan 1760 (32901, f. 399): 'As your Grace's letter in June last mentions your doing me the honour of settling my affair in a very few days and hopes I will excuse that short delay, your Grace must imagine that six months expectation of your Grace's fulfilling your promise has been of the greatest inconvenience and uneasiness to me'.

[7] See below, p. 461.

[8] Besides p. 462, see 33039, f. 362.

[9] See 33040, f. 23, 'List of Members of Parliament who received private pensions with the arrears due to Michaelmas last 1760'.

enough, this money seems never to have been paid, nor does his pension seem to have been continued under George III.

On 21 August 1760 Whitworth wrote to Newcastle about Minehead at the forthcoming general election : [1]

> Mr. Shiffner who opposed Lord Egremont is I understand very likely to be chosen, and I make no doubt of myself, if your Grace encourages me to carry on, but consideration of what might be the issue, if the contest came between his Lordship and myself, made me submit it to your Grace, since if your Grace should be solicited to desire me to withdraw my pretensions, when I am enter'd into it, I might not have it in my power, as was the case last time.

And next on 1 November : Sir Kenrick Clayton has offered to bring him in at Bletchingley 'without any trouble or expence'. This 'will take off any difficulty your Grace may have relative to my interfering with Lord Egremont at Minehead. But as your Grace may now have an opportunity, I flatter myself your Grace will recommend me to some publick employment. . . .' [2]

In conclusion, it may be added as excuse for Whitworth's importunities, that he had nine children. And he seems to have been fond of children : he was Treasurer of the Foundlings' Hospital, and left the Hospital a fund to provide cakes for the children on New Year's Day ; and before the general election of 1768 he held out as an inducement to the Minehead burgesses that for a pledge to vote for him and his fellow-candidate, they would establish 'proper annual schooling for the education of poor voters' children'.[3]

[1] 32910, f. 198.   [2] 32914, f. 23.
[3] H. C. Maxwell Lyte, op. cit. vol. i, p. 246.

APPENDIX

THE SECRET SERVICE ACCOUNTS OF THE DUKE OF NEWCASTLE

SECRET SERVICE ACCOUNTS, MARCH 21, 1754–NOVEMBER 9, 1756

(33044, ff. 18-26)

[THESE accounts are in the handwriting of John Roberts. Originally, as a rule, only initials were given; most blanks were filled in subsequently, and sometimes the full name was written once more at the end of the entry. Many names remain, however, incomplete but can be identified with the help of later accounts and of other papers dealing with the subject. The book as it stands is a mass of scribbled notes, and there would be no point in reproducing their confusion; it seems preferable to render clearly their contents and sense.

The respectful and picturesque blank opposite the quarterly entries of £1050, which stands for the Duke of Newcastle's own 'additional salary', is, however, preserved.

No explanatory notes are given here for expenditure on elections and constituencies as the subject is dealt with in the chapter on 'The General Elections of 1754 and 1761, and the Nursing of Constituencies', which should be read as a commentary on these entries.]

1754		£	s.	d.
March 21st.	Mr. Dodd for Reading . .	300	0	0
25th.	Mr. Medlycott [1] . . .	500	0	0
26th.	Mr. Talbot's election at Ilchester .	800	0	0
28th.	Mr. Bayntun Rolt for Chippenham .	800	0	0
29th.	Yonge for Honiton . . .	500	0	0
April 1st.	Mr. Clevland for Barnstaple [2] .	1000	0	0
	Mr. T. Leslie [3] . . .	300	0	0
2d.	Mr. Trist for Totnes . . .	200	0	0

[1] About him see pp. 406-9.
[2] There was a previous payment of £1000 for Barnstaple by Pelham, see 32955, f. 107.
[3] For his election expenses in Perth Burghs.

1754				£	s.	d.
April	2d.	Sempil [1]	. . . .	50	0	0
	3d.	Mr. Stewart of Castle Stewart [2]	.	200	0	0
		Capt. Mackay [3]	. .	300	0	0
	4th.	Lord Macclesfield [4]	. .	2000	0	0
		Mr. Charlton, Chairman of Committees [5]		500	0	0
		Col. Mordaunt [6]	. .	200	0	0
	5th.	Lord Home [7]	. .	200	0	0
		Mr. Hitch Young for Steyning	.	1000	0	0
		Mr. Whitworth for Minehead.	.	1000	0	0
		Mr. Martin for Camelford	. .	170	0	0
		Mr. Sewell for Wallingford	. .	780	0	0
		Lord Archer for Bramber	. .	1000	0	0

[1] John Gordon of Sempill, an anti-Jacobite spy; already employed by Sir Robert Walpole, who wrote to Lord Waldegrave, Ambassador in Paris, on 10 Nov 1733 (Waldegrave MSS. at Chewton House): 'I paid this week a bill of £50 drawn by our old freind Sample, pray lett him know no more will be accepted or paid, I think he should not quite starve . . . pay him about £50 p.a. and no more . . . 'tis wonderful, how the fool could think to draw bills upon me by the common post, and with his own hand, and not be discovered.' By the time Newcastle took over the Treasury, Sempill was in receipt of £120 p.a., and his reports show what nonsense will be paid for in the 'secret service'. His name still appears in the Windsor secret service lists of 1763 and 1764, and in Rockingham's list of 'Private Pensions, July 1765', where he is grouped — in an 'authors' corner' one must presume — with Dr. Campbell, Guthrie, Samuel Johnson, and Dr. Francis, and £200 is put against him, besides £50 for his transcriber. But actually no payment to him appears in Rockingham's disbursements — probably he was dead. (For Rockingham's secret service accounts see Fitzwilliam MSS. at Sheffield.)

[2] John Stewart, descended from the third son of James, second Earl of Galloway. His father, William Stewart, had sat in Parliament 1713–41, had been Scottish secretary to George II when Prince of Wales, and subsequently Paymaster of Pensions. The recipient of the pension never sat in Parliament; in 1754 he was appointed King's Remembrancer in Scotland, and his pension stopped. He died in 1768.

[3] George Mackay, of Strathmore, M.P. for co. Sutherland 1747–61; the pension stopped when he was appointed Master of the Mint in Scotland in 1756.

[4] For the Oxfordshire election.

[5] See above, p. 228.

[6] Col. John Mordaunt, M.P., brother of Charles, fourth Earl of Peterborough; he is sometimes confused with his cousin, General Sir John Mordaunt, M.P., who commanded the expedition against Rochefort in 1757. Col. Mordaunt died on 1 July 1767.

[7] William, eighth Earl of Home; entered army 1735; served with distinction in the rebellion of 1745; colonel 1752; 16 Apr 1757, appointed Governor of Gibraltar, where he died, 28 Apr 1761. Succeeded to the peerage 1720; Scottish Representative Peer 1741–61; 'took no active part in politics' (V. Gibbs in The Complete Peerage). His pension was obviously in lieu of office, and stopped on his appointment to Gibraltar.

1754				£	s.	d.
April	5th.	Lord Saye and Sele. 1/2 [1]	. .	300	0	0
	9th.	Sir Duncan Campbell [2]	. .	400	0	0
		Lord Falmouth [3]	. . .	1455	0	0
		Lord Edgcumbe and Mr. Andrews [4]	.	700	0	0
	10th.	Duke of Argyle for Scotland .	.	1000	0	0
	11th.	Mr. Dodd for Reading	. .	200	0	0
		Sir Jacob Downing for Dunwich	.	500	0	0
		Lord Willoughby of Parham [5]	.	200	0	0
	12th.	Mr. Dodd for Reading	. .	400	0	0
	18th.	Lord Leven [6]	. . .	500	0	0
	23rd.	Ld. Ilchester for Shaftesbury [7]	.	330	0	0
	25th.	Mr. Soame Jenyns [8] .	. .	600	0	0
		Pickle [9]	. . .	100	0	0
	26th.	Mr. Hamilton, the Duke's [10] relation	.	100	0	0

[1] See above, pp. 178-80.

[2] Sir Duncan Campbell, of Lochnell, Knt. ; M.P. for Argyllshire 1747–1754. He was replaced in his constituency and pension by his nephew, Col. Dugall Campbell of Ballimore, M.P. for Argyllshire 1754–64 ; see under 14 May 1755, p. 437.

[3] For John Fuller's election at Tregony.

[4] For Grampound.

[5] See above, p. 224.

[6] Alexander Leslie, seventh Earl of Leven (1699–1754) ; one of the Lords of Session 1734 ; High Commiss. to the Gen. Assembly 1741–53 ; one of the Lords of Police 1754 ; Repres. Peer 1747–54. Died 2 Sept 1754.

[7] Payment made for Sir Thomas Clavering. See Newcastle's 'Minutes, March 25th, 1754. Lord Ilchester — Shaftesbury, Sir Thomas Clavering to pay £2,000. The remainder to be paid for him. Lord Ilchester supposes it may come to £300 more.' 32995, f. 126.

[8] S. Jenyns (1704–87), M.P. for Cambridgeshire 1741–54, for Dunwich 1754–58, and for Cambridge Borough 1758–80. A Lord of Trade and Plantations, Dec 1755–Sept 1780 ; on his appointment to that office his pension stopped. He was a friend of the Yorkes ; for his correspondence with Philip, second Earl of Hardwicke, see 35631. His works were published in 1790, in four volumes, by C. N. Cole.

[9] 'Alexander Pickle', cover-name of Alastair Ruadh Macdonnell, of Glengarry, an anti-Jacobite spy ; see Andrew Lang, Pickle the Spy (1897), and The Companions of Pickle (1898).

[10] James Hamilton. He wrote to Newcastle on 11 May 1756 (32864, f. 526) : 'Duke Hamilton some years ago recommended me to the late Mr. Pelham for one of His Majesty's Consulships in the Mediteranean as I had been long in these parts, and had been used to the sea mercantile service, or . . . to some place either in the Customs or Excise . . . which he not only promised . . . but as a proof of his sincerity, procured me an annuity of 200 pounds yearly till that happened . . . ; your Grace's kind continuation of these favours . . . makes me flatter myself your Grace will soon think of me . . .' See also above, p. 230. The pension still appears under the heading 'Compensation' in the 'List of Private Pensions' prepared for Shelburne in August 1782 (P.R.O., Chatham Papers, 30/8/229).

1754			£	s.	d.
May	2d.	Mr. Phillipson for Mr. Bristowe for Shoreham	1000	0	0
		Sir C. Powlett [1] . . .	500	0	0
	3d.	Lord Warwick.[2] 1/2 . .	250	0	0
		Justice Fielding [3] 1/2 to Lady Day .	200	0	0
		Mr. Carmichael [4] 1/2 . .	200	0	0
	7th.	Mr. Ralph [5] 1/2 to Lady Day .	150	0	0
	8th.	Alderman Porter for Evesham .	1000	0	0
	14th.	Mr. Jenison [6] . . .	700	0	0
	21st.	Mr. Southard [7] for Totnes . .	140	0	0
	22nd.	Mr. Talbot for Ilchester . .	200	0	0
	28th.	Col. Pelham [8] . . .	500	0	0
	30th.	Earl of Warrington [9] 1/2 to Michaelmas 1753	750	0	0

[1] Charles Powlett (1718–65), nephew of the third Duke of Bolton, whom his father succeeded in 1754 when C. Powlett became Marquess of Winchester; fifth Duke of Bolton 1759. Served in the army; Lieutenant of the Tower of London 1754–60.

[2] Edward Rich, eighth and last Earl of Warwick of that creation (1695–1759); in 1721 he succeeded to the title, but to none of the family estates; he played no part in politics.

[3] John Fielding, the well-known London magistrate, half-brother of Henry Fielding; see *D.N.B.*

[4] James Carmichael, third son of James, second Earl of Hyndford, M.P. for Linlithgow Burghs 1734–41 and 1748–54. He was not re-elected in 1754, and died the same year. He still appears in these accounts on 27 Mar 1755, but these may be arrears paid to his executors.

[5] James Ralph (1705–62), political writer and historian, of low character but able; had served various masters; since 1753 in receipt of a pension of £300 p.a. See *D.N.B.*, where he is very fully dealt with.

[6] Presumably payment for Ralph Jenison's election at Newport, I.o.W.; see above, pp. 131-2.

[7] A cider merchant who acted as one of Newcastle's election agents at Totnes. His begging letters are usually short and amusing. Here is one of 13 June 1758 (32880, f. 435): 'May it please your Grace, The fruits of thirty-six years service to his Majesty's friends — hath given me a violent gout — I realy wish it had been somthing elce'.

[8] Colonel James Pelham, of Crowhurst, Sussex (died 1761), M.P. for Newark 1722–41, and for Hastings 1741–61; he was a distant cousin of the Duke of Newcastle, was for many years Secretary to the Lord Chamberlain of the Royal Household, and had at all times to be at the service of Newcastle. When during the divisions on the Mitchell election, in 1755, Pelham failed to obey Newcastle's orders, the usual cordial address of 'Dear Jemmy' changed into a formal 'Sir' with advice to quit his seat in Parliament so that the Duke might choose one upon whom he could entirely depend; see series of letters from Newcastle to Pelham, 32853, ff. 23-7; f. 27 should be read first. Besides the secret service pension, he had a sinecure place of £700 p.a., held for him by his nephew John Pelham. (32946, f. 46.)

[9] George Booth, second and last Earl of Warrington (1675-1758).

1754			£	s.	d.
June	1st.	Earl of Radnor.[1] One year . .	800	0	0
		Mr. C. Hanbury's dissenting minister [2]	100	0	0
	4th.	Lord Dudley [3] . . .	600	0	0
		Mr. Henry Fox for Speaker's List [4] .	360	0	0
	6th.	Lord Raymond [5] . . .	800	0	0
		Sir J. Downing's man.[6] 1/2 . .	100	0	0
	7th.	Lord Ilchester [7] . . .	400	0	0
	11th.	Mr. Charlton for Newark . .	1000	0	0
	19th.	Fitzgerald [8]	20	0	0
	20th.	Dr. Hepburn of Lynn [9] . .	100	0	0
		Mr. Guthrie.[10] 1/2 . . .	100	0	0
		Mr. Neale.[11] One year . .	500	0	0
July	2nd.	[12]	1050	0	0
	4th.	Mr. Ashburnham [13] . . .	100	0	0

[1] John Robartes, fourth and last Earl of Radnor of that creation (1686–1757) ; succeeded to the title in 1741 on the death of his cousin, while the estates devolved on the nephews of the third Earl, George and Thomas Hunt.

[2] Capel Hanbury (1707–65), M.P. for Leominster 1741–47, and for Monmouthshire 1747–65. He sympathized with the Dissenters, though not one himself. See A. A. Locke, *The Hanbury Family*, vol. i, pp. 161-9.

[3] Ferdinando, eleventh and last Lord Dudley (1710–57) ; succeeded his uncle in 1740 in the title, while the Barony of Ward, together with the castle and lands of Dudley, devolved on John Ward, sixth Lord Ward.

[4] For the Speaker's List, see above, p. 231.

[5] Robert Raymond, second and last Lord Raymond, s. and h. of Chief Justice Raymond. Born about 1717, died 19 Sept 1756. Took no part in politics.   [6] Unidentified.

[7] Elder brother of Henry Fox ; about his 'additional salary', see above, p. 228.

[8] J. Fitzgerald ; I believe he was a spy.

[9] George Hepburn, M.D., physician to Sir Robert Walpole ; died 1760. E. Pyle wrote to S. Kerrick [n.d.] : 'Poor old Hepburn — to live to 90 years, and leave only £2000 ; with his great opportunities of saving for his children ! He was always a vicious expensive man' (*Memoirs of a Royal Chaplain*, 1729–63, ed. Albert Hartshorne, 1905, p. 325).

[10] William Guthrie (1708–70), political writer and historian ; had a pension of £200 p.a. since 1745. See *D.N.B.* ; also Nichols's *Literary Anecdotes*, vol. 8, p. 241, where he is well described by Charles Godwyn : 'He is a florid writer. . . . What his religion is I know not. He writes for his bread.'

[11] Presumably Robert Neale, of Corsham, M.P. for Wootton Bassett 1741–54. See his letter to Newcastle, 15 Feb 1755, in which he ascribes the loss of his seat, interest, and £1800, to having obeyed H. Pelham's orders and tried to carry both seats (32852, f. 481).

[12] A quarterly instalment of Newcastle's additional salary ; see above, pp. 226-7.

[13] Possibly William Ashburnham, Dean of Chichester, who in 1736 had married Margaret Pelham, a cousin of Newcastle. In 1754 he became Bishop of Chichester, which would account for this being the last payment of the pension to him.

1754			£	s.	d.
July	10th.	Baron Münchhausen [1] 1/2 . .	500	0	0
		Lord Halifax 1/2 . . .	750	0	0
	11th.	Lord Peterborough [2] 1/2 . .	200	0	0
		Mr. Brereton Salusbury [3] . .	500	0	0
		Mr. Leveson Gower's friend [4] .	150	0	0
		Ld. Kinnoull [5] 1/2 . . .	400	0	0
		Ld. Montfort for Cambridge . .	550	0	0
		The Duke of Marlborough for Lord Macclesfield for Oxfordshire .	1000	0	0
	12th.	Mr. Carmichael . . .	200	0	0
	18th.	Mr. Schutz [6] 1/2 . . .	200	0	0
	25th.	Col. Cornwallis and Sir John Crosse for Westminster . . .	1800	0	0
		Pickle	200	0	0
		Carey [7]	100	0	0
		Gordon's transcriber [8] . .	50	0	0
		Sempill	20	0	0
		Mr. Harrison [9] . . .	500	0	0
Aug.		Ld. Drummore [10] . . .	100	0	0
		Mr. Maxwell for Taunton . .	500	0	0

[1] Hanoverian Resident in London ; about his pension see above, pp. 233-4.

[2] Charles Mordaunt, fourth Earl of Peterborough (1710–79).

[3] Thomas Brereton Salusbury, M.P. for Liverpool 1724–56 ; Mayor in 1732. Died 9 Mar 1756. 'Mr. Salisbury receives 500£ a year in lieu of his office' (32995, f. 121 ; see also f. 186).

[4] Unidentified. William Leveson Gower sat for Staffordshire from 1720 till his death in 1756.

[5] George Hay, eighth Earl of Kinnoull (1689–1758).

[6] George, son of Augustus Schutz (who had accompanied George II from Hanover and had been his Master of the Robes and Keeper of the Privy Purse ; he died in 1757). George Schutz owned the estate of Shotover, near Oxford. On 22 Sept 1754, he married 'Miss Dorothea Repp, 20,000l.' (Gent. Mag., p. 483). He was Ranger of Richmond Park, but was displaced on the accession of George III.

[7] Unidentified.

[8] A Mr. Smith ; judging by the reports Gordon had 'the gout' in his head, and the transcriber in his hand.

[9] George Harrison, M.P. for Hertford 1727–34, and from 1741 till his death on 4 Dec 1759. The identification is confirmed by 32997, f. 64.

[10] George Campbell, a London banker, wrote to Newcastle, 20 June 1754 (32735, f. 523) that Pelham, during his time at the Treasury, regularly paid through him to Lord Drummore, a Lord of Session in Scotland, £100 p.a. for the use of Lord Dun ; and he understood from the Duke of Argyll that Newcastle would continue these payments. Hew Dalrymple of Drummore (1690–1755) had succeeded David Erskine of Dun (1670–1758) as a Lord of Justiciary on 13 June 1745 (Brunton and Haig, Senators of the College of

1754				£	s.	d.
Oct.	3d.	Mrs. Cannon [1] . . .		100	0	0
		Fitzgerald		20	0	0
		Lutheran clergyman . . .		20	0	0
	16th.	Col. Mordaunt . . .		100	0	0
		. . . .		1050	0	0
		Mr. Maxwell for Taunton . .		500	0	0
	17th.	Ld. Kinnoull 1/4 . . .		200	0	0
		Mr. Thorpe of Hastings.[2] One year		100	0	0
	24th.	Mr. Ralph 1/2 to Michaelmas. .		150	0	0
		Gordon		20	0	0
	26th.	Earl of Warrington 1/2 to Lady Day,				
		1754		750	0	0
		Mr. Maxwell for Taunton . .		1000	0	0
	28th.	Mr. Hunter [3] for Col. Mordaunt to				
		Michaelmas . . .		300	0	0
Dec.	4th.	Mr. Hamilton, the Duke's relation .		100	0	0
	5th.	Marquis of Winchester [4] . .		500	0	0
	6th.	Ld. Warwick 1/2 Michaelmas .		250	0	0
		Mr. Martin for Camelford . .		570	0	0
	10th.	Sir Jacob Downing's man 1/2 .		100	0	0
	20th.	Mr. Macdonald [5] . . .		100	0	0

Justice, p. 501) and the payments were presumably connected with this replacement.

On Drummore's death Robert Dundas wrote to Hardwicke, 19 June 1755 (35448, f. 267): 'he was at the head of what I must call the clan of Dalrymple, which was in many respects too similar to a Highland clan. . . . I hope this is the last in the Low Country, and if no new head is permitted to rise, the death of Lord Drummore, will, I hope, break that cement.'

[1] Most probably 'Mrs. Cannon, midwife to the royal family', whose death is noted in the *Gentleman's Magazine* under 11 Dec 1754. She appears once more in these accounts under 15 Oct 1755, but that may have been a payment of arrears to her heirs. Her executor and residuary legatee was the father of the famous Arthur Young (see his *Autobiography*, pp. 10-13). 'By her will all her furniture and a great collection of medals, bronzes, shells, curiosities, books on natural history, etc., with money in the funds, came into his possession to the amount of five thousand pounds.' Young describes her as 'a lady highly respected and well known as midwife to the Princess of Wales', and mentions letters to her from Mr. Popple, Governor of Bermuda, asking her to help him to a better government or some employment at home.

[2] I have failed to find anything about him.

[3] T. O. Hunter, M.P. for Winchelsea 1741–59 and 1760–69; Col. Mordaunt was his colleague at Winchelsea 1747–54.

[4] See Sir C. Powlett under 2 May 1754. The pension was now discontinued.

[5] Allan Macdonald, an anti-Jacobite agent on 'the Highland service'; see his letter to H. V. Jones, Newcastle's private secretary, 1 Oct 1755 (32859, f. 299), and to Newcastle, 4 Oct 1755 (*ibid.* f. 382).

			£	s.	d.
1754					
Dec. 20th.	Mr. Ellis for Bryer of Weymouth [1]	.	100	0	0
	Lord Radnor 1/2 Michaelmas	.	400	0	0
	Orford [2] . . .	.	200	0	0
	Gordon . . .	.	20	0	0
1755					
Jan. 8th.	Mr. Dodd for Reading	.	100	0	0
	Guthrie 1/2 . . .	.	100	0	0
	Fitzgerald . . .	.	20	0	0
	. . . .	.	1050	0	0
10th.	Sir W. Middleton.[3] One year to Lady				
	Day . . .	.	800	0	0
	Col. Mordaunt . .	.	50	0	0
	Duke of Grafton for Sir H. Bedingfeld.[4]				
	One year . . .	.	500	0	0
14th.	Ld. Peterborough 1/2. .	.	200	0	0
18th.	Ld. Kinnoull 1/4 . .	.	200	0	0
	Sir G[eorge] L[yttelton] for Mr. Bower [5]		200	0	0
22nd.	Baron Münchhausen 1/2 to Xmas	.	500	0	0
23rd.	Col. Pelham. One year to Xmas	.	500	0	0

[1] Welbore Ellis, M.P. for Weymouth (see *D.N.B.*) ; I have failed to find anything about Mr. Bryer.

[2] See above, pp. 389-401

[3] Sir William Middleton, third Bt. (1700–57), M.P. for Northumberland 1722–57.

[4] Sir Henry Arundell Bedingfeld, third Bt. (died in 1760). He married, 1719, Lady Elizabeth Boyle, eldest daughter of Charles, second Earl of Burlington ; her niece, Lady Dorothy Boyle, married in 1741 Lord Euston, eldest surviving son of Charles, second Duke of Grafton, which may account for the connexion between them.

[5] Archibald Bower (1686–1766), born in Scotland, educated at the Scots Coll. at Douay ; became a Jesuit. Left the order in 1726 ; connected with Lord Aylmer and Sir George Lyttelton. In 1741 he is alleged to have secretly resumed his connexion with the Jesuits, but in 1748 published the first volume of his anti-Romanist *History of the Popes*. The same year he was made librarian to Queen Caroline and in 1754 Lyttelton appointed him 'clerk of the buck-warrants' : the last payment to him appears under date of 2 Nov 1756, the pension not being paid any more on Newcastle's resumption of office in 1757. This may have been in consequence of the disclosure of his relations with the Jesuits made in 1756 ; about Bower see *D.N.B.* E. Pyle wrote to S. Kerrick, on 3 Mar 1756 : 'Sir H. Bedingfield of our county, has shown 5 letters written, as he says, and as the handwriting shows by the said Bower, to one Sheldon, an English monk, deceased. . . . Bower denies the writing of them ; says they are a forgery. . . . How this matter will end God knows, I hear Sir George Littleton his patron, does not give him up yet. He has a place of 200 a year and a pension of 2 more procured by Sir George's means, chiefly' (see *Memoirs of a Royal Chaplain*, 1729–63, ed. by Albert Hartshorne, 1905, pp. 251-3).

1755					£	s.	d.
Jan.	23rd.	Fitzgerald [1]	.	.	20	0	0
	28th.	Ld. Halifax 1/2 to Xmas	.	.	750	0	0
	31st.	Mr. Carey	.	.	100	0	0
Feb.	5th.	Mr. Maxwell for Taunton	.	.	1500	0	0
	10th.	Ld. Hartington for Mr. Rivett [2] 1/2 to Xmas	.	.	150	0	0
		Mr. Schutz 1/2	.	.	200	0	0
	11th.	Mr. Allen by the Speaker [3] 1/2	.		100	0	0
	13th.	Col. Mordaunt by Mr. Hunter 1/2 to Xmas	.	.	150	0	0
	25th.	Mr. Chas. Whitworth 1/2 [4]	.	.	200	0	0
March	7th.	Ld. Saye and Sele 1/2	.	.	300	0	0
		Ld. Peterborough 1/4 to Lady Day	.		100	0	0
		Ld. Home. One year	.	.	200	0	0

[1] On 15 Jan, Fitzgerald had written to Newcastle : 'Permit me . . . to . . . beseech you not to leave imperfect the prospect of happiness you gave me, but please to extricate me thoroughly from the many evils, former debts and misfortunes have involved me. . . . A summe not less than fourty pounds, to me the Indies, to your Grace a trifle, will make me I hope for ever happy' (32852, f. 178). In reply to this appeal he received the above £20 ; on 18 Mar 10 guineas were given 'to bury Fitzgerald'.

[2] Thomas Rivett, M.P. for Derby 1748–54. Horace Walpole wrote to H. Mann, 26 Dec 1748 : 'The families of Devonshire and Chesterfield have received a great blow at Derby, where, on the death of John Stanhope, they set up another of the name. One Mr. Rivett, the Duke's chief friend and manager, stood himself and carried it by a majority of seventy-one' (Rivett 382, Thomas Stanhope 311). Rivett now obtained his pension through Lord Hartington to indemnify him for not standing again. In a memorandum of Newcastle's, of 21 Mar 1754 (32995, f. 115), appears the entry : 'Derby. The D. of D[evonshire] is inclined to bring in Mr. Vernon of Sudbury — Mr. Rivett, the present Member was to have a place in some of the inferior Commissions, and in the meantime 300£ a year'. See also ibid. f. 184, 3 Apr 1754, and f. 186, n.d. : Rivett was asking for '£400 a year or an employment'. On 8 June 1762, after Newcastle's resignation, the following note was sent to Charles Jenkinson by Sir Robert Wilmot, Devonshire's secretary and friend : 'Persons whom the Duke of Devonshire desires may be continued on the List of Pensions. William Hewett Esq. Thomas Rivett Esq.' (Bodleian, Oxford, North MS. c.2. f. 148). They were continued even after the Duke's dismissal. Rivett died on 6 Apr 1763 ; but his name still appears in 1763–4 in the Windsor lists of pensions (not of disbursements) ; and even in Rockingham's list of July 1765 ; though a month later, in a list of 'Pensions saved', Rivett's appears with a query against it. Obviously they were puzzled why he no longer applied for it. There was something peculiarly casual about those lists of 'Private Pensions' : once a person was on it, payment became automatic. The list prepared for Shelburne in Aug 1782 (Chatham Papers in the P.R.O.) is the first to inquire into their origin.

[3] A nephew of Speaker Onslow.

[4] About him see above, pp. 418–25.

				£	s.	d.
1755						
March 11th.	Mr. Andrews for Old Sarum .	.		100	0	0
	Gordon .	. .	.	20	0	0
18th.	To bury Fitzgerald .	.	.	10	10	0
27th.	Lutheran Minister's widow	.	.	20	0	0
	Mr. Hewit.[1] One year	.	.	400	0	0
	Mr. Carmichael. One year	.	.	300	0	0
	Ld. Willoughby of Parham. One year			400	0	0
April 8th.	.	. .	. .	1050	0	0
9th.	Ld. Kinnoull 1/4	.	.	200	0	0
12th.	Mr. Burrowes, Beadle of Cambridge [2].			100	0	0
16th.	Mr. Rice for Radnorshire	.	.	173	0	0
22nd.	Sir F. Poole.[3] One year	.	.	300	0	0
	Capt. Mackay. One year	.	.	300	0	0
	Mr. Medlycott	.	.	600	0	0
	Col. Mordaunt 1/4 to Lady Day		.	200	0	0
	Ld. Ilchester. One year	.	.	400	0	0
24th.	Baron Münchhausen. 1/2	.	.	500	0	0
	Earl of Warrington. 1/2 to Michaelmas			750	0	0
	Mr. Salusbury. One year	.	.	500	0	0
	Sir H. Bedingfeld	.	.	500	0	0

[1] In Newcastle's list for Rockingham of persons recommended for pensions (12 Oct 1765 ; 32970, f. 296), the note is put against his name : 'commonly called Count Hewett'. This suggests foreign extraction — and Francis Thompson, in his *History of Chatsworth*, mentions a Frenchman, 'Monsieur Huet (occasionally anglicized as Hewett . . .)', 'a person of great importance' who 'from 1687 until 1706 . . . supervised the reconstruction of the gardens as of the building' (pp. 36 and 80). Was his son the recipient of the pension ? There is a William Hewett, a close friend also of the Rutland family, from whom letters to the third and fourth Dukes of Devonshire are preserved at Chatsworth. On 3 Sept 1745 he informed the Duke of a 'favour' received from Pelham and prospects of having it settled for life; and in a letter from Paris, 27 July 1749, he writes to Lord Hartington : 'I hope the trees at Chatsworth grow well . . . my spirit of planting remains still as strong as ever, for I have ordered four acres . . . to be sow'd with acorns next year . . . but at present my spirit is of the rambling sort, and I think much more of Rome, Naples, Malta, etc., than of our dear county of Leicester . . .' This is clearly the man who is mentioned in John Nichols, *Leicestershire* (vol. ii, part 2, p. 581), as an intimate friend of Lord Granby, a great traveller, and 'said to have obtained a premium for setting the greatest quantity of acorns, and to have planted his trees in the form of the colonnade before St. Peter's at Rome'. But in Nichols he is given a purely English ancestry. He died at Florence 27 May 1766, aged 73. Is there no connexion between Huet who laid out the gardens at Chatsworth and this William Hewett ?

[2] Thomas Burrowes (1705–67), M.A., esquire-beadle to the University of Cambridge 1734–67.

[3] Sir Francis Poole, second Bt. (1683–1763), M.P. for Lewes 1743–63 ; his wife was Frances Pelham, a first cousin of Newcastle.

1755			£	s.	d.
April 24th.	Sir W. Middleton . . .		800	0	0
	Orford. Rent to Midsummer last .		100	0	0
	Gordon's transcriber . . .		50	0	0
28th.	Mr. Buller.[1] One year . .		200	0	0
	Mr. Till.[2] One year . . .		80	0	0
May 7th.	Lord Raymond . . .		800	0	0
	Mr. C. Hanbury for Minister .		100	0	0
	Mr. S. Jenyns . . .		600	0	0
	Mr. Charlton, Chairman of Committees		500	0	0
	Ld. Warwick 1/2 . . .		250	0	0
	Mr. Andrews for Okehampton .		180	0	0
	Mr. Hamilton, D's R. 1/2 . .		100	0	0
8th.	Mr. Lane.[3] Chairman. One year .		200	0	0
	Lord Morton's Lords [4] . .		250	0	0
	Mr. Ralph 1/2 . . .		150	0	0
14th.	Mr. Neale. Last payment . .		500	0	0
	Mr. Dugall Campbell, Sir Duncan's nephew [5]		400	0	0
	Sir W. Irby for money advanced to Mr. Thomas Pitt [6] . . .		1000	0	0
	Dr. Hepburn . . .		100	0	0
	Lord Radnor 1/2 to Lady Day .		400	0	0
	Pickle [7]		200	0	0

[1] John Buller (1721–86), M.P. for East Looe 1747–86 ; see above, pp. 321-3.

[2] John Till, of the Custom House, Chichester. He wrote to Newcastle on 23 Sept 1757 : 'I intend doing my self the honour of attending your Grace . . . to entreat the continuance of the goodness you have shewn me (ever since the late Mr. Pelham's death)' (32874, f. 252).

[3] Thomas Lane, Chairman of Middlesex Sessions.

[4] Lords Borthwick and Kirkcudbright £50 each, and Lord Rutherfurd £150 p.a.—Henry, fifteenth Lord Borthwick, was the eleventh in possession of the dignity, as some of his predecessors considered that 'a title without a suitable fortune was not eligible' (see Douglas-Paul, *Scots Peerage*). William Maclellan, sixth Lord Kirkcudbright, 'was in poor circumstances, and followed the occupation of a glover in Edinburgh' (see *ibid.*). George Durie claimed the title of Rutherfurd but never incontestably established the claim ; see letter from him to Newcastle explaining his claim to a secret service pension, 32870, f. 167.

[5] See under Sir Duncan Campbell, 9 Apr 1754.

[6] A complicated transaction arising from earlier debts and commitments of Thomas Pitt, the owner of Old Sarum, who had handed over the nomination for this so-called borough to the Government ; the claim arose on the election of Sir William Calvert, 18 Mar 1755 ; see letter from Sir W. Irby, 19 Mar 1755 ; 32853, ff. 378-9.

[7] In a letter to Newcastle, on 4 Apr 1755, 'Pickle' states that while engaged on his work, he had contracted £800 of debt ; 'he . . . hopes that he

1755			£	s.	d.
June	4th.	Mr. G. Harrison. One year [1] . .	500	0	0
		Sir J. Downing's man. 1/2 . .	100	0	0
	11th.	Lord Dudley. One year . .	600	0	0
	18th.	Ld. Dupplin for Cambridge. One year	550	0	0
		Mr. C. Whitworth . . .	200	0	0
		Mr. Hewit 1/2 . . .	200	0	0
		Mr. Rivett 1/2 . . .	150	0	0
	25th.	Gordon	20	0	0
July	2d.	Mr. A. Acourt.[2] Two years to Mid-summer	1000	0	0
		Col. Mordaunt 1/4 . . .	200	0	0
	3d.	Speaker's List to Midsummer. 100 for Bodens [3]	560	0	0
NB.	9th.	Ld. Peterborough 1/4 . .	100	0	0
		Guthrie 1/2 . . .	100	0	0
		. . . .	1050	0	0
		Lord Halifax 1/2 . . .	750	0	0
		Mr. Carey	100	0	0
	23rd.	Mr. Manly of Taunton [4] . .	70	0	0
		Mr. Maxwell for Taunton . .	500	0	0
		Lord Kinnoull 1/4 . . .	200	0	0
		Mr. W. Leveson's friend. One year .	150	0	0
	30th.	Lord Drummore's executors . .	100	0	0
		Mr. Schutz 1/2 . . .	200	0	0
		Mr. Burrowes. Beadle of Cambridge. 1/4.	25	0	0
Aug.	20th.	Gordon	20	0	0

be off hand enabled to pay off this triffile' and that until ampler compensation is given him 'he may relay upon somthing handsome, which he can yearly and regularly relay upon beeing payd him at a fixt time' (33050, f. 422).

[1] Further payments were, it seems, intended, but were never made ; see paper of 20 July 1757 ; 32997, ff. 237 and 330.

[2] Pierce Ashe A'Court (1707–68), M.P. for Heytesbury, his borough, 1734–68. After May 1762 his brother, General A'Court, voted regularly with the Opposition, and so did he on the rare occasions when he was present.

[3] Presumably 'Old Bodens', a friend and dependant of Newcastle. He wrote to Newcastle, 25 Nov 1753 : ' The situation of my affairs cannot be pleasant, as I have had no income this year last past, and at present want my friends to think of me, and give me their assistance' (32733, f. 315).

[4] Mayor of Taunton and Newcastle's election agent. The pension was continued to him under Bute and Grenville. 'I beg you will understand', wrote Lord Thomond to Jenkinson, 7 Sept 1763, 'it was given to Mr. Henry Manley, and not to the mayor of the town' (see N. S. Jucker, *Jenkinson Papers*, pp. 187-8). In Rockingham's accounts his pension still stands at £70 p.a. ; but in Grey Cooper's list of 1770 at £120 (Fortescue, vol. v, p. 467). He no longer appears in Robinson's lists of 1779–82.

1755			£	s.	d.
Aug.	20th.	Mr. Shelvoke [1] for Harwich . .	300	0	0
	27th.	Mr. Andrews for Okehampton .	100	0	0
		Mr. Bower. 1/2 to Midsummer .	100	0	0
Sept.	15th.	Orford Rent. 1/2 to Xmas . .	100	0	0
Oct.	15th.	. . . . .	1050	0	0
		Mrs. Cannon . . .	100	0	0
	17th.	Ld. Peterborough. 1/4 to Michaelmas	100	0	0
	23rd.	Ld. Kinnoull 1/4 . . .	200	0	0
		Mr. Hamilton, the Duke's relation 1/2	100	0	0
	24th.	Dr. Thorpe of Hastings. One year to			
		Michaelmas . . .	100	0	0
		Gordon	20	0	0
Nov.	5th.	E. of Warwick 1/2 . . .	250	0	0
		Mr. Ralph. 1/2 . . .	150	0	0
	14th.	E. of Radnor. 1/2 to Michaelmas .	400	0	0
		Mr. Dodd for Reading . .	500	0	0
		Col. Mordaunt. 1/4. . .	200	0	0
	24th.	E. of Warrington. 1/2 to Lady Day .	750	0	0
	25th.	Sir J. Downing's man. 1/2 to Michael-			
		mas	100	0	0
		Mr. Hewit. 1/2 to Michaelmas .	200	0	0
		Mr. Rivett. 1/2 . . .	150	0	0
Dec.	12th.	Mr. Whitworth. 1/2 . .	200	0	0
	13th.	Guthrie. 1/2 to Xmas . .	100	0	0
		Gordon	20	0	0
	19th.	Ld. Saye and Sele. One year .	600	0	0
1756					
Jan.	1st.	Col. Pelham. One year . .	500	0	0
	7th.	Ld. Kinnoull. 1/4 . . .	200	0	0
		Mr. Burrowes, Beadle of Cambridge.			
		1/4.	25	0	0
		. . . . .	1050	0	0
	14th.	Mr. Schutz. 1/2 . . .	200	0	0
		Ld. Peterborough . . .	100	0	0
		B. Münchhausen 1/2 . .	500	0	0
	15th.	E. of Halifax. 1/2 to Xmas . .	750	0	0
	22nd.	Col. Mordaunt. 1/4 to Xmas .	200	0	0
		Orford Rent. 1/2 . . .	100	0	0

[1] The name is marked S——ck, and the blank is not filled in even in the list of 'Disbursements for Parliament' compiled for Newcastle previous to the general election of 1761 (32999, ff. 34-5). But the identity of the recipient is proved by Roberts's paper of 17 July 1758 (32881, f. 317). Shelvoke (or Shelvock) was Secretary to the Post Office.

1756			£	s.	d.
Feb.	12th.	Mr. Michel. Prussian Minister [1] .	500	0	0
	13th.	Mr. Robert Colebrooke.[2] 1/2 .	300	0	0
		Mr. Allen. 1/2. Speaker's List .	100	0	0
		Justices. One year . . .	400	0	0
	17th.	Mr. Ellis for Bryer of Weymouth .	100	0	0
		Sir H. Bedingfeld. One year . .	500	0	0
	24th.	Mr. Nugent for Bristol . .	1000	0	0
March	2nd.	Gordon	20	0	0
	8th.	Mr. Nugent for Bristol . .	1000	0	0
	10th.	Mr. Colvile. One year . .	300	0	0
	11th.	Mr. R. Colebrooke. Remainder .	300	0	0
	19th.	Ld. Malpas [3]	300	0	0
	23rd.	Mr. G. Brudenell [4] . . .	300	0	0
April	2nd.	Mr. Fox for Hindon . . .	313	11	0
		Mr. Bower. 1/2 to Xmas . .	100	0	0
		Ld. Peterborough. 1/2 to Lady Day .	100	0	0
		Mr. Trist [5] for Totnes . .	100	0	0
		Mr. Charlton, Chairman of Committees	500	0	0

[1] The Prussian Minister in London.

[2] Robert Colebrooke (1718–84), of Chilham Castle, Kent, elder brother of Sir James Colebrooke, first Bt., M.P., and Sir George Colebrooke, second Bt., M.P., both merchants and Government contractors. Robert Colebrooke was M.P. for Maldon from 1741 till defeated at the general election of 1761 ; Minister to the Swiss Cantons, Jan 1762, when the pension stopped. On his return from Switzerland he received as from 21 Dec 1764 a pension on the Establishment of £500 p.a. (T. 38/229), and in 1765 was appointed by the Grenville Administration Ambassador to Turkey, but he never went out, and resigned on promise of another appointment or of having his pension doubled. On 16 Nov 1765 he wrote begging Granby's intercession — 'the circumstances of my finances are most deplorable' — he will have 'to decamp' and 'wait at Calais' (Rutland MSS. at Belvoir Castle). He was given an additional pension of £500 p.a., 18 Dec 1765. But on 25 Mar 1769 he was again writing to Granby that he will have to leave England, and asked for a loan. He died in France, 10 May 1784.

[3] George, Viscount Malpas (1724–64), eldest son of George, third Earl of Cholmondeley, served at Fontenoy and in the rebellion of 1745 ; M.P. for Bramber 1754–61, and for Corfe Castle 1761–64. His father had a pension of £3700 p.a. on the Irish Establishment, £2500 of it for life and £1200 during pleasure (see 32876, f. 17).

[4] George Bridges Brudenell (1725–1801), M.P. for Rutlandshire Dec 1754–61 and 1768–90, for Stamford 1761–68 ; on his father's side nephew of George, third Earl of Cardigan, through his mother nephew of Bartholomew Burton, M.P. for Camelford 1759–68, Governor of the Bank of England. Went with Newcastle into opposition and voted against General Warrants in 1764. He was a great friend of Lord Lincoln.

[5] Browse Trist (1698–1777) of Bowdon and Tristford, Devon ; M.P. for Totnes 1754–63, when he vacated his seat ; Recorder of the borough.

1756			£	s.	d.
April	2nd.	Mr. Maxwell for Taunton . .	675	0	0
	6th.	Mr. Whitworth. 1/2 to Lady Day .	200	0	0
		Mr. W. of R.[1] One year . .	60	0	0
		. . . . .	1050	0	0
	7th.	Dr. Hepburn. One year . .	100	0	0
	8th.	Ld. Willoughby of Parham. One year	400	0	0
	9th.	Sir F. Poole	300	0	0
	13th.	Col. Mordaunt. 1/4 to Lady Day .	200	0	0
		Captain Mackay . . .	300	0	0
		Ld. Kinnoull. 1/4 . . .	200	0	0
	15th.	Mr. T. Leslie . . .	500	0	0
		Gordon	20	0	0
		Orford Rent. 1/2 . . .	100	0	0
	28th.	Mr. Vere of Stoneveers.[2] One year .	400	0	0
	30th.	Mr. Hamilton. D. H's R. 1/2 to Lady Day	100	0	0
May	4th.	Lord Ilchester . . .	400	0	0
	6th.	Lord Home	200	0	0
		Mr. Ralph. 1/2 . . .	150	0	0
		Gordon's Transcriber. One year .	50	0	0
	8th.	E. of Warwick. 1/2 . . .	250	0	0
	21st.	Mr. Burrowes, Beadle of Cambridge .	50	0	0
		Sir W. Middleton. One year .	800	0	0
	27th.	Sir J. Downing's man. 1/2 . .	100	0	0
June	10th.	Mr. Buller. One year . .	200	0	0
		Mr. Till of Chichester . .	80	0	0
	Q.	Ld. Raymond . . .	800	0	0
		Mr. Lane. One year . .	200	0	0
		Ld. Malpas. 1/2 . . .	300	0	0
		Mr. Medlycott.[3] One year . .	600	0	0
		Mr. Hewit. 1/2 to Lady Day .	200	0	0
		Mr. Rivett 1/2 . . .	150	0	0
	11th.	Mr. D. Campbell. One year . .	400	0	0
		Mr. Guthrie. 1/2 to Midsummer .	100	0	0
		Ld. Dupplin for Cambridge. One year	550	0	0
		Mr. A. Acourt. One year . .	500	0	0
		Speaker's List. One year . .	460	0	0
		Gordon	20	0	0
July	2d.	Col. Mordaunt 1/4 . . .	200	0	0
		E. of Warrington. 1/2 to Michaelmas .	750	0	0

[1] Unidentified.
[2] James Vere, of Stonebyres, M.P. for Lanarkshire 1754–59.
[3] See his letter of 9 June (32865, f. 243) and above, p. 407.

1756				£	s.	d.
July	2d.	Ld. Peterborough. 1/4 . .	100	0	0
	6th.	. . . . .	1050	0	0
		Ld. Kinnoull 1/4 . . .	200	0	0
	7th.	E. of Halifax. 1/2 to Midsummer .	750	0	0
		Baron Münchhausen, to Midsummer .	500	0	0
	21st.	Mr. Schutz 1/2 . . .	200	0	0
		Mr. Jenyns [1] for Mr. Holmes . .	600	0	0
		Mr. Manly for Taunton . .	70	0	0
	23rd.	Ld. Warwick 1/4 to Midsummer .	125	0	0
Aug.	5th.	Ld. Morton's Lords. One year .	250	0	0
		Gordon	20	0	0
		Mr. Leveson's friend. One year .	150	0	0
	6th.	Mr. G. Brudenell. Remainder .	200	0	0
	12th.	Mr. Andrews for Okehampton .	100	0	0
Sept.	3d.	Mr. Whitworth. 1/4 to Midsummer	100	0	0
	23rd.	Ld. Dudley	600	0	0
Oct.	6th.	E. of Tankerville [2] . . .	500	0	0
		Mrs. Krahé. 1/2 [3] . . .	25	0	0
	7th.	E. of Peterborough. 1/4 . .	100	0	0
	13th.	E. of Radnor	400	0	0
		. . . . .	1050	0	0
	19th.	Col. Lentulers (?) . . .	500	0	0
		A snuff box	63	0	0
		Justices. One year at Michaelmas .	400	0	0
	26th.	Col. Mordaunt. 1/4 to Michaelmas .	200	0	0
		Gordon	20	0	0
		Orford. Rent and expenses . .	200	0	0
		Ld. Kinnoull. 1/4 to Michaelmas .	200	0	0
	27th.	Baron Münchhausen . .	500	0	0
		E. of Warrington. 1/2 to Lady Day	750	0	0
		E. of Warwick. 1/4 to Michaelmas .	125	0	0
		Mr. Ralph. 1/2 to Michaelmas .	150	0	0

[1] Should be 'Jenison'; Ralph Jenison, M.P. for Newport, I.o.W., acted as intermediary between Newcastle and Holmes.

[2] In Newcastle's 'Mem[s] for the King', 12 Sept 1756 (32867, ff. 290-1), appears the following entry :

Pensions agreed to.	Ld. Tankerville	£800 per ann.
Q. As to the commencement.	Ld. Montfort	800 per ann.
£400 if sufficient, private.	Mr. Watson of Berwick	500 ——
Not yet spoke of.	Mr. Thos. Fane	200 ——

[3] Catherine Margaretha Krahé, 'an old servant of the late Queen Caroline' (32970, f. 296).

1756					£	s.	d.
Oct.	30th.	Mr. Hamilton, D's R. 1/2 to Michaelmas	.	. . .	100	0	0
		Mr. Whitworth. 1/4 to Michaelmas	.	. . .	100	0	0
		Dr. Thorpe of Hastings	.	.	100	0	0
		Mr. Burrowes, Beadle of Cambridge	.		50	0	0
		E. of Cork 1/2 [1]	.	.	400	0	0
Nov.	2d.	Mr. T. Fane. One year [2]	.	.	200	0	0
		Mr. Bower. 1/2 to Michaelmas	.		100	0	0
	4th.	Col. Pelham. One year	.	.	500	0	0
	6th.	Lady Trelawny to Mr. Gashry [3]	.		100	0	0
	9th.	Marquis of Rockingham's friend [4]	.		150	0	0
		Sir F. Poole .	.	.	500	0	0
		Mr. Mallet [5] for his book	.	.	300	0	0
		Mr. Cooke [6] to Mr. Gybbon and Mr. Watson	.	. .	150	0	0
		Mr. Clevland for a clergyman [7]	.		240	0	0

[1] John Boyle, fifth Earl of Cork (1707–62), succeeded in 1753 his distant cousin Richard, fourth Earl of Cork and third Earl of Burlington, in his Irish honours while 'the Barony of Clifford . . . and the large estates of the Clifford and Boyle families' devolved on his cousin's daughter Charlotte, Duchess of Devonshire. Lord Cork had literary ambitions ; Samuel Johnson described him as 'a feeble-minded man' whose 'conversation was like his writings, neat and elegant, but without strength'. Lord Macaulay rightly describes his book on Swift as 'most contemptible trash' (MS. note in his copy, now at the British Museum).

[2] Thomas Fane (1700–71), a Bristol attorney, M.P. for the family borough of Lyme Regis from 1753 till 1762 when he became eighth Earl of Westmorland. The pension was promised when his brother Francis Fane left the Board of Trade in Dec 1755 ; but he waived it in 1758 (see page opposite, footnote (2) under 6 Oct 1756, and pp. 451-2 under 1 July 1758).

[3] The identity of the two, whose names in these accounts are marked with initials only, is established by 32997, ff. 68, 70, and 74. About the payment see above, p. 205.

[4] Neither this friend nor the one added under 20 Feb 1760 is ever named.

[5] David Mallet (1701–65), poet and political writer, served in turn Frederick Prince of Wales, Bolingbroke, Newcastle, and Bute (see *D.N.B.*) ; the book is his pamphlet against Admiral Byng, *Observations on the 12th Article of War* ; about it see P. C. Yorke, *Life of Lord Hardwicke*, vol. ii, pp. 350 and 353-4. In 32997, f. 68, this payment appears as 'Mr. Mallet for the expence of printing — 300'.

[6] Mr. Cooke, of Great Swifts, near Cranbrooke, Kent, who later on always appears as 'Mr. Gybbon's friend' (Ph. Gybbon was M.P. for Rye 1701–62). See Cooke's letter of thanks to Newcastle, 17 Nov 1756 ; 32869, f. 80. 'Mr. Watson' is Lewis Watson, M.P. for Kent, subsequently first Lord Sondes.

[7] This item is expanded in 32997, f. 70 : 'Mr. Clevland, paid for an election to a clergyman for two years, at £120 p.a. — £240'.

					£	s.	d.
Nov.	9th.	Springer [1]	.	.	100	0	0
		Mr. Jones [2]	.	.	1359	14	6

Money received March 1754–November 1756
(33044, f. 27)

1754					£	s.	d.
March 19th.	Ballance	.	.	.	7,367	17	0
April	4th.	.	.	.	10,000	0	0
	7th.	By Ld. Bath [3]	.	.	1,000	0	0
	11th.	.	.	.	5,000	0	0
	24th.	Mr. Fox. Remainder from Malmesbury [4]			356	18	6

[1] Christopher Springer, a Swedish merchant, who in 1746 engaged 'in the English and Russian interest', was seized by the French party and condemned to lifelong imprisonment; escaped after four and a half years to Russia; had to leave Russia as the French demanded his extradition, and escaped to England (see his Memorial to the Duke of Newcastle, n.d.; 33055, f. 187). He states that he has recently received by the Duke's order £20, 'which considering his circumstances has been of very little relief to your Memorialist who unless some certain provision is made for him must remain entirely destitute'. In 32997, f. 68, the figure '20' first appears against his name, but is crossed out and '100' substituted. The pension continues to appear in all available Secret Service lists for the next 26 years, and in the 'List of Private Pensions' prepared for Shelburne in Aug 1782 (Chatham Papers in the P.R.O.) the remark is placed against Springer's name: 'A schemer, and is said at times to have given material information to Government'.

[2] There is an undated memorandum by Newcastle, probably of 3 Nov 1756 (32997, f. 68), closing the accounts: 'I have made up Your Majesty's private account, and shall have the honor to bring you the ballance due to Your Majesty which is £3699 14s. 6d.' On this follow, however, various recommendations; those allowed by the King (see ff. 68 and 74) are obviously the eight last entries in these accounts (Col. Pelham on 4 Nov, till Springer on the 9th), and they make a total of £2040, which would reduce the balance to £1659 : 14 : 6. But possibly the calculation was made on 1 or 2 Nov, or at least without the two payments of 2 Nov being deducted; for the entry 'Mr. Thomas Fane — 200' still appears in the first draft of the recommendations, though subsequently crossed out. Anyhow, the last entry in these accounts means that this was the balance left in John Roberts's hands, which he paid over to H. V. Jones, Newcastle's private secretary, and which Newcastle handed over to the King. But on my calculation the sum total of the money accounted for in this first book is by £400 short of the sum acknowledged as received by John Roberts.

[3] Refund of money paid for Lord Pulteney's seat at Old Sarum.

[4] Henry Fox wrote to the Duke of Devonshire on 1 June 1758 (Devonshire MS. 330.225): 'H.M. in 1750 laid down 1,000£, I therefore thought I had no right at the general election to nominate; and chose those His

1754						£	s.	d.
May 1st.	.	.	.	.	.	7,000	0	0
July 10th.	.	.	.	.	.	10,000	0	0
Nov. 26th	.	.	.	.	.	10,000	0	0
1755								
Feb. 1st.	.	.	.	.	.	10,000	0	0
May 8th.	.	.	.	.	.	10,000	0	0
July 11th.	.	.	.	.	.	6,000	0	0
Nov. 19th.	.	.	.	.	.	10,000	0	0
1756								
March 2nd.	.	.	.	.	.	10,000	0	0
June 4th.	.	.	.	.	.	10,000	0	0
Sept. 22nd.	.	.	.	.	.	10,000	0	0

Received in the whole £116,724 15 6

SECRET SERVICE ACCOUNTS, JULY 15, 1757–OCTOBER 25, 1760

With Accounts of the Arrears for this Period paid off under
George III

[THERE are three copies of these accounts in 33044: the first
copy, ff. 28-65, gives only payments made before George II
died; the second, ff. 67-106, adds the arrears of George II's reign
paid off under George III, and is the copy initialed by him; the
third, ff. 107-77, covers the same ground as the second.]

1757		£
July 20th.	To Lord Halifax, 1/2 a year at Midsummer last	750
	To the Earl of Tankerville, 1/2 a year .	400
	To Mr. Manly, the Mayor of Taunton, as usual, one year	70

Grace of Newcastle from the King named to me [Brice Fisher and Lord
George Bentinck], and when they were elected paid the D. of Newcastle
360£ which was the ballance of the thousand after deducting what H.M.
need not, but chose, to allow the candidates towards their election'. See
also paper on the general election of 1754, marked Newcastle House, 20
Mar 1754 (32995, ff. 104-5). Lastly a paper on 'Elections', drawn up by
Newcastle on 12 Dec 1760 (32999, f. 119), thus refers to that affair:

Malmesbury
Mr. Fox £1,000 given to elect Mr. Fox High Steward.
Ld. Kinnoul Q. Whether the £1000 was the King's money.
To speak to Mr. Fox about it.
Mr. Fisher was chose, and Lord G. Bentinck was
chose, at my recommendation. . . .

1757   £

July 20th.   To Mr. Schutz, 1/2 a year .   .   .   200
              To Col. Mordaunt, one quarter .   .   200
      21st.   To the Earl of Warwick, one quarter .   125
      22d.   To the Earl of Peterborough, half a year .   200
              NB.—My Ld. Peterborough acquainted
              me that the Duke of Devonshire had not
              paid him the Lady Day quarter
              To Mr. Scott [1] — one quarter .   .   125
              To Mr. Holmes, one year, by Mr. Jenison for
              the three Isle of Wight boroughs .   .   600
              To Mr. Andrews — one year for Okehampton   100
      28th.   To Lord Kinnoull, one quarter .   .   200
      29th.   To Lord Rutherfurd, one year .   .   150
              Gordon, two months .   .   .   20
              To Mr. Capel Hanbury, for two years, for the
              Dissenting Ministers in Monmouthshire, as
              usual   200
Aug. 5th.   The Speaker's List   460
              To Mr. Charles Hamilton.[2] Half a year of a
              pension of 1200£ given him by Your Majesty
              as the Duke of Devonshire informs me .   600
Sept. 2d.   To Mrs. Krahé. 1/2 a year due at Lady Day   25
       9th.   Lord Morton's two friends.[3] A year at Mid-
              summer. 50£ each .   .   .   100
      13th.   To Mr. Thorpe's executors at Hastings due at
              Lady Day. 1/2 a year .   .   .   50

---

[1] George Lewis Scott (1708–70), late preceptor to the Prince of Wales
(George III). The last instalment of this pension appears on 19 Jan 1758,
'one quarter to Christmas', Scott being appointed in Feb a Commissioner of the Excise (£1000 p.a.), which office he retained till his death in
1780. About this appointment, demanded in a peremptory way by the
Prince and Lord Bute — the Prince 'thinking derogatory to his dignity, to
suffer a person to remain unprovided for, who once had the honour of being
concerned in his education' — see 32877, ff. 350, 382-3, and 408-9.

[2] Charles Hamilton (1704–86), ninth son of James, sixth Earl of Abercorn ; M.P. for Truro 1741–47, and a Member of the Irish Parliament 1727–
1760 ; in 1743 he was appointed Receiver-General of the King's Revenues
in Minorca ; it was as compensation for that sinecure, which disappeared with
the loss of the island, that he was given the pension. His cause was passionately espoused by Fox — if Charles Hamilton is omitted, he wrote to the
Duke of Devonshire on 1 Nov 1756, 'I can take nothing'. There follows a
series of letters on the subject of 'my old and undone friend Hamilton'
whose claims are pressed with growing heat (Devonshire MS. 330.173, 181,
183, 191, 192). See also Ilchester, *Henry Fox*, vol. ii, pp. 15-17.

[3] This time Lord Rutherford's pension is entered separately ; see above
under 29 July.

1757			£
Sept.	30th.	To Mr. Justice Fielding — 1/2 a year due at Michaelmas	200
		Mr. Justice Lane, Chairman. One year .	200
		Gordon — two months . . .	20
		Mr. Guthrie — one quarter . . .	50
Oct.	11th.	To Mr. Till of Chichester — one year to Michaelmas	80
	13th.	To the Earl of Peterborough — one quarter to Michaelmas	100
		Mr. George Brudenell — one year . .	500
		Retained to myself by Your Majesty's special command — one quarter . . .	1050
	18th.	Paid to Baron Münchhausen by Your Majesty's order — half a year to Christmas next .	500
	19th.	To Mr. Charles Whitworth — half a year .	200
	22d.	To Mr. Scott — one quarter . . .	125
		To Lord Kinnoull — one quarter . .	200
		To Mr. Hamilton, the Duke of Hamilton's relation, half a year . . .	100

N.B.—50 ad-
ditl. to be   To Mrs. Boone,[1] half a year to Christmas next   200
replaced.

Nov.	17th.	To the Earl of Warwick — one quarter .	125
	18th.	Mr. Ralph, half a year at Michaelmas last .	150
	22d.	Mr. Burrowes, Beadle of Cambridge, one year	100
	29th.	To Gordon. Two months . . .	20
Dec.	1st.	To Orford rent, half a year due at Christmas last	100
		Orford expences	100
		Col. Mordaunt, a quarter due at Michaelmas .	200
	7th.	Given by Your Majesty as a present to Major Grant, Aide de Camp to the King of Prussia	500
	20th.	To Baron Münchhausen . . .	1000
		To the Hereditary Prince of Wolfenbuttle .	2000
		To the Earl of Warrington, one year to Michaelmas, and then to cease [2] . .	1500

[1] Anne, wife of Daniel Boone, M.P., daughter and co-heir of George Evelyn, of Rooksnest, Surrey, and widow of Thomas Gregg. Daniel Boone, M.P. 1741–61, had attached himself to Frederick, Prince of Wales, had been a Groom of his Bedchamber, and after his death in 1751 became 'a clerk in the household of the Princess Dowager'. The pension for his wife was presumably obtained through Leicester House influence from the Devonshire-Pitt Administration (see 32999, f. 72). About these additional £50 see under 27 June 1758.

[2] Lord Warrington had written to the Duke of Newcastle on 1 Nov 1757 : 'My years and growing infirmities making me little capable of being

2 G

1757   £
Dec.   23d.   To the Earl of Cork, half a year to Michaelmas   400
              To Mr. Hewit, half a year to Michaelmas   .   200
              To Mr. Rivett, half a year to Michaelmas   .   150

1758
Jan.   10th. Retained to myself by Your Majesty's special
                  command, one quarter   .   .   .   1050
       12th. To Mr. Offley, half a year to make up his place   200
              To the Earl of Kinnoull, one quarter   .   200
              To Mr. Tyrrel, the French officer, who was
                  employed in matters of secrecy by Colonel
                  Lawrence in Nova Scotia [1] — one year at
                  Christmas.   200
                      N.B.—The Duke of Devonshire paid him
                  the same sum last year.
              To Mr. Guthrie, one quarter   .   .   50
       17th. To the Earl of Peterborough, one quarter to
                  Christmas.   100
       19th. To Mr. Scott. One quarter to Christmas   .   125
              To the Earl of Warwick, one quarter to
                  Christmas.   125
              Marquess of Rockingham's friend, one year to
                  Christmas.   150
       20th. To the Earl of Halifax. Half a year to
                  Christmas.   750
       25th. To Mr. Charles Whitworth, one quarter to
                  Christmas.   100
       29th. To Gordon. Two months .   .   .   20
              To the Earl of Tankerville, half a year to
                  Christmas.   400
              To Sir Francis Poole, one year at Christmas .   300

any ways serviceable to His Majesty, I ought not to be longer a burthen to
him : that if your Grace please to clear my affair to last Michaelmass, it will
be the last I shall either ask or expect' (32875, f. 372). Anyhow he would
not have seen another payment as he died on 2 Aug 1758.

   [1] For a memorial of the services rendered in Nova Scotia by 'Monsieur
Pichon, now called Mr. Tyrell', see 32866, ff. 52-7 ; Tyrrell's application is
summarized by Lord Halifax (f. 51) and supported in a covering letter of
6 July 1756 (f. 49). He is mentioned in Newcastle's 'Mems for the King',
12 Sept 1756 (32867, f. 290) as 'the French deserter from Cape Breton' and
a pension of £200 p.a. is proposed for him. This pension was paid to him
till his death in 1781 (see 37836, f. 139 and the 'List' prepared for
Shelburne in Aug 1782). For an account of his life see *Selections from the
Documents of Nova Scotia*, ed. T. B. Akins (1869), p. 229. There is a MS.
vol. entitled 'Tyrrell Papers' in the N.S. Archives.

1758			£
Jan.	29th.	Col. Mordaunt, one quarter to Christmas .	200
		Mr. Robert Colebrooke, in part of an allowance of 600£ pr. ann.	300
		To Col. Pelham, one year to Christmas .	500
Feb.	8th.	To Mr. Ellis for Bryer of Weymouth, one year to Christmas	100
	22d.	To Mr. Schutz, 1/2 a year to Christmas .	200
March	9th.	Mr. Jenison.[1] 1/2 a year to Christmas .	900
		Mr. Charles Hamilton. 1/2 a year to Christmas	600
	14th.	Given by Your Majesty, as a present to Major Marwitz, Aide de Camp to the King of Prussia	500
	15th.	To the Duke of Devonshire for Sir Henry Bedingfeld, one year due at Lady Day last .	500
	17th.	To Mrs. Krahé, 1/2 a year due at Michaelmas	25
		Mr. Colvile. One year . . .	300
	24th.	To Mr. Robert Colebrooke. Remainder of an allowance of 600£ pr. ann. . .	300
		N.B.—He received the same sum last year in the same manner from the Duke of Devonshire.	
	29th.	Gordon. Two months . . .	20
April	6th.	To the Earl of Peterborough, one quarter to Lady Day	100
		To Mr. Justice Fielding, 1/2 a year due at Lady Day	200
		To Lord Willoughby of Parham, one year to Lady Day	400
		To Mr. Guthrie — one quarter to Lady Day .	50
	8th.	Retained to myself by Your Majesty's special command. One quarter . . .	1050
	14th.	To the Earl of Kinnoull. One quarter to Lady Day	200
		To Col. Mordaunt. One quarter to Lady Day	200

[1] Ralph Jenison (1696–1758), M.P. for Northumberland 1723–41, and for Newport, Isle of Wight, 1749–58 ; Master of H.M. Buckhounds, 1737–44 and 1746–57, when Jenison gave up the Buckhounds to Lord Bateman, and as a compensation was offered a pension of £1500 p.a. from secret service funds (see Newcastle to Jenison, 1 July 1757 ; 32872, f. 5). Jenison replied by asking that £1000 of it be placed on the Irish Establishment, as secret service pensions depended upon the life of the King (*ibid.* ff. 39 and 55-7). Obviously as a compromise, the pension was fixed higher, at £1800 p.a . Jenison died on 15 May 1758.

1758   £
April   14th.   Given by Your Majesty's order to Querré, the
                French Pilot [1]   300
                   N.B.—Querré is to have an allowance of
                   100£ pr. ann. to commence from Michaelmas
                   last.
                To Lord Malpas in part of an allowance of
                600£ pr. ann.   300
        18th.   To Mr. Charlton, Chairman of the Com-
                mittees, one year as usual .   .   .   500
                To the Earl of Ilchester. One year .   .   400
        19th.   To Mrs. Krahé, 1/2 a year at Lady Day   .   25
        20th.   To Mr. Charles Whitworth. One quarter to
                Lady Day.   100
                To Mr. Ralph, 1/2 a year to Lady Day   .   150
        22d.   To Col. Pelham, one quarter to Lady Day .   125
                   N.B.—Colonel Pelham desires to be paid
                   quarterly for the future.
May   2d.   Lord Saye and Sele. One year to Lady Day.   600
        4th.   To Mr. Cooke, Mr. Gybbon's friend, 1/2 a year
                from Michaelmas to Lady Day   .   .   50
                   N.B.—Mr. Cooke's allowance has been
                   reduced from 150£ to 100£ pr. an. since he
                   had an employment.[2]
                Lord Montfort. One year to Christmas, of an
                allowance which, by Your Majesty's com-
                mand, was to commence last Christmas was
                a twelvemonth [3]   800

        [1] Joseph Thierry, the French pilot who directed the attack against
Rochefort in 1757. His pension appears in all available secret service lists
till 1782, and was presumably continued to him till his death.
        [2] See letter from Cooke to Gybbon, 18 Jan 1758 (32877, f. 172): 'I am
Agent for Prisoners of War . . . the annual salary is 200£, for which I pay
dayly attendance'. Requests him to ask Newcastle 'to make up the retaining
fee (as he is pleas'd to call it) one hundred pounds'. See also Cooke's letter
of thanks to Newcastle, 5 Feb 1758, ibid. f. 362.
        [3] Thomas Bromley, second Lord Montfort. His father, Henry Bromley,
represented Cambridgeshire, 1727–41, when created Baron Montfort; continued chief Whig manager for Cambridgeshire; committed suicide on 1
Jan 1755. Thomas Bromley, returned for Cambridge at the general election
of 1754, now succeeded to the peerage. On 11 May 1756, he reminded
Newcastle of a promise to give him a pension before the end of the session.
'I hope His Majesty and your Grace will not think £1000 p.a. too much
considering the condition I am left in, incumbered with debts to the amount
of above £30,000, and my estate out of repair and in a very ruinous condition.' (32864, f. 524.) The pension was agreed to in Sept 1756 (see
footnote (1) under 6 Oct 1756).

1758   £

May	11th.	To Mr. Jenison.[1] One quarter to Lady Day	450
	24th.	To Mr. Dodd by Your Majesty's command .	500
		To Mr. Allen, the Speaker's nephew, half a year to Christmas	100
	29th.	Gordon — two months . . .	20
	31st.	Mr. Hamilton, the late Duke of Hamilton's relation, half a year . . .	100
		To the Earl of Warwick. One quarter to Lady Day	125
June	15th.	To Lord Morton's three friends :	

Lord Rutherfurd . £150 ⎫
Lord Borthwicke .   50   ⎬ 250
Lord Kircudbright .   50   ⎭
One year

	16th.	To Mr. Holmes — one year for the three Isle of Wight boroughs . . .	600
		To Mr. Medlycott	600
		To Gordon's Transcriber. One year .	50
		To Mr. Hewet. 1/2 a year to Lady Day .	200
		To Mr. Rivett. 1/2 a year to Lady Day .	150
		To Lord Dupplin, one year for Cambridge as usual	550
		To Mr. Vere of Stoneveers. One year .	400
	23rd.	Mr. Dugall Campbell. One year . .	400
		Lord Home. One year . . .	200
	27th.	Dr. Hepburne. One year . . .	100
		To Mr. Guthrie. A quarter to Midsummer .	50
		To Mrs. Boone. 1/2 a year due at Midsummer	200

N.B.—Mr. Boone promis'd to return 50, if Your Majesty shall not think proper to encrease Mrs. Boone's allowance from 300£ to 400£ pr. ann.

		To Orford rent. 1/2 a year due at Midsummer 1757	100
		To Ld. Malpas. Remainder . .	300
	30th.	Given by Your Majesty as a present to Colonel Reden, dispatch'd by Prince Ferdinand .	500
July	1st.	To Mr. Henry Fane for Lyme as usual [2] .	100

[1] The receipt of this payment is acknowledged by his wife (32880, f. 54), he being too ill to write ; died on 15 May.

[2] Henry Fane wrote to Newcastle on 13 June 1758 : 'I informed my friends of Lyme that your Grace had promised to renew the £100 a year

1758   £

July   6th.   To the Earl of Kinnoull. One quarter to Mid-
              summer   200
              To Colonel Pelham. One quarter to Mid-
              summer   125
              The Speaker's List. One year .   .   360
              Mr. Allen, the Speaker's nephew, half a year
              to Midsummer   100
       7th.   To Mr. Charles Whitworth. One quarter to
              Midsummer   100
      14th.   To the Earl of Peterborough. One quarter to
              Midsummer   100
              To Col. Mordaunt. One quarter to Mid-
              summer   200
              To Mr. Manly, the Mayor of Taunton, as
              usual, one year   70
              Retained to myself by Your Majesty's special
              command — one quarter .   .   .   1050
              To the Earl of Halifax, half a year to Mid-
              summer   750
      17th.   To Baron Münchhausen, 1/2 a year to Mid-
              summer   500
      18th.   To Mr. Andrews, one year for Okehampton .   100
      21st.   Given by Your Majesty's order for a sword
              for Prince Ferdinand of Brunswick .   1500
      28th.   To Mr. Acourt Ashe. One year to Christmas
              was a twelvemonth, there being two years
              due at Christmas last .   .   .   500
      29th.   To Gordon. Two months .   .   .   20
Aug. 11th.   To Mr. Offley, 1/2 a year to Midsummer .   200
      15th.   To Mr. Schutz, 1/2 a year to Midsummer .   200
              Mr. Charles Hamilton, 1/2 a year to Mid-
              summer   600
              The Earl of Warwick, one quarter to Mid-
              summer   125
      29th.   To the Earl of Tankerville, 1/2 a year to Mid-
              summer   400
              To Mr. Acourt Ashe, one year to Christmas last   500

for them, and they are pressing me for the money. . . . But I beg leave
to mention that this must not be looked upon as any new or additional
expence, because till within a very few years it was constantly paid from
1734 (when my uncle first went to that place) and by a stipulation when my
late brother left the Board of Trade [Dec 1755], my brother Thomas was to
have £200 a year which he waves and is therefore a saving' (32880, f. 431).

1758			£
Aug.	29th.	To Mr. Thomas Watson, 1/2 a year . .	400
		To Mr. Justice Lane, one year . .	200
		To the Earl of Cork, 1/2 a year to Lady Day	400
Sept.	5th.	Lord Montfort, 1/2 a year to Midsummer .	400
		Mr. John Ramy, a friend of Mr. Charles Townshend of Yarmouth.[1] One year .	200
	12th.	Given by Your Majesty's order to Garstin, the messenger, for bringing the news of the King of Prussia's victory . . .	50
	19th.	To Mr. Capel Hanbury, for one year for the Dissenting Ministers in Monmouthshire as usual	100
	27th.	To Sir Henry Bedingfeld, one year to Lady Day last	500
Oct.	3d.	To Mr. Guthrie. A quarter to Michaelmas .	50
		To Gordon. Two months . . .	20
	6th.	To Mr. Justice Fielding — 1/2 a year to Michaelmas	200
	17th.	To the Earl of Peterborough. One quarter due at Michaelmas	100
		To Colonel Pelham. One quarter due at Michaelmas	125
		To Querré, the French Pilot, one year due at Michaelmas	100
		To Mr. Till of Chichester, one year to Michaelmas	80
	18th.	To Mr. Ralph, 1/2 a year due at Michaelmas .	150
		To Mrs. Krahé, 1/2 a year due at Michaelmas	25

[1] John Ramey (c. 1718–94), a Yarmouth attorney, started as a Townshend-Walpole agent in the borough. Refused a place in the Customs, he encouraged in 1754 his father-in-law, William Browne, a wealthy Yarmouth merchant, and Richard Fuller, a neighbouring squire, to stand in opposition to that interest. After Fuller had run 'Spanish' Charles Townshend very close at the by-election in Dec 1756, Browne was bought off with a Receivership, and Ramey with the pension 'till an employment falls' (33039, f. 79). He did not apply to Bute for the continuation of his pension, but in 1764, through Lord Orford's influence, was appointed Receiver-General (Orford to Grenville, 26 Mar 1764; Grenville MSS. in the possession of Sir John Murray). He had the sole direction of the Townshend-Walpole interest at Yarmouth, 1758–68, when deposed by a combination of rivals. Thereafter he gradually withdrew from Yarmouth politics, and turned country gentleman. His daughter and co-heiress married in 1768 Alexander, ninth Earl of Home. (Ex inform. Brian Hayes.) Ramey did not apply for his pension to Newcastle's successors ; nor was it renewed by Rockingham.

1758   £

Oct.	18th.	Retained to myself by Your Majesty's special command, one quarter . . .	1050
Nov.	1st.	To Springer, the Swedish merchant, who has suffer'd so much	100
	7th.	To Mr. Chancellor of the Exchequer for Mr. Duckett,[1] one year to Michaelmas last .	500
		To Colonel Mordaunt, one quarter to Michaelmas	200
		To the Earl of Warwick, one quarter to Michaelmas	125
	17th.	To Your Majesty for Monsr. de Münchhausen	500
	22d.	To Orford rents, 1/2 a year due at Christmas last	100
		Orford expences	100
Dec.	7th.	To Mr. Burrowes, Beadle of Cambridge, one year to Michaelmas last . . .	100
		To Gordon — two months . . .	20
	19th.	To Mr. Henry Poole, in lieu of his place [2] at Minorca, which he has lost . .	500
		To Mr. Jeffreys by Your Majesty's order .	500
	20th.	To Mr. Hamilton, the late Duke of Hamilton's relation, 1/2 a year to Michaelmas . .	100

[1] Thomas Duckett (1713–66), a London merchant and patron of the borough of Calne, for which he sat 1754–57 and 1761–66 ; he vacated his seat in 1757 to make room for Dr. Hay, at that time a follower of Pitt, agreeing 'to accept a pension of £500 p.a. till an office of that value can be found for him' (Pitt to Newcastle, 26 June 1756 ; 32871, f. 406). About Duckett see my article in the *Wiltshire Archaeological Magazine*, vol. xliv, June 1928.

[2] H. Poole, son of Sir Francis Poole, M.P. for Lewes (about him see under 22 Apr 1755), and through his mother related to Newcastle, had been Deputy Paymaster at Minorca, which office disappeared with the loss of the island. The family 'are starving by the loss of their place in Minorca', wrote Newcastle about them on 23 Aug 1757 (32873, f. 244). Unless some help was given them, 'it would be impossible for Sir Francis Poole to continue at Lewes', wrote Henry Poole to Newcastle on 14 Jan 1758. 'I have very often endeavour'd to perswade him to represent the situation of his affairs to your Grace, but have never been able to prevail with him' (32877, f. 128). The entry 'Mr. Poole £500' appears in the 'Memds. for the King' on 10 Oct and 17 Dec 1758 (32884, f. 308, 32886, f. 214) ; in the latter the remark is added in the margin : 'Minorca place, starving, the first vacancy in the Customs or Excise — his Minorca place, the late Queen'. Henry Poole was made Commissioner of the Excise in Oct 1760, when the pension stopped. Poole had, moreover, a place at the Exchequer worth £200, which he nominally retained with the Commissionership, but the profits of which, after being appointed to the Commissionership, he had to pay over to H. V. Jones (see 32911, ff. 272-3).

1758   £
Dec. 21st. To Dr. Molesworth [1]   .   .   .   200
             N.B.—Dr. Molesworth is by Your
             Majesty's order to have a pension of 200£
             pr. ann.

1759
Jan. 12th. To Mrs. Boone, 1/2 a year due at Christmas .   200
             To Colonel Pelham, one quarter of a year due
             at Christmas   125
     17th.   Retained to myself, by Your Majesty's special
             command, one quarter   .   .   .   1050
     18th.   To the Earl of Halifax, 1/2 a year at Christmas   750
             To Baron Münchhausen, 1/2 a year to Christmas   500
             To Mr. Allen, the Speaker's nephew, 1/2 a
             year due at Christmas   .   .   .   100
             To Lord Montfort, 1/2 a year due at Christmas   400
             To Mr. Hewet, 1/2 a year to Michaelmas   .   200
             To Mr. Rivett, 1/2 a year to Michaelmas   .   150
             To Lord Tankerville, 1/2 a year due at Christ-
             mas   400
             To Mr. Guthrie, one quarter due at Christmas   50
             To Col. Mordaunt, one quarter at Christmas   200
             To Mr. Tyrrel, the French officer employed in
             Nova Scotia, one year due at Christmas   .   200
             Two years for Harwich from April 1757 to
             April 1759   200
             N.B.—The Duke of Devonshire paid the
             last sum up to abovementioned time.
     19th.   Given, by Your Majesty's order, as a present
             to Baron Hardenberg   .   .   .   600
     23d.   To Mr. Robt. Colebrooke in part of an allow-
             ance of 600£ pr. ann.   .   .   .   300
             To the Earl of Peterborough, one quarter due
             at Christmas   100
     30th.   Given by Your Majesty's order as a present to
             Mor. Alt   200
Feb. 2d.   To Mr. Chas. Hamilton, 1/2 a year due at
             Christmas.   600

---

[1] This was another compensation for a place in Minorca. Dr. Coote
Molesworth, M.D., F.R.S. (1697–1782), sixth son of Robert, first Viscount
Molesworth, was in 1735 appointed physician to the garrison of Minorca ;
see also undated memo., of 1758, but misplaced in 33040 (f. 373) :

His place has ceas'd   Dr. Molesworth, made physician to Minorca by
for this last year   the late Queen, is starving   .   .   . £200

1759   £

			£
Feb.	2d.	To Mr. George Brudenell, one year . .	500
		To Gordon — two months . . .	20
	6th.	To Mr. Ellis for Bryer of Weymouth, one year to Christmas	100
		To Mr. Schutz, 1/2 a year to Christmas .	200
		To the Earl of Warwick, one quarter to Christmas.	125
	9th.	To the Marq^{ss} of Rockingham's friend, one year to Christmas	150
	22d.	To the Earl of Ilchester, one year . .	400
March	1st.	To Mr. Thomas Watson, 1/2 a year . .	400
	30th.	To Mr. Charlton, Chairman of Committees as usual	500
		To Mr. Justice Fielding, 1/2 a year to Lady Day	200
		To Gordon, two months . . .	20
		To Mr. Guthrie, one quarter to Lady Day .	50
April	5th.	To Lord Willoughby of Parham, one year to Lady Day	400
	13th.	To Mr. Ralph, 1/2 a year due at Lady Day .	150
		To the person who sends the intelligence to the Duke of Devonshire . . .	100
	27th.	To Lord Morton's three friends :	

To Lord Morton's three friends :

Lord Rutherfurd .	150£	
Lord Borthwick .	50	} . 250
Lord Kircudbright .	50	

			£
		To Gordon's Transcriber, one year . .	50
		To the Earl of Peterborough, one quarter to Lady Day.	100
		To Col. Pelham, one quarter due at Lady Day	125
May	1st.	To Mrs. Krahé, 1/2 a year, due at Lady Day	25
		To Col. Mordaunt, one quarter due at Lady Day	200
		To Lord Malpas, in part of an allowance of 600£ pr. ann :	300
	3d.	To the Earl of Warwick, one quarter due at Lady Day.	125
		To Mr. Cooke, Mr. Gybbon's friend, half a year to Lady Day . . .	50
	2d.	To Mr. Robert Colebrooke, remainder of an allowance of 600£ pr. ann. . .	300

1759			£
May	2d.	To Mr. Martin towards Camelford election [1].	300
	8th.	To Mr. Medlycott for one year . .	600
	11th.	To Lord Saye and Sele, one year to Lady Day	600
		To Mr. Hamilton, the late Duke of Hamilton's relation, 1/2 a year due at Lady Day .	100
		To Mr. Henry Fane for Lyme as usual .	100
	17th.	To Sir Francis Poole, one year due at Christmas	300
	18th.	To Mr. Dodd, one year . . .	500
	25th.	Retained to myself by Your Majesty's special command, one quarter . . .	1050
		To Lord Malpas, remainder . .	300
	29th.	To Orford, rent, 1/2 a year due at Midsummer last	100
		To Mr. Offley, 1/2 a year to Christmas .	200
June	8th.	To Mr. Reiche,[2] for the French Commissary who gave intelligence to Prince Ferdinand	25
		To Gordon, two months . . .	20
	12th.	To Dr. Hepburne, one year . . .	100
		To Mr. Dugall Campbell, one year . .	400
	15th.	To Col. Clavering, who brought the news from Guadeloupe, by Your Majesty's order	500
		To Mr. Andrews, one year for Okehampton .	100
	19th.	To Mr. Holmes, one year for the three Isle of Wight boroughs . . .	600
	23rd.	To the Earl of Kinnoull, one year for Cambridge as usual . . .	550
July	5th.	The Speaker's List — one year . .	360
		Mr. Allen, the Speaker's nephew, 1/2 a year due at Midsummer . .	100
		To Mr. Hewett, 1/2 a year to Lady Day .	200
		To Mr. Rivett, 1/2 a year to Lady Day .	150
		To the Earl of Cork, 1/2 a year to Michaelmas last	400
	6th.	To the Earl of Halifax, 1/2 a year due at Midsummer	750
		To Mrs. Boone, 1/2 a year due at Midsummer	200

---

[1] See above, p. 343.
[2] Gerhard Andreas von Reiche, Secretary to the Elector of Hanover.

1759   £ s.

			£	s.
July	6th.	To the Earl of Peterborough, one quarter to Midsummer . . .	100	0
		To Mr. Thos. Watson, 1/2 a year to Midsummer . . .	400	0
		To Mr. Guthrie, one quarter, to Midsummer . . .	50	0
	10th.	To Col. Mordaunt, one quarter due at Midsummer . . .	200	0
	17th.	To the Earl of Warwick, one quarter, due at Midsummer [1] . . .	125	0
		To the Earl of Warwick as a gratuity by Your Majesty's particular order .	500	0
		To Col. Pelham, one quarter due at Midsummer . . .	125	0
		To Mr. Vere of Stoneveers, one year .	400	0
	20th.	To Baron Münchhausen, 1/2 a year due at Midsummer . . .	500	0
		To Mr. John Ramy, a friend of Mr. Charles Townshend, of Yarmouth, one year to Midsummer . . .	200	0
		To Mr. Justice Lane, one year . .	200	0
		To Mr. Capel Hanbury, one year for the Dissenting Ministers in Monmouthshire as usual . . .	100	0
		To Mr. Manly, the Mayor of Taunton, one year as usual . . .	70	0
	24th.	To Mr. Schutz, 1/2 a year due at Midsummer . . .	200	0
		To Lord Montfort, 1/2 a year due at Midsummer . . .	400	0
		To the Earl of Tankerville, 1/2 a year due at Midsummer . . .	400	0
		Retained to myself, by Your Majesty's special command, one quarter . .	1050	0
		Paid to Mr. Webb, by Your Majesty's order, for his actual disbursements only on the enquiry in 1757 [2] . .	352	7

[1] See 'Mem^ds for the King', 6 July 1759 (32892, f. 444): 'Poor Lord Warwick — his petition — for 500£ only — a great act of charity'.

[2] This refers to the inquiry into the loss of Minorca, which was concluded in May 1757. For a detailed account of these disbursements see 33039, ff. 5-7. P. C. Webb, M.P., Solicitor to the Treasury, acted on instructions from Lord Hardwicke; two letters relating to the matter are published in P. C. Yorke, *Life of Lord Hardwicke*, vol. ii, pp. 355-7.

1759			£
July	27th.	To Mr. Charles Hamilton, half a year due at Midsummer	600
		To Mr. Fairfax as a gratuity by Your Majesty's particular order . .	500
	31st.	To Mr. Offley, 1/2 a year, due at Midsummer	200
		To Mr. Gordon, two months . .	20
Aug.	16th.	To Mor. Erstorff, Adjutant General to Prince Ferdinand, who brought the account of the great and compleat victory near Minden, by Your Majesty's order . . .	500
		To Col. Fitzroy, Aid de Camp to Prince Ferdinand, by Your Majesty's order .	500
		To Capt. Ligonier, Aid de Camp to Prince Ferdinand, by Your Majesty's order .	500
	25th.	To Mr. Andrews for Mr. Henry Luxmore,[1] of Okehampton, 1/2 a year due at Midsummer	50
	28th.	To Mr. White's friend at Retford by Your Majesty's command [1] . . .	50
Sept.	4th.	To Your Majesty for a George for Prince Ferdinand	1500
	14th.	To Mr. Gybbon, for necessary law charges at Rye, by Your Majesty's order [1] . .	300
		To Davis, of Rye, 1/2 a year to Midsummer last [2]	50
Oct.	2d.	To Gordon — two months . . .	20
	5th.	To Mr. Justice Fielding, 1/2 a year due at Michaelmas	200
		To Mr. Guthrie, one quarter to Michaelmas .	50
	12th.	To Col. Pelham, one quarter due at Michaelmas	125
		To Lady Warwick, one quarter which would have been due to the late Earl of Warwick at Michaelmas	125
	16th.	To Sir Henry Bedingfeld, one year due at Lady Day last	500

[1] See Newcastle's 'Mem[ds] for the King', 20 July 1759 (32893, f. 168):

'Elections	Expences for elections creep on apace.
Rye	Mr. Gybbon 350£ law charges.
	£100 p.a. for one Davis.
Retford	£50 p.a. necessary there to one of their voters.
Oakhampton	£100 p.a. to Mr. Luxmore.'

About the case at Rye see also 32888, ff. 25 and 112-13, and 32893, ff. 54, 84, and 152. White's friend was Alderman Smith of Retford; see below, p. 476, n. 2.

1759

			£
Oct.	16th.	To Mr. Hamilton, the late Duke of Hamilton's relation, 1/2 a year due at Michaelmas last .	100
		To Col. Mordaunt, one quarter due at Michaelmas	200
	23d.	To Mrs. Krahé, 1/2 a year, due at Michaelmas	25
	26th.	To the Earl of Peterborough, one quarter, due at Michaelmas	100
		To Mr. Ralph, 1/2 a year, due at Michaelmas	150
	30th.	Retained to myself by Your Majesty's special command, one quarter . . .	1050
Nov.	6th.	To Orford rent, 1/2 a year, due at Christmas last	100
		To Orford expences . . .	100
	13th.	To Querré, the French pilot, one year due at Michaelmas	100
		To Mr. Chancellor of the Exchequer, one year for Mr. Duckett to Michaelmas last .	500
	21st.	To Col. Robinson, in lieu of his place about the young Princes, one quarter to Michaelmas last [1]	100
Dec.	4th.	To Mr. Thomas Pitt, in consequence of an agreement with Mr. Andrews . .	1000
		To Gordon — two months . .	20
	11th.	To the Earl of Cork, 1/2 a year due at Lady Day	400
	14th.	To Baron Münchhausen, 1/2 a year due at Christmas next	500

1760

			£
Jan.	15th.	To the Earl of Halifax, half a year due at Christmas.	750
		To Mr. Ellis, for Bryer of Weymouth, one year to Christmas	100
		To Mr. Andrews for Mr. Henry Luxmore of Okehampton, 1/2 a year due at Christmas .	50
		Retained to myself by Your Majesty's special command, one quarter . . .	1050
		To Mr. Burrowes, Beadle of Cambridge, one year due at Michaelmas last . .	100

[1] The following appears in Newcastle's 'Memds. for the King' on 24 May 1759 (32891, f. 118):

Col. Robinson £400 *private* till some place can be found for him. The ill consequence (in the present state of the Administration) if this affair should now fail for a *trifle*.

Mr. Pitt — Mr. Legge — Leicester House.

			£
1760			
Jan.	17th.	To Mr. Henry Poole, in lieu of his place at Minorca, one year. . . .	500
		To Mr. Guthrie, one quarter due at Christmas	50
		To Col. Pelham, one quarter due at Christmas	125
	18th.	To Col. Robinson, in lieu of his place about the young Princes, one quarter, due at Christmas	100
		To the Countess of Warwick, one quarter, due at Christmas	75
		To Lady Charlotte Rich, one quarter, due at Christmas.	50
		N.B.—Lady Warwick is, by Your Majesty's command, to have a pension of £300 p^r. ann., and Lady Charlotte Rich of £200 p^r. ann.	
		To Col. Mordaunt, one quarter due at Christmas.	200
	22d.	To Lord Montfort, 1/2 a year due at Christmas	400
	23rd.	To Mr. Tyrrel, the French officer employed in Nova Scotia, one year due at Christmas .	200
		To Mr. Allen, the Speaker's nephew, 1/2 a year due at Christmas . . .	100
N.B.	25th.	To Mr. Whitworth, three quarters at the rate of 200£ pr. ann., in order to make up his Government 400£ pr: ann: . .	150
	30th.	To the Earl of Peterborough, one quarter due at Christmas	100
		To Mrs. Boone, 1/2 a year, due at Christmas	200
Feb.	1st.	To Mr. Reiche for the French Commissary who gave intelligence to Prince Ferdinand, the further sum of . . .	25
	5th.	To Mr. Robt. Colebrooke in part of an allowance of £600 pr: ann: . . .	300
		To the Earl of Tankerville, 1/2 a year due at Christmas.	400
	12th.	To Gordon — two months . . .	20
	15th.	To Baron Münchhausen for the wine merchant Koch, recommended by Prince Ferdinand.	100
	19th.	To Mr. Hewet, 1/2 a year, due at Michaelmas	200
		To Mr. Rivett, 1/2 a year, due at Michaelmas	150
	20th.	To the Marq^{ss} of Rockingham's *two* friends, one year due at Christmas . .	250
	22d.	To Mr. Cooke, Mr. Gybbon's friend, 1/2 a year due at Michaelmas . . .	50

1760

			£
Feb.	29th.	To the Earl of Ilchester, one year . .	400
March	4th.	To Mr. Charles Hamilton, 1/2 a year due at Christmas.	600
		To Lord Malpas in part of an allowance of 600£ pr: ann:	300
		To Mr. Schutz, 1/2 a year to Christmas .	200
	5th.	To Mr. Molesworth, one year . .	200
		To Springer, the Swedish merchant, who suffered so much	100
	11th.	To Your Majesty for Prince Ferdinand's two Aides de Camp, Mo^r Derenthal, and Mo^r Winzingerode [1]	400
	13th.	To Mr. Thomas Watson, 1/2 a year, due at Christmas last . . .	400
	18th.	To Mr. Langford, Mr. Sergison's son in law, 1/2 a year due at Christmas last .	150
		To Davis of Rye, 1/2 a year due at Christmas	50
		To Mr. Charlton, Chairman of the Committees, as usual	500
	19th.	To Sir Francis Poole, one year due at Christmas	300
	21st.	To Mr. Whitworth, the remaining three quarters, at the rate of 200£ pr: ann: in order to make up his Government 400£ pr: ann: .	150
	27th.	To Mr. Justice Fielding, 1/2 a year, due at Lady Day.	200
		For Orford rent, 1/2 a year due at Midsummer last	100
		For Harwich, one year, due at Lady Day .	100
		To Col. Pelham, one quarter, due at Lady Day	125
April	1st.	To Your Majesty, in addition to Prince Ferdinand's two Aides de Camp, Mo^r Derenthal, and Mo^r Winzingerode . . .	200
		To Lord Willoughby of Parham, one year, due at Lady Day	400
		To Mr. George Brudenell, one year . .	500
	3d.	To the Earl of Peterborough, one quarter due at Lady Day	100
		To Mr. Hamilton, the late Duke of Hamilton's relation, 1/2 a year due at Lady Day .	100

[1] Mr. Walter Manners, Lord Granby's biographer, in a letter to me, of 14 May 1929, suggested that this payment was 'for their expenses and 'trouble" in coming to give evidence at the Sackville Court Martial which sat from 7 March till 5 April'.

1760   £

April   3d.   To the Countess of Warwick, one quarter, due
              at Lady Day   75
              To Lady Charlotte Rich, one quarter due at
              Lady Day.   50
              To Mr. Gordon — two months   .   .   20
       10th. To Mr. Guthrie, one quarter due at Lady Day   50
              Retain'd to myself by Your Majesty's special
              command. One quarter .   .   .   1050
       15th. Col. Mordaunt, one quarter due at Lady Day   200
       22d.   To Gordon's Transcriber, one year .   .   50
       24th. To Lord Morton's friends :
              Lord Borthwick .   .   50   ⎫
              Lord Kircudbright   .   50   ⎬ .   150
              and to the widow of the   ⎭
                 late Lᵈ Rutherfurd   .   50
              To Mr. Ralph, 1/2 a year due at Lady Day .   150
May   1st. To Mr. Cooke, Mr. Gybbon's friend, 1/2 a year
              due at Lady Day   50
              To Mr. Robert Colebrooke, remainder of an
              allowance of 600£ pr. ann.   .   .   300
              To Lord Saye and Sele, one year to Lady Day   600
       2d.   To Col. Robinson in lieu of his place about the
              young Princes—one quarter due at Lady Day   100
       7th.   To Mrs. Krahé, 1/2 a year due at Lady Day .   25
       8th.   To Lord Malpas. Remainder   .   .   300
              To Mr. Offley, 1/2 a year due at Christmas .   200
       13th. To Mr. Dugall Campbell, one year .   .   400
       20th. To Mr. Burrowes, Beadle of Cambridge, 1/2 a
              year due at Lady Day last .   .   .   50
              To Mr. Dodd, one year   .   .   .   500
       22d.   To Mr. Medlycott, one year.   .   .   600
       27th. To the Earl of Morton's friend, Mr. Baikie of
              Orkney [1]   200
              To Mr. Fairfax as a gratuity by Your
              Majesty's particular order .   .   .   500

[1] James Baikie, provost of Dingwall during the rebellion of 1745. The
Baikies were a leading family in the Orkneys, and James Baikie's son Robert
was returned for the county in 1780 but unseated on petition. In 1760,
Lord Morton was afraid of his candidate, Sir James Douglas, losing the
election, and James Baikie was given the pension of £200 p.a. to secure it.
See Newcastle's 'Memᵈˢ for the King', 16, 22, and 23 May 1760 (32906, ff.
103, 197, and 235) ; also Baikie's letter of 10 Oct 1760, acknowledging receipt
of the £200, and expressing the hope that the 'bounty' will be continued
(32913, f. 28).

2 H

1760

				£
May	27th.	To Mr. Holmes, one year for the three Isle of Wight boroughs		600
June	4th.	To Mr. Henry Fane for Lyme, as usual .		100
	10th.	To the Earl of Cork, 1/2 a year due at Michaelmas last		400
		To Mr. Andrews, one year for Okehampton .		100
		To Mr. Gordon, two months . .		20
	20th.	To Lord Parker for one year due at Midsummer last		600
		N.B.—Lord Parker is to have an allowance of 600£ pr. ann.		
		To Mr. Keck, for 1/2 a year due at Midsummer next		300
		N.B.—Mr. Keck is to have an allowance of 600£ pr: ann: [1]		
	25th.	To Mr. Cadogan in the absence of the Earl of Kinnoull, one year for Cambridge as usual		550
		To Mr. Hewet, 1/2 a year due at Lady Day .		200
		To Mr. Rivett, 1/2 a year due at Lady Day .		150
		To Mr. T. Watson, 1/2 a year, due at Midsummer		400
July	15th.	Retained to myself, by Your Majesty's special command, one quarter . . .		1050
		To the Earl of Lincoln, as High Steward of Westminster for the expences of the Deputy Steward, and Court of Burgesses, in order to secure the election without any further expence		500
		To Col. Pelham, one quarter due at Midsummer		125
		To Col. Mordaunt, one quarter due at Midsummer		200

[1] A. T. Keck, M.P. for Woodstock 1753–67 ; about him see my note on 'Three Eighteenth-Century Politicians', in the *English Historical Review*, July 1927. In Dec 1759 the Duke of Marlborough unsuccessfully applied for a place for him (32900, ff. 105 and 212). On 2 May 1760, Newcastle in his 'Memds. for the King' suggested a pension of £400 for him (32905, f. 242). On 7 June 1760, Marlborough reminded Newcastle of the pension of £700 p.a. which Keck was to have received as from 1 May he 'till could be otherwise provided for' (32907, f. 66) ; Newcastle replied on 12 June : 'His Majesty was very glad of an opportunity to oblige your Grace, and very readily agreed to give an allowance of 600£ p.a. to the person, mentioned in your Grace's letter. He would not, however, go beyond £600, but agreed to the pension starting as from last Christmas' (*ibid.* f. 176).

1760   £

July   15th.   To Col. Robinson, in lieu of his place about
                the young Princes, one quarter due at Mid-
                summer   100
                Mr. Guthrie, one quarter due at Midsummer   50
                To the Countess of Warwick, one quarter due
                at Midsummer   75
                To Lady Charlotte Rich, one quarter due at
                Midsummer   50
                To Mr. Andrews, for Mr. Henry Luxmore of
                Okehampton, 1/2 a year due at Midsummer   50
                To Mo^r Münchhausen, 1/2 a year due at Mid-
                summer   500
                To the Earl of Halifax, 1/2 a year due at
                Midsummer   750
                The Speaker's List, one year   .   .   360
                Mr. Allen, the Speaker's nephew, 1/2 a year,
                due at Midsummer   .   .   .   100
                Mr. Schutz, 1/2 a year due at Midsummer . 200
                Earl of Tankerville, 1/2 a year due at Mid-
                summer   400
                Mrs. Boone, 1/2 a year due at Midsummer . 200
        25th.   To the Earl of Peterborough, one quarter due
                at Midsummer   100
Sept.   17th.   To Mr. Capel Hanbury for the Dissenting
                Ministers in Monmouthshire. One year as
                usual   100
                To Mr. Manly, Mayor of Taunton. One
                year as usual   70
        19th.   To Mr. T. Leslie, by Your Majesty's order, to
                enable him to secure his election   .   .   500
                To Mr. Offley, 1/2 a year, due at Midsummer 200
                To Mr. Chas. Hamilton, 1/2 a year due at Mid-
                summer   600
        30th.   To Mr. Justice Lane, one year   .   .   200
                To Sir Francis Eyles Stiles [1] by Your Majesty's
                order, to enable him to go abroad for the
                benefit of his health   .   .   .   300

---

[1] Sir Francis Haskins Eyles Stiles, third Bt., F.R.S. ; descended from a
family of Wiltshire clothiers, who, between 1715 and 1742, had the dominant
interest in the borough of Devizes ; his grandfather and father were Lord
Mayors of London. He succeeded to the baronetcy in Mar 1745, and a few
months later sold his estate, Gidea Hall. He was a Commissioner of: he
Victualling Office of the Navy, 1747–62 ; died at Naples in 1762.

			£	s.
1760				
Sept. 30th.	To Mr. John Ramy, a friend of Mr. Charles Townshend at Yarmouth, one year due at Midsummer	. .	200	0
Oct. 3d.	To Mr. Justice Fielding, 1/2 a year due at Michaelmas . . .		200	0
7th.	To Gordon — four months . .		40	0
14th.	To Col. Pelham. One quarter due at Michaelmas		125	0
	To Mr. White's friend, at Retford, one year		50	0
17th.	To the Earl of Peterborough, one quarter due at Michaelmas . . .		100	0
	To Col. Robinson, in lieu of his place about the young Princes, one quarter due at Michaelmas		100	0
	To Mr. Guthrie, one quarter due at Michaelmas		50	0
	To Mr. Hamilton, the late Duke of Hamilton's relation, 1/2 a year due at Michaelmas		100	0
	To the Countess of Warwick, one quarter due at Michaelmas . . .		75	0
	To Lady Charlotte Rich, one quarter due at Michaelmas		50	0
	To Col. Mordaunt, one quarter due at Michaelmas		200	0
	Retain'd to myself, by Your Majesty's special command, one quarter . .		1050	0
21st.	To the Earl of Cork, 1/2 a year, due at Lady Day last		400	0
	To Mr. Ralph, 1/2 a year, due at Michaelmas last		150	0
	Paid away .		114,857	7
	Remains .		5,142	13
	Total receipt .		120,000	0

March 11th, 1761.

I this day receiv'd the King's orders to pay the arrears, due on the private account, up to Michaelmas last, out of the money remaining in my hands as far as that would go; and to have a warrant prepar'd for such further sum, out of the late King's arrears, as should be sufficient to discharge the remainder; which warrant is to be for the sum of . . . . £6352 7s.

1761			£	s.
March 12th.	To Baron Münchhausen, one quarter due at Michaelmas last . . .		250	0
	To the Earl of Halifax, one quarter due at Michaelmas last . . .		375	0
	To the Earl of Ilchester, three quarters due at Michaelmas last . . .		300	0
	To Mr. Langford, Mr. Sergison's son in law, three quarters due at Michaelmas last		225	0
13th.	To Lord Willoughby of Parham, 1/2 a year, due at Michaelmas last . .		200	0
17th.	To Mr. George Brudenell, 3 quarters due at Michaelmas last . . .		375	0
	To Mr. Charles Hamilton, one quarter due at Michaelmas last . . .		300	0
	To Mr. Thomas Watson, one quarter to Michaelmas		200	0
18th.	To Mr. Keck, one quarter to Michaelmas		150	0
19th.	To Sir Francis Poole, three quarters to Michaelmas		225	0
	To Mr. Henry Poole, three quarters to Michaelmas		325	0
	To Lord Saye and Sele, 1/2 a year to Michaelmas		300	0
	To Mr. Schutz, one quarter to Michaelmas [1]		100	0
	To Mr. Robert Colebrooke, 1/2 a year to Michaelmas		300	0
	To Mr. Tyrrel, the French officer employ'd in Nova Scotia, three quarters to Michaelmas		150	0
April 1st.	To the Earl of Tankerville, one quarter due at Michaelmas last . .		200	0
	To Mr. Offley, one quarter due at Michaelmas last		100	0
3d.	To Querré, the French Pilot, one year due at Michaelmas last . . .		100	0

[1] On the accession of George III he lost both his place as Ranger of Richmond Lodge and his pension. For his letters and memorial asking that his pay be extended at least till Christmas 1760, as he had to make up his official accounts to that date, see 32920, f. 426, 32926, f. 384, and 32935, f. 455.

1761			£	s.
April	3d.	To Gordon's transcriber, 1/2 a year due at Michaelmas last . . .	25	0
		To Lord Rockingham's two friends, three quarters due at Michaelmas last .	187	10
		To Mr. Manly, Mayor of Taunton, one quarter due at Michaelmas last. .	17	10
		To Springer, the Swedish merchant, 3 quarters to Michaelmas last . .	75	0
	8th.	To Lord Morton's friends : Lord Borthwick, Ld Kircudbright and Ld Rutherfurd's widow 1/2 a year due at Michaelmas. } each £50 pr. ann. .	75	0
		To Mr. Baikie of Orkney, 1/2 a year due at Michaelmas	100	0
	9th.	To Mr. Davis of Rye, 3 quarters due at Michaelmas last . . .	75	0
		To Mr. Cooke, Mr. Gybbon's friend, 1/2 a year due at Michaelmas last . .	50	0
		To Mr. Allen, the Speaker's nephew, one quarter due at Michaelmas last. .	50	0
	14th.	To Lord Parker, one quarter due at Michaelmas last . . .	150	0
		To Mr. Medlycott, 1/2 a year due at Michaelmas last . . .	300	0
		Orford rent, one year and a quarter to Michaelmas last . . .	250	0
		Orford expences—one year to Michaelmas last	100	0
		To Harwich, 1/2 a year to Michaelmas last	50	0
	15th.	To Mrs. Krahé, 1/2 a year due at Michaelmas last . . .	25	0
		To Mr. Hewett, 1/2 a year due at Michaelmas last . . .	200	0
		To Mr. Rivett, 1/2 a year due at Michaelmas last . . .	150	0
	21st.	To Lord Malpas, 1/2 a year due at Michaelmas last [1] . . .	300	0

[1] See letter from Lord Malpas to the Duke of Newcastle, 10 Mar 1761, asking to have 'his *particular business*' finished before he leaves town on the 12th (32920, f. 86).

1761			£
April	23rd.	To Lord Holmes, 1/2 a year to Michaelmas for the three Isle of Wight burroughs [1] .	300
May	7th.	To Mr. Andrews for Mr. Henry Luxmore of Okehampton — one quarter due at Michaelmas last	25
	22d.	To the Earl of Cork, 1/2 a year due at Michaelmas last	400
June	11th.	To Lord Montfort, three quarters due at Michaelmas last	600
	16th.	To Mr. Burrowes, Beadle of Cambridge, 1/2 a year due at Michaelmas last . .	50
	24th.	To Mrs. Boone, one quarter due at Michaelmas last	100
	25th.	To Mr. Andrews for Okehampton, 1/2 a year due at Michaelmas last . . .	50
		To Mr. Cadogan, 1/2 a year for Cambridge, due at Michaelmas last . . .	275
		To Mr. Molesworth, three quarters due at Michaelmas last	150
		To Mr. Acourt Ashe, two years and three quarters due at Michaelmas last, 1760 .	1375
		To Mr. Charlton, Chairman of the Committees — three quarters to Michaelmas last [2] .	375
July	29th.	To Mr. Henry Fane for Lyme, 1/2 a year due at Michaelmas last . . .	50
		To Mr. John Ramy, a friend of Mr. Chas. Townshend of Yarmouth, one quarter due at Michaelmas last . . .	50
Sept.	4th.	To Mr. Justice Lane, one quarter due at Michaelmas	50
		The Speaker's List. One quarter due at Michaelmas last	90
	8th.	To Mr. Geo. Brudenell, one year, being an old arrear	500
Oct.	29th.	To Capel Hanbury for the Dissenting Ministers in Monmouthshire, one quarter to Michaelmas 1760	25

[1] About this payment see 32922, ff. 95 and 227.

[2] Charlton had written to Newcastle on 18 Feb 1761 (32919, f. 98): 'I shal acknowledge it as a particular favor, if your Grace wil order my allowance for the Chair. I understand, that a double gratuity has been given, the establishment of the Civil List Revenue and the Supplies of the Year being considered as two distinct services. . . .' His claim to this double gratuity was not admitted.

1761   £
Dec.   22d.   To Mr. Dodd, 1/2 a year due at Michaelmas
                  1760   250

1762
May   25th.   To Mr. Duckett, one year to Michaelmas 1760   500
                  To Mr. Ellis for Bryer of Weymouth, three
                  quarters to Michaelmas 1760   .   .   75
                                                        ──────
                              Paid away   .   .   . 11,645
                              Remains unpaid   .   .   850
                                                        ──────
                  (initialed) G. R.   12,495

33044, ff. 107-8

                                                            £
July 15, 1757.   Receiv'd of Mr. West   .   10,000
December 20, 1757.   Receiv'd of Mr. West   .   10,000
March 7, 1758.   Receiv'd of Mr. West   .   10,000
June 15, 1758.   Receiv'd of Mr. West   .   10,000
August 3, 1758.   Receiv'd of Mr. West   .   10,000
January 17, 1759.   Receiv'd of Mr. West   .   10,000
May 1, 1759.   Receiv'd of Mr. West   .   10,000
July 17, 1759.   Receiv'd of Mr. West   .   10,000
September 25, 1759.   Receiv'd of Mr. West   .   10,000
February 16, 1760.   Receiv'd of Mr. West   .   10,000
May 20, 1760.   Receiv'd of Mr. West   .   10,000
September 29, 1760.   Receiv'd of Mr. West   .   10,000
                                                  ───────
                                                  120,000
March 19, 1761.   Receiv'd of Mr. West, being
                        the sum necessary to pay
                        off the arrears due on
                        account of the late King .   6,352   7s.
                                                  ─────────────
                              Total   .   .   126,352   7s.

July 22, 1761.   Receiv'd of Mr. West to pay
                        an arrear to Mr. A'Court
                        Ashe and Mr. George
                        Brudenell   .   .   £1000

'NEW BOOK'

'PRESENT KING'S PRIVATE ACCOUNT' (March 19, 1761–May 25, 1762)

(33044, ff. 178-210 [this is the copy initialed by
George III] ; another copy, ff. 211-43)

			£
1761			
March 19th.	Receiv'd of Mr. West	. . .	10,000
July 22d.	Receiv'd of Mr. West	. . .	10,000
Nov. 11th.	Receiv'd of Mr. West	. . .	10,000
1762			
Feb. 15th.	Receiv'd of Mr. West	. . .	10,000
May 25th.	Receiv'd of Mr. West	. . .	10,000

1761

March 20th.	To Baron Münchhausen, 1/4 due at X^{mas} last	250
	To the Earl of Halifax, 1/4 due at X^s last .	375
24th.	Retain'd to myself by Your Majesty's special command, 1/4 to X^s last . . .	1050
April 3d.	To Gordon — six months . . .	60
8th.	To Lord Morton's friends :	

Lord Borthwick
Lord Kircudbright and } each 50£ } . 75
Ld Rutherfurd's widow } pr. ann.

half a year due at Lady Day

To Mr. Baikie of Orkney, 1/2 a year due at Lady Day.	100
To Colonel Mordaunt, 1/2 a year due at Lady Day	400
9th. To Mr. Hamilton, the late Duke of Hamilton's relation, 1/2 a year due at Lady Day .	100
To the Earl of Peterborough, 1/2 a year due at Lady Day.	200
To Col. Pelham, 1/2 a year due at Lady Day .	250
To the Countess of Warwick, 1/2 a year due at Lady Day.	150
To Lady Charlotte Rich, 1/2 a year due at Lady Day.	100
Retain'd to myself by Your Majesty's special command, 1/4 to Lady Day . .	1050

1761 £

April 9th. To Mr. Guthrie, 1/2 a year due at Lady Day . 100

To Mr. Allen, the Speaker's nephew, 1/2 a
year due at Lady Day . . . 100

10th. To Mr. Justice Fielding, 1/2 a year due at
Lady Day. 200

To Gordon's transcriber, 1/2 a year due at
Lady Day. 25

14th. To Col. Robinson, 1/2 a year due at Lady Day 200

To Mr. Robt Colebrooke, remainder of an
allowance of 600£ pr. ann. . . 300

To Lord Parker, 1/2 a year due at Lady Day . 300

To Mr. Medlycott, 1/2 a year due at Lady Day 300

To Lord Saye and Sele, 1/2 a year due at Lady
Day 300

15th. To Mrs. Krahé, 1/2 a year due at Lady Day . 25

17th. To Mr. Chas. Hamilton, 1/2 a year due at
Lady Day. 600

21st. To Lord Malpas, 1/2 a year due at Lady Day. 300

22d. To Mr. Jeffreys, 1/2 a year due at Lady Day. 250

23d. To Lord Holmes, 1/2 a year due at Lady Day
last for the three Isle of Wight boroughs . 300

May 7th. To Mr. Ralph, 1/2 a year due at Lady Day . 150

To Mr. Offley, 1/2 a year due at Lady Day . 200

To Mr. Andrews for Mr. Henry Luxmore of
Okehampton, 1/2 a year due at Lady Day . 50

To the Earl of Halifax, one quarter to Lady
Day 375

N.B.—This is to be the last payment.[1]

19th. To Mr. Henry Finch, one quarter to Lady
Day 225

22d. To the Earl of Tankerville, 1/2 a year due at
Lady Day. 400

June 3d. To Mr. Keck, 1/2 a year due at Lady Day [2] . 300

16th. To Mr. Burrowes, Beadle of Cambridge, 1/2 a
year due at Lady Day . . . 50

24th. To Gordon.—Two months . . . 20

To Mrs. Boone — one quarter due at Christmas
last 100

[1] He was appointed Lord Lieut. of Ireland, Mar 1761.

[2] Keck wrote to Bute on 7 June 1761 (5726, D. f. 173): 'It was not 'till
within these few days that I knew, from Lady Charlotte Edwin of the
obligations I was under to your Lordship for the continuation of my
pension'.

1761

		£
June 25th.	To Mr. Andrews for Okehampton, 1/2 a year due at Lady Day	50
	To Mr. Cadogan, for Cambridge, 1/2 a year due at Lady Day	275
	To Mr. Molesworth, one quarter due at Christmas last	50
	To Mr. Charlton, Chairman of the Committees, one quarter	125
July 29th.	To Mr. James Brudenell,[1] one quarter due at Midsummer last	150
	To Col. Mordaunt, one quarter due at Midsummer last	300
	To Mrs. Boone, 1/2 a year due at Midsummer	200
	To Mr. Guthrie, one quarter due at Midsummer last	50
	To Mr. Justice Lane, three quarters due at Midsummer last	150
	To Mr. John Ramy, a friend of Mr. Cha[s] Townshend of Yarmouth, three quarters due at Midsummer last . . .	150
	To the Countess of Warwick, one quarter due at Midsummer last . . .	75
	To Lady Charlotte Rich, one quarter due at Midsummer last	50
	To Lord Delamer,[2] one quarter due at Midsummer last	200
	To Colonel Pelham, one quarter due at Midsummer last	125
	To Mr. Henry Fane for Lyme, 1/2 a year due at Midsummer last . . .	50

[1] The pension was presumably to compensate him for the loss of the post of Deputy-Cofferer. It was continued at the same rate under Bute, Grenville, and Rockingham. But by Jan 1779 Brudenell was drawing only £400 p.a. (Windsor Archives); and in Robinson's 'State of Pensions and Payments by Lord North' submitted to the King for his orders which he would 'have continued and handed over' [to Rockingham], there is the entry: 'Lord Brudenell in addition to his office — £400' (37836, f. 137). The pension does not appear in the list delivered to Rockingham, 21 Apr 1782, and to Shelburne, 17 July 1782.

[2] Nathaniel Booth, fourth Baron Delamer (1709–70), succeeded in 1758 his cousin George, second Earl of Warrington (about him see pp. 447-8) in the Barony, while the Earldom became extinct. In Newcastle's 'Mem[ds] for Lord Bute', 6 Mar 1761 (32919, f. 475), a pension of £1000 p.a. was suggested for Lord Delamer.

	1761		£
July	29th.	Retain'd to myself by Your Majesty's special command, one quarter to Midsummer .	1050
Aug.	5th.	To Baron Münchhausen, 1/2 a year due at Midsummer	500
		To the Earl of Peterborough, one quarter due at Midsummer	100
		To Gordon.—Two months . . .	20
	26th.	To Mr. Cooke, Mr. Gybbon's friend, 1/2 a year due at Lady Day . . .	50
		To Lord Montfort — 1/2 a year due at Lady Day	400
Sept.	2d.	To Major Wedderburn, who brought the account of the Battle of Fillinghausen, by Your Majesty's order . . .	500
	4th.	To Lord Willoughby of Parham, 1/2 a year due at Lady Day	200
		The Speaker's List, three quarters due at Midsummer	270
		Mr. Manly, Mayor of Taunton, 1/2 a year due at Lady Day	35
Oct.	1st.	To Mr. Hewett, 1/2 a year due at Lady Day	200
		To Mr. Rivett, 1/2 a year due at Lady Day .	150
		To Gordon — Two months . . .	150
	2d.	To Sir John Fielding, 1/2 a year due at Michaelmas	200
	15th.	To the Earl of Peterborough, one quarter due at Michaelmas	100
	29th.	To the Rt Honble Mr. Mackenzie, 1/2 a year due at Michaelmas last . . .	1000
		N.B.—Mr. Mackenzie is, by Your Majesty's order to have an allowance of 2000£ pr. ann: from Lady Day last.[1]	
		Retain'd to myself, by Your Majesty's special command, one quarter to Michaelmas last	1050
		To Mr. Tyrrell, the French officer, employ'd in Nova Scotia, one year due at Michaelmas	200
		To Mr. Allen, the late Speaker's nephew, 1/2 a year to Michaelmas . . .	100
		To Querré, the French Pilot, a year to Michaelmas	100

[1] The pension was given to him on his relinquishing the Turin Embassy in the summer of 1761, and stopped on his being appointed Lord Privy Seal of Scotland in the Grenville Administration, Apr 1763.

1761			£
Oct.	29th.	To Mr. Guthrie, one quarter to Michaelmas .	50
		To Col. Mordaunt, one quarter to Michaelmas	300
		To Mr. Ralph, 1/2 a year to Michaelmas .	150
		To the Countess Dowager of Warwick, one quarter to Mich^s	75
		To Lady Charlotte Rich, one quarter to Michaelmas	50
		To Lord Delamer, one quarter to Michaelmas	200
		To Mr. Jeffreys, 1/2 a year to Michaelmas .	250
		To Mrs. Krahé, 1/2 a year to Michaelmas .	25
		To Mr. James Brudenell, one quarter to Michaelmas	150
		To Col. Pelham, one quarter to Michaelmas [1]	125
		To Mr. Hamilton, the late Duke of Hamilton's relation, 1/2 a year due at Michaelmas .	100
		To Orford rent — one year to Michaelmas last	200
		To Orford expences, one year to Michaelmas last	100
		To Harwich, one year to Michaelmas last .	100
		To Mr. Hanbury, for the Dissenting Ministers in Monmouthshire — one year to Michaelmas	100
Nov.	5th.	To the Earl of Ilchester, one year to Michaelmas last	400
	17th.	To Mr. Offley, 1/2 a year due at Michaelmas last	200
		To Mr. Watson of Berwick, one year to Michaelmas	800
		To Mr. Chas Hamilton, 1/2 a year to Michaelmas	600
		To the Earl of Tankerville, 1/2 a year to Michaelmas	400
		To Mr. Keck, 1/2 a year to Michaelmas .	300
		To the Earl of Cork, 1/2 a year to Lady Day	400
		To Mr. Burrowes, Beadle of Cambridge, 1/2 a year to Michas. . . .	50

[1] James Pelham died on 27 Dec 1761, and on 3 Mar 1762, Newcastle received the following letter, signed Samuel Wright (32935, f. 168) : 'May it please your Grace, I hope you will pardon my taking this liberty of informing your Grace that as my late good master Colonel Pelham died but a few days before the Quarter Day your Grace will be pleas'd to take it into your consideration to enable me to discharge the demands made on me since his death'. There seems to have been no response to this appeal, at least not from secret service money.

1761   £

Nov.   18th.   To Mr. Bull, Mr. Morris's friend, 1/2 a year to
               Michaelmas   300
               N.B.—Mr. Bull, by Your Majesty's com-
               mand, is to have an allowance of 600£ pr.
               ann. from Lady Day.[1]

Dec.   8th.   To Mr. Geo. Brudenell — one year due at
               Michaelmas   500
               To Lord Parker, 1/2 a year due at Michaelmas
               last   300
               To Gordon — two months   .   .   .   20

       10th.   To Mr. Fairfax, as a gratuity by Your
               Majesty's particular order   .   .   500
               To Mr. Andrews for Mr. Henry Luxmore of
               Okehampton, 1/2 a year due at Michaelmas   50

       17th.   To the Earl of Cork, 1/2 a year due at Michael-
               mas last   400

       22d.   To Mr. Dodd, one year due at Michaelmas
               last   500

1762

Jan.   7th.   To Mr. White's friend at Retford. One year [2]   50

---

[1] Richard Bull of Ongar (1725–1806), the famous print collector (see on
him *Gent. Mag.*, 1806, vol. 1, p. 289); M.P. for Newport, Cornwall, 1756–
1780, returned on the interest of his friend and relative Humphrey
Morice, M.P. Bull was offered this pension by Newcastle on 17 Mar 1761,
but declined : '. . . all Mr. Morice's friends have protested against my
skreening disgrace such as his, under any private advantage of my own';
moreover, Morice had written to him : 'if you find me particularly neglected,
I charge you to accept of nothing from the Duke, except what will give me
an honourable reason for saying I am contented'. 'Now, my Lord,' continued Bull, 'your kind offer to me, being of an uncertain duration, and of
rather too private a nature, I cannot consistent with my own and my friend's
honor accept it' (32920, f. 308). Morice wrote to Bull from Naples on
9 Sept 1761 : 'I shou'd be glad you wou'd let him [Newcastle] know I have
desir'd the King will please to nominate who shall be chose for Newport in
case of Colonel Lee's death, which I fear . . . can't be far off' [he died in
November]. Although Newcastle's treatment of him has been 'extremely
unkind', he does not want the Duke to imagine 'he is to recommend' and
be disappointed (32930, f. 72). Bull forwarded this letter to Newcastle on
26 Oct (*ibid.* f. 70). The pension came three months later, and was continued
for nearly twenty years. It appears in Jenkinson's list of 1763, in the King's
list of 1764, in Rockingham's secret service accounts for 1765–66, and in
Robinson's accounts for 1779–80. It ceased on Bull quitting Parliament
(see Laprade, p. 50). During his twenty years in the House, Bull is not
known ever to have voted against any Government.

[2] William Mellish wrote to Newcastle on 2 Jan 1762 (32933, f. 46) :
'Give me leave to remind your Grace of Mr. Alderman Smith of Retford.

1762

Jan.	7th.	To the Countess Dowager of Warwick, one quarter to X^{mas}	75
		To Lady Charlotte Rich, one quarter to Christmas.	50
		To Lord Delamer, one quarter to Christmas .	200
		Retain'd to myself by Your Majesty's special command, one quarter to Christmas last .	1050
	12th.	To the Earl of Lincoln as High Steward of Westminster for the expences of the Deputy Steward, and Court of Burgesses, one year to Christmas 1760 [1] . . .	500
		To Mr. Cooke, Mr. Gybbon's friend, 1/2 a year due at Michaelmas last . . .	50
	14th.	To Mr. Guthrie, one quarter to Christmas last	50
		To the Marquess of Rockingham's two friends — one year due at Michaelmas last .	250
		To Col. Mordaunt, one quarter to Christmas last	300
	20th.	To Baron Münchhausen, 1/2 a year due at Christmas last	500
		To Mr. James Brudenell, one quarter due at Christmas last	150
	21st.	To Sir Fra^s. Poole, one year to Michaelmas last	300
	27th.	To the Earl of Peterborough, one quarter to Christmas last	100
		To Mrs. Boone,[2] 1/2 a year to Christmas last .	200
Feb.	8th.	To Mr. Hewett, 1/2 a year to Michaelmas last	200
		To Mr. Rivett, 1/2 a year to Michaelmas last	150
		To Gordon — two months . . .	20

Your Grace has been so good to releive him with your bounty for two or three years together; he is a very honest man, and endeavour'd to do without it last year; but, I fear, he is at present in the greatest distress.'

[1] This payment obviously ought to have been made from the 'arrears' and not from the current account. The following entry occurs in New-castle's 'Memorandums' of 5 Nov 1761 (32930, f. 321): 'Lord Lincoln The money for the Westminster Burgesses 500£ pr. ann.' And in the margin appears the remark in Newcastle's own hand writing: 'Mr. Jones to pay 500£ to Ld. Lincoln out of the late King's arrears and 500£ p. the an. for future.'

[2] See 33056, f. 2, for the following receipt:

Newcastle House. Jan. 30, 1762.

Receiv'd of his Grace the Duke of Newcastle, for the use of Daniel Boone, Esq., the sum of two hundred pounds.

for Mr. John Gwilt jun
David Macpherson.

1762   £

Feb.   8th.   To Springer, the Swedish merchant, one year
                to Michaelmas last   .   .   .   100
        17th.   To Mr. Robert Colebrooke, three quarters from
                the 14th of April to the 14th of Jan^{ry} when
                he kiss'd Your Majesty's hand, as Minister
                to the Swiss Cantons   .   .   .   450
                N.B.—This is to be the last payment.
                To Sir Thomas Hales, by Your Majesty's
                order, 1/2 a year due at Michaelmas last [1] .   300
                To Mr. Molesworth, one year to Christmas
                last   200
March   3d.   To Mr. Langford, Mr. Sergison's son in law,
                one year to Michaelmas last   .   .   300
April   5th.   To Lord Holmes for the three Isle of Wight
                boroughs, one year   .   .   .   600
                To Mr. Cavendish. One year to Lady Day [2].   800
                N.B.—Mr. Cavendish was, by Your
                Majesty's order, to have an allowance of
                800£ pr. ann.
                To Sir John Fielding, 1/2 a year due at Lady
                Day   200

---

[1] See above, p. 274. Hales had written to Newcastle on 25 Oct 1761
(32930, f. 30): 'There is now half a year due of the small sum your Grace
promised me in lieu of so large a one which I was so hardly deprived of, I
trouble your Grace to know where I must apply to receive it'. On the
accession of George III he had lost his post of Clerk to the Green Cloth.

[2] Richard Cavendish (1703–69), eldest son of Dr. Edward Chandler,
Bishop of Durham, married Elizabeth, daughter of Lord James Cavendish,
and in 1752 assumed her name. He was a barrister, Prothonotary of Common
Pleas for the County Palatine and Chancellor of the Diocese of Durham,
Solicitor to the Excise, and, since 1737, a Commissioner of the Customs.
At the general election of 1761 he was put up (and returned) for Wendover,
which necessitated his resigning the Commissionership ; in anticipation the
Duke of Devonshire wrote to Newcastle on 7 Mar 1761 : 'The chief reason
of my troubling you is to remind of Mr. Cavendish as he must soon vacate
his Commissioner's place, if he can change it for no employment, he wou'd
be glad of a pension. . . . I am very sorry to be troublesome . . . but
. . . this is a point that I cannot possibly do without and therefore I hope
you will get it done, I am ready to ask it as a favour ; is there nobody that
has a pension that wou'd exchange ?' (32919, f. 501). No exchange was
effected ; Cavendish's place in the Customs was given to John Frederick,
for whom no constituency was found at the general election (see above,
p. 328), and Cavendish was accommodated with a private pension. On 31
Mar 1762 Devonshire wrote to Newcastle 'Mr. Cavendish proposes to
wait on you to morrow for some money, a year as he says being due, if you
are not ready for him, let me know and I will stop him' (32936, f. 237).

1762
£

April 7th. To the Earl of Cork, 1/2 a year due at Lady
Day 400
To Mr. James Brudenell, one quarter to Lady
Day 150
To Mr. Gordon. Two months . . 20
To Lord Delamer, one quarter to Lady Day . 200
To the Countess Dowager of Warwick, one
quarter to Lady Day . . . 75
To Lady Charlotte Rich, one quarter to Lady
Day 50
To the R^t Honble Mr. Mackenzie, 1/2 a year
due at Lady Day 1000
Retain'd to myself by Your Majesty's special
command, one quarter to Lady Day . 1050
To Mr. Guthrie, one quarter due at Lady Day 50
To Mr. Allen, the late Speaker's nephew, 1/2
a year to Lady Day . . . 100
To Col. Mordaunt, one quarter due at Lady
Day 300

8th. To Sir Francis Poole, 1/2 a year to Lady Day 150
To Mr. Hamilton, the late Duke of Hamilton's
relation, 1/2 a year to Lady Day . . 100

20th. To Mr. Offley, 1/2 a year to Lady Day . 200
To Mr. Keck, 1/2 a year to Lady Day . 300
To Mrs. Krahé, 1/2 a year to Lady Day . 25
To Mr. Manly, Mayor of Taunton, one year to
Lady Day. 70
To Gordon's transcriber, one year to Lady
Day 50

21st. To the Earl of Peterborough, one quarter to
Lady Day. 100
To Lord Willoughby of Parham, one year to
Lady Day. 400
To Mr. Bull, Mr. Morrice's friend, 1/2 a year
to Lady Day 300

27th. To Mr. Jeffreys, 1/2 a year to Lady Day . 250
To Lord Parker, 1/2 a year to Lady Day . 300
To Sir Thos Hales, 1/2 a year to Lady Day . 300
To Lord Saye and Sele, one year to Lady
Day 600

May 18th. To Baron Münchhausen, by Your Majesty's
particular order, 1/2 a year to Midsummer
next 500

2 I

1762

			£	s.	d.
May 18th.	To Lord Morton's friends: Lord Borthwick, Lord Kircudbright, and } each 50£ Lord Rutherfurd's widow, } pr. ann. one year to Lady Day	.	150		
	To Mr. Baikie of Orkney, one year to Lady Day . . .		200		
25th.	To the Earl of Tankerville, 1/2 a year to Lady Day . . .	400	0	0
	To the Earl of Ilchester, 1/2 a year to Lady Day	200	0	0
	To Mr. Medlycott, one year to Lady Day [1]	600	0	0
	To Mr. Tho[s] Watson of Berwick, 1/2 a year to Lady Day . . .	400	0	0
	To Mr. Geo: Brudenell, 1/2 a year to Lady Day	250	0	0
	To Mr. Dodd, 1/2 a year to Lady Day	250	0	0
	To Mr. Acourt Ashe, one year and a half to Lady Day . . .	750	0	0
	To Mr. Alderman Dickenson, Chairman of the Committee . . .	500	0	0
	To Mr. Charles Hamilton, 1/2 a year to Lady Day . . .	600	0	0
	To Mr. Hewett, 1/2 a year to Lady Day	200	0	0
	To Mr. Rivett, 1/2 a year to Lady Day	150	0	0
	To Mr. Molesworth, one quarter to Lady Day	50	0	0
	To Mrs. Boone, one quarter to Lady Day	100	0	0
	To Gordon. Two months to the end of May	20	0	0
	To Mr. Justice Lane. Three quart[s] to Lady Day . . .	150	0	0
	To Mr. Henry Fane for Lyme, three quarters to Lady Day . .	75	0	0
	To Mr. Ramy of Yarmouth, three quarters to Lady Day . .	150	0	0

[1] The money was paid into his account at Child's bank; for receipt see 33056, f. 20.

1762		£	s.	d.
May 25th.	To Mr. Cadogan for Cambridge, one year to Lady Day . . .	550	0	0
	The late Speaker's list, three quarters to Lady Day . . .	270	0	0
	To Mr. Tyrrell, the French officer employ'd in Nova Scotia, 1/2 a year to Lady Day . . .	100	0	0
	To Querré, the French Pilot, 1/2 a year to Lady Day . .	50	0	0
	To Mr. Cooke, the late Mr. Gybbon's friend, 1/2 a year to Lady Day .	50	0	0
	To the Marq^{ss} of Rockingham's two friends, 1/2 a year to Lady Day .	125	0	0
	To Mr. White's friend at Retford, one quarter to Lady Day . .	12	10	0
	To Mr. Capel Hanbury for the Dissenting Ministers in Monmouthshire, 1/2 a year to Lady Day . .	50	0	0
	For Harwich, 1/2 a year to Lady Day .	50	0	0
	For Orford rents, 1/2 a year to Lady Day	100	0	0
	For Orford expences, 1/2 a year to Lady Day	50	0	0
	To Mr. Andrews for Okehampton, one year to Lady Day . .	100	0	0
	To Mr. Andrews for Mr. Henry Luxmore of Okehampton, 1/2 a year to Lady Day	50	0	0
	To Mr. Burrowes, Beadle of Cambridge, 1/2 a year to Lady Day .	50	0	0
	To the Earl of Lincoln, as High Steward of Westminster for the expences of the Deputy Steward and Court of Burgesses, one year and a quarter to Lady Day . .	625	0	0
	To Springer, the Swedish merchant, 1/2 a year to Lady Day . .	50	0	0
	To Mr. Langford, Mr. Sergison's son in law, 1/2 a year to Lady Day .	150	0	0
	To Lord Montfort, one year to Lady Day	800	0	0
	To Mr. Fairfax, as a gratuity, by Your Majesty's particular order . .	500	0	0

1762   £   s.   d.

The Duke of Newcastle's arrear from
old Lady Day (April 5th) to the 26th
of this instant, May, following, being
the day of his resignation [1]   .   588 19   2¾

                        Paid away   .   .   48,981   9   2¾
                        Remains   .   .   1,018 10   9¼

                                              50,000   0   0
(initialed) G. R.

[1] The money was paid by H. V. Jones into the Duke's account with
Messrs. Hoare ; for receipt see 33056, f. 19.

INDEX

THE END

PRINTED BY R. & R. CLARK, LTD., EDINBURGH

23625